AMERICA IN THE TWENTIETH CENTURY

AMERICA IN THE TWENTIETH CENTURY

by FRANK FREIDEL

HARVARD UNIVERSITY

 NEW YORK : ALFRED·A·KNOPF

1960

FOR

William Best Hesseltine

PREFACE

FOR ONE WHO WOULD UNDERSTAND the onrushing events of the twentieth century, some knowledge of historical background is essential. Out of an examination of trends can come some realization of where we have been and the direction in which we are heading. From a study of the growth of American institutions and traditions one can detect the patterns of thought and action shaping present-day policies and decisions. Some of the traditions are part of our most cherished and enduring heritage; some others are dangerously anachronistic in the face of modern realities. Thus the democratic tradition has continued vital, while that of hemispheric isolation has become obsolescent; a knowledge of both can contribute to a greater awareness of contemporary pressures and problems.

The purpose of this book is to present a simple, clear survey of some of the significant historical factors that have shaped the present-day United States both internally and in its relationship to the rest of the world. A survey like this rests inevitably upon the painstaking research of scores of historians, and the interpretations growing out of their carefully-reasoned conclusions. The writings of many of the historians are cited in the lists of books for further reading. Without these scholars, a book like this would be impossible. Needless to say, all responsibility for selection of both facts and interpretations is mine. In as tentative a field as evaluation of very recent events, there is much room for error. As time gives perspective, doubtless other facts and new interpretations will give a more valid meaning to some of these topics.

In *A History of the United States,* written with T. Harry Williams and

Richard N. Current, the sweep of American history is surveyed from its earliest European beginnings to the present. *America in the Twentieth Century* is substantially the last third of that work, revised and enlarged. An entirely new beginning chapter sketches the course of events from the Civil War through the Spanish-American War. Another new chapter analyzes intellectual, social, and cultural trends during the Progressive era; throughout the book there is more emphasis upon these factors. The basic focus continues to be upon political and economic development and, in the chapters on more recent decades, increasingly upon foreign affairs as the United States emerged more and more clearly in the forefront of the world arena. Some fifty new illustrations, many of them in the arts, and several new maps and charts have been added.

I am indebted to T. Harry Williams and Richard N. Current for their counsel and encouragement, and to the staff of Alfred A. Knopf for their perceptive editorial advice. I am grateful to the following scholars who generously read and criticized parts of the manuscript: Charles C. Griffin, William B. Hesseltine, Arthur S. Link, Ernest R. May, and Morton White. Miss Josephine Cobb of the National Archives gave valuable aid in selection of illustrations. For assistance I am indebted to Mrs. Elizabeth Forsythe, Mrs. Margaret Stark, and Thomas Griffin. My greatest debt, for many reasons, is to my wife, Madeleine Freidel.

F. F.

CONTENTS

xiii · *Contents*

ILLUSTRATIONS

CHARTS

MAPS

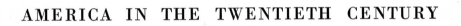

AMERICA IN THE TWENTIETH CENTURY

Chapter *1*

THE LEGACY OF THE
NINETEENTH CENTURY

THE AMERICAN PEOPLE entered the twentieth century with optimistic enthusiasm, looking forward to a future which seemed to hold for them almost limitless potentialities for good. They were proud of their nation's remarkable achievements in the century past, and they confidently expected to build upward from these to new pinnacles. There was little to dim their faith in almost unlimited progress for the American people, and indeed for all mankind. Thus it was that those who took part in the great reform movement of the first years of the twentieth century called themselves progressives.

Pride in past achievement and optimism over the future did not blind the reform-minded to the problems the nation faced. As yet they had no inkling that the century was to bring world conflict and the threat of global destruction; to this extent they lived in a relatively untroubled era. But the challenge that faced them, while it was as yet internal rather than external, seemed sufficiently crucial. In the years beginning with the Civil War they had seen power shift from a broad agrarian base toward a narrow industrial oligarchy. Could they revitalize American institutions decisively enough to counter this threat by preserving and extending democracy? Could they liquidate the liabilities, yet nurture the material assets of the new industrial order? Could they enjoy the best of both the old and the new Americas? Theodore Roosevelt, who led the progressives so vigorously, pointed out that by the end of the nineteenth century the earlier Jeffersonian governmental theories that had fitted an agricultural nation no longer served the intended democratic ends:

> Men who understand and practice the deep underlying philosophy of the Lincoln school of American political thought are necessarily Hamiltonian in their belief in a strong and efficient National Government and Jeffersonian in their belief in the people as the ultimate authority, and in the welfare of the people as the end of Government. The men who first applied the extreme Democratic theory in American life were, like Jefferson, ultra individualists, for at that time what was demanded by our people was the largest liberty for the individual. During the century that had elapsed since Jefferson became President the need had exactly reversed. There had been in our country a riot of individualistic materialism, under which complete freedom for the individual . . . turned out in practice to mean perfect freedom for the strong to wrong the weak. The total absence of governmental control had led to a portentous growth in the financial and industrial world. . . . The power of the mighty industrial overlords of the country had increased with giant strides, while the methods of controlling them, or checking abuses by them, on the part of the people, through the Government, remained archaic and therefore practically impotent.*

The rapid growth of manufacturing in the years since the Civil War had brought for many Americans a high standard of living, and for the entire country many fine cultural assets. It had also left a residue of inequities, especially of rural poverty and urban slum conditions, and seemed at times even to threaten the American democratic system. American reformers were determined to right the wrongs of industrialization without losing the benefits.

The Triumph of Industrialization

THE GROWTH OF INDUSTRY was not a phenomenon limited to America. It was a great shift in Western civilization, a cycle of change that, with all its accompanying blessings and evils, had swept England and Belgium decades earlier, and in the last third of the nineteenth century was remolding Imperial Germany and the United States. In other nations, as in this country, it raised questions concerning the relationships between the new industrialists and government, between capital and labor and agriculture; it brought the unprecedented growth of cities at home, and stimulated the quest for areas for investment and markets overseas. It gave birth to arms

---

* Theodore Roosevelt, *An Autobiography* (New York: Macmillan, 1913) pp. 462–63.

races, and out of the new technology came a volume and fearfulness of weapons never before known. Mankind had never been confronted by such a potential for good or ill; the United States led in this potential.

Between 1860 and 1900, the United States jumped from fourth to first place among the manufacturing nations of the world. Customarily, Americans have attributed this spectacular growth to the Civil War, the "second American Revolution" as the historian Charles A. Beard called it, which shifted the political hegemony from the master of the plantation to the owner of the factory. But the war was as much an effect of previous American industrialization as it was a contributing factor to further growth. This

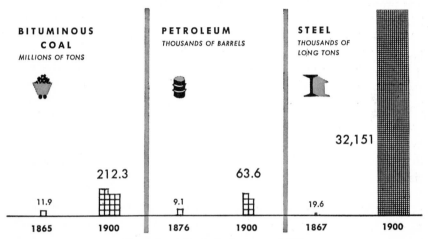

Growth of Basic Industry to 1900

is not to rule out other vital issues that helped bring on the Civil War, especially slavery and states rights, but long before secession, the North, in the rapid expansion of its cities, factories, railroads, and farms, was far ahead of the South. Yet the Southern minority clung to control of the Federal government and managed to perpetuate a national economic program favorable to the interests of the plantation owners. As the North, partly because of its rapidly expanding economy, far surpassed the South in population, it became only a matter of time before it would win control over the Federal government. The instrument was to be the new Republican party.

With the election of Abraham Lincoln in 1860, this triumph seemed close at hand. The South seceded, and in so doing lost its veto in the Senate over national economic policies. During the war, Republican politicians, representing an uneasy coalition of Northern farmers, railroaders, industrialists, and bankers, pushed through Congress the program that the South had so vigorously blocked: a high protective tariff to assist manufacturers, heavy subsidies for western railroad construction which would benefit farmers as well as railroad men, and a Homestead Act promising free farms in the West. In the final analysis, these and similar measures were of less value to farmers than to businessmen, but they helped keep large numbers of Northern farmers in the Republican party. As for the businessmen, legislatively they won the Civil War before the Battle of Bull Run, and they never relinquished their gains. Economically the war was a bonanza, at least for those who profited enough to engage in postwar fortune-building.

After the Civil War, capital, which had always been short in America, was present in the sizable quantities necessary for large scale enterprise. The greater part of it came from the tremendous governmental outpouring of money during the war, whether inflated Greenback paper currency or borrowed funds. The heavy borrowing of the Federal government did not dry up capital within the United States, for nearly a billion dollars of European funds went into government bonds. Additional government bonds which the National Banks bought served as a basis for paper currency. After the war, another half-billion dollars came from Europe to help finance railroads. These European funds, going into what appeared to be safe American investments, released much American capital for risky enterprises which, if successful, would produce huge returns.

The young men who manipulated this "risk capital," as it was called, took tall chances. Many of them gambled and lost, but some won huge fortunes and general acclaim as the builders of industrial America. They became the giants of the age; few poor boys wanted to grow up to be a drab President like Benjamin Harrison when they had the dazzling example before them of a multimillionaire philanthropist like Andrew Carnegie. The heroes of that popular writer of juvenile success stories, Horatio Alger, wound up in the counting-house, not the White House.

These industrial princes won their positions of power because the times were peculiarly ripe for them. The Civil War stimulated business directly through war contracts and indirectly through increased demands for consumer goods. The farmers, for example, met the sudden shortage of hired hands by buying agricultural machinery in unprecedented quantities. Thus the boom spiraled upward in the postwar years. Behind a high tariff wall which kept out competing European goods, the American manufacturer enjoyed the advantages of a rapidly expanding continental market, while the same friendly government which prevented outside competition gave him ready access to the rich resources of America. He made the most of his many opportunities.

Of the several means of making huge fortunes which began to appear, one of the most important was invention or innovation. New types of machinery, new industrial processes, or new railroads opening up trade areas, all could fill essential demands. They gave the person who controlled them the patronage of the public—and edge over competitors—and this in turn led to profits. Although some selfless inventors thought only of the social benefits their achievements might create, behind each inventor there was likely to be a promoter with visions of profits. C. L. Sholes, the inventor of the typewriter, was of this sort, but James Densmore, who was responsible for Sholes's improvement and development of his invention, was sure that there were "millions in it." And so there were, although Sholes himself got little of the money. Profit might be the motive of the promoter, but men like Sholes were right in predicting that these inventions could make profound changes in American life. The typewriter was a relatively minor invention, but without it and the business machines stemming from it, both big business and big government would have been impossible.

There were scores of significant inventions or innovations: steel rails, bridges, and girders of skyscrapers, elevators, electric lights, electric street railways, gasoline engines, telephones, and new industrial and agricultural machines of every sort. Before 1865, the United States Patent Office issued less than 62,000 patents; during the remainder of the century it issued about 600,000 more. The patent gave its owner a monopoly which he could defend in the courts, and despite much confusion, raiding, and litigation at times, the promoter could often make large profits through manufacturing a patented device which was in large demand. Patent monopoly sometimes provided a strong competitive advantage.

The Evolution of Modern Railroads

MANY OF THE MASTERS of capital operated without patent advantages: the railroad builders, for example. They were of several different types, and an examination of them can give some insight into most American industrial development before the turn of the century. There was old Commodore Cornelius Vanderbilt, who forced consolidation of a number of small, inadequate railroads between New York and Chicago to form the New York Central, which could make large profits because it ran over the best route through a thickly populated area. Then there was Jay Gould, less a builder of railroads than a manipulator of their securities to the detriment of unwary investors. In the West there were those who built lines through areas which for years were not able to provide adequate freight; immediate profits could come, if at all, only from the heavy government subsidies for the building, which were in the form of loans and grants of land. This involved, first, the investment of considerable sums in building good relations with Congress in order to obtain the grants; second, continued lobbying to avoid passage of laws forcing repayment of government loans; and finally, liquidation of land grants in as lucrative a fashion as possible.

Federal and state grants totaled about 184,000,000 acres, about one-tenth of the United States—an area greater than that of France, Switzerland, Belgium, the Netherlands, and Denmark combined. The value at the very least was a half-billion dollars, which was considerably more than the worth of the railroads thus constructed. Defenders of the railroad builders extol their vision, and inquire how else the United States could have obtained the many networks lacing the two coasts and North and South long before the nineties. But the critics of more than one western railroad have wondered how under any conditions the nation could possibly have paid a greater price for more flimsily built lines.

The real worth of the railroads was in making possible the rapid settlement of many otherwise inaccessible areas, and in stimulating the economy through the huge expenditures for construction. In the boom years from 1866 to 1873 when the railway mileage in the United States doubled, these expenditures directly and indirectly created heavy orders for a variety of other American industries. As late as the nineties over a fifth of pig-iron production was going into bars out of which rails were manufactured. Consequently railroad construction as it rose or fell ran slightly ahead of other industrial output, and served as an index of economic conditions in the country as a whole.

With railroads, the first large corporations, leading the way, the economic pattern of industrial America began to emerge. The growth of railroads serves as a good example of the way in which most large scale business developed during this era. Like their counterparts in factories, the first railroad builders were hardy men with a knack for "getting things done." They knew how to deal with laborers, politicians, and local citizens; they could command confidence and open sources of credit; with equal adroitness they could fix a wheezy locomotive or a balky legislator. As railroad problems came to center increasingly around finance—the raising of large sums of capital—power often shifted from engineering promoters like Theodore Judah of the Central Pacific, to financial and legal experts like his partner, Leland Stanford. These railroad financiers sometimes, as in the case of Jay Gould, began new construction to win stock exchange battles as well as to beat out rivals for trade areas. Their financial manipulations, although sometimes detrimental to the public interest, did help develop modern stock exchanges and stimulate the growth of investment banking and security brokerage. Another practice of theirs was an American innovation which has continued to be highly important in industry: many of the lines first constructed were so rickety that when profits came in, the railroads, to the distress of stockholders, used much of the money, not for dividends, but for improvement of the lines. Much corporate construction and expansion has come out of profits.

Although the railroads contributed materially to the national wealth, they engaged in many practices which drew sharp protests from shippers. They did provide transportation service for areas which otherwise could not have existed commercially. But they charged such high rates that shippers in these areas, especially farmers, could barely exist commercially even with the railroads. Rate structures were discriminatory if not predatory. There were some instances where they were as much as four times higher west of the Missouri or south of the Ohio. In sections where railroads enjoyed monopoly conditions they charged as much as the traffic would bear, although this sometimes meant that rates were higher for a short haul than for a long one. They could charge more to haul grain from the Dakotas to Minneapolis than the rate by rail and steamship from Minneapolis to Liverpool. Where natural monopoly did not exist and competition ate into profits, they could form pools to divide the traffic and keep rates up. But then there was too much temptation to gain an advantage and more freight by giving secret rebates to large shippers. Pools consequently failed more often than not, and railroads tried the more effective methods of trusts, holding companies, and mergers as a means of seeking the same monopoly ends. The first American holding company, incidentally, was a creature of the Pennsylvania Railroad, the Southern Railway Securities Company, established in 1869. Its president was James Roosevelt, father of Franklin D. Roosevelt.

By the eighties and nineties, railways that had been daring pioneer enterprises only a decade or so earlier had often become mature economic institutions, complex in organization and operation, representing large investments, and committed to perpetuating a safe return on these. The day of the promoter dedicated primarily to the taking of large risks for great gain was waning, and most railroad executives were slowly making their way up through the ranks, or succeeding to their fathers' fortunes, and were concentrating upon maintaining sound, conservative policies. Bankers increasingly took a hand in this institutionalization. During the depression of the nineties chronically mismanaged railroads went into bankruptcy (as did the Erie, which had been so thoroughly looted by Gould and his cohorts), and only Wall Street bankers could command sums of money large enough to restore them to healthy operating conditions. The bankers were willing to provide the capital, but only if they could protect their investors by participating in the management of the railroads. Thus an investment banker, J. P. Morgan, gained a decisive

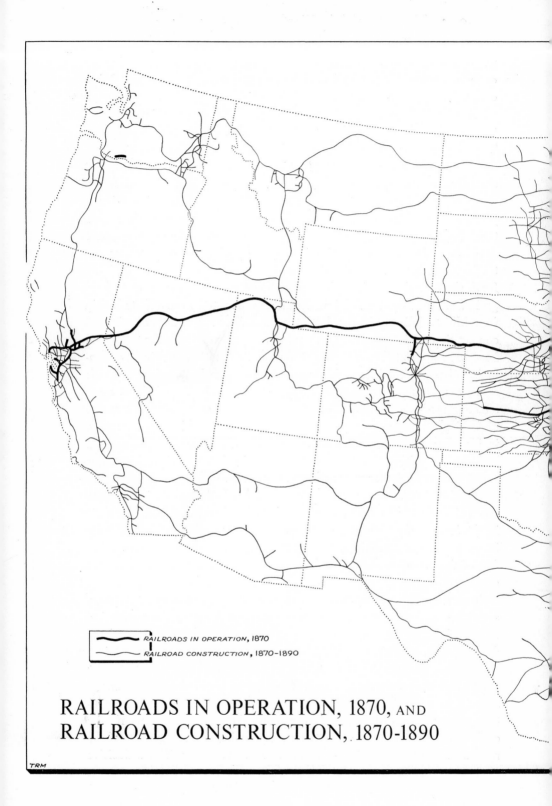

RAILROADS IN OPERATION, 1870, AND
RAILROAD CONSTRUCTION, 1870-1890

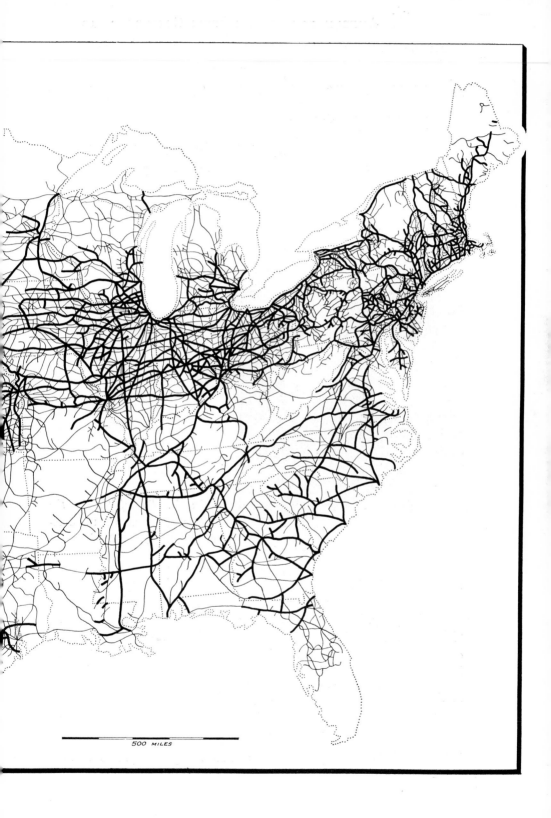

500 MILES

voice in the running of the Erie, and thus Wall Street control came to reach out in every direction and give rise to what reformers in the early 1900's denounced as the "money trust."

The Age of the Trusts

THE CYCLE IN RAILROADS applied to industry as a whole, leading inevitably to concentration and monopoly. Where the innovator or promoter did

John D. Rockefeller in the 1880's (STANDARD OIL COMPANY, NEW JERSEY)

not operate behind the bulwark of a patent or natural monopoly, cutthroat competition could destroy his profits and in time of depression force him into bankruptcy. The way out was to create a monopoly by seizing the "bottleneck" in the industry, whatever this might be, thus getting rid of competitors, and then to raise prices to a highly profitable level. In oil, John D. Rockefeller gained control over transportation and refineries that his competitors had to use and was able to levy or threaten to levy such high charges that in desperation they would sell out to his great Standard Oil trust.

In contrast, Andrew Carnegie became wealthy not through securing a bottleneck, but by selling more iron and steel at greater profits than his competitors through superior salesmanship and lower production costs. If need be, he could sell steel for less than his competitors, because he managed his mills more efficiently and owned the coal mines and coke ovens that supplied them. Then, whenever he had the opportunity, he bought out his rivals. Through building cash reserves in prosperous years, he was able, like most of the other empire builders, to make depressions work for him. Carnegie once explained that, when the Panic of 1873 broke: "So many of my friends needed money, that they begged me to repay them. I did so and bought out five or six of them. That was what gave me my leading interest in this steel business."

By the beginning of the twentieth century, the steel, oil, and other empires were well established, and were following conservative policies that would bring a comparatively modest 10 per cent return on huge investments.

Many people looked askance at the large combinations, fearing that their most conspicuous product was distress rather than prosperity. True, the living standard of the average citizen continued to rise until it was the highest in the world, and for this he could thank the soaring productivity of factories and fields. But consumers felt they were receiving only a relatively small share of the benefits from industrial mechanization and large scale enterprise. Even many middle-class Americans felt this way, and debt-ridden farmers and underpaid laborers had still less reason to be grateful to the large corporations. The Illinois laborer of 1884, earning a dollar and a half a day, had no illusions about Mr. Rockefeller's oil trust, for while bread cost five cents a loaf, and beef roast twelve cents a pound, kerosene for his lamps cost a disproportionately high figure, twenty cents a gallon.

There were vigorous protests against the high railroad rates and monopoly prices from embattled farmers, laborers, and middle-class reformers. Before the turn of the century they were far from successful in their demands because they were seldom able to gain political power. In part this was a failure in methods, in part it stemmed from a reluctance of most Americans to vote for drastic change in the established order.

The fact was that the American people as a whole believed in the system which brought about the domination of the industrialists. Few of these captains of industry during the latter part of the nineteenth century bothered to mask their objectives with sophistries about service or greater good to mankind. They wanted profits, they got profits, and they were generally admired or envied for their success in so doing. For decades most people had no desire to place legal restrictions upon the promoters (except for special sorts of promoters who were doing them personal damage, as the railroad men were doing to the shippers). They favored promoters as a whole because Americans were all promoters at heart. No one was more typical of this spirit than Mark Twain, who brilliantly satirized the land speculation around Cairo, Illinois in his *Gilded Age,* then poured royalties from his books into speculative investment in an invention. He, after all, had all the opportunities of a Rockefeller or a McCormick. If he failed, was it not his own ineptitude as a businessman rather than the system which was to blame? So he reasoned, and so millions of middle-class and laboring-class Americans reasoned.

To add to their traditional faith in profits, individualism, and equality of opportunity, verities in which they had believed since before the election of President Jackson, Americans had a shiny new doctrine to explain why some became multimillionaires while others were penniless. This was Social Darwinism, a concept which was eagerly imported from England where Herbert Spencer, a sort of universal genius, had applied Charles Darwin's biological theory of the survival of the fittest to human affairs. He was attaching the law of the jungle to the existing economic system in a manner which made the system seem divinely ordained. The lions and tigers were delighted, and the rabbits, aspiring to grow as big and powerful as the lions, concurred. Conservatives cited Social Darwinism as an argument for maintenance of the status quo; reformers resorted to the doctrine as a means of urging that a better social order must be evolved.

On the whole, Social Darwinism at this time was a conservative belief. In the struggles of the period, men of small property often opposed those of large property, as did the farmers the railroad presidents, but on occasion both groups co-operated to suppress disorders among the propertyless laborers. Even though the laborers made no threat against the established order comparable to that of the revolutionary proletariat of Europe, citizens of large and small property alike closed ranks against the workers when there were signs of upheaval, as in the Haymarket bombing of 1886 and the Pullman strike of 1894. Middle-class people acclaimed President Grover Cleveland when he called out the troops against the Pullman strikers, and paid little attention to the strikers' serious grievances. As for the agitation of men of small property, it took no more serious form than demands that trusts be dissolved into smaller, competing companies. In other words, the little men favored caging the most ferocious lions, then letting the immutable law of the jungle go on as before.

Social Darwinism was such an effective justification of the actions of the industrial titans that more than one of them took occasion to cite it. Carnegie wrote: "Light came as in a flood and all was clear. . . . 'All is well since all grows better,' became my motto, my true source of comfort." And the pious Rockefeller expounded in a Sunday School address: "The growth of a large business is merely a survival of the fittest. . . . The American Beauty rose can be produced in the splendor and fragrance which bring cheer to its beholder only by sacrificing the early buds which grow up around it. This is not an evil tendency in business. It is merely the working-out of a law of nature and a law of God."

Effects of Industrialization

BOTH THE AMERICAN BEAUTY ROSE of industrialization and the sacrificed buds merit examination. Industrial and technical progress led to the phenomenal growth of American cities as urbanization in America followed close behind that in Europe. In 1860, New York with its 800,000 population (not counting Brooklyn) was next in size to London and

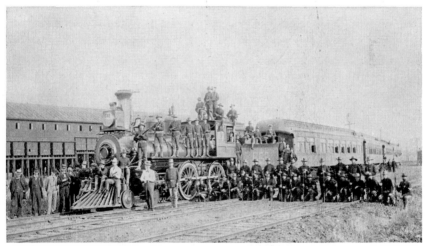

Troops guarding a train during the Pullman Strike (LIBRARY OF CONGRESS)

Paris; Philadelphia was larger than Berlin; but Chicago's population was only 100,000. By 1900, New York (including Brooklyn this time) had 2,500,000 people, which was almost as many as Paris, while Chicago with over 1,000,000 was larger than all but five cities in Europe. Although rural population had merely doubled, that of cities had quadrupled. In 1860, one out of every six persons lived in a city of 8,000 or over; in 1900, one out of every three.

As farm boys swarmed into the cities to seek their fortunes, the cities served as a safety valve to let off some of the steam of rural discontent. There was, and is, a continuing legend, disproven by statistics, that the city was a far more wicked place in which to live. Around melodeons people plaintively sang:

Come, boys, I have something to tell you,
  Come near, I would whisper it low;
You are thinking of leaving the homestead.
  Don't be in a hurry to go.

The city has many attractions,
  But think of the vices and sins,
When once in the vortex of fashion,
  How soon the course downward begins.

Some rural lads no doubt wound up on skid row, and others merely exchanged rural misery for that of the slums. But from these native white Americans who were migrating to cities came a high percentage both of the growing middle class (professional and businessmen) and of the

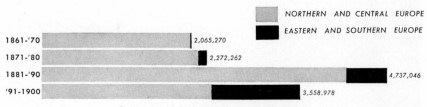

	NORTHERN AND CENTRAL EUROPE
	EASTERN AND SOUTHERN EUROPE
1861-'70	2,065,270
1871-'80	2,272,262
1881-'90	4,737,046
'91-1900	3,558,978

Sources of Immigration, 1861–1900

labor elite (well-paid skilled workers and foremen). These men of farm background maintained many rural ways of thought long after they had been transplanted into the urban civilization. In contrast to these groups which thrived in the cities, millions of non-English speaking immigrants jammed into the slums, and only with difficulty rose out of menial, unskilled, underpaid jobs. For most of the immigrants the fruits of American prosperity were deferred to the next generation.

The cities had many advantages for those fortunate people who earned good livings—not only technological improvements like inside plumbing and telephones, but also, by the end of the century, better sanitary regulations and improved schools. In the cities there was also a flowering of culture of a sort heretofore unknown in America, which existed in Europe only through the patronage of the state or of the wealthy and the nobility. The new American princes of industry, assuming some of the perquisites of European nobility, took over the role of patronage as they endowed universities, hospitals, and symphony orchestras, built libraries, and scoured Europe for art and literary treasures, much of which was trash and some priceless. The first great graduate school and medical school comparable to those in Europe bore the name of a Baltimore distiller, Johns Hopkins, and countless libraries carried the Carnegie name to a

"A Soldier's Farewell" in 1898, showing an American parlor of the period (LIBRARY OF CONGRESS)

generation which had never heard of the Homestead Strike against the lowering of steel workers' wages. This was the American Beauty rose. What of the blighted buds?

First, there was waste. Some present-day economic historians blame it upon the pioneering age rather than the industrial system, but certainly the system did nothing to rectify it. There was the profligate misuse of the natural resources which were so extensive that they seemed beyond possible exhaustion. In the colonial period wood was so commonplace that the colonists applied to its principal product their word for trash, "lumber." This attitude seemed to persist through the decades after the Civil War, even though conservationists were already raising a clamor. In cutting off some of the giant Sequoias in the Sierras, lumbermen wasted 90 per cent of the wood; miners set similar records of despoliation. There was the waste of competitive building of far more mills and factories in boom periods than could operate in a depression, when many stood idle, or were bought up and destroyed by the monopolists. There was the waste of jerry-built railroads and jerry-built cities, and the garish waste of much of the millionaires' expenditures, as in the ornate mansions that existed mainly for conspicuous display. But above all there was the waste of human resources, the waste of so many millions of laborers and farmers condemned to dreary, poverty-stricken lives.

As business grew larger, the bargaining power of the individual workingman declined, and he found it hard to raise his salary or working

The Potter Palmer Mansion, built in Chicago in 1885 (COUR-TESY CHICAGO HISTORICAL SO-CIETY)

conditions even when these cried out for improvement. In 1886, Illinois coal miners were earning an average of only $385.00 per year, which even in an era of five-cent bread and twelve-cent beef roast was scarcely a living wage. There were a fortunate few who could eat steak for breakfast and save a large part of their wages, like the foreman of a roller bar mill outside of Chicago who earned $2,200.00 in 1884. But there were far more who were working as much as sixteen hours a day, seven days a week in Southside sweatshops, sewing trousers for eighteen cents a pair, or finishing coats for four to eight cents each. The average skilled worker in an Illinois factory in 1884 earned less than $2.50 per day; all workers, male and female, adult and child, skilled and unskilled, averaged $1.51 per day.

The workingman may have suffered from deteriorating conditions of work or of life between the Civil War and the Spanish American War, but his wages, while low, remained about constant while prices slowly decreased. He was not content with these conditions, but he seldom turned to a union as the way out. Only one of four Illinois factory workers belonged to a union in 1884. The percentage among all workers was far smaller. The workers themselves, for reasons already suggested, sometimes looked upon unions with suspicion. Some were reluctant to regard themselves as permanent members of a laboring class. There were small class-conscious groups, like the Black International of Chicago, which advocated radicalism and violence, but these were far from representative. Labor movements through American history, typified by the Knights of Labor of the eighties, were marked by a strong interest in middle-class reform, a flirtation with co-operatives or similar schemes, and a reluctance on the part of the leaders to use the strike as a weapon to gain better working conditions. Ordinarily these movements thrived in prosperity years and were wrecked by the first depression. Their principal similarity to more modern labor movements was a tendency toward political action, and that was most likely to drain off into futile third-party movements.

In the nineties a new type of labor movement began to make headway primarily among skilled workers, whose property sense was no less keen than that of other laboring men but who felt they had a valuable possession in their jobs. Earlier, locomotive engineers (who certainly did not aspire to set up railroads for themselves) had formed one of the conservative and long-lived Railroad Brotherhoods. Similarly, in the nineties a variety of skilled craftsmen formed unions which joined together as the American Federation of Labor, a movement following the patterns of organization and operation of the trade unions of Europe. These unionists, holding relatively skilled, well-paid jobs into which it would be difficult to import strikebreakers, aspired only to control their own jobs, not to establish a dictatorship of the proletariat. They did not try to form a third party, and only later, in the early nineteen hundreds, threw their weight to whichever established political party would offer them the most. By 1900, they had become relatively respectable and were well embarked as a lasting force in American history. Still, they embraced only a small part of the working force and had little to offer the large masses of semiskilled and unskilled workers.

In essence, then, by means of craft unions, skilled workers were ready to fight the disadvantages of industrial monopoly by creating monopoly conditions of their own. Labor monopoly might ultimately be able to wrest concessions from industrial monopoly, and perhaps work co-operatively with it.

Agrarian Protest

No such solution seemed possible for the farmer. He was a businessman in that he engaged primarily in the production of goods for the market. Yet because he was so highly individualistic and competitive he had no control over the market. He would not, or could not, band together with other farmers to force monopoly conditions and higher prices. And because the government was under the control of the industrialists, he could not get it to introduce or enforce monopoly conditions and prices for agriculture.

The grievances of the farmer were real enough, although he was usually rather unrealistic in his failure to place the blame in the right quarters. During the Civil War he had been fairly content with his lot because he received high prices, even though manufactured goods were more than proportionately higher. He had mortgaged his land to purchase more land or machinery and had looked to the future with unwarranted optimism. The years that followed from the seventies through the nineties, brought prices that in general were ruinously low. The nadir came when a bushel of wheat that yielded $1.05 in 1870 brought $.49 in 1894, and when the entire cotton crop of 1896, which was six times as large as that of 1866, brought a total of $51,000,000 less.

Basically, the farmer's trouble was that he was overproducing for a world market that was not expanding as rapidly as world farm production. Since he sold the great staples, wheat and meat and cotton, on the world market, the protective tariff was of little use to him. Indeed it guaranteed that while his agricultural products brought low prices, he would have to pay relatively high prices for manufactured goods.

The expected bounty of the Homestead Act proved illusory, since most of the good land in well-watered areas was already gone, and much of the rest for miles on each side of a right-of-way was reserved to the railroads. The West was supposed to function as a safety valve for eastern maladjustments. In popular fancy it was the "Garden of the World," and as the agrarian writer Hamlin Garland pointed out, "All of the associations called up by the spoken word, the West, were fabulous, mythic, hopeful." An historian of agriculture, Fred A. Shannon, has proven by statistical research that the safety valve was no more than an illusion. But it was an important illusion which may well have continued to give hope to many despairing farmers long after any reason for hope was gone. A more important and more real safety valve for them was the city, or, if they stayed on the farm, the rising price of land. It was their only possession which went up in value; obtaining a new and larger mortgage from time to time was what kept some farmers going. By 1890, there were more mortgages than farms in the northern plains states.

It was easy to blame the railroads, which had sometimes turned out to be a scourge rather than a boon. Or the middleman, since the dairy farmer received only about 50 per cent of the consumer's price, and the wheat farmer only 17 per cent. Or the banker, who charged 8 or 12 per cent or more interest on mortgages. Actually, all of these, engaged in the risky business of trying to make money in dealing with poverty-stricken farmers, were sometimes more sinned against than sinning, but in the oratory of the agrarians they all stood condemned as the darkest of villains.

Above all, the farmer tried to bring about inflation, or perhaps one should say that he was trying to end deflation and bring prices back up where they once had been. If he succeeded, he at least would not have to pay back in wheat or cotton too much more on his mortgage than he or his father had borrowed. He hoped to raise prices by getting more money into circulation, and tried first to get legislation to retain or issue paper greenbacks, and then in later years, to mint unlimited quantities of silver dollars. Eastern bankers and merchants denounced as disastrous the agrarian aim to put into circulation fifty dollars per person, although in recent years more than four times this amount per capita has circulated. Since manufactured goods would have advanced in price at least as rapidly as farm commodities, inflation would have offered only limited relief to the farmers' problem, yet the farmers' demand for it was one of the most persistent forces in American history.

In order to obtain inflation, the farmers would have had to gain control of the government and pass enabling legislation. This would be difficult since there were few members of Congress sympathetic toward agrarian demands. In 1870, while 47 per cent of the population derived its living from agriculture, only 7 per cent of the members of Congress had any direct connection with the soil, and many politicians demonstrated a peculiar sensitivity to the requests of industrialists and deafness to those of the farmers.

Political Battles

THE POLITICIANS were not merely the pawns of the industrialists, railroad men, and bankers, although many of them did serve on boards of directors, and almost all of them shared the faith in the Gospel of Wealth and Social Darwinism. At first—during the degrading years of Reconstruction and the Grant regime—politicians from a national down to a city level did seem to function at times as looters and plunderers, indulging in graft and selling legislation to the highest bidder. But this gross age did not last long. Decent people were shocked at revelations of the Tweed Ring, the Gas Ring, and the Whiskey Ring, and corporate leaders felt they were being overcharged for the legislation (or lack of legislation) which they bought. The price could easily become prohibitive; the Central Pacific and later the Southern Pacific had to spend as much as $500,000 per year for lobbying activities.

After 1876 industrialists invested their political funds more prudently. They began to contribute to campaign funds, and in order to hedge, they frequently gave to both parties. This meant that it was not of too much importance to them whether Republicans or Democrats were in office. When, occasionally, the public pressure became too great, Congress would pass some great reform measure, which on careful analysis would turn out to be not much of a reform after all. Thus farmers did get the Bland-Allison Act and the Sherman Silver Purchase Act, neither of which

"History Repeats Itself—The Robber Barons of the Middle Ages and of Today" (Puck, 1889)

brought any real measure of silver inflation. As for the debate over the Sherman Anti-Trust bill, Senator Orville Platt of Connecticut charged:

> The conduct of the Senate . . . has not been in the line of the honest preparation of a bill to prohibit and punish trusts. It has been in the line of getting some bill with that title that we might go to the country with. The questions of whether the bill would be operative, or how it would operate . . . have been whistled down the wind in this Senate as idle talk.

There is scant wonder that by the bleak nineties, many farmers were losing hope of obtaining relief through either major party and were joining a third party, the Populist or Peoples' party. In the farm belt they screamed out their defiance in words that sounded harsh in the East. Mother Lease, the Pythoness of the Prairies, proclaimed in Topeka in

1890, "Wall Street owns the country. It is no longer a government of the people, by the people, and for the people, but a government of Wall Street, by Wall Street, and for Wall Street." Her recommendation was the worst shocker of all: "What you farmers need to do is to raise less corn and more *Hell!*"

The farmers were not alone in suffering acutely during the depression of the nineties. Millions of laboring men were unemployed and, like the farmers, turned to the government in vain. President Cleveland concerned

Mrs. Mary E. Lease (KANSAS STATE HISTORICAL SOCIETY, TOPEKA)

himself with maintaining the credit of the government and the gold standard. When General Jacob Coxey led a march of the unemployed to Washington he was locked up briefly in jail merely for petitioning Congress for a mild sort of work relief program. It appeared when the election of 1896 approached that a combination of workingmen and farmers might win political victory and legislate government aid for themselves. The inflationary or silver forces captured the Democratic party and nominated the young Nebraskan orator, William Jennings Bryan, but the farmers could not muster sufficient labor support. Employed workingmen had little to gain from higher prices, and were frightened by employers' threats of layoffs if Bryan were to win. Consequently, in November the victory went to William McKinley and industrialism.

The depression had frightened many Americans who had not directly suffered from it. For the first time some of them were rather pessimistic about the future, since the great railway network was constructed and its stimulus upon the economy a thing of the past. The historian Frederick Jackson Turner declared the frontier to have been the most significant force in American history, and proclaimed it to be at an end. If it were, where were American industrialists to turn for an expanding market? Would the growing population within the country suffice? And where within the American system were the promoters to find opportunities to take large risks in order to make great profits?

A War of Liberation Leads to Empire

THESE QUESTIONS seemed less important as the country began to recover from the depression soon after the election of 1896, but within two years the Spanish-American War pointed an answer to some of them: one new American frontier lay overseas. Colonial empire could provide a new market for factories, and new opportunities for large profits for the holders of surplus capital.

It was strange that President McKinley, more dedicated to the old order than the new, should establish the bases of the foreign policy of the opening decades of the twentieth century. It was McKinley who reluctantly led the nation into the minor crusade against Spain, forged an American empire out of the spoils of that war, and established an American policy of the Open Door in China. Few presidents have wrought such fundamental changes during their administrations, but because of his caution he has received little attention as a molder of positive policy. Theodore Roosevelt created an indelible image of McKinley when he complained that the President had no more backbone than a chocolate éclair.

The remark was unfair. President McKinley like most Americans was horrified over the destruction, disease, starvation, and carnage being spread by the interminable revolt in Cuba, which lay almost literally at the nation's doorstep. Newspaper accounts, which readers had no way of knowing were grossly exaggerated, claimed that a quarter of the population had already died; the war had begun in 1895 and there was no end in sight. In November, 1897, the Queen Regent of Spain decreed autonomy for Cuba. Rebels, refusing to settle for less than full independence, continued their guerrilla attacks. In Havana and other cities, Spanish-born mobs opposed to independence rioted against even so mild a compromise as autonomy. In the field, neither the Spanish troops nor the Cuban patriots were strong enough to win a clear-cut victory.

As inflammatory newspaper accounts brought public indignation

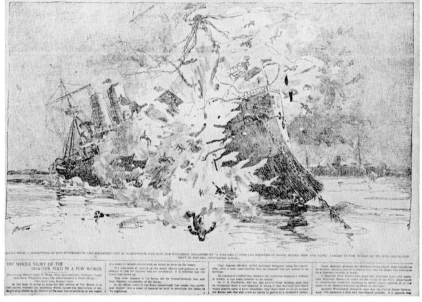
The New York World *a day after the* Maine *blew up*

nearer and nearer to a boiling point, overweighing the cautious counsels
that business leaders were pressing upon Washington, there was the danger that if the Republicans did not act, the Democrats would seize the
issue to win the 1898 election. "If the war in Cuba drags on through the
summer with nothing done," Senator Lodge warned the President, "we
shall go down in the greatest defeat ever known." Further, there seemed
to McKinley the danger that some ambitious European nation might ally
itself with Spain or take advantage of the turmoil in Cuba to intervene elsewhere in the Caribbean. Anarchy in Cuba might be a threat to the Monroe
Doctrine.

Facing these imponderables, McKinley, at the request of the Consul-

General in Havana, sent the battleship *Maine* to Havana harbor on a "friendly visit." Havana was quiet until suddenly on the evening of February 15, 1898, a frightful explosion wrecked the *Maine*, killing 260 of the men aboard. The cause of the explosion was never definitely ascertained—it seems incredible that the Spanish government which was trying to avoid war, was responsible. But this was, in fact, what the American people instantly decided, proclaiming, "Remember the Maine."

On March 26–28, 1898, President McKinley sent in rapid succession three ultimata to Madrid which in total demanded that Spain give full in-

Admiral
George Dewey
(OFFICIAL U.S.
NAVY PHOTO)

dependence to Cuba if it did not wish him to turn the problem over to Congress. Spain did grant an armistice (which would mean little or nothing during the rainy season ahead, when there could be no fighting anyway) but showed no indication that it would at any time concede independence. The American ambassador in Madrid cabled optimistically that independence would follow, but a later scholar, Ernest May, asserts that the administration could see no way of obtaining Cuban independence short of American intervention. So it was that on April 11, McKinley sent a message to Congress asking authority to intervene in Cuba, if need be with armed force. Spain, regarding this as an intolerable insult, severed diplomatic relations. Congress, after several days debate, on April 19 passed a resolution recognizing the independence of Cuba and disclaiming all intention of annexing the island. It authorized the President to use force to liberate Cuba. A formal war declaration followed on April 25.

The Navy, relatively well prepared for the conflict, immediately clamped a blockade around Cuba. In the Pacific, a small squadron under Commodore George Dewey, who had long since been alerted, sailed from Hong Kong to destroy an even weaker Spanish squadron in Manila Bay.

Troops landing at Daiquiri, Cuba (NATIONAL ARCHIVES)

Attacking at daybreak on May 1, the American squadron sank every one of the Spanish vessels without sustaining any serious damage or the death of a single man. When the exciting news reached the United States, President McKinley made the momentous decision to order troops to the Philippines. Had he not done so, Dewey might conceivably have withdrawn later since he had only the tiniest toehold of land at the Cavite naval base. The sending of troops meant that the United States was almost certain to annex at least a base if not the entire archipelago and hence that it would thereafter be a party to Asiatic power politics.

Meanwhile, the blockade of Cuba went badly, since the main Spanish fleet, sent to the Caribbean on an errand of desperation, managed to elude the American searchers and sail safely into the landlocked harbor of Santiago in western Cuba. While the American fleet waited outside the harbor, the War Department hastily sent an expeditionary force of about 16,000 men to capture the city of Santiago and drive the Spanish war-ships out. It was an ill-equipped, utterly mismanaged expedition which escaped disaster only because the Spaniards, while brave, were completely defeatist. The ill-protected transports steamed slowly around Cuba and landed the troops on a mountainous coast without a shot being fired against them. On July 1, the Americans, against fierce opposition, cap-tured the Spanish positions at El Caney and on San Juan hill overlooking Santiago. The troops were decimated but managed to besiege the city. This led the Spanish Governor General of Cuba to order the fleet out of Santi-ago harbor. On July 3, it suddenly popped out single-file, heading west-ward. The pursuing American vessels quickly destroyed them; not a ship escaped. Only one American was killed, and one seriously wounded.

Spain's warmaking potential was gone. In a few days Santiago sur-rendered, and in Puerto Rico, after little fighting, town after town capitu-lated to the American forces. In the Philippines, troops had finally arrived in numbers, but Filipino insurrectionaries under Emilio Aguinaldo had taken over much of the islands long since. Admiral Dewey, after much negotiation with the Spanish commander, on August 13, undertook to fight what was intended to be a bloodless battle for the city of Manila. But the eagerness of the American troops and the energy of the insurrection-aries led to some casualties. At the conclusion, as planned, the Americans were in control of Manila and the resentful Filipino patriots were outside.

Because the cables had been cut, Dewey did not know that the day previously, on August 12, an armistice had been signed. It had come just in time. Troops in camps in the United States were ill with typhoid; in Cuba they were victims of malaria, dysentery, and in a few instances yellow fever. While Spanish bullets accounted for the death of only 460 Americans, disease killed 5,200 men. For the 200,000 men who served in the war, it was a brief but grueling experience, made unnecessarily hard by the confusion and incompetence of the War Department. Men had fought in the tropical heat in heavy woolen uniforms; the ambulances and medical supplies taken to Cuba were grossly inadequate.

Mixed with rejoicing over the defeat of Spain were dark charges against the War Department and hot controversy over which of two naval officers, Admiral William T. Sampson or Commodore William S. Schley, should receive credit for the Santiago victory. The charges against the War Department led to its reorganization between 1900 and 1903 by Secretary of War Elihu Root. He enlarged the regular army to 100,000 men, obtained legislation empowering the Federal government to supervise the National Guard, established a system of officer-training schools, and created a General Staff headed by a Chief of Staff. The Navy, partly because evidence of inefficiency came out of an airing of the Sampson-Schley controversy, underwent a lesser overhaul.

Above all, the end of the Spanish-American War brought a serious debate over imperialism. The United States seemed at a crossroads. Should it imitate the great European powers and acquire a colonial empire with all this would imply? Numerous prominent individuals and groups argued it should not, for a variety of reasons. Some believed holding subject peoples was contrary to the principles of the Declaration of Independence; others feared contamination from the supposedly inferior races. Leaders of labor unions and growers of hemp, tobacco, and sugar feared colonial competition. Pacifists and isolationists pointed to the expense of keeping up imperial defenses and the danger that the United States might be involved in an Asiatic war over the Philippines.

Soon the debate surged only about the Philippines. During the wartime excitement, on July 7, 1898, President McKinley signed an act of Congress ending Hawaii's four-year wait to be annexed. Congress had pledged itself in April not to acquire Cuba; it was a foregone conclusion that Puerto Rico, where there was almost no opposition to annexation, would come under the American flag. The Philippines were different. Aguinaldo and his well-organized followers had hoped the United States was driving out Spain so that they could establish a republic; to hold the islands by force would be to invite a fresh insurrection. But by establishing a strong base in the Philippines, the United States could act so vigorously in the Far East that American business could participate in trade and investment in China. The opportunities in China seemed limitless, and some businessmen who had opposed the war favored keeping the Asiatic spoils. Further, there was the likelihood that if the United States did not annex the Philippines, Germany or another power would, and to nationalists this seemed humiliating. Annexation became popular, and McKinley decided in favor of it. In the Treaty of Paris of December 10, 1898, Spain relinquished her sovereignty over Cuba, and ceded to the United States the Philippines, Puerto Rico, and Guam. The Senate after stiff debate on February 6, 1899, ratified the treaty with only one vote more than the necessary two-thirds.

Two days before the ratification of the treaty, the threatened insurrection in the Philippines broke out. Aguinaldo turned his guerrilla tactics against the Americans with marked success, and in desperation the American troops resorted to Spanish cruelties such as the use of the "water cure" to obtain information, and herded Filipinos into concentration camps. Liberals in the United States, protesting in horror when they learned of these tactics, forced reforms. It was not until 1901 that Aguinaldo was captured by a ruse and the rebellion ended. It had cost far more in money and lives than the Spanish-American War. One result of the insurrection was that the United States established a civil government in the Philippines that began slowly to take the Filipinos along the road to self-govern-

Filipino Insurrectionary Troops (NATIONAL ARCHIVES)

ment, ultimately to independence. By 1913, all the governors of the Christian provinces, 92 per cent of the teachers, 71 per cent of the classified civil service, and four of the nine-man upper house of the legislature were Filipinos.

Both the Philippines and Puerto Rico were governed much as Great Britain had once ruled the thirteen colonies. The governor and upper house of the legislature were appointed from Washington while the lower house was elected in the colony. But Congress was less generous than Parliament had once been, and never conferred United States citizenship upon the Filipinos, and only in 1917 upon Puerto Ricans. The Supreme Court was still less generous, and by complicated reasoning in the Insular cases of 1900–1904, decided that the Constitution did not follow the flag unless Congress so decided. During the Progressive era, Congress did not extend the Constitution to the Philippines and Puerto Rico, but did extend it to Hawaii and Alaska whose inhabitants were granted United States citizenship in 1900 and territorial government in 1912. It was not until 1959 that Alaska and Hawaii became states.

The Open Door for China

ONE OF THE STRONG REASONS for annexing the Philippines had been to maintain equality of commercial opportunities in China. These opportunities seemed seriously imperiled at the end of the century as the European powers and Japan wrested "spheres of influence" and concessions from the weak, chaotic Chinese imperial government. Economically this might have meant the partitioning of China and the exclusion of all but the nationals of each great power from economic activity within its given sphere. The British, who because their trade and investments were larger had even more to lose than the Americans, were anxious to see some halt called. An interested Englishman convinced the advisor to John Hay, President McKinley's Secretary of State, that the United States should call upon the great powers to subscribe to an Open Door policy. Thus it was that Hay in 1899 addressed identical notes to England, Germany, and Russia, and later to France, Japan, and Italy, asking each of them to subscribe to these principles, "eminently beneficial to the commercial interests of the whole world":

> First. The recognition that no power will in any way interfere with any treaty port or any vested interest within any leased territory or within any so-called "sphere of interest" it may have in China.
> Second. That the Chinese treaty tariff of the time being shall apply to all merchandise landed or shipped to all such ports as are within said "sphere of interest". . . . no matter to what nationality it may belong, and that duties so leviable shall be collected by the Chinese Government.
> Third. That [each power] will levy no higher harbor dues . . . and no higher railroad charges . . . on merchandise belonging to citizens or subjects of other nationalities transported through such "sphere" than shall be levied on similar merchandise belonging to its own nationals. . . .

Each of the powers except Russia, which was evasive, sent only a qualified acceptance. Hay, in a move hailed within the country as being brilliant, then sent the powers a second note, declaring that since they had all accepted the Open Door principle, the United States considered their adherence "final and definitive."

An antiforeign uprising in China in the summer of 1900, led by a Chinese secret society known as the Fists of Righteous Harmony, or the Boxers, laid siege to the entire foreign diplomatic corps in the British embassy in Peking. The powers hastily raised an expeditionary force, to which the United States contributed 2,500 men. By August, the siege was lifted, but China was in peril of being partitioned in punishment. Hay again took action, urging the powers to extend the Open Door policy not only to their spheres of influence but to all of the Chinese Empire. Further, the United States, he declared, sought a solution which would preserve the territorial integrity of China. With the backing of Great Britain and Germany, he persuaded the other powers to accept a money indemnity rather than demand new spheres of influence from China. The American share of the indemnity, almost $25,000,000, far exceeded damage done. The United States returned the surplus to the Chinese government, which for many years drew upon it to educate Chinese students in the United States.

In the years that followed, the United States again and again protested against threatened foreign encroachments upon Chinese sovereignty. Other nations did not seem to have committed themselves to much of anything in their answers to Hay's notes, but the United States had added the Open Door in China to the Monroe Doctrine as a basic tenet of its foreign policy. Most Americans, feeling a benevolence toward China reinforced by reports from the missionaries they maintained there, felt pride in Hay's achievements without taking assessment of the risks the nation was assuming in trying to block the aggressions of the great powers in the Far East. They did not weigh the responsibilities against the possible advantages.

Thus it was that before the United States had even entered the twentieth century, it had made some of the most serious of commitments in foreign policy; there would be important consequences to face in decades ahead. As yet there had been no such important shifts in domestic policy. The defeat of Bryan in the election of 1896 had postponed a settlement of the demands for reform by the farmers, laborers, and the middle class—a backlog which made up the agenda of the Progressive era. And in this new age, the politician as well as the industrialist was to become a key figure.

Chapter 2

TECHNICS AND REFORM

THE GREAT QUESTION that faced the American people as they entered the twentieth century was: How could they retain or regain their traditional moral values in an era of rapid technical advance? How could they obtain the high living standards and cultural riches that industrialization could produce without losing much that they cherished in the old order? How could they preserve for the individual his economic opportunity, his right to lead a dignified, decent life? Did this mean, as so many reformers thought at this time, that they must return to the sort of laissez faire individualism that had worked more or less well in an earlier, less complicated society? Or did it mean some new accomodations to the rapid course of industrialization and urbanization?

National prosperity was the dominant note in 1900; the Republican candidates, William McKinley and Theodore Roosevelt, won decisively on the slogan "Four Years More of the Full Dinner Pail." Nevertheless, there was an uneasiness among many of the successful, middle-class young men who for the most part had voted for McKinley—men who were to become the leaders of the progressive movement. In order to understand their uneasiness and their later actions, it is necessary to examine first the rapidly accelerating technical civilization they viewed with intermingled pride and misgivings, then some of the maladjustments the civilization was producing, and finally how they and various other groups of people who coalesced under the banners of progressivism hoped to rectify these maladjustments.

Toward a Technical Millenium

THE VAST CHANGES that had taken place in the United States following the Civil War, as has already been seen, resulted from ever accelerating technical advance. Technics promised still more change in the future. In 1904 Henry Adams, a detached sexagenarian, looked back over his own lifetime and remembered seeing the development of the ocean steamer, the railway, and the telegraph. Might not the next six decades bring still more change? Adams wrote in his famous autobiography, *The Education of Henry Adams:*

> He could see that the new American—the child of incalculable coal-power, chemical power, electric power, and radiating energy, as well as of new forces yet undetermined—must be a sort of God compared with any former creation of nature. At the rate of progress since 1800, every American who lived into the year 2000 would know how to control unlimited power. He would think in complexities unimaginable to an earlier mind. He would deal with problems altogether beyond the range of earlier society.*

Whether the American would be able to control the power, to think in the requisite complexities, or cope with the new problems seemed far from certain two generations later. To well-educated men of the early 1900's, however, the complexities seemed less overwhelming. With a simple faith, they regarded the scientific approach as the key to the ready solution of the manifold problems marring American civilization. They were hopeful that the nation was rushing toward a technical millenium. Most reformers still believed in Social Darwinism—the idea of the survival of the fittest applied to human society—and almost all of them considered this an optimistic faith. It meant in part that, through the application of science and technology, what was new and superior would drive out what was old and inferior. The scientists, engineers, and inventors would lead the way.

American technical achievements by the beginning of the twentieth century were impressive. The steel furnaces of the United States had already for a decade outproduced those of any other nation in the world, and functioned with such efficiency and low cost that Carnegie could have sold steel rails at a profit in Birmingham, England. In the factories the new era

---

* Henry Adams, *The Education of Henry Adams* (Boston: Houghton Mifflin, 1918) pp. 496–97.

meant the rapid introduction of labor-saving machinery. A bottle-making machine patented in 1903 virtually eliminated the hand-blowing of glass bottles; another invention mechanized the production of window glass. A rotating kiln first manufactured in 1899 soon produced huge quantities of cheap, standardized Portland cement, for which the growing movement for paved highways helped provide a ready market.

The nation was shifting to electric power. The first 5,000 horsepower alternating-current generator had been installed at Niagara Falls in 1895,

The Wright Brothers making their first flight (OFFICIAL U.S. AIR FORCE PHOTO)

and within a few years steam generators of 100,000 horsepower had become commonplace. Electricity was entering the home, but even more important, it was becoming a great new source of efficient industrial motive power. In 1899 electricity ran only 5 per cent of the machinery; by 1919, 55 per cent; by 1925, 73 per cent. Large-scale electric power also made possible electrolytic processes in the rapidly developing heavy chemical industry.

A communications revolution, essential to the more efficient conduct of business, was already under way. The Bell system operated 677,000 telephones at the turn of the century; by 1915 the number was nearly 6,000,000, and coast-to-coast lines were in operation. Radio was in its infancy. In 1901 the Italian inventor, Guglielmo Marconi, flying a kite aerial in Newfoundland, caught signals from Cornwall, England. The next year the Marconi Wireless Telegraph Company of America was established, and by 1910 all large ships were equipped with radios.

A transportation revolution was also beginning. In 1903, the Wright Brothers made their first flight at Kitty Hawk, North Carolina. It lasted only twelve seconds and was for a distance less than the wing span of the largest airplanes of fifty years later. Automobiles were in a relatively advanced stage of development: after having been outdistanced by Europeans, Americans by 1900 were producing 4,000 a year. Yet automobiles

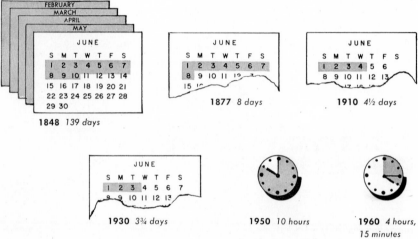

New York to San Francisco, 1848–1960

were still novel enough that perhaps half the population had not seen one. In 1899 William Allen White brought one by rail to Emporia, Kansas, for a street fair—supposedly the first to cross the Missouri River. There had been only four automobiles on the American highways in 1895; by 1917 there were nearly 5,000,000, and the automobile was beginning to remake American life. At the close of the progressive era, automobiles were commonplace among upper-middle-class families, just as telephones were almost essential in middle-class homes.

It was especially in the automobile industry that the new principles of scientific management of production began to find their most spectacular application. This began with the work of an engineer, Frederick Winslow Taylor, who helped revolutionize the machine-tool industry with carbon steel high-speed cutting edges. As soon as Taylor learned how to manufacture tools which could cut efficiently while running white hot, he began to insist that machinists operate their lathes at correspondingly fast speeds. What in effect Taylor was doing was to apply the same sort of scientific techniques to management as to machinery. At first he looked upon work-men much as he did at machines, integrating them into a more efficient in-dustrial system. Fewer men could perform simpler tasks at infinitely greater speed; if not, Taylor would discard them as unhesitatingly as he had the poorer cutting steel.

The whole new industrial system sometimes referred to as Taylorism, based as it was on specialization of men and machines, meant less need for skills among workmen and more monotonous tasks for them. At first organized labor rebelled, and won at least a minor victory when it per-

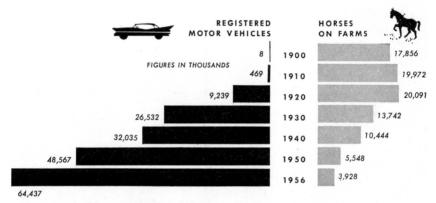

	REGISTERED MOTOR VEHICLES		HORSES ON FARMS	
	8	1900		17,856
FIGURES IN THOUSANDS	469	1910		19,972
	9,239	1920		20,091
	26,532	1930		13,742
	32,035	1940		10,444
	48,567	1950		5,548
	64,437	1956		3,928

Motor Vehicles, and Horses on Farms, 1900–1956

suaded Congress in 1915 to forbid the introduction of efficiency systems into government arsenals or navy yards.

Taylor and his followers regarded themselves as scientific seekers after higher production, and thus after a higher living standard. Before the turn of the century, Taylor had taken a rather ruthless Social Darwinian view. Only one pig-iron handler in eight could make good under his system, but Taylor had felt only the fittest should survive. "All employees should bear in mind," he had written, "that each shop exists, first, last, and all the time for the purpose of paying dividends to its owners. They should have pa-tience and never lose sight of this fact." But by the middle of the progres-sive era, Taylor was talking in more persuasive terms of the greatest good for the entire populace, including even the workers. Indeed, if scientific management were used to eliminate the intolerable inefficiencies in many industries, it could mean not only lower prices for consumers but also higher wages for workers. By the twenties some unions recognized this and were cooperative. As staunch a progressive as Louis D. Brandeis, in argu-ing against a rise in freight rates, asserted that through efficiency systems the railroads could save a million dollars a day.

Industrialists, usually ready to try new techniques, increasingly undertook Taylor scientific management studies of workers' motions. They also brought scientists and engineers into their plants to engage in research for new tools and products. A few years earlier any industrialist who had established a laboratory would have been looked upon as a crackpot. Now laboratories became accepted, partly due to the urging of engineers, partly because of the phenomenal success of some of the pioneering ones. There was, as every schoolboy could proudly cite, the industrial laboratory of

An early industrial laboratory, 1908 (DU PONT)

Thomas A. Edison at Menlo Park, New Jersey, out of which came the incandescent lamp, the phonograph, and scores of other devices. By 1913, Bell Telephone, Du Pont, General Electric, Eastman Kodak, and about fifty other companies had established laboratories with budgets totaling hundreds of thousands of dollars per year.

Out of these new methods and machines came mass production. It required the technology, large supply of raw materials, excellent transportation, and huge markets that the United States could supply in the twentieth century. Specialized precision manufacturing made possible interchangeability of parts even in assembling a machine as complicated as an automobile. Henry Ford began with stationary assembly, earlier used in manufacturing guns, clocks and the like, then gradually changed by 1914 to subdivision of the work and the use of the assembly line. This revolutionary technique cut the time for assembling a Ford chassis from twelve and a half hours to an hour and a half. Mass production had come to the automobile industry. While Ford raised the wages and lowered the hours of his workers, he gradually cut the base price of his Model T from $950 to $290. Other industrialists, following his example, rapidly adopted the assembly line and mass production.

The Ford Assembly Line (FORD MOTOR COMPANY)

By 1914, American manufacturers were producing 76 per cent more goods than in 1899. They were doing so with only 36 per cent more workers, and 13 per cent more establishments. The greater output of goods reflected the rising living standards and the growth of population at home and increased markets abroad. The lower increase in workers demonstrated the greater efficiency of the new technical age; the very low increase in establishments pointed to the rapid growth of industrial concentration.

The Menace of Monopoly

PROGRESSIVE AMERICANS were well aware of the assets and liabilities of twentieth-century industrialism. President Wilson once summed up their thinking when he remarked, "I am for big business and I am against the trusts." What he meant was that he was proud of the size and efficiency of the new corporations, but fearful of their tendencies toward consolidation.

Monopolies could lead to higher prices and higher profits, which were often the basic reasons for the creation of combinations. (Their promoters argued the reverse, that they led to greater efficiency, lower prices, and a higher living standard.) Furthermore, the monopolists could use their great economic strength to wield proportionately great political power. This also the progressives feared.

Despite all the agitation of the progressives in the years between the Spanish-American War and World War I, American industry moved toward greater consolidation and monopoly. Neither the Republican President Benjamin Harrison nor the Democratic Grover Cleveland had demonstrated the slightest real interest in enforcing the Sherman Anti-Trust Act of 1890. With the return of prosperity in 1897, and William McKinley, a businessman's friend, in the White House, combinations began to take shape at a spectacular rate. The Wall Street financiers helped create one giant holding company after another. These gained control over manufacturing and the market by a variety of means: by monopolizing the supply of raw materials, in the case of aluminum; by securing basic machinery patents, in the making of glass bottles; or by sheer overwhelming size, in steel.

From 1887 to 1897 there had been only 86 industrial combinations, and the capitalization of all of these combined had been less than a billion and a half dollars. By 1904, John Moody tabulated 318 so-called trusts with a capitalization of over seven billion dollars. Thus about three-fourths of the combinations with six-sevenths of the capital came into existence at the beginning of the progressive era. They included basic industries like copper, oil, and steel, and industries directly affecting the consumer like sugar and tobacco. Six financial groups controlled 95 per cent of the nation's railway mileage. In the highly competitive steel industry, twenty-one significant mergers between 1898 and 1901 prepared the way for a large scale struggle between Carnegie and J. P. Morgan. When Carnegie announced plans for plants that might be ruinous to Morgan and his associates, they chose to buy him out at his own inflated figure of $447,000,-000, and they then established the nation's first billion-dollar corporation, United States Steel. Although the tangible value of its property was an estimated $682,000,000, it was capitalized at $1,402,847,000. This meant that all of the common stock and a quarter of the preferred stock was "water" with no assets behind it. Yet the earning power of the new behemoth was so great that except for two years it was able to pay dividends upon its common stock. Through a "base-point" system it was able to set standard prices for steel everywhere in the United States—prices from which none of the smaller steel companies dared to deviate.

Whatever pride progressives might have felt over the emergence of these industrial giants was mingled with serious misgivings. It was all too apparent that, regardless of the efficiencies these combinations might effect, often they did not lead to important savings for the consumers. The United States Industrial Commission reported in 1902, "In most cases the combination has exerted an appreciable power over prices, and in practically all cases it has increased the margin between raw materials and finished products. Since there is reason to believe that the cost of production over a period of years has lessened, the conclusion is inevitable that the combinations have been able to increase their profits."

Monopolies may not have raised prices to consumers during the progressive years, but they certainly failed to pass on savings. Whether or not monopolies were to blame, prices were rising so rapidly between 1897 and 1913 that altogether the cost of living went up about 35 per cent. This dismayed progressive Americans. For the considerable number of them who were on fixed incomes, the price rise worked a real hardship. Even for those whose incomes increased, it was irritating, coming as it did after prices had fallen slowly for a generation. They felt that the price increases were eating up their gains and keeping them from advancing economically. Thus higher prices did much to give strong economic incentive to the progressive movement, which came in years of relative prosperity.

To a comparatively minor extent, the public blamed the rising cost of living upon the new labor unions. Consumers winced when the settlement of the coal strike of 1902 forced them to pay substantially more for anthracite. Above all, people blamed industrial consolidation. The handful who pored through the thousands of pages of hearings and findings of the Industrial Commission, published in 1901, and the multitudes who looked at the cartoons in the Hearst newspapers, with their bloated, greedy figures labeled "Trusts," were nearly unanimous in feeling that something was wrong with the economic order.

The Agenda for Reform

POPULISTS, socialists, and the relative few who had followed reform theoreticians like the single-taxer Henry George and the utopian Edward Bellamy no longer were alone in proclaiming that the American economic system was in need of reform. Even the thoroughly conservative Judge Peter S. Grosscup, who had issued the injunction to help break the Pullman strike of 1894, proclaimed in 1905 that the modern corporation was destroying the opportunity for the individual to participate in the proprietorship of the country. This was the recurring complaint of the middle class: that the industrial behemoths had seized political and economic power, and were smothering individual opportunity.

For men like Judge Grosscup this may have been no more than a moral abstraction; for millions of Americans the economic order which had developed since the Civil War meant personal poverty and misery. There was a disparity between the incomes of the wealthy few and the poor multitudes which seemed incredible a half century later. One per cent of the American families owned nearly seven-eights of the wealth; seven-eighths of the families owned only one-eighth. While a fifth of the families were comfortable or even rich, four-fifths lived precariously. A careful

Andrew Carnegie about 1890 (UNITED STATES STEEL CORPO-RATION)

estimate in 1904 indicated that about one-eighth of the people, or a total of ten million, lived in poverty.

The incomes of a handful at the top were enormous. Between 1894 and 1899, Carnegie earned an estimated $10,000,000 per year from his steel company, culminating in earnings of $23,000,000 in 1900. On none of this did he have to pay a cent of income tax. While Carnegie lived comparatively modestly and devoted his millions to worthy causes, many of the very rich created sensational headlines through their ostentatious living. The Vanderbilts, like a clan of feudal barons, maintained, in addition to their many country estates, seven mansions in seven blocks on Fifth Avenue.

These wealthy few often spent incredible sums on parties, accounts of which fascinated, but also angered, readers of yellow journals. The most notorious was the ball upon which Mrs. Martin Bradley spent $250,000; it created such a furor that she and her husband fled to exile in England. A less exceptional dinner, served on gold plates at the old Waldorf-Astoria in 1899, cost $10,000 for forty people, or $250 apiece. At that time, $250 was six months' wages for the average workingman.

In part, the millionaires were able to earn their huge incomes because of the low cost of labor in their factories, and to afford their huge estates and townhouses through the low cost of servants. The middle class, too, benefited from cheap labor. While they did not enjoy the great variety of household appliances of later generations, they were able with the aid of servants to maintain large homes. When Professor Woodrow Wilson was trying to persuade Frederick Jackson Turner of the University of Wisconsin to come to Princeton in 1896, Mrs. Wilson set up a sample budget for a professor on a $3,500-a-year salary. It included two servants, who together would receive $29.00 a month.

Although servants often earned no more than $3.50 or $4.50 a week, at least they were entitled to meals and unheated garret rooms. Working girls could not count upon even these. One woman in five worked, and often for wages as low as $6.00 or $8.00 a week. Unless a girl lived at home, it was almost impossible for her to exist upon these wages. O. Henry was reflecting the widespread indignation of progressive America when he described in his short stories how strong the temptation was for these nearly starving girls to succumb to predatory men. Late in the progressive era, advocates of a minimum wage law to protect women created a sensation in Chicago by bringing several women to a hearing to testify that low pay and poverty had driven them to prostitution. Nevertheless, the Illinois legislature failed to enact a law.

Child labor, which had always existed in the United States, was becoming an increasingly serious problem by the early 1900's. At least 1,700,000 children under sixteen were employed in factories and fields. Ten per cent of the girls between ten and fifteen years old, and 20 per cent of the boys, were gainfully employed. At least 38 states had laws to protect children, but these typically applied only to children employed in factories, and set a minimum age of twelve years and a maximum workday of ten hours. Sixty per cent of the child workers were employed in agriculture, which could mean a twelve-hour day picking or hoeing in the fields. In the cotton mills of the South, children working at the looms all night were kept awake by having cold water thrown in their faces. In canneries, little girls cut fruits or vegetables sixteen hours a day. Some children worked at dangerous machines without safety devices. As these young workers became exhausted at the end of a long day, or night, they might become careless as they leaned over a loom to retie broken threads, have their hair caught in the machinery, and be scalped as it suddenly started up again.

Industrial accidents were commonplace. For most laborers, whether children, women, or men, working conditions were far from ideal. Many women labored in dark, cold, dirty factories or sweatshops without restrooms or fire escapes. For men, working conditions were even worse. As early as 1877, Massachusetts had required safety devices upon elevators and machinery; some states also required mine inspection. But there was little effective enforcement of the laws, if indeed personnel for enforcement existed. In American factories and mines, and on the railroads, the accident rate was higher than in any other industrial nation in the world. In 1901, one railroad employee in 399 was killed, and one in 26 injured. As late as 1907 an average of twelve railroad men a week were killed. In factories, little had been done to prevent occupational diseases such as phosphorus and lead poisoning. Nor was there economic incentive for employers to improve working conditions. Under the common law, if an accident was due to the negligence of an employee himself or a fellow employee, the employer bore no responsibility. Even if the employer were liable under the common law, the courts were slow, and often too expensive for the maimed worker or his widow. Until 1911 there were almost no state workmen's compensation laws.

Cheap labor was one of the reasons for high profits; unrestricted immigration seemed one of the reasons for cheap labor. At the same time that the big industrialists fought against a lowering of the tariff bars, they welcomed in, or even recruited, the low-paid workers of Europe. While the flow of the "old immigrants" from northern and western Europe continued, a new flood, comprising about 72 per cent of the total between 1900 and 1910, poured in from southern and eastern Europe. For the most part they were Italians, Slavs, and Jews. In the single year 1905, over 1,250,000 arrived. In most big cities of the North, immigrants and their children outnumbered the native-born. Bewildered at being thrust into an alien culture, living under conditions far below the level of native Americans (except Negroes), they filled most of the backbreaking unskilled jobs in the new heavy industries, on the railroads, and around the cities. The Jews, many of whom brought their skill with the needle, went into the garment trade, but under just as wretched circumstances.

A United States Immigration Commission report in 1910 claimed on the basis of doubtful evidence that immigrants were depressing the labor market. Isaac A. Hourwitch, who himself had been an immigrant, in reply argued cogently that new labor-saving machines were responsible for the displacement of skilled workers. It was only coincidental that the bulk of

"The Steerage" by *Alfred Stieglitz* (COURTESY MISS GEORGIA O'KEEFFE FOR THE ALFRED STIEGLITZ ESTATE; COLLECTION MUSEUM OF MODERN ART)

the low-paid unskilled workers hired into the factories were immigrants. Nevertheless, both middle-class reformers and union leaders widely believed that unrestricted immigration was to blame.

The American Federation of Labor (whose president, Samuel Gompers, also had been an immigrant) fought to cut off this flood of cheap, unskilled foreign labor, which, it claimed, was keeping wages down and

Mulberry Street, New York City (LIBRARY OF CONGRESS)

hampering unionization. Many Americans, both conservative and progressive, were susceptible to the popular dogma of Anglo-Saxon superiority, and joined in the anti-immigration movement. They feared the high birth rate among immigrants as compared with the low birth rate among natives in the higher-income groups; Theodore Roosevelt warned darkly against "race suicide." They tended to blame the squalor of the slums and the power of the political bosses upon the immigrants, and feel that through restriction could come improvement. In 1907, they succeeded in stopping the immigration of Japanese to the agricultural lands of the Pacific Coast through the "gentleman's agreement" that Roosevelt negotiated with the Japanese government. A series of restrictive laws prohibited various undesirables, ranging from ex-convicts to alcoholics, from entering the United States. In 1917, over the veto of President Wilson, Congress passed a law setting up a literacy test as a means of reducing the number of immigrants.

The attitude of many progressives and mild conservatives was not wholly negative, for they wished to Americanize the newcomers through teaching them English and civics. Within the cities, the social-justice movement focused upon immigrants, not because they were foreign, but because they were poverty-stricken and exploited. Progressives read with sympathy *The Promised Land* (1912), the autobiography of Mary Antin, whose Jewish family had escaped from oppression in Russia, or novels like Willa Cather's *O Pioneers* (1913), dramatizing the heroic struggles of immigrants on the prairies. To many immigrants this interest seemed offensively patronizing, and as much as possible they continued to follow the secure and familiar old-country ways. Their children were much readier to accept new ways and, growing up as Americans, fought to break away from slum living conditions.

For all those, immigrant or native, crowded into city tenements, life was far from enviable. Jacob Riis, the crusading journalist, thought that by 1900 the worst of the New York slums were gone. In their place were a scattering of parks and playgrounds; in some of the worst remaining areas there were privately financed settlement houses to aid the poor. Nevertheless, for millions of city dwellers, housing was barely tolerable. In New York City, two-thirds of the city's three and a half millions lived in tenement houses. Most of them, while by no means slum dwellings, were of the "dumbbell" type, which provided direct light and air for only four rooms of the fourteen on each floor. A report on Boston slums in 1899 applied equally to the blighted areas in every big city: "Dirty and battered walls and ceilings, dark cellars with water standing in them, alleys littered with garbage and filth, broken and leaking drain-pipes, . . . dark and filthy water closets, . . . and houses so dilapidated and so much settled that they are dangerous."

Nor was there any protection for the consumer from insanitary or harmful foods and drugs. The advance of science brought, along with the marvels, many harmful preservatives and adulterants. Much meat and milk was processed or sold under revoltingly dirty conditions. Medicines, purportedly cures for almost any disease from tuberculosis to cancer, contained little but bright coloring, a bitter flavor, and a copious lacing of

Slum dwellers in a tenement room, about 1910 (JACOB A. RIIS COLLECTION, MUSEUM OF THE CITY OF NEW YORK)

alcohol. Syrups did, as they advertised, soothe babies, thanks to the narcotics they contained.

Along with these immediate dangers to the American public were the long-range threats implicit in the reckless exploitation of natural resources, the wasteful and destructive cutting of timber, the pouring of industrial poisons into streams, and the over-grazing or improper cultivation of fields. Hillsides eroded to clog rivers and increase the threat of alternating drouth and flood.

"Our life contains every great thing, and contains it in rich abundance," the new progressive President, Wilson, pointed out in his first inaugural in 1913. The irony was that with the good had come unnecessary evil:

With riches has come inexcusable waste. We . . . have not stopped
to conserve the exceeding bounty of nature. . . . We have been proud
of our industrial achievements, but we have not hitherto stopped thought-
fully enough to count the human cost. . . . The great Government we
love has too often been made use of for private and selfish purposes, and
those who used it had forgotten the people.

The Progressives

WHERE FROM among the American people could there come a movement
forceful and persistent enough to overcome the entrenched economic
power which maintained disgraceful conditions? Populists had vented
their indignation against many of the same evils and had proposed some
concrete remedies. But Populism had been limited largely to the distressed farmers of the West and South. Now, the farmers were enjoying
a renewed prosperity. A traveler reported, "Every barn in Kansas and
Nebraska has had a new coat of paint." Populism and the conditions which
had nurtured it seemed burned out. Yet from its ashes in the prosperous
early 1900's came progressivism, a great drive to destroy the evils of the
machine age and revitalize American political and economic democracy.
It was a vigorous combination of economic determinism and religious
morality. Progressives, to a greater extent than any preceding generation
since the Founding Fathers, were willing to accept an economic interpretation of politics, yet they were emphatic in viewing economic questions
in moral terms. They were proud of the speed with which their nation
had grown, and as the rate of change continued to accelerate, they hoped
to direct America's burgeoning industrial might upward toward lofty
moral ends. They aspired to make the American dream come true within a
measurably few years. William Allen White, the Kansas progressive,
once commented that the progressive leaders had "caught the Populists in
swimming and stole all of their clothing except the frayed underdrawers of
free silver." What was more to the point, the farmers themselves, as prices
rose, discarded the silver issue that had so horrified the East, and by so
doing were able to enter into at least a tenuous alliance with the city middle-class leaders to fight for a wide variety of reforms.

The changed attitude toward reform on the part of White, who was
himself essentially a representative of the urban middle class, indicated
what had happened. He had made his national reputation in the nineties by
penning for the Emporia *Gazette* an editorial entitled, "What's the Matter
with Kansas?" White's vehement answer had been, "The Populists!" He
had written sarcastically: "We don't need population, we don't need
wealth, we don't need well-dressed men on the streets, we don't need cities
in the fertile prairies; you bet we don't! . . . Because we have become

poorer and ornerier and meaner than a spavined, distempered mule, we, the people of Kansas, propose to kick; we don't care to build up, we wish to tear down." In this vein, as the champion of respectability, White and most of his kind had campaigned for McKinley and gloried in the defeat of William Jennings Bryan. Yet White a few years later had become an ardent convert to progressivism, ready to look critically upon his earlier self as "a young arrogant protagonist of the divine rule of the plutocracy." The fact was that White's objectives had not changed. He still wanted wealth, well-dressed men, and cities on the prairies; he had come to view the progressive movement as the means of securing them. A large number of farmers with new painted barns agreed.

So it was with a host of progressive leaders. They were collectively from the urban middle class, to a remarkable extent college-educated self-employed professional men or small businessmen, of native-born Protestant background. For the most part they were about forty years old, financially secure civic leaders who had earlier been McKinley Republicans.

Several studies support these conclusions. Alfred D. Chandler, Jr., examined the social, political, and occupational backgrounds of 260 leaders of the Progressive party of 1912—people who were national committeemen or state chairmen, or who gave time and money. He found 95 businessmen, 75 lawyers, 36 editors, 19 college professors, 7 authors, 6 professional social workers, and a scattering of men in several professions. Only one was a labor-union leader; there was not a single farmer, white-collar worker, or salaried manager for one of the new large-scale corporations. On the whole, Chandler observes, the progressive leaders had retained an individualism free from the restraints of the new corporate institutionalism, and thus represented, "in spite of their thoroughly urban backgrounds, the ideas of the older, more rural America." *

Following these men was a middle class, like their leaders still clinging to the traditional agrarian values, but caught up in the social whirlpool of the new industrial age. The older segment of the middle class, the independent professional and businessmen from which such a high proportion of progressive leaders came, somewhat more than doubled between 1870 and 1910. This meant it grew as rapidly as the population as a whole, which increased about two and a third times. The working class (including farm laborers) trebled; farmers and farm tenants doubled. But there was another group, a new middle class of white-collar workers—the clerks, sales people, and technicians who worked for corporations or service enterprises. It increased almost eight times, from 756,000 to 5,609,000 peo-

---

* Elting E. Morison (ed.), *The Letters of Theodore Roosevelt* (Cambridge: Harvard University Press, 1954), vol. 8, pp. 1462–65.

ple, thus reaching a number almost double the size of the older middle class.

While members of this new white-collar class did not provide leadership for the progressive movement, to a considerable extent they did give it voting strength. Political action was their only outlet for economic protest, since they did not belong to unions or trade associations. Often it was they, on their fixed salaries, who suffered most from rising prices. And basically, like the older middle class, they were urbanites who still expressed the emotions of their rural roots. These two groups, the white-collar class and the older middle class, combined to form the respectable element of the towns and cities who, along with many of the more successful farmers and some of the laborers, were ready to accept the new progressive creed.

The progressive leaders had come out of the Mugwump tradition. Their fathers, or they themselves in their youth, had stood for clean government and the long-established ideals of business morality as opposed to the ruthless code of the new bosses of politics and industry who swept into power in the decades after the Civil War. These progressives joined the cause, not because of economic deprivation, but because they objected to the existing plutocracy. In the past they, or their kind, had backed Horace Greeley against U. S. Grant in 1872, and had temporarily bolted the Republican ticket to vote for Cleveland in 1888. In the early 1900's, back in the Republican party for the most part, they were alarmed by the control the industrial barons were exercising over the country, directly through their economic force, indirectly through their coalitions with the urban political bosses. These bosses frightened the middle classes not only because of their corrupt ties with the industrial moguls, but also because of their hold over the ignorant laboring masses (often largely immigrants) of the cities. Finally, these middle-class people had some fear of the new rising labor unions, since these too threatened to seize power. This was a far less serious fear, since the unions were relatively small and powerless. Gompers, the president of the American Federation of Labor, was diligent in his efforts to prove the respectability and relative conservatism of his organization.

Populist farmers had shared these urban, middle-class suspicions of the moguls and the masses. One of the Populist papers had said the purpose of the party was to serve as a "bulwark against the anarchy of the upper and lower scums of society." Progressives continued the same prejudices. The *California Weekly* proclaimed in 1908, "Nearly all the problems which vex society have their sources above or below the middle class man. From above come the problems of predatory wealth. . . . From below come the problems of poverty and of pigheaded and of brutish criminality." In California, two local political movements began independently in 1906. One was directed against the economic dictator within the state, the Southern Pacific Railroad, the other against the political machine that ran San Francisco, the Union Labor party. Soon these two middle-class movements merged into a single progressive party, which sought not to destroy the railroad or the unions, but to wrest political control from them.

Theodore Roosevelt in his *Autobiography* has stated clearly the reasoning which led him, a conservative young plutocrat of the upper middle-class gentry, to enter politics. The men Roosevelt knew best, cultivated clubmen, warned him that politics was a cheap affair of saloon keepers and horsecar conductors, which gentlemen should shun. "I answered," Roosevelt wrote, "that if this were so it merely meant that the people I knew did not belong to the governing class, and that the other people did—and that I intended to be one of the governing class."

If Roosevelt and others like him, of high intellect and social position, were to win a wide following (as the Mugwumps had not), they would have to modify their conservatism. And so they did. They still clung fundamentally to laissez faire economics as their guiding star, but as a means of returning to it they came to advocate government intervention of varying sorts and degrees. They were of aristocratic tendencies, and certainly had shown no love for the masses, but they became the ardent advocates of more popular government. Above all, they made an appeal not on economic grounds, but upon those of morality. They were more evangelists than economists, and were individualists rather than collectivists. They were realists also, to the extent that when they looked around them they saw much that was grim and sordid and that they wished to change. They were unrealistic, on the other hand, in that most of them were unsophisticated enough to believe that they could legislate their way back to a comparatively simple state of individualism. Only a more urbane few like Charles A. Beard saw that the laws themselves had been shaped to fit the exigencies of the existing order. Most progressives had a simple faith in returning to the old law, or in passing new laws. In greater democratization they saw the way back to the old American utopia, which of course had never been. "The way to have a Golden Age," one progressive novelist wrote, "is to elect it by a . . . [secret] ballot."

By contrast with these views, the business titans and the political bosses, not the progressives, were the realists of the era. It was they who had seen the opportunities implicit in a nation of growing cities still governed by agrarian laws. George Washington Plunkett, the sage of Tammany Hall, was in many respects more pragmatic than many a progressive who had sat in the lectures of William James. Plunkett asserted that the machines were all agreed on "the main proposition that when a man works in politics, he should get something out of it." And so the members of the machines did, dispensing recreation, coal, shoes, and jobs to the immigrant masses, in return for their loyalty at the polls; dispensing large privileges—most often franchises—to the business interests in return for huge gifts. Boss Charles Murphy of Tammany, who was personally puritanical, would not knowingly let his supporters fatten on graft from saloons and prostitutes, but he made the Pennsylvania Railroad pay dearly for the privilege of coming into New York City.

To progressives this was immoral, and being God-fearing men, they felt a personal responsibility to attack such immorality. They felt clearly that it was their duty to gather the power of the business leaders and urban politicos to themselves for the purpose of legislating into existence a new moral order. It was the cult of the hour, W. A. White explained, to "believe in the essential nobility of man and the wisdom of God." Frederic C. Howe wrote, "Early assumptions as to virtue and vice, goodness and evil remained in my mind long after I had tried to discard them. . . . It explains the nature of our reforms, the regulatory legislation in morals and economics. . . . Missionaries and battleships, anti-saloon leagues and Ku Klux Klans, Wilson and Santo Domingo are all a part of that evangelistic psychology that makes America what she is."

Howe was correct; each of these was part and parcel of progressivism. Yet scarcely any progressive would have accepted them all. Various progressives differed in their aims and objectives, for actually progressivism was not a single movement but an aggregate of them, aiming at widely divergent goals. To one progressive, regulation of trusts might be the great end; to another, clean municipal government; to a third, equal rights for women. Certain of the progressive forces would coalesce for different objectives; occasionally they would even oppose each other. Thus some progressives favored imperialism while others fought it bitterly. Out of all these varying drives there emerged two great streams of progressivism: the demand for political reform, and the movement for social justice, as it was called.

The Crusade for Social Justice

THE SOCIAL-JUSTICE MOVEMENT was already well advanced by the turn of the century. It had its roots in European, especially English, reform movements. Englishmen like William Morris and John Ruskin, who were glorifying work with one's hands but also emphasizing the godliness of social reform, were as much its founders as anyone can be said to be. Americans like Beard were profoundly influenced by Ruskin and the Fabian

Socialists. Beard carried one of Ruskin's books with him for years, and was one of the first lecturers at a new workingmen's institution, Ruskin College, established at Oxford, England. Almost every prominent English reformer visited the United States, and conversely almost every American progressive leader fell under the influence of the British. Jane Addams had worked at the newly established Toynbee Hall in the Limehouse section of London; in 1889 she returned to the United States to establish Hull House in Chicago. Young Eleanor Roosevelt, already active in the social-justice movement, while on her honeymoon in 1905 took her husband to lunch with two prominent Fabians, Sidney and Beatrice Webb. Settlement houses, slum clearance agitation, and a great variety of other English reforms quickly had their counterpart in the United States.

The Salvation Army, which had recently come to the United States from England, by 1900 boasted a corps of 3,000 officers and 20,000 privates. It offered aid as well as religion to the dregs of the cities. So did ministers, priests, and rabbis who by the nineties were working in the slums. These men were united in their determination to improve the existence of the miserable people around them. "One could hear human virtue cracking and crushing all around," Walter Rauschenbusch wrote of Hell's Kitchen in New York City. To him the way of salvation for these human souls seemed to be to follow Ruskin and the Webbs into a Christian reform of the social and economic system. Darwinism to Rauschenbusch meant working for a better order on earth. "Translate the evolutionary themes into religious faith," he asserted, "and you have the doctrine of the Kingdom of God." Thus many an American Protestant minister arrived at the social gospel. Catholics like Father John Augustine Ryan joined in the fight for social justice under the authority they found in Pope Leo XIII's encyclical *Rerum Novarum*. It declared that "a small number of very rich men have been able to lay upon the masses of the poor a yoke little better than slavery itself. . . . No practical solution of this question will ever be found without the assistance of religion and the church."

Close behind the ministry were middle-class and upper-class women. In the nineties many of them had seemed restless and discontented, reading more widely than their husbands or brothers, joining literary circles and women's clubs. By the early 1900's these clubs were beginning to display a remarkable growth. The membership of the General Federation of Women's Clubs increased from 50,000 in 1898 to over 1,000,000 by 1914. In the new era the clubwomen agitated for the ballot and legal equality for themselves, and for a wide array of reforms on behalf of children and working women. Especially they took a keen interest in improving standards of public health and safety. At the 1904 convention of the General Federation, the president-elect proclaimed to her fellow members, "I have an important piece of news to give you. Dante is dead. He has been dead for several centuries, and I think it is time we dropped the study of his *Inferno* and turned our attention to our own." The clubwomen heeded her words. On the local level in particular they provided a strong impetus toward social justice. One president of the National Association of Manufacturers urged businessmen to forbid their wives and daughters to join women's clubs where they might be converted to reforms that endangered profits.

A small but significant segment of the social-justice movement was a group of experts who carefully gathered data and statistics on the need for reform. Some of these were social-welfare workers who wrote for *Survey* magazine. Others were frustrated crusaders working for federal or state agencies. In many a state before 1900 there were bureaus of labor which could and did, as in the case of Illinois, compile great quantities of data on deplorable working and living conditions. They could not act directly to ameliorate the conditions, but they could present evidence that dramatized the need for reform. On the federal level, the Industrial Commission undertook a searching investigation of the trusts as they had operated up to 1902; subsequently the Bureau of Corporations carried on similar studies; and because of its investigative powers, the new Department of Commerce and Labor appeared to Theodore Roosevelt as a virtual Department of Sociology. In conservation the same technique was used. It was a scientific age, in which progressives felt that through research they could arrive at the correct answers. But research alone could not gather a great force of public opinion behind the progressive movement. That was the task of the muckrakers and the politicians.

The Muckrakers Publicize Injustices

THE MUCKRAKERS were the many journalists who dramatized the need for reform by writing exposures of what was unsavory in business and government. They began to attract attention toward the end of 1902 and were at their peak of popularity in 1906. There long had been a literature of exposure, from the *Harper's Weekly* crusade against the Tweed Ring through Henry Demarest Lloyd's denunciation of Standard Oil in *Wealth against Commonwealth* (1894). What was new was the scale of the revelations and the rapid attraction of a wide audience. It began almost by accident in about ten of the new popular magazines, selling for ten or fifteen cents, which were then building mass circulation. *McClure's*, already a magazine of broad appeal, began publishing Ida Tarbell's series on Standard Oil, which McClure had not commissioned as an exposure, and which Miss Tarbell did not write to touch off a crusade. Coincidentally, McClure sent a new editor, Lincoln Steffens, out to see the country firsthand; this experience led Steffens to begin a series on municipal corruption. At the same time, Ray Stannard Baker contributed an article belaboring a union for wrongdoing during a coal strike.

McClure had not planned any of these separate attacks, but he saw clearly enough the significance of them—one on a trust, one on government, and one on a labor union. The same theme ran through them all, he pointed out to his readers: the problem of corruption in American life. "Capitalists, workingmen, politicians, citizens—all breaking the law, or letting it be broken," McClure wrote. "Who is left to uphold it? . . . There is no one left; none but all of us. . . . We are all doing our worst and making the public pay. . . . The rest are passing it back to us. We have to pay in the end, every one of us."

This basic theme the muckrakers thrust, year after year, before the eyes of progressive readers: each citizen must bear individual responsibility for what had gone wrong, and must individually do what he could to right the wrongs. On the whole, the muckrakers were optimistic enough to think this possible. Baker remembered, "We 'muckraked' not because we hated our world but because we loved it."

At the height of the muckraking movement, ten journals with a combined circulation of about three million were devoting considerable space to the literature of exposure. In addition, some books like Upton Sinclair's *Jungle* (1906), an exposure of the meat-packing industry, sold over 100,-000 copies. Many newspapers, most notably the New York *World* and the Kansas City *Star*, printed articles by muckrakers. It was exciting for a while, but by 1912 it was over. This was due partly to the hostility of business, which at times withheld credit and advertising from the muckraking magazines, but probably it was more because the public became fatigued. After nine years of sensations, there was little new to whet the public appetite. The rather surprising thing was that the excitement kept going as long as it did.

It was Theodore Roosevelt, at times remarkably able to gauge the public temper, who benefited most from the muckraking movement. It was also he who gave it its name. At a banquet shortly after the appearance of David Graham Phillips's shocking articles on the "Treason of the Senate," Roosevelt arose to liken the writers to the muckraker in *Pilgrim's Progress* who was so busy digging in the muck at his feet that he could not see the heavens above. The cynical, conservative Speaker of the House, "Uncle Joe" Cannon, is supposed to have replied to Roosevelt's remarks, "Yes, you're the chief muckraker." This, as W. A. White commented, was literally true. The great role of the muckraker was to publicize the need for reform. No one succeeded better than Roosevelt in dramatically arousing the indignation of the progressives, and in leading them toward political action.

Chapter 3

ROOSEVELT
PROGRESSIVISM

THEODORE ROOSEVELT exercised long unused powers in the American presidency and assumed flamboyant, strenuous leadership over the emerging progressive movement. Through the prestige of his office, he gave reform a spectacular national impetus, and restored to the presidency a long-lost significance. In the decades since the end of Reconstruction, a succession of dull, elderly politicians had served as chief executive. They had been able enough men, but they had presided more than they had led, leaving largely to Congress the determination of national policies. The most forceful of them, Grover Cleveland, had exerted his stubborn courage to maintain conservative measures against the onslaught of public protest. In part, Bryan was able to stir a furor in 1896 by giving promise of ending the long dynasty of boring Presidents with vigorous positive action. But it was left to Roosevelt to bring excitement and importance back to the presidency.

A leader like Roosevelt inevitably gathered behind him fanatically loyal followers. Not all progressives were ready to be his devotees. There were those Democrats who continued to support Bryan, and the Wisconsin Republicans who rallied behind Governor Robert M. La Follette, but Roosevelt rapidly built the strongest following. Some of those who supported him probably did so blindly, attracted by his personality, indif-

Theodore Roosevelt (THEODORE ROOSEVELT COLLECTION, HARVARD UNIVERSITY)

ferent toward his credo. The aura of excitement around him and his espousal of many a popular but inconsequential cause of the moment may have diverted some of them from the main issues of the period. This was true of only a minority. Most of Roosevelt's men seem to have had a fairly clear idea of the direction in which the nation was heading, toward corporate concentration at home, toward increasing economic and political domination abroad. They were ready to accept Roosevelt's program, both domestic and foreign. They wished to redress the economic balance within the country, as did most of the agrarian followers of Bryan and La Follette. Unlike the agrarians, they cheered Roosevelt as he assumed a firm position for the United States toward the rest of the world.

If Roosevelt progressives were to achieve these aims, they must, despite their nostalgia for the simpler times of their forebears, move toward a stronger federal government and a more powerful chief executive. Therein lay the greatest significance of the emergence of Roosevelt. He brought to the White House strength such as had not been known there since Jackson and Lincoln. He mobilized public opinion behind him in support of progressive measures at home, and operated like a monarch in the realm of world politics. "There adheres in the Presidency," he asserted, "more power than in any other office in any great republic or constitutional monarchy of modern times." This had been true even when he arrived at the White House, and he had gone further, undertaking many new things under the assumption that the President might do whatever was not forbidden by the law or Constitution. "I did not usurp power," he explained afterward, "but I did greatly broaden the use of executive power." Roosevelt was the first really strong President in modern America.

The New President Builds His Strength

ROOSEVELT entered the White House by accident; he became President in September, 1901, when an assassin mortally wounded President McKinley. Nor did he enter it a progressive, even if Hanna, who regarded him as a wild man, lamented, "Now look, that damned cowboy is President of the United States." For when Hanna advised him, "Go slow," Roosevelt replied, "I shall go slow." And he did, through the election of 1904. Like the other men about forty years old who had been McKinley Republicans, Roosevelt needed to be converted to progressivism. As recently as the Pullman Strike of 1894, he had written, "I know the Populists and the laboring men well and their faults. . . . I like to see a mob handled by the regulars, or by good State-Guards, not over-scrupulous about bloodshed." He had regarded Bryan in 1896 as heading "a semisocialist agrarian movement," and concluded, "All the ugly forces that seethe beneath the social crust are behind him."

Why, then, did Roosevelt emerge as a progressive? The answer lies in his background and his times. Born into one of the Knickerbocker families of New York City, he had been brought up among those of comfortable income and assured social position who looked with scorn at the robber barons, and with fear and loathing at the political bosses and their underlings. His generation at Harvard was distinguished by its indifference to all worlds but its own. Roosevelt broke with it, not in its patrician conservatism, but in its aloofness. His background, unusual for an American, rather resembled that of the English Tory reformers of the era. Like them, he plunged into politics when few American gentlemen would do so; like them, he wished to be one of the governing class.

Roosevelt served a lengthy apprenticeship. He was successively a New York State Assemblyman, candidate for mayor of New York, Civil Service Commissioner, New York City Police Commissioner, Assistant Secretary of the Navy, and governor of New York. He learned all of the rules of professional politics, and like the most gifted practitioners, how to break them with profit upon occasion.

Roosevelt's varied and exciting experiences endeared him to his followers. As a rancher, he had helped capture outlaws in the wild West and turn them over to justice; as head of the New York police, he had labored almost superhumanly to try to stamp out crime and vice; as commander of the Rough Riders, he had charged up San Juan hill. It is not surprising that for years after his death he continued to be the Boy Scouts' ideal, for he had lived out the daydreams of many of them. More important, his adventures illustrate his love for direct action and his bellicose morality.

As President, Roosevelt continued to function as though he were a deputy sheriff or a police commissioner or a cavalry colonel dedicated to the upholding of law and order. He did not lose his conservative fear that festering injustice would lead to a bloody upheaval in the United States. Through righting wrongs—the proper sort of police action—he would prevent this cataclysm. Moderate reforms to restrain social malefactors could ease the explosive pressure of malcontent masses. It was for conservative ends that he began to adopt progressive means. He had made a beginning as governor of New York when he signed a bill limiting workers on state contracts to an eight-hour day. It was excellent politics to favor such measures, as he could not have helped seeing. More important in his eyes, it was essential justice. "We Republicans hold the just balance," he explained to Boss Platt, "and set our faces as resolutely against the improper corporate influence on the one hand as against demagogy and mob rule on the other."

Manifestly the kind of progressivism that Roosevelt came to epitomize as President was compatible with conservatism. It was exactly the sort that appealed to the prosperous young men in cities and towns throughout the country. Thus William Allen White, thinking he was undergoing a complete transformation in his beliefs, became Roosevelt's man. The President, working toward the campaign of 1904, accepted the pledge of fealty. "I want it understood," he wrote White, "that the prime movers in forcing my nomination are men like you . . . , like the farmers, small businessmen and upper-class mechanics who are my natural allies."

For Roosevelt, as for White and the multitude of progressives who had reacted strongly against Populism, the conversion to a program of reform was logical. They were ready to try new means to obtain ends in which they had always believed.

As a rather uncertain fledgling President, only forty-three years old in 1901, Roosevelt had little inclination to put a vigorous progressive program into operation. He later admitted, "I cannot say that I entered the presidency with any deliberately planned and far reaching scheme of social betterment." His greatest ambition obviously was to be elected President in his own right. If he were to secure a popular following big enough to return him to the White House he must develop issues. Political logic as well as his own inclination dictated that these issues should be progressive, but they could, and indeed must, come later. He could neither secure legislation from Congress nor win election until he had employed his formidable powers as President to wrest control over the Republican national machinery from Senator Hanna, the Republican National Chairman.

Even had Roosevelt possessed a detailed plan of legislation, he could have done little to forward it in the fall of 1901. Congress, like most of the governmental machinery in the United States from the municipalities up, was under the control of old-style politicians. "Uncle Joe" Cannon, as speaker of the House, operated under the autocratic powers "Czar" Reed had seized in 1890. Though genial, he so firmly controlled appointments to committees and debates on legislation, that the few progressives beginning to appear in the House were obliged either to co-operate or sit as impotent witnesses to Cannon's dictatorship. The Senate was under the domination of an intelligent and competent oligarchy of conservatives. The most commanding of them was tall, austere Nelson Wilmarth Aldrich of Rhode Island, more reserved and less a newspaper personality than Cannon, but even more effective. Aldrich, a wealthy banker, was allied, through his son's marriage, to the Rockefellers. He was as firm in moral principles as any of the progressives, and his principles led him to fight their legislation.

Roosevelt realized how futile it would be to thrust his spear single-handed against these well-organized congressional phalanxes. For the time being, therefore, he was cautious and conciliatory toward their leaders. As he planned his first annual message to Congress, his strategy obviously was to try to attract a wide following without alienating these powerful men. "Before I write my message," he wrote Aldrich in 1901, "I should like to have a chance to go over certain subjects with you." Similarly Roosevelt with sound political logic could draft diatribes against corporate plutocracy, then write Senator Chauncey Depew of the New York Central Railroad, *"How* I wish I *wasn't* a reformer, oh, Senator! But I suppose I must live up to my part, like the Negro minstrel who blacked himself all over!"

With equal logic, Roosevelt dispensed patronage throughout the Middle West in a manner calculated to break Hanna's control over the party, although the policies of the two men were in reality basically similar. It made little difference whether these appointments took Roosevelt to the left or right. In Kansas he backed a former Populist against Hanna's G.A.R. supporter; from Wisconsin, to the chargrin of La Follette, he chose Henry Clay Payne of the Old Guard to be Postmaster General. Payne, through his wide distribution of spoils, helped rally northern right-wing Republicans and Southern Gold Democrats behind Roosevelt. Finally, Roosevelt cemented alliances with businessmen in the North and reshuffled the unstable Republican organizations in the South, using as his agent one of President Harrison's spoilsmen, James S. Clarkson. In the South, he reversed Hanna's "lily-white" policy, to appoint some qualified Negroes to office. Indeed, it was to discuss appointments that Roosevelt took the sensational step of inviting Booker T. Washington to the White House in the fall of 1901.

While playing the game of political patronage, Roosevelt markedly improved the quality of officeholders. Gradually he was able to pull into public service a group of distinguished men, both old and young, of a sort that previously had shunned government work. Henry L. Stimson, who had been earning enormous fees as a corporation lawyer, became United States attorney for the New York City area and brought into his office a group of brilliant and idealistic young lawyers, including Felix Frankfurter. Stimson declared he had "got out where I could see the stars and get my bearings once more . . . and felt that the work was a good deal more worth while." It was significant that at the very time when government was about to play a far larger role in American life, it was beginning to appeal to more men of ambition and high competence.

Partly because Roosevelt had attracted into the government progressives of stature, bound to him by strong ties of personal loyalty, and even more because he had won over or neutralized the Republican machines, he was in firm control of the party by 1904. He had not made it progressive, but he had made it answerable to him. Hanna died early in the year; had he lived and felt the inclination, he could have mustered little strength against Roosevelt at the convention.

Justice for Trusts and Unions

While Roosevelt was quietly taking over the Republican machinery, he was spectacularly building an excited national following. He launched a series of attacks upon the corporate plutocracy—attacks that were vigorous but at the same time moderate. In his first annual message to Congress, December 3, 1901, he set forth his basic policy toward trusts. "Captains of industry . . . have on the whole done great good to our people," he granted. "Without them the material development of which we are so justly proud could never have taken place." In order to protect this advance at home, and to assume a commanding position in the international business world, American industrialists must have as free a hand as was compatible with the public good. "Yet it is also true that there are real and grave evils," Roosevelt pointed out, and as a result:

> There is a widespread conviction in the minds of the American people that . . . trusts are in certain of their features and tendencies hurtful to the general welfare. This . . . is based upon sincere conviction that combination and concentration should be, not prohibited, but supervised and within reasonable limits controlled; and in my judgment this conviction is right.

Specifically, Roosevelt asked for legislation to give the government the right to inspect and examine the workings of great corporations, and subsequently to supervise them in a mild fashion, rather similar to the regulation of banks. What he desired first was the power to investigate trusts and publicize their activities; on the basis of these data, Congress could later frame legislation to regulate or tax the monopolies. Consequently he requested the establishment of a Department of Commerce and Labor, containing a Bureau of Corporations to carry on investigations.

Roosevelt's position on trusts was ready-made for burlesque by Finley Peter Dunne's character, Mr. Dooley: "Th' trusts, says he, are heejoous monsthers built up be th' enlightened intherprise iv th' men that have done so much to advance progress in our beloved country, he says. On wan hand I wud stamp thim undher fut; on th' other hand not so fast." Dunne was satirizing not only the position of Roosevelt but also that of a large number of middle-class Americans. Unorganized in unions or trade associations, powerless except at the polls, they were eager to get control of the government and through it discipline their economic masters. At the same time they did not want to destroy the source of their relatively high living standard.

Congress was unmoved, although Roosevelt had demanded no more than the cautious recommendations of the Chicago Conference on Trusts of 1899. Stalwarts feared these might lead to more drastic controls, and resisted vehemently. Roosevelt capitalized upon this resistance in the summer of 1902 when he took his appeal directly to the people in several speeches. A few months later when Congress was debating whether to create a Bureau of Corporations, he let it be known that the Rockefellers opposed the Bureau. This stimulated the progressive public to pressure their Congressmen successfully. Hence in 1903, Congress established a Department of Commerce and Labor and a Bureau of Corporations. The

Bureau, as Roosevelt had wished, carried on extensive investigations until the Federal Trade Commission absorbed it in 1914. Its twenty-nine volumes of reports on industrial monopolies aided in prosecuting the oil, tobacco, and other trusts. To speed up antitrust prosecutions, Congress also passed an Expediting Act and appropriated $500,000.

Since the fiasco of the sugar decision in 1895, the public had assumed that the Sherman Anti-Trust Act was dead. In effect it was, so far as growth of economic concentration was concerned. But in several less publicized decisions, the Supreme Court had shown a willingness to apply the Sherman Act in cases where interstate commerce was directly and unmistakably involved. The establishment of a great railroad monopoly in the Northwest, after a bitter and spectacular stockmarket battle in 1901, gave Roosevelt an unparalleled opportunity to begin prosecution under the Sherman Act. And so he did, even though his avowed purpose had been to regulate, not destroy, and to stamp underfoot only "malefactors of great wealth," while sparing large corporations that were benign. The new Northern Securities Company had emerged out of the struggle for control of the Northern Pacific between E. H. Harriman of the Union Pacific on the one side, and James J. Hill of the Great Northern and J. P. Morgan on the other. In the eyes of progressives, these men were malefactors. Consequently the prosecution was of sound political value, even though people of the Northwest might not suffer in any way from the railroad merger.

Morgan, feeling his position challenged, hastened to the White House, accompanied by Senators Hanna and Depew. According to Roosevelt, Morgan declared, "If we have done anything wrong, send your man to my man and they can fix it up." Morgan, Roosevelt later remarked, "could not help regarding me as a big rival operator, who either intended to ruin all his interests or else could be induced to come to an agreement to ruin none." Roosevelt was not set upon ruining Morgan, but to the joy of progressives he was using his power as President to discipline industry.

When the Supreme Court in 1904 did dissolve the Northern Securities combine, it in no material way injured Harriman, Hill, or Morgan. But it did convince progressives that Roosevelt, however cautious his avowed policies might be, was a heroic trustbuster. To this extent it served to whet the appetite of progressives for reform and to heighten their enthusiasm for Roosevelt. It also had the intangible but significant effect, as Roosevelt later declared, of establishing "the principle that the government was supreme over the great corporations"—that the government was being injected as a vigorous force in the control of the economy. To this extent, Morgan had been right in his apprehension. The President did not intend to ruin any of Morgan's interests but he did wish to regulate them; he

John Pierpont Morgan (PHOTOGRAPH BY EDWARD STEICHEN)

was in this way a rival operator. It was the first portent that control over the nation's economy was to come from Washington as well as Wall Street.

Trust-busting was popular and proceeded apace. Roosevelt's attorneys obtained twenty-five indictments altogether and instituted suits against the beef, oil, and tobacco combinations. In these, the government was ultimately successful, but the Supreme Court instituted a "rule of reason," declaring in effect that the Sherman Act prohibited only unreasonable restraints upon trade. Even though President Taft initiated ninety more suits and obtained forty-three additional indictments, the results of trust-busting were disappointing. The movement toward industrial consolidation slowed down after 1903 mainly because there were so few fields left in which to build new trusts.

The entrance of the government as a force in the economy could also mean regulation of collective bargaining. This Roosevelt dramatically demonstrated in 1902. Presidential intervention in labor disputes was nothing new—there had been, for example, the Pullman strike—but the government had usually acted as a strikebreaker for the captains of industry. Now Roosevelt was ready instead to make the government an impartial arbiter. Here again, as in dealing with capitalists, he wished the government to be paramount over the conflicting economic forces, and neutral in dealing with them. This became the progressive position. Organized labor, as long as it was well-behaved, did not frighten the progressives nearly as much as did organized capital. The unions were comparatively weak; despite the great upsurge of the American Federation of Labor in the nineties, by 1900 only about 4 per cent of the working force, even excluding agricultural laborers, was organized.

One of the economic areas in which the union leader was most reasonable and personable, and injustice toward the workers most intolerable, was anthracite coal mining. Eight coal railroads dominated by Morgan held a virtual monopoly over the industry. Wages were substandard, hours long, and the accident rate shockingly high. The workers, under John Mitchell, struck in May, 1902, for an eight-hour day, a 20 per cent wage increase, and recognition of the union. Mitchell so effectively presented the miners' claims, and George F. Baer, spokesman for the operators, was so truculent, that public sympathy for the first time in a major strike was aligned with the strikers. Baer foolishly asserted the divine right of the operators to deal with miners as they saw best, thus adding blasphemy to stupidity, in the eyes of many observers. He remained adamant when Roosevelt early in October called operators and miners to the White House to ask them to accept arbitration. In contrast, Mitchell had repeatedly offered to accept it. Roosevelt, who was in a wheelchair at the time, hinted darkly afterwards that he had been tempted to chuck Baer out of the window. He toyed with schemes to send federal troops to take over the mines, but would not have had a shred of authority to do so. The solution was ironic. He persuaded Morgan to force arbitration upon the operators.

Morgan had good reason to act since he wished to keep the Republicans in power. With crisp weather coming, voters might have gone from their cold homes to register their protest in the November congressional elections. (Anthracite was the chief fuel used in heating Eastern residences.) Nor did a settlement harm Morgan's monopoly interests, since the increased wages were passed on to consumers in a higher standard

Powder men in the Perrin coal mine, about 1902 (THEODORE ROOSE-VELT COLLECTION, HARVARD UNIVERSITY)

price for coal. The miners after their long strike failed to gain union recognition and obtained only a 10 per cent wage increase. One of their disappointed number, John L. Lewis, was ready to pattern his own future actions after those of Baer, not Mitchell, regardless of the effect on public opinion.

The coal strike and its settlement were evidence of what has been called "a honeymoon period of capital and labor," stretching from McKinley's inauguration through Roosevelt's first term. Union membership jumped from less than a half million to over two million. Monopolies could well afford to deal liberally with union labor, since they could thus avoid work stoppages in prosperous periods, and pass on increased labor costs to the consumers. It was altogether fitting that Hanna, the high priest of big business, should assume the presidency of the National Civic Federation, which was founded in 1901 to bring about friendly relations between capital and labor, and that Samuel Gompers should become vice president.

This foreshadowed at least dimly an era of monolithic corporations and unions, but it was not the predominant pattern of the early 1900's. Unionism was repugnant to most of the heads of the new trusts, many of whom were utopian capitalists as vehemently antiunion in their principles as was Baer. When a small steel union struck in several mills at the delicate moment when United States Steel was coming into existence, the company was ready to compromise. Union leaders foolishly refused and were crushed. Morgan continued the earlier antiunion policy of the steel industry, and other heavy industry followed his example.

Nor was all labor ready to accept the assumption of leaders like Gompers and Mitchell that differences with capitalists could easily be adjusted around a conference table. The Socialist minority within the American Federation of Labor succeeded in capturing unions of machinists and miners. More radical labor, especially militant western miners, in 1905 founded the Industrial Workers of the World, which tried to organize the great masses of unskilled workers, mostly immigrants, whom the A.F.L. ignored. In the process the I.W.W. employed violent means against which employers retaliated with equal violence. Two episodes, neither the work of the I.W.W., especially outraged orderly progressives. These were the blowing up of a former governor of Idaho, and the dynamiting of the plant of the Los Angeles *Times*, which was militantly antiunion.

Such episodes prompted many progressives to return to their earlier prejudices, and to listen to the antiunion slogans of the National Association of Manufacturers and kindred organizations. The N.A.M., which proclaimed itself against union recognition in 1903, was predominantly made up of men who ran small plants and were dependent upon low labor costs to survive in highly competitive markets. It called the open shop the "American Plan," and the independent workman (strikebreaker) the "American hero." President Charles W. Eliot of Harvard gave formidable support by asserting that nothing was "more essential to the preservation of individual liberty" than protection of the independent workman.

The manufacturers gained much public sympathy. At the same time, what they could not obtain from the President, as they had done in Cleveland's day, they were able to obtain from federal judges, most of whom had been appointed in the earlier era. These judges made the courts the refuge of small business against collective bargaining. The most spectacular court blow against collective bargaining grew out of the Danbury Hatters' strike of 1902. The courts held that the union's efforts to obtain a nation-wide boycott of Loewe hats was a violation of the Sherman Act, and assessed triple damages of $240,000 against the union. Another boycott case, involving the Buck's Stove and Range Company of St. Louis, was even more painful to labor because a federal court issued a sweeping injunction. It forbade the A.F.L. to carry on the boycott, to include the company in a "We Don't Patronize" list in its newspaper, or even to mention the dispute orally or in writing. When Gompers and other A.F.L. officials defied the injunction by mentioning the dispute, they were sentenced to prison for contempt of court. The case dragged on in the courts so long

Samuel Gompers (NATIONAL ARCHIVES)

that the sentences were never carried out, but the principle of the injunction stood. Union officials began a concerted and vigorous campaign to have organized labor exempted from the Anti-Trust Act, and to outlaw antilabor injunctions.

Gompers and his followers wanted simply not to be discriminated against by the government; they were not asking for welfare legislation. Indeed in many instances they did not want it. Explaining his theory of "voluntarism," Gompers once reminisced:

Several times the plain question has been put to me by members of the Senate Committee on Judiciary: "Mr. Gompers, what can we do to allay the causes of strikes that bring discomfort and financial suffering to all alike?" I have had to answer "Nothing.". . . Foremost in my mind is to tell the politicians to keep their hands off and thus to preserve voluntary institutions.

President Roosevelt was to a certain degree sympathetic with the aspirations of the union leaders to organize labor so that it could bargain effectively with organized industry. Labor should "reap the benefits of organization," he declared, and had "a legal right . . . to refuse to work in company with men who decline to join their organizations." He denounced the Buck's Stove decision, and inveighed against court abuse of injunctions. Like most progressives, President Roosevelt was more interested in paternalistic protection for labor, similar to that being proposed in many state legislatures. He asked Congress for legislation to regulate the hours and working conditions of women and children, establish employers' liability for accident compensation, and improve railroad safety measures. For the moment he made no headway. Indeed, if he had, the courts would have invalidated most of Congress's handiwork, for they were striking down most state laws as rapidly as they were enacted. The Supreme Court held, in the Lochner case in 1905, that a New York law limiting hours of bakers, who pursued an unhealthy occupation, to ten a day or sixty a week was unconstitutional, because it violated the right of the bakers to make contracts as they saw fit, under the Fourteenth Amendment. Justice Oliver Wendell Holmes, who had been appointed to the court by Roosevelt because of his enlightened views on labor, tartly dissented: "Some of these laws embody convictions or prejudices which judges are likely to share. Some may not. But a constitution is not intended to embody a particular economic theory, whether of paternalism and the organic relation of the citizen to the state or of laissez faire." Progressives soon won a respite from the Supreme Court's distaste for government regulation, but this came only after Roosevelt had been re-elected and progressivism had won an even greater hold over the American public.

The 1904 Mandate for Reform

ROOSEVELT's rather strange political anxiety had led him to plan exceedingly cautiously for the election of 1904—in some respects too cautiously. Hanna, whom he had undermined so diligently, was dead, and the Republican bosses were either subservient or not openly hostile. At the convention, he was careful not to antagonize the right wing of the party. He allowed the conservatives Root, Cannon, and Lodge to run the convention. They seated the conservative rather than reform factions from all contested delegations, and confined the platform to listing past Republican achievements rather than making promises for the future.

While the Republicans were veering to the right, the Democrats veered even more sharply in the same direction. They abandoned Bryan to nominate Cleveland's former law partner, Alton B. Parker. It was a futile maneuver, for the electorate had no interest in going back to Cleveland, nor would businessmen trust a party which had twice nominated Bryan. When Roosevelt, fearing that Wall Street was putting $5,000,000 behind Parker, allowed his campaign manager to tap the trusts, the money came pouring in. Businessmen might call Roosevelt the "mad messiah," but they were not really afraid of him. Despite the Northern Securities decision, Harriman personally contributed $50,000 and Morgan, $150,000; far more came from their associates. The steel, beef, oil, and insurance trusts, and the railroads all aided. Roosevelt was not altogether aware of the source of all the donations, nor did he feel he was putting himself under obligation, but they were a revealing commentary upon his record.

Roosevelt's apprehensions had been altogether groundless. After a dull campaign, he won by a popular majority of two and a half million votes. While businessmen were convinced he was safe, progressives were confident he would lead in reform. In state elections throughout the nation, progressives were generally victorious. As a sidelight, the Socialists under Debs (often regarded as a left-wing offshoot of the progressives), received 400,000 votes, four times as many as in 1900. Their growth gave Roosevelt a convincing argument that sane and slow reform was essential to forestall a violent upheaval.

Effective Railroad Regulation

UNHESITATINGLY, Roosevelt accepted his 1904 victory as a mandate for progressive reform. Further, he was free from his earlier preoccupation with being elected, since on the evening of his overwhelming victory he publicly announced he would not seek another term. He continued to operate politically from a center position. He so seriously offended the trusts which had contributed to the campaign that Henry Clay Frick, the steel magnate, complained, "We bought the ———— and he didn't stay bought." He equally offended the advanced progressives of the Middle West with his undisguised disdain for "the La Follette type of fool radicalism."

Senator Robert M. La Follette, whose position was in marked contrast to Roosevelt's, felt in turn that the President was betraying progressives with his half-a-loaf policies. By 1905, La Follette had become the most vigorous national advocate of firm regulation of railroads, an advance from his position as a regular Republican congressman from Wisconsin in the eighties. Although he had stayed in the party, by the turn of the century he was championing reforms of a populist nature. In 1901, he was elected Governor of Wisconsin, pledged to fight for a direct primary, tax reform, and railroad control. His votes came largely from a rural constituency, his advice from experts at the University of Wisconsin. Finally at the end of 1905 when he obtained the state legislation for which he had fought, he entered the United States Senate to fight nationally for

Robert M. La Follette campaigning in Wisconsin (STATE HISTORICAL SOCIETY OF WISCONSIN)

the same sort of program. His advocacy of rigorous railroad regulation brought him into conflict with both the Old Guard and President Roosevelt; he entitled a chapter of his autobiography, "Alone in the Senate." La Follette criticized President Roosevelt because he "acted upon the maxim that half-a-loaf is better than no bread." In contrast, La Follette asserted, "I believe that half-a-loaf is fatal whenever it is accepted at the sacrifice of the basic principle sought to be attained." He tried to push the President toward more drastic legislation.

The problem that faced Roosevelt at the beginning of his second term was whether to try to force through Congress a lower tariff or stricter regulation of railroads. The West was clamoring for both of these; the one could mean lower prices for manufactured goods (although the first monopolistic international cartels were already being formed), and the second could mean lower railroad rates. Although La Follette came into the Senate in January, 1905, and numerous progressives were entering the House, it still would be difficult to push a downward tariff revision through Congress. Too many interests in too many sections could combine against it. As for the President, he had written in 1903: "My feeling about the tariff question is, of course, that it is one of expediency and not of morality. There is nothing more intrinsically right or wrong in a 40 per cent tariff than in a 60 per cent one. The question is simply whether the gain to be accomplished by a reduction of some duties is sufficient to offset the trouble that would be caused by a change in the tariff."

On the other hand, Roosevelt felt morally bound to strengthen government regulation over business, not by limiting its profits but by preventing it from doing wicked things. He appalled the conservative members of the Union League Club in Philadelphia in January, 1905, by telling them they should lead in the movement to obtain proper supervision: "Neither this people nor any other free people will permanently tolerate the use of the vast power conferred by vast wealth . . . without lodging somewhere in the Government the still higher power of seeing that this power . . . is . . . used for and not against the interests of the people as a whole." He specifically mentioned unregulated railroad rates; in the eyes of progressives, railroads were still doing many wicked things.

In the eighteen months that followed, Roosevelt ably exercised his presidential leadership to obtain more effective railroad-rate regulation. The courts had practically nullified the Interstate Commerce Act of 1887; rates were high, rebates to favored shippers were large, and short hauls in monopoly areas frequently cost more than long hauls over competitive routes. Western farmers and businessmen alike suffered seriously from these discriminations. Senator Bristow of Kansas pointed out that to transport one hundred pounds of sugar from San Francisco through his home town, Salina, to Kansas City cost 60 cents. To transport it to Salina (a haul 185 miles shorter) cost 89 cents. Frank Norris's novel *The Octopus* (1901), which had vividly portrayed California farmers' struggles with the Southern Pacific, served as another exposure of the situation. A supposed relief measure, the Elkins Act of 1903, was promoted as much by the railroads as the public, and merely outlawed rebates. Someone called the act "a truce . . . to abolish piracy." Real regulation was needed.

By a series of intricate maneuvers, Roosevelt managed to force a new regulatory law through Congress. At one point, he threatened to call for tariff revision, which conservatives feared still more; at another, he seemed to join La Follette in demands for drastic regulation of railroads. La Follette wished to give the I.C.C. power to evaluate railroad property as a base for determining rates; when Roosevelt abandoned him, he felt betrayed. But Roosevelt had been intent only upon obtaining a moderate law. Although the Hepburn Act of June, 1906, was in La Follette's eyes only half a loaf, it was at least the beginning of effective railroad regulation. It empowered the I.C.C. to put into effect reasonable rates, subject to later court review; extended its jurisdiction to cover express, sleeping car, and pipeline companies; separated railroad management from other enterprises such as mining; prescribed uniform bookkeeping; and forbade passes and rebates.

It was a large half-loaf, and La Follette and his supporters in Congress soon were able to obtain the remaining part. In 1910, insurgent Republicans and Democrats in Congress passed the Mann-Elkins Act abolishing the "long-and-short-haul" evil, further extending the jurisdiction of the I.C.C., and strengthening other features of the Hepburn Act. The I.C.C. could suspend proposed new rates up to ten months, and could demand proof from the railroad that they would be reasonable. Finally, in 1913 La Follette's long agitation resulted in passage of a law authorizing the I.C.C. to evaluate railroads, and to set rates to give a fair return of profit on their value.

Conservation of Resources and Health

ONE OF THE MANY reasons for the clamor for lower freight rates had been to cut the rising cost of lumber. The best forests of the Great Lakes area were cut over, and the increasing amounts of lumber coming from the Pacific Northwest had to bear the heavy cost of transportation eastward. Furthermore, trees were being felled faster than they were being grown. It was one of many signs that progressives must abandon the profligate ways of pioneering America. At this point sharp conflict developed between progressives in the West and those in the East. Westerners wanted the government to aid in the rapid development of their resources; the growth of their economy depended upon this. Easterners were more interested in preserving the remaining wilderness; their concern was more aesthetic and recreational.

Roosevelt, ardent sportsman and naturalist that he was, along with his Chief Forester, Gifford Pinchot, and most Eastern progressives, felt that the United States must develop great national forests like those of the European countries. For years Major John Wesley Powell, explorer of the Grand Canyon, and other experts had been advocating new policies for husbanding the public domain. A beginning had come with the passage of the Forest Reserve Act of 1891; under its provisions 47,000,000 acres had been set aside as National Forests. Roosevelt, clothing his actions

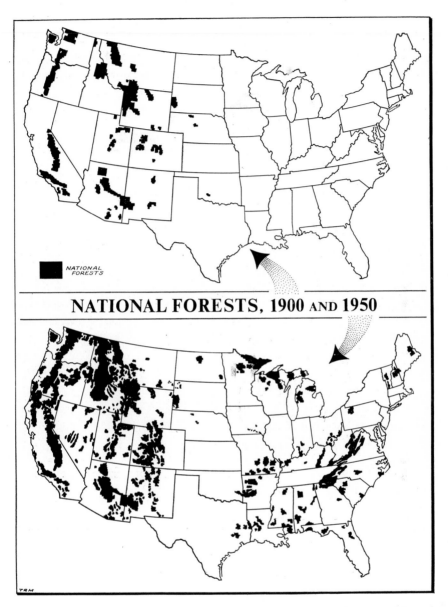

NATIONAL
FORESTS

NATIONAL FORESTS, 1900 AND 1950

with the terminology of the progressive struggle against the vested interests, rapidly extended the government reserves. He had to operate as best
he could, at times with doubtful legality, under existing laws. The very
Westerners in Congress who zealously supported his other policies not
only blocked new legislation but fought to repeal the old. Further, behind
them were not just the big Western business interests, which at times were
not hostile, but often the small businessmen of the towns, and the small
lumbermen, ranchers, and grazers. In 1907 Western Congressmen suc-

ceeded in attaching a rider (unrelated amendment) to an appropriation bill, prohibiting the President from withdrawing further lands. Roosevelt could not veto the appropriations bill without calamitous effects. He acted swiftly, first to withdraw practically all remaining forests in the public domain, and then to sign the bill. All together he added about 125,000,000 acres to the National Forests, and reserved 4,700,000 acres

Roosevelt Dam, Arizona (THEODORE ROOSEVELT COLLECTION, HARVARD UNIVERSITY)

of phosphate beds and 68,000,000 acres of coal lands—all the known coal deposits in the public domain.

Simultaneously Roosevelt prepared the way for a new government policy on electric power by reserving 2,565 water-power sites. These were just the years when expanding private utility companies were interested in obtaining them. Further, he vetoed a bill to permit private exploitation of the power at Muscle Shoals on the Tennessee River, which a generation later became the heart of the T.V.A. This left the way open for government development of huge power projects, a program as popular in the West as the withdrawal of other land was unpopular.

It was not the President, but a Democratic Senator from Nevada, Francis G. Newlands, who proposed an extensive federal reclamation program for the West. Roosevelt endorsed it, and to a considerable extent was able to win political credit for the Newlands Reclamation Act of 1902. It provided that money from the sale of Western lands should go into a revolving fund to undertake irrigation projects too large for private capital or state resources. Eventually, the government built huge dams for the development of power and storage of water, and extensive systems of canals to carry the water to arid lands. Already by 1915 the government had invested $80,000,000 in twenty-five projects, of which the largest was the Roosevelt Dam on the Salt River of Arizona. The principle of government aid in irrigation and power development in the West had become firmly established.

In the same fashion that the progressives were trying to regulate natural resources scientifically, they undertook to legislate the nation into better health. Again, many of the early laws were inadequate, and were of significance mainly for the precedents they set.

Within the Department of Agriculture, Dr. Harvey Wiley had long agitated for the protection of consumers from dangerous foods and adulterants. The muckrakers also had made the public shockingly aware of the disgusting and poisonous things they were sometimes eating. None created a more shocked reaction than Upton Sinclair, who wrote a powerful novel of protest against exploitation of immigrant labor in the stockyards, and incidentally included nauseating descriptions of the preparation of meats. When *The Jungle* appeared in 1906, it hit Americans' stomachs as much as their consciences, even in the White House. "Tiddy was toying with a light breakfast an' idly turnin' over th' pages iv th' new book with both hands," Mr. Dooley declared. "Suddenly he rose fr'm th' table, an' cryin': 'I'm pizened,' begun throwin' sausages ou iv th' window. . . . Since thin th' Prisidint, like th' rest iv us, has become a viggy-taryan."

Roosevelt was indeed horrified, and when a commission verified the descriptions in *The Jungle*, he sought reform. The result was two pieces of legislation passed in June, 1906. One was the Meat Inspection Act, which while fairly ineffective at first, over a period of time did much to bring about eradication of some animal diseases, especially tuberculosis. The other was the Pure Food and Drug Act, which bore the impressive descriptive title, "An Act for preventing the manufacture, sale, or transportation of adulterated or misbranded or poisonous or deleterious foods, drugs, medicines, and liquors, and for regulating traffic therein, and for other purposes." Administration of it went to Dr. Wiley, who established laboratories and sent food inspectors throughout the country. He and his staff became involved in controversies as to whether boric acid and like substances in food were harmful to consumers. Also they were hampered by the weak penalties provided by the law. Nevertheless, they eliminated from drugstores and groceries a wide variety of harmful foods and preparations.

On the local and state levels, laws provided for the inspection of meat and milk, chlorination of water supplies, and the physical examination of school children. Large-scale voluntary campaigns began to eradicate flies, mosquitoes, and diseases like diphtheria and tuberculosis. Advances in medicine and public health were so rapid that the average life span jumped from 49 years in 1901 to 51 in 1910, and to 56 in 1920.

The Panic of 1907: A Warning

ALTHOUGH ROOSEVELT's followers believed he was leading them into the millenium, the panic of 1907 bluntly illustrated the serious flaws still plaguing the American economic structure—and the President's unwillingness to go too far in trying to remedy them. Speculation and mismanagement during the boom years following the Spanish-American War led to a sharp break in prosperity in 1907. It was a rich men's panic at the outset, involving an international tightening of the money market, and the failure of thirteen New York banks and of several railroads. The result was wage cuts and layoffs for large numbers of poor men.

Businessmen were quick to lay the blame upon the "mad messiah" in the White House, the muckrakers, trust-busters, and progressive legislators. This was incorrect; progressive suits, investigations, and laws do not seem to have been responsible. Antitrust suits had not cut corporate earnings, and regulatory laws like the Hepburn Act had so reassured investors in both America and Europe that large funds had poured into Wall Street to enable further promotions. Roosevelt, nevertheless, was sensitive to the criticisms and quick to conciliate Wall Street. Judge Elbert H. Gary and Frick called upon him one morning to tell him that unless United States Steel took over shares of the Tennessee Coal and Iron Company from a New York banking house, it would fail, and thus threaten a widespread industrial smashup. They wanted assurance that the government would not consider the purchase a violation of the Sherman Act. Roosevelt tacitly agreed. United States Steel was thus able to buy out a vigorous competitor at a bargain price, further stifle competition, and hold back the development of the iron and steel industry in the South. It shackled Southern steel to the "Birmingham differential" price scale. This meant that the steel mills in Alabama were forced to charge the same price as Pittsburgh mills, plus a three-dollar-a-ton differential, plus freight from Birmingham.

The real causes of the panic were an inefficient and inelastic credit system, the high degree of "water" in the capital structure of railroads and the new trusts, and the high profits contrasting with the low wages—and thus low buying power—of the workers. By 1909, the economy had swung upward, but continued to wobble between upswings and relapses until war prosperity rescued it in 1915.

The panic of 1907 and the economic instabilities that persisted afterward were alarming to progressives. As they began to investigate the serious flaws in the economic structure, they began to propose more elaborate measures for stabilizing the economy. Gradually many of them were shifting away from their original view that the imposition of a few simple prohibitions would suffice to restore the free flowing of a laissez faire economy. Some began to demand more elaborate machinery even though it would mean an increasing role for the government. These demands would be difficult to obtain, for their proposals not only could not command a majority in Congress, but went considerably beyond the modest limits of Roosevelt, and appealed even less to his successor.

Chapter *4*

THE ASSAULT ON THE OLD GUARD

DURING THE PRESIDENCY of William Howard Taft, a growing wave of progressivism was sweeping the country. At the outset the progressives looked to Taft, who was Roosevelt's handpicked successor, to provide vigorous leadership. When the President did not lead them against the Old Guard, they mounted their own bitter assaults, which in time came to be as much against Taft himself as upon the conservatives in Congress. During these years the progressives won only limited successes in Washington, but at the grassroots they achieved victories which gave promise of ultimate national triumph.

Taft Returns to Traditionalism

As EARLY AS 1904, Roosevelt had tentatively decided that his Secretary of War, Taft, should be his successor, for Taft and Secretary of State Elihu Root, an able, conservative corporation lawyer, were the two men closest to him in the official family. Together they liked to think of themselves as the Three Musketeers—Athos Root, Porthos Taft, and D'Artagnan Roosevelt. Had Root accepted Roosevelt's urgings and run for Governor of New York in 1904, perhaps he, not Taft, would have run in 1908, as a frankly right-wing candidate. Had progressive principles

been the real deciding factor, Roosevelt should have chosen Governor
Charles Evans Hughes of New York, who had reformed insurance companies and fought for public-utility regulation and state development of
water power. His policies were as moderate as Roosevelt's and as firm as
La Follette's, but he was too cool and independent to appeal to Roosevelt,
who was obsessed with the desire to leave in the White House a caretaker

Governor Charles Evans Hughes
(HARVARD UNIVERSITY LIBRARY)

for "my policies." Roosevelt was so convinced that these policies were the
only right solution to the nation's problems, and he so loved being President, that he might well have defied the no-third-term tradition had he
thought he could win. As it was, caution led him to support his loyal lieutenant, Taft.

Taft, the son of a prominent politician in Cincinnati, had, despite his
own distaste for politics, risen rapidly in office: judge on the Ohio Superior Court, Solicitor General of the United States, judge on a Federal
Circuit Court, President of the Philippines Commission, Governor General of the Philippines, and Secretary of War. At a time when the nation
was eager for progressive domestic reform, Taft was known less for his
background as a former federal judge than for his notable achievements
as one of the first viceroys of the new American empire. Between 1900
and 1908, he traveled over 100,000 miles on assignment to Manila, Rome,

Panama, Cuba, and within the United States. He was a glamorous figure in an age which admired big men who labored strenuously in distant places. His achievements were almost all in the realm of colonial or foreign policy; he had little to do with Roosevelt's domestic policies, although privately he subscribed to almost every one of them. If he were to the right of Roosevelt, it was only by a hairline. The great distinction was that while he regarded Roosevelt's objectives as justifiable, he felt, as he commented in 1910, that Roosevelt "ought more often to have admitted the legal way of reaching the same ends." This typically turgid way of saying things was another marked contrast between Taft and Roosevelt.

Once again in 1908 Roosevelt suffered from the overcaution that afflicted him in most campaign years; and he had no difficulty in communicating the disease to Taft. The well-greased, conservatively run Republican machinery followed Roosevelt's bidding, and gathered the votes of the delegates: organization men, office holders, and Southern Republicans. Behind the progressive façade at the convention was the granite firmness of the Old Guard. They ignored Taft's specification for a vice-president: "some western senator who has shown himself conservative and at the same time represents the progressive movement." Instead they chose the flatly uninspiring right-winger, "Sunny Jim" Sherman of New York. They elaborately constructed the platform to appeal to progressives without threatening real damage to conservatives.

At one point the platform construction failed. Taft, with Roosevelt's approval, drafted a labor plank clearly condemning "the reckless use of ex parte injunctions." Under pressure from the National Association of Manufacturers, he and Roosevelt agreed to compromise upon a weaker plank. It did not entirely satisfy the N.A.M., and led Gompers of the A.F.L. to announce that labor had been "thrown down, repudiated and relegated to the discard by the Republican party." Furthermore, Taft in his earlier judicial career had been one of the pioneer foes of the secondary boycott (union exhortations not to buy the products of struck plants). Labor leaders in 1908 began to look to the Democrats. The swing was of little significance in votes cast that year, since union membership was relatively small and often failed to register the leaders' opinions at the polls. The long-range effect was more noteworthy: this shift was the beginning of one of the most vital alignments in twentieth-century politics.

Business moguls had no difficulty in choosing the gingerly progressive Republican candidate over the more forthright William Jennings Bryan, running forlornly for a third time. Rockefeller wired Taft congratulations on the nomination; Morgan remarked, "Good! good!" Carnegie sent a campaign contribution of $20,000. This did not mean that Taft had capitulated to Wall Street; indeed he was more careful about accepting corporate campaign contributions than Roosevelt had been in 1904. He lamented that his campaign treasurer thought "that the place to get money is confined to a narrow strip of street in New York." The Republicans raised only $1,600,000 as compared with the $2,200,000 they had gotten in 1904.

Taft campaigned as the champion of smaller business interests. In his acceptance address he promised that he would perfect the machinery for restraining lawbreakers and at the same time interfere with legitimate

William Jennings Bryan (HARVARD UNIVERSITY LIBRARY)

business as little as possible. Most important, he appealed to small-business and middle-class concern over the rising cost of living by firmly promising a reduction in the tariff. Forty per cent of the members of the National Association of Manufacturers, at this time predominantly a small-business organization, favored a lower tariff. So did both urban and rural progressives, who looked upon it as the one practical way to cut the excessive profits of monopolies and trim prices to consumers.

This program seemed sound, but compared with Roosevelt's crusades, it was not very exciting. The whole campaign ran on a lower key, even though the dynamic Bryan whipped up far more enthusiasm for the Democrats than had the cautious Parker in 1904. This was especially true in the rural areas where year after year he was one of the stellar attractions in the Chautauqua series of tent lectures. In the West, both parties presented their candidates as progressives, although even there Republican progressives warned that, compared with the safe Taft, Bryan was dangerous. Bryan's continued thumping at railroads and banks still appealed to farmers, but still frightened those progressive business and professional men who had earlier rallied to support McKinley against him.

The result was a foregone conclusion, a sweep for Taft. The electoral vote was 321 to 162, but there were portents of national unrest in the victory. Taft's lead over Bryan was only half the size of Roosevelt's plurality in 1904; several Western states shifted to Bryan, and several others in the Middle West elected Democratic governors even though they gave their electoral votes to Taft. Clearly a considerable majority of the people

President William Howard Taft playing golf (HARVARD UNIVERSITY LIBRARY)

by 1908 wished progressive reform, whether from the Republicans or the Democrats. Republican progressives, pleased at the outcome, proclaimed, "Roosevelt has cut enough hay; Taft is the man to put it into the barn." Republican conservatives, taking a different view, rejoiced that they were rid of the "mad messiah." John Wanamaker declared, "It will be such a comforting thing to have old times restored again."

Certainly Taft's intention was to load Roosevelt's hay into the barn, but it soon was drenched by violent political storms. Partly this may have been due to Taft's lethargy; it had never been his nature to move rapidly, whether because of his judicial temperament or his corpulence. An unfriendly critic once wrote during his administration that Taft was "a large, good-natured body, entirely surrounded by people who know exactly what they want." The implication that Taft did not know what he wanted is not correct. But it is true that either he lacked the political skill to obtain it, or he looked upon use of his great executive power to this end as being unprincipled. Later when Roosevelt reminisced, "I did not usurp power, but I did greatly broaden the use of the executive power," Taft warned that this was an unsafe practice.

At times Taft's methods seemed those of the judge rather than the politician. Thus he expected the greatest problem of his administration would be to cope with corporations, and felt lawyers could best do this. So he filled six of his nine cabinet positions with lawyers. He apparently forgot that he had pledged himself to retain any of Roosevelt's cabinet who might wish to stay; he replaced the conservationist Secretary of the Interior, James R. Garfield, who in his zeal had gone beyond the law, with a Seattle lawyer, Richard A. Ballinger, who was ready to apply the strict letter of the law, even though it might deal a blow to conservation.

Taft himself was well aware of the great contrast between himself and his predecessor. He wrote a revealing farewell letter to Roosevelt, embarking for an African big game tour:

> When I am addressed as 'Mr. President,' I turn to see whether you are not at my elbow.
>
> I have no doubt that when you return you will find me very much under suspicion by our friends in the West. . . . I knew . . . I should make a capital error in the beginning of my administration in alienating the good will of those without whom I can do nothing to carry through the legislation to which the party and I are pledged. Cannon and Aldrich have promised to stand by the party platform and to follow my lead. . . .
>
> I have not the facility for educating the public as you had through talks with correspondents, and so I fear that a large part of the public will feel as if I had fallen away from your ideals; but you know me better and will understand that I am still working away on the same old plan.

Had Taft been the most skilled of presidential leaders, he would have had trouble putting the "same old plan" into execution. Part of the fault was Roosevelt's, because in his last months in office, he had outlined to progressives exciting proposals that the conservatives in Congress had ignored. His dazzled following blamed the nonenactment of these proposals upon the Old Guard congressional leadership, especially that of Aldrich in the Senate and Speaker Cannon and the rules committee in the House. One progressive Congressman asserted in 1908, "President Roosevelt has been trying to cultivate oranges for many years in the frigid climate of the Committee of Rules, but what has he gotten but the proverbial lemons?"

At campaign time, "Uncle Joe" Cannon was a homespun, tobacco-spitting man of the people; in the House he was the reactionary friend of corporate interests. Progressives resented his power, and a growing number of them in the House were ready to revolt against him. Taft per-

sonally sympathized with them, but they were not yet powerful enough
to succeed in their revolt, so on the advice of Roosevelt he did not encourage them. Characteristically, he went still further, and told newspapermen he had conferred with Cannon and was confident of his good faith.
Taft privately objected to Cannon's "vulgarity and blackguardism," but
could not find the slightest fault with Aldrich, cultivated and gentlemanly
in his conservatism. Indeed he developed such a warm admiration for

"New Wine in Old Bottles" by
*J. N. Darling, for the Des
Moines* Register

Aldrich that he once wrote, "I long for your presence. I feel as Scott said
of Rhoderick Dhu—a blast upon your bugle horn were worth a thousand
men." Even from the outset Taft seemed incapable of negotiating with
the Old Guard as had Roosevelt, without giving the impression that he
had joined them. To the progressives this seemed betrayal.

Insurgency, the Tariff, and Conservation

THE FIRST BETRAYAL, in the eyes of progressives, was the fiasco that occurred when Taft called Congress into special session to enact a lower
tariff. "I believe the people are with me," he had written in January, 1909,
"and before I get through I think I will have downed Cannon and Aldrich
too." But having proclaimed a tariff crusade, he remained behind while
Middle Westerners carried their lances into battle. They were not "free
traders" like some Southern Democrats, but they did want to thwart trusts
by exposing them to foreign competition. The way to do this, they thought,
was to lower rates substantially—the "Iowa idea," this was called. They
thought the President was behind them, but he failed to send Congress

a fighting message or to intervene with his patronage powers when Congressmen began to succumb to the blandishments of lobbyists or logrollers.

The Payne bill went through the House embodying substantial downward revision from the Dingley tariff. Taft did intervene sufficiently at this point to obtain the placing of hides, coal, and iron on the free list. The raw materials bloc was incensed, but Old Guard leaders assured it confidentially that the Senate would restore the rates. One Democrat in the House commented cynically that there was no point in spending further time on the bill, since the one to be enacted was yet to be written by Senator Aldrich. So it was, for Aldrich's Committee on Finance introduced the bill in the Senate with 847 amendments, most of which were increases. He claimed that his bill would reduce the Dingley tariff, but La Follette produced tables to indicate that it was about 1.5 per cent higher, and went on the offensive. La Follette and a group of Middle Western senators divided the complicated Aldrich amendments. Working night after night, they threaded their way through their alloted portions of the involved figures, then on the floor of the Senate launched detailed analyses against Aldrich and the high-tariff bloc. Throughout the Middle West, indignation sizzled over the dramatic import of the progressives' figures. They demonstrated how the tariff wall enabled manufacturers of almost every kind of product from steel to linoleum to make high profits at the expense of the consumer. Senator Cummins of Iowa presented statistics to show that if United States Steel were to reduce its prices $9.00 per ton, it could still pay a 6 per cent dividend upon its heavily watered stock.

The progressive senators said they were fighting on behalf of the consumers, who were suffering from fluctuating prosperity and rising prices. But Senator Aldrich, stinging from the progressive onslaught, retorted, "I ask who are the consumers? Is there any class except a very limited one that consumes and does not produce? And why are they entitled to greater consideration?" He asserted that the Republican party had made no promise to revise the tariff downward, and proceeded to pass, over progressive protests, one after another of the high schedules. The only compromise he would make was to lower duties on several relatively trivial items: white lead, bronze powder, brocades, Christmas tree decorations, and knives and forks.

The progressives tried to bring Taft openly into the fight. Senator Beveridge appealed to him in a speech, citing his campaign promises, but the next day when Beveridge visited the White House, "a refrigerator was a bake-oven in comparison." Perhaps this was because Taft did not care for the crude or demagogic ways the Middle Westerners sometimes assumed. He was ready in theory to link himself with the small businessmen rather than the corporate moguls, but he found the representatives of small business less pleasant than the suave spokesmen of Wall Street. Thus Taft regarded Beveridge as a "selfish pig," La Follette as objectionable, and the Iowa senators as blatant demagogues. He seems to have placed more faith in personal polish and reliability and in a respect for legalities than he did in political principles. In any event, he snubbed the Midwestern senators, preferring to work privately to wrest whatever concessions he could from Aldrich and his cohorts. This caused the progressives to feel betrayed, and made the public think Taft had joined the Old

"Revising the Tariff Downward (?)" by J. N. Darling for the Des Moines Register

Guard. It was quite unnecessary for him to have acted this way, but throughout his Presidency he seemed to have an almost puritanical aversion to doing whatever was popular, even when it was right.

Taft's main contribution was to persuade the conservatives, who had thrown an inheritance tax out of the Payne bill, that they must accept a compromise. Otherwise the progressive Republicans would join with the Democrats to vote an income-tax law. The compromise was an immediate 2 per cent tax on corporate incomes, and the submission to the states of an income-tax amendment to the Constitution. In the end the income-tax amendment came to have major significance, for it was ratified during the progressive upsurge of 1911 and 1912, and opened the constitutional gates to revolutionary changes in the American tax and economic structure. At the time it seemed a matter of lesser significance than Taft's success in returning hides to the free list and in obtaining reductions in duties on shoes, lumber, coal, and iron ore.

Over the votes of Midwest Republicans, the Payne-Aldrich tariff passed Congress, and was signed by Taft on August 5, 1909. He said it was not a perfect bill, but that it did represent "a sincere effort on the part of the Republican party to make a downward revision." Indeed, estimates of the complicated schedules do seem to indicate that it brought the rates down to 37 per cent ad valorem compared with the 40.21 per cent of the Dingley tariff (and 41.77 per cent of the Aldrich bill). Also it provided for a Tariff Commission which was to make scientific studies of rates—an appealing approach to some progressives, who felt that the tariff, like most problems, should be determined scientifically and taken out of politics.

Nevertheless, the Payne-Aldrich tariff seemed to favor Senator Aldrich's New England and the Far West, at the expense of the rest of the country. Muckraking magazines and many newspapers (perhaps because the tariff kept the price of newsprint high) launched bitter attacks upon it. They brushed aside Taft's defense that it decreased rates on goods valued at $5,000,000,000 a year while increasing them on only $600,000,000 worth, half of them luxury goods. Above all, the Midwest was incensed. It was a gauge of Taft's bad political judgment that on a swing around the country in the fall of 1909, he tried to defend the new tariff in a hastily prepared speech delivered in the heart of the area of resentment, Winona, Minnesota. One line from that speech made damaging headlines against the President. He said, "On the whole . . . the Payne bill is the best bill that the Republican party ever passed." The remainder of the trip through the Midwest, wrote a reporter, was "a polar dash through a world of ice."

Again in 1911 Taft further alienated Middle Westerners over the tariff issue when he took an economically liberal position. He submitted to the Senate a reciprocal trade agreement with Canada which in effect would bring the two countries into an economic union. Many Eastern manufacturers, seeing larger Canadian markets for their goods, were enthusiastic, but the Middle Westerners, fearing a flood of competing Canadian farm products and raw materials, were bitterly hostile. La Follette proclaimed, "It singles out the farmer and forces free trade upon him, but it confers even greater benefits upon a few of the great combinations sheltered behind the high rates found in the Payne-Aldrich tariff." He and his cohorts formed a strange alliance with die-hard members of the Old Guard, but were defeated by Eastern Republicans and Southern free-trade Democrats. The Senate approved the treaty, 55 to 27. In Canada, nationalistic voters, frightened by talk that this was the first step toward annexation by the United States, voted out the Liberal government that had negotiated the agreement, and thus killed reciprocity.

The significance of the tariff battle was that it widened dangerously the rift between Middle-Western progressive Republicans and the Old Guard Easterners. Taft had been able to do nothing to bridge the growing gulf, and himself seemed marooned on the Eastern brink. Even among Eastern consumers he seemed not to be taking the most effective way to lower living costs. He was even more vigorous than his predecessor in prosecuting trusts; he continued the cases against the tobacco trust and Standard Oil, and secured their dissolution. It was his misfortune that the courts carrying out these dissolutions were meticulously careful not to injure the corporate interests. In consequence the public, which had been so bedazzled by Roosevelt's fustian in battling the trusts, came to view the results with some disillusion. The process of dismantling a trust has been likened to trying to unscramble eggs. Certain it is that the consumers were having to pay as much as ever for the new omelettes the courts had cooked for them, and were not pleased. By the campaign of 1912, Taft was reduced to pointing out consolingly that prices were going up all over the world, and "we are more prosperous than we have ever been."

Long since, the progressive Republicans of the Midwest had cut loose from Taft. They had blamed him, unjustly, for their failure to oust Speaker Cannon in 1909. By 1910, without his blessing, they were strong enough to make a fight. Under the leadership of George W. Norris, on March 15, they breached Cannon's formidable parliamentary defenses and opened a fierce debate which raged for nearly thirty hours. It ended with Cannon's removal from the Rules Committee, which henceforth was to be elected by the House. He remained as speaker, however, and the conservative Republicans continued to control committees. The immediate change was not great but it gave impetus to the progressive movement. Taft, who was doubtless sympathetic toward Norris, received none of the credit; indeed it heightened the insurgent onslaught against him. The progressives even charged that his proposal for a Postal Savings Bank system, to be used by small depositors suspicious of banks, was Wall-Street inspired, although actually it was fought by the American Bankers' Association. Taft, convinced that the Middle Western insurgency was determined to destroy him, openly allied himself with the conservatives of the section, seeking through patronage to root out the insurgents in the elections of 1910.

Meanwhile, through the sensational Ballinger-Pinchot controversy, Taft had lost the sympathy of most of Theodore Roosevelt's following in the urban East and the Far West. The basis of the trouble was that Taft had replaced Roosevelt's Secretary of the Interior with a man who wished to distribute the natural resources in the public domain to private interests for development. The viewpoint of the new Secretary, Richard Ballinger, was the one that was dominant among businessmen of the West, who wished themselves to prosper and to see their region grow. But Taft had left in charge of the Forestry Service in the Department of Agriculture Roosevelt's ardent admirer, Gifford Pinchot of Pennsylvania, whose zeal, like that of most Eastern nature lovers and sportsmen, was to preserve the public domain unspoiled, as a part of the nation's heritage. A violent clash between these two men was almost inevitable, and indeed had been foreshadowed in the Roosevelt administration, in which they had both served.

The occasion was the spectacular charge of a twenty-five-year-old investigator in the Department of the Interior, Louis R. Glavis, that Ballinger was conniving to turn over valuable coal lands in Alaska to a Morgan-Guggenheim Syndicate. Glavis, rebuffed by Ballinger, had gone outside of the Interior Department to Pinchot, who sent him directly to the President. Taft, accepting Ballinger's rebuttal, publicly exonerated him and endorsed the dismissal of Glavis. Immediately not only Pinchot but Roosevelt progressives throughout the country championed Glavis as the defender of the national domain against the corrupt onslaught of big business. Pinchot, by going over the President's head directly to Congress, in effect forced Taft to discharge him for insubordination. A Congressional committee investigated, and since the Old Guard dominated it, reported in favor of Ballinger. His victory was slight, for Glavis's brilliant attorney, Louis D. Brandeis, through his adroit questioning had proved that Ballinger, while not dishonest, was thoroughly out of sympathy with conservationism. Newspapers and magazines, especially *Colliers*, heralded these revelations to scandalized progressive millions. To the end, Taft stood by his Secretary of the Interior, whom he correctly considered to be an honorable man. But in refusing to dismiss Ballinger as an anti-conservationist, Taft drove a rift between himself and the Roosevelt following that was as wide and deep as that separating him from the La Follette supporters.

None of the notable achievements of the Taft administration could protect the President from the progressives' scorn. He received no credit for the considerable extension of conservation, even under Ballinger; the passage of a $20,000,000 bond issue for irrigation projects; or the considerable array in other areas: nearly eighty antitrust suits, the postal savings system for small depositors, the establishment of parcel post, the extension of civil service to lesser postmasterships, the creation of the Federal Children's Bureau, a Commerce Court, and a commission to promote efficiency and economy in government, and the signing of the Mann-Elkins Act providing much stricter regulation of railroads. Compared with what Roosevelt had achieved as President it was a notable record, but compared with what progressives now wanted, it was inadequate. The railroad act, for example, fell seriously short of progressive expectations. As early as the tariff fiasco in 1909, progressives had begun looking to the African wilderness for their next presidential candidate.

The Democratic Victories in 1910

IN THE MIDDLE OF JUNE, 1910, loaded with trophies from Africa and fresh impressions of reform from Europe, Roosevelt returned. Since he had emerged at Khartoum he had maintained a Sphinx-like silence,

"Back in the Old Place" by Nelson Harding for the Brooklyn Eagle

and had promised friends he would make no public statement until he had studied the situation. He was as good as his word, but observers noted that his first hello was to Pinchot, and that he did not accept Taft's invitation to the White House. Actually, he had already met Pinchot in Europe, bearing messages from progressives, and had come to the conclusion that Taft had "completely twisted around the policies I advocated and acted upon."

Roosevelt arrived just in time to observe the internecine war among progressive and conservative factions of the Republican party in the 1910 primaries. Cannon and his supporters were denouncing the progressives as prophets of discord and socialistic demagogues who were "Elphadonks" rather than Republicans. "Taft Republicans" in Kansas, financed by Aldrich's corporation fund, were crying "Death to the progressives." Progressives retaliated by charging dishonesty against Aldrich and claiming that the conservative Senator Lodge was "a slave of the steel trust." In primary after primary west of the Mississippi, the progressives whipped the regulars. They defeated forty-one incumbent Republican congressmen and won almost every senatorial and gubernatorial contest.

Although Roosevelt was furious with Taft for helping bring about the split in the party, he determined to do all he could to reunify it. He told reporters he was seeing all Republicans—"regulars and insurgents, party men and independents." He also refused to participate in primary contests even though he assured several insurgents that he secretly sympathized with them. Rather, he tried whenever possible to bring about compromises between the factions so that they could defeat the Democrats in November.

In New York Roosevelt did take sides to fight with the progressive faction against the reactionary Republican boss and the remnants of the notorious "black-horse brigade," presumably because here he could strike the Old Guard, yet side with Taft. Unfortunately, in the complex political in-fighting Taft wound up on the conservative side. Consequently, it was in an excited state of mind that Roosevelt set out on a Western speaking trip in late August. He was still ready to support all Republican candidates —the conservative Warren G. Harding in Ohio as well as progressives elsewhere—but at Osawatomie, Kansas, on September 1, he delivered a speech which returned him to command of the progressives.

At Osawatomie, Roosevelt proclaimed the doctrines of the New Nationalism, emphasizing that social justice could be attained in the nation only through strengthening the power of the federal government so that the executive could be the "steward of public welfare." The judiciary must not disrupt this stewardship; contrary to its traditional position it must "be interested primarily in human welfare rather than property." Indeed, this must be the position of the American nation. Men thinking primarily of property rights and personal profits "must now give way to the advocate of human welfare, who rightly maintains that every man holds his property subject to the general right of the community to regulate its use to whatever degree the public welfare may require it."

Beyond these generalizations, in themselves so frightening to the Old Guard, Roosevelt outlined his "square deal" program: graduated income and inheritance taxes, workmen's accident compensation, regulation of the labor of women and children, tariff revision, and firm regulation of corporations through a more powerful Bureau of Corporations and Interstate Commerce Commission. To Roosevelt this program was undoubtedly part of his basic conservatism, reflecting as it did much of what he had advocated as President, reinforced by what he had learned earlier that spring in England of the Liberal party reforms. In effect he was ready to bring the Lloyd George budget of 1909 to the United States. From the Mississippi westward, progressives were ready to acclaim him as the next presidential candidate, but among his right-wing enemies, Lodge warned him, he was regarded as "little short of a revolutionist."

Characteristically, Roosevelt, having lit a prairie fire among the progressives, tried next to stamp it out. He tried to regain the confidence of the regulars through commending Taft in his subsequent speeches, and by election day was complaining privately with equal heartiness of "the wild irresponsible folly" of the insurgent vanguard and the asininities of the "Bourbon-Reactionaries." Everywhere, he saw, the two factions "intend to cut the throats of the other at the polls." Even as he predicted, the regular Republicans, laboring under the handicap of party schism, the Payne-Aldrich tariff, and the Ballinger-Pinchot controversy, were submerged by Democrats in much of the East and Midwest. At the same time progressives won in nine states, from Wisconsin west, where they controlled the Republican party machinery. Throughout the East also, the progressive vote had been heavy, and while many men of property had moved into the Democratic party, so had many progressives, in order to elect men like the new governor of New Jersey, Woodrow Wilson. The Democrats also captured the House of Representatives.

For the moment, Roosevelt was in political eclipse at Oyster Bay, since all but two of the Republican candidates for whom he had spoken in the East had been defeated. Further west, progressive Republicans, freshly victorious, hoped they could wrest the presidential nomination from Taft in 1912. In January, 1911, a group of them formed the National Progressive Republican League to work for the nomination of La Follette, but a great majority of the progressive Republicans continued to hope that Roosevelt could be persuaded to run.

The Crusade Against City Bosses

While on a national level the relentless quarrel went on between progressive and regular Republicans, progressivism made giant strides on the state and local planes. Muckrakers aroused progressives to fight against the corruption and vice still all too common in urban centers.

The Shame of the Cities was the title Lincoln Steffens gave to his notable series of exposures which first appeared in *McClure's*, and shame was what civic-minded progressives felt. They tried to wrest control of their city governments away from the machines, reorganize the governments scientifically, and use them as instruments of economic and social reform. Banded into civic associations, they fought with the aid of women's organizations, many of the churches, and the crusading segment of the press. Part of their support—as long as they were fighting for clean, inexpensive government—came from real estate and other business groups that had favored this type of reform since the onslaught against Boss Tweed's Tammany in the seventies. But much of this faction was equally fervent in its hostility toward the reforms of the social-justice movement, because these would increase taxes.

Arrayed in the opposition were the bosses, and behind them those interests so abhorrent to the progressives, the saloons and brothels, and various businesses which could gain more from the bosses than from clean government. Allied with the bosses were some newspapers that ridiculed the progressives as either killjoys or scoundrels. Finally, there was the great constituency of city working people, mostly of immigrant origins. To them the bosses were friends who could be counted upon to help them when they ran afoul of the law in some minor way, or were in need of jobs or food. The bosses, to an extent which sometimes surpassed the progressives, did keep in close touch with the common man; their records were not merely ones of unmitigated evil. Progressives, on the other hand, seemed to be do-gooders who were trying to take away the saloon, the poor man's club, and to deprive him of his amusements from prize-fighting to Sunday baseball. What could be more logical than the laborer's readiness to deliver his vote to the boss?

Many progressives, finding it difficult to grasp the relationship between the bosses and their constituents, saw the problem in simple moral and legal terms. Bad government, they thought, came from bad charters. They should seize the municipal governments and through reforming the charters usher in the urban millenium. For a time they seemed remarkably successful.

The beginning grew out of tragedy in Galveston, Texas, where the old, ineffective government broke down in the wake of a tidal wave. The citizens replaced it with a commission of five, whose members by 1908 were jointly enacting ordinances and were singly running the main city departments. In 1907, Des Moines adopted the commission plan with modifications to make it more democratic, and other cities followed. Another variation was the city-manager plan to place a trained expert, similar to the manager of a business, in charge of the city, and make him responsible to the commission or the mayor and council. Staunton, Virginia, hired a city manager in 1908; the new device attracted national attention when Dayton, Ohio, adopted it in 1913 to speed rehabilitation from a serious flood. By the end of the Progressive era some 400 cities were operating under commissions, and another 45 under city managers.

Whether through old or new city machinery, progressives fought to destroy economic privilege on the municipal level. During these years it meant primarily trying to prevent the sale of streetcar franchises, or to force exorbitantly high fares downward. The most notable of the reform mayors was Tom Johnson of Cleveland, who had invented the streetcar fare box. He was a traction magnate converted to the ideas of Henry George. As mayor, Johnson fought to raise the ridiculously low assessments upon railroad and utility property, introduce city planning, and above all, lower streetcar fares to three cents. After his defeat and death, his brilliant aide, Newton D. Baker, was elected mayor, and helped maintain Cleveland's position as the best governed American city. In almost every city, leaders in the social-justice movement were fighting to destroy slums and replace them with parks and playgrounds, establish free kindergartens, improve sanitary conditions, and raise standards of public health.

Many of the urban gains of progressivism were permanent, but in some cities, as soon as progressives relaxed, the old forces recaptured the city hall. Cities seemed to require periodic cleanups. In other municipalities, state control over city government made reform almost impossible. Cities derived all of their powers from the state, and many a state legislature granted new charters only reluctantly, or controlled a large city within the state through special legislation. In the state of New York, which functioned this way, the reform mayor of Schenectady complained, "Whenever we try to do anything, we run up against the charter. It is an oak charter, fixed and immovable." Consequently, a municipal home-rule movement spread, to try to obtain state laws allowing cities to write their own charters. Much of the difficulty with state legislatures was even more serious. Many a reformer, like Johnson in Cleveland, or Joseph W. Folk in St. Louis, found himself helpless in the cities because the trail of corruption led back to the legislature.

The Attacks on State Machines

Hiram Johnson in California, Folk in Missouri, and other progressives moved on from cities where they had been crusading district attorneys to become progressive governors. It was only by taking this step that Folk, for example, was in a position to break the bosses and control the big corporations behind them. It was Johnson's avowed purpose as governor of California to end the political hold of the Southern Pacific Railroad upon the state, a hold so firm that some years earlier, at a banquet eighteen months before an election, Edward H. Harriman, president of the railroad, had been able to predict accurately that an obscure congressman would become the next governor.

At the state level, progressives enacted a wide array of legislation to increase the power of crusading governors, give the people more direct control over the government, and decrease, sometimes almost to the point of insignificance, the functions of legislators. It was these ill-paid, relatively inconspicuous men who were being exposed by muckrakers as the villains in many a state. William Allen White in *McClure's*, December, 1905, described the Missouri legislators:

> The legislature met biennially, and enacted such laws as the corporations paid for, and such others as were necessary to fool the people, and only such laws were enforced as party expediency demanded. . . . Boodling, bribe-giving, public blackmail, legislative hold-ups, corrupt political deals and combinations carrying thousands of dollars with them flourished, and politicians who benefited thereby were accounted shrewd.

This view of the legislatures led progressives to circumscribe and circumvent them in almost every conceivable way. The most important of the devices, the initiative and the referendum, were first enacted in Oregon in 1902 as a result of the quiet but persistent advocacy of the secretary of several voters' organizations, William S. U'Ren. The initiative enabled voters to short-circuit the legislature and vote upon measures at general elections; the referendum forced the return of laws from the legislature to the electorate. By 1918, twenty states had adopted these schemes. A number had also limited their state legislatures through prescribing a wide variety of matters upon which the state could act only through constitutional amendments that the voters must approve. From 1900 to 1920, the electorates voted upon a total of about 1,500 constitutional amendments, and approved some 900. In some states, these devices created long ballots crammed with technical measures which plagued voters at elections long after the Progressive era. A half-century later the crowded California ballot was forcing voters to be what one commentator called "do-it-yourself legislators."

Although progressives threw part of the legislative burden back onto the electorate, they also tried to obtain better officials. They tried to eliminate machine choice of candidates through the direct primary, first instituted in Mississippi in 1902 and adopted in some form by every state by 1915. Unfortunately, if they were not vigilant, machines operated one step further back and dominated the primaries. Another way many progressives hoped to thwart the machines was through giving the vote to women. For decades this had been the keystone of the women's rights movement, since women felt that once they obtained this they could vote in their other rights. As early as 1897, Colorado women obtained the right to vote, at a time when those of Kentucky still could not legally even make wills. By 1914, women could vote in twelve states, all west of the Mississippi; in 1916, Montana elected the first woman to the House of Representatives. During the first World War, Congress finally gave in to the suffragists, and in 1919 the Nineteenth Amendment was added to the Constitution. It made no spectacular change in voting patterns. In 1920, when for the first time all American women could vote in a presidential election, a large majority of them seem to have voted for Warren G. Harding.

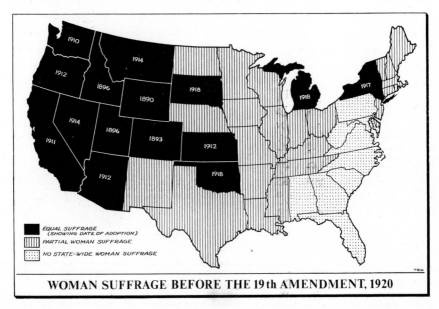

WOMAN SUFFRAGE BEFORE THE 19th AMENDMENT, 1920

A more controversial and less widely used device for obtaining better officials was the recall, which made possible removal from office through a special election to be called after sufficient numbers of the electorate had signed petitions. It became a national issue when President Taft vetoed a bill admitting Arizona as a state because its constitution authorized recall of judges. Horrified conservatives approved of the veto, but soon after Arizona entered the union without the offensive provision the state's voters restored it.

Undoubtedly all these devices did bring about a greater degree of democratization. Progressives used them to obtain control of states, and then eradicated corruption and passed reform legislation. La Follette in Wisconsin obtained firm regulation of railroads, compensation for workmen injured in industrial accidents, and graduated taxation of inheritances. Hughes in New York obtained a commission to regulate public utilities. When Wilson, fresh from the presidency of Princeton University, became governor of New Jersey in 1911, he obtained from the legislature a substantial array of measures to transform the state from the backward "mother of trusts" into one of the progressive leaders.

Nevertheless, much social-justice legislation came only late and after much struggle. New York failed to enact factory-safety legislation until it was shocked into action by the Triangle Shirtwaist Factory fire in New York City in 1911, in which 148 people, mostly young women, were helplessly trapped and killed in a few minutes. When factory bills were introduced, several of the Tammany legislators, especially Alfred E. Smith and Robert F. Wagner, were active in their behalf. Boss Charles F. Murphy had found that Tammany gained many votes by supporting an earlier law limiting women to 54 hours of work a week, and now was ready to put his machine behind welfare legislation on behalf of his working-class constituents. It was something different from the progressive movement; it was the beginning of a basic shift in American politics which reached a climax in the New Deal, when urban organizations furnished strong support for national reform legislation.

Throughout the era, progressive legislators ran the risk that the Supreme Court would invalidate their handiwork, for it never became really progressive. Even the great iconoclast on the Court, Holmes, was ready during the Taft administration to apply the "rule of reason" to trust-busting, and was reluctant to allow the I.C.C. to regulate railroad rates. Nevertheless the Court made one great, although temporary, shift toward progressivism. This came in 1908 when Brandeis argued before it on behalf of an Oregon law to limit women workers to a ten-hour day. He presented a brief in which he devoted only 2 of 104 pages to the legal precedents and the remainder to proofs that Oregon's police power was necessary to protect the health and general welfare of the mothers, and thus of all mankind. The Supreme Court accepted this arguing, although in effect it was moving toward the "sociological jurisprudence" which Dean Roscoe Pound of the Harvard Law School advocated. This, Pound was explaining, was a movement to adjust "principles and doctrines to human conditions they are to govern rather than to assumed first principles."

Progressives engaged in state reforms looked nationally not only to the Supreme Court but also to the Congress and the White House. Here obviously rested the ultimate power for the control of the many problems that crossed state lines. They obtained from the Congress in 1910 several laws to reinforce state legislation. The Webb-Kenyon Act, passed over Taft's veto, prohibited the interstate shipment of liquor into dry areas; the Mann Act outlawed the interstate transportation of "white slaves," and thus helped in the progressive fight to break up prostitution syndicates, one of the main sources of underworld income.

It was also at the state level that progressives fought to liberalize the United States Senate through the direct election of Senators. State legislatures were occasionally open to bribery, and much too often they elected conservatives who did not represent the public choice. David Graham Phillips in his sensational articles, "The Treason of the Senate," scourged the body as a rich men's club; a California Senator replied that there were only ten millionaires in the Senate. Lord Bryce had written in 1888, "Some, an increasing number, are senators because they are rich; a few are rich because they are senators."

By 1902, the House of Representatives had already five times passed resolutions for a constitutional amendment for direct election of Senators; each time the Senate blocked the amendment. Impatient progressives in various states developed techniques for circumventing the Constitution and providing in effect for direct election. By 1912, twenty-nine states had adopted these devices. In 1911, Governor Wilson of New Jersey gained renown by blocking the legislative election of a party boss, while at the same time in New York, Franklin D. Roosevelt, just 29, won his political spurs by leading legislative insurgents against Tammany's hand-picked candidate, a Buffalo traction magnate. That same year, the Senate ousted one of its members, Boss William E. Lorimer of Chicago, for vote-buying. In the wake of the public indignation that followed, the Senate in 1912 passed the Seventeenth Amendment, and by 1913 the requisite number of states had ratified it. The new amendment did not startlingly modify the nature of the Senate, since most progressive states had already elected Senators of a new mettle.

Neither did another progressive reform measure, the preferential presidential primary, have much consequence. This was begun in Oregon in 1910 and had spread to twenty states by 1920, but it by no means eliminated the maneuvering in conventions. Its main effect was to conduct a series of state-wide popularity contests among leading candidates in the months before the convention. These were of a spectacular nature in 1912, not to be equalled for a score of years, for they were one of the opening battles in the progressive revolution of that year.

Chapter **5**

THE NEW FREEDOM
TRIUMPHS

As the election of 1912 approached, the progressive movement had grown so strong that it gave promise of capturing both the presidency and the Congress. A decided majority of the American electorate seemed to favor the sort of legislative program that President Roosevelt had not been able to wrest from Congress, and which President Taft had been too conservative or too inept to try to obtain. The makeup of Congress had become decidedly more progressive; with encouragement from the White House, it was ready to produce a harvest of national legislation.

What was not as yet apparent was whether a national progressive program would come under Republican or Democratic auspices. If the Democrats ran a progressive for the presidency and the Republicans renominated Taft, the Democrats might win. Among the Republicans, progressive sentiment was building to such an explosive point that it was likely either to carry the nomination or blast the party. President Taft by the fall of 1911 had reached such a state of pessimism that he publicly admitted he would probably be defeated the following year. The prediction was more of a credit to Taft's skill as a prophet than his ability as a politician. As further indication of how little he had learned about politics, he was vigorously prosecuting the trusts and making progressive appointments, an action which offended his conservative supporters without winning back the progressives. Nevertheless he had properly distributed patronage to guarantee himself a heavy majority of delegates at the Republican convention.

The Promise of the New Nationalism

AT THIS POINT Roosevelt seems to have lost touch with political realities. After the 1910 debacle he had been depressed to the point of considering himself a complete political has-been. As he recuperated, he at first viewed with relative equanimity the prospect that Taft would be renominated and go down to defeat, then began to fear that a Democratic victory, whether of foolish radicals or "Bourbon reactionaries," would be a national calamity. With Roosevelt receptive, many of La Follette's supporters switched to him indecently quickly after La Follette on February 2, 1912, exhausted and worried, delivered a rambling, repetitive talk. Roosevelt thus acquired new recruits as he moved toward what he later called Armageddon, but he also won the undying hatred of La Follette and his loyal Middle Western progressive following. Nevertheless, in the primaries Roosevelt demonstrated that he was overwhelmingly the presidential choice of Republican voters. Further the Republican electorate was topheavily progressive, for Roosevelt and La Follette together polled twice as many votes as Taft. Unfortunately for Roosevelt, only a minority of the delegates were elected by primaries; the majority were chosen by state conventions, for the most part dominated by Republican regulars. Some politicians thought Roosevelt would win the nomination at the convention, but it would depend upon the seating of the delegates; more than a third of the seats were contested. The Republican National Committee, made up almost entirely of loyal Taft supporters, allowed Roosevelt only 19 out of 254 contested seats, and thus in advance counted him out of the nomination.

Roosevelt himself came to direct his forces at the convention. The night before it opened, he told a hysterically cheering throng of 5,000 that he would not be bound by the convention if it failed to seat his contested delegates. He concluded thunderously, "We stand at Armageddon, and we battle for the Lord." As good as his word, he bolted, leaving the conservatives in complete command at the Republican convention. With Roosevelt's onetime friend Elihu Root presiding, Warren G. Harding, one of the most regular of the regulars, mellifluously nominated Taft. This seemed to symbolize what the Republican party had become. Taft was chosen on the first ballot, amidst bitterness and gloom.

It was in a different atmosphere that the Progressive party came into existence. During the Republican convention, Roosevelt agreed to its formation when Frank Munsey, the newspaper magnate, and George W. Perkins, of United States Steel and International Harvester, promised him financing. Roosevelt, agreeing publicly to run, remarked that he was as fit as a bull moose, giving the party a symbol as well as a name. When the Progressives met at Chicago in August to nominate Roosevelt formally, the conclave was far more symbolic of progressivism than of ordinary American politics. It was important primarily for the program it presented, one of the basic manifestoes in the history of American reform. Most of the Republican progressives who were in control of their state party machinery, or who were running for re-election, were not there. Missing were La Follette and his following, five of seven governors who had signed a call for Roosevelt in January, and such notable Republican insurgents as Norris of Nebraska and William E. Borah of Idaho. There were present a few of the old line bosses and a handful of well-established politicians like Hiram Johnson of California, but the rank and file was made up of fervent middle-class reformers from the cities, like Jane Addams of Hull House, and aspiring urban progressive politicians, like Harold L. Ickes of Chicago. An ambitious young mining engineer, Herbert Hoover, sent a campaign contribution from London.

The reformers dominated the proceedings so that the convention bore more resemblance to a camp meeting than the gatherings to which Roosevelt was accustomed. The delegates sang "Onward Christian Soldiers," and closed the convention with the "Doxology." Roosevelt seemed to a newspaperman to appear bewildered as he acknowledged their almost fanatical, hymn-singing welcome, because "they were crusaders; he was not." If so, this disparity was not openly apparent, for in his "Confession of Faith," he castigated both of the two old parties as representing "government of the needy many by professional politicians in the interests of the rich few." He offered his followers the full array of advanced progressive reform—all the changes in the machinery of government; all the economic and social legislation. Once more he singled out the courts for attack. At the end of the campaign he asserted in words foreshadowing a great struggle a quarter-century later, "We stand for the Constitution, but we will not consent to make of the Constitution a fetish for the protection of fossilized wrong."

What was distinctive and different about Roosevelt's program was his willingness to accept big business, provided it should be regulated through a national industrial commission. A Federal Securities Commission should police stocks and bonds. In the program of New Nationalism there was much to appeal to the progressives of the cities, whether reformers or businessmen, but little of interest to farmers, and much paternalism but no guarantee of collective bargaining for organized labor. In an effort to win disgruntled Southern businessmen away from the Democratic party, Roosevelt endorsed a lily-white Progressive party for the South.

Altogether, Roosevelt's New Nationalism represented the ultimate in urban progressivism. When the votes were counted, Roosevelt had run 10 per cent better in the eighteen largest cities than in the country as a whole. His program owed much to the thinking of Herbert Croly, who in the *Promise of American Life* blue-printed a powerful federal government that would regulate in the interest of the whole nation the forces of big business and small, agriculture, and labor. It owed much also to the enlightened capitalists like Munsey and Perkins, who saw the solution of the monopoly program in regulation rather than destruction. Its basic significance was in firing the imaginations of young men who a score of years later tried to put the program into effect in the early New Deal.

For the moment, the Progressive insurrection spelled political disaster for Roosevelt personally and for his zealous followers. Why had he, who had always been "regular," split from his party? Perhaps he was carried away by the excitement of the moment. Perhaps he was gambling that the Democrats might nominate a Bourbon, and that consequently their progressive wing might defect and elect him. Perhaps it was his strenuous philosophy of sportsmanship which led him to charge to defeat in 1912 rather than retreat to ultimate victory in 1916 or 1920. "I wish to Heaven I was not in this fight," he wrote privately, "and I am in it only on the principle, in the long run a sound one, that I would rather take a thrashing than be quiet under such a kicking." It was misplaced gallantry, for like an unwitting Pied Piper he had led the idealistic young Progressives out of the Republican party, and the Old Guard were not disposed to let them back except on terms of unconditional surrender. W. P. Hepburn exulted at the time of the exodus that it would eliminate "the guerillas and insurgents" and restore the Republican party to its old conservatism. Thus Roosevelt's candidacy relegated progressives to a weak minority in the Republican party.

The Appeal of the New Freedom

BETWEEN THE PROGRESSIVE bolt of the Republican convention and their nomination of Roosevelt, the Democratic party met at Baltimore, exultant with the heady knowledge that, although they were a political minority, they almost certainly were nominating the next President. Bryan, who long had dominated the party, stood aside while four contenders battled for the nomination. They were Governor Woodrow Wilson of New Jersey, Speaker Champ Clark of Missouri, the right-wing Governor Judson Harmon of Ohio, and Representative Oscar W. Underwood, the champion of Southern conservatism and a low tariff. Wilson's spectacular reform achievements in New Jersey had early made him the favorite of Democratic progressives in Eastern cities, and he took a quick lead for the nomination as he crisscrossed the nation to make hundreds of inspiring speeches denouncing special privilege and heralding the new progressive order. Yet, in 1912, he emerged from the primaries and state conventions with only 248 delegates to Clark's 436. Underwood swept most of the South.

Why did the dynamic Wilson lag so far behind the uninspiring, heavy-drinking Clark, whose only redeeming feature was progressive regularity? The answer was that Clark had the party professionals and most state organizations, the Hearst press, and most of Bryan's old agrarian following (although not Bryan himself) behind him. Professionals preferred dealing with professionals rather than with the little group of Southerners migrated North who served as Wilson's leaders. It was little short of a miracle that Clark, who had the rural Democrats and most of the bosses behind him, and who obtained more than a majority of the votes on ballot after ballot, nevertheless failed to win the nomination. The main reason for the miracle was that the Wilson and Underwood forces stood firm, blocking Clark's nomination while Wilson's managers negotiated deals with the machines and the Underwood following. To some slight extent it may have been due to Bryan, who fought for a progressive keynoter, and received the unequivocal endorsement of only Wilson. Partly it may have been the intangible factor that the bibulous Clark with his threadbare "Signs of the Times" lecture and "Ol' Hound Dawg" song would have been a slow-footed warrior to send into the fray against Roosevelt at Armageddon.

A crusade requires a crusader, and this the Democrats obtained at last on the forty-sixth ballot when they nominated Wilson. This lean, lantern-jawed son of a Southern Presbyterian preacher looked as well as acted the part of a crusader. Born in the Valley of Virginia, brought up in Confederate Georgia and the South Carolina of Reconstruction, Wilson had matured in an atmosphere of romantic nostalgia for the lost cause and Calvinistic ardor for what was right and moral. In his emotions he was deeply devoted to his kinfolk and fervently religious. His aspiration had always been to become a political leader, but when as a beginning lawyer in Atlanta he had found the road rough, he had taken a doctor's degree at Johns Hopkins. He had become a professor of political economy, and later president of Princeton University. At Princeton, his lectures, evoking images of the selfless founding fathers, inspired his students with a respect for an idyllic American past. His graceful writings were also more inspirational than analytical. Wilson drew his own intellectual strength from the Bible, and from the political essays of the English conservatives, especially Edmund Burke and Walter Bagehot. The British parliamentary system was his ideal, and as President he was to pattern himself more on Gladstone than on Jefferson.

President Woodrow Wilson (NATIONAL ARCHIVES)

Both as president of Princeton and as governor of New Jersey, Wilson demonstrated the courageous strength and alarming weaknesses that would characterize his Presidency. Both times he fought through major reform programs, and then, because of personality difficulties, lost control. He had the vision to inspire multitudes, but was dogmatic and distant with individuals. He could lecture an opposition in high moral terms, but his sense that he and he alone was absolutely right prevented him from stooping to necessary political negotiations. His sense of virtue, backed by stubbornness, could lead him away from political accommodation into bitter deadlock. Out of the same characteristics came the glory of Wilson and his ultimate tragedy.

In 1912, and for some time thereafter, only the glory was apparent. Wilson had won the nomination without badly splitting the party. Backed by a progressive platform, he appeared before the electorate in armor at least as shiny as Roosevelt's. The distance between the positions of the Democratic party and the new Progressive party was not as great as campaign oratory made it out to be, just as personality more than principle separated Wilson from Roosevelt. Nevertheless, the differences in platform were significant in the campaign and in Wilson's future program as President.

Wilson's New Freedom emerged as the campaign unfolded. His conversion to progressivism had come only two or three years before, and he had continued to cling to the state-rights position that the task of the federal government was the purely negative one of destroying privilege. Thus Wilson hoped to restore the good old days, which in reality had never existed, to re-create full opportunity for the small enterpriser. Brandeis, the leading spokesman for regulation on behalf of small businessmen, met with Wilson at the end of August, and helped him develop this as the main theme of his campaign. Roosevelt's New Nationalism, Wilson charged, would mean the federal licensing of the juggernauts of big business to crush the American people. In contrast, Wilson proclaimed his New Freedom as the fight for the emancipation of the small businessman, the "man on the make." He proclaimed, "If America is not to have free enterprise, then she can have freedom of no sort whatever." Roosevelt retorted that this was "Rural Toryism." Roosevelt's labor program, Wilson declared, would substitute federal paternalism for freedom. The Democrats, in contrast, had promised freedom from the restraints of the Sherman act so that unions could bargain collectively. This, not welfare legislation, was what organized labor had been clamoring for, and the unions openly supported Wilson. For the first time they helped bring the Democrats into power.

Wilson's appeal was greatest in the hinterland. He was able during the campaign to win over Bryan's rural and small-town following with the same religious appeal, the same excoriation of the Wall Street money trust and extolling of the little man that the "Great Commoner" had always used. There was more hint of stained glass and less of the camp meeting in Wilson's phrases, but this was all to the good. Some well-educated people who had always scorned Bryan as a fool came to revere Wilson as a saint.

Thus Wilson was able to hold Democratic progressives within his party, and Roosevelt was able to pull only progressives out of the Republican party. As for Taft, after several sad speeches, so conservative that they might have been written by Aldrich, he lapsed into silence. The Socialists, at the peak of their strength that year under Eugene V. Debs, attacked the fundamental acceptance of the established order by all three major candidates. The main effect of the Socialists was to serve as a bugaboo for progressive leaders, who could warn that the only alternative to their safe, moderate programs would be the drastic remedies of Socialism. Even in 1912, the Socialists' heyday, they attracted only 901,000 votes, 6 per cent of the total cast.

Because of the three-cornered contest, Wilson carried the electoral college overwhelmingly, with 435 votes to 88 for Roosevelt and only 8 for Taft. In popular votes, Wilson polled 6,293,000; Roosevelt, 4,120,000; and Taft, 3,485,000. Wilson had received less than 42 per cent of the popular vote, less than Bryan in any of his three campaigns, but in terms of the combined Democratic and Bull Moose totals, the vote was an overwhelming progressive mandate.

Enacting Wilson's Program

FEW PRESIDENTS have taken more seriously their electoral mandate or worked more effectively to transform it into law than did Wilson. He brought back into the White House a firm belief in positive presidential

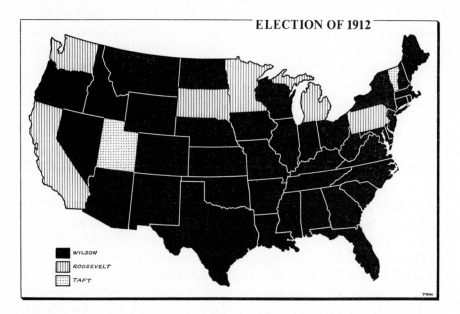

ELECTION OF 1912

WILSON
ROOSEVELT
TAFT

leadership. As he assembled a cabinet and advisers, his only shortcoming was his tendency to gauge his subordinates by their complete, unquestioning willingness to accept his point of view. Senator John Sharp Williams once declared, "He was the best judge of measures and the poorest of men I ever knew."

The closest of Wilson's advisers was the shrewd and ubiquitous Colonel Edward M. House, who, through intelligent service and the refusal to accept a cabinet position, virtually shared presidential powers as Wilson's alter ego until 1919. He served as agent for Wilson in negotiations first with the men of economic power in America, and later with those of political power in Europe. His discretion and anonymity were so consummate that one contemporary remarked, "He can walk on dead leaves and make no more noise than a tiger." It was House who gathered data for Wilson on the cabinet choices.

The cabinet, as was politically necessary, represented the wide range of factions within the Democratic party. Bryan had to be offered the appointment as Secretary of State in recognition of his long leadership of the party. William Gibbs McAdoo, an energetic, ambitious New York entrepreneur from Georgia, became Secretary of the Treasury; Albert S. Burleson, an adroit Texan, as Postmaster General became the political expert in the cabinet. Representative William B. Wilson, earlier Secretary-Treasurer of the United Mine Workers, became the first Secretary of Labor, establishing a twenty-year precedent that the office should be filled by a labor leader. It was the most Southern cabinet since the Civil War; half of its members were Southerners, at least by birth. To the disappointment of progressives there was one omission from the cabinet, Brandeis, whom Wilson did not appoint because of the protests of financiers and Boston machine politicians.

Over his cabinet and Congress, Wilson exerted strong leadership as though he saw in himself the personification of the will of the people. He remarked that first summer, "No one but the President seems to be expected . . . to look out for the general interest of the country." In this spirit, he cajoled and drove the Democratic majority in Congress into writing the New Freedom into law. A good many of these men were energetic, responsible progressives new to the Congress who took no urging, but above them in many important committee chairmanships were the Bourbons. They too were ready to co-operate with Wilson, although less enthusiastically, because they realized that the only opportunity for the Democrats, a minority party, to stay in power was to enact a positive program. Thus Wilson possessed what Roosevelt had lacked, a congressional majority behind him. What he added to Roosevelt's presidential leadership was firm control over the party majority in Congress. Wilson did not wield his patronage powers as young progressive Democrats would have liked, to remodel the party by destroying conservative Democratic control in the many states where it persisted. Since this would have jeopardized his legislative program, he accepted the advice of Burleson and rewarded the faithful old-line Democrats in Congress even though this helped stifle progressivism in several Southern states. In effect he occasionally sacrificed progressive men in order to obtain immediate progressive measures. Wilson may not have been too displeased with this state of affairs, since the fervent young progressives were less manageable than the older and more conservative Democrats. "My head is with the progressives in the Democratic party," he once told his secretary, Joseph Tumulty, "but my heart, because of the way they stood by me, is with the so-called Old Guard. They stand without hitching."

From this formidable position, Wilson undertook what Roosevelt had avoided and Taft had foundered upon, a substantial lowering of the tariff. On the day he took office he called a special session of Congress. When it met, he spectacularly broke a precedent in effect since Jefferson's administration and appeared before both houses in person. His short graphic message was aimed less at them than behind them at their constituents. It brought to a blaze the sentiment for real tariff reform. With the President's active support, Underwood introduced a bill in the House providing for tariff cuts substantial enough to bring European manufacturers into competition with Americans. The bill passed the House by an overwhelming 281 to 139 majority, but Senators, especially those from states producing sugar and wool and backed by the lobbyists of a score of special interests, threatened to engage in the familiar practice of logrolling sabotage. Wilson brought direct pressure upon the recalcitrants and created a sensation by publicly denouncing the "extraordinary exertions" of the "industrious and insidious" lobby. The Midwest progressive Republicans picked up the cue, and to embarrass the administration proposed an investigation. La Follette's investigation aided rather than harmed Wilson, however, for it exposed the innumerable lobbies and the substantial personal economic interests of protectionist Senators. Those Senators who had dutifully revealed their holdings capitulated, and voted for an even lower tariff schedule than the House bill.

To make up for the loss of revenue under the new tariff, Representative Cordell Hull drafted for the bill a section providing, under the new Sixteenth Amendment, for a graduated income tax. Hull cautiously set the rates exceedingly low. To his delight, progressive Republicans and Democrats in the Senate forced substantially higher rates upon the conservatives and the administration. This first modern income tax imposed upon individuals and corporations a tax of 1 per cent on all income over $4,000, and an additional surtax of 1 per cent on income over $20,000, ranging up to a maximum of 6 per cent on income over $500,000. It was the beginning of a great change in the American tax structure. More slowly than England and some other nations, the United States was beginning to place upon those of large income a proportionately greater share of the cost of the government. In so doing, it was beginning to chip away at the enormous disparity in incomes in the United States.

Proud of their handiwork, the Democrats proclaimed that the Underwood-Simmons tariff would cut the cost of living. The law brought the rates down from the Payne-Aldrich level of about 37 per cent to 29 per cent, and added many imports to the free list. The economic upheavals of war came too soon for any proof that it aided consumers or did not injure business. Conclusively, the measure did demonstrate that the Democrats could unite to enact against great hazards a significant piece of reform legislation.

Rather than lose momentum, President Wilson held Congress in session through the sweltering summer to begin work on banking reform. In 1911 he had declared, "The great monopoly in this country is the money monopoly. So long as that exists, our old variety and freedom and individual energy of development are out of the question." A House investigating committee headed by a Democrat, Arsene Pujo, early in 1913 published frightening statistics to back Wilson's accusation. These figures, to which Brandeis gave wide circulation in a series of articles entitled "Other People's Money," indicated that small banks were depositing their surpluses with larger ones, which in turn deposited with a few great investment bankers concentrated on Wall Street. These bankers with their enormous capital, representing the aggregate savings of millions of people, were able to demand control over corporations in return for granting them financing, "the life blood of business." The Morgan-Rockefeller empire held "in all, 341 directorships in 112 corporations having aggregate resources or capitalization of $22,245,000,000." This was in 1913, when the entire national wealth was estimated at less than ten times this figure. The tightness of the control through these directorships was illustrated by the remark of a railroad president in 1905: "Wherever Morgan sits on a board is the head of the table even if he has but one share."

To President Wilson, evidence like this indicated a need to break the money trust. At the same time, paradoxically, one of the serious ills of the American banking system was its decentralization and independence, except through the loose tie of urban clearing houses. This, and the defective functioning of the national banking system, meant that in time of financial crisis and deflation, it was hard for banks to draw upon their reserves or to expand their currency. After the panic of 1907, Congress passed the Aldrich-Vreeland Act as a makeshift to permit greater expansion of the currency in time of economic distress. Aldrich recommended, through the National Monetary Commission in 1912, a broader base for currency and the establishment of a great central bankers' bank under bankers' control. To Wilson and the even more vehemently anti-Wall Street Bryan wing of the Democrats, this seemed to threaten a strengthening of the money trust. But Democrats and Republicans alike agreed that banking reform was needed; both parties had promised it in their platforms.

The conservative Democrat Senator Carter Glass proposed a system with perhaps twenty privately controlled but decentralized bankers' banks (reserve banks). Bryan and his followers favored decentralization, but they did want firm government control. It was no easy task for Wilson to satisfy the agrarians without frightening the bankers, especially since he wished to cap the system with a supervisory board. A great struggle developed over whether it should be under banker or government control. Under the influence of Brandeis, Wilson accepted the minimum progressive specifications, that the federal government exercise exclusive control over the Federal Reserve Board, and stand behind the Federal Reserve notes.

This was not sufficient to appease some Southern and Western agrarians, who demanded the rediscounting of short-term agricultural notes and a provision against interlocking directorates. Wilson promised later legislation against the directorates, and accepted the rediscounting, which would provide easier agricultural credits. Eastern papers sneered at it as "cotton currency" or "corn-tassel currency." With Bryan mediating, and Wilson brandishing every presidential power in his armory, the measure finally went through both houses and was signed by the President on December 23, 1913. It was the most important piece of domestic legislation in his administration.

The Federal Reserve Act created twelve regional banks. Each was to serve and be owned by the banks of its district. The Federal Reserve bank would rediscount their notes, issue a new type of paper currency, Federal Reserve notes, and fulfill other banking functions for member banks and the government. The Act required National Banks to become members, and encouraged other banks to do so. Although the American Bankers' Association had criticized the legislation, nearly half the nation's banking resources were represented in the system within its first year of operation, and four-fifths by the late twenties. Nor did bankers have any cause to fear the Federal Reserve Board, to which Wilson appointed conservative, sympathetic men. When the list was announced, a progressive Republican Senator exclaimed that it looked as though the President of the National City Bank had selected it.

The Federal Reserve system was a notable advance in banking regulation, providing as it did for a more elastic currency, essential at harvest time in agricultural areas, and in periods of crisis throughout the nation. It did not destroy the so-called money trust, but it did mark a significant start toward a decentralization of capital in the United States. It did not serve as a safeguard against panic and depression, although it could to some extent counteract deflationary flurries. Its cautious board failed at times to regulate the discount rate and use its other powers properly; many of the important regulations which the Pujo committee had prescribed had not been enacted. Thousands of banks outside of the system were to fail, and the

Federal Reserve was to demonstrate its impotence to cope with the great crash of 1929 before new reform legislation was enacted to strengthen it.

There remained the over-all problem of the trusts. Wilson had promised to accept legislation abolishing interlocking directorates, but on January 2, 1914, only a few days after he had signed the Federal Reserve Act, the House of Morgan proclaimed that it was voluntarily relinquishing thirty directorships. Wilson decided to go ahead with the legislation anyway, but neither he nor various factions of Democrats in Congress could agree upon where to go. A strong agrarian minority wanted drastic legislation: strict stock exchange regulation, destruction of the interlocking ties of the "money trust," limitation of production by each trust to a third of the product of the particular industry; and a graduated corporation tax so stiff that it would destroy giant combinations. Organized labor, on the other hand, was insistent that it be completely exempted from antitrust legislation. Wilson was strongly opposed to such drastic solutions. Since he felt most businessmen were public-spirited, he sought no more than clear rules for their guidance.

Consequently, as several antitrust bills began their course through Congress in 1914, Wilson shifted to follow the lead of Brandeis away from the rather negative court approach earlier envisaged in the New Freedom, toward the regulatory solution of the New Nationalism. He gave his strong support to a bill outlawing unfair trade practices and establishing a Federal Trade Commission to prohibit unfair methods of competition such as price discrimination or exclusive dealing contracts. The Commission would police business through cease-and-desist orders, engaging in prevention as well as punishment. Thus Wilson intended to stop monopolistic practices at an early stage and protect legitimate business, small as well as large.

Simultaneously, Wilson lost interest in the Clayton Anti-Trust bill. Conservatives in Congress put qualifying clauses around the sections outlawing interlocking directorates or stockholdings and exclusive selling contracts, so that the clauses, as a progressive Republican Senator complained, did not have enough teeth to masticate milk toast. Labor, as the American Anti-Boycott Association reported with satisfaction, gained nothing of practical importance from the bill. It contained no more than a platitude that labor was not a commodity and a declaration that unions were not conspiracies in restraint of trade. Although the clause did not cover such activities of unions as the secondary boycott, President Gompers of the A.F.L. chose to hail the Clayton Act as "Labor's Magna Charta," and insist that organized labor was now exempted from antitrust prosecution. This assumption served merely to make bitterness and resentment the greater when courts continued in the twenties to follow their earlier inclinations. The Sherman and Clayton Acts might be impotent against trusts, but they were a stout club for disciplining boycotters and strikers.

In practice, Wilson's antitrust program was much like those of his predecessors. In the Federal Trade Commission he had accepted the principle of regulation as opposed to dissolution, but the men he appointed to it were so inept or so sympathetic toward business that Brandeis dismissed them as a "stupid administration." Wilson's Attorney General, James C. McReynolds, as an assistant attorney general in the Roosevelt administration and special counsel in the tobacco suits, had come to favor consent decrees over trust-busting. He continued the policy of the Taft administration, and announced that large corporations doubtful about their legality could straighten out their affairs with the friendly co-operation of the Department of Justice. By December, 1913, he had thus obtained a spectacular settlement with the American Telephone and Telegraph Company, which dropped control of the Western Union Telegraph Company. Prosecutions continued, but their main effect was either political (to placate anti-Wall Street sentiment) or persuasive (to bring about consent decrees). The appropriation and staff were too small for effective regulation or prosecution. With more men and money, the Department of Justice would still have lost in the courts, for the Clayton Act had done nothing to counteract the Supreme Court's limiting "rule of reason."

The debate over antitrust legislation during the first half of 1914 coincided with a deepening depression. It came because the United States, still a debtor nation easily affected by European money markets, suffered from credit restrictions growing out of European pessimism over the Balkan wars and the likelihood of a bigger war. Within this country, businessmen blamed the depression upon the Underwood Tariff, and the other legislation of the New Freedom. Wilson tried to placate business titans through friendly conferences and mild administration of his new reform legislation. He assured the leaders that he opposed only business that expanded "by methods which unrighteously crushed those who were smaller." From its inception the New Freedom had been a comparatively limited, state-rights, negative program, aimed at eliminating the economic evils of America so that free enterprise could flourish. Progressives in Congress had forced Wilson further than he had intended to go in the basic legislation of his first eighteen months in office. By the fall of 1914, when business at home was unsettled and war had broken out abroad, he was ready to proclaim the completion of the New Freedom. The future would be one of business co-operation under the new regulatory legislation.

Through 1914 and 1915, to the disappointment of many advanced progressives, Wilson again and again applied the brakes to reforms. With a state-rights answer he turned aside the plea for woman suffrage. He condoned the actions of his Southern cabinet members when they introduced Jim Crow into the administration to an unprecedented degree. Only the angry protests of Northern liberals brought some reversal. He opposed a bill to establish federally backed land banks to ease credit to farmers, declaring it went beyond the proper scope of the government. He gave no

Suffragette being arrested for picketing the White House, July 4, 1917
(NATIONAL ARCHIVES)

aid to a child labor bill because he thought it unconstitutional. With marked misgivings, he studied the La Follette Seamen's bill of 1915, the work of the eloquent president of the Seamen's Union, Andrew Furuseth, which freed seamen of the fetters of their contracts and improved safety regulations. Wilson "finally determined to sign it because it seemed the only chance to get something like justice done to a class of workmen who have been too much neglected by our laws."

A Final Burst of Reform

FOR WILSON, the New Freedom might be complete, but not for the progressive Democrats in Congress. At times they expressed their sharp dismay, but they did not have to engage in warfare with him as had the

Republican insurgents with Taft. When the election year 1916 opened, two things were apparent. The Progressive party, which had never been much more than a Roosevelt vehicle, was disintegrating. Unless the Democrats, who were normally a minority, presented a new, strong progressive program they would be swamped at the polls by the reunited Republicans. Wilson saw this reasoning and went beyond the New Freedom, allying himself with the progressives, farmers, and laborers to accept a

Child at spindles in a Carolina textile mill, 1909 (PHOTOGRAPH BY LEWIS HINE; GEORGE EASTMAN HOUSE COLLECTION)

series of laws which in some respects enacted the Progressive party program of 1912. From a negative policy of restriction he moved to a positive one of vigorous Federal intervention in the economy and society. Strangely, this came at a time when Roosevelt had moved to the far right and no longer supported his 1912 proposals.

In January, 1916, Wilson appointed Brandeis to the Supreme Court, and weathered the conservative uproar to obtain his Senate confirmation. In May, he accepted a farm-loan bank system in the Federal Farm Loan Act. At the urging of progressives, he applied pressure upon the Democratic leaders in the Senate to obtain a workmen's compensation system for federal employees. He also accepted the first federal child-labor law, the Keating-Owen Act of 1916, which prohibited the shipment in inter-state commerce of products manufactured by under-age children. It marked not only a significant reversal on the part of Wilson but also a new assumption of federal control over manufacturing through the commerce clause of the Constitution. When the Supreme Court invalidated it in 1918 by a 5-to-4 decision, Congress passed an act levying a heavy tax on the products of child labor. This too President Wilson signed, and this too the Supreme Court ultimately invalidated, with Taft, who in 1921 became Chief Justice, writing the decision.

Despite the setback in prohibiting child labor, this second wave of legislation in the Wilson administration further enlarged the regulatory function of the federal government. After Wilson had failed to mediate a dispute between the railroad brotherhoods and the railroads, he signed an emergency measure, the Adamson Act, to prevent a nationwide railroad strike that would have paralyzed commerce. The measure provided for an eight-hour day at the previous ten hours' pay for all railroad workers. While it attracted national attention, other less known pieces of legislation brought about even greater changes. Without attracting much attention, they undermined state rights by granting subsidies on a dollar-matching basis for states to undertake various types of programs. Another effect of these laws, in combination with the new income tax, was to take money out of the wealthier northeastern areas and redistribute it in the South and West. The first of these laws was the Smith-Lever Act of 1914, which provided money for states to establish extension work in agricultural education. This made formal and national the new system of county agents to advise farmers, and facilitated the rise of the powerful American Farm Bureau Federation. It was followed by the Smith-Hughes Act of 1917 which subsidized vocational courses in secondary schools. Most important of all, the Federal Highway Act of 1916 appropriated $75,000,000 to be spent for road building over a period of five years.

Altogether the first Wilson administration had gone far beyond the limited reform program of the New Freedom in this impressive array of regulatory legislation, built upon the efforts of all the progressives for a decade and more. To a considerable extent it represented the fruition of most of the main progressive objectives. Wilson was justified in his boast that the Democrats had come close to carrying out the platform of the Progressive party as well as their own. Like many of the products of the progressive spirit, some of the laws were limited and cautious in conception and application. Few of the next generation would accept the exaggerated view of a New York Congressman who denounced one of the measures (the Adamson Act) as "the first step away from the old democracy of Thomas Jefferson and the federal policy of Alexander Hamilton to the socialism of Karl Marx."

Altogether the progressives had achieved much. They had introduced genuine regulation of railroads, a lower tariff, a better credit system, and the income tax. They had refused to give organized labor the weapon of unlimited collective bargaining, but had favored much paternalistic labor legislation. They had failed to curb the growth of large corporations, but had established the principle of corporate regulation. Through federal subsidies they were undermining state barriers in order to secure standard reform legislation. Within states, progressives passed laws regulating

Stuck on the Lincoln Highway in 1915 (BUREAU OF PUBLIC ROADS, DE-PARTMENT OF COMMERCE)

the working conditions of women and even of men, providing workmen's compensation insurance, preventing child labor, and protecting social welfare in a wide variety of ways. On both national and state levels they had made advances in the fields of public health and conservation. Also, progressives had put the businessman on the defensive so that he gave at least a semblance of acting in the public interest. No mogul was likely now to snarl at a reporter, as William H. Vanderbilt had done earlier, "The public be damned." The National Association of Manufacturers lobbied against almost every progressive measure; nevertheless corporations moved toward an era of welfare capitalism. Judge Elbert H. Gary wrote in 1926, "To my personal knowledge many men of big affairs have completely changed their opinions and methods concerning ethical questions in business." Progressivism had played a large part in whatever change had taken place.

In the area of social justice, progressives had failed to legislate a golden age but had wiped out some of the most vile abuses of the nineteenth century. Their improvements to the machinery of government at times creaked or broke down, or responded as readily to bosses as to progressives, but they had unquestionably made governmental institutions, except for the Supreme Court, much more susceptible to popular will. In the next great wave of reform, the leaders did not have to spend years winning control of the machinery of government.

Chapter 6

MILITANT PROGRESSIVISM

THE MILITANT MORALITY of the American people during the Progressive era was not limited to domestic affairs. Police action and government regulation as a means of righting wrongs at home had as a logical concomitant the belief in using threats of armed intervention to obtain justice overseas. A few progressives like President Theodore Roosevelt were ready to throw American force into the preservation of what appeared to be a just power balance in Europe; many more were willing to see the nation risk war to keep a balance in Asia; almost all favored the strongly paternalistic policies in Latin America. A decided majority seems to have favored maintenance of an American empire; a vociferous minority opposed it. These divisions split conservative Americans as well as progressives; thus votes in the Senate on naval bills and expansionist treaties did not run along progressive versus Old Guard lines.

The ardent moralistic nationalism that had so much to do with America's entrance into the war with Spain in 1898 continued to be present. Most Americans, whether their inclinations were militaristic or pacifistic, whether they were from the city or the country, whether they were ill-educated or well-educated, accepted the nationalistic credo of the times. This faith superimposed upon the old spread-eagle Fourth-of-July Americanism the new, supposedly scientific racist doctrines so popular in both the United States and Western Europe. These notions also explain much of the opposition to the "new immigrants," in the absence of any valid data that they were in any way inferior. (There was data capable of such an interpretation, but enlightened members of a later generation labeled it unscientific rubbish.) The popular racist doctrines gave justification for the new colonialism, compounded of equal parts of the old "Manifest Destiny" and Kipling's new "White Man's Burden." This was why a sophisticated Easterner like Roosevelt, who looked toward England as a model, and a simple Populist like Mother Lease, who hated England, both could glory in the new American empire.

Nationalism meant that most Americans during the progressive era did not object too strenuously to naval construction that they thought was purely for national defense. Advocates of a strong navy, in fact, had no stancher friend than the conservative Chicago *Tribune*. Almost everyone accepted without much question strange adventures in the Western Hemisphere. Thus, at the time Marines landed in Vera Cruz, Mexico, Senator William E. Borah of Idaho, usually labeled an "isolationist," proclaimed: "This is the beginning of the march of the United States to the Panama Canal." Most nationalistic Americans also did not object to a strong policy toward east Asia, particularly China. In this area as well as Latin America, they felt that the United States as a matter of historic right had an interest.

Progressives, who cheered as the government put down malefactors at home, were often ready to applaud just as loudly when the government extended its police power overseas. Some, like Jane Addams of Hull House, were pacifistic—indeed, among most progressives there was the optimistic feeling that great wars were not only un-Christian but also outmoded—but there seemed none of the urgency about foreign policy that there was in domestic matters. Hence most progressives, preoccupied by reform at home, allowed the Presidents to conduct foreign policy little observed, and little checked. Walter Lippmann, who had graduated from Harvard into the progressive vanguard in 1910, wrote years later, "I cannot remember taking any interest whatsoever in foreign affairs until after the outbreak of the First World War. . . . I remained quite innocent of the revolutionary consequences of the Spanish-American War."

When progressives did note foreign policy, many of the most idealistic applauded as the United States—through its missionaries, its businessmen, or even its armed forces—brought religion and medicine, economic progress, law and order, and (it was hoped) American democratic institutions to backward areas. Involved in this was the exhiliration of moral adventure, seemingly without risk of major war. It was progressivism by the sword.

Along with these militant moral ideas, most Americans of the Progressive era still clung to the reassuring illusion of being somehow safely isolated from any war that might break out in Europe. They would have been incredulous if anyone had suggested that they were drifting toward the twentieth-century maelstrom of world conflict. It is easier to see in hindsight that the industrial and technological revolutions in the Western world had brought, along with their economic benefits, heightened competition among the great powers for markets, sources of raw materials —and sheer national prestige. The first years of the twentieth century were marked not only by great social gains among industrial nations, but also by a frightening arms race, intensified as these countries split into two rival alliances. Even if the United States had not entered the Spanish-American War it scarcely could have remained long disentangled, since it was the greatest industrial nation in the world. Its emergence from the war with colonies in the Caribbean and the Pacific guaranteed its involvement.

Roosevelt's Foreign Policy

ONE PROGRESSIVE who could see the risks, as he brought the United States into the dangerous business of world power politics, was Theodore Roosevelt. As much as any other progressive, he liked to engage in moralizing about the position of the United States in the world. His most often repeated theme was, as he once put it:

> The just war is a war for the integrity of high ideals. The only safe motto for the individual citizen of a democracy fit to play a great part in the world is service—service by work and help in peace, service through the high gallantry of entire indifference to life, if war comes on land.

This kind of talk rallied the support of many progressives, even those who were revolted by Roosevelt's blatant militarism—and his equally incessant extolling of the soldierly virtues as "the most valuable of all qualities." Beyond and above all this talk, of infinitely more significance, was Roosevelt's realistic conduct of foreign policy as President. In this realm he was an even stronger President than in the domestic area. This was not, as once used to be suggested, because the Old Guard Republicans made a tacit deal with him, giving him freedom there in return for restraints on internal matters. Rather, on foreign policy he could carry with him most of his party, whether to the left or the right, when most questions came before Congress. On other vital questions—and here he created precedents of fateful significance in the twentieth century—the President could act decisively without the need of congressional affirmation, or before matters became known publicly. In one of the most controversial of his acts as President, Roosevelt apparently threatened Germany with naval action if she did not comply with his request, yet made his threat so quietly that most historians regarded his later revelation of the affair as a gross exaggeration.

Roosevelt's concept of the role of the United States in world politics emphasized sea power. Now that the United States had colonies, it needed to build a navy powerful enough to keep the sea lanes open to them. It also needed to build an Isthmian canal so that naval units could sail quickly from one ocean to another, and not have to make a lengthy and difficult transit around Cape Horn, as had the *Oregon* during the Spanish-American War. In addition it needed to protect the Caribbean approaches to the canal from encroachment. All this predicated a strong naval policy at a time when the key to strength in the world was a powerful fleet. It meant a navy second only to that of Great Britain.

These were the views of President Roosevelt at the time when Kaiser Wilhelm II was launching Germany upon a gigantic naval race with Great Britain. The German fleet laws of 1898 and 1900 committed Germany too to a navy second only to England's, and set forth plans for one that could even challenge England. As Britain in 1905 picked up the gauntlet by beginning construction on the first dreadnought, both Germany and the United States embarked upon an intense naval race, amidst increasing alarums of war. There was no real fear of war in the United States, but naval and political leaders regarded each new German battleship as a possible threat in the Western Hemisphere. The progressive period was punctuated with war scares over Japan, which the navy could safely represent to the public as the most likely foe. The power the United States actually was building against was Germany.

Under the strong urging of President Roosevelt, who was himself the most effective of naval lobbyists, Congress between 1902 and 1905 voted for ten battleships and four armored cruisers. These were far stronger than the relatively light vessels of the nineties which had been built primarily to defend the American coastline. The two battleships authorized in 1905 were equal to the dreadnought in firepower and the one or two a year begun from 1906 through 1913 were full dreadnoughts. The fleet became even more effective through revolutionary improvements in gunnery during the Roosevelt administration. The gunnery had been so bad at the Battle of Santiago that the fleet, firing 9433 shots at close range at four Spanish ships, had scored only 122 visible hits. By 1906, *Jane's Fighting Ships* rated the United States Navy as second only to England's, but in the next few years it fell to third place behind Germany.

Even some congressmen who had regularly voted for naval appropriation bills became alarmed as the ships grew larger and larger and the annuals outlays more costly. For several years, the United States spent more on its navy than did Germany, France, Russia, and Japan combined. Critics warned that this would lead to unbridled militarism, and lamented that the money was not going into schools, roads, and public works.

The new navy, extolled in the Sunday supplements more than it was lamented by pacifists, gave President Roosevelt and his successors the armed might with which to back up, if they chose, a strong foreign policy. Roosevelt so chose.

Policing Weak Neighbors

ROOSEVELT'S preoccupation with the American strategy of defense in the Caribbean—especially his almost obsessive fear of German penetration—betrayed him into becoming a stern policeman toward small coun-

"Here No One Dares Lay a Hand but Myself" by Mayol, for the Buenos Aires Caras y Caretas

tries to the South. He did not want to annex them, but he did come to feel that he must police them to keep them from falling prey to expanding European powers.

The new policy first unfolded in Cuba. At the close of the Spanish-American War, the island was in such a chaotic condition that it took several years of paternalistic rehabilitation under General Leonard Wood to prepare it for self-government. Americans took pride in the way the

Army had supervised the building of roads and schools, wiped out diseases, and maintained order so that the blighted economy could re-establish itself. Capital poured in, reaping profits for American businessmen and creating relative prosperity for the Cubans. Since the Cuban people were assured that the occupation was preparing the way for independence, they were relatively content under it. Understandably enough, throughout the Progressive era the administrations in Washington looked to the pattern of Cuban military government as the device for bringing peace, prosperity, and ultimately democracy to revolution-wracked small neighbors to the South.

As General Wood completed his task in Cuba, the question was, how could the United States withdraw without running the risk that Cuba would slip back into anarchy or come under the influence of a European power? The answer was to make Cuba partially a protectorate of the United States. Before Cuba could gain a relative degree of independence, it had to write into its new constitution a series of stipulations, and in 1903 had further to accept them in a treaty with the United States. Among these provisions, first included in the Platt Amendment to the army appropriation bill of 1901, were:

1. Cuba must never enter into a treaty with a foreign power which would impair its independence or permit the establishment of a foreign base.

2. Cuba must not incur a debt larger than could be repaid by the ordinary revenues of the government.

3. Cuba conceded to the United States "the right to intervene for the preservation of Cuban independence, [and] the maintenance of a government adequate for the protection of life, property, and individual liberty."

4. Cuba agreed to allow the United States to maintain bases on the island.

Under the terms of the Platt Amendment, President Roosevelt withdrew the troops from Cuba in 1902, but there was intermittent turbulence and, in 1906, serious revolution. "Lo and behold," Roosevelt complained, the Cubans "may get things into such a snarl that we have no alternative save to intervene—which will at once convince the suspicious idiots in South America that we do wish to interfere after all, and perhaps have some land-hunger." At the end of 1906, the United States did send troops to restore order.

One reason why South American countries looked upon American intervention in Cuba with such deep suspicion was the impetuous way in which President Roosevelt had used his might to start work on a canal in Panama. Even before Roosevelt became President, the McKinley administration was negotiating with England to remove an old obstacle, an 1850 treaty agreeing that the two countries would jointly construct a canal. In 1901 the British, eager to court American friendship, consented in the Hay-Pauncefote treaty to exclusive American construction of a canal—but it had to be unfortified. When the Senate blocked ratification, the British gave way on that point too; the canal could be fortified and thus be made a key part of the American defense system.

The next question, over which serious trouble arose, was where to build the canal. There were two possible routes. The shortest canal would be across the Isthmus of Panama, but the rights there were owned by a French company that had taken over the assets of Ferdinand de Lesseps' earlier bankrupt enterprise. The French company wanted $109,000,000 for its franchise, which would make a canal at Panama more expensive than the longer Nicaraguan route. Consequently a commission, Congress, and President Roosevelt all favored the Nicaraguan route. But the French company had expert agents in Philippe Bunau-Varilla, who had been chief engineer under de Lesseps, and in William Nelson Cromwell, an attorney who had contributed heavily to the Republican campaign fund in 1900. Hastily they cut the price of their rights to $40,000,000 as well they might, since the rights would expire in 1904, and unless sold to the United States and sold quickly, would be worthless. This price cut, and a volcanic eruption in Nicaragua, caused Congress and the President to change their minds.

Impatient to begin digging the canal, Roosevelt put pressure upon Colombia, which included Panama, to conclude a treaty authorizing the United States to dig a canal. In January 1903, Secretary of State Hay signed one with the Colombian chargé d'affaires Tomás Herrán which was most unfavorable to Colombia. It authorized the United States to construct a canal in return for a payment of only $10,000,000 and an annual rental of $250,000, as compared with the $40,000,000 the French company was to receive. Moreover, Colombia must not try to exact money from the French company. Not surprisingly, Colombians were thoroughly disgruntled, since they had hoped to receive much more. If they delayed only one year, all the rights of the French company would revert to them. The Colombian Senate, as it had every right to do, rejected the treaty.

Roosevelt was too furious to give thought to niceties or to the value of a friendly policy toward Latin America. Fuming that the Colombians were "inefficient bandits," he considered seizing Panama through twisting a technicality in an 1846 treaty with Colombia (then New Granada) guaranteeing the neutrality and free transit of the Isthmus. Roosevelt's intended seizure became unnecessary, because Bunau-Varilla helped organize a Panamanian revolution. There had been many such revolutions, all failures. But at the outset of this one, the United States landed troops from the U.S.S. *Nashville*, and, invoking an old treaty obligation to maintain order, prevented Colombia troops from putting down the revolution. Three days later the United States recognized Panama, and within a few days negotiated a treaty paying Panama the sum Colombia had rejected, in return for the grant of a zone ten miles wide. The minister from Panama who arranged the treaty was Bunau-Varilla.

Work on the canal proceeded smoothly and efficiently. The elimination of tropical diseases in the area, the digging of the tremendous cuts, and the installation of huge locks at a total cost of $375,000,000 filled Americans with patriotic enthusiasm. The achievements demonstrated that the United States like other nations could undertake enormous projects in the tropics and, indeed, could succeed where the French had failed. The canal opened in 1914.

Amid the general self-laudation in the United States, some Americans were ashamed of Roosevelt's ruthlessness. He righteously asserted that his every action had been "in accordance with the highest, finest, and nicest standards of public and governmental ethics," but in 1911 he could not resist boasting, "I took the Canal Zone and let Congress debate; and while the debate goes on the Canal does also."

Undoubtedly Roosevelt's principal concern was with perfecting the over-all defense strategy of the United States, not with forcefully stripping Colombia of its greatest national asset. Another indication of his preoccupation with defense was the sharp warning he delivered to Germany over the Venezuelan blockade. At the outset the blockade had appeared to be typical European demonstration on behalf of bankers to force a deadbeat dictator to pay his country's debts. Such demonstrations always aimed at seizing the custom house in the principal port, since it was almost the sole source of revenue of each of these governments. Roosevelt the year before had written a German friend, "If any South American State misbehaves toward any European country, let the European country spank it." But by January 1903 the nominally Anglo-German-Italian intervention was overwhelmingly German; Americans were upset over the Germans' bombardment of a Venezuelan port and their apparent unwillingness to accept arbitration. At this point, Roosevelt, fearing that taking over a custom house to collect debts could lead ultimately to the establishment of a base, took a firm position. He claimed later that he warned the German ambassador that Admiral Dewey had the fleet on maneuvers in the Caribbean, and that the United States would use force if Germany tried to acquire territory anywhere in the area.

The Germans wished no incident, and quickly agreed to arbitration. One result was that up into World War I, the Americans were even readier than before to suspect the Germans of plans to acquire a foothold in this or that area to the south. There was equal reason to be suspicious of the French, but because of other factors not related to the Caribbean, more antipathy was felt toward the Germans. There was, in particular, a persistent fear that the Germans might try to acquire the Danish West Indies. In 1902 the Senate ratified a treaty for their purchase, but the Danish parliament rejected it. Finally in 1917 the United States acquired the poverty-stricken little islands, which were then renamed the Virgin Islands, for an exorbitant $25,000,000. Their value was negative: the United States wanted to make sure they were not in the possession of any potentially hostile power. Even after the outbreak of the World War, when the British had bottled up the German fleet, the State Department still cited alleged German plots as the reason for strong action in the Caribbean.

An even more important development of the Venezuela crisis was a strengthening of the Anglo-American ties that European politics were making vital for the British. This crisis demonstrated to the British that they could not afford to defy the Americans or co-operate with the Germans in the Caribbean if they wished to retain their over-all friendship with the United States. After 1903 they heightened their courtship of the Americans.

Within the United States, the main innovation as a result of the Venezuela incident was a new Caribbean policy usually called the Roosevelt corollary to the Monroe Doctrine, although it was a broad departure from that historic dogma. The Hague Court declared that the powers that had attacked Venezuela had prior claim on payment of their debts; this increased the likelihood of European intervention in the future in the Western Hemisphere. For Roosevelt, who still believed that small nations must pay their just debts, the only way out seemed a drastic new device. If these little countries could not behave themselves, the United States reluctantly would police them and collect debt payments from them in order to forestall European intervention. In effect, Uncle Sam would act as a bill collector for European bankers. Roosevelt declared to the Congress in 1904 that the United States might be forced "however reluctantly, in flagrant cases of . . . wrongdoing or impotence, to the exercise of an international police power."

The occasion for putting the "Roosevelt corollary" into operation was the defaulting of Santo Domingo on about $22,000,000 of its debt to European nations. France and Italy threatened to intervene. In effect, the United States established a receivership, taking over Dominican customs, paying 45 per cent of the receipts to the Dominican government and the rest to foreign creditors. The American Receiver General increased revenue to an amazing extent, and at the same time persuaded the outside creditors to scale down their claims to a manageable $12,407,000. After two years, the senate ratified a treaty embodying the system, which with modifications remained in effect until 1941. Roosevelt limited his intervention to this financial administration; it improved the economic status of the Dominican Republic but irritated local politicians, since the customs house was no longer a prize for successful revolutionaries.

As a part of an American strategy of defense, Roosevelt's Caribbean policy was doubtless successful. As a means of securing the support and co-operation of nations to the south, it left much to be desired. Roosevelt's tactics inspired fear rather than friendship.

The "Big Stick" in the Far East

IN THE FAR EAST, Roosevelt could not ride roughshod, but he could and did make effective demonstrations of America's new naval strength. He liked to quote an African proverb, "Speak softly and carry a big stick." This certainly expressed his course of action in the Far East, as well as in the Caribbean. But in the Orient he intervened diplomatically first, and later engaged in a display of force to try to maintain a balance of power.

At the time that Roosevelt became President, following his announced plan still meant trying to make the Open Door policy effective against Russian expansion in Manchuria. Although for a moment in 1903 Roosevelt expressed much indignation over the "treachery" and "mendacity" of Russia and toyed with the idea of going to "extremes" with her, his practical policy was sympathy toward Japanese efforts to check the Russian drive. When these efforts took the form of a Japanese surprise attack upon the Russian fleet at Port Arthur, Manchuria, in 1904, like most Americans he cheered. He warned the French and Germans against aiding Russia, but he did not wish to see the Japanese totally victorious in the war since this might "possibly mean a struggle between them and us in the future."

Roosevelt pursued this same policy in the peace negotiations. The Japanese, even after winning a series of spectacular victories, faced such serious financial difficulties that they asked Roosevelt to mediate. He agreed, but with a justifiable reluctance, for at Portsmouth in the summer of 1905 he brought down upon the United States the wrath of the Japanese public because he would not back Japanese demands for an enormous indemnity. The end result was hostility in spite of Roosevelt's aid to Japan during the war and his acceptance at the conference of Japan's control over southern Manchuria and Korea, and its annexation from Russia of the southern half of Sakhalin Island. Shortly before the Portsmouth conference opened, President Roosevelt dispatched Secretary of War Taft from Manila to Tokyo to reach a Far Eastern understanding with the Japanese. In the resulting Taft-Katsura executive agreement of July 1905, the Japanese acknowledged American sovereignty in the Philippines, and the United States recognized the suzerainty of Japan over Korea.

Roosevelt's role in helping negotiate the 1905 Treaty of Portsmouth won for him the Nobel Peace Prize. His actions did indeed contribute to preservation of the peace by retaining the power balance between Russia

The "Great White Fleet" sails around the world, 1908 (OFFICIAL U.S. NAVY PHOTO)

and Japan on the Asiatic mainland. But in Asiatic waters Japan had risen to a new ascendancy through its destruction of the Russian fleets. It refloated and repaired many of the vessels, and in the following years built new ships rapidly. Japan undoubtedly had become powerful enough to seize the Philippines (which Roosevelt came to regard as an Achilles heel) because the American fleet would have had trouble fighting effectively over such long distances. Unfortunately, at this very time the people of Japan and the United States became angry with each other.

Within a year after Japan's victory over a great European power, the San Francisco school board, in October, 1906, ordered the segregation of Oriental school children. This was the outcome of Californians' resentment over a trickle of 500 to 1,000 Japanese immigrants coming in each year, and their excitement over lurid "Yellow Peril" articles in the Hearst and other newspapers. Resentment in Japan flared high, and jingos in each country fanned the flames hotter.

Roosevelt worked skillfully to douse the flames. He persuaded San Francisco to desegregate its schools, and in return in 1907 he negotiated a new, more effective "gentlemen's agreement" with Japan to keep out agricultural laborers. Then, lest the Japanese government think he had acted through fear, he launched a spectacular naval demonstration. He sent sixteen battleships of the new navy, "the Great White Fleet," on an unprecedented 45,000-mile voyage around the world. It gave the navy invaluable experience in sailing in formation (and demonstrated a dangerous dependence upon foreign coaling vessels). Most important, the Japanese invited this formidable armada to visit Yokohama, and gave it a clamorous welcome. Thus Roosevelt came to feel that through brandishing the big stick he had helped the cause of peace.

For the moment, the United States had demonstrated sufficient naval strength to restore an unsteady balance in Asiatic waters. In 1908, before the fleet had returned home, Japan negotiated the comprehensive Root-Takahira Agreement, as she probably would have done anyway. Both countries agreed to support the Open Door in China. The United States tacitly seemed to give Japan a free hand in Manchuria (where rivalry with Russia continued) in return for an explicit guarantee of the status quo in the Pacific. It was a precarious equilibrium, and might be destroyed by any future upset in the naval ratios.

A Perilous Balance in Europe

AT THE SAME TIME that the United States was directly engaged in balancing Japan in the Pacific, Roosevelt was participating somewhat less directly in trying to maintain a balance in Europe. There the great powers were engaging in an arms race, and two great rival alliances were taking form and solidifying. American relations with Britain were increasingly cordial. In 1903, the British agreed to the establishment of an Alaskan boundary commission on terms highly favorable to the United States, and then voted on the tribunal against almost all the Canadian claims. After the settlement, the British pulled a majority of their fleet units out of the Caribbean, allowing it to become virtually an American lake. Toward Germany, Roosevelt was outwardly friendly but had reservations because of its vigorous efforts to expand overseas.

When the European powers quarreled over Morocco, Roosevelt was reluctant to involve the United States. "We have other fish to fry," he told Taft in 1905. But in the final analysis he would throw the weight of the United States into the balance if he thought he could thus help prevent war. He resolved to try "to keep matters on an even keel in Europe." Consequently he intervened on behalf of the Kaiser to persuade France and England to attend an international conference for establishing the status of Morocco. Germany was protesting because the French were excluding foreign economic interests there. Roosevelt insisted that a conference be held, to forestall the danger of war.

At the conference, which was held at Algeciras, Spain, the United States played a less decisive role, but did vote with the British and the French as they defeated the Germans at the conference table. This alignment boded ill for the next European crisis, but for the moment the United States had helped avert, or at least postpone, a war into which it might ultimately be dragged.

The Fiasco of Dollar Diplomacy

PRESIDENT TAFT was no readier in foreign affairs than at home to exert strong personal leadership as Roosevelt had done. For the most part he left the State Department to his Secretary of State, a former corporation lawyer, Philander C. Knox. Nor was Taft, despite his years of experience in the Philippines, successful in maintaining Roosevelt's foreign policies. He made no real effort to maintain a balance of power either in Europe or Asia. Rather, he and Secretary Knox concentrated upon promoting American banking and business interests overseas during these years when capitalists were keenly interested in foreign expansion. Taft declared in 1910:

> While our foreign policy should not be turned a hair's breadth from the straight path of justice, it may well be made to include active intervention to secure for our merchandise and our capitalists opportunity for profitable investment which shall insure to the benefit of both countries concerned. . . . To call such diplomacy "dollar diplomacy" . . . is to ignore entirely a most useful office to be performed by a government in its dealings with foreign governments.

In Far Eastern relations, this policy brought to the forefront young Willard Straight, an agent of American bankers, formerly consul general at Mukden, Manchuria. He argued that dollar diplomacy was the financial expression of the Open Door policy, that it would make "a guaranty for the preservation, rather than the destruction of China's integrity." Taft, therefore, was ready to ignore Roosevelt's tacit arrangement with Japan that the United States would stay out of Manchuria, and to support the right of Americans to invest in both China and Manchuria. When British, French, and German bankers formed a consortium to finance railroads in China, Secretary Knox insisted that Americans should also participate. In 1911 they were admitted (but in 1913 Wilson helped them to withdraw). Next Secretary Knox proposed that an international syndicate purchase the South Manchurian Railroad in order to neutralize it. This led the rivals Russia and Japan to sign a treaty of amity in 1910, and jointly close the Manchurian door in Taft's face.

In the Caribbean there were no other great powers to block the amateur-ish American operations. As a result, a new pattern emerged there of interventions, going far beyond Roosevelt's limited ones, to establish firm military, political, and, above all, economic control over several un-stable republics to the South. It could be argued that American investors

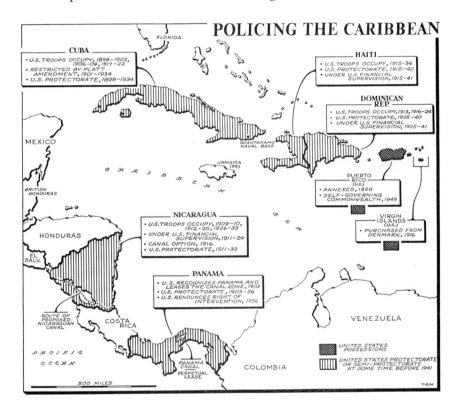

POLICING THE CARIBBEAN

CUBA
- *U.S. TROOPS OCCUPY, 1898–1902, 1906–09, 1917–22*
- *RESTRICTED BY PLATT AMENDMENT, 1901–1934*
- *U.S. PROTECTORATE, 1898–1934*

HAITI
- *U.S. TROOPS OCCUPY, 1915–34*
- *U.S. PROTECTORATE, 1915–40*
- *UNDER U.S. FINANCIAL SUPERVISION, 1915–41*

DOMINICAN REP.
- *U.S. TROOPS OCCUPY, 1913, 1916–24*
- *U.S. PROTECTORATE, 1905–40*
- *UNDER U.S. FINANCIAL SUPERVISION, 1905–41*

PUERTO RICO (U.S.)
- *ANNEXED, 1898*
- *SELF-GOVERNING COMMONWEALTH, 1949*

VIRGIN ISLANDS (U.S.)
- *PURCHASED FROM DENMARK, 1916*

NICARAGUA
- *U.S. TROOPS OCCUPY, 1909–10, 1912–25, 1926–33*
- *UNDER U.S. FINANCIAL SUPERVISION, 1911–24*
- *CANAL OPTION, 1916*
- *U.S. PROTECTORATE, 1911–33*

PANAMA
- *U.S. RECOGNIZES PANAMA AND LEASES THE CANAL ZONE, 1903*
- *U.S. PROTECTORATE, 1903–36*
- *U.S. RENOUNCES RIGHT OF INTERVENTION, 1936*

FLORIDA, MEXICO, GUANTANAMO NAVAL BASE, JAMAICA (BR.), BRITISH HONDURAS, HONDURAS, EL SALV., ROUTE OF PROPOSED NICARAGUAN CANAL, COSTA RICA, PACIFIC OCEAN, PANAMA CANAL PERPETUAL LEASE, COLOMBIA, VENEZUELA, 500 MILES

UNITED STATES POSSESSIONS
UNITED STATES PROTECTORATE OR SEMI-PROTECTORATE AT SOME TIME BEFORE 1941

must be invited in and supported in order to supplant European investors who otherwise might in time bring about European control. This was a logical step beyond the Roosevelt corollary. Bryan (who unwittingly continued much the same policy) incisively complained against it to President Wilson in the summer of 1913:

It is pathetic to see Nicaragua struggling in the grip of an oppressive financial agreement. . . . We see in these transactions a perfect picture of dollar diplomacy. The financiers charge excessive rates on the ground that they must be *paid* for the risk that they take and as soon as they col-lect their pay for the risk, they then proceed to demand of the respective governments that the *risk* shall be eliminated by government coercion.

No wonder the people of these little republics are aroused to revolution by what they regard as a sacrifice of their interests.

The new policy began in 1909 when Knox tried to arrange for American bankers to establish a financial receivership in Honduras; in 1910 he persuaded New York bankers to invest in the National Bank of Haiti. Then, in 1909, he sent marines to Nicaragua to protect revolutionaries, sponsored by an American mining company, who were fighting to overthrow a hostile dictator. Knox negotiated a treaty with the new friendly government giving the United States financial control, but the United States Senate failed to ratify it. American bankers, less reluctant, accepted Knox's invitation to move in. By 1912 the new pro-American government was so unpopular that revolution against it broke out. Taft sent marines to crush the uprising, but the populace remained so anti-American that the United States continued to occupy the country into the Coolidge administration.

Even more than Roosevelt's policies, those of Taft tended to alienate America's neighbors to the south. The dollars reaped were far surpassed by the harvest of ill will.

Gunboat Benevolence

PRESIDENT WILSON brought to the determination of foreign policy a flair for idealistic pronouncements. He was never unsure of his moral position, but was often uncertain about the way to reach it. He and his Secretaries of State and the Navy, William Jennings Bryan and Josephus Daniels, were all three devoutly religious, war-hating men of goodwill, who profoundly disapproved of the exorbitant money-making sometimes connected with dollar diplomacy. But the temptation to make use of the force at their disposal to uplift their brothers to the south was too great to resist. The need to do so seemed compelling to them, because like their predecessors they felt that they must maintain an American-sponsored stability in the Caribbean as a vital part of national defense. Hence they succumbed to a policy of benevolence backed by the United States Marines and American gunboats. The administering marine and naval officers and enlisted men had had little schooling or background to prepare them for dispensing progressivism abroad. To the recipients, who did not always understand why they were being uplifted, the new policies did not seem appreciably different from the repudiated dollar diplomacy.

President Wilson expounded his new policies in a speech at Mobile, Alabama, in the fall of 1913, aiming his remarks especially at Mexico, but encompassing the small republics as well. He utterly disavowed imperialist intent. "The United States will never again seek one additional foot of territory by conquest," he declared. Rather, he sought "the development of constitutional liberty in the world." As for economic penetration, while he denounced the extortion of unfair interest rates and concessions, he encouraged American businessmen to be active overseas, in an ethical fashion. As at home, he favored the small enterpriser on the way up, of the sort who would obey the rules. Indeed, Wilson remained dependent upon American bankers and enterprisers. Bryan suggested that the United States government should itself fund the external debts of the Caribbean and Central American nations, but Wilson rejected this as too radical. Private American capital, closely watched by Bryan, had to undertake the task.

The Wilson administration not only regularized through treaty the continuing occupation of Nicaragua, but also initiated new interventions into Santo Domingo and Haiti. In spite of American customs control, revolution after revolution had swept through and impoverished Santo Domingo. The United States took over all Dominican finances and the police force, but the Dominicans would not agree to a treaty establishing a virtual protectorate. In 1916, Wilson established a military government. During the eight years that it continued, the United States forcibly maintained order, trained a native constabulary, and promoted education, sanitation, and public works.

On the other end of the island of Hispaniola, the Negro republic of Haiti was even more revolution-wracked, the violence culminating in 1915 when a mob cut an unpopular president into small pieces. Wilson again sent in the marines, established another military government, and began the task of improving living conditions in Haiti. The marines demonstrated their efficiency in 1918 when they supervised an election to ratify a new American-sponsored constitution. The vote for it was 69,377 to 355. Nevertheless, that year they had to put down a serious revolt, in the process killing some hundreds of Haitians. When the young Assistant Secretary of the Navy, Franklin D. Roosevelt, visited Haiti, he was most enthusiastic over the way the country had been cleaned up and roads built. During the campaign of 1920, he unwisely boasted that he had written the new constitution of Haiti. In point of fact, he had not written it, but his many subsequent denials never entirely caught up with the original boast. In later years, Roosevelt came to look upon the intervention in Haiti as a failure; it finally came to an end in his Presidency.

President Wilson's always idealistic but sometimes ill-informed program for bringing democracy and stability to southern neighbors ran into serious difficulties in Mexico. This was partly because Mexico was too large a country for resistance to crumple upon the appearance of a warship or two and the landing of a few companies of marines. It was also partly because Wilson at times based his moral policy upon incomplete information about Mexican movements and leaders. Finally, under strong conflicting pressures at home, the President occasionally had great difficulty in making up his mind.

American business interests had invested about a billion dollars in Mexico during the regime of a friendly dictator, Porfirio Díaz. They owned over half the oil, two-thirds of the railroads, and three-fourths of the mines and smelters. Popular though Díaz was in the United States, he came to be hated in Mexico because, while he encouraged foreigners to amass huge profits, he suppressed civil liberties and kept the masses in peonage. For the average Mexican, there was little of the progress toward democracy or economic security that President Wilson desired. In 1910 the aged Díaz was overthrown by a democratic reform leader, who in turn was murdered by the reactionary Victoriano Huerta just before Wilson took office. Wilson turned a deaf ear to American investors who saw in Huerta an opportunity to return to the "good old days." Rather, he refused to recognize "the government of butchers."

Years of tedious complications followed. Wilson hoped that, by abandoning the traditional policy of the United States government since Jefferson's administration and refusing *de facto* recognition to Huerta's government, he could bring about its collapse and the development of constitutionalism in Mexico. Since this course of action alone did not suffice, he offered in June 1913 to mediate between Huerta and the opposing Constitutionalists of Venustiano Carranza. Both sides rejected Wilson's efforts to interfere, and Wilson developed a sharp dislike for Carranza, who offered the best hope for orderly reform in Mexico.

For several months, Wilson pursued a policy of "watchful waiting," but when Huerta in October 1913 established a full military dictatorship, Wilson began to bring increasing pressure against him. First he persuaded the British (who were obtaining most of their naval oil from Mexico) to stop supporting Huerta. Next he offered to send American troops to the aid of Carranza, but again was rebuffed since all Carranza wanted was the right to buy arms in the United States. In February 1914 Wilson revoked President Taft's arms embargo, but still the Carranzists did not win. Republicans in the House sneered that Wilson's Mexican policy made the United States "the laughing stock of the world."

Wilson was in a difficult dilemma: he might have to choose between recognizing Huerta, stronger than ever, or intervening with armed force, which could mean war against all the Mexican factions. Off the coast of Mexico, the commanders of American fleet units, engaged in watchful waiting, became increasingly restless. The precipitate action of one of them gave Wilson a way out. In April 1914 one of Huerta's officers arrested several sailors who had gone ashore at Tampico. A superior officer quickly released them and apologized, but the American admiral demanded in addition a twenty-one gun salute to the United States flag. At this Huerta balked. Wilson, deciding to back the admiral, sent all available warships to Mexican waters and asked Congress for authority to take drastic action. Then, determined to prevent a German ship loaded with munitions from reaching Huerta's forces, Wilson, without waiting

for Congress to act, ordered the Navy to seize Vera Cruz. It did so, on April 21 and 22, 1914, but not in the bloodless way that Wilson had anticipated. The Mexicans suffered 126 killed and 195 wounded; the Americans, 19 killed and 71 wounded.

Wilson, shocked by the unexpected bloodshed, seemed to a reporter a day or so later "preternaturally pale, almost parchmenty." While jingoists were urging him onward into Mexico, humanitarians protested. Wilson seemed to some to have incurred the loss of life over a minor bit of punctilio. At this difficult point, Argentina, Brazil, and Chile offered to mediate. With relief, Wilson accepted, and sent his delegates to confer with Huerta's at Niagara Falls, Canada, from May to July 1914. As the negotiations went on and on, the Carranzists advanced on Mexico City, bringing finally in mid-July the result Wilson wished, the abdication of Huerta.

The coming into the presidency of Carranza should have ended the Mexican muddle; instead affairs entered a new, more protracted, and more serious phase. By September 1914 civil war was again devastating

Mexico, as a former general of Carranza's, Francisco ("Pancho") Villa, tried to overthrow him. Villa, who was actually little more than a bloodthirsty bandit chieftain, made gestures of friendship toward the United States and tried to give the appearance of being a reformer. Wilson and Bryan, displaying bad judgment, favored him. Carranza in the spring of 1915 decisively defeated Villa and his plunderers, but in the process so much property was destroyed and the Catholic church was so injured that jingoes and many Catholics in the United States urged Wilson to intervene again. Wilson would have liked to eliminate Carranza, but not

General John J. Pershing in Mexico (NATIONAL ARCHIVES)

at the risk of a general war with Mexico, especially at a time when the United States was preoccupied with German submarine warfare. In October, 1915, the United States gave *de facto* recognition to Carranza's government.

This new friendliness was distasteful to Villa, who was still roaming northern Mexico. He tried to bring about a war between the United States and Mexico through shooting sixteen Americans he seized from a train in January 1916. When that failed, in March he raided Columbus, New Mexico, just across the border, killing nineteen more Americans. Wilson retaliated by ordering a punitive expedition under Brigadier General John J. Pershing to hunt down Villa. Wilson tried not to offend Carranza, but as Villa led the American forces 300 miles into Mexico, two skirmishes occurred with Mexican troops which almost led to war. Again the peace forces outweighed the jingoes in the United States, and again Wilson accepted compromise. Carranza suggested on July 4, 1916, the appointment of a Joint High Commission to consider the problem. It debated into January 1917, when it broke up without establishing a basis for the withdrawal of American troops. By then the United States was so close to war with Germany that it withdrew the troops nevertheless, and in March 1917 gave *de jure* recognition to Carranza's government.

Nothing but trouble had come out of Wilson's long and muddled intervention in Mexico. His bad tactics had built up hostility among the Mexican people which did not dissipate for years. On the other hand, he had tried to act in their best interests. "My ideal is an orderly and righteous government in Mexico," he explained in 1914, "but my passion is for the submerged eighty-five per cent of the people of that Republic who are now struggling toward liberty."

In other respects President Wilson and his Secretary of State were slightly more successful in improving relations between the United States and Latin America. During 1913 and 1914 they negotiated a treaty with Colombia expressing "sincere regrets" for the Panama incident and paying an indemnity of $25,000,000. Roosevelt thundered that it was a "blackmail treaty," and his Republican friends in the Senate blocked it until after his death. Finally, in 1921, Congress voted to pay the indemnity but omit the apology.

In 1915, Wilson and Colonel House formulated an international treaty which would, in effect, have turned over enforcement of the Monroe Doctrine to all the American nations through a joint guarantee of their independence and territorial integrity. Chile and Peru, because of their quarrel over the nitrate fields of the Tacna-Arica area, balked, and Wilson became preoccupied with the European war. At its close he wrote this protection of territorial integrity into the Covenant of the League of Nations, to cover all nations of the world.

In spite of difficulties and setbacks, Wilson was sufficiently successful in his over-all Latin American policy so that the entire area, except perhaps Argentina, was sympathetic toward the United States during the World War. At the invitation of the United States in 1917, eight declared war against Germany and five additional countries broke off diplomatic relations with her.

Wilson "Cools Off" Japan

AT THE OUTSET of his administration, Wilson was preoccupied with domestic reform. "It would be the irony of fate," he had remarked shortly before his inauguration, "if my administration had to deal chiefly with foreign affairs." He seemed more concerned with asserting a moral position for the United States in the world than in using its naval strength to firm up power balances. On July 4, 1914, he declared typically, in an address, "America will come into the full light of day when all shall know that she puts human rights above all other rights and that her flag is the flag not only of America but of humanity."

Bryan, before taking office as Secretary of State, suggested to Wilson a scheme for "cooling off" treaties with all the nations of the world. These would provide that disputes should go to permanent commissions for a one-year investigation before either party could strengthen its armaments or go to war. This proposal was in keeping with the progressive theory that war was unthinkable, and that all disputes could be settled through reasonable discussion. Bryan negotiated thirty such treaties with large nations and small.

This was the attitude with which Wilson and Bryan approached a new crisis with Japan which seriously threatened war in the spring of 1913. The California legislature was threatening to pass a law disqualifying aliens ineligible for citizenship (Japanese) from owning land. As jingo newspapers in Japan whipped up a froth of war excitement, Wilson and Bryan could do little with the Republican legislature and the Republican Governor of California, Hiram Johnson, who signed the bill. Wilson was rather inept in his negotiations, both with the Californians and the Japanese, but fared better with the Japanese. He assumed correctly that they did not want war, and in a fashion quite in contrast with Roosevelt's tactics, sternly ordered the Navy to refrain from fleet movements that Japan might misinterpret. Then he undertook long, deliberately unspectacular negotiations that continued without result until Japan terminated them in June 1914.

With the outbreak of war in Europe in August 1914, Wilson feared that Japan would take advantage of the preoccupation of the Western powers to expand in the Orient. He reverted to a balance-of-power policy to try to stem the Japanese tide as much as possible. Japan declared war upon Germany and seized the German holdings on the Shantung peninsula of China; this the United States could not criticize. Next Japan at the beginning of 1915 tried to impose upon China a treaty embodying twenty-one demands that virtually would have changed it into a protectorate. At this point, the United States, with the aid of the British, brought such strong pressure to bear upon Japan that it abandoned the treaty.

Japan continued to try, through economic penetration into China, to achieve what it had failed to gain diplomatically. To counter the penetration, Wilson withdrew his disapproval of American participation in a bankers' consortium to supply capital to China. New conversations between the State Department and Japan resulted, in which there was such wide divergence of position over China that an agreement could be reached only through resort to ambiguous language. In the Lansing-Ishii Agreement of November 2, 1917, the United States recognized that Japan had "special interests in China, particularly in the part to which her possessions are contiguous." In return Japan joined in disavowing any purpose to infringe upon "the independence or territorial integrity of China" or to shut the "open door" to commercial and industrial development. In a secret clause, Japan promised not to take advantage of the war "to seek special rights or privileges in China which would abridge the rights of the subjects or citizens of other friendly states."

The Japanese were pleased, because they could translate the ambiguous document into strong Chinese. Soon they engaged in yet another intervention, into Siberia. The Secretary of State was satisfied because he felt he had protected China for at least the duration of the European war. For both nations, if they held to their policies, there was trouble ahead, since an Asiatic balance was difficult to maintain.

The problem of the European balance gave Wilson at least slight concern early in 1914 when he authorized Colonel House to sail abroad in May to try to bring an end to the arms race. Within a few months, Europe became Wilson's greatest cause for anxiety, as fate directed his administration toward an overwhelming concern with foreign affairs.

Chapter 7

THE NEW ENLIGHTENMENT

DURING THE TWO GENERATIONS between the Civil War and the First World War, the United States underwent an intellectual as well as a material revolution. Even more than technological advances, the evolutionary theories of Charles Darwin had helped introduce a scientific age, similar to the way in which Isaac Newton's new conceptions of the physical universe had early ushered in the eighteenth-century Enlightenment. In the closing years of the nineteenth century, educated Americans, whether they were conservative or liberal in their leanings, widely accepted Darwin's biological theories as an explanation of the functioning of human society. It was an age in which scientific method, whether it was applicable or not, seemed supreme in almost every field of learning.

Adjustments had to be made to accommodate the new scientific dogmas to the old religious faith. Some of the adjustments were theological; others were social. For conservatives, social reconciliation seemed to come with the nineteenth-century Gospel of Wealth which preached that the rich (whose acquisitive prowess theoretically represented a working of the law of survival of the fittest) should exercise Christian stewardship of their wealth. To religious progressives this was far from adequate. As has been seen, by the turn of the century they were advocating the

Social Gospel, which meant placing upon themselves the responsibility for evolving the Kingdom of God on earth in the foreseeable future.

The Evolution of Pragmatism

As FOR PHILOSOPHERS, in the latter part of the nineteenth century many of them, like Josiah Royce, had helped transplant German idealism to the United States. Idealism in various forms persisted, but by the early 1900's it was attracting far less attention than the distinctly American pragmatism. The dominant philosophy of twentieth-century America, pragmatism remarkably fitted the progressives' need for an essentially scientific system of thought which could encompass their militant morality. Throughout American history, philosophers had alternated between religious-idealistic views and scientific-naturalistic ones. The Great Awakening of the eighteenth century and the transcendentalism of the nineteenth century had grown out of the former; the Enlightenment and Social Darwinism out of the latter.

Scientific method was uppermost in the thinking of a brilliant, eccentric, mathematical logician, Charles Sanders Peirce, when in 1878 he published in *Popular Science* an essay entitled, "How to Make Our Ideas Clear." In this paper, which established pragmatism, he developed a method for explaining the meaning of ordinary words (nouns and adjectives) as they are used by scientists. "Let us ask what we mean by calling a thing hard," Peirce suggested. "Evidently that it will not be scratched by many other substances." This type of experimental approach could easily be adopted by scientists in laboratories or engineers in factories, but it was not readily applicable for the testing of moral or religious values.

Peirce's pragmatism did not attract much attention until the turn of the century; it was a twentieth-century philosophy. In the early 1900's it was William James who modified and gave wide currency to pragmatism. James, the son of a transcendentalist and mystic, and the brother of the expatriate novelist Henry James, had left medicine, to become a famous psychologist. It was he who in the nineties had done most to establish psychology as a natural science. James sought to reconcile religion and science by developing a pragmatic theory of truth. His pragmatism, he claimed, "can remain religious like the rationalisms, but at the same time, like the empiricisms, it can preserve the richest intimacy with facts." Morton White has explained in *The Age of Analysis* (1955), "The test of scientific, metaphysical, and theological truth was made uniform by James. If you want to know whether a theory of any kind is true, try believing it and see whether satisfactory results ensue: that is the brief summary that led some to hail James as a savior and others to caricature him brutally." Many critics of James were outraged by his suggestion that the truth of a belief depended on its value for the individual believer, as it seemed to undermine the possibility of objective truth.

James's contemporary, John Dewey, who was active in several fields and left an indelible impress upon education, emphasized the moral aspects of pragmatism. Dewey had first become excited over Darwinism when he was a junior at the University of Vermont, and through years of hard work he had become a master of philosophy. At the turn of the century he was one of the brilliant younger scholars who helped to build the University of Chicago along modern, pragmatic lines. Ultimately he moved to Columbia University. Living to a patriarchal age of ninety-three, he was always fundamentally the hard-headed son of a Vermont grocer; never in the troubled years of the thirties was he deluded, as some

William James
(BROWN BROTHERS)

of his fellow intellectuals were, by the totalitarian sirens of fascism and communism. Unlike the withdrawn Peirce and the patrician James, Dewey was looking for a philosophy of reform, one that would help guide the way to the good society. While Peirce sought meaning, and James truth, Dewey's quest was for more precise ways to determine what was good.

Dewey felt that what was good, or had value, could be ascertained through carefully conducted experiments of the sort Peirce had advocated. He wrote:

> Judgments about values are judgments about the conditions and the results of experienced objects; judgments about that which should regulate

the formation of our desires, affections, and enjoyments. For whatever decides their formation will determine the main course of our conduct, personal and social.

In turgid prose, through 36 books and 815 articles, Dewey plotted the pragmatic way toward an ideal society. Justice Oliver Wendell Holmes once commented privately, "Although Dewey's book is incredibly ill-written, it seemed to me after several rereadings to have a feeling of intimacy with the inside of the cosmos that I found unequaled. So methought God would have spoken had He been inarticulate but keenly desirous to tell you how it was." Dewey, despite his writing style, provided progressives with the philosophical system they required. "We were all Dewey-ites before we read Dewey," declared a progressive political scientist, "and we were all the more effective reformers after we had read him."

Changes in Schooling and Scholarship

IN EDUCATION, pragmatism was especially influential. Psychologists emphasized the importance of proper early environment and training. Educators led by Dewey insisted that the schools could best provide the proper environment and training for curing the ills of society. Through their emphasis upon "progressive education" they touched off a debate which was still continuing vigorously a half-century later. Dewey attacked the prevalent classical education for the elite with its emphasis upon memorization and proposed more democratic methods of "learning by doing." Schools should develop not merely knowledge but also adjustment to life.

Some of Dewey's more zealous followers fell into excesses, but that his influence did solidly extend education during the era is undeniable. Kindergartens spread rapidly. The number of public high schools nearly doubled between 1900 and 1914 and the number of students increased two and a half times. In 1900 the average elementary schoolchild attended a one-room school for about half the 143-day school year, and was taught by rote by an untrained teacher who received about $38.00 per month. By 1914 the average child attended 86 days of the 158-day school year and was taught rather better by a teacher who received about $66.00 per month. Total schooling, however, averaged 6.16 years.

Enrollment in higher education more than doubled during the progressive years, and by 1910 reached a total of 355,215. Scholarship was of a level undreamed of at the time of the Civil War. Colleges and universities had moved from the rigid, classical curriculum into a wider course-offering and the elective system. At 34 leading institutions in 1901 students could choose more than 70 per cent of their courses. Weighing against the merits of the elective system was its failure to provide students with a common core of fundamental knowledge within the traditional intellectual disciplines, and to keep some from pursuing merely a narrow vocational training. It was not until the thirties that the pendulum swung back to the system of requiring certain general courses.

Professional and graduate schools generally improved to such a degree that in some respects they rivaled those of Europe. New universities boasting distinguished graduate faculties had sprung into existence: Johns Hopkins (1876), Clark (1889), Stanford (1891), and Chicago (1891). When at the beginning of the nineties Rockefeller poured millions of dollars into the University of Chicago, its president, in some respects emulating its benefactor, was able to raid Clark University of several of its most distinguished professors by offering fabulous salaries. Professional associations had also come into existence: the American Historical Association (1884), the American Economic Association (1885), and the American Sociological Society (1905), to mention a few.

The prevailing spirit in higher education after the Darwinian winds had swept across the nation was scientific. It brought remarkable improvements in some areas and certain excesses in others. For the social sciences, it meant all too often merely a painstaking collecting of data, much as in the cataloging technique of botany and zoology. Broad-sweeping national histories by American historians gave way to history monographs that imitated the work of German scholars, whose methods were influencing American scholars even more than was Darwinian theory.

In the nineties a young University of Wisconsin historian, Frederick Jackson Turner, broke away from the prevalent fashion of tracing American institutions back to Anglo-Saxon origins, and within the Darwinist framework returned American historical writing to broad, nationalist interpretations. He accepted an evolutionary theory of the growth of American society, but felt that the development had been a distinctly American phenomenon which had taken place through the impact of the American frontier. During the progressive era, Turner's became the dominant school of American historians. James Harvey Robinson, of Columbia University, likewise conceived of American history as an evolutionary development, but expanded its scope beyond the merely political themes to encompass the history of Western culture. It was Charles A. Beard who, accepting the nationalism of Turner and the broad cultural interests of Robinson, introduced into American historical interpretation the factor of "economic determinism." Beard's *Economic Interpretation of the Constitution* (1913) suggested that the Founding Fathers had had a substantial economic interest in their handiwork.

Appearing at a time when the Supreme Court tended to apply constitutional restrictions upon the progressive program, the book was hailed by reformers and damned by conservatives. Undoubtedly, Beard exaggerated the economic motives of the Founding Fathers, for much of his data has not stood up under re-investigation, but he did inject into American historical writing the previously disregarded ingredient of economic interest. For a generation, American historical writing showed the strong influence of Turner, Robinson, and Beard.

Among economists, the most devastating employer of the new scientific methodologies was Thorstein Veblen, a shambling misfit who had intimately known hardship and privation. He was the son of immigrant Norwegian parents who had homesteaded on a Wisconsin farm. To the study of the American economy he brought many of the prejudices of Populism and a devastating iconoclasm of his own. The prevailing laissez faire approach was to him no more than a romantic bulwark of the status quo. In "Why Is Economics Not an Evolutionary Science?," which appeared in 1898, Veblen attacked numerous orthodoxies. In *A Theory of the Leisure Class* (1899) he employed with wry irony his own pragmatic, broadly institutional analysis. Where Veblen himself stood was not always clear. His few contemporary readers were influenced toward progressive reform, and his many readers of the next generation toward the New Deal.

Like Veblen, the eminent jurist Oliver Wendell Holmes presented to his contemporaries an uncertain picture of himself. The witty attacks he sometimes made upon long-established institutions endeared him to progressives and seemed to make him one of them, but he frequently disappointed progressives when in his judicial capacity he failed to act according to their expectations. In his private writings and in his decisions and dissents as a Justice on the Supreme Court, he punctured the assumptions of conservatives even while he expressed his skepticism about the reformers. In his famous dissent in the *Lochner* decision (1905) invalidating a New York law limiting the hours of work of bakers, Holmes had invoked judicial noninterference:

> This case is decided upon an economic theory which a large part of the country does not entertain. If it were a question whether I agreed with that theory, I should desire to study it further and long, before making up my mind. But I do not conceive that to be my duty, because I strongly believe that my agreement or disagreement has nothing to do with the right of a majority to embody their opinions in law.

Roscoe Pound, as has already been seen, was ready to go well beyond Holmes in developing a theory of sociological jurisprudence. "Law is not scientific for the sake of science," Pound declared. "Being scientific as a means to an end, it must be judged by the results it achieves, not by the niceties of its internal structure. . . . The sociological movement in jurisprudence is a movement . . . for the adjustment of principles and doctrines to the human conditions they are to govern rather than to assumed first principles."

A revolution in legal training had already been wrought by Pound's predecessor at Harvard Law School, Dean Christopher C. Langdell, who had supplanted the passive text and lecture technique with the inductive give and take of the case method. Langdell argued that since Anglo-American law is firmly based on Common Law, which in turn is developed by the decisions given on cases brought before the courts, the training of lawyers ought to center around the study of cases. The case method of legal training assumes that the main function of the lawyer is to serve in court and to be able to predict the action of the court on cases which he brings before it. Holmes declared in 1897, "The prophecies of what the courts will do in fact, and nothing more pretentious, are what I mean by the law." In the early 1900's, even as law schools were adopting the case method, increasing numbers of lawyers were being employed as corporate counsels or in other ways which require little or none of a lawyer's time in advocacy before a judge. The use of the case method increased, however, until by 1928 three-fourths of the leading law schools employed it, even as pressure was being applied for a further modification of legal training in order to meet the legal realities of the thirties.

The experience of the universities in training lawyers and social scientists by means of case and laboratory methods was utilized subsequently in the areas of politics and public service. As Richard Hofstadter has pointed out:

> The progressive program, with its positive body of state legislation, involved continual research and consultation with the university's economists, political scientists, and agricultural specialists. Further, state regulatory commissions were often manned by university teachers and a veritable system of interlocking personnel was evolved between the university and the state government. Just as it was welded into the life of the state at the top, the university developed warm relations with the people of the state not only through its technical work in agriculture but also through an exceptionally widespread system of extension education. By its opponents the university was occasionally accused of "ruling the state." In fact the university deserves whatever credit may attach to introducing into our political culture the "brain trust" idea. *

---

* Richard Hofstadter and C. D. Hardy, *The Development and Scope of Higher Education in the United States* (New York: Columbia University Press, 1952), pp. 47–8.

Science and Medicine Move into the Laboratory

IN THEIR SCIENTIFIC LABORATORIES the universities were beginning to support a certain degree of pure research. Josiah Willard Gibbs of Yale had published in 1876 a paper on the Rule of Phase, which founded the field of physical chemistry, but he was almost alone among Americans in making a fundamental scientific advance. Most of the great discoveries were still being made in Europe: the quantum theory in the field of physics, by Planck, in 1900; the theory of relativity, by Einstein, in 1905. The strength of Americans was in applied science and engineering, and in the training of an ever increasing number of technicians required by America's industry.

Science applied to agriculture caught the imagination of farmers. In 1869, the President of the University of Michigan had complained, "The great and insuperable trouble is to inspire farmers with the belief that science has anything to offer them." Farmers had long been suspicious of the land-grant colleges, and only slowly took advantage of the federal experiment-station system established in 1887. In the early 1900's, resistance broke down. M. L. Wilson, one of the founders of the New Deal agricultural program, recalled:

> Shortly after the twentieth century began, science began to work a revolution among the mass of farmers. When I went to Ames to study agriculture, in 1902, . . . I was the first boy from that [Iowa] neighborhood to go to an *agricultural* college. Ten or fifteen years later it was becoming an accepted thing for all who could afford it.

By 1900 medical education at a few medical schools, and notably at Johns Hopkins, opened in 1893, had reached a level that compared favorably with that in Edinburgh, Vienna, and elsewhere in Europe. At Johns Hopkins, William H. Welch assembled a brilliant array of doctors who taught in laboratories and clinics by the inductive method. Their approach was pragmatic, but they were inspired not by the pragmatism of James or Dewey, but by the scientific tradition of the German scientists and of teachers like "Darwin's bulldog," Thomas Henry Huxley. Scientific medicine, dedicated in one of its goals to the ending of the scandalously high rate of infant mortality and to the preservation of health for the weak and the aged, ran athwart the natural selection principle of Social Darwinism and demonstrated the importance of humanitarianism over dogma. At Johns Hopkins students did not merely sit in clinics or visit hospitals as had long been commonplace, but served as part of the working staff. The hospital itself functioned as an integral part of the medical school. There was no finer training anywhere. Unfortunately, many mediocre and worthless medical schools were in existence throughout the country. When Abraham Flexner in 1910 made a survey for the Carnegie Foundation for the Advancement of Teaching, he discovered that the "library" at one school possessed no books, and that the dissecting room at another doubled as a chicken yard. The report forced almost half of the medical schools out of existence and helped prod others toward the standards of Johns Hopkins.

The nation had attained excellence in applied medicine, but its record in medical research was considerably below that of Europe. One beneficent outcome of the Caribbean adventures of the United States, beginning with the Spanish-American War in 1898, had been the great discoveries in tropical medicine made by American medical scientists. In 1900, Dr. Walter Reed and his associates proved conclusively that a striped mosquito carried and transmitted yellow fever. Reed's work as head of the United States Army Yellow Fever Commission illustrated the manner in

Major Walter Reed (NATIONAL ARCHIVES)

which groups of doctors, attacking health problems through laboratory and clinical study, could make spectacular advances. In the nineties, Reed persuaded the army to station him in Baltimore so that he could study the new science of bacteriology in the laboratory of Professor Welch at the Johns Hopkins medical school. When typhoid fever raced through army camps in 1898, Reed, studying it, discovered that flies to a considerable degree were the transmitters. In 1900, when American troops in Cuba caught yellow fever, he and a group of doctors tested the hypothesis advanced as early as 1854 that the striped Stegomyia mosquito (since called *Aëdes aegypti*) was the carrier. They induced twenty-two cases of yellow fever; one of the experimenters, Dr. Jesse W. Lazear, was accidentally bitten by an infected mosquito and died. Having proved that the mosquito was the carrier, the army began a widespread extermination program in 1901. As a result, yellow fever cases decreased from 1,400 in Havana alone in 1900 to 37 in all Cuba in 1901.

During the digging of the Panama Canal, Major William C. Gorgas applied the new knowledge so thoroughly that not one case of yellow fever originated there, and malaria was virtually eradicated. In Puerto Rico, Major Bailey K. Ashford discovered that the cause of the widespread anemia was hookworm, for which he developed an inexpensive cure.

All this knowledge was valuable in the southern United States. In 1909, Rockefeller gave a million dollars for the eradication of hookworm in the South, where almost 60 per cent of the school children had some infestation. With chemicals and vaccines, some of which were important European developments, the nation made encouraging progress in combating venereal diseases, typhus, typhoid, and diphtheria. Sanitariums and a national association successfully combatted tuberculosis. Campaigns against mosquitoes and flies, improved sanitation, milk inspection, and, beginning in 1908, the chlorination of water supplies reflected the new vigor of the state and municipal boards of health. To cap the entire program, the marine hospital service expanded in 1902, and in 1912 became the United States Public Health Service. The national death rate dropped from 17 per 1000 in 1900 to 13.2 in 1920. The boundaries of medical science had advanced far beyond the relatively narrow limits of the day of Dr. Oliver Wendell Holmes, poet, physician, and father of the jurist. Dr. Holmes was not by these standards professionally lax at the doctoral degree examination of William James at Harvard Medical School when, after James correctly answered the first question, declared: "If you know that, you know everything. Now tell me about your dear father."

Letters: From Back Bay to Greenwich Village

THE PROGRESSIVE GENERATION of intellectuals had as vigorously moved beyond Holmes's genteel literary traditions as its doctors had moved beyond the confines of medical knowledge of Holmes's day. Ohio-born William Dean Howells, the last of the great Boston literary arbiters, had left the Back Bay for the brownstone fronts of New York in 1881, bringing with him a polite realism, a careful, simple rendering of what he saw.

The most talked-about American novelist was another polite realist, Henry James, who, when he came for a visit in 1904, had not been in the United States for a score of years. While expatriates like the painter James McNeil Whistler and others broke ties with their American origins, James had never abandoned interest in his own country. He examined the interaction of the representatives of America's newer culture with the sophisticates of the older culture of Europe. In his works of the opening years of the twentieth century—*The Wings of the Dove* (1902), *The Ambassadors* (1903), and *The Golden Bowl* (1904)—he raised the novel to a level of art it had seldom before reached in the English language. James's novels commanded only a limited number of readers in the United States since to many they seemed to be intolerably involved in style and concerned with little more than the interplay of polite, well-to-do people in drawing rooms. In his novels there was but slight hint of the age. Rather, the remarkable structuring of them and his art in probing into the actions of his protagonists gave his novels an agelessness. Directly and indirectly he influenced several generations of European and American novelists, those of the early 1900's to a lesser degree than those of later years. James was in, but scarcely a part of, his age.

The age brought naturalism into the arts. Between 1910 and 1917, New York's Greenwich Village became a gathering place for artists and intellectuals seeking an American renaissance. Toward the still-flourishing genteel and popular writers this new group expressed unbounded scorn. Henry L. Mencken in his first critical article, which appeared in *Smart Set* in 1908, sneered that "American manufacturers of fiction, having the souls of fudge-besotted high-school girls, behold the human comedy as a mixture of a fashionable wedding and a three-alarm fire with the music of Chopin."

Popular magazines of the period had built huge reader circulation on the publication of light, romantic fiction, interspersed for several years with "muckraking" articles that exposed real or alleged corruption in politics and other areas. The popularity of romantic historical fiction was so high that Howells, in 1901, lamented,

> I find duels and battles set forth as the great and prevalent human events; I find pride and revenge worshipped as right and fine, but no suggestion of the shame and heartache which have followed the doers of violence in all times and countries since the stone age. There is such a spilth of blood that you might almost expect to see it drip from the printed page.

Before 1898, few American novels had sold 100,000 copies; by 1901 such sales were commonplace. Edwin Wescott's homespun *David Harum* reached 520,000 copies. Two historical novels of the American Winston Churchill, *Richard Carvell* and *The Crisis*, sold 420,000 and 320,000, respectively. By 1904, the predilection for historical fiction gave way to the hairy-chested stories of Jack London and Rex Beach, the sentimentalism of Kate Douglas Wiggin and Alice Hegan Rice, and the shrewd limning of American life, whether middle class or genteel, of Booth Tarkington and Edith Wharton. Popular fiction was for the most part American in theme, and some of it became progressive in overtone. London lost a good part of his audience when he turned from adventure to socialism, but Churchill kept his when he attacked the railroads in *Mr. Crewe's Career* (1908). Tarkington's first best-seller, *The Gentleman from Indiana* (1899) portrayed an idealistic small-town editor, almost a progressive prototype.

The writers who survived for later generations, along with the then currently popular authors, reflected much of the spirit of the times—Social Darwinism—with emphasis upon racism and imperialism, and preoccupation with success and its reverse image, failure. A present-day critic, Kenneth S. Lynn, has tarred the leading novelists of the progressive era with William James's remark that "the exclusive worship of the bitch-goddess SUCCESS . . . is our national disease."

Literature raced rapidly down the path of realism or naturalism, far beyond Howells and James, leading deep into the scientific age. Realism, as its detractors pointed out, merely photographed American society in its lower, if not lowest, strata, in sharpest contrast to the romantic literature of the period. Naturalism grew out of the drive of the French novelist Emile Zola and his followers to rip away the curtains of superstition. "A novelist," Zola specified, "must be only a scientist, an analyst, an anatomist, and his work must have the certainty, the solidity, and the practical application of a work of science."

Inhibited by American moral standards, some American novelists who had in part embraced naturalism had, like Howells, heeded the admonition that "literature must be suited to maiden eyes and ears." Increasingly, younger novelists strained against this restriction, one of their number complaining, "The female reader is the Iron Madonna who strangles in her fond embrace the American novelist." In 1900 Theodore Dreiser tried to break away from the literary iron maiden to portray, in *Sister Carrie*, a poor girl who, far from suffering punishment for her liaisons with two men, used them to achieve success as an actress. The book was suppressed on the insistence of the publisher's wife, and did not reappear for twelve years. Dreiser himself, rising from poverty and failure, and looking, as Sinclair Lewis saw him, "more like a wholesale hardware merchant than a properly hollow-cheeked realist," had become meanwhile the prosperous editor of a trio of women's magazines. Forced by a personal scandal to resign his editorship, Dreiser returned to his own writing. In a tumbling, awkward style he hewed out a series of massive novels that established naturalism in American literature. *Jennie Gerhardt* (1911) was similar in theme to *Sister Carrie*, and franker in some of its aspects. *The Financier* (1912) and *The Titan* (1914) formed the saga of a ruthless Chicago magnate who destroyed his business competitors and made unscrupulous use of his wealth.

Dreiser's contemporaries, who for the most part did not approach European naturalism as closely as he did, presented American realities in the harsh spirit of revolt. Hamlin Garland ripped the agrarian dream with his sketches of the bleakness of farm life. Although by the early 1900's he had abandoned the prairie populist leanings which had made his *Main-Travelled Roads* (1891) so influential, as late as 1914 he commented in his autobiographic *A Son of the Middle Border:* "Most authors in writing of 'the merry merry farmer' . . . omit the mud and the dust and the grime, they forget the army worm, the flies, the heat, as well as the smells

Frank Norris (HARVARD UNIVERSITY LIBRARY)

and drudgery of the barns." Garland remembered the realities as well as the idyllic pleasures of working close to nature throughout the seasons.

Frank Norris, as a well-to-do young man, went to Paris to learn to paint; but he returned to America to write. Influenced by Zola and Kipling, his writing blended a powerful naturalism with overtones of romanticism. In *McTeague* (1899), the tragedy of an educated but brutish man and his masochistic wife, both destroyed by avarice, Norris explored the dual nature of his protagonists by the effective use of symbolism. Striving for a "big, epic, dramatic thing," Norris embarked upon a trilogy, but died at the age of thirty-two before he could complete the third volume. The first volume, *The Octopus* (1901), told of the struggle between the wheat ranchers and the railroad interests of the San Joaquin Valley. The action of the second volume, *The Pit* (1903), shifted to the grain markets of Chicago.

Ellen Glasgow, four years younger than Norris (she was born in 1874), succeeded where Norris failed, by carrying to completion a large-scaled fictional project. Indeed, she executed a scheme as grand as that of Balzac or Zola, in a series of twelve novels that systematically examined the changing ways of the American South. The daughter of a socially prominent Richmond family, she consciously broke with Southern womanly tradition by publishing in 1897 *The Descendant*, the hero of which was of illegitimate birth and poor-white background. In later years, Miss Glasgow reminisced:

> Whether people liked what one wrote, or failed to like it, was no great matter. But that one should write the truth of life with a single mind and a single conscience appeared to me, at the moment, to matter profoundly. So I determined that I would write, not merely about Southern themes, but a well-rounded social record of Virginia from the decade before the Confederacy down to the period in which I was then living.*

Writing in the tradition of Howells, in an urbane, supple style, she regarded her works as instruments of a culture rather than products of the laboratory.

Though few of the leading poets sang the themes of progressivism, the new stirrings wrought changes in poetry. In the nineties, Edward Arlington Robinson, living in secluded poverty, superbly mastered the techniques of the complicated verse forms being imported from France, and developed a dignified and beautiful blank verse in which he expressed his questioning about man's struggles against an unkind destiny. His poetry reflected the afterglow of fading Puritanism and transcendentalism as much as it did the dawning pragmatism. He received from President Roosevelt, an admirer of his verse, an appointment to the New York Custom House that provided him a livelihood while he carried on with his writing.

Robert Frost, ignoring in his poetry both progressive reform and poetic fashions, wrote of New England folk and countryside and was in turn ignored by American publishers. In 1912 Frost sold his farm and moved to England where, as he said, he might "write and be poor without further scandal in the family." *A Boy's Will* (1913) and *North of Boston* (1914), written and published in England, brought him a renown that spread back to the United States. He returned in 1915, to write and to lecture at colleges and universities for many decades.

"A poem begins with a lump in the throat; a homesickness or a love-

---

* Ellen Glasgow, *A Certain Measure* (New York: Harcourt, Brace, 1943) p. 59.

sickness," Frost declared. "It is a reaching-out toward expression; an effort to find fulfilment," culminating "in a clarification of life."

In the main current of American literature floated Vachel Lindsay. His visionary poetry, when analyzed layer by layer, seemed to reveal no more than the evanescent bubbles of a child's dreams, but in about a score of his poems he caught something more: the rhythms and cadences of the revival tent, the street parade, and the carnival. In 1913 he published *General Booth Enters Heaven and Other Poems*, and for the rest of his life he toured schools and colleges declaiming "The Congo" and other of his chants of mysticism, rhythm, and excitement.

Robert Frost (NATIONAL ARCHIVES)

Carl Sandburg, in his free verse, caught even more of the cadence and movement of the common people. Like Walt Whitman he saw broad democratic vistas behind and ahead, but he was less the mystic and more the recorder of the multitude of voices in modern America. Besides writing poetry, he was a collector of folksongs and the author of a six-volume biography of Lincoln (1926–39), whom he helped elevate still higher than before in the hierarchy of folk heroes.

The first magazine to publish Sandburg and many another American poet of the era was *Poetry: A Magazine of Verse*, which Harriet Monroe founded in Chicago in 1912 for the publication of poetry of both a traditional and an experimental nature. The first number published two poems by an expatriate in London, Ezra Pound, who thereafter continued to proclaim in *Poetry* the dogmas of a small London group calling themselves the Imagists, who sought to create a new type of sharp, severe free verse. Amy Lowell went from Boston to London and eventually took command of the movement, and Pound moved on to other experiments in poetry.

The work of expatriate American artists in London and Paris was less exciting in American terms than the "Little Renaissance" that had begun among poets, novelists, playwrights, and artists in Chicago and spread to New York and other American cities. In the closing years of the Progressive era, many brilliant young writers and artists were serving their apprenticeships in Greenwich Village. John Butler Yeats wrote in 1912, "The fiddles are tuning as it were all over America."

Music, Painting, Architecture, and the Cinema

ALTHOUGH AMERICAN COMPOSERS during the Progressive era failed to make a niche for themselves comparable to that of the writers and artists, musical performance moved into golden years. If a concertgoer of today could go back and attend the performances at the new Symphony Hall in Boston in October 1900, he would find that little has changed in the decades following that opening. Modeled after a Greek theater by Charles F. McKim of the New York firm McKim, Mead, and White, this concert hall was the first in the world to be constructed in conformity with acoustical research. The observer from a later day would find everything familiar except the costumes of the women at the first regular concert. The Boston Symphony Orchestra, opening its twentieth season, played Weber's Overture to *Euryanthe*, Handel's Organ Concerto No. 4 in D Minor, the ballet music from Schubert's *Rosamunde*, and Beethoven's Fifth Symphony.

Throughout the nation, distinguished symphony orchestras came into existence, and galaxies of performing stars made memorable the concert and opera seasons. In the years since the Civil War symphony orchestras had become permanent organizations, able to give an increased number of concerts and expand their repertoires. The works of Beethoven continued to dominate orchestra programs throughout the first half of the twentieth century, but did drop from about a quarter of the repertoire to about an eighth, making room for the romantic Wagner and Tchaikovsky, who soared to a high peak of popularity in 1906–10. Brahms, Mozart, and Bach were trailed by a galaxy of the modern composers, with an occasional American composer at the bottom. Even then, the Boston Symphony led all other orchestras in performing American music, allotting it about 6 per cent of its repertoire. Americans hoped that at last they had acquired a great composer in Edward MacDowell, whose *Indian Suite* was first per-

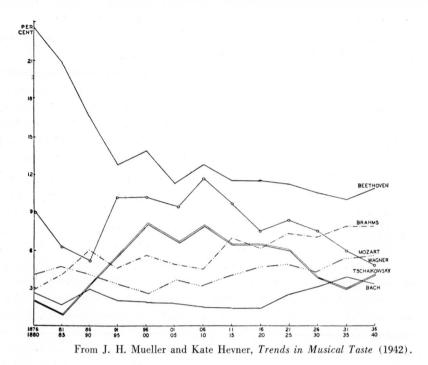

From J. H. Mueller and Kate Hevner, *Trends in Musical Taste* (1942).

Trends in Musical Taste: (above) eight American symphony orchestras, 1876–1941; (below) eleven orchestras, 1880–1950

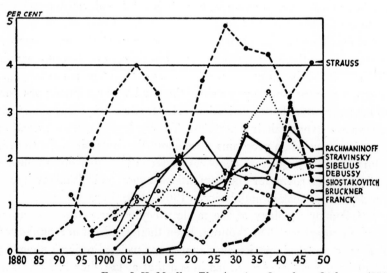

From J. H. Mueller, *The American Symphony Orchestra* (1941).

formed in 1896. During the 1900's MacDowell's music was performed more often than that of any other American composer, but failed to impress critics as being comparable to the best European work.

Victor Herbert, born in Dublin in 1859 and trained in Germany, established himself in America as an orchestra conductor and as the composer of a long series of excellent light operas: *Babes in Toyland* (1903), *Mlle. Modiste* (1905), *Naughty Marietta* (1910), and many others. Musical comedy, even further removed from opera, was developing rapidly, with hits like George M. Cohan's *Forty-five Minutes from Broadway* (1906), and in this field American music proved to be eminently successful.

During these years jazz was in its infancy and was confined to New Orleans. It did not burst upon the nation until about 1917. Ragtime, one of the elements of jazz, had become the national musical passion by the turn of the century, but it was at the point of being forgotten when in 1911 Irving Berlin briefly revived it with *Alexander's Ragtime Band.*

The trends in art nearly paralleled those in literature. One critic wrote in 1902 that the underlying theme of that art which was not official, commercial, or fashionable "is sadness, heart-searching, misgiving, melancholy—now spiritual, now sensuous—revolt against surrounding circumstance." It was a revolt against the prevailing academic style, typified at its best in the fashionable, lively portraitures by John Singer Sargent. Earlier, in the period of the eighties, Sargent had been influenced by impressionist contemporaries, as is shown by the color and line of some of his paintings like *El Jaleo.* But the exciting quality of his earlier work was lost in the conventional forms and colors that characterized, for example, the murals he executed for the Boston Museum of Fine Arts. Even as late as 1925, the year of Sargent's death, his work represented what was generally most admired in American art.

Parallel to Sargent in the early 1900's were several well-established painters: the romantic realist Thomas Eakins, who was painting dark and sober portraits that seldom pleased the sitters; and the popular Winslow Homer, who was delighting both the critics and the middle-class public with his pictures of the sea and the sky. Another painter, a romantic visionary who worked almost unnoticed, was Albert Pinkham Ryder. Ryder had executed a number of supernatural and obscure canvases, like *The Flying Dutchman,* but from about 1900 until his death in 1917 he did little beyond reworking some of his earlier paintings and inspiring a small group of younger men who called themselves the Introspectives.

It was out of romantic realism and French impressionism that the most effective painters of the Progressive era developed. By the early 1900's the work of several of the French impressionists had become accepted in the United States: masters of light, form, and color like Renoir, Monet, and Pissaro. Impressionism had touched Sargent; it dominated Mary Cassatt and Childe Hassam. Hassam had painted New York's Union Square as Monet had painted Les Grands Boulevards of Paris. Robert Henri developed a more distinctly American impressionism, painting urban scenes and portraits in the manner of Pissaro and Franz Hals, respectively, while employing Sargent's broad, descriptive brush-strokes. "What is necessary for art in America as in any land," wrote Henri, "is first an appreciation of the great ideas native to the country and then the achievement of masterly freedom in expressing them." Henri gave instruction and leadership to a new school of American painters whose work has often been compared to that of the contemporary progressive novelists. These "dark impressionists," as an art critic, John I. H. Baur, has called them, were more popularly called the "Ashcan School" because of their insistence upon portraying the grimmer sides of American life. Most of them at one time or another had earned their livings as newspaper and magazine illustrators; one of their number, George Luks, was the illustrator of a comic strip, "Hogan's Alley." Their debt to Hogarth and Daumier was almost as great as to the impressionist Henri. In revolt, in 1908, against the National Academy's refusal to countenance their work, they organized as "The Eight," and held an exhibition in New York. Some critics denounced them as "the Revolutionary Black Gang," more by reason of their subjects than their techniques. Other critics readily acceded that the group was "creating a national art."

Four painters who most often had the epithet "Ashcan School" tied to them were John Sloan, George Luks, William Glackens, and Everett Shinn. To soften the dreariness of the slums he painted, Sloan used a touch of satire in portraying its men and women, as in *The Hairdresser's Window*. Luks dramatically and wittily portrayed individuals, as in *The Spielers*. Glackens painted larger canvases in which people as a group seem to form the subject pattern, as in *Roller Skating Rink*. In an era when it was boldness to do so, Shinn painted an actress showing her shapely ankle in *The Revue*. A pupil of Henri's, George Bellows, caught the vigor and violence of the era in his paintings and drawings of prize fights. In 1910, the Eight and their followers held a second successful exhibit, but they were already at the peak of their reputations as revolutionizers of American art, about to lose their place to even more modern and daring artists.

Americans had become used to the Impressionists and the artists whom they had influenced; they were ill-prepared for Cézanne, Van Gogh, Gaugin, Picasso, Matisse, and the nonrepresentational painters. The work of these artists came as a bombshell. It was a gifted photographer, Alfred Stieglitz, who as much as anyone else helped detonate it among painters. The walls of his small gallery at 291 Fifth Avenue exhibited one shock after another: in 1908 Rodin and Matisse, followed in the next three years by Toulouse-Lautrec, Cézanne, and Picasso. A sympathetic American, Gelett Burgess, viewing the work of some of these painters, assured Americans that the artists were not degenerates, even though Matisse's work did remind him of "what a particularly sanguinary little girl of eight, half crazed with gin, would do to a whitewashed wall, if left alone with a box of crayons." Stieglitz also encouraged an equally advanced group of American artists, among whom were John Marin, Max Weber, and Georgia O'Keeffe, whom he married.

Taking unparalleled photographs at night and during rain and snow storms, Stieglitz demonstrated how an art form could take advantage of

The Armory Show, New York City, 1913 (MUSEUM OF MODERN ART)

technical advances (in this instance, photographic emulsions). When crossing the Atlantic in 1907 he photographed a scene he called *The Steerage* (see page 45), showing the ship's immigrants as he came upon them crowded into the cheapest quarters. His intent was not to document by means of pictures. Rather he was trying to utilize photography as a form of creative expression, as an art in itself and not an imitation of other arts.

Only a small number of artists and art-lovers were aware of what was going on at Stieglitz's "291" gallery until, in 1913, modernism burst upon the American public through a huge exhibition assembled by the Association of American Painters and Sculptors at the Sixty-ninth Regiment Armory in New York. Most of the 1,600 exhibited works were conservative, but a group of French moderns left the critics wide-eyed. "American art," wrote one of the promoters of the exhibit, "needs the shock that the work of some of these men will give." Certainly the classicists reacted strongly. An outraged Academician, Kenyon Cox, asserted that Cézanne was "absolutely without talent and absolutely cut off from tradition" and Van Gogh "too unskilled to give quality to an evenly laid coat of pigment." As for Matisse: "It is not madness that stares at you from his canvases, but leering effrontery." Cubism fared even worse. Cox complained that in the lines of the nonrepresentational painters (all lumped together by him as cubists) there was "a total destruction of the art of painting." The public was

"*Augustus Saint-Gaudens*" *by Kenyon Cox* (METROPOLITAN MUSEUM OF ART)

less outraged than the critics by pictures like Marcel Duchamp's *Nude Descending a Staircase,* in which the appearance of movement is suggested by the arrangement of line. Theodore Roosevelt, who felt that he saw better cubism in his Navaho rug than in the exhibited pictures, nevertheless expressed his pleasure with the exhibit in that it did contain so much that was different, and some of it of striking merit. The Metropolitan Museum purchased one of the exhibited Cézannes, the first public museum to acquire a Cézanne painting. Despite the disapproval of the American Academy of Arts and Letters, much of the work that seemed so intolerable to Cox and other conservative critics was becoming familiar and respectable to the public. The total effect of the Armory show and Stieglitz's exhibits was to lead many young artists far beyond the Ashcan revolt to explore the fields of expressionism and abstraction.

The trends in American sculpture paralleled those in painting, but perhaps because the American public's acquaintance with sculpture was limited to its civic and national monuments, done for the most part in the classic style, these trends moved more slowly than in the medium of painting. While the paintings of the Academician Cox and some of the other traditionalists seemed to a later generation little more than politely watered-down imitations of Titian, the sculptures of Augustus Saint-Gaudens, although in the tradition of the Florentine Renaissance, secured him an undiminished reputation. He was known by such works as an enormous equestrian statue of General William Tecumseh Sherman in New York City. Well past 1908, when the Corcoran Gallery in Washington assembled a large memorial exhibit of Saint-Gaudens's works, his was the style of most of the monuments, fountains, and pediments of buildings being erected throughout the United States.

Classic forms similarly continued to dominate architecture. "The White City" of the Chicago Columbian Exposition of the 1890's had exalted the reputation of Charles F. McKim and had established the Greek or Roman temple as the model for public buildings. Louis Sullivan won few followers when he proposed types of architecture he regarded as better suited to America, in which "form follows function." While Sullivan continued into the early 1900's designing commercial structures, his gifted assistant, Frank Lloyd Wright, had left him in 1893 to follow his own bent in domestic architecture.

In 1900, Wright built the first of the "prairie houses," thus achieving, according to H. R. Hitchcock, an expert on modern architecture, "something of as much consequence in the history of dwelling as the architects of the fifteenth century who turned the defensive castle into the residential mansion." For his own home and studio, Wright built *Taliesin* (in Welsh, "shining brow") around a Wisconsin hillcrest. Wright has written of it:

> The buildings became a brow for the hill itself. . . . *Taliesin* was to be an abstract combination of stone and wood as they naturally met in the aspect of the hills around about. And the lines of the hills were the lines of the roofs, the slopes of the hills their slopes, the plastered surfaces of the light wood walls, set back into shade beneath broad eaves, were like the flat stretches of sand in the river below and the same in color, for that is where the material that covered them came from.*

* Frank Lloyd Wright, *An Autobiography* (New York: Duell, Sloan and Pearce, 1943) p. 171.

In designing public buildings and factories, as well as homes, Wright tried to make his architecture fit the surroundings, both in appearance and in historic spirit, yet he used modern materials and the newest engineering techniques. Thus the Imperial Hotel in Toyko, designed in 1915–22, harmonized with Japanese traditions and yet was such a triumph of modern engineering that it withstood the devastating 1923 earthquake. "After the industrial revolution . . . had driven architecture to take refuge in applied decoration," wrote Bruno Zevi, Wright "effected a completed artistic synthesis." Nevertheless, until the late twenties Wright's designs influenced European architecture more than that of the United States. The most that can be said for Americans is that they did revert to the grace-

Frank Lloyd Wright's Taliesin East, 1911

ful colonial styles for their homes; they refused, for the time being, to accept modern architectural design.

Like architecture, the American theater during the progressive era leaned more to the commercial interests than to the esthetic. It was an expanding business, dominated by a nationwide syndicate which prospered on romantic plays, popular vaudeville, and matinee idols. Experimental realism had made a beginning, but only in the realm of little-theater groups like the Provincetown Players and the "47 Workshop" of Professor George P. Baker of Harvard, later of Yale. These could hardly appeal to wide audiences, who were soon to be won over to the motion picture. At first, to theater-goers and the theatrical world in general, the idea of the motion picture offering serious competition to the stage appeared ludicrous. The first film to tell a continuous story was the melodrama, *The Great Train Robbery*, produced in 1903. Vachel Lindsay in *The Art of the Moving Picture* (1915) wrote, without any intent of humor, this synopsis of a movie popular at that time:

> One of the best Action Pictures is an old Griffith Biograph, recently reissued, the story entitled *Man's Genesis*. In the time when cavemengorillas had no weapons, Weak-Hands (impersonated by Robert Harron) invents the stone club. He vanquishes his gorilla-like rival, Brute-Force (impersonated by Wilfred Lucas). Strange but credible manners and customs of the cavemen are detailed. They live in picturesque caves. Their half-monkey gestures are wonderful to see. But these things are beheld on the fly. It is the chronicle of a race between the brain of Weak-Hand and the body of the other, symbolized by the chasing of poor

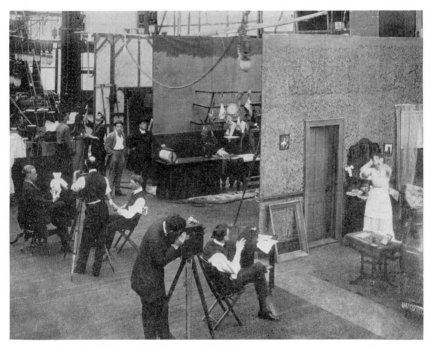

On the Edison Studio set, 1914 (MUSEUM OF MODERN ART)

> Weak-Hands in and out among the rocks until the climax. Brain desperately triumphs. Weak-Hands slays Brute-Force with the startling invention. He wins back his stolen bride, Lily-White (impersonated by Mae Marsh). It is a Griffith masterpiece, and every actor does sound work. The audience, mechanical Americans, fond of crawling on their stomachs to tinker [with] their automobiles, are eager over the evolution of the first weapon from a stick to a hammer. They are as full of curiosity as they could well be over the history of Langley or the Wright brothers.*

---

* Vachel Lindsay, *The Art of the Moving Picture* (New York: Macmillan, 1916), pp. 9–10.

This stage of motion picture development was short. By 1915 the lengthy, impressive feature film had arrived with *The Birth of a Nation*. It was as significant in marking the coming of age of a new art form as it was deplorable in its glorification of the Ku Klux Klan. A motion picture monopoly movement had begun in 1909 and had been smashed by the government in 1914, but motion pictures had become a multimillion dollar industry and were moving into large and ornate theaters.

Thus in many ways the first years of the twentieth century swept Americans far beyond the old nineteenth-century patterns of life. The First World War was to sweep them even further.

Chapter 8

TO MAKE THE WORLD
SAFE FOR DEMOCRACY

THE PROGRESSIVE GENERATION felt few qualms over the use of armed force to police the American periphery, or even to uphold in the Far East what they conceived of as the nation's interests and international morality. Thus far and no further a majority of Americans were willing to go. The great war which broke out in Europe in the summer of 1914 seemed almost incredible; that the United States might become involved seemed inconceivable. Yet in less than three years the nation reluctantly embarked upon the great crusade President Wilson called upon them to undertake "to make the world safe for democracy."

The outbreak of war among the great powers was a cataclysm which had threatened for so many years that almost no one thought it would occur. There had been no war in western Europe since 1871, which was longer ago than most people could remember. Despite the hectic building of alliances and armaments, few in the United States thought there would ever be another major conflict. Consequently they had paid little attention to the minor alarms that followed the assassination of the Austrian Archduke in Sarajevo, Bosnia, at the end of June. Balkan crises were familiar and boring news, less sensational than events in Mexico where Carranza was driving out Huerta. Even when Austria-Hungary declared war on Serbia on July 28, Americans were not shocked, but the week that followed left them stunned. The declaration of war against Serbia triggered among the alliances a chain reaction of threats and counterthreats, commitments and countercommitments. It detonated an explosion no one seemed really to want, but no one seemed able to avoid. By August 5, England, France, and Russia were at war with Germany and Austria-Hungary. The explosion had blown to bits the comfortable, optimistic Europe that had seemed so safe and stable.

Bewildered Americans congratulated themselves that at least the explosion could not extend to their shores, that the New World was still secure. What the war was about they had no idea. Senator John Sharp Williams reflected the thinking of millions when he said he was "mad all over, down to the very bottom of my shoes, and somewhat sick and irritable too," at the "outbreak of senseless war, setting all Europe aflame." Nevertheless, Americans took sides. A sizable number, who were of German ancestry or had been educated in German universities, automatically saw the war as a valiant German struggle against the cruel despotism of Czarist Russia. But the vast majority had greater educational, economic, or sentimental ties with England and France, and were shocked by the German invasion of Belgium in defiance of a treaty. They would have agreed more or less with young Franklin Roosevelt who hoped the Allies would "force peace at Berlin!"

This predisposition of most Americans did much to shape the future actions of the United States, but it by no means meant that even a small minority of the pro-Allied Americans wished to see their country intervene. They were pro-Allied without being at all sure what the war was about. In the months and years ahead they were ready to accept the interpretations of Allied propagandists as confirming their earlier inclinations, but even this did not make them want to fight. None of them in August 1914, and few of them for long thereafter, favored American entrance into the war. There was no clear call for an American democratic crusade.

Controversies over Neutral Rights

President Wilson distracted by the death of his wife, issued a conventional proclamation of neutrality and an appeal to the American people to be neutral in thought as well as deed. He too was rather pro-Allied in his thinking but as late as 1916 referred to the war as "a drunken brawl in a public house." He felt justice and a restoration of international equilibrium could come only with a negotiated peace. During these crisis years from 1914 to 1916, Wilson increasingly concentrated his attention upon foreign policy as he sought for a means to bring the struggle to an end and meanwhile to defend the traditional neutral rights of the United States.

The immediate problem for Wilson was domestic: to bolster the economy, which was staggering under the impact of war. As European nations sought to liquidate their investments in the United States, Wilson closed the Stock Exchange to prevent panic, and discouraged loans to belligerents in order to preserve the gold reserve. (Secretary Bryan asserted such loans by banks would be unneutral.) Congress passed legislation to promote the shipping of American produce to Europe. One act permitted foreign vessels to transfer to American registry, and another provided marine insurance at standard rates through the War Risk Insurance Bureau. Bankers and businessmen, partly through government assistance, were able to get through the first six months or so of depression without overly serious effects. After that, war orders began to turn the panic into a boom.

Farmers, heavily dependent upon all their European markets, were less fortunate. The British control of the high seas nearly cut these markets in half. The decline in exports to Germany and Austria-Hungary from $169,000,000 in 1914 to $1,000,000 in 1916 hit the cotton farmers of the South especially hard. The price of cotton fell to half what it had been, but Wilson failed to advocate any effective aid to the growers.

Since cotton was not contraband of war under the first British listings, many congressmen hoped that, through the new Ship Registry Act, vessels could be obtained to carry it to central Europe. They soon learned that the British would countenance no neutral trade with Germany even if the commodities were not on a contraband list. President Wilson acquiesced, though not without protest, as the British developed and tightened their system of control of the seas. The United States could have retaliated with an embargo, which would have been far more effective a means of coercion than it had been in Jefferson's day. An embargo would have forced the British to make concessions through hampering their power to make war, though at home it would have hurt industry and created additional economic distress among farmers. But what made so drastic a step as an embargo unthinkable was less the damage it would inflict upon the United States than the basically pro-Allied sympathies of the administration and a great majority of the people. This is why the United States accepted the British blockade of the Central Powers but was not so ready to condone a German counterblockade.

Blockade warfare became essential to the strategy of both the British and the Germans. The development of rapid-firing cannon and of machine guns made frontal assault prohibitively expensive, so that the war in Europe settled down into an exhausting trench warfare between the combatants. The counterpart on the high seas was the blockade. From the outset, Great Britain made use of her superior navy to wage economic warfare against Germany. Gradually she extended the contraband list and the controls so far that she even seized American vessels carrying foodstuffs to neutral countries, on the grounds that such vessels might release within these countries supplies that could go to Germany. Not only did the control over neutral trade become tight, but at some points Americans complained that the British were using their controls to benefit British firms at the expense of American business.

On the whole, the British blockade was not economically too onerous for the United States, since by early 1915 heavy war orders were arriving which more than filled the trade gap it had created. While trade with the Central Powers almost came to an end, that with the Allies jumped between 1914 and 1916 from $824,000,000 to $3,214,000,000—a staggering figure for that time. In March 1915, the government relaxed its regulations to allow the Allies to float huge loans in the United States to finance their purchases.

In effect the United States, embarking upon the greatest boom in its history, was becoming the arsenal for the Allies. This, Germany could not permit. During the first weeks of the war she imposed no blockades, but concentrated upon trying to win a decision in France. The German armies drove deep but were halted short of Paris in the Battle of the Marne in September 1914. Although on the Russian front great armies continued to move back and forth for several years, in the west the war turned into the grinding attrition of trench combat along lines extending from the North Sea to Switzerland. As a relative stalemate developed along the western front, Germany turned toward the submarine as a possible means of breaking the British blockade. Submarines had the advantage of surprise, but were so vulnerable to attack by an armed ship that they could scarcely follow the accepted rules of international law. These rules called for visit-and-search of enemy merchantmen, and allowed sinking only if provision were made for the safety of passengers and crew. The sinking of merchant vessels without warning seemed to Americans to add a new and frightful dimension to warfare.

Beginning on February 4, 1915, this was what Germany set out to do. She announced that she would sink enemy vessels in a broad zone around the British Isles. This policy, the Germans explained, was in retaliation for the British food blockade, which they claimed would starve women and children in Germany. In American eyes the German claim was a gross exaggeration, and the offense against the British was far more heinous. It immediately brought the United States into serious diplomatic controversy with Germany, as German submarines began to sink passenger vessels. The United States, on February 10, declared it would hold Germany to "strict accountability" for unlawful acts. The first sign of a crisis came in March with the torpedoing of the *Falaba*, in which one American was killed. President Wilson and the State Department tried to devise a policy to protect American rights yet not provoke a serious crisis with Germany.

The crisis soon came, for on May 7, 1915, a submarine fired a torpedo without warning into the Cunard liner *Lusitania*. It went down in eighteen minutes, drowning 1,198 people, including 128 Americans. Of 129 children aboard, 94 were lost. This act was utterly contrary to what Americans considered to be civilized warfare—and they still equated warfare with civilization. "An act of piracy," Theodore Roosevelt called it. A few days earlier, April 22, the Germans had launched against the Allied lines at Ypres a new weapon of frightfulness, poison gas. On May 13, American newspapers carried lengthy excerpts from an official British report on almost unprintable alleged German atrocities in Belgium. Although it bore

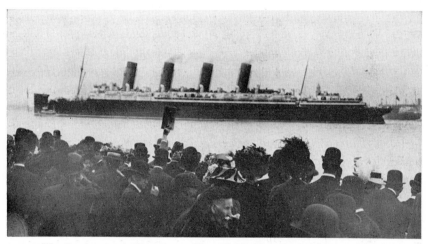

The Lusitania *sailing from New York City* (BROWN BROTHERS)

the respected name of the former Ambassador to the United States, Lord Bryce, the report contained fabrications. Few Americans questioned its authenticity, for by this time most people were ready to believe almost anything against the Germans. Yet even in their revulsion, they were not ready to fight. The British Ambassador, Sir Cecil Spring-Rice reported, "At the bottom the people desire to keep out of the European struggle and will do so if they possibly can." Only a minority of militants jeered when President Wilson declared on May 10, "There is such a thing as a nation being so right that it does not need to convince others by force that it is right."

Nevertheless Wilson came close to the point of coercion in the ensuing exchange of notes with Germany. In his first message he virtually demanded that Germany end its submarine blockade. When the Germans sent an argumentative reply, he drafted a still stronger second note—so strong that the peace-minded Secretary Bryan resigned rather than sign it. Wilson appointed the Counselor of the State Department, Robert Lansing, ·an expert in international law, to be the new Secretary. Lansing was ready to take an adamant position. Wilson had said, "There is such a thing as a man being too proud to fight," yet he was ready to risk war rather than to surrender to Germany what he considered to be American maritime rights. A new sinking, of the *Arabic* on August 19, 1915, brought the crisis to a head. Wilson was determined to obtain concessions from Germany or sever diplomatic relations. He won. The German Ambassador pledged that there would be no more surprise sinkings of passenger liners.

New trouble developed in the early months of 1916 when the Allies began arming merchantmen and ordering them to attack submarines. On February 10, 1916, Germany gave notice that it would sink them without warning. Wilson reiterated his doctrine of "strict accountability," and on March 24, when the channel steamer *Sussex* was torpedoed, he threatened to break off diplomatic relations if Germany did not abandon its unrestricted submarine campaign. He made the threat at a time when Germany still lacked sufficient submarines to maintain a tight blockade and did not wish to bring the United States into the war. Consequently, on May 4, the German Foreign Office pledged that submarine commanders would observe rules of visit-and-search. The President had won an even more remarkable diplomatic victory than before, and relations with Germany became less tense during the eight months that followed.

A National Defense Program

THE EASING OF TENSION did not mean that the sympathies of the American public switched toward Germany. Allied progaganda probably did not play an enormous role in influencing their thinking, but it had reinforced their prejudices. The clumsiness of German propaganda, intrigues in Mexico, and sabotage in the United States had all helped create tension. Lurid books like Hudson Maxim's *Defenseless America*, hypothecating the invasion of the United States by a Germany fresh from a European victory, had a frightening effect. All this and the crises over submarine warfare had brought Americans not to the point of wishing to fight, but at least to an acceptance of a national defense program.

With the outbreak of war, generals and admirals, who in peacetime attracted little attention, began to gather followings as they raised a hue and cry for increased defenses. President Wilson through his pacifist Secretary of the Navy, Daniels, was able to muzzle the navy rather effectively. Its demands for a huge fleet-building program and its warnings of the catastrophe that faced America if the British Grand Fleet collapsed appeared for the most part indirectly through friendly politicians and publicists. (Maxim's sensational book bore a marked resemblance to the Navy's "Black Plan" of defense against the Imperial German Navy.)

Roosevelt's close friend, Major General Leonard Wood, who had just finished a term as Chief of Staff, was not so easy to silence. The Secretary of War, Lindley M. Garrison, was a zealous advocate of preparedness, and several influential civilians like Roosevelt constantly made the headlines with their warnings. Also, the army was much less ready than the navy to fight a major war. The establishment of the General Staff and other administrative reforms had come into effect in the Roosevelt administration, but the older officers were still antagonistic toward most changes. The quartermaster corps in 1913 was thinking about using trucks, but as yet had not seriously tested them. The air force, consisting of seventeen planes, was part of the signal corps; its 1913 appropriation was $125,000. The Army numbered less than 80,000 men, a major part of whom were required to maintain the posts within the United States. The National Guard was somewhat larger, but was scarcely professional.

President Wilson opposed new armaments, and so did the public, until the crisis over submarine sinkings frightened the nation into preparedness. In November 1915 the President proposed a long-range program which by 1925 would give the United States a navy second to none and would increase and reorganize the army to provide the nation with a reserve force of 400,000 men. This proposal touched off a vehement debate in Congress and throughout the country. Old progressive-conservative lines in Congress disappeared and re-formed, as large numbers of those who had been agrarian progressives of the West and South rallied behind the House majority leader, Claude Kitchin of North Carolina, to block the army program. Throughout the country, the pleas of Bryan and peace organizations strongly appealed to farmers and workingmen. Wilson took the issue to the country in a series of speeches in January and early February 1916, but the House would not budge.

Wilson had to compromise. He accepted the resignation of Secretary of War Garrison, and appointed in his place Newton D. Baker, an able Ohio progressive who only a few weeks earlier had opposed preparedness. Ultimately Congress passed legislation providing for substantial increases in the army, the navy, and merchant ships. The Merchant Marine Act of 1916 established the United States Shipping Board, which was empowered to own and operate vessels and to regulate shipping.

Conservatives wished to finance the defense expenditures through bonds, but the administration proposed new, heavier taxes. Progressives denounced the tax proposals as falling too heavily upon the masses, and in Congress fought through a tax measure frankly aimed at making the wealthy, whom they blamed for preparedness, pay the bill. The new income and inheritance taxes of the Revenue Act of 1916 for the first time in American history levied heavily upon the rich.

The 1916 Election: "He Kept Us Out of War"

IN 1916, Democrats and Republicans fought the presidential campaign over the issue of foreign policy before a seriously divided people. Before the campaign got under way, President Wilson had already secured the support of most progressives through sponsoring much new legislation in the domestic field. At the Democratic convention, Wilson wished the theme to be Americanism, but the keynoter found it evoked little response from the delegates. Then the keynoter began citing Wilson's interchanges with Germany, and the crowd whooped with enthusiasm. "What did we do? What did we do?" it would chant, and the keynoter would proclaim, "We didn't go to war, we didn't go to war." Out of the convention came the direction for the campaign and the slogan (which Wilson himself never used) "He kept us out of war."

Armed with a slogan Wilson did not really want, the Democrats went into the campaign far stronger than had been expected of a minority party battling against the reunited Republicans. Many of the ex-Bull Moosers, Republican farmers in the Midwest, and workers who had once voted for a full dinner pail now favored the Democrats. In part they did so because of Wilson's progressive domestic policy, but still more because of their hope that the President could continue to keep the country out of the war.

As for the Republicans, Roosevelt was not only back in the party but apparently in its Old Guard wing. He could not obtain the nomination himself, partly because of his earlier Bull Moose sins, but still more because of his unpopular rampant interventionism. When during the convention he finally realized this, he wanted either of two ultraconservatives, Wood or Lodge, to receive the nomination. The Republican leadership was too wise to nominate a man as closely linked with intervention as Wood, or with reaction as Lodge. Rather they persuaded Charles Evans Hughes, who had an impeccable progressive record, to resign from the Supreme Court and accept the nomination.

Primarily because of the whooping of Roosevelt, Lodge, Wood, and others on the sidelines, the Republicans gradually began to look like the war party. True enough, the Chicago *Tribune* had proclaimed that Roosevelt was the only real prophet of peace, but Roosevelt in 1916 spoke with no restraint, as he tried to drive Hughes into a bellicose position. He complained to newspapermen that the cautious Hughes would not accept advice but just "withdraws into his whiskers." Roosevelt even made veiled references to the "bearded lady." Hughes, under such pressure, wired Roosevelt congratulations on warlike speeches. These telegrams and Hughes's own remarks led voters to believe that he was more likely than Wilson to adopt a militant policy. On domestic matters, Hughes was for the most part either negative or conservative. In California, a critical state, the Old Guard Republicans took him into such tight custody that he did not even meet the progressive Hiram Johnson while they were in the same hotel. Hughes probably would have lost California on the issues anyway, since these above all were against him, but the bad management of his campaign and his own negative lackluster performance also helped make votes for Wilson. The Hughes of 1916 demonstrated little of the outstanding statesmanship that distinguished him earlier and later.

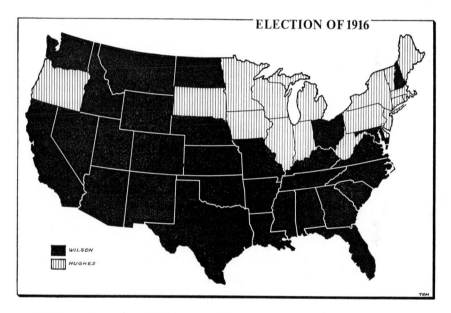

ELECTION OF 1916

WILSON
HUGHES

Wilson campaigned boldly on the progressive issues, and warned that a Republican victory would mean intervention in Mexico and war in Europe. The lure of progressivism and peace were still so irresistible in 1916 that the Democratic party, though normally a minority, squeezed through to victory. On election night, returns from the East were so solidly for Hughes that he appeared elected; then, as returns from the West came in, Hughes began to lose his lead. But it was not until Friday that Wilson's election was certain. He had received 9,130,000 votes to 8,538,000 for Hughes—three million more than he had gotten in 1912. The Socialist vote had dropped 300,000. In the electoral college, Wilson had a majority of 23; the West and the South had re-elected him. The Democrats also retained a precarious control over both houses of Congress.

U-Boats Plunge America into the War

So FAR AS elections can be regarded as national plebiscites, Wilson had received a narrow mandate to continue along the path of progressivism and peace. Undoubtedly he intended to follow such a course. Even before the summer of 1914, he had tried through Colonel House to bring an end to the armaments race. Since the outbreak of the war he had repeatedly sought means to bring the warring nations into a peace conference. But both sides had invested too heavily in the conflict, and were still too hopeful of realizing upon their investment, to feel able to talk of a negotiated peace. During the summer and fall of 1916, after their military offensives had failed, they intensified their blockade warfare against each other on the high seas. Wilson, thoroughly irritated with the further British encroachment upon American maritime rights, had veered toward a vigorously neutral frame of mind. He had come to feel that only a negotiated peace which brought a draw between the two sides could be just.

Immediately after the election, in November 1916, Wilson renewed negotiations looking toward a settlement. Germans, successful on the eastern front, for a while were encouraging. The Chancellor thought of using Wilson to bring about a conference, then acted on his own. The top German generals did not want any conference at all, and in the middle of the arrangements succeeded in reducing the Chancellor to a cipher. Although the British, in contrast, promised to negotiate on a generous basis, the German attitude doomed Wilson's scheme. Nevertheless, on January 22, 1917, he spread his plan before the Senate, calling for a lasting peace that the American people would help maintain through a league of nations. It would be a peace with freedom of the seas, disarmament, national self-determination for subject peoples, and equality among nations. "Peace among equals" could come only through "peace without victory."

The time when either side would accept "peace without victory" was long since past. The possibility that the United States could stay out of the war had almost disappeared before Wilson spoke, for on January 9 the military leaders who had come to dominate Germany had decided upon one final cast of the iron dice. They had agreed to return to unrestricted submarine warfare even though it would bring the United States into the war. They hoped that they could crush France on land and starve Britain from the sea before America could make its weight felt. On January 31, the German Ambassador announced that beginning the following day submarines would sink all ships, enemy or neutral, in a broad zone around the Allied countries. One conspicuously painted American liner a week would be let through to Falmouth, if it carried no contraband. At the same time,

Germany announced peace terms that they knew the Allies would accept only if they were crushed.

President Wilson was impaled on a dilemma of his own making. He had in effect during the previous eighteen months drawn a narrow line—the right of American citizens and vessels to travel on the high seas in time of war—and threatened Germany with war if she transgressed it. How could Wilson take the United States into a war against Germany for such a limited end, and still bring about the sort of peace he wanted, a just peace among equals, a peace without the victor dictating to the vanquished?

The President found no ready answer in February and even into March. He immediately broke off diplomatic relations with Germany and waited for sinkings, but he still hoped for peace. He did arm merchant vessels under an old statute after a group of antiwar Senators filibustered a bill to death. Wilson called them "a little group of willful men," but he himself blocked the Navy from recalling ships from the Caribbean to refit themselves for immediate war. When his impatient Assistant Secretary of the Navy, Franklin D. Roosevelt, protested, Wilson explained, "I want history to show not only that we have tried every diplomatic means to keep out of the war; to show that war has been forced upon us deliberately by Germany; but also that we have come into the court of history with clean hands." The moral position of the United States deeply concerned him. As late as March 20, when Burleson asserted in a cabinet meeting that unless he called Congress the people would force action, Wilson replied, "I do not care for popular demand. I want to do right, whether popular or not."

Gradually events carried Wilson toward war. On February 25, the British turned over to him an intercepted note from the German Foreign Secretary, Arthur Zimmerman, proposing that in the event of war Mexico should attack the United States and receive in return her lost provinces north of the border. Americans were infuriated. At about the same time, the Russian revolution eliminated one of the moral problems in Wilson's mind by replacing a despotism among the Allies with a constitutional monarchy. (It lasted only until November 1917, when Lenin and the Communists came into power). It seemed increasingly clear to Wilson—despite the horrors and losses of war, and the way in which it would bring brutality even at home and damage progressive reforms—that American participation would be worthwhile. He believed the German cause to be unrighteous, and had faith that if the United States sat at the conference table, it could bring about a just and lasting peace.

On March 18, 1917, news came that submarines had torpedoed three American ships. On March 20, the cabinet unanimously advised the President to ask Congress for a declaration of war. The following day Wilson issued a call for Congress to meet April 2, and began work on his war message.

Why was the American nation, poised on the brink of war, about to enter it? For two decades afterwards the question was widely debated. The most generally accepted conclusion was that Allied propaganda, and the machinations of Wall Streeters and American industrialists who had an enormous stake in an Anglo-French victory, were basically responsible, and that a narrow interpretation of maritime rights precipitated the United States into the war. Yet while Americans from the outset had been preponderantly pro-Allied, there is no clear indication that either these leanings or Allied propaganda led a majority of them to favor war in

The sinking of the Illinois, *March 18, 1917* (OFFICIAL U.S. NAVY PHOTO)

April 1917. As for the economic titans, while many of them were emotionally extremely pro-Allied, they apparently had no fear of an Allied collapse in 1917, and would have had much of their enormous neutral profits taxed away from them if the United States entered the conflict. In any event, there is no evidence that they had any influence on Wilson during the crisis. The United States seemed to be entering the war solely to fight for its rights as a neutral. The acquiescence of much of the public and almost all of Congress in this course may have been partly due to an illusion that the American role would be no more than heightened industrial production on behalf of the Allies and the waging of a naval war against German submarines. Few people knew that the General Staff was already working on plans for conscription.

On the evening of April 2, 1917, President Wilson delivered his war message to Congress. He enumerated the German transgressions of

American neutral rights, placed a strong emphasis upon these American rights, and expounded highly idealistic war aims. He declared:

> It is a fearful thing to lead this great peaceful people into war, into the most terrible . . . of all wars. . . . But the right is more precious than peace, and we shall fight for the things which we have always carried nearest our hearts—for democracy, . . . for the rights and liberties of small nations, for a universal dominion of right by such a concert of free peoples as shall bring peace and safety to all nations and make the world itself at last free.

Four days later, Congress passed the war declaration and the President signed it. So war had come, but more through the basic decision of Germany than through that of the American people. Americans had merely acquiesced in President Wilson's establishment of a policy on the high seas which could lead to war if Germany violated it. Germany did, and the President and Congress decided to fight. It still remained for the American people to learn what this would entail, and realize the broad aims for which they were struggling. No people had ever embarked upon a crusade more reluctantly.

The Great Economic Mobilization

IN THE MONTHS that followed, Americans came to accept Wilson's idealistic war aims, and to acquire some less idealistic ones of their own, too. Opposition or apathy changed to enthusiasm and even hysteria. The contribution the United States was obliged to make turned out to be a colossal one as, clumsily at first but steadily and impressively, the unprepared nation built a gigantic war machine. In the process it made almost revolutionary changes in the fabric of what had been progressive America.

The changes progressivism had wrought were results of a philosophy; those of the war were responses to an emergency. Much as the wartime measures went against longstanding American prejudices, much as they were derived from European rather than American precedents, in two respects they were in keeping with American ways. They were means of getting things done in a hurry, and they were, for the most part, practical. To this extent they were part of the prevailing philosophical current of pragmatism. Most of the public, unlike Wilson, thought of the wartime innovations in rather simple terms as conditions of a dangerous, unpleasant adventure upon which one could embark with the expectation of later returning to things as they had been. Few people realized that the nation had not crossed such a divide since the Civil War and that little could be the same afterwards.

Roosevelt, elderly and ill, still seeming to think in terms of the Spanish-

American War, fought for permission to take a volunteer division to the Western Front. A clique of Republican Senators backed him. Speaker Champ Clark was so incensed at the prospect of a draft that he asserted from the floor of the House during debate, "In the estimation of Missourians there is precious little difference between a conscript and a convict." For weeks the debate went on, but in the end Roosevelt was blocked, and the Selective Service Act was passed.

During the debate it had become clear what a large figure in both money and men the President must write into the blank check which Congress (and the American people) had signed. When a distinguished economist suggested that in the first year the nation would spend at least $10,000,000,000, it seemed incredible, for even in the three previous defense years the government had spent an average of only $718,000,000 on armament. In April, British and French missions arrived and made clear for the first time their desperate need for money, men, and ships if they were to stave off imminent defeat. In London, Admiral John Jellicoe revealed to Admiral William S. Sims, an American who had been hurried over, that the Germans were sinking 900,000 tons of ships per month and would win unless these losses could be stopped, and stopped soon. Before long, army officers arriving in France discovered that the French army, bled almost beyond repair, was groggy and defeatist.

Massive measures were necessary at once if the Germans were not to win their gamble by starving out the British and knocking out the French. Without fully informing the public of the perils facing the Allies, the administration, obtaining the requisite legislation from Congress, began moving rapidly. The Navy Department stripped the fleet of destroyers for antisubmarine duty and the War Department worked on plans for an American Expeditionary Force. Congress voted to the Treasury Department the necessary authorization to borrow seven billion dollars, of which three billion were to go as loans to the Allies.

From this start the United States had to build in a few months a war organization comparable to those that the other belligerents had spent three years developing. This country had to create machinery like theirs to regiment the national economy, manpower, and ideas and attitudes as never before in American history, even during the Civil War. Americans did not like regimentation, and even at the height of the reform spirit during the Progressive era had been slow to accept measures which would give greater control to the government. Under the exigencies of war, President Wilson was able to establish numerous government agencies, and, when necessary, obtain authorization for them from Congress.

During the preparedness period, in August 1916, Congress had approved the establishment of a Council of National Defense, consisting of six cabinet members, and an Advisory Commission made up of representatives of industry, transportation, business, and labor. Even before the United States entered the war, the distinguished members of this council discussed conscription, food control, and the organization of industry. Although an alarmed congressman was moved to refer to them as "the secret government," their power was mainly advisory. In the spring of 1917, they persuaded the armed forces to establish a Munitions Standard Board, shortly reorganized as the General Munitions Board, to supervise purchasing running into billions of dollars. Since the new Board merely proliferated additional weak advisory committees, the Council, on July 8, 1917, established a new, more centralized War Industries Board to co-ordinate government purchases. It too lacked power at first, and its first two chairmen resigned in despair.

By the winter of 1917–1918, the American economic mobilization seemed a failure. A Senate investigator charged that the military establishment "has almost stopped functioning . . . because of inefficiency in every bureau and in every department of the Government." When Secretary of War Baker appeared to testify, the hue and cry was, "We need a butcher, not a Baker." Republicans demanded a coalition war cabinet like England's, which in effect would wrest the direction of the war from the President. A year earlier Wilson had privately expressed his opposition to bringing Republicans into high administrative positions, calling them "the *Junkerthum* [German aristocracy] trying to creep in under cover of the patriotic feeling of the moment." He acted boldly by sending Congress a bill to confer upon him almost unlimited economic power, the Overman Bill, which was passed in April 1918. Before Congress could act he overhauled the War Industries Board, conferring upon it sweeping powers to co-ordinate industry, and appointing as chairman a Wall Street broker previously on the Board, Bernard Baruch.

Even in this strengthened form, the War Industries Board did no actual buying except for the Allies and continued to be primarily advisory and organizational. Baruch marshaled a brilliant group of about a hundred businessmen and armed-forces officers who, largely through moral suasion and their near-monopoly on information, were able to establish their authority over American industry and to locate supplies and establish realistic priorities for them. They also eliminated duplication and needless articles, thus cutting the sizes and styles of plows from 376 to 76, and removing the steel stays from women's corsets. For a while in 1918 they reduced automobile production 75 per cent. Because they were primarily interested in expanding production, they did little to control prices, and consequently profits, except on some raw materials and steel.

Already, before the American entrance into the war, considerable wartime inflation had taken place. Metal prices in July 1917, averaged three and one half times more than those of 1913. This hurt, and the War Industries Board received some of the blame. Congress complained that dollar-a-year men in Washington on loan from industry were over-tender toward the companies from which they had come, so Baruch shuffled them to put them in charge of different commodities. By the end of the war, the United States had achieved fairly effective industrial regulation.

Food was almost as vital as munitions for the Allies. At the suggestion of the Council for National Defense, a Food Administration was set up by the President. It was later authorized by Congress, after vigorous debate, in the Lever Act of August 10, 1917. Its administrator was one of the most spectacular civilian heroes of the war, an American mining engineer, Herbert Hoover, who had supervised the relief feeding of Belgium. His task was to increase food production, cut waste, substitute plentiful for scarce foods, and protect consumers from speculators. Hoover, in keeping with his experience in Belgium, wished to be an administrator, not a dictator, and to run his program as far as possible on a voluntary basis. To a remarkable degree he was able to enlist the patriotic support of the public in conserving food and observing meatless and wheatless days. One of his effective strategies was to distribute posters reading, "Food will win the war."

The shortage of wheat was especially critical because 1916 had been a bad crop year. Hoover encouraged wheat production by guaranteeing the purchase of the entire 1917 crop at $2.20 per bushel, a figure not as high as the price might later have risen on a free market, but sufficient to assure farmers a substantial profit. Unfortunately, 1917 was another bad crop year. In 1918 and 1919, the farmers outdid themselves, selling their mules to the army, purchasing tractors, and plowing up the pastures. They also planted wheat on semiarid lands on the Great Plains. Wheat acreage jumped from 45 million in 1917 to 75 million in 1919, and the land produced bumper crops. The government purchased the wheat through a new flexible device, a government-owned corporation chartered in Delaware, the United States Grain Corporation. Similarly, the Food Administration nearly doubled hog production to meet the fat shortage through setting the price 43 per cent above what was normally profitable.

In effect, the American farmers received five billion dollars in compensation from 1917 to 1920 to produce enormous quantities of food for Europe. Shipments jumped from less than 7,000,000 tons in prewar years to 12,300,000 tons in 1917–18 and to 18,600,000 tons in 1918–19. While Europeans were thus kept from starvation, Americans were able to avoid rationing. They did have to buy substitutes for wheat flour, and sometimes to do without scarce commodities. Hoover opposed retail price-fixing, which he thought would lead to black markets, but did protect consumers from speculation. Food costs went up gradually. Wholesale prices were already up 80 per cent over 1913 when the Food Administration began operation in August 1917; by November 1918 they had increased 20 per cent more. Hoover was criticized for having allowed so much profit to food processers, especially meat packers, and conversely for not having allowed more profit to farmers. On the whole, because he narrowed the gulf between what farmers received and what consumers paid he and the Food Administration ended the war remarkably popular.

The Lever Act which established the Food Administration also authorized a Fuel Administration, which fixed the price of coal high enough to bring submarginal coal mines into operation and increase bituminous coal production by about 50 per cent. In spite of this increase, the fuel shortage became so acute that the Fuel Administration had to order a series of coal holidays for eastern industries in the early months of 1918.

In order to guarantee war production in German-owned factories in this country, especially those producing chemicals, these and all other German assets came under the custody of an Alien Property Custodian, A. Mitchell Palmer. The Trading-with-the-Enemy Act of October 6, 1917, provided for their seizure and administration. Palmer obtained additional authority to sell German property, which he utilized especially to license dye and chemical patents to American industry. This was punitive toward the Germans, immensely profitable for some American businessmen, and helpful for the development of a strong chemical industry in the United States. Under the same piece of legislation, a War Trade Board licensed imports and exports in order to conserve shipping space, obtain supplies for the United States, and hamper enemy trade.

Increased production and stringent economy within the United States would be of no avail unless supplies could be delivered to Europe. Into the winter of 1917–18, two acute transportation bottlenecks plagued the nation. Railroads could not get raw materials to eastern factories or munitions to ports, even through cooperation with a voluntary Railroad War Board. On December 28, 1917, Wilson put the railroads under a Railroad Administration headed by Secretary of the Treasury McAdoo. He utilized expert railroad men to run the lines as one unified system. Railroads could draw upon a half-billion-dollar revolving fund for improvements, and received rent equivalent to their average earnings in 1914–1917. The transportation snarl was so effectively untangled that a freight-car shortage of 150,000 in 1917 was transformed into a surplus of 300,000 by the end of 1918.

Shipping was a still greater and more continuing problem. By the

Launching the first freighter at Hog Island, August 1918 (NATIONAL ARCHIVES)

summer of 1917, submarines had sunk nearly a quarter of the British merchant fleet. The number of American vessels was relatively small, and they were mainly committed to coastal trade. It seemed essential to build a "bridge of ships" to Europe if the war were not to be lost, but the iron out of which to build it had not been mined, and the trees for its timber had "birds still nesting in their tops." The Emergency Fleet Corporation under the Shipping Board faced long and difficult tasks, not made easier by the quarreling of early leaders. After July, 1917, under a new, ener-

Manufacturing Curtiss OX-5 airplane engines (NATIONAL ARCHIVES)

getic chairman, Edward N. Hurley, it began to make remarkable progress in building new shipyards to turn out 1,700 ships of steel and 1,000 of wood. Designing them took months; the first keel at the huge Hog Island yard at Philadelphia was not laid until February 12, 1918, and the first ship not delivered until nearly a month after the armistice. Had the war lasted into 1919, as had been anticipated, ships aplenty would have been provided.

As it was, the Shipping Board had to solve its problems with existing tonnage—that seized from the Germans and the Dutch, and that already under construction for the Allies in American shipyards. By September 1918 it had accumulated a fleet about half as large as that of the British. Through pooling these ships, scientifically planning their loading, and cutting their turn-around time in half, the Shipping Board improvised, out of what had already existed, the essential "bridge of ships."

Other wartime construction agencies shared difficulties similar to those of the Fleet Corporation. The Aircraft Production Board failed to produce a promised 22,000 airplanes by July 1918—a ridiculous figure, since neither side on the Western Front ever had as many as 2,500 planes at one time. The failure to fulfill this over-optimistic promise led to harsh criticism. By the time the armistice was signed, the United States had delivered in France 1,185 De Haviland bombers and 5,460 Liberty motors.

A galaxy of war agencies dealt with labor. Several commissions and boards helped adjust disputes in different industries and areas. In April 1918 President Wilson established the National War Labor Board to serve as a sort of supreme court for labor disputes. Labor and industry each provided five representatives for the board; the public was represented by the two co-chairmen. One was ex-President Taft, a conservative; the other, Frank Walsh, was sympathetic toward labor. The War Labor Board would not countenance strikes or lockouts but recognized the right of unions to organize and bargain collectively. It favored the eight-hour day, the establishment in any given area of the wages prevailing in it, the maintenance of a basic living standard for workers, and equal pay for women who did equal work. Like some other war agencies, it had to function through persuasion or use of the President's war powers rather than through its own legal authority. It could commandeer plants of recalcitrant employers or threaten stubborn workers with the draft. Altogether it heard 1,251 cases involving 711,500 workers. Since the Board was primarily judicial, one other labor agency came into existence in May 1918 to co-ordinate and unify the policies of all the many labor boards and agencies. This was the War Labor Policies Board under Felix Frankfurter.

President Gompers of the A.F.L. did much during the war to enhance the prestige of organized labor. He sat with industrialists on the Council of National Defense, and in return for recognition of unionism and wage increases, he pledged that there would be no strikes. Gompers also co-operated in the government onslaught against labor radicals, which meant the Industrial Workers of the World, who were engaging in sabotage in the West. The I.W.W. almost disappeared, while membership in all unions jumped from 2,716,900 in 1914 to 3,104,600 in 1917 and 4,169,100 in 1919. Still, this was no more than one-eighth of all wage earners.

Financing the War

ONE OF THE GREATEST of the tasks of the administration, financing the war, was the duty of Secretary of the Treasury McAdoo. He faced firmly the problem of trying to raise as much of the staggering sum as possible

Women working on fuses for artillery shells (NATIONAL ARCHIVES)

through taxes rather than loans. Morgan wished to limit funds acquired through taxation to 20 per cent of the total to be raised, as in England, but the Midwest progressives would have liked to obtain 100 per cent through taxes, in order to make the rich finance the war. McAdoo raised about one-third of the thirty-two-billion-dollar total through taxes, a ratio he felt was as high as possible without placing a heavy burden on the lower income groups. The War Revenue Act of 1917 imposed a great variety of excise taxes, and raised income taxes to an unprecedented peak, two-thirds of a $2,000,000 income. The 1918 law, which did not go into effect until after the war, raised the ceiling to 77 per cent. Altogether, the taxes on individual and corporate incomes, excess profits, and inheritances provided 74 per cent of the war tax revenues. There was one conspicuous loophole: many corporations distributed to their stockholders stock exempt from taxes, rather than giving them dividends.

Also through loan policy, McAdoo tried to keep the burden of the war from falling too heavily upon the poorer people. He sought to sell as many Liberty Bonds as possible to them so that they, not richer people, would reap the ultimate profit. The bonds carried interest rates lower than ever before, and, except for the first series, provided more benefits for small holders. Despite the emphasis upon selling to a wide public, those with moderate incomes (under $2,000 a year) probably purchased no more than 30 per cent of the twenty-three billion dollars worth of bonds sold.

War finance progressed more smoothly than it had in the Civil War, but it still left much to be desired. Taxes and bond sales did not sufficiently

Fourth Liberty Loan Parade, New Orleans (NATIONAL ARCHIVES)

drain off purchasing power. Too much of the financing came from inflationary expansion of bank credit through the Federal Reserve System, which became in effect an arm of the Treasury. The member banks bought huge quantities of war bonds, and on the basis of these increased the amount of Federal Reserve notes by 500 per cent. The new money in circulation created an irresistible pressure upon prices, and thus caused trouble after the war.

Two finance agencies emerged, of interest for the precedents they set. Congress in April 1918 created the War Finance Corporation to make loans to munitions industries, and the Capital Issues Committee to police new security issues and prevent waste of loans upon nonessentials.

Altogether nearly 5,000 war agencies worked in countless areas. They brought an unprecedented degree of economic control and regimentation to American life. On the whole, the public disliked them, was ready to blame the discomforts of the war upon them, and was impatient to dissolve them at the end of the war. By the late fall of 1918, they were unpopular symbols of "un-American regimentation." On the other hand, some of the agencies seemed to work miracles, and, like the Food Administration, received a good press. These agencies later seemed, to the economic groups they benefited, to offer a way out of postwar difficulties, and when new crises arose a decade later, certain groups clamored for the reinstatement of the agencies.

At the beginning, in the spring of 1917, Washington had tried to meet the unprecedented war demands by falling back upon what was usually called the "British experience." By the close of the war, these innovations had become part of the American experience—an unpleasant, drastic, but nonetheless rather effective means of meeting national emergency. Something new and of the utmost significance had been added to the American political tradition, and thereby the tradition had undergone a sharp modification.

Chapter **9**

VICTORY AND
ISOLATION

WHILE THE AMERICAN PEOPLE were transforming their nation's vast resources into the sinews of war, the armed forces were striving to tip the scales of battle against Germany on the high seas and along the battle line in France. A third great mobilization, that of the minds of the people of the United States, brought an almost hysterical support for the war. President Wilson and the administrators in Washington intended to teach them the significance of the war and the necessity to build a just and lasting peace. Many Americans of both major parties viewed the war and the peace that was to follow with truly Wilsonian dedication, but among many others the indoctrination seemed to lead to conformity rather than understanding, and to engender more hatred than idealism. This threatened tragedy, for while the course of the war on the battlefield was determining its military conclusion, its path in men's minds was helping shape its ultimate outcome. What victory would mean to either the world or the United States was far from clear as the battles unfolded, yet in the conduct of the war were to be found some of the clues to the peace.

Countering the Submarine Menace

FOR MANY MONTHS after April 1917 it seemed quite possible that the Allies would lose the war. The Germans had acted to provoke American

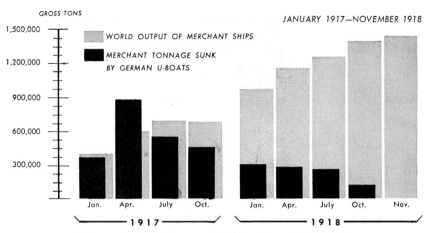

GROSS TONS   JANUARY 1917—NOVEMBER 1918

1,500,000

☐ WORLD OUTPUT OF MERCHANT SHIPS

1,200,000   ■ MERCHANT TONNAGE SUNK
                    BY GERMAN U-BOATS

900,000

600,000

300,000

Jan.   Apr.   July   Oct.   Jan.   Apr.   July   Oct.   Nov.

\———— 1 9 1 7 ————/   \———— 1 9 1 8 ————/

Submarine Sinkings and Shipbuilding, 1917–1918

entrance, taking the calculated risk that they could destroy the French armies and starve the British people before the United States could intervene decisively. They came close to making good on this risk.

None of the huge mobilization of men and matériel in the United States would benefit the Allies until it had reached the Western Front. For every American soldier in France there would have to be about four tons of shipping in continuous operation; there must be a "bridge of ships" across the Atlantic. Yet German submarines were sinking ships faster than they could be built. In the second quarter of 1917, one out of every

A convoy in the danger zone, and (inset) *a camouflaged warship* (OFFICIAL U.S. NAVY PHOTOS)

four ships that left Great Britain on a transatlantic crossing never returned. If this continued, by October 1917 there would not be sufficient tonnage to carry on the war. The British had no solution. Fortunately, the United States navy was able to bring both fresh resources and an effective defense scheme. It sent all the destroyers to Queenstown, Ireland, to aid in the antisubmarine patrols; by July 1917 there were already thirty-five stationed there. At home, the navy suspended building battleships to begin construction of 250 destroyers and 400 submarine chasers.

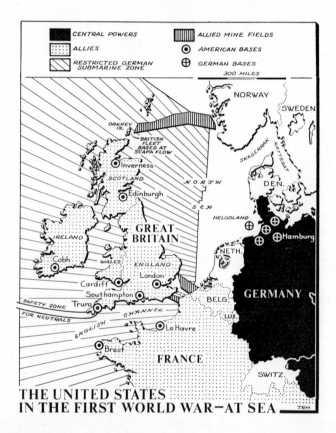

THE UNITED STATES IN THE FIRST WORLD WAR—AT SEA

Later one squadron of five battleships helped keep the Imperial German navy bottled in the North Sea, while another of four battleships guarded against surface raiders.

The solution to the sinkings by submarines came primarily through the establishment of convoys. The British admiralty had opposed such convoys, and kept most of its destroyers as a curtain to protect the Grand Fleet and the channel ferries. Eventually, however, the American Admiral Sims, with aid from home, broke down the resistance of the admiralty so that a convoying system was well established by August 1917. The American navy developed other types of antisubmarine defense. The most spectacular was the project to plant a barrage of mines across the North Sea from Scotland to Norway. This was a distinctly American project, which Sims as well as the admiralty opposed, but it was well on the way to completion by November 1918. Perhaps it was of some value, since in its short period of existence it destroyed eight submarines, but the convoy was the main device that counteracted the submarine.

Sinkings, which had totaled nearly 900,000 tons in April 1917, had dropped to 350,000 tons by December 1917, and to only 112,000 tons by October 1918. This was primarily a British achievement, but the United States contributed to it substantially. The British provided 70 per cent of the escorting ships and the French 3 per cent, compared with 27 per cent provided by the United States.

This is not to minimize the significant part played by the United States in the Allied victory. The navy, after a slow start—in keeping with Wilson's policy of neutrality, it had not been on a war footing in April, 1917 —grew enormously in size and efficiency. By the time the armistice was signed it had 200,000 men and 834 vessels engaged in convoying across the Atlantic or serving in European waters, and had expanded in total to 533,000 men and 2,000 ships. Under its protection, the "bridge of ships" came into existence and performed great feats in moving men and supplies across the Atlantic.

The Margin of Victory in France

THE WAR DEPARTMENT was as ill-prepared as the Navy Department for large-scale intervention. The General Staff, the agency charged with devising war plans, had not been informed by the President that national policy might lead to involvement in Europe, nor had it been instructed to prepare for possible operations in the European theater. American strategic plans were drawn up after the country entered the war, and essentially they were concocted in France at the headquarters of the commanding general of the American Expeditionary Force. This was General John J. Pershing, a highly intelligent officer and a driving personality who conceived of his position as being that of General in Chief in the field. Because of Pershing's concept and because the command relationship between a commanding general and the General Staff had never been sharply defined, Pershing engaged in almost constant bickering with the Chief of Staff, Peyton C. March, who attempted to exercise a supervisory control over field operations. Pershing was also bitterly critical of the bureau chiefs who, under the supervision of the General Staff, were supposed to direct the flow of supplies to the zone of battle. The chiefs seemed unable to adjust their thinking to the demands of modern war, and the supplies failed to reach France. At one point, in the summer of 1918, the shortages were so great as to threaten disaster. Finally the crisis was met by assigning the service of supply directly to the General Staff.

Pershing's goal was to build an American force in France numbering a million men by June 1, 1918. Many an obstacle stood between him and his objective, as he came to realize after he arrived in Paris on June 14, 1917. The dispirited Allies stood on the defensive against the desperately aggressive enemy. They wanted fresh American troops, but wanted to use them piecemeal as reinforcements along their own weary lines. They did not like Pershing's insistence that the Americans should operate as a

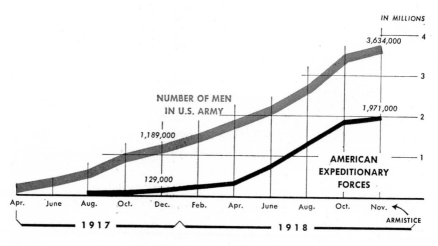

The U.S. Army in World War I

separate army along their own sectors, since they had no reason to trust the untried American soldiers or their leadership. In truth, there had been nothing in American military activities during the Spanish-American war and the Mexican intervention to warrant confidence. But General Pershing stood firm, with President Wilson behind him, and consequently the Allies were reluctant to find ships for the A.E.F. and its mountains of supplies.

After a few months the serious need for American troops overweighed these misgivings. In the fall of 1917, the Germans in effect knocked the Russians out of the war; in November, Lenin and his followers in Russia overthrew the constitutional government of Kerensky and opened peace negotiations. With the Austrians, the Germans delivered a near-fatal blow to the Italians at Caporetto. The stunned Allies for the first time organized a Supreme War Council, and looked to the United States for manpower. Meanwhile Pershing gradually had been building port facilities, running railroads across France, and constructing training camps and supply dumps. As a trickle of troops began to arrive, he tried to give them three months' training before putting them into combat. While the number was small, he was willing to brigade his units temporarily among the Allies to give them experience and to meet emergencies. Thus the First Division went into action with the French in Lorraine in October 1917, and took over a quiet sector of its own near Toul in January 1918.

In the early months of 1918, Germany moved troops from the east and slammed them against the Allies in a series of great offensives de-

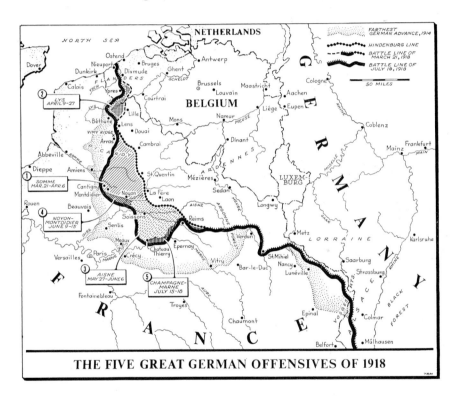

THE FIVE GREAT GERMAN OFFENSIVES OF 1918

signed to end the war before the Americans had arrived in numbers. In March 1918, the Germans smashed through the British and French lines where they met in the Somme, and thus made a gain of thirty miles. They launched a second mighty blow in Flanders in April. The Allies were staggered, but managed to stabilize their lines, and for the first time appointed a Commander in Chief for all their armies, Marshal Ferdinand Foch. They asked the United States to supply as many soldiers as possible in the shortest possible time. Out of fear of defeat, the British found the transports for the troops, and the trickle turned into a flood. At the beginning of the German offensives in March, less than 300,000 American soldiers were in France; by July 1, Pershing had his million. This meant that by late spring, the fresh American manpower for the first time could be a significant factor, since both the Allied and German armies were low on reserves. The Americans distinguished themselves in battle on May 28, 1918, when they captured the strategic town of Cantigny in the Somme sector and held it against several German counterattacks.

Fourteen-inch railway gun firing at railroad and troop center (NATIONAL ARCHIVES)

The preceding day, May 27, 1918, what turned out to be the great climactic struggle of the war had begun. The Germans mounted a final giant offensive through rough hills, across one river valley, and on to the next, until on May 30 they crossed the Marne River at Château-Thierry and threatened Paris fifty miles away. American and French troops, under French command, fought to blunt the German drive. After a week of bitter attack, the Americans recaptured Belleau Wood, and thus helped stabilize the line. A little further south at Reims, in the great bulge toward Paris, the Germans tried on July 15, the morning after Bastille Day, to crash through the French lines. Some 85,000 American troops helped repel the German thrust. By July 18, the German offensive was over; and

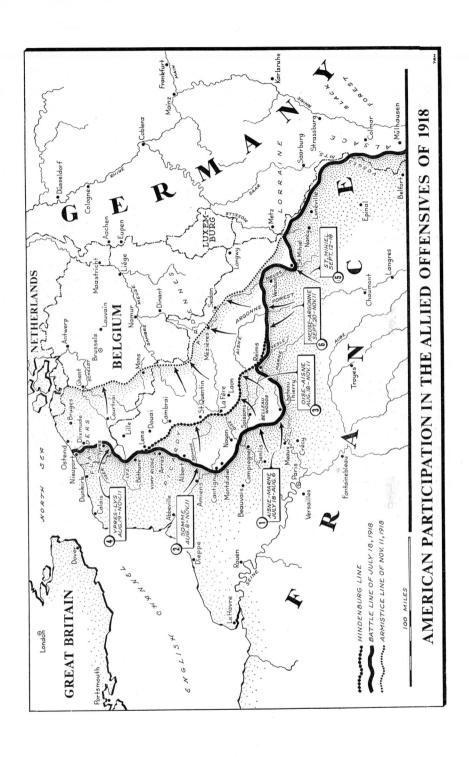

AMERICAN PARTICIPATION IN THE ALLIED OFFENSIVES OF 1918

the Allies began a counteroffensive, with American divisions participating, to liquidate the Marne salient (outward projection in the battle line). By August 6 it was gone.

In the months that followed, as American troops disembarked at a rate averaging 263,000 per month, the reinvigorated Allies pressed the exhausted Germans from Lorraine to the North Sea. On August 10, Pershing for the first time launched an offensive under his own command. He directed the First Army, consisting of 550,000 American troops, against the St. Mihiel salient protruding south of Verdun. Within 36 hours it was wiped out.

For the advancing Americans it was a nightmare. During the St. Mihiel drive one soldier, Norman Roberts of Alexandria, Virginia, wrote in his diary on September 12:

> Bullets, millions of them, flying like rain drops. Rockets and flares in all directions. Shrapnel bursting the air and sending down its deadly iron. . . . Every minute looking for the next to be gone to the great beyond. A mad dash for 50 feet and then look for cover. A stop for a minute and then the barrage would lift to a farther point and then another mad rush. Always leaving some of your comrades cold in the face of death. . . . The field of dead a terrible sight. Both Americans and German. A day never to be forgotten.

Pershing would have liked to push on through rugged terrain against the vital German fortress of Metz, but Foch wanted the First Army to attack instead north of Verdun in the Meuse–Argonne area. The American assault along a twenty-four mile front in the Argonne forest began on September 26, 1918, as part of a grand offensive along two hundred miles of the front. The terrain was as difficult as that protecting Metz. The offensive bogged down, had to be reorganized, then continued for a total of forty-seven days. The American troops fought through what Pershing has described as a "vast network of uncut barbwire, the deep ravines, dense woods, myriads of shell craters, and a heavy fog." The Allied high command had not imagined the Americans could make much progress against these obstacles, but after October 4 the regrouped army again advanced. By the end of the month it had overrun almost all of the enemy's fixed positions, was beyond the Argonne forest, and was driving toward vital German communications. On November 7, the Americans established bridgeheads across the Meuse River, planted their guns looking down on the famous fortress of Sedan, and cut the railroad which carried German supplies to the front. It had been the greatest battle in which American troops had ever fought. The 1,200,000 soldiers had used a greater weight of ammunition than had all of the Union forces through the four years of the Civil War.

Other American divisions had been deployed at the same time on other sectors of the front. Altogether Americans participated in thirteen major operations, of which only two were under Pershing's command.

American-trained squadrons of aviators had begun operations in April. The first of these to engage in combat was the 94th Pursuit Squadron, more popularly known as the "Hat-in-the-Ring" squadron, under the command of Captain Edward V. Rickenbacker. The over-all record of the Americans, who engaged for the most part in individual combat against Germans flying the superior Fokker planes, was not impressive. At the armistice they constituted only 10 per cent of the Allied airpower. Individually they were brave to the point of foolhardiness—they refused to wear parachutes. The exploits of the seventy-one American aces (those

Captain Edward V. Rickenbacker (center) *and other pilots of the 94th Pursuit Squadron* (NATIONAL ARCHIVES)

who destroyed five or more enemy airplanes) were followed eagerly at home by newspaper readers hungry for heroes. Captain Rickenbacker, who shot down at least twenty-six German planes, became more famous than most generals.

By early November, the weight of American troops, which then numbered two million in France, was becoming irresistible. All along the front, millions of Allies had pushed back the Germans. The German reserves were gone, their regiments weakened, and their communications threatened. Invasion of their country, which the Germans could not repel, was imminent. For weeks they negotiated for an armistice—a temporary cessation in the fighting. Pershing was convinced that the Allies should demand surrender instead, and he would have liked to push his armies on toward Berlin to make the Germans really feel the war. The day after the Americans reached Sedan, German envoys crossed the lines to meet Foch and receive armistice terms from him—terms so stiff that a resumption of hostilities would be impossible. The Germans accepted, and on November 11, 1918, the armistice went into effect.

Rejoicing Americans were ready to credit their armies with winning the decisive battles, and in subsequent years felt they had won the war for the Allies. Beyond question they had supplied the margin of victory. During the frightful March offensives, the Germans had outmanned the Allies by 300,000 soldiers; by June, arriving American troops tipped the balance toward the Allies; by the time of the armistice the Allied lead was

Stanford University Section of the American Ambulance Field Service leaving for the front (NATIONAL ARCHIVES)

a decisive 600,000 men. Further, the raw American troops had made up for their ignorance with their vigor, valor, and quickness to learn. On the other hand, the really crushing burden of the war had not fallen upon them or the American people. They had fought bitterly, but only for a few months. The United States lost 112,000 men from enemy action or disease; 237,000 more were wounded. By comparison 1,385,000 French died, and 900,000 British. Only 7 per cent of the Americans in the services were casualties, compared with 73 per cent of the French, and 36 per cent of those from the British Empire.

The Struggle for Men's Minds

EVEN BEFORE the armistice, the thoughts of Americans were turning from war to peace. The conduct of the war had depended upon production at home and operations of the armed forces abroad. The pursuit of a satisfactory peace depended—in a democratic nation like the United States —upon a much more subtle and difficult factor, the temper of the American people. Since the hesitant entrance into the war, both official agencies and private publicists and organizations, from President Wilson and the Committee on Public Information to the yellow press, had sought to mold the minds of Americans. In conflicting ways they had tried to explain the significance of the war, encourage Americans in its vigorous pursuit, and prepare them for the peace to follow. As is all too easy in such circumstances, Americans had learned readily to hate the Germans and all those at home whom they might consider German sympathizers but had prepared themselves less well to assume a commanding role in maintaining a just peace in the postwar world. This in the end was to be the tragedy of President Wilson, of the American people, and consequently of all mankind.

Even before America entered the war, President Wilson had begun his idealistic series of addresses outlining the nature of the postwar world he wished to see emerge. He had talked then of "peace without victory," and about the right of the several submerged nationalities in Europe to organize governments of their own choosing. He had asserted too that the American people would be willing to join a postwar league of nations. Many Americans of goodwill, like the members of the League to Enforce Peace, had thrilled to Wilson's words. But his speeches had remained merely words, since Wilson had not bound the Allies to his conditions as a basis for American intervention. In fact, until his war message he had not even expounded his idealistic views to the American people as grounds for American entrance. He had instead placed the entrance of the United States upon the negative basis of German violations of American maritime rights, and he seemed to perpetuate this distinction between the United States and the Allies through the fiction that we were fighting Germany separately as an "associated power."

After American entrance, Wilson had discovered that the Allies had made secret treaties among themselves. These were agreements buying the intervention of several nations neutral at the beginning of the war, and arrangements designed to avoid postwar friction. Only the Anglo-Japanese agreement affected Germany, the only power with which the United States was at war. The new Bolshevik government of Russia publicized some of the treaties, to the embarrassment of Wilson since their terms seemed to run counter to the idealism for which he was exhorting Americans to fight. Wilson was sure in time he could counteract the treaties and force the British and French to accept a just peace. Meanwhile he unilaterally expounded his own war aims on January 8, 1918, in a speech before a joint session of Congress. He outlined his peace program in fourteen points. The first five of these were general, providing for open diplomacy, freedom of the seas, equality of economic opportunity, the reduction of armaments, and adjustment of colonial claims. These were to apply to all nations, victor and vanquished alike. Then he set forth formulas for given countries and areas in keeping with his previously expressed principle of national self-determination. Finally, Wilson placed emphasis upon his fourteenth point, which was basic to all the rest —establishment of "A general association of nations . . . affording mutual guarantees of political independence and territorial integrity to great and small states alike." The Fourteen Points, coming when all the belligerent peoples were overwhelmingly weary of the war, met with an enthusiastic response among liberals and working people in the United States, in the Allied nations, and among suppressed people throughout the world. Even many Germans welcomed them (and a later clarification of them, "the five particulars,") as the promise of a democratic Germany which could assume a position of equality in the community of nations. They were the most stirring and effective piece of propaganda the war produced.

While President Wilson meant the Fourteen Points as the war-weary peoples accepted them, as a blueprint for peace, there was no assurance that the Allied leaders would agree to them. Nor was there any clearcut proof that Wilson had the American people behind him, even though his Committee on Public Information had been engaged in a large-scale effort to sell the war. George Creel, a progressive newspaperman who had worked in the 1916 presidential campaign, headed the Committee. He persuaded newspapers to engage in voluntary self-censorship, an idea not entirely palatable to them, since it seemed to mean at times suppressing information less because it would be valuable to the enemy than because it might reveal unpopular facts about the administration and armed forces. On the positive side, the Committee disseminated countless tons of propaganda, and enlisted the services of 150,000 writers, lecturers, actors, and artists. Throughout the country 75,000 such volunteers arose to speak on almost every conceivable occasion; throughout the United States and the world 75,000,000 pieces of printed matter carried the American view of the war. Much of what the Creel Committee disseminated was idealistic, in keeping with Wilson's speeches and the Fourteen Points, depicting the war as a great crusade for humanity. Much also, unfortunately, appealed more to fear and hate than to a spirit of altruistic sacrifice. The Committee emphasized the menace of the Germans, and while it balked at the further dissemination of German atrocity stories, private organizations like the National Security League had no such scruples.

Dr. Ernst Kunwald, former conductor of the Cincinnati Symphony Orchestra, being arrested as an enemy alien (NATIONAL ARCHIVES)

A hysterical wartime hatred of all that seemed not to conform spread throughout the country. Congress passed several stern measures for the protection of the country from disloyal individuals. The Espionage Act of June 15, 1917 provided penalties running up to a $10,000 fine and twenty years' imprisonment, not only for those engaged in espionage, sabotage, and obstruction of the war effort, but even for those who should "willfully cause or attempt to cause insubordination, mutiny, or refusal of duty . . . or . . . willfully obstruct the recruiting or enlistment service." It also empowered the Postmaster General to ban from the mails any matter which in his opinion was seditious. The Trading-with-the-Enemy Act of October 6, 1917, established censorship over international communications and the foreign-language press (in addition to authorizing various types of economic warfare against the Germans). These measures were vigorously, and at times capriciously, enforced, but the administration sought still greater punitive powers to discipline the disloyal.

Congress responded with the Sabotage Act of April 20, 1918, aimed primarily at the I.W.W., and the Sedition Act of May 16, 1918. The Sedition Act, modeled after a Montana statute for supressing the I.W.W., was harsh beyond any previous legislation in American history. The reason for the law was to meet the public demand that those who were making disloyal remarks be punished. Many such people had been arrested and subsequently released because their remarks were not illegal. An Illinois mob lynched one such German-American before he could be released from jail. Senator Albert Fall warned his colleagues that they must define crimes clearly if they were to avoid direct action by the people. The Senate took his advice.

The enforcement of these laws was almost stern as any lynch mob would desire. Over 1,500 were arrested for seditious utterances, though only 10 were taken into custody for sabotage. The force of the laws continued unabated after the armistice. In the fall of 1918, after a four-day trial, the Socialist leader Eugene V. Debs, who had been pacifist, not pro-German, was sentenced to ten years in a federal penitentiary under the Espionage Act, and after the armistice, in March 1919, the Supreme Court upheld his conviction. Whatever pacifist or pro-German offenders escaped the Federal net were likely to be caught in the meshes of state sedition laws, or to suffer the wrath of vigilantes. The furore at its mildest was rather ludicrous, as sauerkraut became "liberty cabbage" and hamburger, "liberty sausage." It was a bit less funny in some communities to ban all German music, including the compositions of Mendelssohn and Beethoven. It was not funny at all to suspend Bruno Walter, the conductor of the Chicago Symphony Orchestra, because he had not become an American citizen; to ban the study of German in some public schools, as in Ohio; or to dump all books in German out of some public libraries, as in Los Angeles. And it was frightening when a vigilance committee in Minnesota, having forbidden a pastor to speak German, caught him praying at the bedside of a dying woman who spoke only German, tarred and feathered him, and rode him out of town on a rail.

At the same time, right-wing detractors of the war effort went unpunished, and for the most part uncriticized. George Harvey, with the encouragement of Senator Lodge, called the war administrators "mannikins," and labeled the Secretary of War a "cooty" who was "shockingly and dangerously unfit for his job." Theodore Roosevelt continued his bombast unabated in the Kansas City *Star*. The Postmaster General considered taking action, but did nothing. In the closing days of the war, Roosevelt thundered, "Let us dictate peace by the hammering of guns and not chat about peace to the accompaniment of the clicking of typewriters."

Sadly, at the time of the armistice there was more of this bellicose feeling than of the spirit of the Fourteen Points abroad in the United States.

The Reaction Against Wilson

MORE THAN WAR HYSTERIA was affecting the American people. Many of them were upset by the dislocations the war brought. There was the great migration of labor to war industries, and the resulting suspicion of strangers, especially of the Negroes who were migrating into the North. There were the businessmen and their employees who were engaged in the manufacture or retailing of nonessentials and who had consequently suffered from the emphasis upon war production. There were all those other businessmen whose profits of the neutrality period had been drained off by heavy wartime taxes. Some munitions makers did fatten on the war, but the real incomes of all manufacturers and property owners scarcely increased between 1913 and 1918, while seven-eighths of the new high income taxes fell upon them. Below these groups, the white-collar workers and all others with fixed incomes suffered annoyances and even hardships as their incomes failed to keep up with rising prices and they had to put up with wartime scarcities or substitutes. Here were the audiences for right-wing critics of the management of the war.

Many laboring men did fare better during the war than they had previously. The real income of factory and transport workers and coal miners jumped 20 per cent between 1914 and 1918. The vaunted prosperity of some shipyard workers who, according to wild rumors, bought silk shirts with huge wages they made tossing rivets into the water, and the glaring headlines the few strikes received in most newspapers, reinflamed the old prejudices of the middle class. They felt that workers were getting rich while they and their sons in the army and navy were making sacrifices. Added to their grievances against the administration was a feeling that it was too soft toward labor.

All things considered, farmers benefited more than any other group. Their real income after taxes was 25 per cent higher in 1918 than it had been in 1915. Even they were not all satisfied; while they enjoyed the new high farm prices, they disliked the new high prices of what they bought in town. Grain farmers in the Midwest and on the Great Plains were unhappy because the Food Administration had pegged wheat at $2.20 a bushel, which was below the free market, while cotton farmers of the South suffered no price peg to prevent them from reaping a full bonanza as cotton rose to 36 cents per pound. Further, many of the farmers of German origin in the Middle West who had voted for Wilson in 1916 because he had kept the country out of war were not disposed to follow him in 1918 or thereafter.

Thus, although the war had raised the living standards of millions of Americans in lower-income brackets, the Wilson administration did not benefit from their votes in the congressional election of 1918. The only possible exception was in the East, where the Democrats lost only two House seats compared with 21 lost in the remainder of the nation. Within his own party, Wilson had faced dissension throughout the war, as some of his congressional leaders of agrarian progressive background had fought drastic war measures, helped impose heavy taxation on the more well-to-do, and hurried through wartime prohibition and a prohibition amendment to the Constitution. City Democrats were particularly unhappy over losing their beer. Southern Democrats prevented a ceiling on the price of cotton, and as a result the grain belt, which had a pegged price on wheat, reacted angrily against all Democrats.

Even before the 1918 election, it seemed likely that these factors would influence voters more than the Fourteen Points. Nevertheless, with the war obviously almost over, the President put the election on the basis of high international policy. He succumbed to the pleas of Democratic Congressmen, and on October 24 declared, "The return of a Republican majority to either house of the Congress would . . . be interpreted on the other side of the water as a repudiation of my leadership." This outraged those Republicans who had supported him in his foreign policy, since he had earlier declared "politics is adjourned" for the duration of the war. The fact that the Republicans captured both houses of Congress in 1918 would itself have had a serious effect on foreign policy; the effect was exaggerated even more by Wilson's ill-considered appeal.

In reality, there had been no question of a vote of confidence on the terms of peace, but the President had called for one and European observers were ready so to interpret the situation. Lest they not do so, Theodore Roosevelt, in one of his last public statements before his death, asserted, "Mr. Wilson and his fourteen points and his four supplementary points and his five complementary points and all his utterances every which way have ceased to have any shadow of right to be accepted as expressive of the will of the American people."

The Background of Versailles

SHARP PARTISANSHIP and the inference of repudiation created a sad atmosphere for Wilson's assumption of peace negotiations. The President, like the nation, was tense and tired, but he was ready to drive ahead. He strove to pull his own country and the reluctant Allies with him in his determination to make the Fourteen Points, and especially the fourteenth —the League of Nations—become a reality.

The pulling and hauling with the Allies went on through most of October 1918, during the negotiations which led to the armistice. The Germans sought through Wilson an armistice based on the Fourteen Points and their modifications. The Allies denied even knowing what these points were, for they were by no means ready to give up their claims for reparations and annexations. Only after Wilson had twice threatened to negotiate a separate peace were they willing to present a united façade. The Allies seemed to agree to the Fourteen Points in entirety, except for explicit reservations on reparations and freedom of the seas, and this apparent agreement led the Germans to expect generous treatment. Further misunderstanding developed because, while the Allies laid down military and naval terms that would make it impossible for the Germans to resume warfare, they used the term "armistice," which meant a negotiated pause in hostilities, rather than the word "surrender." What followed at Versailles was a conclave of victors dictating to a vanquished country, not a negotiated peace or the peace without victory that Wilson had once recommended.

The armistice which went into effect on November 11, 1918, provided that the Allies would negotiate peace on the basis of the Fourteen Points. The Germans agreed to withdraw their forces from France and Belgium to a zone well to the east of the Rhine, and to surrender huge quantities of matériel. They accepted what was virtually the unconditional surrender of their fleet. Finally, while the peace was being drafted, the Allied blockade continued.

To the Allies, as they assembled in Paris, there seemed no need to consult Germany on the nature of the peace. Indeed, the only block between them and the kind of postwar world they had planned in their secret treaties was President Wilson. That was a serious block indeed, for Wilson made the precedent-breaking decision of leaving the United States to attend the peace conference in person. House and other advisers urged him not to go. In retrospect, weighted against his failure to stay in command of domestic policies in the United States, was his undoubted ability, through his great prestige and firm insistence, to gain many otherwise impossible concessions at Paris. He paid little attention to the serious problems of reconversion and concentrated instead upon the molding of the peace. He miscalculated in thinking that at Paris he had the overwhelming support of public opinion, both in the United States and Europe. He paid no attention either to the results of the 1918 election at home, or to the "khaki election" in England which Lloyd George won with hints that he would make Germany pay for the war, or to Clemenceau's similar overwhelming vote of confidence in the French Chamber of Deputies. Rather, Wilson declared, "There is a great wind of moral force moving through the world, and every man who opposes . . . that wind will go down in disgrace." The reality, which held such ill promise for the future, was that the peoples of the great powers, the United States included, were still animated by fear and hatred of Germany as well as by their desire to build a new world order.

Wilson also seriously miscalculated in refusing to take with him as one of the Peace Commissioners a leading Republican like Elihu Root or William Howard Taft. He would have done well, too, to have included one of the powerful Republican Senators, since it would take many Republican votes to muster the requisite two-thirds majority for the treaty in the Senate. Nevertheless, Wilson took only a nonpolitical Republican diplomat, Henry White, and relied neither upon him nor upon the other commissioners.

Wilson did consult a remarkably knowledgeable group of experts, including Bernard Baruch and Herbert Hoover, both of whom accompanied him to Paris. In 1917, Colonel House had assembled a group of scholars to undertake what was called "the Inquiry." When they sailed for Paris, William Allen White reported they were carrying along "all sorts of literary crowbars with which to pry up the boundaries of Europe and move them around in the interests of justice, as seen through the fourteen points." On shipboard, Wilson declared to them, "Tell me what's right and I'll fight for it; give me a guaranteed position." If they did not exactly accomplish this exalted purpose, they at least helped Wilson work in various technical ways toward a scientific peace.

Wilson, arriving in Europe in December 1918 before the other European leaders were ready to confer, toured France, Italy, and England. Wherever he went, hysterically cheering crowds greeted him; everywhere boulevards and plazas were renamed for him. The cheering millions reinforced this feeling that he was the spokesman for humanity. He was not aware that in each nation these masses looked to him to obtain for them much that ran contrary to the Fourteen Points. A little later, when he fought against some of their national claims, their adulation evaporated into disillusion.

The Clashes at the Conference

THE SESSIONS AT PARIS began January 12, 1919, in an atmosphere of idealism tinctured with national aggrandizement, amidst glittering scenes reminiscent of the Congress of Vienna. Just beyond, to the east, however, there was an urgency born of imminent starvation and the threatening spread of Communism. Hoover, trying to get food into central Europe to fend off both threats, declared, "The wolf is at the door of the

Red Cross official supervising the unloading of American flour in eastern Poland (NATIONAL ARCHIVES)

world." Later Lloyd George told Parliament, "I am doubtful whether any body of men with a difficult task have worked under greater difficulties— stones crackling on the roof and crashing through the windows, and sometimes wild men screaming through the keyholes." One of the greatest difficulties was that Russia, where Bolsheviks were still fighting White armies, was entirely unrepresented.

It has been entirely too easy to accept the contemporary caricatures of Wilson and his fellow peacemakers, and thus to overlook how conscientiously each sought to protect the interests of his own country and yet arrive at a peace acceptable to others. Here were serious statesmen, the fatigued representatives of exhausted nations, laboring against such extreme obstacles that the wonder is less that they failed to negotiate a settlement both just and lasting than that they were able to draft any treaty at all.

The caustic brilliance of the pen of a thirty-five-year-old British economist at the Conference, John Maynard Keynes, created a stingingly adverse picture of Wilson: "He had no plan, no scheme, no constructive idea whatever for clothing with the flesh of life the commandments which he had thundered from the White House. . . . He not only had no proposals in detail, but he was in many respects, perhaps inevitably, ill-informed as to European conditions. And not only was he ill-informed—that was true of Mr. Lloyd George also—but his mind was slow and unadaptable." Keynes concluded. "It was harder to de-bamboozle this old Presbyterian than to bamboozle him." These stereotypes clung to Wilson for decades, although the British Foreign Secretary, Arthur Balfour, who sat at the meetings of the Big Four, declared that Wilson was "firm, modest, restrained, eloquent, well-informed, and convincing." To Balfour's surprise, Wilson was "as good round a table as he was on paper." General Jan Smuts of South Africa declared that Wilson was "the noblest figure, perhaps the only noble figure in the history of the war."

Neither is the stereotype correct that Wilson was so preoccupied with the drafting of the League Covenant and getting it embodied in the Treaty that he allowed the Allies to draft a German settlement a great deal harsher than that proposed in the Fourteen Points. Much of what he permitted was either out of compromise or his own fervent desire to limit the future German war-making potential. Some of the terms resulted from his own ignorance and that of his experts. When he discovered that millions of Germans lived in the Sudetenland area awarded to Czechoslovakia, he exclaimed, "Why, Masaryk did not tell me that."

At the outset Wilson had to fight to prevent a division of spoils under the secret treaties. He tried to block the Japanese from obtaining permanently the German treaty rights in the Shantung Peninsula of China and the former German islands north of the Equator in the Pacific, which could be Japanese strongholds. He had to give way, however, to the insistence of the British that they honor the treaty promising the islands with which they had lured the Japanese into the war. Wilson with more success persuaded the Allies to hold former German colonies and Turkish territories on a basis of trusteeship responsible to the League of Nations. This was the new and unprecedented "mandate" system.

Simultaneously, Wilson worked on the drafting of the League Covenant. He insisted that it form the first part of the treaty, and be inseparable from it, and he labored long and hard fabricating it in meticulous detail. In the League Covenant he saw the one possible way of overriding the vengeful selfishness which seemed dominant among the victorious nations. Whatever imperfections and inequities there were in the Treaty he thought could be rectified through the League: through it and it alone, the world could avoid future wars. In the League he envisaged the con-

The "Big Four" in Paris: (left to right) *David Lloyd George of Great Britain, Vittorio E. Orlando of Italy, Georges Clemenceau of France, and President Wilson* (NATIONAL ARCHIVES)

stitution of a potentially powerful (but not armed) international organization through which the nations of the world could share responsibility in maintaining the security of all against any aggressor.

At the end of February 1919, as Congress prepared to adjourn, Wilson came home to sign bills. He brought with him the League Covenant, determined that he would force the Senate to accept it without compromise. The acclaim with which Bostonians greeted him, the friendliness of editorials in most newspapers, and the energy with which large and influential organizations advocated the League, all encouraged him to think public sentiment overwhelmingly behind him. When Colonel House warned him he must be prepared to compromise with the Senate, he had retorted, "I have found that you get nothing in this world that is worthwhile without fighting for it."

A stiff fight was taking form. In the Senate, on March 4, 1919, Lodge produced a round robin signed by thirty-seven Senators, a number sufficient to block the treaty, announcing they would not accept the Covenant in its existing form. Wilson, about to re-embark for Paris, retorted angrily. But back at the Conference, on the advice of Taft he did obtain some of the reservations for the United States upon which the Senate would obviously insist. These provided that a nation need not accept a mandate against its will, that a member could withdraw with two years' notice, that the League would not regulate immigration and other internal matters, and that it would not infringe upon the Monroe Doctrine. To obtain these, Wilson had to trade concessions with the Allies. He made little progress toward conciliating the Republican Senators. Many of them saw in the struggle over the Covenant a means of embarrassing Wilson, stripping him of some of his glory, and developing a winning issue for the campaign of 1920. There was no good political reason for them to be generous, so despite the concessions they continued to harass him.

While Wilson was obtaining revisions to the Covenant, the Conference was also grappling with the critical problem of Germany and the remaking of the European map. Together with Lloyd George, Wilson resisted the French proposal to carve western Germany into buffer states. He did sanction the return to France of Alsace-Lorraine, and the establishment of a strong Poland and Czechoslovakia on Germany's borders, all in keeping with the national self-determination clauses of the Fourteen Points. He also supported German demilitarization, long-term Allied occupation of the west bank of the Rhine, and an Anglo-French-American mutual defense pact. If maintained, these security provisions should have prevented the resurgence of Germany as a military menace to the West. Elsewhere the remapping of Europe proceeded rather fitfully. Italy obtained the Brenner Pass area in which 200,000 Austrians lived, then was outraged at not also receiving Fiume, which Wilson felt must be a port for the new nation of Yugoslavia. In this region and others, the economic needs of nations and the principle of national self-determination of peoples often ran counter. Back in the United States, ethnic groups were ready to clamor for more for their native countries. And the Irish-Americans insisted that Wilson should fight for national self-determination for Ireland, wracked by civil war. Wilson took up the matter privately with Lloyd George but did not make a public stand.

Wilson's most important departure from the Fourteen Points was his acceptance of British and French demands for heavy reparations from the Germans. Even before the armistice, he had partly conceded to their insistence that Germans must make payment for civilian damages, although such a proposal ran counter to his negotiations with the Germans. At the Conference, he permitted these claims to cover even pensions for veterans. The astronomical sum was to be set later by a reparations commission. Meanwhile, although Wilson himself for years had taken an economic-determinism view of the origins of the war, the other powers insisted that Germany must accept sole responsibility for starting it. The "war guilt" clause and reparations stuck in the craw of Germans as a betrayal. Even in the United States, the harsh peace meted out against Germany disillusioned many liberals and alienated them from Wilson. They regarded the treaty as a "hell's brew" which would ultimately lead to another war.

The defects in the Treaty of Versailles should not obscure the over-all achievements of Wilson, for while he had not obtained a treaty entirely in keeping with the Fourteen Points he had forced the drafting of one far more lenient toward the vanquished nation than the Allies would have drawn up without the influence of the United States. Also there was the crucial factor that he had obtained the League, through which in time might come a rectification of the blemishes of the treaty and the maintenance of a just peace.

Rejection in the Senate

WILSON returned to the United States confident that the Senate, despite the difficulties Lodge was creating, would ratify the treaty. On July 10, 1919, when he presented it to the Senate, he brushed aside a reporter's question whether he would accept reservations. "I do not think hypothetical questions are concerned," he remarked. "The Senate is going to ratify the treaty." He had commented in private conversation that some of the Senators with their "pygmy minds" were ignorant of public opinion, "as far from the great mass of our people as I am from Mars." Yet it was the overwhelming pressure of American public opinion for some sort of a League of Nations—as far as one could measure it by all the media of that era—that Wilson counted upon to bring senatorial recalcitrants to heel. He overlooked how independent of momentary public pressure were Senators elected for six years.

When Wilson presented the treaty to the Senate, he asked rhetorically, "Dare we reject it and break the heart of the world?" To Wilson, such a prospect was unthinkable. In retrospect it also seems to have been unnecessary, since Wilson—by exercising all of the presidential powers which he had used so skillfully to bring about the enactment of his New Freedom program years before—could through a combination of coercion and compromise have brought about ratification. Why did not Wilson again practice his old crafts? Part of the answer may have been overconfidence, and part of it his seriously deteriorating physical condition. Throughout the war he had grappled with great masses of exhausting detail; he had continued to do so at Paris. He not only had worked endless hours over the Treaty but had even drafted messages to Congress on his portable typewriter. He was suffering from hardening of the arteries, and in March, while in Paris he had been so ill that he may have been close to a stroke. His physical condition robbed him of his political suppleness, so that instead of using patience and tact, he was more likely to shower his opponents with self-righteous anger. He had ignored House, who had reminded him of Burke's words, "to govern is to compromise."

Nor were Wilson's opponents in the Senate ready to put statesmanship ahead of partisanship, regardless of the needs of their nation or the world. Those easiest to justify are the fourteen who were irreconcilables. They were men of conscience, of Middle Western or Far Western progressive tradition, like Republicans Johnson of California and La Follette of Wisconsin, and Democrat James Reed of Missouri. They acted out of deep conviction that their nation could best be served by staying out of the League. Other opponents with less conviction were more concerned with constructing a winning issue for the Republicans in the 1920 election than they were with the future of the world. Behind them were constituents assuming that the United States would enter the League but far more concerned with their immediate reconversion problems at home. And there were the many foreign-born Americans, angry because Wilson had not done more for the Old Country, whether Ireland or Macedonia. There were many of both these groups in a state like Massachusetts, where twenty-six Democratic members of the legislature had petitioned President Wilson to come home from Paris to cut the high cost of living, "which we consider far more important than the League of Nations."

From Massachusetts also came Senator Lodge, applying all his brilliant intellect to his loathing of Wilson. Lodge, as Chairman of the Senate Foreign Relations Committee, was ready to use every possible tactic to obstruct or delay the treaty. It can be argued upon his behalf that he was anxious to prevent the irreconcilables from seceding from the Republican party and making the 1920 election another 1912. It also can be argued that, at least at the outset, he did not expect to defeat ratification but only wanted to wipe some of the luster from Wilson's reputation. He succeeded beyond his dreams, and is known by his success.

Public sentiment, as good politicians know, can be maintained at a high point of enthusiasm for only a short time. Public sentiment favored ratification of the treaty, and Lodge needed time to marshal forces against it. Consequently, he spent the first two weeks after it reached the committee reading aloud every word on its nearly three hundred pages. Next, he held six weeks' of public hearings, listening to the complaints of every disgruntled minority. Meanwhile wealthy opponents of the League supplied funds to pour hostile propaganda into the hinterland. Lodge's badgering began to have an effect.

From the White House, Wilson did some conferring with Republican Senators. He explained to a group of them that he considered the collective-security provision of Article X to be more of a moral obligation upon the United States than a legal one—but to Wilson moral obligations were the more important. The Senators were not impressed. It began to appear that Wilson would have to accept some of Lodge's reservations if he wished to obtain ratification. When one Senator told him this, he retorted, "Never! Never! . . . I'll appeal to the country!"

So it was that Wilson, at the end of his physical resources, against the stern warnings of his physician, undertook a cross-country speaking tour, writing his speeches as he went along, delivering them night after night. In twenty-two days he traveled over 8,000 miles, giving thirty-six speeches averaging an hour in length. At first the halls were not entirely filled nor were his speeches always too polished. As the tour proceeded, he gained larger and more enthusiastic audiences, and grew more eloquent in his moral fervor. Had it been possible to sway the United States Senate through public opinion, the tour might have been a success. But Wilson became more and more frail. Finally after speaking at Pueblo, Colorado, on September 25, he suffered such acute headaches that he had to cancel the tour and return to Washington.

At the White House on October 2 President Wilson suffered an acute stroke which partially paralyzed his left side. For two weeks he was close to death, and for six weeks more he was so seriously ill that he could attend only to what little business his devoted wife and doctor thought would not unduly upset or fatigue him. When some officials tried to see the President on vital matters, Mrs. Wilson turned them away, saying, "I am not interested in the President of the United States. I am interested in my husband and his health."

The public had no knowledge of how ill and incapacitated the President was. Yet it was at this critical period that the Senate Foreign Relations Committee finally reported the treaty, recommending forty-five amendments and three reservations. Lodge managed to marshal the Republican Senators so well that in November he obtained passage of fourteen reservations. By this time Wilson had recovered sufficiently to give stern directions to the Democratic minority: they must vote only for the treaty without any reservations. Although none of the Lodge reservations would have devitalized the League, Wilson preferred no ratification of the treaty to ratification with reservations. While he was by no means his old self, he was able to exert power enough to maintain discipline over the loyal Democrats. On November 19, 1919, when the vote came, 42 Democrats joined with the 13 Republican irreconcilables to vote down the treaty with reservations. Next, the Senate voted on ratification of the treaty without reservations. There were 38 Senators, all but one of them a Democrat, who voted for it; 55 voted against it.

The defeat of the treaty seemed preposterous to public leaders throughout the United States. Representatives of twenty-six organizations, together with numerous influential newspapers, demanded compromise between Wilson and Lodge. Wilson would not budge, and the Republican irreconcilables (even if perhaps not other factors) kept Lodge from compromising. In spite of this, on the day of the final vote, March 19, 1920, when the Senate considered the treaty with fifteen reservations, it came within seven votes of receiving the requisite two-thirds. By this time, President Wilson was ready to look to the campaign of 1920 as the opportunity for a solemn referendum on the League issue. There could be no "referendum" of this sort, for the American people were already preoccupied with domestic problems.

So it was that the United States, almost by accident, failed to join the League of Nations, and thereby weakened the frail organization upon which the prevention of a new world conflict depended. Blame can be assessed against both Senator Lodge and President Wilson, but behind them were millions of Americans not yet ready to see the United States assume a decisive role in a world organization. Nor would that organization necessarily have been effective if the United States had co-operated within it, for there was even greater tension, hatred, and bitterness in other nations that did join the League.

Wilson had declared when he submitted the Versailles treaty to the Senate, "Our isolation was ended twenty years ago. . . . There can be no question of our ceasing to be a world power. The only question is whether we can refuse the moral leadership that is offered." The United States did refuse, until another quarter of a century had elapsed and the world had gone through a still more devastating war.

Chapter *10*

THE NEW ERA

IN TIMES OF STRESS, Americans dream of the "good old days." And so it was that, as they emerged, disillusioned, from the First World War, they looked backward to the mirage of a happier past. They were sick of war-time regimentation, and of talk about world responsibilities which isolationists warned would mean involvement in future wars. They rejoiced in the speed with which wartime regulations were scrapped, and at the polls in 1920 overwhelmingly voted away the Wilsonian order of things. But nothing could restore what had once been, for both progressivism and the war had brought lasting changes.

The Legacy of Progressivism and the War

AMERICAN POLITICAL LIFE in the twenties was not a break from previous developments; it was more, too, than a reactionary interlude between the New Freedom and the New Deal. Much of what Wilson had stood for remained, for the pattern of the twenties grew out of American experience in the war and the Progressive era. A good bit of the progressivism that persisted in the twenties represented the dark side, the narrowness and even hatreds that could sometimes be involved in the movement. Many a man who had voted for Bryan or Roosevelt was now determined to fight for his cherished smalltown way of life, and if the ballot failed he would resort to the bedsheet of the Ku Klux Klan. Much of the positive side of progressivism survived as well, in the persisting demand throughout much of the South and West for government regulation or dissolution of monopolies, development of water power, and similar reforms. Men like La Follette and Norris still proclaimed these objectives in the Senate, where they formed an impotent but vocal minority. Progressivism persisted in the urban East also, in drives for more efficient government and better service to communities. Men like Governor Alfred E. Smith of New York led these campaigns on the state level; Secretary of Commerce Herbert Hoover was one of their champions in the national government. Progressivism had disappeared from the White House and could no longer command a majority in Congress, but it remained a significant force through the twenties.

As for the war, it had raised the living standard of factory workers and built a powerful labor movement; it had created great shifts in population and accompanying tensions. It had given a temporary bonanza to the farmer, stepped up mechanization of agriculture, and brought the plow to tens of thousands of acres of semiarid prairie grasslands. Much of this transformation had been painful, and led to further difficult adjustments in the twenties. The war also had changed styles and fashions, and molded consumer demands into new channels. In little ways (such as the introduction of wrist watches for men, shorter skirts for women, and cigarettes for both) and in major ways that involved basic shifts in the economy, it was changing the patterns of life for most Americans.

A new literature, born of the disillusion of war, led to new styles of thought among the intelligentsia. There was much criticism of what was supposed to be a jazz generation of flappers with bobbed hair and men with coonskin coats and hip flasks. That small minority who made the most of being "lost," from the Left Bank in Paris to Greenwich Village in New York, savagely attacked the industrial civilization of the United States. Most Americans were deaf to these assaults; they reacted against the war, but voiced no disillusionment with the twenties, except as a fashionable pose.

The wartime production miracles and the clever new writings of American public relations experts and advertising men renewed the nation's faith in business. Even before the war, the Supreme Court's "rule of reason" had so impressed the masses that they were beginning to make distinctions, illusory though they might be, between virtuous large-scale businesses of which they should be proud, and the wicked trusts they should police. The worship of science and technology continued unabated, but now Americans felt that the new knowledge could best be applied by business. The heroes of the twenties were the business leaders in the great industries. The bright young men no longer flocked to Washington, nor did they hurry to establish their own small businesses. Rather they aimed for the board room or the industrial laboratory of a large corporation.

Business moguls, for their part, had abandoned their open contempt for the public, and talked the new language of "service." The way they had gone to Washington to serve their country for a dollar a year, while their factories had poured out the munitions to win the war, received wide and respectful attention in the popular press. The former "robber barons" and "malefactors of great wealth" became again "industrial statesmen." They occupied, as *Nation's Business* pointed out, "a position of leadership which the businessman has never held before." They, not the Wilson administration, received the credit for the wartime rise in the living standards of millions of people in the lower income brackets. And they promised to create even higher living standards in the years ahead. The price they asked was simple—merely that the government aid and protect them, and not interfere with them. This the government was ready to do. "This is a business country," Calvin Coolidge proclaimed, "and it wants a business government." Thus the nation once again embarked into a business age. This phase was called simply the New Era.

The pattern of the New Era unfolded slowly and hesitantly in the years after the war. There were some who would have made it quite the reverse of an age of big business, who would have liked to see the continuation of wartime government regulation or even ownership. At the close of the war the government owned most of the nation's commercial radio facilities (used as yet only for sending messages), commanded a vast merchant fleet, and controlled the railroads. McAdoo proposed that the government should continue to run the railroads until 1924 to test in peacetime the benefits of unified operation. Labor leaders wished to go even further: government ownership should provide for the workers a share in both policy-making and profits. Thus the Railroad Brotherhoods endorsed the plan of their lawyer, Glenn E. Plumb, to nationalize the lines; the A.F.L. in convention voted that the Plumb plan be applied to other industries; and the United Mine Workers proposed the nationalization of mines.

This call for nationalization frightened many Americans, and went beyond the old progressive bounds. Congress was not willing to go so far, but still had sufficient impetus left to legislate typically progressive solutions for most of these problems. While Congress did not enact the Plumb plan, it did pass the Esch-Cummins Transportation Act of 1920, establishing over railroad rates and securities Federal control as tight as any progressive had ever visualized. In addition, the Interstate Commerce Commission was to plan railroad consolidations in order to continue wartime efficiencies; enforced competition was to give way to enforced monopoly under government supervision. In practice, supervision was rigorous, but the consolidations did not take place because strong railroads did not wish to absorb weak ones. Throughout the nation, railroads suffered from the new rigorous competition of motor vehicles and other carriers. They were not as a rule able to earn the 6 per cent return the I.C.C. allowed them.

Shipping did remain in part under direct government ownership, because private operation had to be heavily subsidized one way or another in order for American companies to compete successfully with those of other countries. Operating and capital costs were higher than those of foreign merchant fleets; financing and insurance arrangements were poorer. The Navy Department strongly favored maintenance of a strong merchant marine as a continuing defense measure. Consequently, while much of the 16,000,000 tons of American shipping afloat in 1920 was not suitable for peacetime use and was tied up to rust, at the end of the decade 7,000,000 tons were still in operation. Most of this carried cargo between American ports, a segment of the shipping trade that was limited by law to American shippers. Some companies engaged in international trade, subsidized by very low prices and easy terms in buying ships and by liberal mail contracts. The Merchant Marine Act of 1920 authorized the sale and operation of these ships. Under authority of the same act the Merchant Fleet Corporation operated, at a loss, a number of government-owned lines. In contrast, Congress refused to allow the navy to continue to operate commercial radio communications, and as a result the navy reluctantly sold its stations to the newly established Radio Corporation of America. In this instance the government turned its monopoly over to a private corporation without regulatory strings attached except to insist that it be American-controlled rather than British-dominated.

Western progressives obtained two measures to stave off corporate onslaughts in their area. One, the General Leasing Act, was intended to protect the naval oil reserves from oil companies that for some years had been trying to obtain them. It also authorized the leasing of other mineral and oil lands on terms favorable to the government. The other measure, the Water Power Act of 1920, was a first tentative step toward federal regulation of power. It established a Federal Power Commission (consisting of the Secretaries of War, the Interior, and Agriculture) to license the construction and operation of hydroelectric plants on public lands and to regulate rates on power from these plants when it passed across state boundaries.

Soon after the war, Congress helped bring to fruition two other progressive dreams. In June 1919 it approved the women's suffrage (Nineteenth) amendment, which was ratified by August 1920. In October 1919, over the veto of President Wilson, it passed the drastic Volstead Act implementing the prohibition (Eighteenth) amendment, submitted by Congress in December 1917 and ratified by January 1919. Several states had passed laws outlawing hard liquor but permitting the sale of weak beer, which might have been a successful sop to the millions of urban opponents of prohibition. The Volstead Act prohibited all liquors containing more than ½ of 1 per cent of alcohol. To jubilant members of the Anti-

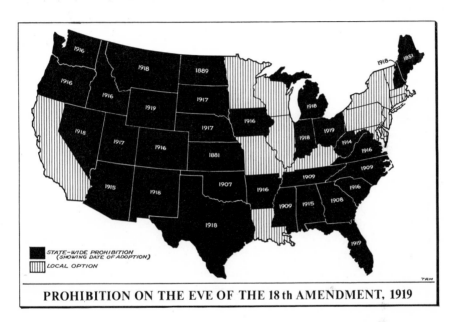

PROHIBITION ON THE EVE OF THE 18th AMENDMENT, 1919

Saloon League and the W.C.T.U. this meant the enforcement of morality; to opponents it meant an unjustifiable infringement upon their personal liberties. Prohibition soon became unpopular among a large minority, and some of its unpopularity rubbed off on progressivism.

In total, these pieces of legislation seemed to be the last surge of progressivism as the new order emerged. The rapid scrapping of the wartime controls pointed the main direction the twenties were to take. President Wilson himself, in what little attention he gave to domestic problems, seemed to be assuming the lead. "The moment we knew the armistice to have been signed we took the harness off," he declared in his Annual Message to Congress in December 1918. This indeed had happened. The War Industries Board ceased operations so quickly, and so completely without plan, that it left many of its employees stranded in Washington; Baruch paid their fares home out of his own pocket. Throughout the country, the government canceled war contracts without any provision for reconversion, injuring businessmen and workers alike. Farmers were not yet dumped, but their jolt came in May 1920, when basic commodities lost their price guarantees.

"It is surprising," Wilson declared in his 1918 message, "how fast the process of return to a peace footing has moved." The government, he said, needed do no more than "mediate the process of change," except for creating some mild measures to meet the expected unemployment among returning servicemen. He recommended that these men be aided with a public works program and with the creation of new farms by irrigating arid Western lands. But Congress heeded the voice of businessmen who wanted economy rather than public works and of farmers who did not want competition from new Western acres. It did nothing.

Troops returning on the Leviathan, *December 1918* (NATIONAL AR-CHIVES)

When President Wilson called a conference of governors and mayors to meet at Washington in March 1919 to work out plans for remedying the expected heavy unemployment, it too showed no disposition to act. Governor Calvin Coolidge of Massachusetts served in effect as its spokesman when he declared that 90 per cent of the boys were able to take care of themselves. As 4,500,000 servicemen rushed through separation centers, most of them before the end of 1919, they and the former munitions and shipyard workers were able to find jobs. Unemployment reached the 3,000,000 mark in February 1919, but by summer a boom, especially in the automobile industry, was absorbing the workers. Americans were spending their wartime savings; Europeans were importing three times more than before the war. Planless reconversion seemed to work—for the moment.

The Red Terror

THE SUDDEN DROPPING of controls allowed prices to soar, to the dismay of consumers and organized labor. On the price index (in which 1913 prices had an index of 100), manufactured goods rose from 198.4 in 1918 to 239.5 in 1920; food prices kept pace. The rising cost of living further hurt and irritated white-collar workers and other middle-class people. There was little way they could take out their resentment except at the polls, and they became bitter against organized labor because it did have a more direct means of combating rising prices. Union workers tried to preserve their wartime economic gains by striking for higher wages as living costs went upward. A great wave of strikes spread across the country, involving in 1919 some 4,000,000 workers. In many of these strikes, such as those conducted by longshoremen, printers, and laborers in the clothing, textile, telephone, and other industries, the strikers succeeded even in raising their living standards. In the process they alienated much of the public, which was quick to accept the industrialists' explanations that higher wages were responsible for higher prices, and that the strike leaders were radicals. Early in 1919 the mayor of Seattle fought a general strike, which had begun in the shipyards, as though he were fending off Bolshevism.

The outbreak of a steel strike in September brought antilabor feeling to a boil. The grievances of the workers were serious. They were working an average of nearly 69 hours per week for bare subsistence wages and were becoming so discontented that the A.F.L.'s organizing committee made rapid headway among them. United States Steel discharged all union men and refused to negotiate with Gompers or any other union official. Some 343,000 men struck in the Chicago area, and additional workers went on strike in other areas. Why did the men go on strike? The Interchurch World Movement quoted from an open-hearth worker's diary: "You lift a large sack of coal to your shoulders, run toward the white hot steel in a 100-ton ladle, must get close enough without burning your face off to hurl the sack, using every ounce of strength, into the ladle and run, as flames leap to the roof and the heat blasts everything to the roof. Then you rush out to the ladle and madly shovel manganese into it, as hot a job as can be imagined." And this, another worker wrote, one did twelve hours a day, except Saturday night when one worked seventeen hours, a weekly total at Carnegie Steel of 87 hours! Half the employees worked the twelve-hour day; half of these the seven-day week. Semiskilled workers were earning less than $2,000 per year, and unskilled workers less than

$1,500 (the minimum subsistence level for a family of five in 1919.)

Despite the workers' valid claims, United States Steel was able to swing public sentiment away from the strikers by claiming that the leaders were Communists. William Z. Foster, the main organizer, had once been a follower of Bryan and was to emerge in 1924 as the presidential candidate of the Communists. His leftist tendency did not make the grievances of the workers any less valid, but it did give the company a better opportunity to ignore them. The company also tried to stir up trouble between Italian and Serb strikers, and brought in Negro strikebreakers. State and federal troops prevented picketing; in rioting at Gary, Indiana, eighteen strikers were killed. Within a few weeks, tens of thousands of strikebreakers under armed protection were operating the plants at three-quarters capacity, and by January the workers were starved out. Steel remained unorganized for another decade and a half.

Public opinion turned even more firmly against organized labor when a police strike broke out in Boston. The policemen were working long hours on prewar salaries under unpleasant conditions. After their organization, the Boston Social Club, obtained an A.F.L. charter and threatened to strike, a Mayor's Citizens Committee prepared to meet their demands except for recognition of their union. The Police Commissioner, responsible only to the Governor, refused and dismissed nineteen leaders. In response, the police struck. As mischief makers and rowdies took over, horrified citizens put on their wartime uniforms and, armed with rifles and shotguns, began patrolling the streets. The mayor mobilized state troops and restored order. The following day, Governor Coolidge, who although it was within his power had previously done nothing to prevent the strike or preserve the peace, suddenly acted after the crisis was over. He ordered in outside troops and backed the decision of the Police Commissioner never to re-employ any of the strikers. When President Gompers of the A.F.L. appealed to Coolidge, the Governor wired back, "There is no right to strike against the public safety, anywhere, anytime." Even President Wilson sent Coolidge his congratulations. This one telegram made Coolidge a formidable contender for the Republican presidential nomination in 1920.

In Washington, Attorney General A. Mitchell Palmer was becoming a leading candidate for the Democratic nomination through his war on both labor and radicals. When the new president of the United Mine Workers, John L. Lewis, took the bituminous coal workers out on strike in November 1919, Palmer smashed the strike with federal court injunctions. The coal strike, Palmer contended, was in violation of the Lever Act, the wartime food control measure. The claims of the workers, however, had some justification, since they had received no wage increase since August 1917. Consequently the government, and later an arbitration commission, awarded them substantially higher pay.

Palmer attracted even more attention with his crusade against Reds. Throughout the country the violent suppression of pro-German persons during the war had been continued in the persecution of the I.W.W., the Socialists, and all other left-wingers. Both Congress and the New York state legislature denied seats to Socialists. By 1920, a third of the states had enacted criminal syndicalist laws to punish radicals. The New York law prohibited "advocating, teaching, or aiding and abetting the commission of crime and sabotage, or unlawful acts of force and violence or unlawful methods of terrorism as a means of accomplishing a change in industrial ownership or control, or affecting any political change."

Bombings and attempted bombings captured the headlines. A bomb damaged the front of Palmer's home in June 1919; bombs addressed to a number of government leaders were discovered in the mails; a year later an explosion on Wall Street killed 38 people. Four members of the newly founded American Legion were killed in an attack on I.W.W. headquarters in Centralia, Washington, on Armistice Day, 1919. These incidents furnished the material out of which the newspapers, with some aid from Palmer, built a great national panic. Within the country there were numerically very few radicals to undertake a revolution: I.W.W. membership was down to 35,000 and continued to decline; the Socialist party numbered 39,000 and was not revolutionary anyway; the Communist Labor party (left-wing Socialists) had 10,000–30,000 members; and the Communist party, organized September 1, 1919, had 30,000–60,000.

Palmer's goal was to ferret out and eliminate the Communists. He proposed a sedition bill so drastic that Congress would not enact it, then he proceeded anyway without it. The Labor Department had already arrested and deported to Finland 249 Russian Communists. Nevertheless, Palmer, without advance notice to the Labor Department, conducted a great Red roundup on January 1, 1920, jailing some 6,000 suspects. Communists who were United States citizens he turned over to states for prosecution. The aliens came under the jurisdiction of the Labor Department, which gave them fair treatment. The Commissioner of Immigration, Frederic C. Howe, later wrote:

> I had to stand against the current. . . . Most of the aliens had been picked up in raids on labor headquarters; they had been given a drumhead trial by an inspector, with no chance for the defense; they were held incommunicado and often were not permitted to see either friends or attorneys before being shipped to Ellis Island. In these proceedings the inspector who made the arrest was prosecutor, witness, judge, jailer, and executioner. He was a clerk and interpreter as well. . . .

I refused to railroad aliens to boats made ready for their deportation. . . . I faced a continuous barrage from members of Congress, from the press, from business organizations and prosecuting attorneys. Yet day by day aliens, many of whom had been held in prison for months, came before the [United States] court; and the judge, after examining the testimony, unwillingly informed the immigration authorities that there was not a scintilla of evidence to support the arrest.*

Only 556 proven Communists were deported.

In Massachusetts, a payroll robbery and murder in April 1920 led to the trial and conviction of two anarchists, Nicola Sacco and Bartolomeo

Vanzetti and Sacco being taken into court, 1927 (BROWN BROTHERS)

Vanzetti. Many believers in civil liberties felt that the two men were being prosecuted more on the basis of their radicalism than on that of the criminal evidence. Ultimately, throughout the country, and even in western Europe, outraged liberals and radicals demanded the release of the two men, but in August 1927 they were executed. The Sacco and Vanzetti case was the *cause célèbre* of the twenties. One of the counsels for the two men who did not "belong even remotely to [their] school of thought," warned, after the execution, of "minds that are closed by deep prejudice or transient passion." "If," he declared, "the local hostility was inflamed by

* Frederic C. Howe, *Confessions of a Reformer* (New York: Scribner's, 1925) pp. 274–75.

foolish words of their sympathizers or wicked deeds of their exploiters, this also is a fact to be recollected." The publisher of the conservative Boston *Herald,* which had called for an impartial commission to review the case, asserted: "The momentum of the established order required the execution of Sacco and Vanzetti, and never in your life or mine, has that momentum acquired such tremendous force."

As for Attorney General Palmer, he proudly declared the month after his great Red raid of January 1920 that he had averted open revolt. "Like a prairie-fire, the blaze of revolution was sweeping over every American institution of law and order a year ago," he wrote. If there had been a

A Ku Klux Klan meeting—not in the Twenties but in 1948 (NATIONAL ARCHIVES)

blaze of revolution, which was improbable, it was indeed under control, but the backfire of intolerance had swept out of control and was blackening the country. Not only radicals, but labor organizers, aliens, Catholics, Jews, and Negroes all became its victims.

No group suffered more severely than the Negroes. For hundreds of thousands of them, the war had offered an opportunity to break out of the narrow caste structure of the South. Some 400,000 served in the army, half of them in Europe, which drew no color line. Several hundred thousand more moved into the industrial North, where there was less discrimination against them than in the South. Even in the North, however, they suffered from wretched housing, low pay, and the animosity of unskilled white workers who feared their competition. Many Negroes in the North and South alike began to follow the militant leadership of the National Association for the Advancement of Colored People, which demanded larger economic opportunities and greater civil rights for Negroes.

In both North and South, Negroes faced explosive resentment against them. In order to intimidate Negroes back into their old subservience, Southerners resorted to the terrorism of the Ku Klux Klan, which grew by 1919 to a membership of 100,000, and to lynchings, which increased from 34 in 1917 to more than 70 in 1919. Terrible race riots broke out, beginning in July 1919, in twenty-six towns and cities. Hundreds of persons were killed or wounded, and millions of dollars worth of property was destroyed. The worst of the outbursts began on a Chicago bathing beach and continued through thirteen days of pillaging and burning in the Negro district; 23 Negroes and 15 whites were killed, 500 were injured, and 1,000 families, mostly Negro, were left homeless. These terrors led millions of Negroes to follow a persuasive charlatan, Marcus Garvey, founder of the Universal Negro Improvement Association. In return for their contributions, he promised to take them home to an African empire. In 1923 Garvey was convicted of swindling and sentenced to federal prison, but Negro nationalism nevertheless persisted.

The onslaught against all Americans who did not conform, against any who might disturb the status quo, reacted strongly to the advantage of business leaders, who already basked in the public favor. They were able to establish again in the minds of many people the feeling that unionism was somehow un-American. In 1920, they began a great open-shop movement to break unions and reduce wages, under the alluring slogan, "The American Plan"; aided by depression, they succeeded in erasing some gains that unions had made during the war and in 1919.

President Harding's "Normalcy"

AMID THESE STRUGGLES and alarms, the 1920 election took place. Domestic tensions made impossible a solemn referendum on a League of Nations; only an ill man sequestered from the flow of events, as President Wilson was, could have expected it. The situation made a Democratic victory so improbable that the Republican leaders felt no compulsion to put forth any of their strong candidates. Herbert Hoover, the choice of many liberals in both parties, and the most popular of the potential nominees, did not announce himself a Republican until February, 1920. It was easy for the party managers to ignore him. Another progressive, Senator Hiram Johnson of California, could not command much of a following.

The two leading contenders were Leonard Wood and Frank O. Lowden. General Wood, an ardent conservative nationalist, commanded most of Roosevelt's former following, and collected a campaign chest of startling proportions ($1,773,000), with which he battled Lowden for delegates. Lowden, favorably known as an efficient governor of Illinois, also commanded large campaign funds, totaling $414,000. Progressive Republican charges that both contenders were deeply indebted to big business helped enable party managers to ignore them when the two deadlocked at the convention. Instead, a Senate cabal led by Henry Cabot Lodge late one night in a smoke-filled hotel room turned to one of the most regular and pliable of their colleagues, Warren G. Harding of Ohio. The convention nominated Harding on the tenth ballot and chose as his running mate the hero of the Boston police strike, Calvin Coolidge. They were thoroughly conservative candidates running on a thoroughly conservative platform.

The Democrats assembled at San Francisco rather confused because President Wilson, who could have easily designated a candidate, seemed to be waiting with pathetic coyness to be renominated for a third term. This was patently impossible. For thirty-eight ballots, two of Wilson's cabinet members, his efficient son-in-law McAdoo, and his superpatriotic Attorney General Palmer battled for the nomination. In the end the urban bosses stepped in and secured the nomination of an antiprohibition candidate who might salvage their city tickets for them. This was the former progressive Governor of Ohio, James M. Cox. As a gesture toward the Wilsonians, Assistant Secretary of the Navy Franklin D. Roosevelt was nominated for Vice President.

Despite the nature of Cox's nomination, he and Roosevelt campaigned arduously to try to make the election the referendum on the League that Wilson wished it to be. Everywhere they won the enthusiastic support of small groups of intellectuals, and to this extent probably did service to the League ideal. Most people outside of the big cities were indifferent, had little understanding of the League covenant, and assumed the United States would enter some sort of a League in any event. Within the cities, large groups of foreign-born voters were so hostile toward the League that they were ready to desert the Democratic party. The bosses in New York City almost completely ignored the national ticket in their desperate effort to salvage something from the coming debacle. Most voters, rural or urban, had come to dislike Wilsonianism, had been infected with the anti-Red hysteria, and were unhappy over rising living costs and the plummeting prosperity of 1920. As a result, urban workers, Western farmers, small businessmen, and isolationist progressives, all reacting against Wilson, voted for the very group they had so long abhorred, the right-wing Republicans. In voting against Wilsonianism they unheedingly voted for big business.

Harding, following the advice of his managers, made few speeches and took few positions on the issues of the day except to promise a return to what he earlier had called "normalcy." In an address on May 14, 1920, he had asserted alliteratively, "America's present need is not heroics, but healing; not nostrums, but normalcy; not revolution, but restoration; not agitation, but adjustment; not surgery, but serenity; not the dramatic, but the dispassionate; not experiment, but equipoise; not submergence in internationality, but sustainment in triumphant nationality." McAdoo joked that Harding's speeches were "an army of pompous phrases moving across the landscape in search of an idea." Certainly Harding displayed an ambivalence that was politically most successful. On the League

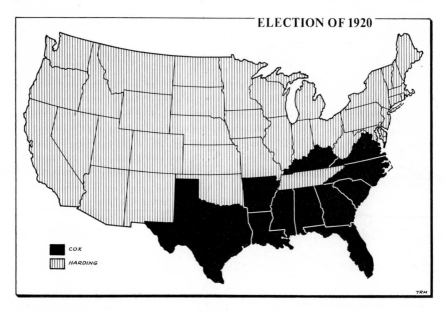

ELECTION OF 1920

COX

HARDING

he at first gave the impression that he favored adherence, then as city resentment against it flared, he gave the impression he was against it. Then, lest Cox's crusade for the League win away Republican votes, thirty-one distinguished Republicans, including Hughes, Stimson, Root, and Hoover, signed a statement declaring that a vote for Harding was a vote for American entrance into the League with reservations. In most other campaign years Harding would have been a hopelessly weak candidate. Even many Republican newspapers had expressed disgust at the time of his nomination. In 1920, he had merely to wait for the landslide against Wilson and the Democratic party.

The landslide exceeded even the expectations of the Republicans.

Harding received 16,152,000 popular votes, 61 per cent of the total, and carried every state outside of the Solid South. He even won Tennessee. Cox received only 9,147,000 popular votes. Debs, running from the Atlanta penitentiary on the Socialist ticket, received 920,000 votes. The sweep brought a Republican majority in the Senate of 22, and in the House of 167.

In voting against Wilsonianism, the electorate brought into power a weak, amiable conservative. For years Harding had been editor and publisher of the Marion, Ohio, *Star*, an undistinguished smalltown newspaper. Because of his regularity and his ingratiating ways, he had risen in the Republican party hierarchy, until in 1914 he had achieved his life's goal, election to the United States Senate. The ambitions of his wife and of his campaign manager, Harry Daugherty, together with luck, elevated him

President Harding speaking on his Western trip (NATIONAL ARCHIVES)

to the Presidency. Daugherty once explained how he had happened to work for Harding: "He looked like a President." This was Harding's main qualification.

The new President was a distinct departure from the gentleman reactionaries in the party. The confused meandering of his campaign speeches had been far too indicative of his thought processes; he was too unsystematic in his thinking to be a steady reactionary. Also he was too much a man of good will. Alice Roosevelt Longworth, daughter of a President and wife of the speaker of the House, reared in the genteel tradition of Republican politics, could not forget the sight of a poker session in the President's study. "Harding was not a bad man," she commented. "He was just a slob." Hughes and Hoover, invited to one of these all-night sessions, remained aloof and were never asked again.

Much of the atmosphere of a rural courthouse permeated the White House, as a group of smalltime politicians, the "Ohio Gang," moved into power with Harding. With singularly bad judgment he placed a number of his poker-playing and drinking companions into positions of trust where they betrayed him and the American people.

Fortunately, Harding in his appointments did more than honor old cronies. He wished to surround himself with the best-qualified men, and in part he succeeded. When he was persuaded that his friend Albert B. Fall was not of a caliber to be Secretary of State, he placed Fall, a notorious anticonservationist, in charge of the Interior Department. However, he then appointed the brilliant and distinguished Charles Evans Hughes to be Secretary of State. He placed Hoover, the friend of small enterprise and expert on efficiency, in charge of the Commerce Department, and made Henry C. Wallace, spokesman for the Midwest farmers, Secretary of Agriculture. Andrew W. Mellon represented big business as Secretary of the Treasury. These able men, pulling in several directions, together with the congressional leaders formulated government policies.

Substitutes for League Membership

The problem of developing Republican alternatives to the Wilsonian foreign policy fell largely on the shoulders of Secretary Hughes. He had signed, and perhaps written, the round robin of the previous fall, proclaiming that a vote for Harding was a vote for American entrance into a world organization. But Hughes had criticized Article X of the League Covenant, and never really believed in collective security. The lukewarm attitude of the electorate in the campaign of 1920 and the stubborn determination of the irreconcilable "battalion of death" in the Senate led him to abandon the League. Hughes could not persuade Harding to fight for it, and in any event there was little chance of winning the battle. He had to choose between abandoning the League and resigning. His decision was to stay on to develop an essentially nationalistic but nevertheless positive foreign policy.

Hughes's policy involved first of all ending the war with Germany by an act of Congress, which was signed July 2, 1921. He then negotiated separate peace treaties with the former Central Powers, to secure for the United States the benefits without the responsibilities of the Paris treaties. In time, Hughes permitted American delegations to participate in League conferences on minor matters as long as they did not make commitments. Throughout his years as Secretary of State he was chilly toward every European proposal for collective security, but he did, in February 1923, persuade President Harding to recommend that the United States join with reservations the World Court, an almost completely powerless body. But the World Court was an instrument of the League, and while internationally minded Americans ardently favored joining, the irreconcilables in the Senate violently fought it. Each succeeding President through Franklin D. Roosevelt advocated American adherence to the League; each time, through 1935, the Senate blocked it.

By calling the Washington Arms Conference, Republicans made it appear that they were taking positive steps to preserve the peace. This was in effect a Republican substitute for entrance into the League. Senator Borah, in May 1921, had introduced a resolution requesting a conference to reduce armaments, but the basic impetus for the meeting came from the British, who feared a three-way naval race with the Americans and the Japanese. Japan had emerged from the war stronger than before in China and with troops still stationed in Siberia. It threatened to expand still further, to shut the "Open Door" in China, and to arm its new island possessions in the Pacific. American public opinion saw an even more serious threat in the Anglo-Japanese alliance. Hence the British, wishing to strengthen their amicable relations with the United States, proposed the conference. Hughes seized the initiative; President Harding issued invitations to a conference.

The arms conference opened on November 12, 1921, the day after burial rites for the Unknown Soldier at the Arlington Cemetery. The American public at the time was demonstrating its overwhelming desire for continued peace. Hughes, in his opening speech, startled the delegates and won enormous acclaim by dramatically presenting a concrete plan for the reduction in size of the fleets of the United States, Great Britain, and Japan. He proposed a ten-year moratorium on capital-ship construction (battleships, cruisers, and carriers) and the scrapping by the three powers of nearly 1,900,000 tons of ships already built or under construction. A British observer declared, "Secretary Hughes sunk in thirty-five minutes more ships than all the admirals of the world have sunk in a cycle of centuries."

In the negotiations that followed, Japan agreed to limit her capital ships to a total of approximately 300,000 tons compared with 500,000 tons each for the United States and Great Britain. In addition the United States pledged itself not to increase its fortifications in Guam and the Philippines. Japan and Great Britain made similar pledges. Thus the Naval Limitation Treaty of February 6, 1922, provided a ratio of 5:5:3, and of 1.75:1.75 for France and Italy, stopping what otherwise could have become a disastrous armaments race. Two other treaties aimed at guaranteeing the status quo in the Far East. The Nine Power Pact pledged a continuation of the "Open Door" in China. Japan restored to China full sovereign rights in the Shantung Peninsula, and promised to withdraw her troops from Siberia. The Four Power Pact, among the United States, Great Britain, France, and Japan, was a mutual guarantee of insular rights in the Pacific. Upon its ratification, Japan relinquished her alliance with Great Britain.

At the time and subsequently, American naval experts vehemently attacked the Washington treaties as weakening the American position in the Far East and thus helping lead to an ultimate war with Japan. Contemporary evidence was quite to the contrary. The naval supremacy Hughes relinquished was a paper supremacy that the United States could have achieved only through continued expensive building, which Congress would have been most reluctant to finance. Congress also would probably have appropriated little or no money for the strengthening of fortifications in the western Pacific, judging by its reluctance in the late thirties, when the threat of Japan was much stronger and more imminent.

Meanwhile, the United States stood in a powerful defensive position, with the over-all strength of its fleet much greater than that of Japan's. Likewise, Japan, thousands of miles removed from American naval bases, had nothing to fear. The Washington treaties lowered the tensions between the two nations for nearly a decade. Their one unfortunate result was that the United States relinquished the physical force with which to impose its will in the Far East but retained its moral, economic, and political objectives in the area. The Senate came close to rejecting the Four Power Pact for fear it would commit the United States to some collective security arrangement in the Orient. On the other hand, the popularity of the Naval Limitation Treaty at the time is shown by the fact that only one Senator voted against its ratification.

One unpleasant episode marred the new, more cordial relations with Japan. In 1924, Congress under the leadership of Lodge insisted upon passing overwhelmingly an act abrogating the Gentlemen's Agreement in a backhanded way by excluding all aliens ineligible to become citizens. This meant the Japanese and other Asiatics. It was an unnecessary insult to the Japanese, since the Gentlemen's Agreement had worked well, and the application of a quota system to Japan would have allowed only a tiny trickle of immigrants. Indignation in Japan was so extreme that Hughes lamented privately, "It has undone the work of the Washington Conference and implanted the seeds of an antagonism which are sure to bear fruit in the future."

Toward Latin America Hughes also tried to extend the goodwill of the United States. During the 1920 campaign, when Franklin D. Roosevelt had inaccurately and unwisely boasted of writing the constitution of Haiti, Harding had attacked the Democrats for running Haiti at the point of a bayonet. In the Republican administration, the marines stayed on in

Haiti, but Hughes moved toward a new policy. During his first months in office, he was decidedly influenced by Sumner Welles, later one of the chief molders of the Good Neighbor policy. By 1924, Hughes had ended the marine occupation of Santo Domingo and prepared for its end in Nicaragua. He felt that the occupation was still necessary in Haiti.

Hughes moved away from the progressive policy of intervention and tried wherever possible to substitute nonrecognition of undesirable governments for the landing of the marines. Neither he nor his successor in the Coolidge administration was ready to give up intervention entirely, but in August 1923 he disclaimed any right on the part of the United States "to superintend the affairs of our sister republics, to assert an overlordship . . . and to make our power the test of right in this hemisphere." For a time during the Coolidge administration, trouble with Mexico over the rights of American oil companies and renewed Marine intervention in Nicaragua seemed to indicate a retreat to the old policies. By 1928, however, Coolidge and his Secretary of State, Frank B. Kellogg, were pursuing a more liberal policy in Latin America.

The extent to which the Senate recalcitrants could force a tinge of unrealism into the new Republican foreign policy became most clear in negotiations over reparations and war debts. The failure of the United States to join the League had most serious repercussions on this problem, since the Reparations Commission, which was not under the chairmanship of an American as had been expected, set astronomically high sums for Germany to pay. This high reparations payment, it has been argued, helped bring the runaway German inflation, the impoverishment of the German middle class, and, out of the depression and disillusion that it fostered, the rise of Hitler. This is clearly an exaggerated view, but it is true that the United States had slipped into a new and critical economic role in Europe. Reparations payments depended to a considerable degree upon American aid to Germany; war-debt payments from the Allies to the United States depended almost entirely upon reparations. The American public insisted that the Allies should repay the ten billion dollars the United States had loaned during the war. Coolidge later epitomized the popular view when he remarked simply, "They hired the money, didn't they?"

In 1923, Secretary Hughes futilely tried to prevent the disastrous French effort to collect reparations by force in the Ruhr. By the end of the year the Reparations Commission was willing to accept a subterfuge he had suggested and invite private American financial experts to devise a payments plan. The result was the rather indefinite Dawes plan, the handiwork of General Charles G. Dawes, a Chicago Banker, and Owen D. Young, head of the General Electric Company. It provided for an international loan to Germany, a stabilization of her currency, and a schedule of payments based on Germany's ability to pay. In 1929, Young headed a new committee which set a final reparations figure of approximately two billion dollars, to be paid by 1988.

The Congress pressured the former Allies, through a World War Foreign Debt Commission, to negotiate long-term schedules of debt payments. Between 1923 and 1926 the Commission reached agreements with the Allies (which the United States government insisted bore no relationship to German reparations payments). The administration did not worry about how Germany, France, Italy, and the other debtors could make payments over the high tariff wall which the United States was raising

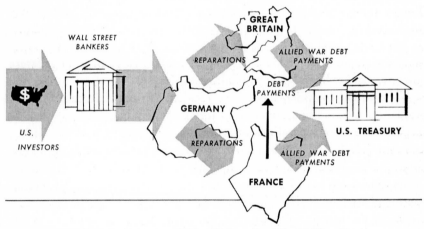

Private Loans and War Debts after World War I

against their exports. Nor did Secretary Hughes voice any protest against the passage of the Fordney-McCumber tariff in 1922.

What kept the system going during the twenties was the huge total of private American loans pouring into German governmental units or corporations—about $2,500,000,000 between 1923 and 1930. Germany paid about $2,000,000,000 in reparations, and the former Allies about $2,600,000,000 in war-debt payments. It was an arrangement which the United States government refused to recognize and which could work only as long as prosperity continued. It was part of a larger world system in which the United States was pouring out goods and building up huge investments abroad, yet through a protective tariff slowing down the reciprocal flow of goods into this country. It was a remarkable system while it worked, but it could not work for long.

Appearances in foreign policy had to be less internationalist than realities, because of pressure from parts of the electorate and especially from a dominant group of Senators. The United States was apparently assuming no responsibilities while, politically as well as economically, it was actually undertaking the part of a dominant power. In the reparations question it served as the honest broker at Lausanne between Germany and the Allies. In disarmament it could more openly take the lead, especially in the naval meetings at Geneva and London. What was of paramount political importance within the country was that the United States must at no time make any international commitment which could conceivably lead to the use of armed force.

This approach reached its peak in the Coolidge administration when millions of Americans (many of them isolationists) signed petitions urging the United States to promote a multilateral treaty outlawing war. The French foreign minister, Aristide Briand, had proposed a treaty of this sort between France and the United States. Secretary Kellogg agreed, and at Paris in 1928, most civilized nations, including the United States, signed a treaty solemnly condemning war as an instrument of national policy but providing no machinery whatever for enforcement. The United States added reservations exempting defensive wars and the Monroe Doctrine. The treaty evoked much enthusiasm within the country, for it seemed to offer collective security without any risks. Only a few critics were disturbed, pointing out that it lulled the public into regarding itself as secure from war when really the pact provided no security whatever.

Democrats in Congress made little criticism of the Republican foreign policy, for they too were intimidated by their own isolationist wing. The nation had a tacit bipartisan foreign policy led by those who felt that the United States must participate in world affairs, but not too openly. Foreign policy was no real issue in the elections from 1924 through 1932.

Barring Imports and Immigrants

THE OPTIMISTIC NATIONALISM of the New Era spilled over into areas adjacent to foreign policy. As soon as the Republicans came into power in the spring of 1921, they enacted an emergency tariff measure to raise the low Underwood rates. In 1922 they passed the Fordney-McCumber Act providing protection especially for agriculture, the chemical industry, and manufacturers threatened by Japanese and German competition. The tariff gave agriculture little real protection, but it did provide industrialists with several benefits. It accepted the principle that, when foreign firms had lower costs of production than their American competitors, the tariff should be high enough to offset the differential. It prohibited most competing imports and led to higher prices at home. Democrats complained that as soon as the aluminum duty went up from two to five cents per pound, Mellon's Aluminum Company of America raised its price three cents a pound. Neither the price of pots and pans nor the heavy profits of sugar producers proved to be effective political issues. Other nations followed the American lead in economic nationalism; by 1928, some sixty countries had raised their tariffs.

The high tariff did not wreck foreign trade because of heavy American loans overseas. Year after year there was a balance of exports over imports, ranging from $375,000,000 in 1923 to over $1,000,000,000 in 1928—the reverse of the normal balance for a creditor nation.

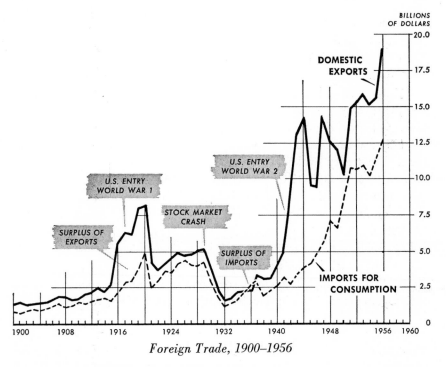

Foreign Trade, 1900–1956

Along with high walls against competing goods, Congress finally succeeded in erecting barriers against incoming foreigners. The movement to curtail immigration came to a spectacularly successful climax with the beginning of the Harding administration. Racist objections to the "new immigrants," and the unionists' fear that the newcomers were perpetuating a pool of cheap labor in the United States, were reinforced by the new allegation that some of them were radicals. This led employers who had previously favored immigration to switch to the restrictive side. In the spring of 1921, Congress passed an emergency immigration act, setting up a quota system: immigrants from any country could not exceed 3 per cent of the number of persons of their nationality who had been in the United States in 1910.

This cut the number of immigrants from 800,000 in the year ending June 30, 1921, to about 300,000 in the following twelve months. Racists still were not satisfied, so Congress in 1924 enacted the National Origins Act. This measure not only banned the people of East Asia entirely, but set a quota of 2 per cent for Europeans, and this on the basis of the 1890 census. It cut the yearly total to 164,000, heavily weighted in favor of those from northwestern Europe. On July 1, 1929, new smaller quotas based on the 1920 census went into effect, but during the entire depression decade of the thirties the total net immigration was less than 70,000.

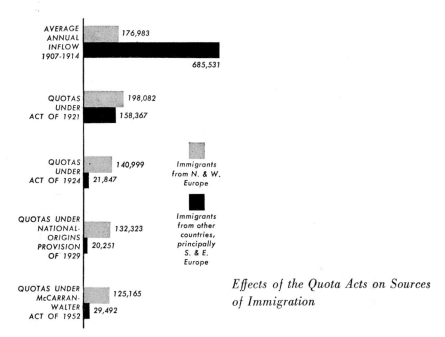

AVERAGE ANNUAL INFLOW 1907-1914 — 176,983 / 685,531

QUOTAS UNDER ACT OF 1921 — 198,082 / 158,367

QUOTAS UNDER ACT OF 1924 — 140,999 / 21,847

QUOTAS UNDER NATIONAL-ORIGINS PROVISION OF 1929 — 132,323 / 20,251

QUOTAS UNDER McCARRAN-WALTER ACT OF 1952 — 125,165 / 29,492

Immigrants from N. & W. Europe

Immigrants from other countries, principally S. & E. Europe

Effects of the Quota Acts on Sources of Immigration

The great flood of so many decades had been cut to a few drops. In the years that followed, the effects within the United States were profound.

The Harding Debacle

ALTOGETHER, the Harding administration seemed to stand for a businessmen's nationalism. In domestic as in foreign policies, the President seemed to be carrying out his campaign slogan, "Less government in business and more business in government." The Democrats made strong gains in the 1922 elections, reflecting continuing hard times, but the return of prosperity soon afterwards darkened their prospects for 1924 and heightened Harding's popularity. He continued to "look like a President," and occasionally was even vigorous in his humanity. He took a step Wilson had curtly declined when on Christmas Day, 1921, he pardoned the Socialist Eugene V. Debs. At the urging of Hoover, he pressured the steel companies into granting an eight-hour day to their workers. The press of the country, overwhelmingly Republican, created the illusion among most of the public that Harding was an exceptionally fine President.

Behind the façade, rot had set in which sickened Harding with worry. His cronies were betraying him. "My . . . damn friends," he complained to William Allen White; "they're the ones that keep me walking the floors nights!" Probably Harding never knew in detail how shockingly they were looting the government, but he knew enough to be heartsick. One of the "Ohio Gang," Attorney General Harry Daugherty's friend Jesse Smith, had been engaging in large-scale "fixing" in the Department of Justice. After Harding ordered him out of Washington, Smith committed suicide. The Director of the Veterans' Bureau, Charles R. Forbes, engaged in such colossal thievery that the total loss ran to nearly $250,000,000. When Harding received intimations of the corruption, he allowed Forbes to flee the country and resign. Ultimately Forbes served a two-year penitentiary sentence for defrauding the government.

The most spectacular fraud involved the rich naval oil reserves at Teapot Dome, Wyoming, and Elk Hills, California. Secretary of the Interior Fall persuaded Harding to transfer them to his department, then secretly leased them to Harry F. Sinclair and Edward L. Doheny. Fall, who had been in financial straits, suddenly became affluent. An investigation headed by Senator Thomas J. Walsh of Montana during the fall and winter of 1923 and 1924 uncovered the reason. Sinclair had loaned Fall $308,000 in cash and government bonds and a herd of cattle for his ranch; Doheny had loaned $100,000 more. In 1929, Fall was convicted of receiving a bribe, fined $100,000 and sentenced to a year in a federal penitentiary.

In the summer of 1923, Harding journeyed to Alaska. Tired and depressed, he responded wanly to the cheering throngs, who had no inkling of the mess in Washington. At the last moment he had taken Hoover rather than Daugherty with him, but on the boat he played bridge endlessly instead of seeking counsel. One day he did query Hoover: "If you knew of a great scandal in our administration, would you for the good of the country and the party expose it publicly or would you bury it?" Hoover urged him to publish it and at least get credit for integrity. Harding feared this might be politically dangerous.

He never had to face the storm, for upon his return to Seattle he became ill. It was reported that he had been poisoned by seafood, but he had suffered a serious heart attack. He seemed to improve, so he continued to San Francisco. There he had a second attack and suddenly died. Harding was buried a popular hero, but in the months that followed, as exposure after exposure crowded the headlines, his reputation collapsed. By his sudden death he had escaped certain ignominy, and had spared it for his party. His successor, Coolidge, was all that he was not, a man of impeccable integrity and efficient conservatism. In many respects Harding had symbolized the years immediately after the war. Just as his fine presidential appearance had covered appalling weakness, so the notion of "normalcy" had covered much that was cruel, greedy, or shortsighted.

Chapter *11*

A PRECARIOUS PROSPERITY

THE MIDTWENTIES were a golden interlude of prosperity for a large part of the American people. The generation which had been young then looked back upon these years with a justifiable nostalgia, for they were rich years, both materially and in cultural advance. It was a short boom, not lasting much more than five years, and it was a precarious one, in which millions of people did not share. The flaws in these years require critical examination, but their substantial contributions also should be remembered.

Coolidge Takes the Nation Further Right

IT WAS the singular good fortune of Calvin Coolidge to become President of the United States at the only time since the nineties when his largely negative custodial approach to the Presidency could bring him popularity rather than disaster. He came to be Chief Executive through a curious mixture of luck, political regularity, and Yankee shrewdness. If it was mainly luck that elevated him to the White House, it was mainly shrewdness that kept him so well established there. Even more than Harding, Coolidge had gone up the ladder of respectable political regularity, missing few of the rungs from minor officialdom in Northampton, Massachusetts, to the Vice Presidency: he had been councilman, solicitor, representative in the legislature, mayor, state senator, lieutenant-governor, and governor, where he probably would have stopped had it not been for the Boston police strike. Unlike Harding, he had a clear-cut conservative philosophy; he always co-operated whole-heartedly with the big interests because he believed in them, and he fought unwaveringly for what he believed. His Secretary of Commerce, Herbert Hoover, has reminisced with wry humor:

> Mr. Coolidge was a real conservative, probably the equal of Benjamin Harrison. He quickly dissolved our controls over foreign loans. He was a fundamentalist in religion, in the economic and social order, and in fishing. On one of his summer vacations, when he started in that art to which he was a stranger, he fished with worms to the horror of all fly fishermen.*

To the older circle in Washington, Coolidge's personality was not especially appealing; Alice Roosevelt Longworth remarked that he had been weaned on a dill pickle. To the American public, however, there was an infinite appeal and security in his folksy virtues, so lavishly detailed and praised in the nation's press. Coolidge reinforced this folksy appeal with little homilies drawn from his Vermont boyhood—exhortations (in which he fervently believed) to thrift, hard work, and respect for business. It was the old Puritan ethic in homespun terms, sermons couched in the phrases of the "good old days," urging an acceptance of the new economic oligarchy. For millions of middle-class urban people, only a generation or two away from rural backgrounds, there was a strong attraction in this country philosophy refurbished for the machine age.

The Coolidge philosophy began with echoes of Cotton Mather: "If society lacks learning and virtue, it will perish. . . . The classic of all classics is the Bible. . . . The nation with the greatest moral power will win." Applied to the economy, it sounded like Poor Richard brought up to date:

> What we need is thrift and industry. . . . Let everybody keep at work. . . . We have come to our present high estate through toil and suffering and sacrifice. . . . The man who builds a factory builds a temple. The man who works there worships there. . . . Large profits mean large payrolls.

On the role of government, Coolidge resembled the moderator of a Vermont town meeting:

> The law that builds up the people is the law that builds up industry. . . . The Government can do more to remedy the economic ills of the

---

* *The Memoirs of Herbert Hoover* (New York: Macmillan, 1952) vol. 2, p. 56.

people by a system of rigid economy in public expenditure than can be accomplished through any other action. . . . If the Federal Government should go out of existence, the common run of people would not detect the difference in the affairs of their daily life for a considerable length of time. . . . The business of America is business.

There is no clearer indication of the eagerness of middle-class Americans to fit old verities to the New Era than the seriousness with which most of them accepted the pronouncements of Coolidge, and the echoes of his statements by the publishing and advertising world. These were the years

President Coolidge in Vermont (HARVARD UNIVERSITY LIBRARY)

that marked the birth of that phenomenal publishing success, *Reader's Digest*, which endlessly elaborated similar themes. In 1925–26, the top nonfiction best-seller was Bruce Barton's *The Man Nobody Knows*, a businessmen's life of Christ, sprinkled with allusions to Lincoln. According to Barton, Jesus "picked up twelve men from the bottom ranks of business and forged them into an organization that conquered the world. . . . Nowhere is there such a startling example of executive success as the way in which that organization was brought together." This was not sacrilege, but reassurance to American businessmen that in accepting the doctrine of service they were following in the path of the Founder of modern business.

The sober, taciturn President was far more the prophet of the New Era than any of the clever cynics. Leaders of business, the press, and the Republican party accepted with relieved gratitude the regime of what the *Literary Digest* called the "High Priest of Stability." In his first message to Congress in December 1923, Coolidge called for a continuation of the conservative Republican domestic and foreign policies: tax cuts, only limited government aid for agriculture, and aloofness from the League of Nations. Chief Justice Taft declared that it was "great in the soundness of its economic statesmanship."

Under this comforting moral leadership, the men of power in the United States could take a calm and even incredulous view of the Harding scandals as one by one they came to light in the winter of 1923–24. Indeed, they and the respectable press showered indignation less upon the corrupt officials than upon those pressing the investigations. The two progressive Democratic Senators Thomas J. Walsh and Burton K. Wheeler appeared to the New York *Times* to be "assassins of character," and to the *Herald-Tribune,* "Montana scandal-mongers." Throughout much of the press, the investigations seemed a "Democratic lynching-bee," a work of "poison-tongued partisanship, pure malice, and twittering hysteria," at bottom the machination of Reds and subversives.

Under Coolidge the Republicans seemed so patently incorruptible that the exposures appeared if anything to backfire against the exposing Democrats. Ultimately Coolidge forced Attorney General Daugherty to resign and helped clean up the scandals. There was no possibility they would be repeated; and, as the election of 1924 approached, they seemed to be doing no appreciable harm to the Republican party. The nation seemed committed in advance to "keep cool with Coolidge."

For the Republican party meeting in convention in 1924, there was nothing to do except nominate Coolidge. While Lodge sat impotently in his hotel room, businessmen took over from the old senatorial cabal of four years earlier. But the platform they drafted was no different. It pledged a continuation of things as they were and, at the insistence of Coolidge, included a mild endorsement of the World Court. For the Vice-Presidential nominee, after Senator Borah declined, the convention chose General Charles Gates Dawes, a Chicago banker. It was a dull convention, lasting only three days, but the Republicans had no need for greater fanfare for their candidate or platform.

The Democrats, meeting at Madison Square Garden, should have been in a strong position to challenge the conservative Republicans. After their shattering defeat in 1920, they had made a strong comeback in the 1922 elections, cutting the Republican majority in the Senate to 8, and in the House to 18. Further, throughout the Midwest and West, insurgent Republicans had made such sweeping gains that, together with the Democrats, they were in control of Congress. If the Democrats could offer a candidate and platform which would capture this insurgent spirit beyond the Mississippi, they might recement the coalition of 1916 and win. But the Democratic party was badly split between its rural and urban wings. Rural Democrats were advancing as their candidate William Gibbs McAdoo, the competent heir to Wilsonianism. Strangely, the Teapot Dome scandal, which did no harm to the Republicans, tarnished McAdoo's reputation because he had served as lawyer to Doheny, the California oil magnate. On the other hand, much of the Ku Klux Klan strength in the Democratic party was coalescing behind him. As for the urban wing of the party, it was advancing the candidacy of the equally competent liberal governor of New York, Alfred E. Smith, who was the son of Irish immigrants and had made his way upward from the lower East Side of New York. Because of his background, and because he was a Catholic and a wet, he was the idol of many new Americans, and anathema to the Southern and agrarian Democrats.

Although these two candidates and wings of the party basically agreed upon the sort of progressivism a considerable part of the electorate wanted, they canceled each other out at the convention in a bitter, two-week-long clash. Separating the two men were the festering issues of the Ku Klux Klan, which by a fraction of a vote the convention failed to repudiate, and the even more troublesome question of prohibition, already a failure in the cities but still an ideal among godly people in the country. Smith, through the two-thirds rule, commanded sufficient votes to block McAdoo but not to effect his own nomination. He was never able to rise beyond 368 votes, nor McAdoo beyond 530. Finally both contenders withdrew, and on the 103rd ballot the exhausted delegates nominated a compromise candidate, John W. Davis. It no longer made much difference, so intense had the anger and hatred of the Democratic factions toward each other become, and the party itself was a national laughingstock. As one delegate wrote, it had been a sort of a wake at which "the crêpe was hung on the door before the election instead of after . . . as is the custom."

Davis, originally a West Virginian, had as Solicitor General under Wilson ably defended the legislation of the New Freedom before the Supreme Court. In the years since, he had become lawyer for J. P. Morgan and some of the great corporations and had amassed a fortune. Davis was a man of superior ability, but neither he nor the compromise Democratic platform offered much competition to the Republicans. Early in 1924 Davis had boasted of his clients. "They are big institutions, and so long as they ask for my services for honest work I am pleased to work for them," he declared. "Big business has made this country what it is." Davis became the forgotten man of the campaign.

While the Democratic convention had dragged on, insurgent Republicans and allied representatives of labor had held a third convention to organize a Progressive party and nominate La Follette and Wheeler. Their platform reasserted an advanced progressive position, attacking monopoly and promising reforms for the farmers and workingmen. Their support came from agrarians, chiefly on the Great Plains, who had earlier formed the Non-Partisan League and the Farmer-Labor party, and from the railroad brotherhoods and the A.F.L. Here, apparently, was a real contrast to the Republican and Democratic tickets, and it served as a made-to-order

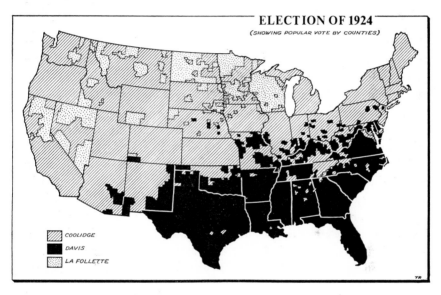

ELECTION OF 1924
(SHOWING POPULAR VOTE BY COUNTIES)

COOLIDGE

DAVIS

LA FOLLETTE

target for the Republicans. They campaigned to frighten the electorate into choosing Coolidge as the only alternative to the "red radicalism" of La Follette. Before election day, labor became lukewarm toward La Follette; Republican farmers, as crop prices rose, decided to stay within the party. In its last thrust, the old Middlewestern insurgency carried only Wisconsin, and secured 16.5 per cent of the popular vote throughout the country. Coolidge polled 54 per cent, and Davis only 28.8 per cent. The electoral vote was Coolidge, 382; Davis, 136; and La Follette, 13.

The bleak showing of the Democrats was due less to the La Follette bugaboo than to Davis's failure as a personable conservative to attract voters away from a dour conservative. Only 52 per cent of the electorate bothered to go to the polls. Further, Congress remained under the control of dissident Republicans and Democrats. Coolidge won his lopsided victory mainly through default of the Democrats, and because, as Franklin D. Roosevelt commented at the time, "the people will not turn out the Republicans while wages are good and the markets are booming."

Businessmen's Government

In his inaugural speech, March 4, 1925, President Coolidge declared that the nation had achieved "a state of contentment seldom before seen," and pledged himself to the maintenance of things as they were. Walter Lippmann wrote: "Mr. Coolidge's genius for inactivity is developed to a very high point. It is far from being an indolent inactivity. It is a grim, determined, alert inactivity which keeps Mr. Coolidge occupied constantly. . . . Inactivity is a political philosophy and a party program with Mr. Coolidge." It was as well that he did not seek positive legislation beyond tax cuts and economy, for he could not have pushed a conservative program through the relatively progressive Congress. While Congress fumed and fulminated, Coolidge turned over the reins of government to business and slept as much as twelve hours a day.

Coolidge continued the conservative policies begun by the more able cabinet members of the Harding administration, but his power was mainly negative. Again and again he vetoed legislation he considered undesirable. In 1924, he unsuccessfully vetoed the veterans' bonus bill, strongly backed by the American Legion, which provided additional compensation for veterans in the form of twenty-year paid-up endowment insurance policies. Harding's veto of it had stuck, but Coolidge's came in an election year, so Congress repassed it over his veto. Later, in 1927 and 1928, Coolidge vetoed the McNary-Haugen farm relief bills, and Congress failed to override his vetoes.

In effect this was government by deadlock, as the power issue best illustrated. Through the twenties, millions of liberal Americans of both parties ardently shared the dream of Senator George Norris that the government might develop the nation's great water resources to provide cheap electric power. Millions of others accepted the educational program of the utilities companies, which spent twenty-eight to thirty-five million dollars per year combating the idea of a national power program. The battle centered around the great dam at Muscle Shoals on the Tennessee River, which had not been finished in time to provide nitrates during the war. Coolidge and the conservatives wished to sell it to Henry Ford for private development; Norris and his cohorts in Congress blocked them. Norris wished to make Muscle Shoals the center of a great regional development on the Tennessee River; Coolidge pocket-vetoed his bill in

1928. In 1931, Hoover again vetoed it, and the deadlock continued until the New Deal began.

Another way in which Coolidge could exercise his executive power negatively was through appointments. He continued, as Harding had done, to place on the federal bench judges of conservative leanings who were quick to use the antilabor injunction. In making an appointment to the Supreme Court, however, he slipped. Coolidge appointed his Attorney General, Harlan Fiske Stone, who, once on the Court, began joining in dissents with Holmes and Brandeis. Norris and other progressive Senators had tried unsuccessfully to block the appointment of Stone, whose liberalism neither they nor Coolidge suspected. They did succeed in blocking the man proposed as Stone's successor as Attorney General, an able lawyer connected with the sugar interests. It was the first time in half a century that the Senate had rejected a cabinet appointment. The progressives had done so out of indignation over Coolidge's many appointments of enemies of regulation to the Interstate Commerce Commission, Federal Trade Commission, and Tariff Commission. Norris asserted that these appointments were "an indirect but positive repeal of Congressional enactments, which no Administration, however powerful, would dare to bring by any direct means."

Big government continued. The progressives had created it, and then, during the war, the dollar-a-year men had moved in. After the war, they had eliminated the progressives, and proceeded to run the government in accordance with somewhat different objectives. One goal remained the same: the achievement of scientific efficiency. Both Republicans and Democrats had promised during the 1920 campaign that they would apply it to the government. The Republicans in 1921 passed the long-debated Budget and Accounting Act. This created a Bureau of the Budget, nominally under the President, to compile for the first time a single, unified budget for the federal government. The act also established an auditing agency with quasijudicial powers, the General Accounting Office, under a powerful Comptroller General to be appointed for a fifteen-year term, and not removable by the President. Fear of the Comptroller General had led Wilson to veto a similar measure. Conflict between the President and the Comptroller General did indeed develop during the New Deal. When the office became vacant in 1936, Roosevelt left it unfilled for a long time. The Bureau of the Budget, under its able first director, Charles Dawes, did promote greater efficiency in the government, even though it did little to shorten battles in Congress over appropriations.

Working conditions for government employees improved in the twenties through the extension of civil service and some increase in salaries and pensions. At the beginning of the decade, the top career civilian employee in the Navy Department received only $3,000; in the Department of Commerce, some employees after sixty years' service were receiving only $720 and had no pension rights. Ultimately Congress authorized pensions and a minimum wage of $1,200 with increases for seniority. Higher salary ceilings attracted more competent workers into government employ.

During these years of prosperity, as revenues came pouring in, the federal government did not greatly enlarge its services. It spent nothing in such areas as public housing, and little for farm relief or public works. Arms expenditures were a relative pittance. Consequently the budget varied little between 1923, when it was $3,250,000,000, and 1929, when it was $3,300,000,000. Meanwhile the national debt dropped by nearly a quarter, from $22,400,000,000 to $17,000,000,000.

Andrew Mellon, the Pittsburgh aluminum baron who served as Secretary of the Treasury from Harding's inauguration into the Hoover administration, was widely hailed as the greatest Secretary of the Treasury since Hamilton. His main function seemed to be to preside over tax cuts; cartoonists routinely pictured him slicing tax melons. So far as Mellon could do so, as a matter of principle, he divided these cuts among the wealthy to give them the incentive to earn more money. When Representative John Nance Garner asked him in 1922 why he would not exempt those earning less than $5,000 from the income tax, Mellon asserted, "As a matter of policy nothing brings home to a man the feeling that he personally has an interest in seeing the Government revenues are not squandered, but intelligently expended, as the fact that he contributes a direct tax, no matter how small, to his Government." Democrats like Garner and insurgent Republicans, the "sons of wild jackasses," as they were later called, managed to frustrate Mellon in the House of Representatives from 1921 through 1925 by voting cuts more favorable to lower-income groups. Finally in 1926 they capitulated to allow drastic slashes at the top also. Millionaires paid less than a third the taxes of a year before. Mellon himself saved over $800,000, a sum, Norris said, greater than the aggregate for almost all the taxpayers in Nebraska. In addition, during the twenties Mellon refunded three and a half billion dollars in one manner or another. He declared, "A decrease of taxes causes an inspiration to trade and commerce." The serious question was whether the tax "melons" were enlarging the economy or being squandered in inflationary speculation. But there could be no question that the great business moguls had a powerful patron in the Secretary of the Treasury.

How Business Fared

SMALLER BUSINESSMEN also had a strong champion in the government, Secretary of Commerce Hoover. In his own spectacular rise as an international mining engineer, Hoover epitomized the self-made businessman. Denouncing both the radicalism and reaction he had seen in Europe, Hoover set forth his own credo in 1922 in a small book entitled *American Individualism.* It extolled the equality of opportunity which enabled Americans to succeed on their own merits, and the "rising vision of service" which led them to develop community responsibility rather than merely to seek "the acquisition and preservation of private property." This had been Hoover's own way of life. He had made a fortune while still a young man, then turned to public service, from which he never took a cent for his own use. He hoped the high standards of voluntary service he set for himself would dominate the business community. Conversely, he felt the government should aid business in many practical ways while putting as few restrictions upon it as possible. He himself took a lead in developing these ways. He accepted a cabinet office under Harding only upon the assurance that he might participate in all making of economic policy, whether or not directly under the Commerce Department. He continued to operate broadly under Coolidge, to the irritation of the President, who thought him nosey, and complained that while Hoover was Secretary of Commerce he tried to be undersecretary in all other departments.

Hoover to a remarkable extent made Commerce the most spectacular of the departments, as he sought to aid small business to become as efficient and profitable as big business. Through commercial attachés whom he sent to American embassies, he sought foreign orders for American industry at the same time that he favored the tariff to protect it from overseas competition. The Assistant Secretary of State told exporters at a convention in 1928, "Mr. Hoover is your advance agent and [Secretary of State] Kellogg is your attorney." Through the National Bureau of Standards, Hoover performed innumerable scientific services for industry such as setting simplified standards and eliminating waste by means of the techniques introduced by the War Industries Board. At a time when scientific management and the industrial laboratory were becoming indispensable to big business, the Commerce Department was helping make them available to small business as well. It also helped improve transportation, develop private electric power, and arbitrate industrial disputes.

The most significant of the ways to help small business was the sponsorship of voluntary trade associations similar to the committees of the War Industries Board. By 1921 some 2,000 were in operation. These associations, free from government regulation, could establish codes of ethics, standardize production, establish efficiency, and make substantial savings. They could serve even better than government prohibition of evil practices, Hoover has pointed out, to secure "cooperation in the business community to cure its own abuses." They could also, although Hoover did not seem to contemplate this, arrive indirectly at higher standard prices that would bring them good profits. Their real value to highly competitive smaller businesses was to eliminate competition through setting up standardized

"The Traffic Problem in Washington, D.C." by J. N. Darling for the Des Moines Register

schedules of quality (and prices). The trade associations faced two difficulties. One was that the Supreme Court, although disinclined to dissolve United States Steel, tended to crack down upon them. The other was that in many of the voluntary associations members failed to abide by the regulations. For example the head of the American Construction Council, Franklin D. Roosevelt, found that this association could do little to bring order into the chaotic building industry.

Voluntarism was at the heart of all of Hoover's projects. As the new field of commercial radio broadcasting began to develop, Hoover fostered voluntary self-regulation for it. Only when the efforts to keep stations off each other's wave lengths completely broke down did he move toward compulsory government regulation through the Federal Radio Commission, established in 1927. In the same way, the Department of Commerce finally took over regulation of commercial aeronautics through the Air Commerce Act in 1926.

The ups and downs of the business cycle were of peripheral interest to Hoover. In 1921 at the President's Conference on Unemployment (which he had persuaded Harding to call), he took the view that depression was inevitable, planning illusory, and government spending worse than useless. Nevertheless, he gave at least nominal support to schemes to cut back public-works expenditures in boom times and to accelerate them when depression threatened.

On the whole, business thrived during the New Era. In part, this was due to benign governmental policies: Hoover's laudable efforts to bring about increased standardization and efficiency took the economy further away from free competition and contributed to the increased profits of business and consequently to the concentration of wealth. Secretary Mellon's tax policies helped the rich to become richer, while incomes of poorer people advanced little if at all. The tendency of the courts to frown upon trade-association price schedules helped stimulate mergers. And mergers helped to sustain the trend toward concentration of business which had begun after the Civil War. In the twenties, eight thousand mining and manufacturing companies disappeared into combinations; by 1928, five thousand public utilities were swallowed, mostly by holding companies; by 1929, chain stores were selling more than a quarter of the nation's food, apparel, and general merchandise. The two hundred largest nonfinancial corporations owned nearly half of all corporate wealth, and 22 per cent of all national wealth. Their combined assets, matching the growth in national wealth, soared from twenty-six billion dollars in 1909 to forty-three billion in 1919, and eighty-one billion in 1929.

Because of better machinery and management, industry functioned more efficiently. The productivity of labor rose about 50 per cent in the decade, while the labor cost per unit of output fell 9.5 per cent. Only a small amount of the savings went to consumers, so that the cost of living had risen slightly by the end of the twenties. Industrial labor fared better than before the war; wages went up 33 per cent between 1922 and 1929. In comparison, white-collar salaries increased 42 per cent; corporate net profits, 76 per cent; and dividends to stockholders, 108 per cent.

Increased productivity did mean a higher living standard for the nation. Consumers purchased 23 per cent more in 1929 than six years earlier, and bought 33 per cent more durable goods like automobiles and furniture. Through their governmental units, they spent three times more for education than before the war. These were some of the substantial rewards of the over-all prosperity of the twenties.

The industrial growth of the decade centered around the automobile and other consumer durable goods. Automobile production jumped from a million and a half cars in 1921 to four and three fourths millions in 1929.

By then, automobiles were responsible directly or through countless ramifications for the employment of over three million persons.

Many economists thought it deplorable that Secretary Mellon's policies were leading to such a great concentration of wealth. Stock dividends were rising much more rapidly than wages. Although corporate leaders boasted of the broad ownership of stocks, one third of one per cent of the population received 78 per cent of these dividends. The 503 persons with the highest incomes were receiving as much money as the total wages of 615,000 automobile workers. Mellon's argument was that wealthy individuals and corporations to whom he granted tax relief would be able to save money and pour it into expansion of industry and thus continue prosperity. But only relatively well-to-do people were able to save much money. The 2.3 per cent of families with incomes of $10,000 per year or over accounted for two thirds of all personal savings, and those with incomes under $2,000 only 1.6 per cent. Corporations accounted for 40 per cent of total savings of all sorts. Altogether, savings amounted to eight or nine billion dollars per year in 1923, and fifteen billion by 1929. Unfortunately, only about five billion a year went into industrial expansion or investments, and the remainder into foreign loans and investments.

In some respects, business was faring too well in the twenties. It was saving or investing overseas or engaging in speculative enterprises at a greater rate than it was expanding productivity. Nor was it making full use of existing productive capacity, which was about 19 per cent greater than output even in 1929. This may have been even more significant than the failure to put more dollars into workers' pay envelopes. Some economists feel that increased production was needed more and would have been difficult to achieve. What was wrong in business generally and in certain sick industries in particular would have been hard to set right.

Welfare Capitalism Undermines Unions

THE PATERNALISTIC POLICIES of welfare capitalism, combined with a continued crusade against the open shop, led to a decline in union membership during the twenties. Many companies greatly improved working conditions by installing safety devices and improving sanitation. They raised their workers' morale by building attractive cafeterias and promoting athletic teams. Company welfare workers looked into the laborers' family problems. By 1926, nearly 3,000,000 workers could look forward to pensions upon retirement. In some companies they could buy stock below market value. Altogether they owned less than 1 per cent, but it did much to change some workers' attitudes. Further, they could voice their grievances through company unions or workers' councils, which were often effective safety valves for the employer. Through devices like these, companies helped fend off unionism from the new mass-production industries like automobile manufacturing.

Within the skilled crafts, the A.F.L. continued quietly and conservatively under the presidency of William Green. Its leaders seemed more interested in maintaining labor monopolies, especially in the building trades, than in organizing industrial workers. Membership in the United Mine Workers dwindled after unsuccessful strikes in 1922, but its president, John L. Lewis, called in 1928 for the election of Hoover, "the foremost industrial statesman of modern times." Union membership declined from over five million in 1920 to four and a third million in 1929.

In some industries, like coal mining and textiles in the South, hours were long and wages were pitiful. At Elizabethton, Tennessee, in 1929, mill girls were working 56 hours a week for sixteen to eighteen cents an hour. Behind the harried workers was always the threat of legal action if they sought recourse in unions. Federal courts were granting injunctions to break boycotts, or to enforce antiunion ("yellow dog") contracts. For most workingmen, however, conditions of labor had improved and living standards were up. Real wages increased about 26 per cent between 1919 and 1929, though they still were far from adequate. The average was less than $1,500 at a time when it was estimated that $1,800 was required to maintain a minimum decent living standard. Workers were able to purchase automobiles, vacuum cleaners, radios, and furniture through installment buying. More of them than ever before bought their own homes through monthly payments. But the amount one could buy on installments was limited, and sooner or later most workingmen had frugality forced upon them. During the twenties, American labor was on the road to plenty, but was still some distance from the goal.

The Clamor for Farm Relief

WHILE THE INCOME of most Americans advanced during the twenties, that of the farmers drastically declined. In 1920 they lost their price supports at the same time that the bloated wartime European market contracted. At home, as machines released workingmen from heavy manual labor and middle-class people tried to become slimmer, consumption of starches sharply dropped. The farm price index plummeted from 215 in 1919 to 124 in 1921. Land prices tumbled, and again farmers found themselves caught in a deepening morass of mortgages and taxes. The real income of farmers by 1921, on the basis of 100 for 1910–1914, was down to 75. It improved slightly as prosperity returned, but never passed the high point of 93 in June 1928.

Within agriculture there were great variations. To lump all farmers together is almost like lumping all businessmen. Truck gardening more than doubled, and dairying and citrus growing increased a third, reflecting the shifts in eating habits. Many of such farmers enjoyed satisfactory incomes. At the same time, those on marginal or submarginal lands suffered so acutely that in the five years after 1919 thirteen million acres were abandoned. These farmers were unable to compete with new, expensive machinery, which especially helped contribute to the glut of wheat. The number of tractors in use increased from 230,000 in 1920 to 920,000 in 1930, displacing 7,450,000 horses and releasing an additional thirty-

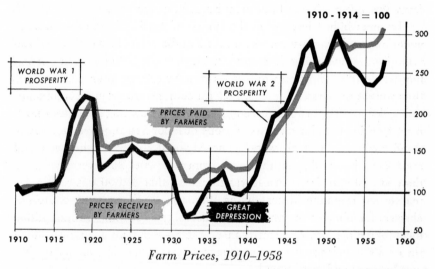

Farm Prices, 1910–1958

five million acres of land for crops. On the high plains, speculators bought the lands of bankrupt farmers and grew wheat on it with improved tractors and combines. In the Texas panhandle alone, nearly three million new acres were ploughed. The success of the big operators made the desperation of small farmers the more acute. In the year ending June 30, 1927, the income of all 6,300,000 farmers averaged only $548, and out of this farmers had to meet a variety of pressing obligations. It is not surprising that agricultural population dropped three million between 1921 and 1928. Those who remained on their farms began to agitate militantly for relief.

Even during the bonanza years of the war, agrarian agitation had stirred the Great Plains. In 1915, wheat growers of North Dakota had organized the Non-Partisan League, pledged to strict regulation of railroads and banks and state ownership of grain elevators and farm credit agencies. It won control of the North Dakota government in 1916, then began to organize in adjacent states, and in 1920 joined with other radical groups to form the Farmer-Labor party. The new party had some success in the congressional election of 1922, but by 1924 even La Follette would not accept its support. It was too radical for most of those American farmers who were earning $1,000 to $4,000 a year.

These men, the middle 40 per cent of the farmers in terms of income, produced 46 per cent of the farm products, and were solid citizens in their communities. Acting often through the Farm Bureau Federation or the Grange, they sought some means of capturing the government to obtain protective legislation. Many of them had chafed under the government price ceilings during the war; now they sought government price supports. From the outset they had powerful strength in the Congress. During the special session of Congress in the spring of 1921, Midwestern congressional leaders from both parties, meeting in the offices of the Farm Bureau Federation, organized a farm bloc. It was so strong that for years it was able to frustrate or harass Mellon's tax policies and force upon the administration an array of agricultural legislation. One such piece of legislation, the Emergency Tariff Act of 1921, gave not very effective tariff protection to farmers; later the Fordney-McCumber tariff placed a duty of 42 cents a bushel on wheat. The Packers and Stockyards Act and Grain Futures Act of 1921 protected farmers from exploitation by monopolists and speculators. The Agricultural Credits Act of 1921 and the Federal Intermediate Credit Act of 1923 offered financing to distressed farmers; by the end of the twenties farmers had borrowed three billion dollars from the various credit banks. The Capper-Volstead Co-operative Act of 1922 exempted farm co-operatives from the Sherman Act, and greatly stimulated their growth.

None of these measures gave the middle group of American farmers the better prices they sought. As early as 1921, Senator Norris proposed in effect the re-establishment of the Food Administration to buy surplus produce, ship it abroad in the Shipping Board fleet, and sell it cheap to deprived Europeans. The Harding administration, Eastern Republicans, and even Hoover, the former Food Administrator, opposed this proposal. Soon a new scheme replaced it in farmers' thinking. This scheme was the suggestion of two former administrators of the War Industries Board, George N. Peek, president of the Moline Plow Company, and the company's general counsel, General Hugh S. Johnson. "You can't sell a plow to a busted farmer," Peek once remarked to Johnson. They suggested that behind the tariff barrier, the American protected price for crops should be raised to a "fair exchange value" based on the price of the crop during ten prewar years compared with the general average of all prices during the same period. This price concept was called "parity." The means of obtaining parity prices for farmers within the country would

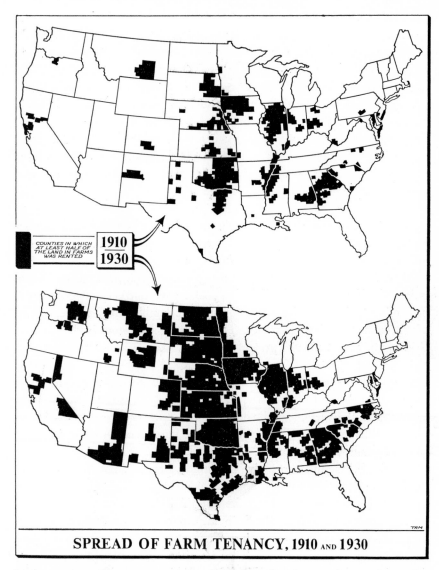

COUNTIES IN WHICH AT LEAST HALF OF THE LAND IN FARMS WAS RENTED | 1910 | 1930

SPREAD OF FARM TENANCY, 1910 AND 1930

be for a government corporation or farm board to buy up the surplus at the high American price, and sell it abroad at whatever it would bring on the world market. To make up for the loss, an equalization fee or tax would be charged the farmers on their entire crop.

Hypothetically, this meant that if the nation could consume only 650,000,000 bushels of an 800,000,000-bushel wheat crop, the domestic price could be raised to the world price of, for instance, $1.00 plus the 42 cents tariff. Thus the farmer would receive a gross return of perhaps 40 cents a bushel more than otherwise for his wheat. The 150,000,000 bushels of surplus wheat could be dumped over the tariff wall at the world price. Then an equalization fee on all wheat of perhaps 10 cents a bushel would pay for the dumping, yet leave the farmer about 30 cents ahead.

Between 1924 and 1928, Senator Charles L. McNary of Oregon and Representative Gilbert Haugen of Iowa promoted this scheme in Congress. In 1924 the McNary-Haugen bill covered only grain, and was defeated in the House, but in 1926 the addition of cotton, tobacco, and rice brought Southern support. In 1927, Congress passed it, but President Coolidge coldly vetoed it as being preferential legislation contrary to the principles of laissez faire. (On the same day he signed an order raising the tariff on pig iron 50 per cent.) A year later, Congress again passed the McNary-Haugen bill, and Coolidge again vetoed it.

Obviously the McNary-Haugen program had defects. At home it would have stimulated great commercial farmers to produce still more of the unwanted surpluses, and overseas would have forced world market prices still lower, as world production of the surpluses mounted. This would have led to greater retaliation against the United States. Many agricultural economists began to seek for some alternative program which would cut production at home. Some of them began to develop crop-restriction schemes foreshadowing the later New Deal domestic-allotment program. Professor Rexford G. Tugwell of Columbia University wrote in 1928, "The problem of immediate farm relief is . . . that of limiting production, not to the nation's or the world's needs, but to the buying capacity of the farmers' market." In 1928, economists might have reached this conclusion, but it was still academic. Farmers, because of the weight of their votes in electing members of Congress, could continue to maintain a bloc large enough to vote farm legislation and harry the friends of the industrialists. While general prosperity prevailed, they could not capture the Presidency. In 1928, Northern farmers tried to obtain the Republican nomination for Frank O. Lowden of Illinois, and failed ignominiously.

Farmers were well organized, and indeed were on the threshold of victory, but they could not win until they had put into the White House a President, either Republican or Democratic, sympathetic to their program. In 1928, the Democratic Smith accepted the farmers' proposals, but few were as yet ready to bolt their party even to obtain price supports. As long as the country as a whole was prosperous, the farmers seemed doomed to be depressed. Farm income had been 15 per cent of the national total in 1920; by 1929 it was only 9 per cent.

New Ways of Life

FOR THOSE who enjoyed the prosperity, and for those content to share vicariously in the frolics and foibles of the wealthy through tabloid newspaper accounts, it was a wonderful era. The national wealth of the United States was almost as great as that of all of Europe, and this was the impression newspaper readers and visitors received. It was the era when Florida realtors hired Bryan to lecture on the climate. Even though only an infinitesimal portion of Americans bought real estate in Florida during the land boom of 1924–1925, the impression was that most people were dabbling in the speculation. So too with the stock market later in the decade. Millions shared in the national frenzies, but most of them did so only vicariously while living sober, quiet lives.

The average American family owned an automobile. There were 23,000,000 cars in use by 1929, and on Sundays it seemed as though they were all out on the new concrete highways. At home, people listened to the radio. The first commercial station, KDKA, broadcast the news of Harding's election in November 1920; by 1924, the National Broadcasting Company had organized a nationwide network of stations; by 1930 over 12,000,000 American families had radios. Millions more had electric vacuum cleaners and washing machines; many were beginning to buy electric refrigerators. Household appliances were supplanting the housemaid and the hired girl. Food and clothing accounted for only 44 per cent of the family expenditures, compared with 58 per cent in 1899—a clear indication of the rising living standards.

New ways of life, alarming to the older generation, swept America. Women seemed to have lost their modesty as they cut their hair, applied lipstick, donned short skirts and silk stockings, and unblushingly began using words previously reserved for males. Younger people talked frankly and openly about sex. It was talk that frightened their elders, and was made doubly frightening by the disappearance of chaperons and the availability of automobiles. Compounding the evil in the eyes of elders were the many new roadhouses and speakeasies, where young people flaunted Prohibition by drinking beer or cocktails. There, too, they listened to jazz and danced the new steps like the Charleston, which some preachers denounced to their flocks as lascivious. It seemed to many critics that Gertrude Stein had correctly labeled this the "lost generation"; these people could not believe that in time it too could mature into censorious middle age.

Motion pictures flamboyantly heralded the new moral code and, together with tabloid papers, helped fabricate false stereotypes of the New Era. An estimated 50,000,000 people a week went to theaters to see the "It" girl, Clara Bow, the glamorous Rudolph Valentino, the comedian Charlie Chaplin, gangster pictures, westerns, and great spectacles like *The Ten Commandments*. These helped standardize American habits, and not always in the most edifying way. Further, since nine-tenths of the world's motion pictures were made in the United States, they brought to other countries curiously distorted notions of American culture. In 1927 a revolution struck the motion picture industry when the first important all-talking picture, *The Jazz Singer*, starring Al Jolson, was a phenomenal success. Motion pictures began to carry American speech also around the world.

Detail from mural "City Life" by Thomas Hart Benton (THE NEW SCHOOL FOR SOCIAL RESEARCH)

In journalism, the twenties brought an even greater sensationalism than the nineties in some mass-circulation city papers. From England came the idea of the half-sized tabloid, which led to the founding of the *News, Mirror,* and *Graphic* in New York City, and similar papers throughout the country. Tabloid journalism came to mean what "yellow journalism" had meant earlier, with the addition of a strong emphasis upon serial comic strips and sensational photographs. Millions of readers followed the gang wars in Chicago and murder trials in New York. Even the dignified *New York Times* had to capitulate to reader demands and lavish front-page space upon one spectacular murder trial. For the most part, however, the huge circulation of the sensational papers was largely among a new semiliterate audience; the older, less exciting, more responsible press went on much as before.

Among magazines, the *Saturday Evening Post*, with its conservative editorials and well-written stories, mirrored the era as faithfully as President Coolidge. Close behind it in capturing the popular spirit was a reprint magazine founded in 1921, *Reader's Digest*, which filled its readers with inspiration and optimism, and guided them effortlessly through what they might consider difficult, serious subjects. It was the beginning of predigested reading. Much the same formula went into *Time*, the first of the news magazines, founded in 1923. In cleverness, *Time* was one of the magazines tailored for the college graduates of the twenties. Another was the gay, sophisticated *New Yorker*, founded in 1925, which soon eclipsed the older *Life* and *Judge*. The magazines which best typified the iconoclastic spirit of the intelligentsia and its rejection of middle-class values were *Smart Set* and the *American Mercury*. Their editors, Henry L. Mencken and George Jean Nathan, ridiculed the shibboleths of the decade, but, more than that, they introduced to their readers many of the most vigorous writers of the era, from D. H. Lawrence and James Joyce to Theodore Dreiser and F. Scott Fitzgerald.

Renaissance in Babylon

IN LITERATURE and the arts, as in politics, there was many an echo of the prewar progressive era. Many of the older established realist novelists continued to publish and to grow in the mastery of their craft. Before the war, Dreiser had exploited a typical progressive theme in exploring the inner thinking of a business magnate. In 1925 he published his greatest popular success, *An American Tragedy*, in which he continued his emphasis upon psychological and environmental factors but, more in keeping with the twenties, demonstrated how they led a young man to consider drowning his mistress. Willa Cather, whose model had been Flaubert, by the end of the progressive era was chronicling the struggles of hearty immigrants to subdue the rolling grasslands of Nebraska (*O Pioneers*, 1913), and of their daughters to fit into the American mold (*My Ántonia*, 1918). She continued to depict the impact of harsh environment on good men but shifted the locale to New Mexico in her masterpiece, *Death Comes to the Archbishop* (1927), and to Quebec in *Shadow on the Rocks* (1931). In 1922 she advanced firmly her ideas on literary craftsmanship:

> There are hopeful signs that some of the younger writers are trying to break away from mere verisimilitude, and, following the development of modern painting, to interpret imaginatively the material and social inves-

titure of their characters; to present their scene by suggestion rather than by enumeration. The higher processes of art are all processes of simplification.

In a frequently fumbling way, Sherwood Anderson was trying to develop both simplicity and psychological insights. In 1912, after suffering a nervous breakdown, he had quit as manager of an Ohio paint factory to devote his life to writing. A perceptive critic, Howard Mumford Jones, has written, "The myth which pictures Sherwood Anderson walking out of his office in the midst of dictating a letter is historically false but sym-

Sinclair Lewis (NATIONAL AR-CHIVES)

bolically true. When he discovered his purpose in life was not money-making but writing, the discovery was absolute." Anderson was in his forties when his *Winesburg, Ohio* (1919) made its impact upon the postwar generation. His direct, almost psychoanalytic probing into the minds and spirit of small-town individuals was offensive to genteel tradition and exciting to youthful rebels discovering Freud. Relatively few of Anderson's stories long endured, but his influence upon young writers made him as significant an advance agent of the postwar generation as Howells had been of the progressive realists.

A little closer to the new generation, but closer still to bygone progressivism was Sinclair Lewis, satirically exploiting the Midwestern town and metropolis with a sure ear and a dramatic sense that won him a large audience. Lewis, who had grown up in Sauk Center, Minnesota, and once lived in a New York settlement house, tried in *Main Street* (1920) to epitomize small-town America. He had, as he later wrote, "spent a good deal of time in Midwestern villages and . . . I still felt that the ghetto-

like confinement of small towns could be . . . a respectable form of hell."
As he attacked philistinism in one or another of its forms in novels like
Babbitt (1922), whose very titles went into the American language, his
philistine readers tingled with mild shocks of delight as they recognized
their neighbors. Lewis was too much like them, and at heart too sympathetic, for them to be really horrified. He fed their cultural aspirations,
and perhaps he taught them better manners.

The talented younger writers were much more upsetting. They were
rebels in a different sense than their progressive predecessors in that
they were aligned against many of the intellectual values as well as what
was materially ugly in American civilization, and they sought a way out in
hedonism rather than reform. They fancied themselves outcasts in a
dollar-grubbing Babylon. Some fled to that earlier refuge of the unconven-
tional, Greenwich Village; others tried to create their own Greenwich
Villages wherever they were; the most conspicuous among them fore-
swore the United States to seek inspiration in Europe. In Paris, especially,
they could find an ancient and sophisticated civilization, cheap living costs,
the legal liquor which symbolized freedom to Americans chafing under
Prohibition, and above all encouragement from a talented coterie of writers. T. S. Eliot, who became a permanent expatriate, wrote from the perspective of the late fifties:

> The situation is different for the young men of today compared with
> the earlier part of this century. I don't know what Prohibition had to do
> with it. Certainly it was easier then for youngsters to earn a living over-
> seas. And the American literary scene didn't offer them much encourage-
> ment. That was a very dull period.
>
> In Europe there was a desire to aid younger people. Pound introduced
> me to Yeats. I got to know Virginia Woolf. People were interested in my
> poetry. I had never experienced such interest at home. But now the trend
> seems to be in the other direction. Young Americans go back and find
> they can make a living teaching in colleges, that there is genuine interest
> in them. A young writer needs the society of other writers, both his con-
> temporaries and benevolent older writers whom he can respect. There are
> more of these now in the United States.*

Eliot, one of the most distinguished and influential writers in his generation, felt despair even in Europe. The frightening emptiness of *The
Wasteland* (1922), a long, brilliant, gloomy poem, brought responsive
echoes from the young intellectuals of two continents. Eliot's world, as he
wrote in *The Hollow Men* (1925), threatened to end not with a bang but
a whimper. To Eliot's early comrade-in-poetry, Ezra Pound, the solution

---

* *New York Times,* March 30, 1959.

before the end of the twenties seemed to be to migrate to Italy and accept the frightening discipline of Mussolini's fascism. For Eliot, as intellectuals were plunged from self-indulgence into the sobering hardships of depression, the only way out was through faith. The world was dropping into new Dark Ages, he warned in 1931. Faith alone could "renew and rebuild civilization and save the World from Suicide."

The sense of emptiness and disillusion dominated the work of many of the young Americans both in Europe and at home. Among the expatriates there was Ernest Hemingway, as much the symbol and hero of his

Ernest Hemingway (NATIONAL ARCHIVES)

group as Byron had been of the nineteenth-century Romantics. Hemingway carried with him the pleasant memories of boyhood hunting and fishing in northern Michigan and nightmare recollections of the military debacle at Caporetto on the Italian front. From these experiences he fashioned stories written in a terse, lean style learned in part from Sherwood Anderson, Ezra Pound, and Gertrude Stein. What he had to say was his own: that man, faced with the cruelty, violence, and death inevitable in the world surrounding him, might as well withdraw himself from the responsibility for trying to change things and enjoy what sensual pleasures he could before he met fate. This was the theme of *The Sun Also Rises* (1926), the novel of the lost generation in Paris, and of his polemic against war, *A Farewell to Arms* (1929). Violence filled his writing, and he sought to learn the meaning of the "moment of truth" in the Spanish bull-ring. He went on safari to face the perils of shooting big game in Africa, displaying the same sort of anxious virility as Theodore Roosevelt but, unlike Roosevelt, trying to escape from American values and duties. The United States had been fine, he wrote in *The Green Hills of Africa* (1935), but "we had made a bloody mess of it and I would go, now, somewhere else as we had always had the right to go somewhere else and as we had always gone. You could always come back." Later Hemingway, unlike many of the expatriates and some of those who had never left home, did come back.

At home, the romantic young hero among the writers was F. Scott Fitzgerald. As a Princeton undergraduate he had remarked to his fellow student, Edmund Wilson, "I want to be one of the greatest writers who ever lived, don't you?" In an officers' training camp in the United States, he had written *This Side of Paradise*, and when it appeared in 1920, he seemed to be on his way. In his novels and in his personal life, he spoke for the "sad young men" whose idealistic dreams had been blunted by the jazz age into somewhat cynical, narcissistic pleasure-seeking. No other end seemed possible. *The Great Gatsby* (1925) told of a young hero who had gone off to war like a knight with his lady's scarf on his sleeve, and had reappeared to live near her on Long Island like an opulent baron. But the heroine was married to someone else, and the hero was a baron of rum-runners. All of Fitzgerald's central characters, and Fitzgerald himself, were "the beautiful and the damned."

When William Faulkner, a Southerner who had fought in the British and Canadian air forces, returned to Oxford, Mississippi, he seemed in his life and writing to follow the familiar pattern of the twenties. He too was encouraged by Sherwood Anderson, and he too published a bitter war novel. There the similarities ended. He attracted so little attention in the twenties that for a while after publishers had rejected *Sanctuary* he worked shoveling coal at the University of Mississippi power plant. But recognition came when he published *The Sound and the Fury* in 1929, followed by *Sanctuary* in 1931. In these novels he had begun analyzing the South with morbid intensity in the abstruse stream-of-consciousness style that led critics to place him in the top rank among American novelists.

In the drama, these were the golden years of Eugene O'Neill, who drew from Ibsen, Strindberg, and Freud to develop American plays that were both critical and popular successes. *The Emperor Jones* (1920), *Anna Christie* (1922), *Strange Interlude* (1928), and other plays won O'Neill three Pulitzer Prizes in the decade, and helped maintain him in the forefront of American dramatists for many years. A number of other young playwrights wrote for the experimental stage, which flourished at scores of colleges and cities, even while motion pictures were superseding the old legitimate-theater circuits.

Although American writers were beginning to attract a world audience, competent composers and artists still had trouble gaining recognition even at home. Painters continued to produce along lines that in many cases had been pioneered before the war, and continued to battle against resistance to modern art. John Sloan, with finer brushwork, was profiting by what he had learned from the French postimpressionists; George Bellows achieved the peak of his talent in *Dempsey and Firpo* (1923). As early as 1915, Max Weber had experimented with totally abstract art, but abandoned it by 1920, not to return again until the early forties. Several of the most interesting artists of the twenties were working in

Eugene O'Neill (NATIONAL ARCHIVES)

semiabstraction. John Marin put into his seascapes what Winslow Homer had never seen along the Maine coast. It was "the purest, most forceful abstract expressionism we have yet produced," John I. H. Baur, of the Brooklyn Museum, has written. "The explosive intensity of his emotion is most spontaneously embodied in a series of brilliant water colors in which the slashing strokes, the sudden angular distortions, and the calculated tensions of arbitrary color tug against the flat surface of the paper and the boundary of the frame without ever destroying their autonomy."

About 1920, Georgia O'Keeffe and Charles Sheeler turned from abstraction or semiabstraction to a sharp, precise realism in which abstract design was dominant. Into the paintings of bleached skulls of cattle or the interiors of lilies which Miss O'Keeffe rendered in bright colors and meticulous detail, critics could read attractive abstract patterns, or, if they chose, a wealth of feminine symbolism. Sheeler, working with lens as well as brush, explored the artistic potentialities of industrial forms.

He objected when people considered his work photographic and over-looked its abstract qualities. Thomas Craven, the art critic, commented, "What he evidently looks at and strives, successfully, I believe, to put down, is the structural character—the inherent qualities of its materials, the meaning of its forms."

Some of the surplus wealth of the twenties poured into European painting; Mellon matched his ingenuity in keeping taxes down with his

"River Rouge Plant" by Charles Sheeler (WHITNEY MUSEUM OF AMERI-CAN ART)

lavish purchases of Old Masters, some of them from the dollar-hungry Soviet Union. By 1930, American art galleries owned two billion dollars worth of paintings. Along with this went a rapidly widening popular ap-preciation of fine art. Similarly, schools and colleges introduced musical training and music appreciation courses. Innumerable Americans de-veloped an interest in good art and fine music.

Architecturally, the United States went on much as it had since the Columbian Exposition, building its public structures in classic or gothic forms, and erecting taller and taller skyscrapers in its cities. The ultimate, in 1931, was the Empire State Building, thrust up to a height of eighty-six stories and topped by a dirigible mast. In the growing suburbia, architectural styles varied from Georgian to Spanish. Only modern styles, which banks were reluctant to finance, remained a curiosity. Frank Lloyd Wright was in eclipse throughout the decade. At least American architecture was substantial and comfortable, and in various of the functional

Louis Armstrong's Hot Five, about 1927: Johnny St. Cyr, banjo; Kid Ory, trombone; Louis Armstrong, trumpet; Johnny Dodds, clarinet; Lillian Armstrong, piano (NATIONAL ARCHIVES)

forms like the factories and grain elevators that Sheeler liked to paint, there was a utilitarian artistry.

What was most exciting in music was the rise of jazz, at the time widely denounced as being degenerate but, in the decades since its advent, ever more widely acclaimed as a great American cultural contribution. Jazz gradually evolved out of the improvisations of New Orleans Negro and white bands during the decades after the Civil War, and seems to have made its first appearance in the North when one of the groups, "Brown's Dixieland Jazz Band," played in Chicago in 1915. The new music rapidly spread in popularity as many of the early talented

George Gershwin (NATIONAL ARCHIVES)

musicians went from New Orleans to Chicago, New York, and Paris. During the twenties the popular songwriters of legendary Tin Pan Alley imitated the new rhythms and techniques, turning out tunes which saxophones wailed on thousands of dance floors throughout the land. Millions of young people danced to these strange rhythms, and to older people, jazz seemed to be taking the younger generation to perdition. But the new music continued to flourish so spectacularly that to many the twenties became known as the "jazz age."

Devotees of jazz regarded the greatest of these musicians, such as Bix Beiderbecke, "King" Oliver, "Jelly Roll" Morton, and Louis Armstrong, with the awe and devotion that symphony patrons lavished on Toscanini and Beethoven. Some of the most talented young composers took jazz seriously. George Gershwin wrote:

It is difficult to determine what enduring values, aesthetically, jazz has contributed, because "jazz" is a word which has been used for at least five or six different types of music. It is really a conglomeration of many things. It has a little bit of ragtime, the blues, classicism, and spirituals. Basically, it is a matter of rhythm. After rhythm in importance come intervals. . . . One thing is certain. Jazz has contributed an enduring value to America in the sense that it has expressed ourselves. It is an original American achievement which will endure, not as jazz perhaps, but which will leave its mark on future music in one form or another.

Gershwin himself, born in 1898, had won fame in the twenties as a composer of popular tunes and of scores for musical comedies. Paul Whiteman commissioned him to write a composition utilizing jazz components in symphonic form. The result, first played in 1924, was *Rhapsody in Blue*, which drew from the classic tradition as much as from jazz. There followed *An American in Paris* (1928) and, in 1935, Gershwin's last and most significant work, *Porgy and Bess*, which has been the most vital and successful of American operas. Gershwin died in 1937.

Aaron Copland, born in 1900, was a student of the same harmony teacher as Gershwin. After serious training in Paris he "was anxious," he has written, "to write a work that would immediately be recognized as American in character." In a suite, *Music for the Theater* (1925), and a concerto, he introduced jazzlike rhythms; in the thirties and forties he turned more to folk songs as his inspiration and a careful simplicity as his mode in compositions like *El Salón México* (1936) and *Appalachian Spring* (1944).

Gershwin and Copland were both born in Brooklyn, but a third composer emerging in the twenties as a writer of American music, Roy Harris, was born in a log cabin in Oklahoma in 1898, drove a milk truck in California for four years, then like Copland studied in Paris under the distinguished Nadia Boulanger. He too combined the new muscial techniques of Europe with American themes. In 1934, the Boston Symphony Orchestra performed his First Symphony, which the conductor, Serge Koussevitzky hailed as "the first truly tragic symphony by an American." When his Third Symphony appeared in 1939, it received numerous performances; the Boston Symphony alone played it ten times in a year. Harris wrote an overture, *When Johnny Comes Marching Home*, in 1934, a *Folk Song Symphony* in 1941, and much more music drawing firmly from American roots. At the same time, Harris was a serious and creative composer. He declared: "I have become increasingly convinced that music is a fluid architecture of sound and that all the elements of music—melody, harmony, counterpoint, dynamics, orchestration—must be coordinated into a swift-moving form which fulfils itself from the root idea to its complete flowering in organic ornamentation."

One of the remarkable achievements of this trio of composers and some of their fellows was that they were creating American music which was being taken relatively seriously and which was increasingly being heard by American audiences. It was interesting too that these composers and a group of artists (who are discussed in Chapter 14), were already in the twenties drawing upon popular American folk themes and were receiving popular approbation. Several years later, a baseball manager is supposed to have written Harris after hearing the Third Symphony, "If I had pitchers who could pitch as strongly as you do in your Symphony, my worries would be over."

The Search for New Values

IN CONTRAST to the musical and artistic glorification of the popular, many intellectuals were in revolt against American civilization. In both letters and arts there was a seeking for values that would be something more than the advertising man's apotheosis of the mass-production culture, something less than President Coolidge's platitudinous evocation of the old verities. This is why so many of the younger writers were rejecting the standards of the United States for those of Europe, which did not seem to them as yet caught in the new commercial maelstrom.

A group of talented young Southerners, remaining within the country, thought the solution was to reject the machine. A dozen of them collaborated in 1930 upon a joint denunciation of the industrialism encroaching from the North. Among them were the notable literary figures John Crowe Ransom, Allen Tate, and Robert Penn Warren. In their statement of principles, *I'll Take My Stand*, they declared:

> How far shall the South surrender its moral, social, and economic autonomy to the victorious principle of Union? That question remains open. The South is a minority section that has hitherto been jealous of its minority right to live its own kind of life. . . . The younger Southerners, who are being converted frequently to the industrial gospel, must come back to the support of the Southern tradition. They must be persuaded to look very critically at the advantages of becoming a "new South" which will be only an undistinguished replica of the usual industrial community.

Not all Southern thinkers agreed with them. One historian, William B. Hesseltine, retorted, "at no time in its history . . . has the American South been other than a horrible example of the spiritual failure of agrarianism." It seemed unrealistic to blame all the failings of American society upon industrialism, and to hope that through rejection of factories it could be purified.

Others were trying to appraise American society with the psychological tools suggested by Freud, or the economic determinism stemming from Marx.

Among ministers, publicists, philosophers, and economists seeking to interpret the new order, there was some confusion. The fundamentalist ministers went on much as before, although they became the butt of national ridicule in 1925 when their champion, William Jennings Bryan, matched wits with the agnostic Clarence Darrow in the famous Scopes trial involving a Tennessee law forbidding the teaching of evolution. Ministers to the middle class who earlier had so exurberantly preached the Social Gospel or the great crusade in Europe, had been beaten down in 1919 when they took up the cause of the striking steel workers. Many businessmen were ready to adopt paternalistic policies and label them "Christian industrialism," but they denounced the militant Social Gospel as Bolshevism. Ministers further lost their hold on their following as middle-class reaction spread against two of the causes in which they had been so deeply involved, the war in Europe and prohibition. Many of them tended, consequently, to concentrate upon the building of fine churches and the development of a sophisticated theology embracing the new psychological concepts.

Many of the most popular publicists were negative in their view of government. Mencken and Irving Babbitt launched some of their most scathing epigrams against the American democratic system because it could produce the New Era. They were ready in the process to sneer social justice out of existence. Walter Lippmann, who had been so deeply involved in the New Nationalism and New Freedom, became aloof and brilliantly analytical in his observation of American society. The mature man must be strong not through hard resolves, "but because he was free of that tension which vain expectations beget." The Socialist candidate for President in 1928, Norman Thomas, remarked, "The old reformer has become the Tired Radical and his sons and daughters drink at the fountain of the *American Mercury*."

Nevertheless, many of the most influential philosophers and social scientists continued to write in modified progressive terms. John Dewey, at the peak of his influence, was expounding a socialized pragmatism: man through science and technology could develop an organized social intelligence which could plan a rational and fruitful future society. The aged Veblen was placing a similar faith in science: engineers, as opposed to businessmen, could bring forth an economic utopia. This doctrine, carried to its ultimate conclusion, engendered the technocracy movement of the early thirties. Other economists would not go this far, but some of them accepted Veblen's emphasis upon the producers, who unlike businessmen would not raise prices and restrict markets. Around them could develop an economy of still greater abundance. Together with the agricultural economists who were thinking in opposite terms of restriction, they looked forward to an age of social and economic planning. Among a wider group of readers, Charles A. Beard was disseminating some of these ideas. In his and Mary Beard's *Rise of American Civilization* (1927), expressing mild economic determinism and emphasizing social and cultural factors, he did much to perpetuate progressive thinking among the new generation of intellectuals. Vernon L. Parrington's *Main Currents of American Thought* (1927), tracing the same themes in literature, helped create a Jeffersonian cult. Writing on a popular level, Claude Bowers developed similar ideas. Franklin D. Roosevelt, reviewing Bowers's *Jefferson and Hamilton* in 1925, declared, "Hamiltons we have today. Is a Jefferson on the horizon?"

In the schools and colleges of the twenties the way was being prepared for another Jefferson if the New Era should fail. There instructors who had come to maturity in the progressive era continued to expound the old ideas reshaped to the new order. There too the international vision of Wilson remained alive. Simultaneously, in the technical schools and the laboratories, the physicians, scientists, engineers, and managers to run American society were being turned out in greater numbers and were better educated than ever before.

The prosperity of the twenties spilled over into the educational system. The per capita expenditure per pupil jumped from $24 in 1910 to $90 in 1930. Free elementary education had become established throughout the nation; illiteracy dropped from 7.7 per cent to 4.3 per cent. Enrollment in high schools increased 400 per cent, and universities grew nearly as rapidly.

How Prosperous?

ONLY A NATION as rich and prosperous as the United States in the twenties could have built so rapidly its educational systems, art museums, symphony orchestras, and little theaters. Only in such a nation could an automobile have seemed a necessity of life. The twenties were a decade of much material and intellectual gain. Sadly enough, the positive achievements tended to be obscured by the garishness and banality of the surface of American life. Many observers were ready to follow Mencken in seeing

American society as consisting only of the "booboisie." Too many were ready, on the other hand, to overlook the unevenness of American prosperity, especially the dangerous disparity between rural and urban incomes. It was a rich and fruitful era, but it carried within itself the seeds of its own destruction.

Chapter *12*

THE GREAT ENGINEER
AND THE
GREAT DEPRESSION

To MANY AMERICANS, a simple and effective way of perpetuating the
Coolidge prosperity after 1928 seemed to be to put the "Great Engineer,"
Herbert Hoover, in the White House. His policies as Secretary of Commerce apparently guaranteed an indefinite continuation of businessmen's
government, and of boom without bust. Hoover himself shared this faith.
In his acceptance address in August 1928, he proclaimed, "We in America
today are nearer to the final triumph over poverty than ever before in the
history of any land." He backed his assertion with so many statistics that
it seemed irrefutable. "Given a chance to go forward with the policies of
the last eight years," he promised, "we shall soon with the help of God
be in sight of the day when poverty will be vanished from this nation."
Yet, fifteen months later the stock market crashed, and sent the nation
careening down into the blackest depression in its history. Hoover applied
all the techniques and skills he had perfected during the years of prosperity, and in desperation turned to new methods. All was to no avail.

Rum, Romanism, and Prosperity

No ONE could have guessed in 1928 that businessmen's government so soon would be in ill repute. When President Coolidge had announced the previous summer, "I do not choose to run," a scramble had begun for the Republican nomination as a prize sure to bring four if not eight years in the White House. Hoover, who had done so much to bring efficient government aid to business, was immediately in the forefront of the contenders, even though neither Coolidge nor professional politicians cared much for him. He was easily nominated on the first ballot to run on a platform emphasizing prosperity and straddling the troublesome issues of farm relief and prohibition. Second place on the ticket went to a Senator from Kansas, Charles Curtis.

Prosperity was also the decisive issue affecting the Democrats. The experienced politicians were still almost as badly divided as in 1924, but they saw no reason to turn their convention into another brawl when their candidate had no chance of winning against Republican prosperity. Even those who were ardently dry and Protestant raised no barrier against the wet Catholic governor of New York, Alfred E. Smith. He was nominated on the first ballot to run on a platform not much more positive than that of the Republicans. It did, however, include a plan offering the farmers McNary-Haugenism.

More important, Smith promised, despite a compromise plank on prohibition, that he would favor relaxing the Volstead enforcement act. This forced prohibition into the forefront of the campaign. It probably would have been there anyway, since there was relatively little else except that and religion to campaign about. Both Hoover and Smith were self-made men and proud of it. Hoover's path had been from an Iowa farm through Stanford University, and had been marked by a phenomenally successful rise as a business and government executive. Smith's had been from the East Side of New York through the Fulton Fish Market and the Tammany hierarchy to the governorship of New York. There he had demonstrated a consummate political and administrative skill; he had reorganized the state government, fought to build schools, parks, and parkways, and struggled for public development of the great power sites. All this, and especially his forthright distaste for prohibition, won him the support of many liberals and intellectuals. It also brought him the enthusiastic backing of some people who called themselves liberals but in the twentieth-century meaning of the word were liberal only in their opposition to prohibition. On the other hand, Hoover, although personally reserved and not nearly as skilled in politics as Smith, had the support of other liberals and old progressives. Both candidates were mild progressives dedicated to perpetuating the intimate ties between business and government. The *Wall Street Journal* forthrightly announced this. Smith made his position amply clear by naming as his campaign manager John J. Raskob of Du Pont and General Motors. Smith apparently was trying to woo business, but in thus appointing a wet Catholic Republican prominent in two of the largest

Secretary Hoover the day he was nominated for President (NATIONAL ARCHIVES)

corporations in the nation, he further offended agrarian and progressive Democrats.

This contest between two men of high character degenerated into one of the lowest mud-slinging campaigns in American history. Hoover himself campaigned on prosperity, popularly translated into the notion of a chicken in every pot and two cars in every garage. This left the political storms to sweep around Smith, who evoked more enthusiastic loyalty and venomous hatred than any candidate since Bryan. In the American cities, prohibition had never been popular, and by 1928 it seemed the rankest farce. Some well-to-do Republicans, like Raskob, whose sole notion of liberalism was the repeal of prohibition, poured money into the Smith campaign. Millions of the urban masses, mostly themselves of immigrant and

Catholic background, saw in Smith their spokesman, their great hero. His reception in cities like Boston was unprecedented in its noisy enthusiasm.

In reverse, in the Protestant South, belief in prohibition was still almost an act of faith, and the Ku Klux Klan was still boisterous in its anti-Catholicism. Fiery crosses greeted Smith near Oklahoma City, where he courageously denounced the Klan. It was impossible to counteract the vile, crude handbills, typewritten doggerel, and whispered dirty jokes. One handbill in Georgia declared that if Smith were elected, the marriages

Alfred E. Smith (NATIONAL ARCHIVES)

of Protestants would be voided and their children would thus become illegitimate. Smith had no effective defense against the religious and prohibition issues; they overrode rural Americans' disgust with Hoover's coldness toward their demands. Anyway, Smith with his East Side accent promising McNary-Haugenism was no more convincing than Hoover with his Iowa intonation pledging a special session of Congress to enact "sane" farm relief. Borah, influential in the West, unexpectedly campaigned for the Republican ticket.

The Hoover landslide far exceeded expectations. In the North, Smith carried only Massachusetts and Rhode Island; in the previously solid South, Hoover swept Virginia, North Carolina, Florida, Kentucky, Tennessee, Oklahoma, and Texas. The popular vote was 21,391,000 for Hoover, compared with 15,016,000 for Smith; the electoral vote, 444 to 87. This lopsided result obscured both the weaknesses of the Republican

organization, which had done badly in congressional years, and the growing strength of the Democrats. Smith, doubling the vote of Davis four
years previously, had brought to the polls so many Americans of recent
foreign background that for the first time the Democrats carried most of
the big cities. In some Midwestern agricultural areas, the Democratic
vote doubled. These symptoms were unimportant only as long as prosperity lasted.

Although to some observers, the 1928 election seemed to be a great
referendum in favor of prohibition, this national restriction was not to last

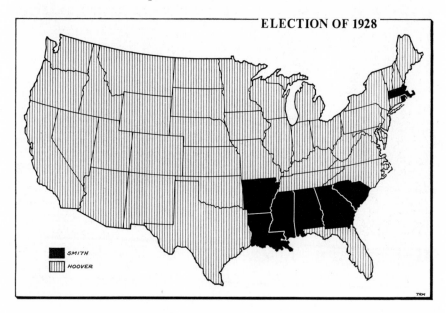

ELECTION OF 1928

SMITH
HOOVER

much longer than prosperity. During the campaign, Hoover had referred
to prohibition as the "noble experiment," but enforcement was breaking
down so badly that Congress stiffened the penalties for violating the
Volstead Act, and authorized the new President to appoint a National Law
Enforcement Commission. This commission, headed by a former Attorney General, George Wickersham, and including such distinguished
members as Newton D. Baker and Roscoe Pound, ultimately reported in
1931 that prohibition was not only not being enforced but was virtually
unenforceable.

Enforcement had begun with naive optimism. The first Prohibition
Commissioner had proclaimed, "We shall see that [liquor] is not manufactured, nor sold, nor given away, nor hauled in anything on the surface
of the earth or under the earth or in the air." He undertook all of this during the first five years on a budget of about $8,000,000 a year, with 3,374
agents—who were for the most part inefficient and underpaid political

employees. With whatever aid they could muster from state and local authorities, theirs was the task of patrolling 18,000 miles of coastline, guarding against the diversion of 57,000,000 gallons of industrial alcohol, overseeing hundreds of millions of medical prescriptions, and checking on 20,000,000 homes to prevent the concoction of home-brew, wines, or "bathtub gin."

It was an opportunity readymade for gangsters, who switched to the large-scale smuggling or manufacture and distribution of liquor, and the

Prohibition officers at Detroit on the seized tug "Geronimo," June 1928
(NATIONAL ARCHIVES)

subverting of law enforcement officers. In Chicago, "Scarface" Al Capone built an underworld empire; based on beer and extending out into slot machines, laundries, and labor unions, it grossed about $60,000,000 per year. He guarded it against interlopers with an army of 700 to 1,000 gunmen. Between 1920 and 1927, over 250 gangsters were killed in Chicago warfare alone. Capone miraculously survived both his rivals and the forces of the law, until finally in 1931 he was convicted of federal income tax evasion.

Rampant gangsterism and the open flaunting of the law by millions of otherwise respectable citizens convinced many thoughtful Americans that prohibition was not worth its price in lawlessness. With the coming of the depression, some well-to-do people, already banded into organizations like the Crusaders, redoubled their efforts in the hope that repeal would bring lower income taxes and greater prosperity. By the time of the campaign of 1932, prohibition, compared with the depression, had evaporated as a serious issue and the Democrats bluntly advocated repeal. In February 1933 Congress submitted to the states the Twenty-First Amendment repealing prohibition; by December it had been ratified, and the experiment was at an end.

Hoover's Program for Agriculture

As HERBERT HOOVER took his oath of office in March 1929, editorial writers throughout the nation enthusiastically predicted that the government under his sane and scientific management would help create new high levels of comfort and prosperity for the American people. Hoover seemed ideally fitted for the Presidency. He presented the appealing spectacle of an orphaned Iowa farm boy who through intelligence, energy, and self-reliance had worked his way upward. He was the first student to enroll at Stanford University, where he studied mining engineering. He was so successful in managing mining enterprises in far parts of the world that by the time he was forty in 1914, he was independently wealthy. Thereafter, he devoted himself to public service: organizing war relief in Europe, administering the wartime food program in the United States, and serving as Secretary of Commerce. At the time of his inauguration in 1929, Americans hailed him as a great humanitarian and engineer; he was at the height of his popularity.

No problems more serious than prohibition and farm relief were on President Hoover's agenda. In his inaugural he pledged himself to protect the health and education of children. More than that, he declared:

> Our first objective must be to provide security from poverty and want. . . . We want to see a nation built of home owners and farm owners. We want to see their savings protected. We want to see them in steady jobs. We want to see more and more of them insured against death and accident, unemployment and old age. We want them all secure.

This was a far departure from the taciturn conservatism of Coolidge, but Hoover meant that the American people themselves rather than their government should provide the security. The task of the government seemed to be (as in the Progressive era) to establish commissions to compile and collate relevant data. Hoover appointed competent members to several commissions, which in time produced notable reports. The President wanted the data, but, as William Allen White once gibed, there he stopped, rather like an adding machine.

Hoover's immediate positive step was to call Congress into special session in April 1929, to enact farm-relief legislation and raise the tariff. Hoover's program, embodied in the Agricultural Marketing Act of 1929, established, for the first time in peacetime, large-scale government machinery to aid the farmer. The program was, as Hoover insisted, voluntary, and did not include any of the price-fixing schemes for which farm organizations were lobbying. In keeping with Hoover's long-established ideas, it encouraged the voluntary combination of farmers to help themselves under government auspices. The machinery for this was a Farm Board of eight members to administer a revolving fund of $500,000,000. It could loan this to national marketing co-operatives, or itself establish corporations to buy surpluses and thus raise prices.

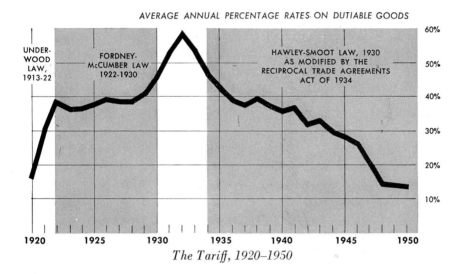

AVERAGE ANNUAL PERCENTAGE RATES ON DUTIABLE GOODS

The Tariff, 1920–1950

Within six months the depression precipitated farm prices toward new lows. Until the summer of 1931, the Wheat Stabilization Corporation and the Cotton Stabilization Corporation were able to keep prices a bit above world levels. By 1932, their funds were spent, their warehouses full, and world grain prices at the lowest point since the reign of Queen Elizabeth I. The Farm Board had operated on too small a scale, and had no power to reduce production. When President Hoover later called for voluntary reduction of the wheat crop, acreage dropped only 1 per cent in Kansas, and that probably would have happened anyway. The Farm Board experiment thus underscored the futility of a voluntary crop-control program, and prepared the way for a more drastic measure.

Congress took advantage of President Hoover's proposal to raise agricultural tariffs, and prepared an over-all measure, the Hawley-Smoot bill, which contained 75 largely futile increases on farm products, and 925 on manufactured goods. It raised the average ad valorem duty from the 26 per cent of the Fordney-McCumber Act to a new high of 50 per cent. By the time it was ready for the President's signature in the spring of 1930, a thousand members of the American Economic Association had signed a petition urging him to veto it as an unwise piece of economic nationalism. He ignored such warnings and signed the measure. Other nations in reprisal placed high tariffs on American goods. In a time of world depression, rampant economic nationalism was perhaps inevitable, but it was unfortunate and unnecessary for the United States to lead the way.

The Great Crash and Downward Spiral

As IN THE CASES of farm relief and the tariff, almost every other action of the Hoover administration also revolved around the depression which was touched off by the collapse of the stock market in the fall of 1929. For several years stock prices had been rising so rapidly that they had little relation to the earning power of corporations; the New York Stock Exchange had become for many speculators a great national gambling casino, where everyone won almost all of the time. Many of the most frequently quoted financial sages predicted this would go on almost endlessly. In August 1929, Raskob was quoted in the *Ladies' Home Journal,* "I am firm in my belief that anyone not only can be rich, but ought to be rich." All that was necessary was to put $15 per month into good common stocks. At the end of twenty years, Raskob predicted, one would own an investment of $80,000 yielding an income of $400 per month.

Relatively few Americans were buying stocks, and only part of them were speculating on the market. Only 1,500,000 people had accounts with brokerage houses, and only 600,000 were purchasing on margin (making down payments of a fraction of the cost of the stocks). During the summer of 1929, while speculators blithely pushed stock prices ever higher, there were many disquieting signs that the prosperity, so long gone for the farmers, was coming to an end for business. Construction had passed its peak in 1926, and by 1929 had declined drastically; automobiles were filling dealers' garages; business inventories of all sorts were three times larger than a year before; freight carloadings, industrial production, and wholesale prices were all slipping downward.

Wise operators began quietly unloading their holdings, but the many small ones buying on margin pushed the stock market higher and higher, until by September 3 United States Steel was up to 261 3/4, General Electric up to 396 1/4, and the Dow-Jones industrial average up to 381.17. Then the market turned soft and nervous. Within a month securities values dropped two and a half billion dollars amidst the optimistic statements of the pundits. On October 21, 1929, the market dropped sharply, and two days later the big crash began. Temporarily, J. P. Morgan and Company and other big bankers managed to stave off disaster, but on October 29, their efforts failed. Sixteen million shares were sold that day. Total losses for the month reached sixteen billion dollars. For two weeks more the market continued to drop until stocks had lost over 40 per cent in value.

The great crash was more than a spanking for speculators; it marked the cataclysmic close of the New Era. The stock-market collapse was not the cause of the depression but did precipitate it, through replacing the inflationary spiral with a deflationary one equally hard to stop. It brought to

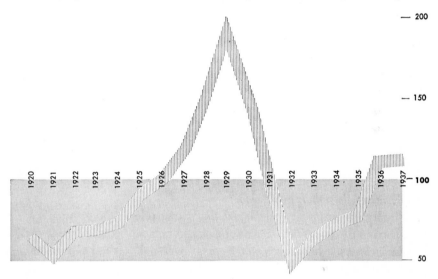

Prices of Common Stocks, 1920–1937

an end a decade of business optimism and opened one of almost unalleviated pessimism. Bewildered businessmen saw their only hope in retrenchment, and the more they retrenched, the worse conditions became.

For years afterward economists, businessmen, and political leaders debated the causes of the depression. Something had gone shockingly wrong; just what it was they could not agree upon. A later generation of economists, differently trained from their predecessors and having the advantage of hindsight, came to these conclusions: There were serious defects in the economy which could not easily have been remedied. In the twenties, as production rose, too little of the profits went to farmers and other raw-materials producers, or to the workers. Too much went to the top 5 per cent of the income group, which received a third of all personal income, or into the building of new plants. As long as the expansion of capital facilities continued, it stimulated the economy, but it created more plant space than could be used. As a result, factories by 1929 were pouring out more goods than consumers could purchase. This did not mean Americans would not have consumed more had they had more income, for in 1929 only one family in six had an automobile, only one in five a fixed bathtub or electricity, and only one in ten a telephone.

Part of the huge corporate investment had been built up overseas as exports continued to exceed imports in the traditional American pattern, even though the United States was now a great creditor rather than debtor nation. Through the twenties the rest of the world had been far from prosperous. The inability of other nations to develop a healthier foreign trade with the United States contributed to their lack of prosperity, and in the end also limited the markets for American goods.

The stock crash started the downward spiral because the economy was unsound and confidence in prosperity destroyed. Once the spiral began, the unwieldy and often inefficient structure of American business and finance, which had done much to make the period of prosperity unsound, contributed to the collapse. In addition, holding companies tended to drain off funds earmarked for expansion from companies they controlled, and to use the money for dividend payments. On the other hand, banks were not well enough organized, and the crash of one was likely to lead to runs on others and then their crash also.

Finally, government had played the wrong role in the economic system. During the twenties the tax policies had helped increase the inequalities in incomes, whereas greater equality would have had the desirable effect of increasing consumption. The tariff policies had meant that foreign trade could continue only as long as overseas loans were high. The economic policies encouraged concentration, and thus resulted in rigidly high prices. The government had done nothing to check speculation or regulate the securities market during the boom, and nothing effective to restore the buying power of farmers. In retrospect, critics of the government policies of the twenties asserted that it was not sufficient for the business of the government to be only business; it should have embraced all classes of the American people.

In facing the depression, the government, in the view of critics a generation later, continued to do the wrong things. It concentrated upon balancing the budget and keeping the nation upon the gold standard, both of which were deflationary, when the country was suffering from too much deflation. Blame for these policies should not fall solely upon President Hoover; they were the ancient formulas for the conduct of government during a depression, and were urged upon the President by leaders of both parties and of business, and by experts in economics. Times had changed; these policies not only would not work but were destructive.

Hoover Resorts to Government Intervention

PRESIDENT HOOVER was far more energetic and imaginative than any previous American President in trying to develop a program to combat the depression. His Secretary of the Treasury, Mellon, remembering the panic of 1873, was ready to see the economy go through the wringer in the old laissez faire fashion; he was a "leave-it-alone liquidationist" who thought a thoroughgoing cycle of bankruptcy and deflation would be healthy. Hoover did not agree; he pointed out that only 30 per cent of the people lived on farms where they might weather such a depression by living on their own produce, compared with 75 per cent in the seventies. He determined that the government should intervene positively but in a very limited way, seeking the voluntary co-operation of business and labor. His philosophy and techniques were the same as they had been when he was secretary of Commerce.

First, to restore confidence, Hoover announced to the nation, "The fundamental business of this country, that is production and distribution of commodities, is on a sound and prosperous basis." Most of the business moguls echoed him. Next, he held a number of highly publicized meetings of business, farm, and labor leaders in Washington to try to rally the country into a voluntary program. Business participants pledged themselves not to cut payrolls or production; labor leaders, not to ask for better wages or hours. Julius Rosenwald predicted to reporters after a conference that there would be a labor shortage. In addition, Hoover used the government to fight deflation. He announced a significant tax cut, and arranged for the Federal Reserve to provide liberal credit for business, and for the Farm Board to prop up farm prices. He asked Congress for an increase of $423,000,000 in public works—a huge sum for the period—and called upon mayors and governors to engage in the "energetic yet prudent pursuit" of them. Beyond this, Hoover stood for a balanced budget and sound money; it would have seemed unthinkable and unnecessary for him to have acted otherwise. The Boston *Globe* declared that the nation was aware "that it has at the White House a man who believes not in the philosophy of drift, but the dynamics of mastery."

During the first months after the stock crash it seemed as though these positive though mild steps might be sufficient. The pattern of the deflationary spiral became apparent only slowly as, with the gradual cancellation of orders, business leaders found they could no longer keep their full-employment pledges and began to lay off workers or put them on part time. The public gradually became aware that more than paper profits were sinking. The index of industrial employment had remained as high as 96.3 in April 1930, but dropped to 84.6 by November. The President established a committee to find work for the unemployed, and requested a still larger public-works appropriation.

Democrats, finding in the growing depression the issue so conspicuously lacking two years earlier, campaigned vigorously in the fall of 1930. They barely won the House of Representatives, and with the aid of Republican progressives, took effective control of the Senate. From this point on, Congress began seriously to harass Hoover, demanding that he move from voluntary measures to large-scale federal relief and spending. Hoover would not budge, but it seemed in the spring of 1931 as though conditions were improving. The depression to this point had not been much more serious than that of 1921; perhaps it was nearly over.

Instead, the nation was dragged down into far worse conditions as the repercussions of European panic hit these shores. Since the flow of long-term American loans to central Europe had slackened several years previously, Germany and Austria had depended upon short-term credit. French bankers cut this off in March 1931, and by May the largest bank in Austria had in effect collapsed. This disaster threatened to wreck the financial system of Germany and nations further west. Germany, appealing to the United States in June, obtained from President Hoover the proposal of a one-year moratorium on reparations and war debt payments, but France destroyed much of its good effect through its delay in accepting the plan. By September, England and most other nations of the world went off the gold standard. The crisis in western Europe hit the United States severely in the spring of 1931, as European gold was withdrawn from American banks and European holdings of American securities were dumped on the market. As other nations devalued their currency in going off the gold standard, American trade with them declined disastrously.

From May 1931 to July 1932 the economy sank lower and lower. Security and commodity prices collapsed; bankruptcies and bank failures multiplied; unemployment soared. Hoover still hoped to bring recovery through voluntary means. In September 1931, when the head of General Electric proposed a plan that was the prototype for the subsequent National Recovery Administration, the President rejected it indignantly as "the most gigantic proposal of monopoly ever made in history." Rather, he hoped to persuade banks to establish voluntarily a $500,000,000 emergency credit pool, and insurance companies not to foreclose mortgages. By December 1931, when Congress met, conditions were so frightening that President Hoover abandoned his reliance upon voluntary measures, and proposed direct governmental action of an unprecedented sort to combat the depression: (1) establishment of a federal loan agency like the War Finance Corporation; (2) additional credit for farmers faced with foreclosure; (3) reform of the banking system to safeguard deposits; (4) reform of bankruptcy laws to aid in the speedy reorganization of businesses and the settlement of overwhelming debts; (5) the loan of $300,000,000 to states for direct relief; (6) further expansion of public works; (7) drastic economy in the federal government.

Some Democrats in Congress denounced the program as inadequate, and proposed spending sums as large as forty billion dollars over a period of five years in order to bring about recovery. Hoover retorted, "We cannot squander ourselves into prosperity." The Republican progressives and Democrats in Congress were so slow to act that Hoover felt they were deliberately sabotaging his program, that they did not want to bring about recovery before the election of 1932. Slowly they passed some of his measures.

In January 1932, Congress created a giant loan agency, the Reconstruction Finance Corporation, which during 1932 loaned $1,500,000,-000, mostly to banks, railroads, and businesses. Hoover, trying to parry criticism that he had set up a bread line for big business, asserted that its purpose was to stop deflation and thus increase employment, mainly by helping smaller businesses. Later, when he was abused because the R.F.C. (quite correctly) loaned $90,000,000 to bolster a Chicago bank dominated by General Dawes, who had been head of the R.F.C., Hoover pointed out that the ramifications of its failure would have been felt by 26,500,000 depositors in 21,755 banks! To a considerable degree the R.F.C. was successful in bolstering the basic economic structure. It remained the key finance agency of the New Deal, of the Second World War, and of the period of reconversion.

President Hoover also obtained some reform of the Federal Reserve system and establishment of home loan banks, together with further capital for existing loan banks, to help prevent mortgage foreclosures. On the issues of very large-scale public works and direct relief, he clashed bitterly with progressives and Democrats in Congress. In July 1932 he vetoed their bill as being impractical and dangerous; he felt that direct relief was a state and local responsibility. Subsequently, he signed a bill he had recommended authorizing the R.F.C. to lend $300,000,000 for relief, and another $1,500,000,000 for self-liquidating public works.

As early as February 1931 Hoover had stated his strong feeling that while people must not go cold and hungry, feeding them was a voluntary and local responsibility. "If we start appropriations of this character," he had declared, "we have not only impaired something infinitely valuable in the life of the American people but have struck at the roots of self-government." It was hard to impress the niceties of distinctions like this upon desperate people. Hoover, who for so many years had been one of the most popular of American heroes, became the scapegoat for the depression. His opponents charged him with callousness and inaction, accusations which obviously were untrue. But he was more susceptible to criticism for attacking those who were ready to go somewhat beyond him in degree, as though they were undermining the foundations of the republic.

In the progressive tradition, President Hoover had developed mildly positive programs, first voluntary, then more vigorous, for combating the depression. He had created many of the precedents for the New Deal and its lasting changes in the role of government in American society. He received little or none of the credit. Congress had been able to maneuver him in the summer of 1931 into approving funds for the feeding of cattle in areas suffering from drouth at the same time that he refused funds for humans. He had never mastered the art of politics, and his lack of suppleness during his last two years in the White House made him an easy target for the opposition. He administered the government in an atmosphere of gloom; his spirit was as depressed as that of the nation. Secretary of State Henry L. Stimson wrote in his diary in the fall of 1930, "How I wish I could cheer up the poor old President."

World Depression Shapes Foreign Policies

IN FOREIGN AFFAIRS as in domestic matters, the depression and its repercussions were the dominant theme. Before the end of the Hoover administration, at least at one point (relations with Japan), the depression threatened the major foreign-policy objective he had set forth in his acceptance address, the pursuit of peace. At that time he had declared, "We have no hates; we wish no further possessions; we harbor no military hreats."

Toward Latin America, Hoover moved still further toward what under . is successor became the "Good Neighbor" policy. Before his inauguration he toured much of the hemisphere, promoting good will; during his administration he prepared for the removal of marines from Haiti, and did finally withdraw them from Nicaragua. He refused to intervene in Cuba, which was restless under a dictatorship. Throughout Latin America, as depression toppled about half the regimes, he recognized de facto regimes without questioning the means by which they had come into power. Even when several countries defaulted on their obligations in October 1931, he did not press them to pay or threaten to seize their custom houses.

American policies toward Europe became increasingly important as economic conditions sagged. The moratorium on war-debt and reparations payments, begun in June 1931, aided temporarily. Secretary Stimson wished it to lead to a general cancellation of these hampering obligations but could not convince the President, who considered them sacred. Hoover was willing to extend the moratorium but would go no further; behind him he had the wholehearted support of Congress and the public. He condemned an agreement European powers made at Lausanne, Switzerland, in June 1932 scaling down German reparations to $714,000,000. The inevitable developed nonetheless. Germany ceased reparations payments, and within a year, nations owing the United States, except for Finland, began to default or make mere token payments. As payments stopped, neither Europe nor the United States gained in either trade or prosperity, since economic nationalism became rampant. Particularly in depressed Germany, the portents were evil, as increasing numbers of suffering people turned to Hitler to lead them out of the economic morass.

With respect to Japan, whose warlords tried to solve the nation's economic crisis by conquests on the Asiatic mainland, President Hoover and Secretary Stimson did not agree on policy. Stimson wished to use strong deterrents—sanctions and whatever they might lead to; Hoover insisted the United States should not go beyond expressions of moral disapproval. Unstable conditions in China continued throughout the twenties, and the United States was in a weak position to try to protect China from the encroachments of strong nations. As Russia became stronger, she built up her forces in eastern Siberia, and in 1929, when China tried to oust her from Northern Manchuria, fought an undeclared war to retain her foothold. Stimson tried to invoke the Kellogg-Briand pact outlawing war and to bring about mediation; he failed, demonstrating the weakness of the pact.

Japanese military leaders, feeling that their treaty rights in Southern Manchuria were being threatened both by the Russians and the Chinese Nationalists under Chiang Kai-Shek, wrested the initiative from Japan's Foreign Office in a manner little short of mutiny. In September 1931, they launched a large-scale military campaign in Manchuria at a time when the United States and Great Britain were preoccupied with the monetary crisis. For several weeks Stimson was moderate, in the hope that the civilians in the Japanese cabinet could regain control; the British were even less disposed to pursue a strong policy. The Japanese Foreign Office engaged in conciliatory talk but was unable to alter events as the army plunged deeper into Southern Manchuria. By January 2, 1932, the conquest was complete.

As early as October 1931, Stimson had felt the United States might have to co-operate with the League of Nations in imposing economic sanctions against Japan even though these might lead to war. Hoover strongly opposed such action, and in cabinet meetings discouraged Stimson by referring to the Washington treaties and the Kellogg-Briand pact as scraps of paper. He learned from the British that they too opposed sanctions. Hoover was willing to allow Stimson to exert moral suasion against the Japanese, and suggested that he apply the doctrine of nonrecognition against territorial changes brought by force of arms. When the British seemed not to concur even in this, Stimson issued a declaration unilaterally, on January 7, 1932. The statement, which came to be known as the Stimson Doctrine, asserted that the United States would not admit the legality of any changes brought about by force in China to the impairment of its territorial or administrative integrity or the open-door policy. Less than two weeks later, the Japanese attacked Shanghai. This brought the League of Nations to Stimson's position; the British were already amenable to it. When the League in February 1933 requested Japan to withdraw from Manchuria, Japan instead withdrew from the League. The League took no further action.

Expansionists remained in control in Japan, but the Manchurian crisis had brought a momentous change in American foreign policy. This nation had at last assumed strong world leadership in co-operation with the League of Nations, heaping moral opprobrium upon Japan for its aggressions. The American stand was a long way from collective security based upon economic and military pressure, but it represented a move in that direction. It also pointed the possibility, as Stimson gloomily predicted in his diary, March 9, 1932, that if Japan persisted in her course the ultimate result would be an armed clash with the United States.

In the early thirties, when the depression made the use of economic coercion seem especially undesirable, Hoover's firm position against such coercion represented overwhelmingly the prevailing public sentiment. The American people were eager to see the United States assume moral leadership against war, and nothing more. Their ideal was international disarmament, not policing. Hoover took affirmative action in trying to bring about this objective. After the Geneva Conference of 1927 had failed to extend quotas to destroyers, cruisers, and submarines, the United States had threatened to begin a substantial building program. Hoover, fearing a naval race, called a conference that opened in London in January 1930. There the United States, Great Britain, and Japan agreed not to build the capital ships authorized under the Washington treaty, and even to scrap some existing ships. They also agreed to ratios on smaller ships, to continue until 1936. Hoover had avoided a new naval race and saved taxpayers at least $300,000,000. Big-navy proponents were displeased. They charged that Hoover's subsequent failure to build smaller vessels up to treaty strength allowed Japan to become relatively stronger at a time when the United States was trying to halt its ventures in China.

Hoover's ultimate goal was general military disarmament. The United States participated vigorously in the World Disarmament Conference that opened under League sponsorship at Geneva in February 1932. With the Japanese attacking Shanghai, and Hitler daily winning new converts to his militaristic Nazi movement in Germany, the French firmly demanded an international army and compulsory arbitration rather than disarmament. In June 1932 Hoover tried to break the deadlock with a proposal to abolish immediately all offensive weapons such as bombing planes and tanks, and cut all land and naval forces approximately 30 per cent. Despite much enthusiasm for the proposal, it failed. The tide of militarism was already rising too rapidly to be halted. By January 1933 Hitler was in power, and in October 1933 he withdrew German delegates from the League of Nations and the Disarmament Conference. Along with depression, the world faced the threat of dictatorships and wars.

The Nation Suffers Privation

As the depression deepened, there were surprisingly few signs of social disorder or outbursts of violence within the United States. Communists agitated, and won a few converts among intellectual leaders, but they made almost no impact upon the masses. Nor was there any threat of a fascist movement as times became increasingly desperate. A few riotous hungry farmers broke into a store in Arkansas in July 1931, but this was exceptional.

The chain reaction of unemployment slowly spread from 1930 into 1933. At first those in marginal or poorer jobs were hit hardest, as those who had been in better jobs moved downward. In time, millions who had never been unemployed for any lengthy period of time in their lives were jobless and unable to find work of any sort. They were bewildered, for they had been brought up in the sturdy tradition of self-reliance, and during the twenties had accepted the doctrine of rugged individualism—that opportunities were limitless if only one had the ambition and energy to take advantage of them. Now they were humiliated and baffled at not being able to provide for themselves and their families. As they remained idle for months and then years, they were in danger of losing their skills as well as their morale; physical and moral erosion threatened.

Care of the unemployed was a responsibility primarily of private charity, and for several years the President and governors exhorted citizens to contribute to the Red Cross or to emergency funds. But the task

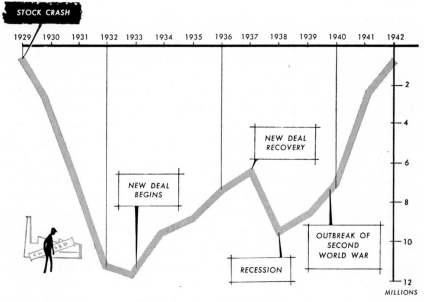

Unemployment, 1929–1942

was far too great for private charity to handle. By 1931, the Red Cross could provide only 75 cents a week to feed each hungry family in southern Illinois. The Secretary of War recommended a scheme: restaurants should scrape leftovers from diners' plates into clean five-gallon containers that could be given to the worthy needy. Edmund Wilson, as incisive a reporter as he was a literary critic, described in the *New Republic* in February 1933 the almost incredible scenes he had been witnessing in Chicago:

> There is not a garbage-dump in Chicago which is not diligently haunted by the hungry. Last summer in the hot weather when the smell was sickening and the flies were thick, there were a hundred people a day coming to one of the dumps. . . .
>
> One widow with a child of nine who had formerly made $18 a week in a factory and who has since been living on $4 a week relief and two or three hours' work a day at fifty cents an hour, has tried to get along without garbage but has had to fall back on it frequently during a period of three years. Another widow who used to do housework and laundry, but now had no work at all, fed herself and her fourteen-year-old son on garbage. Before she picked up the meat, she would always take off her glasses so that she couldn't see the maggots.

In most states, poor relief was a county obligation, and the poorhouse a byword for degradation. In several states, the poor laws were based on one that had been enacted in England in the reign of Queen Elizabeth I. Cities began dispensing relief, but soon they too reached the limit of their resources.

Although several European nations had maintained unemployment insurance programs for decades, not a single state in the United States enacted such a law until January 1932, when Wisconsin passed one. Even as the distress grew greater, many magazines and newspapers proclaimed that any permanent system of direct unemployment relief like the British dole would bankrupt the government and undermine the moral fiber of the recipients. It was not until September 1931 that the New York state legislature, at the insistence of Governor Franklin D. Roosevelt, established the first relief organization of any state, the Temporary Emergency Relief Administration, which became the model for other states and the prototype of the later federal relief agency. Roosevelt insisted that it be established on a pay-as-you-go basis but within six months was forced to advocate borrowing. The T.E.R.A. offered relief to nearly 10 per cent of the families in the state, providing them with an average of approximately $23 per month. In the ensuing six years it aided, at one or another time (bolstered by federal funds), some five million people, about 40 per cent of the population of the state. By 1937, 70 per cent of these no longer needed government aid.

To some unemployed who had recently moved to cities, the solution seemed to be to return to the farm; the migration away from farms was reversed. But farm prices fell so low that once again on parts of the plains farmers burned corn to keep warm. A rancher sold seven lambs in the Denver livestock market, and after paying commissions and fees received a check for 75 cents. In a railroad diner, two lambchops cost the same amount. Prices of manufactured goods were relatively so high that it took ten bushels of wheat to buy a cheap pair of shoes. In drouth areas farmers lacked even sufficient food.

This is what had happened to farm prices:

	COTTON, per pound	CORN AND WHEAT, per bushel	
1919	$ .353	$1.51	$2.16
1929	.167	.79	1.03
1932	.065	.31	.38

Some bewildered farmers around Sioux City, Iowa, in 1932 embargoed milk bound into the city, because they were receiving two cents a quart and it retailed for eight cents. Many more Iowa farmers participated in

Milo Reno's militant Farmers' Holiday Association to block all farm products from the market until prices went higher. But this was a futile gesture. Most farmers waited for the election of 1932.

Through the summer of 1932, some twelve to fourteen thousand unemployed veterans began to congregate in Washington demonstrating for the immediate payments of their bonus for wartime service, not due until 1945. For weeks they lived in squalor in abandoned tenements, and in shanties on the mud flats of the Anacostia River. After Congress failed to

General MacArthur watching the burning of the bonus encampment (UNITED PRESS PHOTO)

pass a bonus bill, about half of them, discouraged, went home. The remainder, who would probably have left ultimately, alarmed Hoover and many Washingtonians. After a riot, the President called upon the army to oust them. Under the personal command of General Douglas MacArthur, with tanks, gas masks, and fixed bayonets, the army did so. "That was a bad-looking mob," MacArthur declared. "It was animated by the essence of revolution."

Surprisingly enough, apparently it was not. Nor, as was later charged, was it Communist-led. The hundred-odd Communists in the Bonus Expeditionary Force were too inept to take over leadership, and received rough treatment from their fellows. Like other unemployed, the bonus marchers were ready to wait for the election.

The farmers' strike and the bonus march were symptomatic of the times. They frightened the administration and helped contribute to its unpopularity, but they did not really threaten revolution. Even in this period of extreme despair, Americans were ready to turn to the ballot box. There was little doubt how a sizable majority would vote. Throughout the country, the President had become the butt of every depression joke. Every shanty settlement of unemployed was called a "Hooverville," and the newspapers under which its inhabitants tried to keep warm were "Hoover blankets."

1932: Protest at the Polls

REPUBLICANS MEETING in Chicago renominated Hoover in a spirit far from jubilant; they had few illusions about what the outcome of the election would be. The Democrats, assembling later in an excited, expectant mood, saw almost certain victory after twelve years out of power. Almost anyone they nominated was sure to be elected.

Well over a majority of the candidates came pledged to vote for Governor Roosevelt of New York. Roosevelt, who astutely had been working for the nomination for years, to a considerable degree had bridged the gulf between the urban and rural Democrats. He was ready to emphasize economic issues and ignore the earlier divisions over prohibition and religion. His opponents, who hoped to keep him from obtaining the necessary two-thirds vote in the convention, were an unstable coalition of the urban followers of Al Smith, Eastern conservatives, and the Southwestern supporters of Speaker John Nance Garner of Texas. Had the "Allies" stood firm they could have deadlocked the convention and nominated a compromise candidate, probably Newton D. Baker, Wilson's Secretary of War. But Garner, wishing no repetition of the 1924 fiasco, on the fourth ballot swung his delegates and the nomination to Roosevelt. To placate the Texans, Garner accepted nomination for the Vice-Presidency, although he would have preferred to remain in the more powerful speakership.

Roosevelt, breaking precedent, flew immediately to Chicago to deliver his acceptance address before the convention. He endorsed the Democratic platform, which except for a promise of prohibition repeal was not much bolder than that of the Republicans, and in his peroration declared, "I pledge you, I pledge myself, to a new deal for the American people." Thus the Roosevelt program acquired a name before the electorate had more than the haziest notion of what it might embody.

Nor did they learn much during the campaign, for Roosevelt astutely confined himself to warm generalities which would offend few, yet suffice to bring him the enormous vote of protest against Hoover. Early in the campaign he was so cautious that the Republican press, hinting that his health was none too good, warned against his running mate, Garner, as an inflationary prairie radical. This was bad prophecy, for Garner in turn was privately warning Roosevelt against radical schemes. Through Roosevelt's speeches ran many of the old progressive themes, together with the new suggestions of economic planning. An able team, largely of university professors under the leadership of Raymond Moley, helped devise policies and draft speeches for him. Newspapermen dubbed them the "Brain Trust." Most of what Roosevelt said was their handiwork carefully balanced to meet his campaign needs. At the Commonwealth Club in San Francisco, he broke most sharply with the past by insisting that the government must assist business in developing an economic constitutional order. "Private economic power is," he declared, ". . . a public trust as well." Everyone had a right to a comfortable living; the nation's industrial and agricultural mechanism could produce enough and to spare. If need be, to achieve this end, government must police irresponsible economic power. Roosevelt felt he was doing no more than restate the objectives of Jefferson and Wilson in terms of the complexities of the thirties when he proposed that government should act as a regulator for the common good within the existing economic system. So far as Roosevelt explained the New Deal during the campaign, this was its essence.

To each of the main groups within the United States Roosevelt pledged something. At Topeka, Kansas, he delivered his main farm speech, so phrased that it would seem to promise to the Farm Bureau the new domestic allotment scheme, and to other farm groups their pet panaceas, yet all so ambiguously that it would not upset Easterners. At Portland, Oregon, he spoke more forthrightly in favor of strict public utility regulation, and public development of power in some areas as a yardstick to measure private rates. It was the doctrine for which Senator Norris and progressive Republicans had battled vehemently but futilely through the twenties; to many of them it was the paramount issue in the campaign. Roosevelt's strong position on public power, based upon his equally firm stand as governor of New York, brought him the support of Norris and most of his following.

To the business community, and to conservatives within his own party, Roosevelt pledged at Pittsburgh that he would cut government spending 25 per cent and balance the budget. (He left the loophole that he would operate the government at a deficit if starvation or dire want necessitated it). Roosevelt charged that the budget had gone up approximately a billion dollars, or roughly 50 per cent, between 1927 and 1931, "the most reckless and extravagant past that I have been able to discover in the statistical record of any peacetime Government anywhere, any time." Ludicrous as this seems in retrospect, Roosevelt was thoroughly serious. He believed in government economy as essential to recovery.

President Hoover, tired and grim, took to the road in October to warn the populace that without his program things might be infinitely worse. His speeches were earnest, but dull and dreary in both style and delivery compared with Roosevelt's breezy, optimistic performances. Hoover was the last of the Presidents to scorn the aid of speechwriters. He placed much emphasis upon the protective tariff, and ridiculed Roosevelt's many equivocal tariff statements as being like a chameleon on plaid. Hoover's own tariff pronouncements seemed equally ridiculous when he charged that if the Democratic policies were introduced, "The grass will grow in the streets of a hundred cities, a thousand towns; the weeds will overrun the fields of millions of farms."

The President also pressed Roosevelt hard on sound money; to Hoover the gold standard was vital and he was alarmed over rumors that Roosevelt meant to abandon it. And of course Hoover reiterated his determination to balance the budget. Thus he chose to emphasize those parts of his own program for combatting the depression which later-day economists would regard as negative or deflationary. Although he had extended the economic responsibilities of the government further than any previous President, he proclaimed his alarm because Roosevelt was hinting that they should be extended slightly further. Hoover warned that the election was a contest between two rival philosophies of government and that Roosevelt was "proposing changes and so-called new deals which would destroy the very foundations of our American system."

Few intellectuals agreed with Hoover. Some of them were disappointed because they could detect little difference between Roosevelt's program and Hoover's, and turned to Norman Thomas and the Socialists or to William Z. Foster and the Communists, but in this year of despair the Socialists polled only 882,000 votes, and the Communists 103,000. American voters might not be able to see any vast difference between Hoover and Roosevelt, but they supported Roosevelt by a heavy majority. He received 22,822,000 popular votes, or 57.4 per cent, to 15,762,000 (39.7 per cent) for Hoover, and carried the electoral college 472 to 92. The Democrats carried both houses of Congress by topheavy majorities. Roosevelt had won an overwhelming mandate—but for what?

Actually, there had been discernible differences between the two candidates and their programs other than the obvious one that Hoover was a worn, discredited President and Roosevelt a buoyant candidate. Hoover had seen the depression as worldwide in origin and development; rather inconsistently he was ready to combat it internationally through currency stabilization, and nationally through raising the tariff still higher if need be. Roosevelt chose to regard the depression as domestic, specifically Republican, in origin. During the campaign, Hoover had forced him to equivocate on the old Democratic low-tariff position; Roosevelt was ready (as both his record as governor and his speeches indicated) to move toward economic nationalism. Like Hoover, he believed in economy and a balanced budget, although these would run contrary to his advocacy of social and economic planning. Unlike Hoover he was so far from being doctrinaire that inconsistencies in his program would bother him little.

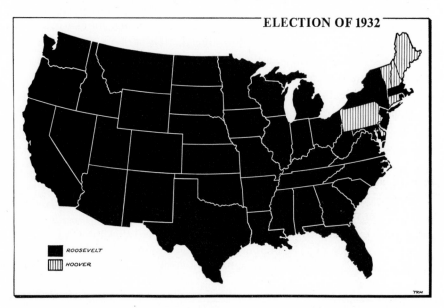

ELECTION OF 1932

ROOSEVELT
HOOVER

There was little doubt that the positive aspects of his program would win out, and that, once in office, he would translate his campaign speeches into the New Deal.

The Crisis of the Interregnum

PRESIDENT HOOVER faced an agonizing four months before Roosevelt would take office on March 4: Norris's Twentieth ("lame duck") Amendment to end this long carryover of a defeated President and Congress was not ratified until February 1933. As the economy plummeted once again Hoover ascribed the drop to lack of business confidence in the incoming President. There had been a brief economic upswing in the spring months of 1932, reaching a peak in July. (Economists later ascribed this rise to Hoover's own brief plunge into deficit financing through public-works spending and Reconstruction Finance Corporation loans.) Hoover felt he was bringing an end to the depression and that only the threat of unsettling measures from Roosevelt was preventing continued recovery. Hence, in a series of interchanges with Roosevelt during the winter of

1932–1933, he tried to bind the President-elect to economic orthodoxy.

The first negotiations were over the question of European debts. Both Hoover and Roosevelt opposed cancellation, but Hoover wished to use the debts as a lever to re-establish an international gold standard. Tied in with this was the proposed International Economic and Monetary Conference, which Hoover hoped would restore financial stability. Roosevelt would make no commitments in these areas, but did carry on friendly conversations with Secretary of State Stimson in which he endorsed the administration's Far Eastern policy.

By February 1933 an acute banking crisis had developed. Bank resources and deposits had been declining at an alarming rate. In the previous three years 5,000 banks had failed, and one after another was collapsing as depositors lined up to withdraw their deposits. To prevent failures, governors began proclaiming banking holidays in their states, beginning with Michigan on February 14; by March 4, banking was at a halt or drastically restricted in all states but one.

President Hoover penned a lengthy longhand letter to Roosevelt, charging that the crisis was due to "steadily degenerating confidence" in the President-elect, and calling upon him to give prompt public assurance that there would be no tinkering with the currency, no heavy borrowing, and a balanced budget. Hoover explained elsewhere that Roosevelt must disavow the underwriting of mortgages and public works, and the development of the Tennessee Valley. "I realize that if these declarations be made by the President-elect," Hoover wrote "he will have ratified the whole major program of the Republican Administration; that is, it means the abandonment of 90 per cent of the so-called new deal." Roosevelt did not even answer the President's letter for eleven days; he had not the slightest intention of abandoning his plans. Had Roosevelt accepted the repudiated program of his predecessor, it is hard to see how this would have stemmed the banking panic. Depositors were worried about the strength of individual banks, not the gold standard. In any event, on March 4, President Hoover, glum and exhausted, left office, the problem of the depression still not solved. Could Roosevelt and the New Deal do better?

Chapter *13*

THE ROOSEVELT
REVOLUTION

IN A PERIOD of one hundred days following the inauguration of Franklin D. Roosevelt in March 1933 the Congress embarked on one of the largest and most remarkable legislative programs in American history. As the White House sent one bill after another to the Capitol for action, the government for the first time tried to utilize its full powers to pull the nation out of the depression. The direction of the recovery program was not new—indeed, President Hoover had already tried to persuade business and agriculture to head along the same path voluntarily. The Roosevelt program still emphasized voluntarism but provided far stronger positive incentives and negative penalties. It was based on the principles of progressivism and the techniques of the agencies of the First World War. But in breadth and scale the early New Deal went so far beyond Hoover's tentative measures and anything else previously known in peacetime that a Washington newspaperman, Ernest K. Lindley, with some reason entitled his account of it *The Roosevelt Revolution*. Under the first Roosevelt the government had begun to assume a significant role in the economy; under the second Roosevelt it took command in time of crisis.

Roosevelt's Leadership

AS THE AMERICAN ECONOMY careened dizzily downward in the winter of 1932–33, the one hope was that somehow the new President would be able to bring a return to prosperity. By the time Roosevelt took office in March, most of the nation's banks were closed and the industrial index had sunk from 64 in December (compared with 1929) to a low of 56. At least thirteen million people were unemployed, and several hundred thousand were homeless wanderers living in shanty towns on dumps or under bridges. Millions of farmers faced foreclosure of their mortgages; many others had already lost their land. The measures of Hoover, despite their novelty and scope, had done little to rejuvenate the nation's economy.

Few people had much idea what to do about the situation. In February 1933, when the nation's business and financial leaders testified before the Senate Finance Committee, banking, insurance, railroad, and steel magnates had nothing to suggest except perhaps more economic orthodoxy. "Balance budgets," advised the financial sage, Bernard Baruch. "Stop spending money we haven't got. Sacrifice for frugality and revenue. Cut government spending—cut it as rations are cut in a siege. Tax—tax everybody for everything." Democratic leaders in Congress seemed bent upon defining the New Deal in advance for Roosevelt by enacting a conservative program including a deflationary sales tax. Leaders outside of Congress thought similarly. The Democratic party, declared Al Smith, should free itself of "the populists . . . with their free-silver and other economic heresies . . . [and] the mountebanks with their cloutish antics and their irresponsible ravings against millionaires and big business." In addition, Smith hinted, the nation should follow the precedent of the World War, wrap up the Constitution and lay it on the shelf until the crisis was over.

Roosevelt chose to repudiate both courses, that of economic orthodoxy on the one hand and that of drastic dictatorial action on the other. He would not accept a sales tax, nor would he upset democratic processes. What he would do of a positive nature was not yet clear. Neither he nor his advisors were any more clear in their thinking than the conservatives. What was important was that Roosevelt, while basically rooted in the older economics and the social-justice tradition of the progressives, was ready to experiment. His program would be flexible, not doctrinaire; the new economic theories would grow from it, not it from the theories. When one of the brain trusters warned of perils ahead, Roosevelt declared, "There is nothing to do but meet every day's troubles as they come." This was Roosevelt's political pragmatism, and out of it grew the New Deal economic policies.

Pragmatism also guided Roosevelt in the selection of his cabinet, in which he balanced diverse political, sectional, and economic interests. For Secretary of the Treasury he had to turn first to that Democratic financial conservative, Senator Carter Glass, architect of the Federal Reserve system, but he did so refusing to pledge orthodoxy. When Glass declined, he turned to an amiable Republican businessman, William Woodin, acceptable to Wall Street yet long Roosevelt's supporter. For Secretary of State he chose Senator Cordell Hull, an ardent low-tariff advocate who had been his stanchest Southern ally. For Secretary of Agriculture, he picked a young farm editor from Iowa, Henry A. Wallace, son of Harding's Secretary of Agriculture and candidate of the Farm Bureau Federation. Although a Republican, Wallace had supported Smith in 1928, and Roosevelt during the 1932 campaign. For Secretary of the Interior Roosevelt wanted another Republican progressive. Ultimately he took a former Bull Mooser from Chicago previously unknown to him, Harold L. Ickes.

In recognition of the growing importance of women in politics, Roosevelt wished to put a woman in his cabinet for the first time in American history. The logical department was Labor, although previously a sinecure for some unionist, because it performed most of the social welfare functions of the government. Roosevelt chose Frances Perkins, who had served brilliantly as Industrial Commissioner in New York. For Attorney General he chose Senator Thomas J. Walsh of Montana, who had led in exposing the Harding scandals. When Walsh died just before Inauguration Day, Roosevelt turned to an old Wilsonian, Homer Cummings, who had helped obtain his nomination. For Postmaster General, he appointed his energetic "political drummer," James A. Farley. Other cabinet appointments went to Southerners and a Westerner. Subordinate positions went to deserving Democrats, and to brain trusters, some of whom did much to shape the New Deal. Roosevelt, who himself was not much of an intellectual, was ready to draw upon the talents of men of learning. In the first exciting days of the New Deal, thousands of brilliant young men and women flocked to Washington to work with a degree of energy and dedication reminiscent of the Bull Moose movement.

No one could have guessed in those black days that the incoming President would set his mark on the age as have few American chief executives. He alarmed even those closest to him with his amiability, his ready acceptance of suggestions, his quick "Fine, fine, fine." New Yorkers, fearful that his jaunty buoyancy, his facility at compromise, and his skill at political maneuver were a façade for weakness, sometimes had referred to him as "the Grin," or the "Boy Scout Governor." They did not as yet see the en-

President and Mrs. Roosevelt returning to the White House from the inauguration, 1941 (FRANKLIN D. ROOSEVELT LIBRARY)

ergy and persistence with which he applied himself, or the cold iron sometimes not far beneath the charm. His physical courage they realized, for after his polio attack in 1921 he had indomitably stayed in politics, refusing to surrender to his infirmity. He had subordinated it so thoroughly that most people regarded him only as somewhat lame, and never thought of him as using a wheelchair. Again he demonstrated this trait at Miami in February 1933 by remaining astoundingly calm when an insane assassin missed him but mortally wounded the Mayor of Chicago sitting beside him. Somehow Roosevelt was able to transmit some of this personal courage to the nation in March 1933.

Few Presidents have been better trained for the White House. Roosevelt had served in the New York state senate, been wartime Assistant Secretary of the Navy, and had been twice elected governor of New York. He was skilled in both legislative and administrative techniques as well as in practical politics. As a youth he had spent much time in Europe, and maintained a continuing interest in foreign affairs. Roosevelt's ideology was progressive, molded by his wife's uncle, Theodore Roosevelt, whom he adored, and his former chief, Woodrow Wilson, whom he revered. Frequently political exigencies forced Roosevelt beyond progressivism; at other times, to the dismay of some of his followers, he seemed more a progressive than a New Dealer.

The New Deal Begins

THERE WAS LITTLE NEW or startling in the beginnings of the New Deal. On March 4, 1933, at his inaugural, President Roosevelt addressed himself to all the American people. "This great Nation will endure as it has endured, will revive and will prosper," he declared. "So, first of all, let me assert my firm belief that the only thing we have to fear is fear itself." Somehow these words, although they said nothing new, helped inspire the American people. From their depths of helplessness they were ready for the moment to be commanded, and in Roosevelt they saw someone ready to take strong leadership. In his Inaugural Address he promised it. If Congress did not act, he asserted, he would ask for "broad executive power to wage a war against the emergency, as great as the power that would be given to me if we were in fact invaded by a foreign foe." For the moment, with the banking crisis at its height, he might well have taken drastic steps: nationalized the banks or even, perhaps, set aside the Constitution. The temper of the American people was such that they would not have long tolerated such drastic measures; the background of Roosevelt was such that he resorted to only the mildest of expedients.

During his first days as President, Roosevelt seemed bent above all upon restoring the confidence of businessmen. His initial program differed little from what they had been advocating. First he solved the banking crisis in a manner pleasing to the banking community. He issued a proclamation on March 6, 1932, closing all banks and stopping transactions or exports in gold for four days until Congress could meet in special session. On March 9, he sent it a conservative bill which would bolster the stronger banks. It authorized the Federal Reserve system to issue notes against their assets, and the Reconstruction Finance Corporation to make them loans. The bill dealt a death blow to weaker banks; inspectors would deny them licenses to reopen. It stopped the ebb of gold from the Treasury and the country through prohibiting hoarding and exportation. In effect, the country went off the gold standard (officially it did so April 19, 1933). Congress passed the bill within four hours of its introduction. In the House, a rolled-up newspaper substituted for it, since there had not been time to print copies; in the Senate, seven Western progressives opposed it as strengthening the Wall Street monopoly. This was indeed a conservative measure to promote recovery rather than a reform bill. New Dealers began almost at once to plan banking reform, but it came later.

On March 12, in the first of his "fireside chats" over the radio, the President, speaking in a warm, intimate manner, told the American people that the crisis was over. "I can assure you," he declared, "that it is safer to keep your money in a reopened bank than under the mattress." And so indeed it was; by this simple legislation and his confident leadership, Roosevelt had averted the threat to banks and the capitalist system. Three-fourths of the banks in the Federal Reserve system reopened within the next three days; a billion dollars in hoarded currency and gold flowed back into them within a month. During the next two years the R.F.C. loaned a billion dollars to shaky banks; the Treasury Department refused to license another 1,772 of them. Practically all unsafe banks were out of business; altogether the crisis had closed a total of 2,352. There were very few new failures in the years that followed.

On the morning after the passage of the Emergency Banking Act, Roosevelt further reassured business by sending Congress an economy bill, to balance the budget by cutting salaries of government employees and pensions of veterans as much as 15 per cent. It was, Roosevelt declared, the only way to avoid a billion-dollar deficit. This bill too passed almost instantly, although with such fierce opposition from veterans' organizations that it carried the House only with Republican votes. Pressure from veterans soon led Congress to rescind the pension cuts over Roosevelt's veto, but the President slashed drastically the regular expenditures of the government. Services of many agencies like the National Bureau of Standards were seriously curtailed; its budget was cut in half within two years, and did not return to the 1931 level until 1940. The Department of Agriculture dismissed 567 workers on scientific projects, and salaries of some scientific and specialized employees dropped to little better than work-relief levels. Thus Roosevelt balanced his regular budget, and took pride in keeping it balanced. He did so in the only way possible at the time, by reducing many valuable government services. Parallel to the regular budget, Roosevelt established an emergency budget, and this was another matter.

On March 13, 1933, Roosevelt proposed legalizing beer of 3.2 per cent alcoholic content, pending repeal of the prohibition amendment. This, he felt, would stimulate recovery and bring in needed taxes. (It also rescued millions of law violators from the rigors of home brew and gangster-made beer).

Thus far, except for the gold clause in the Emergency Banking Act, the program of the new administration might have been that of a Hoover with a smile. It had to a startling degree restored the confidence of bankers and businessmen. The stock market had gone up 15 per cent. However, this was no more than anticipatory of real recovery to follow, since for the moment nothing had been improved but the confidence of the American nation.

The nation, hysterically relieved and grateful over the ending of the banking crisis, looked to Roosevelt for leadership. Public opinion, the press—even the Chicago *Tribune*—and a heavy majority of congressmen were his to command. Roosevelt was expert enough in politics to know that this was the psychological moment to push through Congress a comprehensive program, and he was clever enough in manipulating legislators to know how to maintain their support. He did not need to undertake the tedious task of building a New Deal party, even if he had known what that might be. The existing majorities in the Congress were his; old-line Democratic conservatives and unruly Republican progressives, together with uncertain Democratic freshmen, were all ready to vote his bidding. He could be slow about dispensing patronage, again of great weight in this time of unemployment, could exercise all the arts of personal persuasion, and, through his radio fireside chats, could whip up public support like a prairie fire. This was an unprecedented opportunity, and Roosevelt took full advantage of it. He decided to keep Congress in special session, and in the next hundred-odd days pushed through it a remarkable array of legislation. Thus the New Deal took form.

The most important of this legislation aimed at recovery. As with the banking measure, Roosevelt felt that he was acting in a time of economic emergency, little different from the seriousness of war. Through his emergency program, he hoped to bring about recovery in a matter of months. Meanwhile, he felt the federal government must itself intervene to keep people from starving and losing their homes and farms. He therefore proposed much relief legislation. In addition, he wished long-range measures that would eliminate the evils responsible for the depression and would make future depressions impossible. Some legislation of this nature was passed during the hundred days, but much of it would take lengthy planning. Consequently, in the spring of 1933 the emphasis was upon recovery and relief rather than reform.

Roosevelt began bombarding Congress with messages and draft bills proposing, on:

March 16	—	*an agricultural recovery program;*
March 21	—	*unemployment relief;*
March 29	—	*federal supervision of investment securities;*
April 10	—	*creation of a Tennessee Valley Authority;*
April 13	—	*prevention of mortgage foreclosures on homes;*
May 4	—	*railroad recovery legislation;*
May 17	—	*an industrial recovery program.*

By June 16, 1933, with the passage of the National Industrial Recovery Act, Congress had enacted all the proposed legislation.

Enacting Relief and Recovery Measures

THE FIRST STEP, even ahead of recovery, was to feed the millions of hungry unemployed. While Roosevelt subscribed to his predecessor's maxim that relief was primarily the task of states and communities, he proposed that the federal government provide grants rather than loans to states. Congress established the Federal Emergency Relief Administration, and appropriated an initial half-billion dollars for it. Roosevelt appointed the director of the New York state relief agency, Harry Hopkins, whom he hardly knew as yet, to run the federal program. Hopkins was a dedicated social worker with a lively tongue and a keen sense of professional ethics. To the exasperation of Farley and many Democratic party leaders, Hopkins appointed the men he considered best qualified regardless of their party affiliations. He labored zealously to establish high professional standards throughout the state emergency relief administrations in return for their federal grants. Hopkins ardently believed in work relief rather than direct relief, but in the spring of 1933 everyone hoped recovery was at hand so that relief would be needed only for a few months.

Congress also created an organization that reflected Roosevelt's keen interest in preserving natural as well as human resources, the Civilian Conservation Corps. It received a grant of $300,000,000 to enroll 250,000 young men from relief families and 50,000 veterans and woodsmen to work at reforestation and flood control. Ultimately the C.C.C. enrolled 500,000 young men, but this was only a fraction of the unemployed youths in the nation. Almost alone among the New Deal agencies it received a highly favorable press through the thirties. Roosevelt also visualized public-works construction as a means of putting large numbers of men to work, but this came to be tied in with his industrial recovery program and developed more slowly.

Mortgage relief was a pressing need of millions of farm owners and home owners. Roosevelt quickly consolidated all farm credit organizations into a new Farm Credit Administration. Congress voted such large additional funds for it that within two years it had refinanced a fifth of all farm mortgages in the United States. For farmers who had already lost their farms, the Frazier-Lemke Farm Bankruptcy Act of June 1933 made recovery possible on reasonable terms. Unfortunately, these measures came too late to save many farmers; by 1934, a quarter of them for one reason or another had lost their property. A comparable Home Owners' Loan Corporation, established in June 1933, in a three-year period loaned three billion dollars to refinance the mortgages of over a million distressed

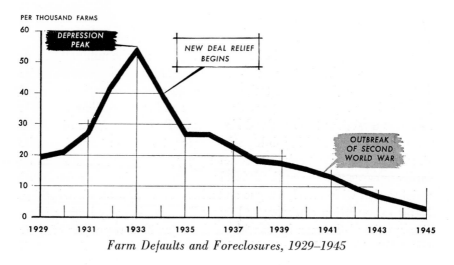

PER THOUSAND FARMS

Farm Defaults and Foreclosures, 1929–1945

householders. Altogether it carried about a sixth of the nation's urban mortgage burden. A year later, Congress established a Federal Housing Administration to insure mortgages for new construction and home repairs —more properly a recovery than a relief agency. All these mortgage agencies not only rescued mortgage holders, but also eased the burden on banks and insurance companies, thus filling a recovery function.

Under the New Deal, the Reconstruction Finance Corporation continued to function as the key loan agency. The Democratic Congress, which had inveighed against the R.F.C. policy of making large loans at the top which would provide aid to the individual only by trickling down, broadened its loaning powers. It could, and indeed did, lend to small businessmen. Under the conservative management of a shrewd Texan, Jesse Jones, it continued to make most of its loans to large enterprises and governmental units, on sound security and with a high percentage of ultimate repayment. Between its establishment in 1932 and the defense crisis in 1941, it poured fifteen billion dollars into the American economy.

Altogether these relief and recovery agencies spent unparalleled sums during the thirties and thus, in the view of later economists, contributed substantially to recovery. However, public spending was not their primary aim at the time they were established.

Two other agencies came into existence to undertake the fundamental task of recovery. These were the Agricultural Adjustment Administration and the National Recovery Administration, at the heart of the early New Deal program. The one applied to agriculture and the other to industry, but they were both based on the premise that one of the basic reasons for

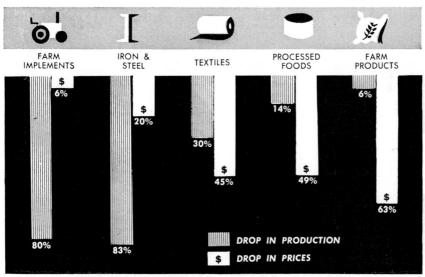

FARM IMPLEMENTS	IRON & STEEL	TEXTILES	PROCESSED FOODS	FARM PRODUCTS

DROP IN PRODUCTION
$ DROP IN PRICES

Adjustment of Various Industries to the Depression

the continued depression was overproduction. During the campaign of 1932 Roosevelt had asserted, "Our industrial plant is built; the problem just now is whether under existing conditions it is not overbuilt. Our last frontier has long since been reached." Manufacturers of heavy equipment and consumer durable goods of most sorts had cut production drastically and maintained relatively high prices. Other manufacturers and the farmers had maintained high levels of production, but their prices had fallen disastrously. The task seemed to be to cut production in areas like textiles and farm products in order to bring prices back in line with those of durable goods. This procedure, it was argued, would bring a return to prosperity, and with greater prosperity, production could again expand.

There could be no doubt how drastic deflation had become. Here are some prices advertised by a market in the Los Angeles area on September 6, 1932:

Bread, 1-pound loaf	5¢
Tomatoes, 8 pounds	5¢
Lettuce, per head	1¢
Sliced bacon, per pound	10¢
Spring lamb chops, per pound	12½¢
Choice sirloin steak, per pound	20¢

The pressure upon the New Dealers to raise prices was most persuasive. But one serious difficulty in the way of raising prices was the low purchasing power of consumers. Few people could afford to eat lamb chops or steak, even at the prices of 1932–1933. They would be able to buy more only if their purchasing power went up more rapidly than prices, but producers rather than consumers drafted the plans for the A.A.A. and N.R.A. These recovery agencies took Roosevelt only one step beyond the conservative so-called Jeffersonian Democrats. Aside from limited public-works expenditures, Roosevelt wanted a recovery program that would not be a drain on governmental finances. Neither the A.A.A. nor the N.R.A. were. Both of these programs reflected not the progressivism of the first years of the century, but the progressive methods of regulating production during the First World War. In other words, these agencies were to provide regulation that would as far as possible protect both producers and consumers, both employers and employees. This was the ideal of the New Dealers too. Roosevelt especially wished the New Deal to benefit everyone in one fashion or another. Unlike wartime measures, the new agencies were to reduce output in most areas rather than raise it, and encourage price increases rather than restrain them. Thus, waging a war on the depression was in some ways the reverse of waging one on a foreign foe.

Limiting Crops to Raise Farm Prices

THE AGRICULTURE ADJUSTMENT ADMINISTRATION, created in May 1933, marked the triumphant conclusion of the farmers' struggle for so many decades to obtain aid from the government. It was the logical climax to the Granger and Populist movements, and the drive for farm relief in the twenties. Henceforth, although the farmers formed a diminishing fraction of the population, they received preferential treatment from the government. Partly this was because of a growing realization of Roosevelt's paraphrase of Lincoln, "This Nation cannot endure . . . half 'boom' and half 'broke.'" Mostly it was because farmers had formed such an integral part of Roosevelt's victorious coalition that the Republicans could win them back only if they promised comparable benefits.

Among the farmers, Roosevelt looked especially to the relatively substantial ones, such as the 300,000 who even in 1933 were paying dues of
$10 a year or more to the Farm Bureau Federation. These and the Grange
wished a domestic-allotment program to limit crops. Poorer members of
other farm organizations like the Farmers' Union and the National Farmers' Holiday Association opposed production cuts, seeking instead direct
relief and, above all, inflation. Roosevelt could not ignore them altogether.
As he had proposed in his farm speech in the 1932 campaign, he tried to
develop a farm program which would fit the Farm Bureau formula, yet
not drive poorer farmers into new revolt. In effect, Roosevelt let the farm
organization leaders devise their own program. Fifty of them met in Washington early in March 1933 and drafted an omnibus bill which contained
scraps and reworkings of most of the old schemes. Primarily it provided
for the "domestic-allotment" plan. Producers of seven basic commodities
(wheat, cotton, corn, hogs, rice, tobacco, and milk and dairy products)
were to receive benefit payments if they cut acreage or production. Funds
for these payments would come from a processing tax upon the commodities. This meant taxing consumers to subsidize the farmer to grow less.
In addition, the consumers would have to pay higher prices. For the
farmer, prices were to be brought up to "parity," which in this instance
was the average for the years 1909–1914 when the price relationship of
farm products to manufactured goods had been particularly favorable.

"The sole aim and object of this act is to raise farm prices," declared
the first head of the A.A.A., the Republican George Peek, as he took office.
This remained the basic objective not only of Peek but of the Farm Bureau
Federation and the Grange, which made their influence felt strongly both
in the Department of Agriculture and with Congress. The spokesmen of
the poorer prairie farmers were active too in pressing their inflationary
ideas. As the agricultural bill went through Congress, Senator Elmer
Thomas of Oklahoma added to it an amendment permitting the President
to inflate the credit and currency in six different ways. This, Thomas felt,
was the way to raise farm prices. Peek did not worry about monetary un-
orthodoxy as a means of inflation, even though it did not impress him.
He remarked, "We can use gold or brass or tin or buffalo chips."

The debate over how best to improve the farmers' lot carried over into
the A.A.A. There the agrarians, mostly of farm background, seeking little
more than higher prices, fought the liberals who believed also in agricultural reform and protection of consumers. Peek called the liberals the
"boys with their hair ablaze," and the agrarians liked to whisper that
one of their chief opponents knew so little about agriculture that he wanted
to aid the macaroni growers. Subsequent attacks upon the liberal wing
of the A.A.A., because it included a small group of radicals and even Com-

munists, were more damaging. With the sanction of Wallace, many of the liberals were driven from the A.A.A. in February 1935.

Because the 1933 farm season was well under way when the A.A.A. began operations, large-scale destruction was necessary to cut surpluses. Six million pigs and 220,000 sows about to farrow were slaughtered. Nine tenths of their weight was inedible and processed into fertilizer, but they did provide 100 million pounds of pork for needy families. Opponents of the New Deal long cited this slaughter as one of its prime iniquities. To the relief of Wallace, bad weather so drastically cut the wheat crop that the A.A.A. did not have to intervene and then "explain the logic of plowing under wheat while millions lacked bread." Beginning in August, cotton farmers destroyed a quarter of their crop—but it was the poorest quarter and they so intensively cultivated the rest that thirty million acres produced somewhat more than thirty-six million had done the previous year.

Despite continued high cotton production, a short textile boom sent the price up from 5.5 cents per pound to 10.6 cents in the summer. Then it began to sag again, and was held to 9.6 cents in November only through another device. A subsidiary of the R.F.C., the Commodity Credit Corporation, loaned 10 cents per pound to cotton farmers who would agree to take additional land out of production the next year. Since the loan was in excess of the market value of cotton, the government in effect was buying the crop at a premium price upon the promise of drastic cuts in production. In this way cotton farmers received double the cash in 1933 that they had in 1931.

Farmers in other crop-reduction programs did not fare as well, although corn producers too could obtain commodity loans in the fall of 1933. The total income of all farmers went up only a fifth over 1932, and still lagged behind 1931. Rising prices of manufactured goods wiped away most of the farmers' gain in real income. In the following two years, through the marketing quotas set under the Bankhead Cotton Control Act of 1934, cotton production was cut from 13,000,000 bales to 9,600,000 in 1934 and 10,600,000 in 1935. After that, production began to soar again. Drought more than production quotas similarly reduced the output of wheat and corn and hogs. The cash income of farmers jumped from $4,700,000,000 in 1932 to $8,700,000,000 in 1936, and was even higher the following year. The relative position of the farmer improved. On the parity yardstick of 100 for the years 1909–1914, the ratio of prices of farm products to those of manufactured goods increased from 61 in 1932 to 86 in 1935. But it was a depressed parity the farmers were achieving, since farm income did not exceed the quite inadequate 1929 amount until 1941.

Apparently the A.A.A. was of only negligible help in bringing national recovery. The government payments of $1,500,000,000 through 1936 could not have had much effect on the economy as a whole, since through the processing taxes they were collected from the consumers, whose buying power was diminished accordingly. The droughts, which cut production and helped liquidate accumulated farm surpluses, contributed as much as the A.A.A. in bringing the farm nearer to parity.

"The Cotton Pickers" by Thomas Hart Benton (METROPOLITAN MUSEUM OF ART, THE GEORGE A. HEARN FUND)

At the same time, quite contrary to the wishes of liberal New Dealers, the A.A.A. actually hurt many of the smaller marginal and submarginal farmers. In the cotton belt, especially, it did little to help them. Two Southern authorities on sharecropping, T. J. Woofter, Jr. and Ellen Winston, wrote in 1939:

Total family incomes in a good year (1934 with a fair cotton crop at twelve cents a pound) averaged on the efficient plantations $312 for croppers and $417 for other share tenants. This included food raised and consumed by the family. . . . The 18,000,000 bale crop of 1937 so reduced the price that it is probable that the average cropper did not have more than $75 in net cash at the end of the year and the lowest fourth either came out in debt or did not have enough to replace the overalls and brogan shoes worn out in working the crop. Living standards as expressed in the miserable shacks that croppers and other share tenants occupy, the shoddy clothing they wear, and the inadequate diet they consume are indefensible. Here are over a million families who cannot in any real sense be considered a part of the American market. They live in a climate which will produce an amazing variety of sustenance. Yet they can barely exist in good years and know hunger in poor years.

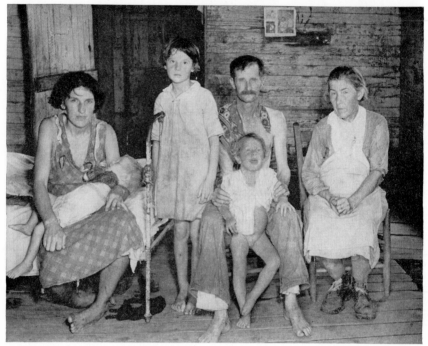

A sharecropper's family, 1936 (LIBRARY OF CONGRESS)

To add to the afflictions of the sharecroppers, at times the A.A.A. indirectly dispossessed them, because planters in reducing their acreage to A.A.A. levels on occasion found it profitable to evict tenants and to fire field hands. The A.A.A. tried unsuccessfully to stop evictions through prohibitory clauses in the acreage-reduction contracts. Thus the A.A.A. helped continue the great migration away from sharecropper cabins; rapid mechanization and the "Dust Bowl" on the Great Plains gave it impetus. One Oklahoman explained, "In '34 I had I reckon four renters and I didn't make anything. I bought tractors on the money the government give me and got shet o' my renters."

Despite these serious shortcomings, the early A.A.A. program so improved the relative position of most farmers that it was popular among them. The Farm Bureau Federation and the Grange strongly supported it and favored more, not less, regulatory legislation. As for the submarginal farmers, floundering in desperate poverty, especially in the South, the New Deal seemed the only hope—except perhaps for the roseate promises of Senator Huey P. Long of Louisiana. When they were "tractored off the land," at least they could go on relief.

The N.R.A. Business Recovery Program

BOTH HARD-PRESSED BUSINESSMEN and suffering workers sought measures providing for government stabilization of business. The A.F.L. favored limiting hours of work to thirty per week in order to spread employment. Their bill, backed by Senator Hugo L. Black, passed the Senate in April. The Black bill frightened business leaders and worried New Dealers, who feared it would obstruct recovery. As for businessmen, leaders of the United States Chamber of Commerce and others had since 1931 been urging an antideflation scheme which in effect meant price fixing through trade associations. This plan would have necessitated suspension of the antitrust laws. President Hoover, who earlier had given such strong impetus to the trade-association movement, indignantly opposed price-fixing schemes. His Attorney General forced five leading trade associations to dissolve, and the Federal Trade Commission forced revision of the trade-association codes for 62 industries.

In the spring of 1933, businessmen sought from Roosevelt what Hoover had refused them. Many of them had reached such a degree of desperation that they also demanded government enforcement of their agreements in order to raise prices and stabilize production. The New Deal was ready to give them what they wanted if they would accept wages-and-hours regulation and other concessions for labor. As a consequence of such an arrangement, prices and wages would go up. Consumers' buying power might lag and thus defeat the scheme. Therefore the New Dealers drafting the great recovery bill added another ingredient for which there was much pressure: a large-scale public-works spending program to prime the economic pump. This was the genesis of the National Industrial Recovery Act, which passed Congress in June 1933.

A new era of government alliance with business for the common good seemed to be opening. Roosevelt, as he signed the act, called it "the most important and far-reaching legislation ever enacted by the American Congress." On the same day the President appointed as Administrator the volatile, colorful General Hugh S. Johnson, who had pictured himself as a sort of benign Mussolini presiding over the economy. He expected on the one hand to negotiate codes, and on the other to pour public-works money into areas where it was most needed. Roosevelt refused to give such tremendous economic power to one man, especially a rather unstable one. Also the President took a more conservative view of public-works spending. He turned over the $3,300,000,000 for public works to Secretary of the Interior Ickes, who slowly and methodically began to gather plans for projects, checking each carefully to make sure it would be really worthwhile. The need was for heavy spending in the next few months, but it was four years before Ickes' Public Works Administration pumped appre-

The N.R.A. Eagle: Jolting "Old Man Depression" in 1933 (left, by Talburt for the New York World-Telegram) and, in 1935, nailed to the wall by the Supreme Court (by Fitzpatrick for the St. Louis Post-Dispatch)

ciable amounts of money into the economy. Rather, the National Recovery Administration staked everything upon the willingness of businessmen to put the nation's welfare and their own long-range well-being ahead of immediate advantage for their individual enterprises. Johnson was well aware how difficult this undertaking would be. "It will be red fire at first and dead cats afterwards," he remarked upon taking over. "This is just like mounting the guillotine on the infinitesimal gamble that the ax won't work."

First came the red fire, as the President and Johnson called upon an excited nation to accept an interim blanket code, providing minimum wages of 30 or 40 cents an hour, maximum working hours of thirty-five or forty per week, and the abolition of child labor. All employers who agreed with the code were to display the N.R.A. blue-eagle symbol; all consumers who co-operated were to sign pledges that they would buy only from blue-eagle establishments. In much the spirit of 1917, the nation participated in N.R.A. parades and rallies. The blue eagle with its slogan, "We Do Our Part," went up almost everywhere, and as Johnson began negotiating codes with big industries, recovery seemed really imminent.

Factory production had already shot up spectacularly, from an index figure of 56 in March to 101 in July. The index of employment rose from 58.9 to 71.5. Roosevelt's campaign theme song, "Happy Days are Here Again," seemed indeed to be coming true. Unfortunately, this little boom was based merely on anticipation of the inflation the recovery measures were expected to bring. Manufacturers had rehired employees, bought raw materials, and raced to produce goods at relatively low cost; wholesalers had bought them speculatively, all in anticipation of the higher prices and limited production the N.R.A. was supposed to establish. Payrolls had risen, but only from an index figure of 37.1 to 50.8. Neither from relief nor any other source had sufficient buying power been pumped into the economy to sustain the anticipated rise in production and prices. Industrial stocks had risen from an average of 63 in March to 109 in July, then crashed on July 21. Three days later the administration hastily proclaimed the plan for a blanket code, in order to prevent the collapse of recovery. Already Johnson was at work presiding over code negotiations for the major industries. The imminence of collapse hastened the process, and even the most trivial of the nation's industries clamored for codes. By the beginning of September 1933, codes for most of the big industries were in operation; by the following February, code-making was complete, with 557 basic codes and 208 supplementary codes approved.

In the drafting of all the codes, Johnson had tried to serve as arbiter to balance the conflicting interests of business, labor, and the consumer. All three had been represented at the bargaining table, and to some degree received protection in the codes. Basically, the codes all guaranteed minimum wages and maximum hours (usually 40 cents an hour and forty hours a week in industry), prohibited child labor, and reaffirmed the right of labor to bargain collectively [section 7(a) of the National Industrial Recovery Act]. They also in theory protected consumers through a Consumers' Advisory Board and code stipulations against substandard or harmful merchandise. Johnson tried to fight rises in prices which would outdistance buying power. "Keep prices down—for God's sake, keep prices down," he warned in January 1934. "That and that alone is the royal road to recovery." Nevertheless the real power in drafting the codes went to the businessmen themselves, and to the leaders within each industry. Representatives of consumers were voting members on only three authorities, and those of labor on only thirty-seven. The real benefits in the codes likewise went to the businesses, and to the already dominant firms, as they flocked to Washington and in the urgency of the moment rewrote their old trade-association agreements into new N.R.A. codes. Some codes were almost word for word the same as the agreements. These codes often contained provisions that, while laudable, were difficult for small units in the industry to maintain. Basically, most of them provided for limiting production and, although often in disguised form, for price-fixing.

Production continued to skid downward during the fall of 1933, from an index figure of 101 in July to 71 in November, even as prices began to creep upward. The brave words and great N.R.A. demonstrations of the spring and summer had not brought recovery. The New Deal honeymoon was over, and even as General Johnson had predicted, the dead cats began to fly.

What was wrong? Basically it was the fallacy that the way to bring recovery was primarily at the production end, by limiting output and raising prices, rather than at the consumer end, by raising buying power. Added to this was the naive faith that businessmen in a desperate period would not, to use Johnson's word, "chisel" each other, labor, and consumers. Finally, the whole system had almost immediately become impossibly complicated and unenforceable. Rather than limit itself to straightening out prices and production in a few starving industries like textiles and bituminous coal, the N.R.A. authorized codes even for the mopstick manufacturers, and put the force of federal law behind such code prohibitions as the marketing of egg noodles in yellow cellophane. There was really almost no machinery for the enforcement of N.R.A. codes. Of 155,000 cases docketed by N.R.A. officials, less than one in four hundred reached the courts. General Johnson inveighed against chiseling and monopoly practices, but businessmen became well aware that his was "a velvet hand in an iron glove."

In the spring of 1934, a National Recovery Review Board under the famous iconoclastic lawyer Clarence Darrow reported that the N.R.A. system was dominated by big business, and hinted that what was needed was socialism. In the ensuing storm of vituperation between Johnson and Darrow, the N.R.A. lost still further prestige. Johnson tried to make the N.R.A. more acceptable to small business, but was forced to resign in September 1934. For some months thereafter, the N.R.A. limped along under a five-man board.

For organized labor, the N.R.A. was also disappointing. In a few industries like textiles the codes did improve working conditions and eliminate child workers; in many industries it did establish the forty-hour work week. But after the establishment of the codes, wages failed to rise, and the workers had little success in forcing them up through collective bargaining. Section 7(a) of the National Industrial Recovery Act, drafted by President William Green of the A.F.L., guaranteed workers the right to bargain collectively through unions of their own choosing. Unions began militantly to seek new members as John L. Lewis of the United Mine Workers sent out organizers who spread the garbled doctrine, "President Roosevelt wants you to join a union." Membership in unions increased from 2,857,000 in 1933 to 3,728,000 in 1935, and the new union members frequently tried to obtain through bloody strikes what they were failing to gain from N.R.A. codes. Employers conversely fought doggedly for the open shop.

President Roosevelt, again drawing upon a wartime precedent, established a National Labor Board, headed by Senator Robert F. Wagner of New York. The most significant thing about this first board was that it created a precedent for peacetime federal intervention in industry-wide collective bargaining. The board had little power except through the N.R.A. and the Department of Justice, and its members tended to throw this bit on the side of management, compromising disputes rather than settling them in keeping with section 7(a). When the Board failed, the President replaced it in July 1934 with the National Labor Relations Board, which was not much stronger. Senator Wagner became convinced that labor could organize successfully, against the powerful opposition of entrenched anti-union employers, only if it received stronger federal protection. He introduced a bill which would outlaw the unfair practices of employers.

Both business and labor assailed the N.R.A. As early as September 1933, Secretary Woodin reported that the big financiers feared it would put the country entirely in the hands of labor. Newspapers accused the President of fomenting class warfare. Yet union men were soon wise-cracking that N.R.A. stood for "National Run Around."

Experiments with Inflation and Work Relief

AS COLD WEATHER APPROACHED in 1933 and the economy continued to edge downward, Roosevelt turned seriously toward managed currency as another device to bring recovery. Some of his advisers argued that producers of farm products and other commodities that had dropped drastically in price must receive more income. Only in this way could they pay their debts and buy durable goods like automobiles which had remained relatively high-priced. If production cuts failed to bring higher prices, currency inflation might. In the spring, Roosevelt had made political concessions to the inflationary congressmen by accepting the Thomas amendment to the Agricultural Adjustment Act, and he had taken the country off the gold standard.

By the summer of 1933, Roosevelt was ready to follow the reasoning of two Cornell University agricultural economists that if the price of gold were increased, the prices of other commodities would rise in rough proportion to the increase. If the nation purchased quantities of gold, and cut the gold content of the dollar (as authorized by the Thomas Amendment), prices would automatically go up. When financially orthodox treasury officials refused to make the purchases, Roosevelt turned to the head of the Farm Credit Administration, Henry Morgenthau, Jr., who began purchasing gold every day along with wheat, corn, and oats. Soon he replaced Woodin, who was seriously ill, as Secretary of the Treasury. The manipulations of the so-called "commodity dollar" impressed few economists; the Brookings Institution called it a "fickle price aid." Perhaps it did stem the fall of prices at home; probably it helped foreign trade by devaluating the dollar to the level of other currencies on the world market. At home, it infuriated holders of certain securities who could no longer claim repayment in gold, and thus obtain a depression bonanza. Al Smith was speaking for them when he denounced the "commodity dollar" as the "baloney dollar."

The silver-purchase program was of much the same purpose and effect as the "commodity dollar." From the seven silver-producing states with their fourteen Senators came strong pressure for it, reminiscent of the Populist era, culminating in the Silver Purchase Act of 1934. This measure nearly tripled the price of silver at home, serving as a subsidizer for the mining interests comparable to the A.A.A. for agriculture. It also sent up the world silver price and wrought havoc in nations whose currency was on a silver standard. Secretary Morgenthau administered the measure as conservatively as possible, and it did little or nothing to bring inflation in the United States.

Roosevelt quickly stabilized the currency. He explained to a critical congressman, "I have always favored sound money, and do now, but it is 'too darned sound' when it takes so much of farm products to buy a dollar." In January 1934, he obtained legislation and stabilized the gold content of the dollar at 59.06 per cent of its former value. Altogether, the resort to managed currency did create new precedents for government action and thus, like the income tax a generation earlier, helped bring about in time an economic revolution. But it had little immediate effect upon recovery.

Some new way had to be found to care for the unemployed through the winter of 1933–1934. Relief Administrator Hopkins persuaded the President to establish a temporary work relief program, the Civil Works

Administration. Between November and April it put four million people to work at emergency projects. Sometimes it was made-work like leaf raking, to which critics applied an old Texas term, "boondoggling." Some of the projects, despite lack of funds for materials and tools, made substantial improvements. The output was of secondary importance; the work raised the morale of the unemployed, and increased their buying power by $950,000,000. The purchasing power thus injected into the economy was probably responsible for the wavering recovery, as the index

Harry Hopkins (NATIONAL ARCHIVES)

of production rose once more from 71 in November 1933, to 86 in May 1934. But Roosevelt capitulated to fierce conservative criticism and liquidated the program in the spring of 1934.

Through 1934, the President was still trying to hold the support of businessmen and bankers. As late as October he told the American Bankers' Association, "The time is ripe for an alliance of all forces intent upon the business of recovery. In such an alliance will be found business and banking, agriculture and industry, and labor and capital. What an all-American team that would be!" There was little chance of it. In August 1934, conservative businessmen and self-styled Jeffersonian Democrats founded the American Liberty League to fight for free enterprise, state rights, the open shop, and an end to New Deal bureaucracy. Motivated partly by dislike of the recovery measures, partly by fear of reform, it gave a point of focus to the growing business opposition to the New Deal.

Reforming the Utility Magnates and Financiers

ALTHOUGH RECOVERY OVERSHADOWED IT in the early New Deal, reform was there. Increasingly New Dealers turned their attention to measures which would remedy conditions they felt had helped bring the depression, and would make future depressions less likely. Their indignation burned especially hot against the private power interests, which they felt had gulled investors and overcharged consumers. The cataclysmic failure of the great Insull utility empire in the Middle West lent credence to their charges. Thus the first and most spectacular of the New Deal reform measures was the creation of the Tennessee Valley Authority in May 1933. It

Senator George Norris at TVA (UNITED PRESS PHOTO)

brought to fruition Senator Norris's dream that the Wilson dam at Muscle
Shoals on the Tennessee River should bring greater abundance to the
four and a half million people in an area rich in resources but subnormal
in its living standards. Basically, the T.V.A. was a project to prevent the
devastating floods that all too frequently had rolled down the rivers of the
area, and to provide cheap, plentiful electricity as a yardstick for the measurement of private rates. More than this it became a great experiment in
regional planning and rehabilitation.

Under a three-man board of directors with wide powers, the T.V.A.
in the next twenty years improved five existing dams and constructed

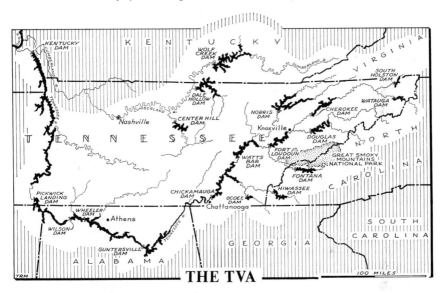

THE TVA

twenty new ones. It stopped floods in the largest heavy-rainfall region in
the nation, and by holding back the water, provided an inland waterway
system with a nine-foot channel 652 miles long, soon heavy with traffic.
From the water power, and increasingly with steam plants, it became
the greatest producer of electric power in the United States. T.V.A. also
manufactured low-cost phosphate fertilizers. It taught farmers how to use
them, how to farm in order to restore the fertility of their soil, and how to
contour-plow and reforest as a means of ending erosion. T.V.A. worked
no miracles, but it did bring a higher living standard to the farmers of the
area. It brought new light industry and increased business. When the war
came, it produced indispensable power for the production of munitions,
aluminum, and plutonium.

In its "yardstick" function, T.V.A. drove down the price of power in
the area from 10 cents a kilowatt-hour to 3 cents. Throughout the country,
because of T.V.A. and other pressures, the residential rate dropped from

5.52 cents in 1933 to 3.67 cents in 1942. While the power that was used increased 63 per cent throughout the country, it almost doubled in the T.V.A. area. To private power companies it seemed a grossly unfair "yardstick," and they claimed the T.V.A. did not set its rates on the basis of true costs. T.V.A. officials claimed that they did, including payments to local and state governments comparable to property taxes assessed against private power companies. The spokesman of private power was the vigorous, personable president of the Commonwealth and Southern Corporation, Wendell Willkie. After losing in the courts, in 1939 he sold his company's facilities in the area to T.V.A., and himself emerged as one of the most effective opponents of the New Deal.

Other great public power and irrigation developments were underway in the West during the same years. On the Colorado River, the Hoover Dam was finished in 1936, and on the Columbia River the Bonneville Dam in 1937 and the Grand Coulee Dam in 1942. Norris in 1937 proposed the creation of six additional regional authorities like the T.V.A.; Congress failed to act, and the decades-long debate over public versus private development of power continued.

To combat drouth conditions in the West, Roosevelt in 1934 by executive order set aside fifteen million dollars to build a "shelter belt" of trees on the Great Plains, to break the wind, collect moisture, and harbor wild life. Critics scoffed, but somehow the trees grew where no one had believed they would. A Soil Erosion Service (later Soil Conservation Service), using much Civilian Conservation Corps manpower, was active especially in the West. Homesteading on the range, which meant dry-farming under almost insuperable difficulties, came to an end with the passage of the Taylor Grazing Act of 1934, which withdrew overgrazed land and set regulations for the use of public rangeland. Spoliation of Indian lands came to at least a temporary halt with the passage of the Indian Reorganization Act of 1934, intended to preserve the tribal domain, customs, and civil liberties of the Indians.

Roosevelt, turning his attention to the East, fostered some mild reform of banks and brokerage firms. After the passage of the emergency banking measure at the outset of the New Deal, he proposed, as he had pledged in his inaugural, measures to preserve the temple of American civilization from further malpractices by the money-changers. In June 1933, he signed the Glass-Steagall Act aimed at curbing speculation by banks, although it also established the Federal Deposit Insurance Corporation, which he had not favored. The F.D.I.C. guaranteed small deposits up to $2,500, and functioned so successfully that the guarantee was raised by successive stages to $10,000 by 1950. It was a longer task to work out a comprehensive overhauling and strengthening of the Federal Reserve system to remedy the defects that had appeared during the depression. This was accomplished through the Banking Act of 1935, which established a seven-man Board of Governors with firm, direct power over discount, or interest, rates and key functions of the Federal Reserve banks.

To protect investors further, Congress passed the so-called "Truth in Securities" Act of 1933, requiring corporations floating new securities to register them with the Federal Trade Commission, and provide full and accurate information on them. In June 1934 Congress went further and established the Securities and Exchange Commission to police the stock-markets. Wall Streeters protested, but their complaints lost some of their effect when the former head of the New York Stock Exchange was sentenced to Sing Sing for larceny.

The 1934 Election: Thunder on the Left

IN MANY AN AREA reform measures were enacted or were in the making in 1934: the Communications Act establishing the Federal Communications Commission to regulate radio, telegraph, and cable operations; the Air Mail Act, establishing tight controls in the awarding of contracts; and the Railroad Retirement Act, providing pensions for workers. Most significant of all, the President had appointed a Committee on Economic Security to develop an over-all plan for national social security.

But it was recovery that dominated American politics as the congressional elections of 1934 approached. Or rather, it was the very slow progress of recovery, and its failure to bring more than subsistence to underprivileged millions. Conservatives could not see this; within the Liberty League and without, they campaigned against the New Deal on the grounds that it was destroying the constitution and driving the country toward bankruptcy. All they succeeded in doing was to drive the dispossessed millions toward the New Deal. No matter how dissatisfied with it they were, it seemed better than its alternative, and they had faith in the President's good intentions. A North Carolina mill worker, after complaining about the N.R.A., remarked, "I do think Roosevelt is the biggest-hearted man we ever had in the White House."

Instead of the shift back toward the Republican party which would have been normal in a mid-term election, the Democrats gained an additional ten seats each in the Senate and House. It was "thunder on the left," commented the historian, Charles A. Beard. Roosevelt heard the thunder. In addition, he was coming to feel more and more betrayed by the business community in his efforts to achieve recovery. His emphasis was shifting perceptibly toward reform, perhaps because this seemed the means of obtaining recovery and certainly because he believed strongly that reform was necessary. One of the most ardent New Dealers, Rexford G. Tugwell, noted in his diary after a conversation with Roosevelt in that month of November 1934: "He is convinced that he can transform the country physically and morally in his time and do it without great changes in government structure or in democratic processes."

Chapter *14*

THE NEW DEAL SHIFTS
TOWARD REFORM

By 1935 the New Deal was outgrowing the moderate premises of the Progressive era and was emphasizing massive government intervention on behalf of the underprivileged. President Roosevelt still wished to maintain a balanced program providing for the welfare of each of the economic and political groups in the country, but realities were forcing him to shift toward reform as he became the champion of the emerging political coalition of farmers, laborers, and millions of poor people.

In part, Roosevelt changed because he felt that large business had defected, that it had betrayed his recovery program and was fighting politically to destroy the New Deal. He had to counteract the threat of this opposition, numerically not frightening but carrying with it powerful means of influencing voters' opinion. Aligned against him were some 70 per cent of the newspaper publishers and most of the large contributors of campaign funds. Roosevelt's quite human reaction was to regard this opposition as reckless and unprincipled, and to force reform upon it for its own good.

Far more important was the threat from the left, and it was this which was mainly responsible for the gradual shift in the New Deal. In undermining this threat, Roosevelt's political pragmatism combined with his humanitarian inclinations to carry him along the road to reform even

further than the progressives had dared venture, toward positive government action on behalf of the general welfare. "We have not weeded out
the overprivileged," he told Congress in January 1935, "and we have
not effectively lifted up the underprivileged." To do so became the goal
of the New Deal.

The Rise of Demagogues

THROUGHOUT THE NATION leaders had emerged who were promising
much to those despairing people whom the New Deal had not yet rescued.
An elderly physician in California, Dr. Francis E. Townsend, attracted
a following of five million destitute old people with his plan to obtain a
federal pension of $200 per month for everyone over sixty. This would
have cost nearly half the national income but, its proponents claimed,
since the pensions would have had to be spent within the month, "the
velocity of money" would have solved the depression. The immediate
political realities of the movement were that its promoters raised nearly
a million dollars in two years and commanded a formidable block of votes.

Among restless people in northern cities, Father Charles Coughlin's
politico-religious broadcasts attracted a wide following. Starting with a
mixture of Papal encyclicals and populism, he at first supported then went
far beyond Roosevelt. Coughlin advocated silver inflation, and nationalization of banks, utilities, and natural resources. Ultimately, in 1938, he
founded the antidemocratic, anti-Semitic Christian Front. In January
1935 he was able to demonstrate his power by inspiring an avalanche of
letters and telegrams to Senators protesting against the World Court.
His program was vague, but the discontent he was able to tap was concrete.

From the South, Senator Huey P. Long of Louisiana succeeded in
launching a far more telling assault upon the New Deal. He was a skillful
politician who was able to build a powerful organization in Louisiana and
a rapidly growing following that spilled out first into neighboring states,
then by 1935 into the Middle West, the Pacific coast, and indeed, to at
least a slight extent, into every part of the country. Within Louisiana, he
had delighted his poverty-stricken supporters by immobilizing their traditional enemies through his strong-armed techniques. Within the state, he
built bridges, roads, hospitals, and a modern educational system. It was
an era of dictators in Europe, and it was easy to assail the self-styled Louisiana Kingfish with ambitions to be a Fuehrer, although his techniques
were the time-honored ones of the American political boss. He was ambitious to become President and lured the masses by offering them more
than Roosevelt. His "Share the Wealth" program promised through
confiscatory taxes on great fortunes to provide every family with what in

those depression years seemed in itself a fortune: an income of $2,500 per year and a homestead worth $5,000. Even in Iowa, farmers guffawed when he called the Secretary of Agriculture, "Lord Corn Wallace." The New Dealers' political tactician, Farley, estimated in the spring of 1935 that Long could poll three or four million votes on a third-party ticket, and possibly even throw the 1936 election to the Republicans.

The "thunder from the left" was so ominous early in 1935 that many despairing New Dealers, chafing at Roosevelt's apparent inertia, predicted defeat in 1936. Roosevelt, who never liked to explain his tactics, remarked confidentially that he had no intention of engaging in public debate with the leaders of the "lunatic fringe." Rather, he quietly went about stealing their thunder with the reform programs the New Dealers had long been planning. Without the pressure from the left upon Congress, these might never have been enacted. As Roosevelt moved to meet this pressure, abandoning his earlier, more cautious program of economic nationalism, he saw less and less of earlier advisers like Raymond Moley, who had been the chief braintruster, and more and more of men like Harry Hopkins, head of the relief program. After the election of 1934, Hopkins had declared:

> Boys—this is our hour. We've got to get everything we want—a works program, social security, wages and hours, everything—now or never."

The Reform Counterattack

OF ALL THIS panoply of reform, the least debatable and probably the most significant was social security. Frances Perkins had accepted a cabinet position only with Roosevelt's pledge that he would support a social-security program. For several years, she and a group of New Dealers sought to win converts in the cabinet, in Congress, and throughout the country to their view that a social-insurance program would not only aid the unemployed but would also help prevent future depressions. Pressure from the Townsendites led them to include old-age insurance in the proposed measure. By the time a social security bill was introduced in January 1935, congressional and public sentiment heavily favored it. The sums it would provide indigent old people, or even those who contributed for years to pensions, were small compared with the Townsend promises, but the bill (and a congressional investigation exposing some of the greedy Townsend lieutenants) served to stem that movement.

The Social Security Act of August 1935 provided two types of assistance for the aged. Those who were destitute could receive federal aid up to $15 per month, depending upon the matching sums states provided.

Those who were working could receive upon retirement annuities provided from taxes upon their earnings and their employer's payroll. The 1935 law specified payments, to begin in 1942, ranging from $10 to $85 per month, and excluded wide categories of workers from the program—but it was a beginning. The act also provided for unemployment insurance, aid for the blind and crippled, and assistance for dependent mothers and children, all such funds to be administered by the states in keeping with minimum federal standards. A Social Security Board supervised the entire system.

As the designers of the Social Security program knew, the 1935 act was incomplete and not entirely effective, but it was a most significant start toward guaranteeing the well-being of the American people. From the outset most Republicans as well as almost all Democrats in Congress had favored the measure. Serious opposition had come only from the die-hard National Association of Manufacturers. Nine out of ten persons polled in 1938 believed in old-age pensions.

Social Security could not help those already unemployed in 1935; to aid them, Congress in April voted $1,400,000,000 to supplant direct relief with the Works Progress Administration. Work relief was more expensive, but was essential to prevent the moral erosion, and if possible to save the skills, of the unemployed. "We have a human problem as well as an economic problem," Roosevelt had declared in his January message to Congress. "To dole out relief is to administer a narcotic, a subtle destroyer of the human spirit."

The W.P.A. under Harry Hopkins did much to "help men keep their chins up and their hands in." It enrolled an average of 2,100,000 workers between 1935 and 1941 on a wide variety of projects. Since the W.P.A. workers were, theoretically at least, the less employable segment of the working force, and since almost all W.P.A. money went for wages rather than tools and materials, their undertakings could not compare in efficiency with private construction projects. Many people tended to forget this and regard W.P.A. as a politically inspired paradise for loafers. Considering the handicaps under which the W.P.A. operated, and despite a certain amount of parasitism, and in 1938 of politicking, the tangible output of W.P.A. was impressive. Four fifths of the W.P.A. projects were in public works and conservation. Among the great variety of undertakings W.P.A. built nearly six hundred airports and built or rebuilt 110,000 public buildings, more than a half million miles of roads and streets, over a hundred thousand bridges, a half million sewers, and over a million privies. In the realm of art, music, and the theater it gave opportunities to a remarkable proportion of the nation's talented people; its writers, for example, produced a useful set of state guidebooks.

W.P.A. paid wages on a "security" level, between relief payments and prevailing wages, ranging from $15 per month in the rural South to $90 for professional workers in New York City. The National Youth Administration, established in June 1935 as a sort of "junior W.P.A.," aided young people between 16 and 25, seven eighths of whom received student aid in schools and colleges. The billions thus poured into the economy led to a marked and sustained upswing beginning in the late summer of 1935. The workers themselves felt a pride in being off relief, and a gratitude toward the New Deal. It was not necessary to pressure them to vote for Roosevelt; their strong inclination was to do so.

For those fortunate enough to be employed, Roosevelt preferred a paternalistic program of wages-and-hours guarantees, and social-security benefits. Union leaders wanted to use collective bargaining to gain these advantages for their workers, so they would look to the union, not to the government. They had gained much of what they wanted just before the advent of the New Deal, with the passage in 1932 of the Norris-LaGuardia Act. This had prohibited the courts from issuing injunctions against most ordinary collective-bargaining practices, and had made unenforceable any "yellow-dog contracts"—pledges from employees that they would not join unions. The Norris-LaGuardia Act in effect stopped Federal courts from interfering on behalf of employers in struggles with employees. It left management and the unions free to bring economic pressure upon each other as best they could in collective-bargaining procedures. But in the depression years, employers were usually stronger than unions. Also, strikes could interfere with economic recovery. Hence in 1933, section 7(a) of the National Industrial Recovery Act affirmed the right of labor to bargain collectively, and led to a government agency, a National Labor Board, to settle disputes arising under section 7(a). The result, as has been seen, was a relatively weak board, tending at first to be favorable to employers. Labor was disgruntled.

Although Roosevelt had always maintained cordial relations with labor leaders, he was little inclined to give them firm collective-bargaining guarantees in place of the weak section 7(a) in the National Industrial Recovery Act. Congress, under the leadership of Senator Wagner, felt differently; in May 1935 the Senate passed his bill providing strong government protection for the unions.

While Congress was moving toward the left, the Supreme Court was heading to the right. A case involving the code and collective-bargaining systems of the National Recovery Administration had finally reached the Court. The constitutional basis for the N.R.A. was the right of Congress to regulate commerce among the states, but the test case involved alleged code violations by the Schechter brothers, who were operating a wholesale poultry business in Brooklyn. Among the charges against them were the selling of poultry not in good condition and the unfair treatment of employees. The Court unanimously held that the Schechters were not engaged in interstate commerce, and that Congress had unconstitutionally delegated legislative power to the President to draft the codes. It thus invalidated the code system and section 7(a).

Several days before the decision, President Roosevelt, bowing to the inevitable, endorsed the Wagner bill. In July 1935 he signed the measure. What he had reluctantly accepted became one of the mainstays of the New

Workers balloting at a National Labor Relations Board election, Ford Plant, 1941 (LIBRARY OF CONGRESS)

Deal. The Wagner Act, passed at a time when unions were relatively weak, outlawed a number of the "unfair practices" by which management had been bludgeoning them, and created a powerful National Labor Relations Board to police the corporations. Militant labor thus obtained the governmental backing essential to its drive to unionize the great mass-production industries. As organized labor began to grow in size and power, it looked to the New Deal as its ally and benefactor.

The "sick chicken" decision holding the N.R.A. code system unconstitutional outraged Roosevelt. Partly he saw in it a threat to the whole New Deal, and lashed out at the judges for cutting back the federal power to regulate commerce to that of the horse-and-buggy era. Further, he feared that little businessmen and laborers would suffer, as indeed they did, from unfair cutting of prices and wages. But the decision was more of a blessing than a catastrophe for the New Deal, since it ended the decrepit N.R.A. code system with its tacit suspension of the antitrust laws. "It has been an awful headache," Roosevelt confessed privately. It was politically more comfortable for him to return to the old progressive antitrust position and at the same time promote positive protection for smaller business.

Much of the N.R.A. program that had benefited smaller business and overcompetitive producers was now enacted piecemeal to form a "little N.R.A." As early as February 1935, in response to the Supreme Court invalidation of legislation to prevent the overproduction of oil, Congress passed the Connally Act prohibiting the shipment of "hot oil" in interstate commerce. The Guffey Act of August 1935 virtually re-enacted the N.R.A. bituminous-coal code, fixing prices, limiting production, and protecting labor. When the Supreme Court threw out the new coal-control law in 1936, Congress passed the second Guffey Act of 1937. Roosevelt feared a wages-and-hours law would be unconstitutional, but did sign the Walsh-Healey Act of August 1936, covering wages and hours on work done on federal contracts. In order to protect small retailers, the Robinson-Patman Act of 1936 prohibited wholesalers or manufacturers from giving preferential discounts or rebates to chain stores or other large buyers; the Miller-Tydings Act of 1937 fortified state "fair trade" price-fixing laws.

As yet Roosevelt did not resort to vigorous use of the antitrust laws, but he did advocate tightening the regulation of various segments of big business. In March 1935 he recommended passage of an act to prohibit after five years the pyramiding of utility holding companies, which had led to such flagrant abuses in the twenties. In the thirties, thirteen companies still controlled three fourths of the nation's electric power. They fought desperately through the summer of 1935 against what they viewed as a threatened "death sentence." One company alone spent $700,000 lobbying against the measure. In the Holding Company Act of August 1935, the companies gained a partial victory since the Act permitted two strata of holding companies above the operating companies.

In addition, Congress passed a series of other laws between 1935 and 1940 stiffening federal regulation. These strengthened the Federal Power Commission, brought trucks and carriers on inland waterways under the supervision of the Interstate Commerce Commission, created in 1936 a new Maritime Commission to subsidize and regulate a merchant fleet, and in 1938 set up a Civil Aeronautics Authority (later Board) to regulate airlines.

One of the most effective ways to regulate was to tax, and in June 1935 Roosevelt proposed democratizing the federal tax structure by placing far higher levies upon big corporations and wealthy people. He pointed out that a person receiving $6,000 per year paid twice the tax levied upon one receiving $4,000, yet the tax upon a $5,000,000 income was at the same rate as on $1,000,000. His enemies immediately charged that his recommendations were political rather than fiscal, for he was accepting the program of the younger Senator Robert M. La Follette and other Republican progressives whose support would be valuable in 1936. More important, he was undercutting Huey Long's "Share the Wealth" platform. Conservative newspapers immediately attacked his proposal as a "soak the rich" tax scheme, but it passed Congress in August 1935. It wiped away the last vestiges of Secretary Mellon's influence on tax policy, as it established the highest rates in history at the top: a maximum 75 per cent income tax, 70 per cent estate tax, and 15 per cent corporate-income tax. It was an important step toward redistribution of American income.

In answer to protests that the New Deal was punishing business, Roosevelt pointed out that the purpose of the new tax program was:

> . . . not to destroy wealth, but to create a broader range of opportunity, to restrain the growth of unwholesome and sterile accumulations and to lay the burdens of Government where they can best be carried. This law affects only those individual people who have incomes over $50,000 a year, and individual estates of decedents who leave over $40,000. . . . Taxes on 95 per cent of our corporations are actually reduced.

In agriculture, since the first strong protests in 1934, the New Dealers had been attempting to reshape policies to give more aid to smaller farmers. Modification of the A.A.A. crop contracts had not greatly helped. In January 1936, the A.A.A. processing-tax scheme ran afoul of the Supreme Court, and the administration switched to a soil-conservation basis for the program. The new contracts provided that landlords must share with their tenants and sharecroppers the payments for withdrawing land from production. Nevertheless in 1937, while the average plantation operator was grossing $8,328, of which $833 came from the soil conservation program, the average tenant family received only $385, of which $27 came from the government.

Meanwhile a new misfortune was afflicting farmers on the Great Plains. While those in the Southeast still suffered from the soil washing away, in the West it began to blow away. Beginning late in 1933, years of extreme drought and high winds made life unbearable for farmers in the "Dust Bowl," an area centering around eastern Colorado and New Mexico and the panhandles of Texas and Oklahoma.

To aid submarginal farmers in West and East alike, the Resettlement Administration, established in 1935, entered into a great variety of projects. They received spectacularly adverse publicity and aided only rela-

Father and sons walking in the face of a dust storm, Cimarron County,
Oklahoma (LIBRARY OF CONGRESS)

tively few farmers. In 1937, the Farm Security Administration, which
replaced it, faced similar difficulties. The Resettlement Administration had
planned to move 500,000 farm families; it actually resettled 4,441. However, by 1944 it and the F.S.A. had made 870,000 short-term rehabilitation loans and 41,000 long-range loans for the purchase of farms. The
large farm organizations, concentrating upon price supports, took little
interest in the rehabilitation work, which if successful would raise production at a time when they were trying to lower it. In the old battle between
agrarians and liberals in the Department of Agriculture and on Capitol
Hill, the agrarians seldom lost a skirmish.

One reform program upon which both factions could agree was the
Rural Electrification Administration, established in 1935 to extend power
lines to farms through co-operatives. Since its activities stimulated pri-

vate power companies also to extend into the country, it was effective both directly and indirectly. Power lines had reached only 4 per cent of the farms in 1925; they reached a quarter by 1940.

By 1936, the New Deal could still count upon the support of most substantial farmers. At the same time it had allayed through its relief and public-works programs much of the discontent, if not the suffering, of those who were poorer.

The 1936 Landslide

THE VIGOROUS REFORM PROGRAM, enacted in its main outlines by 1936, left little doubt that Roosevelt would win re-election by a wide margin. Many millions felt that their personal lot had been improved by the New Deal. The violent attacks upon it from the right, and the cries of anguish over such measures as the "soak the rich" taxes, convinced them the more that the President was their friend. Despite the misgivings of many conservatives within the party, the Democratic convention in 1936 renominated Roosevelt and Vice-President Garner by acclamation. His control was so complete that he even obtained abrogation of the rule requiring a two-thirds majority to nominate a candidate through which minorities had so often hamstrung Democratic conventions. Roosevelt's campaign technique was simple: to tour the country asking people if they were not better off than four years before.

As for the Republicans, they nominated their strongest candidate. Ignoring ex-President Hoover and the right wing, which was crying calamity, they chose a one-time Bull Mooser who had never strayed far from the 1912 Progressive position. This was the competent governor of Kansas, Alf M. Landon. His running mate was another Bull Mooser who had moved well to the right, the Chicago publisher Frank Knox. The Republican platform promised to do most of what the New Deal was undertaking —but more competently, constitutionally, and without running a deficit. This was Landon's position, which he expounded in his speeches. In addition, Landon tried hard to make Roosevelt state his intentions toward the Supreme Court. But Roosevelt did not need to commit himself; the New Deal record was sufficient to re-elect him. Landon's dry voice could not match Roosevelt's radio pyrotechnics, and Landon had to fight to protect his moderate position from the militant Republican right.

The election did demonstrate the degree to which the New Deal depended upon a coalition of farmers, union men, and the poor. The unions were the heaviest Democratic campaign contributors, providing a million dollars. Negroes switched en masse from the party of Lincoln to that of Roosevelt. The "lunatic fringe" coalition against Roosevelt stirred hardly a ripple. Long had been assassinated the year before; the Union party candidate was "Liberty Bell" William Lemke—who was "cracked," said wiseacres. His ticket polled only 890,000 votes; the Socialists, 190,000; the Communists, under 80,000.

Surprisingly, a postal card poll by the *Literary Digest* showed Landon would win by a big margin. How could it be so wrong? The answer seemed to be that it was because the names and addresses of those polled were taken from old telephone directories. A majority of people who could afford telephones and had not been forced to move favored Landon. In

Alf M. Landon (NATIONAL ARCHIVES)

the election, Landon received 16,680,000 popular votes compared with 27,477,000 for Roosevelt, and got the electoral votes of only Maine and Vermont.

The Fight to Reform the Supreme Court

PRESIDENT ROOSEVELT in his inaugural dedicated his second administration to reform. He was at the zenith of his power, and seemed to have the support in Congress to enact a sweeping new program. He had carried with him into the Congress many a freshman legislator pledged firmly to his support. These had reduced further the already small Republican minorities. By the close of the campaign, Roosevelt had become vehement in his retorts to those right-wing opponents whom he labeled "economic royalists." "Never before in all our history have these forces been so united against one candidate as they stand today," he declared. "They are unanimous in their hate for me—and I welcome their hate. . . . I should like to have it said of my second Administration that in it these forces met their master."

It seemed to Roosevelt that regardless of the outcome of the elections, these forces would be in control as long as the Supreme Court continued to hold New Deal legislation unconstitutional. Foes of the Coal Act, the Holding Company Act, the National Labor Relations Act, and the Social Security Act were openly flaunting them and resorting to the courts, confident that these measures would be destroyed like the N.R.A. and the first A.A.A. The Supreme Court, through its narrow interpretation of the federal power over commerce and taxation, and its broad interpretation of freedom of contract in the Fourteenth Amendment, seemed to have created an economic no-man's land within which neither the federal nor state governments could act.

Many critics of the Court had been urging passage of some sort of constitutional amendment to provide the federal government with more extensive economic powers. Roosevelt's opinion (which subsequent Supreme Court decisions were to sustain) was that the Constitution granted adequate powers. All that was wrong was the Supreme Court's antiquated interpretation, he felt, but the four or five justices firmly opposed to the New Deal enjoyed excellent health and showed no signs of resigning. Consequently Roosevelt decided to propose adding to the Supreme Court, and to lower federal courts also hostile to the New Deal, new justices (presumably sharing his viewpoint) to match superannuated ones. At this point Roosevelt's political sixth sense deserted him and instead of presenting his proposal frankly and firmly in terms of its economic implications, he enclosed it in a larger scheme. Without informing congressional leaders in advance, in February 1937 he sent a surprise message proposing a needed general overhauling of the federal court system, which would include the appointment of as many as six new Supreme Court justices. His nearest approach to frankness was a statement that the addition of younger blood would revitalize the courts and help them meet the needs and facts of an ever-changing world.

There was little question about the constitutionality of Roosevelt's proposal, since Congress had from time to time changed the number of justices on the Supreme Court. But it aroused a furor throughout the country. By 1937, Americans were thoroughly frightened by the rise of Hitler in Germany and the impending threat of a second World War. Many thoughtful people who had supported Roosevelt in 1936 heeded the warning of conservatives that it was through such constitutional shortcuts that dictators came into power. Roosevelt obviously had no such leanings, but they feared that some successor of his might. Besides, economic conditions had been improving steadily for several years and many people were well enough off to worry about constitutional principles as well as economic necessities. Within Congress, the controversy cut across party lines as some Democrats like the progressive Senator Burton K. Wheeler of Montana and conservative Senator Carter Glass of Virginia fought against the "packing" of the court, while the Republican progressive Senator La Follette supported the President. Social and economic as well as constitutional questions entered the debate. La Follette declared the Court had already been "packed" for years "in the cause of Reaction and Laissez Faire." Glass warned with remarkable foresight that a Roosevelt Court might rule against segregation in the South.

Since much of the electorate for the first time sided with the conservatives, some of the old-time Democratic leaders, especially from the South, who until now had gone along with the New Deal mainly because of party loyalty and pressure from their constituents, broke loose. They joined with the bulk of the Republicans to form a new conservative coalition in Congress. Roosevelt fought back by openly proclaiming his reasons for wanting the measure, and by using every device of party discipline to round up votes in Congress. He might have succeeded in obtaining at least a compromise measure had not the Supreme Court itself eliminated the necessity for one.

The justices, including Brandeis, the oldest and most liberal, had been indignant over charges that they were too old to handle the business of the court. Chief Justice Charles Evans Hughes even wrote a letter insisting that the Court was not falling behind in its work. Several of the justices apparently feared that Roosevelt's plan would rob the Court of its prestige, as had happened during Reconstruction. Four of them, far to the right, were of no disposition to take a broader view of the Constitution. Three of them took a more progressive if not a New Deal view, and Chief Justice Hughes on occasion voted with them; on the other hand, Justice Owen J. Roberts more often voted with the conservative four. Just before the President sent his court plan to Congress, Roberts joined with Hughes and the three more liberal justices to validate, by a five-to-four decision in the case of *West Coast Hotel* v. *Parrish,* a state minimum-wage law. This reversed a five-to-four decision of the previous year invalidating a similar law. "You may have saved the country," Hughes jubilantly told Roberts. The decision was announced March 29, 1937. Two weeks later, the Court, again five to four, upheld the Wagner Act, and in May, the Social Security Act. Since there was no longer any need for a court plan, the new conservative alliance in Congress easily dealt Roosevelt a spectacular personal defeat. At the same time, the shift of the Supreme Court's interpretation of the Constitution was the New Deal's most significant victory.

Almost at once the older justices began retiring, and Roosevelt replaced them one by one with his appointees. In the next decade the Roosevelt Court rewrote large sections of constitutional law. The new justices were sharply divided among themselves, but usually upon technical matters. In the main they interpreted the commerce and tax clauses so broadly and the Fourteenth Amendment so narrowly that they laid few restrictions upon economic regulation by either the federal or state governments. For several years they tended to restrict governments in their interference with organized labor, but by the end of a decade labor too was subject to firm restraints. Thus they removed almost all constitutional impediments to government regulation of the economic system. While they tore away the Fourteenth Amendment as a shield to protect corporations from state authority, they began to restore it to racial minorities. In decision after decision they ruled against discriminations, as they moved gradually toward the principle that all citizens are equal before the law. In these ways the Supreme Court helped give permanence to the great changes of the New Deal era.

The Government Fosters Unionization

In the summer of 1937, as Roosevelt's prestige was pricked by the collapse of the court reform program, it was suffering still another jab as apprehensive people blamed him for the violence of the union drive to organize the steel, automobile, rubber, and other huge industries. Even before the enactment of the Wagner Act, union membership had jumped from a depression low of less than 3,000,000 to 4,200,000. A group of leaders of industrial unions (that is, those offering membership to everyone within an industry) had chafed under the conservatism of the craft unions (which took in only those working at a given trade). Men like the head of the United Mine Workers, John L. Lewis, and the leaders of the two great garment unions, Sidney Hillman of the Amalgamated Clothing Workers and David Dubinsky of the International Ladies' Garment Workers, in 1934 had forced President William Green of the A.F.L. and the craft unionists to agree to charter new industrial unions in the big unorganized industries.

In 1935, with the passage of the favorable Wagner Act, organization of these industries began. It led to violent opposition not only from the corporations but also from the A.F.L. craft unions, which feared they would be submerged by the new giant unions. Jurisdictional fights led to a schism between the A.F.L. and the industrial unionists, who formed a Committee for Industrial Organization in November 1935. Industrial warfare followed, as both the A.F.L. and the C.I.O. mounted great rival organizational drives.

President Roosevelt and a few industrial leaders were inclined to be favorable toward industrial unionism. Gerald Swope of General Electric told Roosevelt that his company could not conceivably negotiate with a large number of craft unions but might find advantages in contracting with a single industrial union. This was an unusual view in the spring of 1936; the point was still far off when big business could see advantages in

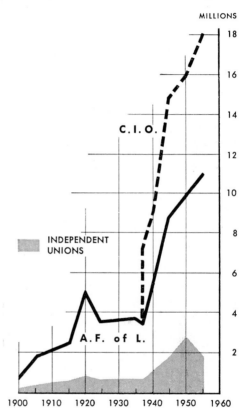

Organized Labor, 1900–1956

big labor. Vigorous young organizers had to battle it out, often by physical force, with "loyal" strong-arm squads, occasionally with the police, and sometimes with rival organizers. The great difference between this and earlier periods of labor warfare was the aid the federal government provided unions through the National Labor Relations Board. Unions could take complaints and cases to the Board whenever employers engaged in the unfair labor practices forbidden by the Wagner Act (National Labor Relations Act of 1935). It was illegal for employers:

To interfere with employees in their right to self-organization, to form, join, or assist labor organizations, to bargain collectively through representatives of their own choosing, and to engage in concerted activities, for the purpose of collective bargaining or other mutual aid or protection.

To dominate or interfere with the formation or administration of any labor organization or contribute financial or other support to it.

By discrimination in regard to hire or tenure of employment or any term or condition of employment to encourage or discourage membership in any labor organization.

To discharge or otherwise discriminate against any employee because he has filed charges or given testimony under this Act.

To refuse to bargain collectively with the representatives of his employees duly chosen pursuant to other provisions in the Act.

Despite these firm prohibitions, many managements engaged in drastic tactics to fend off union organizers. National attention focused upon the organizing drives in the automobile and steel industries. Through 1936, the United Automobile Workers gained recruits despite vigorous company opposition. There was good reason, for in 1934, at about the time the organizing drive began, 45 per cent of the auto workers were receiving less than $1,000 per year. General Motors alone, in an effort to keep down union organization, spent almost a million dollars on private detectives between 1934 and 1936. In the first two months of 1937, seventeen General Motors plants were struck through the device of the sit-down strike, as the workers stayed within the plants by their machinery. In February, General Motors recognized the U.A.W.; gradually in the following years, other automobile companies recognized the union. Rubber and other industries were similarly organized. Newspapers darkly saw in the sit-down strikes a menace to private property of a sort radicals had tried in Italy in 1919; courts outlawed sit-down strikes, and much of the public became thoroughly alarmed.

Bloody warfare in the steel industry heightened their fears. In 1936, the C.I.O. voted a half-million-dollar fund to organize the industry and began its great onslaught, winning tens of thousands of workers from company unions. United States Steel chose to capitulate rather than face a long strike just as prosperity seemed to be returning. In March 1937, to the amazement of the nation, one of the company's subsidiaries signed a contract with the Steel Workers' Organizing Committee. For the first time, "Big Steel" was organized. The triumph was quickly blunted when three of the "Little Steel" companies, under the moral leadership of Tom Girdler of Republic Steel, who violently disapproved of unions, fought furiously. At the Republic plant in South Chicago on Memorial Day, 1937, the police killed ten strikers. Republic Steel, according to the prolabor La Follette committee, was the largest purchaser of tear gas and sickening gas in the United States; Youngstown Sheet and Tube Company owned an arsenal of over a thousand weapons. The strikers lost completely, to the relief of middle-class Americans, who, like the newspapers they read, blamed the unions for the strife, and behind the unions, the New Deal.

Roosevelt, forgetting the strong labor support he had received in 1936, was so irritated by the private war between Girdler and Lewis that he ex-

Police battling Republic Steel strikers, South Chicago, May 30, 1937
(UNITED PRESS PHOTO)

claimed, "A plague on both your houses." Lewis retorted, "It ill behooves one who has supped at labor's table and who has been sheltered in labor's house to curse with equal fervor and fine impartiality both labor and its adversaries when they become locked in deadly embrace." In his anger, Lewis, who had earlier been a Republican, returned to his party in 1940 even though it meant supporting a candidate who had hailed Girdler as one of "the true heroes of America." But Lewis could not carry the C.I.O. or even the United Mine Workers with him. Labor and the New Dealers continued to sup at the same table; industrial unionism was firmly established, and the era of big labor was dawning. By 1941, union membership totaled about 9,500,000. Accompanying this phenomenal growth was a marked middle-class return to the Republican Party.

The Lesson of the Recession

A THIRD GREAT BLOW to the New Deal was the sharp recession that developed in the fall of 1937. It came just as many economists were fearing an inflationary boom that might get out of hand. There had been a remarkable recovery by the summer of 1937. The national income, which had dropped from eighty-two billion dollars in 1929 to forty billion in 1932, was back up to nearly seventy-two billion. Farm prices were up 86 per cent, and the real income of farmers was about the same as the unsatisfactory 1929 level. Industrial production, still 7.5 per cent below 1929, was 77 per cent greater than in 1932. Dividends were up to 90 per cent of 1929. Those workers who were employed were working fewer hours than before the depression (38.6 in 1937) and were receiving real wages about 10 per cent higher than in 1929. Average weekly wages had advanced from $17.57 in 1933 to $25.14 in 1937.

Two serious flaws marred this remarkable picture of recovery. One was the continued unemployment, for although employment was higher than the 1929 peak, the population had grown. There were still 7,500,000 unemployed and nearly 4,500,000 families on relief. The second factor was closely interrelated to the first: there had been no upsurge of capital investment and business expansion as in the 1920's. New issues of stocks and bonds had averaged five billion dollars a year in the twenties; they totaled only a billion and a quarter in 1937.

Economists who have subsequently analyzed the 1937 recovery note the increased farm buying power, a good bit of which went into machinery. Above all, they emphasize that heavy government spending started the nation back toward prosperity. The enormous sums spent on work relief, the gradual momentum of the public-works program, and the loans to farmers, combined with the payment in 1936 (over Roosevelt's veto) of the veterans' bonus, powerfully stimulated the economy.

Out of this experience emerged new economic theories, centering around the concept that the government could by liberal spending in hard times help pull the nation out of a depression. As a corollary, the government could help curb inflationary booms by means of restrictive policies. With all of their ramifications, these new economic theories came to be known as Keynesianism, after the famed British economist John Maynard Keynes. The United States was Keynes's main laboratory, but the economic policies that developed in this country grew peculiarly and pragmatically out of the American experience. The name "Keynesian" was a popular label, even though not too accurate a description for the economics of the thirties. A score of years later, the popular label was still being applied, although most of the nation's leading economists had progressed well beyond Keynesianism.

Although within a decade most leaders of both the Republicans and Democrats had come to accept government spending as a means of combating depressions, in 1937 Roosevelt as much as his Republican opponents abhorred a deficit and worried about the mounting national debt, which had risen to thirty billion dollars. He actually feared another disastrous boom like 1929. Acting therefore in terms of the older economics, he had the Federal Reserve tighten credit even though the upswing had been sound rather than speculative. More important still, he tried to balance the budget and drastically cut government spending. Between January and August 1937, he cut the W.P.A. in half, sending a million and a half workers on unpaid "vacation." And since, with the ending of the drought, a huge farm surplus was again imminent, produce prices fell drastically. The fragile new boom collapsed and sent the economy plummeting. The index of production dropped from 117 in August 1937, to 76 in May 1938; four million additional workers were thrown out of employment. It seemed like 1932 all over again.

Businessmen of course blamed the New Deal: its spending policies, the mounting cost of labor, and incessant reforms were destroying the economy and making it impossible for them to have confidence in the future. Roosevelt equally naturally blamed the businessmen: the percentage cost of labor had not gone up; the new crash was due to the selfish manner in which business had sabotaged the recovery program. Especially, through monopoly practices it had kept for itself a disproportionate share of the returns. In October 1937 the President called Congress into special session to renew heavy public spending, and to reform the "selfish interests" he blamed for the recession. Congress passed an emergency appropriation of five billion dollars; the public-works and work-relief programs once again poured these large sums into the economy, and by June 1938, the recession was melting away. The "spending school" had won a point, and the government seemed to have assumed a new role in warding off threatened economic disaster.

A Last Burst of Reform

So IT WAS that the New Deal entered into its final stage of reform, combining what was as new as Keynesianism with what was as old as progressivism. The trend had seemed to be toward big government, big labor, and big business. Big government had come with the active intervention of the New Deal into so many aspects of the economy; the number of civilian government employees jumped from 588,000 in 1931 to 1,370,000 by

1941. Big labor grew out of union militancy protected by the Wagner Act. Big business had long existed, but seemed to have grown bigger through New Deal inadvertence. The N.R.A. relaxation of the antitrust laws had given large corporations an opportunity to grow at the expense of smaller business. In the two years after the end of the codes, the Attorney-General initiated fewer antitrust suits than during the N.R.A. period.

Throughout the country, the old progressive element with its mistrust of bigness was threatening to defect from the New Deal. Since the New Dealers could not or would not reverse the trend toward big government and big labor, that left only big business for them to attack in order to placate their progressive allies. Senators like the Republicans La Follette and Borah and the Democratic Joseph C. O'Mahoney were relighting the old antitrust fires, and threatening to wrest the power of industrial regulation away from the administration and vest it in Congress. Once again, Roosevelt demonstrated his skill in stealing issues.

In April 1938 the President sent Congress a message vehemently denouncing the unjustifiable concentration of economic power. Less than 5 per cent of all corporations in 1935 owned 87 per cent of all the assets, he declared. This was leading to such a serious maldistribution of income, he pointed out, that in 1935–36 the upper 1.5 per cent of the population had a share of the national income as great as the 47 per cent at the bottom—and these had less than $1,000 per year per family. The remedy, Roosevelt proposed, was to study economic concentration and enact more modern antitrust laws to cope with the newer techniques of monopoly. In response, Congress established the Temporary National Economic Committee under the chairmanship of Senator O'Mahoney. It conducted lengthy public hearings and published 39 volumes of reports and 43 scientific monographs by the end of 1941. By that time the national attention was entirely engrossed elsewhere; legislation never followed.

While congressional progressives held hearings, Roosevelt launched an immediate militant program in 1938 through Thurman Arnold, whom he appointed head of the Anti-Trust Division of the Department of Justice. Arnold, who felt there was adequate power in existing legislation, made new and sophisticated use of the Sherman and Clayton Acts as he undertook 215 major investigations and 92 test cases. He tried to break restraints of trade in the distribution of goods in order to lower prices to consumers. His campaign operated largely through industry-wide consent decrees which could prohibit practices harmful to consumers and encourage those helpful to industries suffering from overcompetition. The consent decrees combined the old and the new, for in some respects this antitrust program was more like a negative N.R.A. than the antithesis of the N.R.A. It was well publicized and popular with Congress and the public until the national emphasis changed to defense production.

Roosevelt genuinely believed in the antimonopoly program. Also, it helped him retain control over a majority in Congress as the new conservative alliance battled against his reform proposals. The conservatives won several victories, most notably narrowly defeating his government reorganization bill, which would have brought some of the reforms which came only after the war with the establishment of the Hoover Commission. On the whole the New Deal forces in Congress held together surprisingly well despite Roosevelt's serious loss of prestige since 1936.

Agricultural interests pressed for a new A.A.A. to cope with the enormous threatened surplus. The end of the drouth, increased mechanization, and other improvements like the rapid spread of hybrid corn in the Middle West outmoded the crop controls in the 1936 legislation. The Agricultural Adjustment Act of 1938 provided a number of devices to cut back production: soil-conservation payments, marketing quotas, export subsidies, and crop loans. Surpluses of five nonperishable commodities upon which farmers received loans would be stored under government seal until needed in lean years, thus creating what Secretary Wallace termed an "ever normal granary." The surpluses so stored were of vital aid in feeding allies during the war years. The 1938 act also established a Surplus Marketing Administration to channel surpluses to needy persons and provide food for school lunches. Under this legislation, farm income by 1940 was back to the 1937 level.

From the beginning of the New Deal, the Department of Agriculture put increasing emphasis upon soil conservation. Farmers were constantly being warned of the damage of soil erosion; Pare Lorentz's documentary film "The River," made for the Resettlement Administration in 1938, dramatized the washing away of three billion tons of soil a year. In October 1933 the government established the Soil Erosion Service, later the Soil Conservation Service, which began to establish demonstration projects, building checkdams and contour-plowing fields, throughout the farming areas. By 1951, 2,383 soil conservation districts had been organized by state laws, covering approximately 80 per cent of the nation's farmlands. With government instruction and subsidies, such extensive soil conservation work was being carried out that from the air the appearance of many farming areas had drastically changed.

For the protection of workers, Federal regulation of wages and hours and of child labor became possible since the Supreme Court would no longer raise serious questions of constitutionality. In June 1938, New Dealers fought through Congress the Fair Labor Standards Act. This established a minimum wage of 25 cents an hour (to be raised gradually to 40 cents by 1945) and a maximum work week of forty-four hours (to be lowered to forty) for most labor, excepting agricultural, domestic, and maritime workers. It also forbade employment of children under sixteen in most areas except agriculture. Low though these standards were, they raised the pay of 300,000 workers and shortened the work week for 1,300,000. In subsequent years the standards were raised repeatedly and broadened to include more categories of workers.

The enormous new outlays for public works in 1938 had as their primary purpose the quick liquidation of the recession. More than that, these

Strip and contour farming in Georgia (U.S. DEPARTMENT OF AGRICULTURE PHOTO)

projects, and especially public housing, filled a reform function begun early in the New Deal and receiving increasing emphasis. All together, the Public Works Administration, before it came to an end in the forties, spent over four billion dollars on over 34,000 projects. These included the speed-up of the completion of Hoover Dam and the New York Triborough Bridge, and also such socially vital construction as school and university buildings, and hospitals containing more than 120,000 beds.

From the outset, in June 1933, the P.W.A. through an Emergency Housing Division began for the first time federal sponsorship of public housing. It cleared some of the nation's most notorious slum blocks, replacing them with some fifty developments containing almost 22,000 family units. The rent was an average of $26 per month, too high during these years for many previous slum dwellers to meet. Congress in 1937 finally passed Senator Wagner's bill creating the United States Housing Author-

ity, which with $500,000,000 (later in 1941 increased to $1,600,000,000)
took over and expanded the housing program to 511 projects including
161,000 units for the truly poor. Almost a third of the units went to Negroes—one of the largest pieces of federal aid they had ever received. It
was at least a beginning toward solving a problem which would continue
to occupy the nation for decades to come.

Together with the other measures already discussed, Congress had
passed a remarkable amount of reform legislation in 1937 and 1938. The
several spectacular setbacks and Roosevelt's waning popularity had obscured the continued surge toward reforms which would long endure.

Nevertheless, Roosevelt himself worried about the strong negative
power the conservative coalition was developing in Congress. In many
states, the Democratic party was under conservative leadership; Farley
had done little to aid New Dealers who had tried to challenge this leadership, and indeed himself seemed in sympathy with the conservatives. Roosevelt in the 1938 campaign intervened in several primaries, mostly in the
South, to try to defeat powerful conservative Democrats who headed congressional committees. Since the conservatives had strong organizations
behind them and his New Deal candidates were relatively unknown, the
conservatives won in almost every contest. More important, the November
election reflected the degree to which the prestige of Roosevelt and the
New Deal were waning. The Republicans gained eighty seats in the
House and seven in the Senate, and together with the conservative Democrats could dominate Congress.

By the end of 1938, the New Deal was close to its ideological limits,
and implementing legislation was needed more than basic reforms. It was
harder to exhort the electorate to a crusading zeal for this more technical
sort of measure, and the nation was swinging to the right. More important,
the threat of a second World War was beginning to overshadow even the
most critical domestic problems. The new Congress, as Vice-President
Garner remarked with some relish, gave Roosevelt his roughest ride. The
President could drive the Southern committee chairmen in the direction of
strong defense legislation and a vigorous foreign policy only if he compromised with them by abandoning reform. From this point on, he made concession after concession on domestic matters in order to gain their aid in
overriding the large minority of militant isolationists in Congress. In his
message to Congress in January 1939, Roosevelt declared: "We have now
passed the period of internal conflict in the launching of our program of
social reform. Our full energies may now be released to invigorate the
processes of recovery in order to preserve our reforms." And he went on
to address himself to the world crisis. He had not abandoned the New
Deal, but it was in abeyance.

A New Pride in American Culture

TO MANY INTELLECTUALS the New Deal was a stimulating challenge. Old progressives during the first years saw the coming to fruition of many of their dreams, but most of them were disturbed by the increased reliance upon Federal regulation, subsidization, and planning that swept the New Deal well beyond the basically laissez faire current of progressivism. Some one-time progressives came to regard Roosevelt's course as the high

Grant Wood (NATIONAL ARCHIVES)

road to "statism"—whether socialism or communism. Most progressives accepted the New Deal, though with misgivings.

As for younger New Dealers, most of them were impatient because Roosevelt did not go further and frequently compromised. They chafed under his essential conservatism, but they too, except for a tiny percentage, wished only to regulate, not to revolutionize. Like their counterparts in the Progressive era, they participated vigorously in shaping the new program. Perhaps for this reason, their spirit and the prevailing spirit of the thirties, unlike the cynical negativism of the twenties, was singularly enthusiastic and optimistic. This was true even though these young reformers exposed the cruel realities of privation in these depression years. They developed new concepts in economics, sociology, and political theory. Beyond this, they took an intense interest in a resurgence of American arts and culture.

Even before the establishment of the Federal Art Project, which came to enroll 5,000 persons, the government had aided artists through an

"American Gothic" by Grant Wood (THE ART INSTITUTE OF CHICAGO)

earlier relief project and the commissioning of extensive murals for new public buildings. Some of these artists painted leftist subjects comparable to those of the highly popular Mexican muralists. Many turned their attention, sometimes satirically, to the American scene.

This was the heyday of Grant Wood, with his patterned Iowa landscapes and austere rural portraits. Wood, born in 1892, in the twenties brought back to Cedar Rapids, Iowa, the bright colors and stylized forms with which he had experimented during his art studies in Paris. His careful, sympathetic interpretation of the Iowa countryside and people

John Steuart Curry (NATIONAL ARCHIVES)

was easy for his generation to understand, and won him wide acclaim during the thirties. His *American Gothic* was the most popular painting at the Chicago Century of Progress Exposition of 1933. The art historian Oliver W. Larkin has written, "If his faces looked rather stony and his rounded hills monotonous and hard, Iowans explained that these qualities were indigenous ones in a country where a hen's shadow at noon fell sharp as a cut silhouette on the barnyard."

John Steuart Curry, born in 1897, equally represented the nationalistic school of painting of the thirties. He was the son of a stockman on the Great Plains and, after training in Chicago, Paris, and New York, turned back to the plains for his major theme: the struggle between man and the forces of nature. The art critic Thomas Craven, who helped build

Curry's reputation, commented, "He paints the barnyard, the wheat fields, the tornado, rustic burials, and baptisms in the open air; the sultry Kansas wind blows through his cornfields; and in his characters, all drawn with strange tenderness, there is the pathetic loneliness and the sinewy courage of the pioneer." There was in Curry's work something of the same glorification of the struggling Americans that had run through the writings of Professor Frederick Jackson Turner. A generation later than Turner, Curry also taught at the University of Wisconsin, as artist-in-residence at the College of Architecture.

"Homesteading and Building Barbed Wire Fence" by John Steuart Curry
(MURAL IN DEPARTMENT OF INTERIOR BUILDING, WASHINGTON, D.C.)

The spirit of the thirties was reflected most strongly in the work of Thomas Hart Benton, who with dramatic sympathy portrayed sharecroppers and Negroes. Benton was born in 1889, the grandnephew of the first senator from Missouri (whose name was also Thomas Hart Benton). He studied at the Chicago Art Institute and then in Paris, where he experimented with half-abstract styles. By the end of the twenties, Benton was rooting his work firmly in his Midwest background, and proclaiming vigorously the virtues of a distinctly American art. In 1932, he declared, "No American art can come to those who do not live an American life, who do not have an American psychology, and who cannot find in America justification of their lives." The critic Craven in 1934 added greatly to Benton's luster by declaring, "The rushing energy of America, the strength and vulgarity, the collective psychology, are embodied in his art. The subordination of artistic tradition to actual experience with American life has enabled Benton to create the outstanding style in American painting, perhaps the only style."

In sculpture, typifying the new government aid and the resurgent nationalism, Gutzon Borglum finished the enormous heads of Washington, Jefferson, Lincoln, and Theodore Roosevelt spread across a mountainside in the Black Hills. Altogether, thousands of artists and sculptors worked during the depression years; never before had America possessed so many who were competent and promising.

Appreciation of the arts took a strong upturn, partly through art classes sponsored by the Federal Art Project, partly through the building of new

Thomas Hart Benton (NATIONAL ARCHIVES)

art museums. In 1941, the National Art Gallery in Washington opened, displaying collections of European art valued at thirty-five million dollars, the gift of Andrew W. Mellon. Samuel H. Kress added four hundred Italian paintings. More people than ever before visited galleries, or bought reproductions of the old masters and of the French impressionists, especially Vincent Van Gogh.

Although jazz more than held its own, interest in classical music likewise increased. The Federal Music Project employed 15,000 persons. They brought concerts to one hundred million people, and gave free music lessons to over a half-million pupils, most of whom could have afforded neither concerts nor lessons. Much of the music they played was that of American composers, such as Roy Harris's Third Symphony and Aaron Copland's *Music for the Theater*. Through new high-quality radio receivers and recordings, many additional millions listened to fine music, especially the symphony broadcasts conducted by Arturo Toscanini and the Metropolitan Opera performances. In 1940, listeners contributed over $300,000 to help "save the Met." But to the great mass of Americans, music meant either sweet popular songs played by bands like Guy Lombardo's or jazz like Benny Goodman's which came surging back into favor in 1934.

After depression and competition from motion pictures had thrown most actors and old vaudeville performers out of work, the Federal Theater Project found employment for 12,500 of them. It brought performances to millions who had never previously seen a stage production. Some of these were highly successful as entertainment, some were of an advanced experimental nature, and some were so far to the left that they kindled the wrath of Congress. It killed the project in 1939. Many of the Broadway playwrights, impervious to Congress, also took a critical look at social problems, as did Lillian Hellman in *The Little Foxes*. Robert E. Sherwood, who illustrated another trend, stopped writing light comedies to dramatize the impotence of the intellectual (*The Petrified Forest*, 1936) and the menace of war (*Idiot's Delight*, 1936). Later, in the pressure of world events, he reversed themes, and glorified the intellectual fighting totalitarian aggression (*There Shall Be No Night*, 1940). Meanwhile, Thornton Wilder wrote *Our Town* (1938) and Eugene O'Neill, who in 1936 won a Nobel Prize, labored quietly on a lengthy cycle of plays.

Novelists were likewise divided into those who, like Faulkner, seemed to be largely unaffected by the era, and others like Ernest Hemingway, who paralleled Sherwood's cycle from 1929 (*A Farewell to Arms*) to 1940 (*For Whom the Bell Tolls*). Thomas Wolfe richly and poetically portrayed the world swirling around him in these years in *Of Time and the River* (1935) and *You Can't Go Home Again* (published posthumously in 1940). Many other novelists turned out proletarian themes from Marxist molds. John Steinbeck sentimentalized his suffering protagonists in his best-selling novel on the Oklahoman trek to California, *The Grapes of Wrath* (1939). The lure of romantic escape and the bargain of the sheer bulk helped make spectacular best-sellers of Hervey Allen's *Anthony Adverse* (1933) and Margaret Mitchell's *Gone With the Wind* (1936).

Reading was one of the most inexpensive pursuits of the depression years, and although libraries suffered from slashed funds, book circulation increased 40 per cent by 1933. Depression likewise cut the cost of radios and enlarged the size of audiences. Twelve million families owned radios in 1929; twenty-eight million families, comprising 86 per cent of the population, had them by 1940. This fact in part explained why Roosevelt was able to campaign so successfully with at least 70 per cent of the metropolitan newspaper circulation opposing him. A radio serial, *Amos and Andy*, was so popular that Huey Long took the name of one of its characters, the Kingfish, as his sobriquet. Motion picture audiences dropped a third early in the depression, then by 1939 box-office totals

Drought refugees stalled on the highway, New Mexico, 1937 (LIBRARY OF CONGRESS)

boomed, with a yearly average of $25 per family. Like radio serials, motion pictures dispensed mostly escape. Because of the vigor of the Catholic-led Legion of Decency, founded in 1934, it was less sexy escape than in the twenties. Theaters also dispensed two movies rather than one, and offered giveaways of a wide variety in order to bolster the box office. As yet television, the coming threat to the movies, was still in the engineering laboratory, a curiosity exhibited at the World's Fair of 1939. It was too expensive for commercial development during the depression.

Education and Science in the Depression

THE TWO depression factors of lack of funds and excess of leisure operated also in education. A third of the unemployed, it was estimated in 1935, were young people. Many went to school for lack of an alternative, and high-school enrollment went up a third between 1929 and 1935. In spite of this rise in enrollment, economy-minded chambers of commerce and citizens' committees led the drive for cuts in school budgets so deep that they carved out educational sinew along with the fat. Colleges and universities dropped in enrollment until 1935, then more than recuperated but continued to suffer budgetary crises. Vocational education was strongly emphasized at both high-school and college level, but serious students also explored social and economic questions so energetically that frightened civic and patriotic organizations warned that "pinks" were taking over the educational systems.

Alarmists feared "pinks" were taking over the churches also, for ministers responded as enthusiastically to the new demands for human welfare as they had once to the "social gospel." Of 20,000 ministers polled in 1934, nearly a third favored socialism, and three fifths, a "drastically reformed capitalism." The main intellectual current among ministers was toward neoorthodoxy. Reinhold Niebuhr, without disavowing political and social liberalism, found powerful psychological pressures driving man toward sin, from which he could be rescued only by faith, that is, submission to God.

The depression seriously cut funds for medical research; nevertheless the thirties were another decade of advance. Ironically, by 1935, when the American Medical Association was warning that twenty million people were suffering malnutrition or were close to it, highly publicized discoveries in vitamin research were leading the well-fed to consume a variety of vitamin-fortified foods, and swallow vitamin pills in quantities second only to laxatives. Sulfa drugs, typhus vaccine, blood plasma, and the "artificial lung" all came into use. Life expectancy increased from fifty-six years in 1920 to sixty-four in 1940, but malnutrition, illness, and sometimes lack of good medical care wrought a heavy toll during the depression. Army medical examiners rejected almost half the first two million young men Selective Service called up in 1940–41. Yet doctors were ill-paid (even in 1929 half of them netted less than $3,000), and were idle much of the time. When some relief units and the Farm Security Administration offered medical aid to the destitute, the demand was overwhelming. Senator Wagner in 1938 introduced a national health bill, but it met stern opposition from the American Medical Association. Voluntary group health and hospitalization plans spread rapidly in some sixty cities and gained three million or more subscribers.

While scientists suffered serious cuts in research funds, university budgets and industrial research funds were back at a peak level by 1936, federal expenditures by 1940. Thus the decade was one of increasing scientific research. The need for reorganization and reinvigoration of some of the government's scientific agencies led to the creation in 1933 of a Science Advisory Board, which futilely tried to obtain a New Deal for science. In 1935 the National Resources Committee (succeeding several similar planning agencies) took over the problem and prepared a study, *Research—A National Resource* (1940). The way was being prepared for centralized scientific planning and establishment of a scientific organization, but they were far from being a fact during the New Deal.

The thirties were years of marked scientific achievement in both basic and applied research in many fields. A chain of basic discoveries by men of many nationalities opened the way to the applications of nuclear fission. In 1931, Harold C. Urey of Columbia discovered a heavy isotope of hydrogen, deuterium, which combined with oxygen atoms to form "heavy water." Bombardment of deuterium atoms by various types of "atom smashers" brought new knowledge about the nature of the atom which could lead to revolutionary applications. Science, a neglected stepchild of the New Deal, was to become the salvation of a nation at war.

Chapter **15**

AMERICA FACES
THE WORLD CRISIS

WHEN THE ROOSEVELT ADMINISTRATION first took office, the threat of a second World War already darkened distant horizons. Gradually through the thirties the threat became more and more immediate, until most Americans came to feel there was little likelihood war would be avoided. At the same time, they and their President were determined that the United States should not become involved. There was no question most people wished the nation to remain a neutral bystander, but there was no certainty that the United States could avoid being pulled into the vortex of the world crisis.

Even as Roosevelt took his oath of office on March 4, 1933, the existing world order was crumbling. That was the day that the Japanese occupied the capital of the Chinese province of Jehol. The next day the last free elections in Germany consolidated Hitler in power; before the end of the month, brown-shirted Nazi storm troopers were harassing Jews. Neither Roosevelt nor many other Americans harbored illusions about what lay ahead. The President was well aware of the menacing nature of Nazism, and in one of his first cabinet meetings warned that the United States might become involved in a war with Japan. But such an eventuality seemed most unlikely, because Roosevelt was ready to lead the nation in the direction it wanted to go, and for years that was toward greater isolation.

As the American people struggled to extricate themselves from the disaster of depression, they abhorred war as an even worse disaster. They entered the new era of reform full of nationalistic fervor, determined to set the country right regardless of what might go on in the rest of the world. Unlike the progressives earlier, they had no predilection for police actions to bring the New Deal to less enlightened areas; above all they were determined that no matter what horrors Hitler might perpetrate, there should be no second crusade in Europe. Yet less than nine years later, they were involved in war with both Germany and Japan.

President Roosevelt ardently admired the foreign policy of Theodore Roosevelt, with its emphasis upon vigorous action backed by a powerful navy, and in some respects functioned similarly. But the current of the times was against him for a full four years or more. Essentially he operated in the field of foreign policy as he did in domestic affairs, by making daring proposals, then accepting an accomodating middle way between extremes. He had once thrilled to the imperialistic adventures of the Progressive era, and in 1920 had campaigned earnestly for the League of Nations. During the twenties he had come to feel that imperialism was a mistake, and by the early thirties had lost his faith in the faltering League. He still had basic leanings toward a strong foreign policy involving collective security, but during his first years in office was preoccupied with the economic nationalism of the New Deal.

In the molding of foreign policy, Roosevelt took seriously his position as chief of state, as the superior of prime ministers and the co-equal of royalty. He enjoyed conferring with foreign potentates, and it often seemed to him that he could solve dangerous international problems if only he could confer with Mussolini or Prince Konoye or others face to face across a conference table. He made the bland optimistic assumption that he could deal with foreign antagonists as he would with political rivals at home, charming them into friendship, arriving at vague agreements with them which later could be honed into viable settlements. This assumption was one of the major weaknesses of his conduct of foreign affairs, especially in his negotiations with the Russians.

Quite correctly, Roosevelt regarded the ambassadors as his personal envoys, but he often created difficulties for the State Department by communicating with them or with foreign ambassadors without keeping the Secretary of State fully informed. While Roosevelt was ready to experiment and even to take chances in foreign affairs, Secretary Hull, from his Wilsonian moralistic position, frequently counseled caution. Roosevelt thoroughly respected Hull, who had an intimate knowledge of Congress, and allowed him to act as a sort of balance wheel. The President also respected the powerful isolationist Senators, and, if anything, overestimated their strength. He never forgot the fiasco of the Versailles Treaty, and was well aware that no foreign policy could be effective without the support of Congress and the public. As in domestic matters, he was keenly sensitive to public opinion.

As a whole, Roosevelt's part in foreign policy was that of a strong, flexible leader, forever toying with daring innovations but ordinarily moderating his actions to fit the more cautious views of the Secretary of

Secretary of State Cordell Hull
(KARSH, OTTAWA)

State, Congress, and the public. At certain critical times, the result seemed to be rather lumbering and even contradictory as Roosevelt moved with considerably less than the decisiveness and directness credited to him by both his friends and his foes. Like the New Deal domestic program, foreign policy developed in directions little anticipated in March 1933. Because it evolved largely in keeping with majority opinion in the United States, for better or worse it was basically democratic.

Withdrawing into the Western Hemisphere

AT THE OUTSET of the New Deal, depression issues dominated foreign policy. With regard to Europe, Roosevelt had inherited from the Hoover administration the problems of war-debt settlements, disarmament, and economic stabilization. He failed to share Hoover's view that the proper settlement of these questions was a key to recovery. Like his predecessor, however, he was willing to see the United States assume a leading moralistic part in world affairs as long as this involved no hampering economic or military commitments.

Roosevelt was well aware of the unwillingness of Congress and the public to scale war-debt payments down to a size payable during the depression, and he took no action. Thus he missed an opportunity to use the debts for bargaining purposes. Most nations were making only token payments. In April 1934 Roosevelt signed an act sponsored by Senator Hiram Johnson, forbidding private loans to any defaulting nations; thereupon all payments, except those of Finland, stopped altogether. Much of the public and press looked upon the defaulting Europeans as deadbeats, rather than regarding the loans as part of the American contribution to the First World War. It was particularly hard to convince Americans that the Europeans could not afford to pay when, after Hitler came into power, these same nations began to increase their outlay for armaments. The United States continued to assert a strong moral position to try to bring about substantial disarmament. It tried to keep the disarmament conference at Geneva functioning, and in May 1933 even pledged itself in the event of disarmament to what at that time was a collective security position, "to consult with other nations in the event of a threat to the peace." But Hitler was bent upon arming, and in October withdrew from both the conference and the League of Nations. The new arms race was underway.

In the same months that the hopes for an arms settlement collapsed, hopes for international economic stabilization went the same way, and the blame this time was assessed against Roosevelt. He had agreed to co-operate in a World Economic Conference which President Hoover had called to meet in London in June 1933. He gave vague assurances to the representatives of eleven countries who visited him in advance that he favored currency stabilization, and announced on May 16 that it was essential in order to "establish order in place of the present chaos." This was the policy under which Secretary Hull, a firm believer in international economic co-operation, and the American delegation went to London. After their arrival President Roosevelt, changing his mind, decided that currency stabilization would be disadvantageous until the dollar had fallen to a competitive position on the world market. There had been little likelihood that the conference would succeed amid the economic sniping among leading nations; Hoover had already ruled off the agenda the critical questions of tariffs, war debts, and reparations. As the boat departed with the delegation, reporters called it the "Funeral Ship." Whatever chance of agreement there had been disappeared when Roosevelt on July 3,

1933, cabled Hull a "bombshell message" disavowing currency stabilization. The conference limped on for three weeks, but Roosevelt's confused and contradictory policy had ended what little possibility there had been at the conference of achieving international co-operation toward economic rehabilitation.

Early in the New Deal, the Roosevelt administration, fearing the economic competition of other nations, continued to look with some suspicion upon the dictatorships and democracies alike. Within a year or so, as the totalitarian countries, especially Nazi Germany, began to bring economic pressure upon the democracies, the Treasury Department switched quickly to form a common front with England and France. Undoubtedly by 1933 America's share of foreign trade had suffered somewhat through the competitive lowering of currencies by other nations. When England had gone off the gold standard, depressing the value of the pound sterling, it had given economic incentive to importers in other nations to buy the cheapened pounds, and with them purchase British goods, rather than to obtain the more expensive dollars for American goods. In the winter of 1933–34, the devaluation of the gold content of the dollar, intended primarily to raise prices at home, did have the effect of making dollars comparatively easy to buy on the world market. It became more advantageous for importers in other nations to buy dollars than it had been previously. After January 1934, when this point was reached, the administration was ready to work toward relative stabilization of the dollar in its relationship to British pounds and French francs. By 1935, as the economic pressures of the dictatorships upon the democracies increased, Secretary of the Treasury Morgenthau worked for *de facto* stabilization as a means of countering it. If France and Great Britain were not to be undermined financially, their currencies must be kept firm. In September 1936, when the franc was seriously threatened, the United States accepted a new French devaluation and signed a tripartite pact with Great Britain and France formally underwriting stabilization. Thus the threat of the dictatorships had taken the United States far from its nationalistic currency position during the London Economic Conference.

The use of foreign policy to further economic improvement at home led President Roosevelt to reverse the policy of his predecessors and recognize Soviet Russia in November 1933. Since the revolution of November 1917 the Russian government had gone unrecognized while a number of irritating questions between the two nations continued to fester. Americans, hungry for what they unrealistically dreamed would be a substantial Russian trade, were eager for recognition. In 1932, trade had dropped 89 per cent from the $114,000,000 of the year before. Even Senator Johnson, for all his isolationist tendencies, declared it was economic idiocy to withhold recognition when "there are billions of dollars' worth of future orders in Russia for American workers to fill."

The Russians had even stronger motives for obtaining recognition, for they were afraid of being attacked by Japan. Maxim Litvinov, the Russian Foreign Minister, after discussions with Roosevelt at the White House, agreed that Russia would end its propaganda activities in the United States, guarantee religious freedom and protection in the courts to Americans resident in Russia, and would negotiate a settlement of debts and claims. Roosevelt was mistaken in trusting to the good faith of the Russians and not negotiating a firm settlement of the claims of American citizens against the Soviet before granting recognition. Several months later the United States established an Import-Export Bank to facilitate exchange and made plans to extend credit to Russia, but the Russians balked over the claims settlement and continued to propagandize through the Communist Party. The large trade did not materialize and relations between the two countries remained cool. The United States did gain from maintaining an embassy staff in Moscow where the men who were to become the State Department Russian specialists could study the techniques of the Soviet government.

By January 1934 Roosevelt was ready to heed Hull's emphatic recommendation that tariff barriers be lowered in order to improve foreign trade. With the President's support, Congress in June 1934 passed Hull's cherished program, the Reciprocal Trade Agreements Act. It authorized the administration to negotiate three-year reciprocity agreements, lowering tariffs on specified goods coming in from individual nations by as much as 50 per cent in return for arrangements to take certain American goods. These agreements did not have to be ratified by the Senate, and through most-favored-nation clauses came to apply to most countries. Thus Secretary Hull was able to negotiate a controlled lowering of the tariff schedules without the traditional pitched battles with the logrollers within Congress and the lobbyists without. Technically the new measure was an amendment to the Hawley-Smoot Tariff.

The immediate effect of the reciprocal trade agreements is difficult to estimate. During the depression years they were drafted carefully to cover only products not competitive with American industry and agriculture. By 1939, Hull had negotiated agreements with twenty-one countries, ranging from Cuba to the United Kingdom. These lowered the tariff an estimated 29 per cent, at the same time that they gained concessions for American exporters, especially growers of cotton and tobacco. By the end of 1938, American exports to the sixteen nations with which it then had trade agreements had increased nearly 40 per cent. The reciprocal trade program was working a quiet revolution in tariff policy.

At the Inter-American Conference at Montevideo in December 1933, Hull won such acclaim with his proposals for reciprocity that President Roosevelt gave him full support upon his return home. To small nations like Cuba, dependent upon exports to the United States, reciprocity seemed a way out of the depression. At the same time that Hull offered economic succor, he reiterated to the people of Latin America at Montevideo (while Roosevelt said the same thing in Washington) that the United States was opposed to armed intervention in Latin America. Most important of all, Hull signed a convention declaring, "No state has the right to intervene in the internal or external affairs of another." This, unlike American policy declarations, was a binding position.

Thus Hull took the United States a step further than the Hoover administration, which had unofficially disavowed the Theodore Roosevelt corollary to the Monroe Doctrine, but had reserved the right to intervene in self-defense. Limited intervention seemed to be the American policy as late as the summer of 1933 when revolution exploded in Cuba. Sumner Welles, one of the chief draftsmen of the new Latin American policy, was sent into Cuba, rather than the Marines, to offer the "good offices" of the United States, but had American lives been seriously threatened, troops would have followed. Welles helped bring pacification without intervention. In 1934, when a more conservative government came into power in Cuba, the United States gave up its right of intervention under the Platt Amendment. It also withdrew the last Marines from Haiti, and in 1936 negotiated a treaty (not ratified until 1939) relaxing the restrictions upon Panama.

The new Good Neighbor policy of nonintervention received a severe testing in 1938 when Mexico expropriated all foreign oil holdings, including property valued by its American owners at $200,000,000. The United States conceded the right of expropriation but at first contended that the price the Mexicans wished to pay was so trivial as to be confiscation. Nevertheless when in 1942, after years of involved controversy, a commission evaluated the property at $24,000,000 the State Department told the protesting oil companies that they must accept the settlement or receive nothing. This reversal of Dollar Diplomacy, the self-denial of the right to intervene to protect American property in Latin America valued at hundreds of millions or even billions of dollars, had a corollary. Along with nonintervention, the Good Neighbor policy was emphasizing cooperation toward mutually advantageous ends. In terms of trade it was of immediate benefit. As the threat of war in Europe increased, it came to mean also mutual defense, and this became paramount.

Latin peoples watched with especial interest the policies of the United States toward its Spanish-speaking colonies, Puerto Rico and the Philippine Islands. The troubles of overcrowded Puerto Rico, with its impoverished population of 1,800,000 and absentee ownership of farm lands, were little noted in the United States but made headlines as far south as Buenos Aires. When militant nationalists assassinated the American police chief in Puerto Rico, Senator Millard Tydings was able to chasten the Puerto Ricans by introducing an independence bill, since freedom from the United States would bring even greater economic disaster. In the late thirties, Governor Rexford G. Tugwell helped provide Puerto Ricans with aid for the underprivileged, public works, and encouragement to manufacturers. The Jones Act of 1917 had given Puerto Ricans American citizenship and a popularly elected legislature, but it was not until 1949 that they could elect their own governor, and 1952 before they could assume what in effect was commonwealth status.

As for the Philippines, primarily the depression and secondarily isolationism brought them the long-sought but economically dubious blessing of independence. American producers of sugar, fats, and oils were determined to thrust their Filipino competitors outside the tariff wall; isolationists were eager to drop this dangerous Far Eastern military commitment. The Tydings-McDuffie Act of 1934 thrust upon the Philippines complete independence rather than the dominion status they sought. In 1935 the Philippines entered upon a transitional commonwealth period; on July 4, 1946 they became a fully independent republic. The United States was demonstrating that it was trying to rid itself of possessions rather than seize new ones.

The gravest of diplomatic problems continued to be relations with Japan. While Roosevelt accepted the Stimson doctrine of nonrecognition of Manchukuo, as the Japanese called Manchuria, he did not press it, and for the next several years, Hull periodically exchanged friendly assurances with the Japanese. On the surface, tensions seemed to have relaxed, but beneath it, the Japanese government continued steady pressure for a free hand in China—for a "Japanese Monroe Doctrine." There were occasional disquieting bits of jingoism; in 1934, realistic displays in Osaka department stores depicted the coming war with the United States. The State Department paid no attention; Hull politely, mildly, but nonetheless firmly, stood by the Open Door policy.

In an equally unspectacular fashion, President Roosevelt kept the fleet stationed at Pearl Harbor in the Pacific, rather than in the Atlantic, and began the considerable task of modernizing and building it toward treaty strength. Pacifists and budget balancers were horrified over the enormous sum of one billion dollars necessary to bring the Navy to parity and the additional hundred million required annually for replacements. Big-navy advocates asserted the expenditure was essential, since not a single new ship had been authorized during the Hoover administration. Roosevelt quickly demonstrated where he stood by earmarking $238,000,000 of the first emergency-relief appropriation for the construction of thirty-two ships. He justified these as public works that would stimulate recovery, since 85 per cent of the money would go into wages in almost every state, but Congress stipulated in 1934 that no more public-works money should go to the navy. Under the effective pressure of the President and the congressional naval committees, Congress in March 1934 passed the Vinson-Trammell Act, which authorized both the immediate construction of four cruisers and a long-range large-scale building program to bring the navy to treaty strength by 1942.

At the London Naval Conference of 1935, the Japanese withdrew after they failed to obtain equality with the Americans and British in place of the 5:5:3 ratio, and thus opened the way for competitive naval building. So it was that in the isolationist years of the thirties, the United States built the fleet with which it was to fight the opening battles of a Pacific war.

Neutrality Legislation

THE BREAKDOWN of the naval status quo and alarm over the threatened aggressions in both Asia and Europe convinced most Americans that at all costs they must stay out of impending wars. Many leaders of the peace movement who had been dedicated Wilsonians and advocates of the League had become disgusted with its inability to stop Japanese aggression. They reasoned that internationalism had failed, and that therefore they must fall back upon isolationism to maintain the peace. Others, taking an economic-determinist view of wars, felt that the machinations of Wall Streeters and munitions makers, combined with Wilson's legalistic insistence upon outmoded neutral rights on the high seas, had trapped the nation into the First World War. Senate investigators, under the progressive Republican Gerald P. Nye of North Dakota, revealed exorbitant wartime profits and tax evasion, and claimed that bankers sought war to rescue their loans to the Allies. President Roosevelt, himself impressed by the Nye investigation, wrote privately his regret that Bryan had left the State Department in 1915.

The Nye Committee findings and similar sensational popular writings convinced a large part of the public that entrance into the First World War had been a frightful mistake. The way to avoid its repetition seemed to be to legislate these pitfalls out of existence. As Mussolini openly prepared to conquer Ethiopia in 1935, Americans feared that a general European war might develop. They felt the way to avoid involvement was not to participate in strong deterring pressure against Italy, since Mussolini might strike back. Rather it was to isolate the nation through neutrality legislation.

President Roosevelt also favored legislation, but he and Hull wanted, as Hull had proposed in 1933, a law that would enable Roosevelt to embargo war supplies to the aggressor and allow their sale to the victim. He might thus have been able to co-operate with the League in coercing Mussolini to remain at peace. The line was this thin between collective security and isolation, but Congress did not dare risk even a mild gesture. Instead it passed a neutrality act providing a mandatory embargo against both aggressor and victim, and empowering the President to warn American citizens that they might travel on vessels of belligerents only at their own risk. This first Neutrality Act of August 1935 was temporary legislation that expired at the end of February 1936, and was then renewed, with even stronger isolationist provisions, to May 1937.

When the attack upon Ethiopia came, in October 1935, the League branded Italy an aggressor and voted sanctions against it. England and France made gestures against Italy, but showed no inclination toward stronger action even before Hitler created a new threat by militarizing the Rhineland. The German threat further restrained them from imposing an oil embargo against Italy, since they did not dare risk war in the Mediterranean for fear it would leave them vulnerable to Hitler. Also they feared alienating Russia, which supplied oil to Italy. Hull imposed a "moral embargo" upon oil which was not very effective; even had the League taken strong action, neutrality legislation would have kept him from doing more. The outcome was that Mussolini easily conquered his African empire, withdrew from the League, and in October 1936 joined with Hitler to form a new Rome-Berlin axis. Collective security had suffered a new, staggering blow and events were moving rapidly toward a European war.

The fiasco seemed to strengthen the determination of the American people to stay out of war. The new public opinion polls, based on samplings of only 1,500 to 3,500 people, with a probable error of 4 to 6 per cent, indicated top-heavy opinion against involvement. A typical poll in November 1935, after the attack on Ethiopia, queried, "If one foreign nation insists upon attacking another, should the United States join with other nations to compel it to stop?" The answer: yes, 28 per cent; no, 67 per cent; no opinion, 5 per cent. The 28 per cent answering yes were queried further as to what measures they would favor. They replied:

Economic and nonmilitary measures only	65%
Military if necessary	31%
No opinion	4%

This antiinvolvement sentiment continued to be the mood of the nation when a new danger arose in July 1936, as General Francisco Franco and the Falangists (modeled after the Fascists) revolted against the Republican government in Spain. Hitler and Mussolini sided with Franco; Russia, France, and, to a lesser extent, Great Britain favored the Loyalists. To prevent the Spanish civil war from spreading into a general European conflict, England and France agreed to send no aid to either side. Roosevelt tried to co-operate, but could impose only another "moral embargo" since the second Neutrality Act did not cover insurrections. In January 1937 Congress remedied this defect. The result was that the United States and other Western nations denied aid to Republican Spain. At first, Communists were only a trivial minority within it; there had not been a single Communist member in the Spanish Cortes (legislature). As the Republican government came to depend increasingly upon Russia for what little aid it received, gradually in the following three years Communists became more dominant. As for Franco, he received massive aid from Mussolini and Hitler, who violated their nonintervention agreement with impunity and ultimately crushed the Loyalists.

American feelings became inflamed over the invasion of Ethiopia and the Spanish civil war, but President Roosevelt voiced the majority attitude in August 1936, a month after the outbreak of the war in Spain, when he asserted, "We shun political commitments which might entangle us in foreign wars; we avoid connection with the political activities of the League of Nations. . . . We are not isolationists except in so far as we seek to isolate ourselves completely from war." He emphasized, "I hate war."

In this spirit, Congress enacted the third Neutrality Act of May 1937, which, while it increased the President's discretionary power, tightened the previous laws and relinquished American claims to freedom of the seas in wartime. Congress had legislated against the factors that had precipitated the nation into the First World War. This action had the advantage within the United States of placing questions of war and peace on issues more vital to the national interest than technicalities involving neutral rights. It had the serious disadvantage of serving notice to both totalitarian aggressors and democratic nations that in case of attack the democracies could expect no American aid. To this extent the neutrality legislation contributed to the steady deterioration of the peace. The third Neutrality Act came as Japan was about to plunge into China, and Germany was already taking aggressive steps against Austria and Czechoslovakia.

Moving Toward Collective Security

NEITHER PRESIDENT ROOSEVELT nor Secretary Hull wished the United States to be so uncompromisingly isolationist; consistently they had favored neutrality legislation that would give the President the discretion of favoring the victims of aggression in applying embargoes. There was some possibility that they could win public opinion to this point of view, since the nation abhorred totalitarianism. The great obstacle was a small group of powerful isolationist Senators in key positions. Previously Roosevelt had capitulated to them without serious struggle. In 1937 came a change.

The great Japanese drive into the five northern provinces of China began in the summer of 1937. At first the State Department pursued a "middle-of-the-road" policy, favoring neither country. Since Japan carefully avoided declaring war, President Roosevelt did not invoke the Neutrality Act; private American ships at their own risk could carry arms and munitions to both belligerents.

By October 1937, the administration was ready to take a firm position against Japan. The British proposed a joint arms embargo which seemed to involve no great risk. At this time and during the next four years, the consensus of the experts was that Japan was a mediocre military power. Hull persuaded Roosevelt to make a statement to counteract isolationism. The President, speaking at Chicago facing the Chicago *Tribune* tower, went beyond his advisors and declared:

> The peace-loving nations must make a concerted effort in opposition to those violations of treaties and those ignorings of humane instincts which today are creating a state of international anarchy, international instability from which there is no escape through mere isolation or neutrality.

War, he asserted, was a contagion, which like a disease must be quarantined by the international community.

There is evidence that Roosevelt had in mind nothing more drastic than a collective breaking off of diplomatic relations, that he did not favor economic or military sanctions. Immediate press reaction and White House mail was favorable, but within a few days, as the Chicago *Tribune* and Hearst press continued to draw sinister implications from the speech, it plunged the nation, as the *Tribune* reported, into a "hurricane of war fright." Hull, dismayed, felt it set back the campaign for collective security at least six months. It also set back Roosevelt in his thinking. In November 1937 he sent to Brussels a delegate to an international conference to consider the Japanese aggression, but instructed him not to take the lead, or be a tail to the British kite.

Japan had no need to fear economic or military reprisals from the United States. On December 12, 1937, young Japanese aviators bombed and sank the United States gunboat *Panay* on the Yangtze River. At the time, and in years since, the aviators claimed they bombed it in error, but visibility was excellent and an American flag was painted on the deck. As at the time of the sinking of the *Maine* in 1898, a wave of excitement swept the country, but this time it was fear that the nation might become involved in war. The United States quickly accepted the profuse Japanese apologies and offers of indemnity.

At the end of 1938, Japan was in military and economic control of almost all of eastern China. As it supplanted the Open Door with the New Order, it was making conditions almost untenable for Americans in China. But the United States would not recognize any new status in China, and in the interior, the armies of Chiang Kai-shek continued to fight. The relations of the United States with Japan were becoming gradually more critical, but the threat of war in Europe overshadowed the Asiatic impasse.

As President Roosevelt tried to swing Congress and the people toward collective security, he had his greatest success in building a system of mutual defense in the Western Hemisphere. The traditional American isolationism, as exemplified by Hearst editorials or the speeches of several Senators, involved strict nonintervention toward Europe but a considerably more active role in Asia—no sanctions, but an insistence upon the Open Door in China. Within the Western Hemisphere, toward both Canada and Latin America, these isolationists were ready to give the President almost a free hand. Indeed there were no more devout exponents of the Monroe Doctrine than they. The term "isolationist" was really a misnomer for them; they were really a narrow sort of American nationalist.

Roosevelt took full advantage of these prejudices to inaugurate policies within the hemisphere which he could later apply across the Atlantic and Pacific. In December 1936 he traveled all the way to Buenos Aires to put his personal prestige behind a pact to change the Monroe Doctrine into a mutual security agreement. Henceforth, if any outside power threatened the American republics, instead of the United States acting unilaterally they would all consult together for their own protection. The machinery also covered disputes among the republics themselves, but was specifically aimed at meeting the threat of the Axis. It provided that the members would consult "in the event of an international war outside America which might menace the peace of the American Republics." In December 1938, with war in Europe imminent, the republics, at a meeting in Lima, Peru, established a means of consultation. Roosevelt also extended hemispheric security to the north in August 1938, when he issued a declaration of solidarity with Canada.

By 1938, Hitler had rebuilt such a strong German army and air force that he was ready to embark upon a course of intimidation and conquest. In March, he proclaimed union with Austria and paraded triumphantly through Vienna. This union put western Czechoslovakia into the jaws of a German vise. Hitler began tightening it with demands on behalf of the minority of 3,500,000 Germans in Czechoslovakia. In September 1938, Hitler brought Europe to the brink of war with his demands for the cession of the Sudeten area in which the minority lived. The Czechs, who had a strong army, were ready to fight rather than submit, but the people of other Western nations, appalled at the threat of another world conflict, were eager for a settlement on almost any terms. Roosevelt joined in the pleas to Hitler for a peaceful solution, but this was of minor significance. At Munich on September 29, the French and British signed a pact with Hitler granting his demands in Czechoslovakia. "This is the last territorial claim I have to make in Europe," he declared.

Within a few weeks, the once strong Czechoslovakia was whittled down to impotence. In March 1939, Hitler took over the remainder of it as German protectorates, thus demonstrating speedily the worthlessness of his Munich pledge. In April, he began harassing Poland. The British and French, seeing clearly that appeasement had failed, gave firm pledges to Poland and other threatened nations. They made half-hearted gestures toward Russia, which had been left out of the Munich settlement, but Stalin instead in August signed a nonaggression pact with Hitler. It freed Hitler to attack Poland if he could not frighten the country into submission. When Poland stood firm, Germany invaded it on September 1, 1939. Great Britain and France, true to their pledges, on September 3 declared war on Germany. The Second World War had begun. Americans wondered if they could stay out.

The Outbreak of War: Limited Aid

As HITLER had moved toward war in the spring and summer of 1939, President Roosevelt tried to persuade Congress that the arms embargo would encourage Hitler, and that American security demanded that it be modified to assure arms to Great Britain and France. Senator Borah, claiming superior sources of information, asserted that there would be no war, and Congress took no action.

With the outbreak of war, Roosevelt issued a neutrality proclamation pointedly different from Wilson's 1914 plea for Americans to be neutral in thought as well as action. "This nation will remain a neutral nation,"

Roosevelt stated, "but I cannot ask that every American remain neutral in thought as well." The great majority of the American people did not want to become involved in the war, but also did not want the democracies to lose. This, according to every gauge of public opinion, was the American attitude from the invasion of Poland until Pearl Harbor.

Roosevelt called Congress into special session, and despite a heated debate was able to muster the votes for a revision of the Neutrality Act. The 1939 measure still prohibited American ships from entering the war zones, but it did allow belligerents to purchase arms on a "cash-and-carry" basis. Had England and France been able to restrain Hitler with this limited assistance, Roosevelt probably would have asked for nothing more. Indeed, during the quiet winter of 1939–40, after the quick Nazi overrunning of Poland, overoptimistic American publicists asserted that the Allies were calling Hitler's bluff, and after a long and boring blockade on sea and land would triumph. During these months of the "phony war," American indignation flared hottest over the Russian invasion of Finland. The administration applied a tight "moral embargo" on shipments of munitions to Russia, but went no further.

During these months of relative quiet, President Roosevelt made only modest requests for increases in armaments. Army and navy appropriations went up only about 50 per cent in the two years ending June 30, 1940. In May 1938, after the German annexation of Austria, Roosevelt had obtained with some difficulty a 20 per cent increase in the naval program. Congressional isolationists pointed out that the navy was already the largest in history. In November 1939, Representative Carl Vinson announced another large four-year naval program to cost $1,300,000,000. In January 1940, Roosevelt asked for moderate increases in armaments expenditures, but the House Appropriations Committee cut $12,000,000 for an air base in Alaska, and slashed the 496 recommended airplanes to only 57. By the time the bill reached the Senate, events in Europe had made it obsolete.

The Fall of France: All-Out Aid

OPTIMISTIC ILLUSIONS about Hitler's weakness turned into panic in the spring of 1940 when the Nazis invaded Denmark and Norway, then swept across Holland and Belgium deep into France. On May 16, Roosevelt asked Congress for an additional billion in defense expenditures and obtained it quickly. On the premise that the United States must build great air armadas to hold off the Nazis, he set a goal of at least 50,000 airplanes a year.

On June 10, 1940, Mussolini joined the Germans by attacking France,

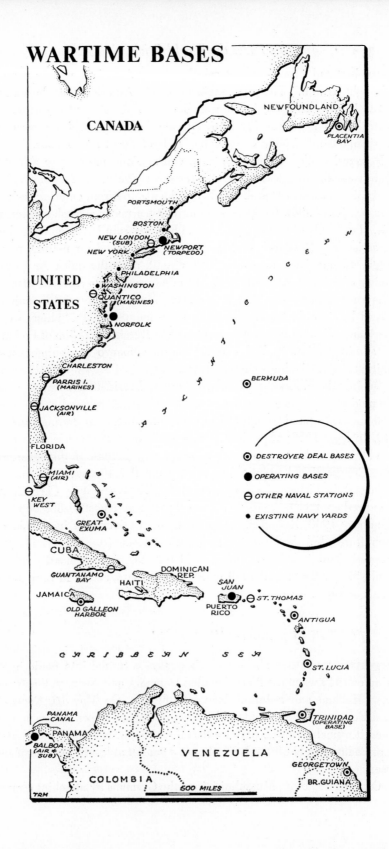

WARTIME BASES

CANADA

NEWFOUNDLAND

PLACENTIA
BAY

PORTSMOUTH

BOSTON

NEW LONDON
(SUB)

NEWPORT
(TORPEDO)

NEW YORK

PHILADELPHIA

WASHINGTON

QUANTICO
(MARINES)

UNITED

STATES

NORFOLK

CHARLESTON

PARRIS I.
(MARINES)

BERMUDA

JACKSONVILLE
(AIR)

FLORIDA

MIAMI
(AIR)

KEY
WEST

GREAT
EXUMA

BAHAMAS

CUBA

GUANTANAMO
BAY

DOMINICAN
REP.

HAITI

SAN
JUAN

ST. THOMAS

JAMAICA

OLD GALLEON
HARBOR

PUERTO
RICO

ANTIGUA

C A R I B B E A N   S E A

ST. LUCIA

PANAMA
CANAL

PANAMA

BALBOA
(AIR &
SUB)

TRINIDAD
(OPERATING
BASE)

V E N E Z U E L A

GEORGETOWN

COLOMBIA

BR. GUIANA

◉ DESTROYER DEAL BASES

● OPERATING BASES

⊖ OTHER NAVAL STATIONS

• EXISTING NAVY YARDS

500 MILES

TRM

despite an earlier strong plea from Roosevelt to "withhold your hand." Roosevelt, speaking that evening, asserted, "The hand that held the dagger has struck it into the back of its neighbor." And, with France tottering from the German onslaught, he proclaimed that the United States would "extend to the opponents of force the material resources of this nation." He was taking the United States from a status of isolation to one of non-belligerency on the side of the democracies.

Twelve days later France fell, and in all western Europe only the shattered remnants of the British army that had been retrieved from Dunkirk opposed the Nazis. Already the new prime minister, Winston Churchill, was showering Roosevelt with requests for destroyers and arms of all kinds to help the British man their bastion. The odds against the British were heavy, but Roosevelt made the bold and dangerous decision to "scrape the bottom of the barrel" and turn over to them all available matériel of war. This plan was carried out to such an extent that, as late as 1941, some American troop units were maneuvering with pieces of telephone pole substituting for artillery that was in England. The United States also promised the British 14,375 airplanes by April 1942. Most spectacular of all, as the air softening-up for the invasion of Britain began, Roosevelt gave fifty over-age destroyers to the British in return for 99-year leases on eight bases from Newfoundland to British Guiana. It was, as Churchill later wrote, "a decidedly unneutral act."

As Roosevelt threw the resources of the United States behind the British as completely as Congress would let him, he did so with the feeling that an Axis victory would mean disaster to the nation. He believed the Germans, through either military or economic means, would encircle and destroy the United States. A large part of the public seemed suddenly to have changed its mind and to agree. In March 1940 only 43 per cent of those polled thought a German victory would be a threat to the United States; by July, 69 per cent did. In May 1940, only 35 per cent favored aid to Britain at the risk of American involvement; four months later, 60 per cent did. Yet no more people than previously wished to enter the war; as late as the month before Pearl Harbor, only 20 per cent of those polled favored a declaration of war against Germany. Roosevelt and the American public seemed to share incompatible aims. They wished to bring about the defeat of the Axis without involving the United States in a shooting war. Some time in the next eighteen months, Roosevelt probably came to feel that American entrance was desirable; the public never did.

All America was pulled into a great debate on the issue of war versus peace. William Allen White, the Kansas newspaper editor, headed a Committee to Defend America by Aiding the Allies, often called the White Committee. White himself (like a large percentage of Americans) favored merely aid, but a minority wanted to go further and declare war. This group, in April 1941, founded the Fight for Freedom Committee. On the antiinvolvement side, a Yale student, R. Douglas Stuart, Jr., organized an America First Committee under the chairmanship of a leading Chicago businessman, General Robert E. Wood. It drew upon the oratorical talent of the aviation hero Charles Lindbergh, General Hugh Johnson, and Senators Nye and Wheeler. It won the editorial support of the Hearst and other large newspapers, and appealed to a considerable segment of patriotic Americans. Inevitably it also attracted a small fringe of pro-Nazi, anti-Semitic, and American fascist fanatics. The statements of its principal speaker, Lindbergh, often aroused violent controversy. In April 1941 Lindbergh asserted that Britain was defeated, and several weeks later joined with Senator Wheeler in calling for a negotiated peace. In September, he declared, "The three most important groups which have been pressing this country toward war are the British, the Jewish, and the Roosevelt Administration." Roosevelt so curtly denounced Lindbergh as an appeaser and defeatist that Lindbergh resigned his colonelcy in the Army Air Force.

It was a bitter fight, and through the summer and fall of 1940, it was complicated by a presidential election.

The 1940 Election

During the winter of the "phony war" it seemed likely that Roosevelt would retire at the end of his second term and that the Republicans would nominate either of two young men who were courting the isolationists, Senator Robert Taft of Ohio or a reforming New York City district attorney, Thomas E. Dewey. Also, a Republican victory seemed imminent. The German blitz ended these possibilities.

The Republicans met at Philadelphia in June 1940, as the sickening black shadow of the collapse of France sank over the nation. National defense was suddenly the most important issue. Roosevelt underscored this, and stole headlines from the Republican convention on June 20 by appointing to his cabinet two of the most distinguished Republicans. He made the elder statesman Henry L. Stimson Secretary of War, and appointed as Secretary of the Navy the 1936 Vice-Presidential candidate and sharp critic of the New Deal, Frank Knox.

The chagrined Republicans at Philadelphia promptly read Stimson and Knox out of the party but could not ignore the defense issue. They succumbed to the grass-roots pressure, which had been built through a careful advertising campaign, and nominated a young internationalist, Wendell Willkie. It was a startling blow to the isolationist majority among the Republican politicians, but provided them with a tousle-haired, personable candidate who could win hysterical devotion from the amateur party workers. Willkie, the son of a prosperous lawyer and landowner in Elwood, Indiana, had been considered a red-sweatered campus radical at the University of Indiana. As a rising corporation lawyer in the twenties, he remained a Democrat, but after 1933, when he became president of the Commonwealth and Southern utility company at a salary of $75,000 per year, he found it hard to retain his old party loyalties. As he challenged

Wendell Willkie (NATIONAL ARCHIVES)

T.V.A. on behalf of private utilities, he managed to retain both the language and appearance of a rural radical. "It is an asset in my business to look like an Indiana farmer," he remarked, leading Secretary Ickes to sneer that Willkie was "a simple barefoot Wall Street lawyer." Willkie appealed enormously to many middle-class Americans as a liberal Republican who would retain the New Deal reforms but encourage business and investment. The Republican domestic planks and Willkie's campaign orations ran in this direction. He was a forerunner of the modern Republicans. On foreign policy, both the platform and Willkie pledged that the nation would be kept out of war but would aid peoples fighting for liberty.

By the time the Democrats met in mid-July, it was a foregone conclusion that they would renominate Roosevelt. Shrewd politician that he was, he had kept so silent about a third term that newspapers had cartooned him as a sphinx; until the convention nominated him, he maintained complete freedom of action. White House mail indicated that voters were little concerned with the no-third-term tradition, and at the Democratic convention Roosevelt could command the solid support of Northern liberals and city bosses, and most of the rank and file. He was even able to force the Democratic politicians to swallow his choice for Vice-President, Secretary of Agriculture Henry A. Wallace, who by this time was considered an advanced New Dealer.

Willkie embarked upon an appealing but slightly amateurish campaign, whistle-stopping so vigorously that he nearly lost his voice, denouncing the bad management of the New Deal rather than its basic program. Numerous right-wing Democrats and even some early New Dealers like

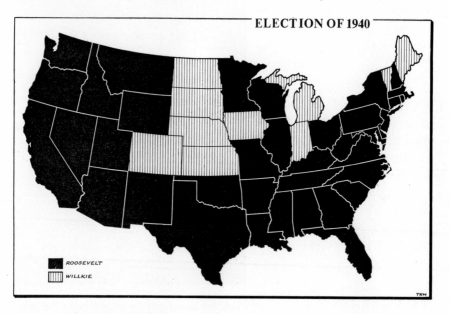

ELECTION OF 1940

ROOSEVELT
WILLKIE

Moley and General Johnson supported him. John L. Lewis threatened to resign as President of the C.I.O. if Willkie were not elected, a possibility that did not seem to frighten organized labor.

Roosevelt, a wily old campaigner, tried to give the appearance of not campaigning at all. Defense problems were so acute, he insisted, that he had to spend his time instead touring army bases, munitions plants, and shipyards, along routes which somehow took him through innumerable cities where he cheerily greeted quantities of voters. Willkie was trying to prove that Roosevelt was not shoring up defenses fast enough, and the President was conspicuously functioning as Commander in Chief; Willkie was trying to show that the New Deal had not brought prosperity, and thousands of workers were being hired in munitions plants and shipyards. Then to cap Willkie's trouble, Roosevelt launched into a series of vigorous campaign speeches defending the New Deal.

No matter how much Willkie and Roosevelt talked about it, the campaign did not center around the New Deal. Rather, foreign policy was paramount. On this, they both had much the same views: Willkie approved of the destroyers–bases agreement. Both made fervent antiwar statements to placate the isolationists. Willkie declared that if Roosevelt's promise to stay out of a foreign war was no better than his pledge to balance the budget, the boys were "already almost on the transports." This was an effective campaign issue which cut into Roosevelt's support. At Boston, Roosevelt (making the mental reservation that any attack upon the United States would not be a foreign war) picked up the challenge in words the isolationists were to mock incessantly:

> I have said this before, but I shall say it again and again and again:
> Your boys are not going to be sent into any foreign wars.

No matter what Willkie's principles and Roosevelt's protestations, a large part of the vote of those opposing aid to the Allies went to Willkie. At the same time, a considerable part of those favoring vigorous aid or even intervention (including many who fervently opposed New Deal domestic policies) voted for Roosevelt. They preferred Roosevelt's sure leadership to Willkie's inexperience. It was a relatively close vote: 27,244,000 for Roosevelt, and 22,305,000 for Willkie; 449 electoral votes to 82. The combined third-party vote was less than 200,000. Within a few weeks, Willkie was on his way to England with a letter from Roosevelt to Churchill in his pocket.

Building an Arsenal of Democracy

IN ADDITION TO POLITICKING, in the months after the fall of France Roosevelt had to build makeshift defense machinery. With Willkie's aid, he pushed through the Burke-Wadsworth bill, passed in September 1940, which inaugurated the first peacetime selective service in American history. This was the summer when he arranged to send destroyers to England, turned back new airplanes to the factory to be ferried across the Atlantic, and somehow ran the gauntlet of several anti-British, isolationist chairmen of Senate committees.

By mid-December, the British had so nearly exhausted their financial resources that they had practically stopped letting new contracts, yet Churchill warned Roosevelt that their needs would increase tenfold in the future. The Neutrality Act of 1939 and the Johnson Act forbade American loans; a request for repeal would have reawakened the old furore about unpaid war debts. Roosevelt, cruising in the Caribbean after the election, thought of a formula. The United States should lend goods rather than money, "to eliminate the dollar sign." If one's neighbor's house caught fire, he explained, one would lend a garden hose to prevent the fire from spreading to one's own house. Lend-Lease would create an "arsenal of democracy" as a means of protecting the American nation, he explained. The bill went into the congressional hopper at the right moment to bear a significant number: it became House Resolution 1776. The fierce debate over Lend-Lease shocked the country. Senator Wheeler charged that it was "the New Deal's triple A. foreign policy; it will plow under every fourth American boy." That, Roosevelt retorted, was "the most untruthful, as well as the most dastardly, unpatriotic thing that has ever been said." The bill went through Congress by a wide margin, and in March 1941 was signed by the President. It empowered him to spend an initial seven billion dollars—a sum as large as the controversial loans of the First World War.

Lend-Lease committed the United States formally to the policy the President had been following since the fall of France, pouring aid into Great Britain to help it withstand the German onslaught. Since Lend-Lease shipments had to cross the Atlantic to be of aid, the United States acquired a vital interest in keeping the Atlantic sea lanes open against the formidable wolf packs of German submarines, which in the spring of 1941 were destroying a half-million tons of shipping a month, twice as much as shipyards could produce. The President did not dare openly convoy vessels to England as Secretary Stimson urged; isolationists in Congress were too powerful. Instead he fell back upon the device of "hemispheric defense." The American republics had proclaimed an Atlantic neutrality zone in 1939; Roosevelt in 1941 extended it far to the east, almost to Iceland, and ordered the Navy to patrol the area and give warning of aggressors. This meant radioing to the British the location of Nazi submarines. The United States occupied Greenland in April 1941 and Iceland in July, and began escorting convoys as far as Iceland.

In secret, the United States had gone even further, for in the spring of 1941 American and British officers in Washington reached agreement on the strategy to be followed if the United States entered the war. President Roosevelt demonstrated publicly in August 1941 how close he had come to carrying the United States from nonbelligerency to cobelligerency with England when he met with Prime Minister Churchill off the coast of Newfoundland. Roosevelt refused to make military commitments but did sign with Churchill a press release on war aims, the Atlantic Charter. It called for national self-determination, greater economic opportunities, freedom from fear and want, freedom of the seas, and disarmament. As Churchill later pointed out, Roosevelt, representing a nation not at war, subscribed to a document that referred to "the final destruction of the Nazi tyranny."

In June 1941, Hitler unleashed an enormous surprise attack against Russia, so powerful that American military leaders predicted that Russia

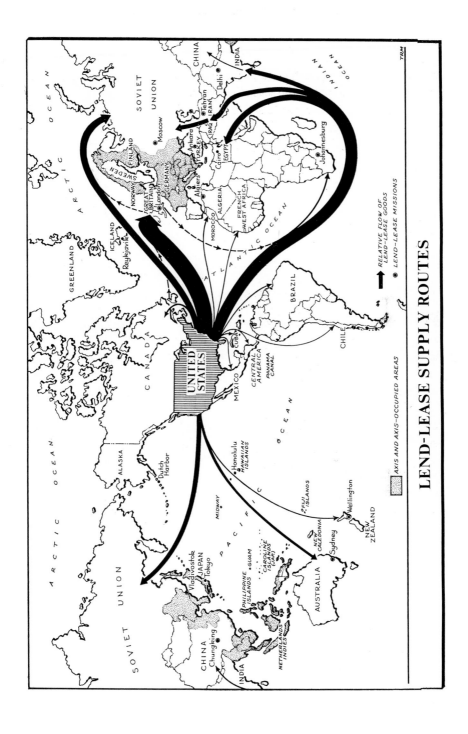

LEND-LEASE SUPPLY ROUTES

would collapse in a few weeks or months. The Russians fell back before the deep Nazi incursions, but continued to fight, and in September Roosevelt, again gambling, extended Lend-Lease to them. This made it even more imperative to patrol the seas effectively.

The German answer was to strike back with submarines. In May 1941 they sank the American ship *Robin Moor* off the coast of Brazil and replied to protests by saying, "Germany will continue to sink every ship with

Lend-Lease supplies for Russia being unloaded on the Persian Gulf (NATIONAL ARCHIVES)

contraband for Britain whatever its name." In September, a submarine attacked but failed to hit the destroyer *Greer*, which was radioing the submarine's position to the British. President Roosevelt, who did not know, or at least did not reveal, what the *Greer* was doing, issued orders to the navy in the future to "shoot on sight." In October, another destroyer was hit, and the *Reuben James* was sunk. Congress voted legislation to arm merchantmen and allow them to sail to belligerent ports. Naval war with the Nazis was underway.

The Chief of Naval Operations, Admiral Harold R. Stark, wrote in his diary that fall that Hitler "has every excuse in the world to declare war on us now, if he were of a mind to." But Hitler did not, and war came from the Pacific, not the Atlantic.

The Path to Pearl Harbor

IN THE MONTHS AFTER the sinking of the gunboat *Panay*, the deadlock between the United States and Japan over the Open Door versus the New Order gradually deepened into an impasse. The Japanese saw in the European crisis an unparalleled opportunity to extend their empire. In the summer of 1939 they forced concessions from the British which demonstrated their intentions. The United States promptly took a most serious step and gave the requisite six months' notice to terminate its 1911 commercial treaty. Beginning in January 1940, it was free to cut off its shipments of oil, scrap iron, and other raw materials; Japan had been depending on the United States for half its supply of such commodities. Japan feared losing these supplies vital for its armed forces, but would not recede. American public opinion violently opposed war with Japan, but increasingly demanded the embargo which might bring war.

The fall of France and siege of England gave global significance to Japanese policy. Japan was eager to take advantage of the defeat or preoccupation of the colonial powers to nibble its way into Southeast Asia, beginning with northern French Indo-China. The United States was determined to restrain Japan, even at the risk of a war. More was at stake than tin, rubber, and other vital raw materials. In September 1940, Japan signed a defensive alliance with Germany and Italy (the Tripartite Pact); any further Japanese thrusts would damage the world status quo to which the State Department was committed. The administration policy toward Japan was inseparably interrelated with that toward Germany, and subordinate to it.

As the United States began to deny Japan supplies essential to her warmaking, the danger that Japan would strike back became imminent. Under the Export Control Act, by the fall of 1940 the United States had placed an embargo upon aviation gasoline and almost all raw materials with military potential, including scrap iron and steel. Already war was close. The Japanese government of Prince Konoye wished to conciliate the United States if it could do so without serious concessions. Negotiations began in the spring of 1941 and dragged on into December. At first the Japanese informally suggested rather generous proposals, but by May were making formal ones that were unacceptable: the United States should ask Chiang Kai-shek to make peace on Japan's terms, it should restore normal trade with Japan, and it should help Japan procure natural resources in Southeast Asia. Also Japan would decide for itself whether the Tripartite Pact bound it to aid Germany in a war against the United States. In return,

Japan promised to expand peacefully and to respect the Philippines. The United States countered with its traditional Open Door, antiexpansionist demands. The gulf between the negotiators was broad, but the United States was gaining valuable time and hoped moderates might win control in Japan.

The contrary occurred. The German attack upon Russia relieved the Japanese of one of their greatest worries, since they no longer needed to fear interference from Siberia. They decided to move into southern Indo-China and Thailand, even though it might mean war with the United

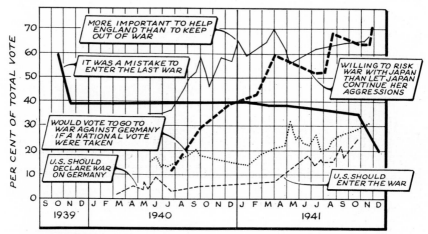

Public Opinion about Intervention, 1939–1941 (Reproduced by permission of Professor Hadley Cantril and the Public Opinion Research Project of Princeton University)

States and Great Britain. The United States had broken the Japanese code, and through intercepted messages knew this move was probably a prelude to attacks upon Singapore and the Dutch East Indies. At the end of July 1941, when the Japanese occupied southern Indo-China, the United States, acting firmly in concert with the British and the Dutch, froze Japanese assets and applied other tight economic sanctions. These put the Japanese into such a desperate plight that they would either have to abandon their aggressions or fight the United States.

Since the Japanese naval leaders wished to avoid a war they feared they might lose, the cabinet sought compromise. Prince Konoye requested a personal meeting with Roosevelt at which he was ready to make some concessions. (Simultaneously Japan prepared for war if agreement could not be reached.) Roosevelt was enthusiastic, since Konoye was ready to promise that Japan would not expand further southward and would not attack the United States in the event it fought a defensive war against Germany. Hull was discouraging because he feared Konoye could not bind the Supreme Command. On Hull's advice, Roosevelt would not meet Konoye without specific advance commitments about China, and these Konoye would not give.

Perhaps a personal meeting between Roosevelt and Konoye could have resulted in a face-saving accommodation which could have avoided war. If so, in being ruled out, the last possibility of peace evaporated. Roosevelt and Hull decidedly did not want war in the fall of 1941, but they seemed to make the foolish error of thinking Japan was bluffing when she was not. Instead of making limited concessions which would have strengthened the Japanese moderates and postponed or avoided a war which the United States was in no position to fight in 1941, they took an adamant moralistic position which played into the hands of the Japanese extremists. If there were to be a showdown over China, the time should be later, not when the United States was fighting German submarines on the Atlantic.

The Japanese made an even more grievous miscalculation by drifting into a war few of their leaders were sure they could win. On September 6, 1941, an Imperial Conference decided to attack if negotiations were not satisfactory by early October. Most leaders had misgivings, but none tried to reverse the decision. Negotiations continued through November, with the Emperor urging that a solution be found, but the Japanese timetable called for a surprise attack in early December.

Each nation refused to budge on the question of China. On November 20, 1941, Japan offered a *modus vivendi* (temporary settlement) highly favorable to herself. Hull rejected it and prepared a *modus vivendi* of his own, involving a three months' truce. It was most unlikely Japan would accept it, but anyway the Chinese objected so strongly and it was so likely to be unpopular in the United States that Hull abandoned it. Instead he replied in the basic American terms. He not only knew Japan would not accept these but knew also, through intercepted Japanese messages, that they had made their last offer and that after November 29 things automatically would happen. "I have washed my hands of the Japanese situation," Hull told Stimson on November 27, "and it is now in the hands of you and Knox, the Army and Navy."

The United States knew that Japan was on the move and that war was imminent. A large Japanese convoy was moving southward through the China Sea. The administration thought an attack upon American territory unlikely, and debated what to do if the Philippines were bypassed. The commanders in Hawaii were routinely warned, but were equally preoccupied. Negligence on their part and in Washington, not diabolical plotting, as was later charged, led to the disaster ahead. Meanwhile, on Novem-

The magazine of the U.S.S. Shaw *exploding during the Japanese raid on* Pearl Harbor (OFFICIAL U.S. NAVY PHOTO)

ber 25, a Japanese naval task force had sailed eastward from the Kuriles.

At 7:55 on Sunday morning, December 7, 1941, the first wave of Japanese airplanes hit the United States naval base at Pearl Harbor, Hawaii; a second wave came an hour later. The attacks were successful beyond Japan's greatest expectations. Within two hours the planes destroyed or severely damaged 8 battleships, 3 light cruisers, 4 miscellaneous vessels, 188 airplanes, and important shore installations. There were 3,435 casualties. The Japanese task force withdrew without being detected, having lost 29 airplanes, 5 midget submarines, and less than 100 persons. In this first strike, the United States was almost rendered impotent in the Pacific, but the bitterly wrangling nation was suddenly unified for the global war into which it had been precipitated.

Chapter **16**

OUTPRODUCING
THE AXIS

IN THE GRIM DAYS following the attack on Pearl Harbor, the United States, along with its allies, seemed powerless before the onslaught of Japan, Germany, and Italy. Yet experts, comparing the potential war production of the United States with that of the Axis, never lost their optimism. They were sure that it was only a question of time before the United States could pour such a weight of armaments into the struggle that the tide would turn.

The American nation was united in the task of producing these armaments and training the men to fight with them. On the Monday after the debacle at Pearl Harbor, millions of Americans listened at their radios as President Roosevelt grimly addressed Congress: "Yesterday, December 7, 1941—a date which will live in infamy—the United States of America was suddenly and deliberately attacked by the naval and air forces of the Empire of Japan." Within four hours the Senate unanimously, and the House 388 to 1, voted for a war resolution against Japan. Three days later Germany and Italy declared war on the United States, and on the same day, December 11, Congress reciprocated without a dissenting vote.

The United States had entered the global war with a unanimity unthinkable before the disaster of December 7. The nation was united in its angry feeling that the war against Japan must be prosecuted with the ut-

most vigor to avenge the attack. Except for a very small minority of pacifists, almost all of the former isolationists called for punishment of Japan
with all the ardor they had previously directed against interventionists.
Some of them concentrated so completely upon hating the Japanese enemy
that they seemed hardly aware that Germany too had declared war on the
United States. They became alarmed and indignant when they discovered
that American military planners months before had decided in the event
of war to concentrate upon the defeat of Germany while holding Japan at
bay. Thus, into the war (and even after), there persisted some of the old
divisions that had rent the nation before Pearl Harbor. Other political
schisms developed out of the emergency.

The Congress Moves Right

AT TIMES the sound and fury in Washington seemed almost to overshadow the struggle against the Axis. Despite platitudinous pleas to put
aside politics in the interest of national unity, the struggles became if anything more virulent during the war. Conservatives saw in the war an opportunity to eradicate hated remnants of the New Deal; some liberals
regarded it as an opportunity to bring Wilson's ideas to fruition, and even
go beyond them to establish a global New Deal. Every one of the great
pressure groups in the country fought to maintain or improve its relative
position; spokesmen for large business and small, farmers and labor,
jockeyed for position in Washington.

The tenor of Congress continued to be conservative, and it was sensitive as always to the demands of organized constituents. Throughout the
war, key committee chairmen who were leaders of the conservative coalition dominated Congress and forced their will upon President Roosevelt.
Through the election of 1942, as the United States and its allies suffered
unparalleled military disasters and the war administration in Washington
seemed to compound confusion, the criticism rose to a crescendo. In the
election, the Republicans gained forty-seven seats in the House and ten in
the Senate. Within both parties the trend was to the right; in Nebraska
the famous liberal Republican, Senator George Norris, lost to the ardently
right-wing Kenneth S. Wherry.

Conservative Southern Democrats and Republicans dominated the
Seventy-eighth Congress even more completely than they had the previous
session. Eugene Cox of Georgia declared in the House, "Government by
bureaucrats must be broken, and broken now," and a Massachusetts Republican Representative asserted it was necessary to "win the war from
the New Deal." Congress abolished relief agencies no longer needed; it
also ended the National Youth Administration, which could have been

used in training for war industry, and hamstrung aid to underprivileged submarginal farmers. In 1943, it abolished the National Resources Planning Board because it had recommended an expansion of Social Security after the war. On the other hand, through wise use of its investigatory power it maintained a salutary check on war agencies and military expenditures. Also, Congress, despite the conservative trend in domestic policy, accepted the principle that the United States in the future must co-operate with other nations to keep the peace.

President Roosevelt, in order to obtain crucial congressional support in prosecuting the war and planning the peace, continued to accept the sacrifice of New Deal measures. He did fight resourcefully, although not always successfully, against inflationary pressures, but seemed to concede the conservatives' position when he remarked that the best name he could devise for the conflict was the "war for survival." Again, at a press conference he proclaimed that "Dr. Win-the-War" had replaced "Dr. New Deal." This did not appease conservatives, even though they failed to notice Roosevelt's implication that once the crisis was over Dr. New Deal would return. Through all the problems of organizing the home front ran a thread of angry political partisanship, which indicated that despite the growth of regulation, once again the nation was waging war in a relatively democratic fashion.

Reshuffling War Agencies

THE DRIVE to build massive war production began with the fall of France and continued during the two defensive years after Pearl Harbor. Turning the United States into a huge machine for the waging of total war was no easy task. In the frightening aftermath of the December 7 disaster, with a large part of the fleet immobilized or destroyed, the United States possessed little armament with which it could have countered a determined Japanese thrust against Hawaii or even against the Pacific coast of the United States. After eighteen months of defense preparations and appropriations greater than those for total American participation in the First World War, rearmament was still largely in a blueprint and plant-building stage. Much of the new flow of war supplies was going on Lend-Lease to Great Britain or Russia. Nevertheless, a basis had been established for war production. The nation was far readier than it had been in April 1917.

Critics, especially the admirers of Bernard M. Baruch, asserted strongly during the war and thereafter that the government should have been still better prepared. They claimed that it would have been had President Roosevelt heeded the recommendations of Baruch, head of the War Industries Board in 1918, and a respected elder statesman in 1939, who had urged that the administrative machinery of the First World War be re-created and headed by an economic czar. This plan, critics claimed, would have enormously speeded war production and eliminated inflation, thus bringing the conflict to an end much earlier at an enormous saving in lives and at half the monetary cost. Here was another shocking indictment of the administration, especially powerful if it were assumed Roosevelt could establish defense machinery without reference to politics during the fierce debate over neutrality from 1939 into 1941. The obvious impossibility of such an accomplishment somewhat blunts the indictment; the fact that conditions in the Second World War were decidedly more complex than in the first blunts it still more. Yet there is no explaining away the sometimes chaotic nature of the defense agencies, reorganized with every turn of the Washington kaleidoscope. The indictment, while not provable in damning completeness, also cannot be dismissed lightly.

Total war made the planning of industrial production as vital as military strategy. "War is no longer simply a battle between armed forces in the field," the Industrial Mobilization Plan of 1939 stated, "—it is a struggle in which each side strives to bring to bear against the enemy the coordinated power of every individual and of every material resource at its command. The conflict extends from the soldier in the front line to the citizen in the remotest hamlet in the rear." Recognizing this, Roosevelt, at the time of the Munich crisis in 1938, had ordered the armed forces to modernize their production plan. Just before the outbreak of war in Europe, in August 1939, he authorized the War and Navy Departments to appoint a civilian advisory committee to survey the 1939 plan. This was the War Resources Board, made up of five leaders of big business together with the presidents of the Massachusetts Institute of Technology and Brookings Institution, and an army colonel. At this point politics began. The unfortunate use of the word "war" rather than "defense" in the title frightened the public, especially after the invasion of Poland when even the existence of such a body seemed a move toward involvement. The firmly anti–New Deal attitude of the Board pained Roosevelt. If he had allowed it to be created in order to show he could co-operate with big business, he had failed in his purpose. He refused to provide funds for it, or to make public its reports. This led at the time to wild rumors, and after the war to the assertion that these recommendations, largely inspired by Baruch, would have infinitely shortened the war.

For the most part the reports were a sober endorsement of the Industrial Mobilization Plan, which itself was a keen analysis of the problems of the First World War but a poor prognosis of what lay ahead. What irritated New Dealers was the Board's recommendation that the patriotic business leaders should administer war production through agencies independent of, and coequal with, executive departments. One alternative in the Plan went even further and suggested what Wilson had successfully headed off in 1918, a single economic administrator who would have seriously encroached upon the President's power. Further, the Board argued that certain social gains, especially labor legislation, must be put aside for the duration of the war. It thus implied that Roosevelt should turn over the conduct of the war to his conservative political opponents and allow them to reverse parts of the New Deal.

New Dealers, union labor, and members of the farm bloc in Congress joined with the isolationists in denouncing the War Resources Board and the Industrial Mobilization Plan. Roosevelt was reported to be saying privately, "If war does come, we will make it a New Deal war." He speedily disbanded the War Resources Board and submitted to the many pressures against substituting any new defense agencies. He did this even though Baruch at his request had provided him with a modified plan that was more flexible, eliminated the possibility of too great military control, and retained ultimate authority in the President. Had Roosevelt put this plan into operation late in 1939 it would have speeded mobilization for defense, but apparently he considered the political risks too great.

With the collapse of France in the late spring of 1940, Roosevelt could delay no longer, even though he was embarking upon a new Presidential campaign and wished to temper isolationist hostility. Rather than ask Congress to create defense agencies, he drew upon a 1916 statute for authority and re-established the Advisory Commission of the Council of National Defense. This time he used the word "defense" rather than "war," and carefully balanced all of the major national interests. He headed it with William Knudsen (General Motors) and Edward Stettinius (United States Steel) to conciliate business; Sidney Hillman (C.I.O.), labor; Chester Davis (A.A.A.), agriculture; Ralph Budd (who had been president of several railroads), transportation; Leon Henderson (a New Deal economist), prices; and Harriet Elliott (a University of North Carolina dean), consumer protection. Closely associated with it as Co-ordinator of Purchasing was one of the nation's biggest buyers, Donald M. Nelson of Sears, Roebuck. At the first meeting, Chairman Knudsen asked Roosevelt, "Who's boss?" The President replied, "I am."

Out of this commission as prototype grew the many defense agencies with their shifting or nebulous lines of authority and often ill-defined powers. Out of it came many of the heads of subsequent war agencies. Out of it too came one clear fact amid the many uncertainties: whatever war agencies developed, Roosevelt was of no disposition to abdicate or share his Presidential powers.

In January 1941, after the Advisory Commission had almost broken down and lost its control over priorities to the military, Roosevelt established a new Office of Production Management under Knudsen and Hillman. In April 1941, he created an Office of Price Administration and Civilian Supply under Leon Henderson. The new improvisations worked little better than the old in controlling priorities; in August 1941 Roosevelt established a new priorities board for the O.P.M. Finally, after American entrance into the war, Roosevelt in January 1942 organized the sort of agency Baruch had long advocated, a War Production Board, under Donald Nelson. Although Nelson was personable and a good organizer, he was not strong enough to force civilian control over priorities, or a more equitable distribution of contracts among smaller manufacturers, or a well-balanced production plan. He remained head of the W.P.B. until August 1944, but as early as October 1942 lost much of his power when President Roosevelt persuaded Justice James F. Byrnes to resign from the Supreme Court to become in effect a sort of assistant president in charge of war production. Byrnes was head at first of the Office of Economic Stabilization, then after May 1943, of the Office of War Mobilization. The O.W.M. developed into a workable war administration.

Building War Plants

MEANWHILE, with the awarding of the first large defense contracts in the summer of 1940, the administration had to face the question of whether or not the United States was to wage a New Deal war. Some manufacturers, still stinging from the "merchant of death" epithet flung at them during the Nye Committee investigations, were reluctant again to risk opprobrium. Others, thinking in depression terms of an economy of scarcity, were reluctant to build new plants that they feared would lead to overproduction after the war. Still others would not accept contracts until they were sure of an adequate profit margin, or a speedy tax write-off on their new plants. It was the initial task of Knudsen, the production genius of General Motors, to persuade manufacturers that it was their patriotic duty to take contracts. As for the new war plants, even if later they should prove to be excess capacity, at least manufacturers need not worry about paying for them: the Reconstruction Finance Corporation received authorization from Congress in June 1940 to finance the construction, expansion, and equipment of plants that it could then lease to contractors. Or, if manufacturers would put their own capital into defense construction, by act of Congress of October 1940 they received a fast, five-year tax write-off. This meant that instead of deducting a normal 5 per cent for depreciation from their taxes on wartime profits, they could deduct 20 per cent of the cost of the plant. Manufacturers who turned to war production were not to suffer economically.

Neither were the war workers. The manufacturers, backed by the War and Navy Departments, wished to abrogate New Deal restrictions on government contracts in order to lengthen the hours of workers without paying overtime. Labor leaders, wishing to increase employment, fought bitterly for double shifts. Ultimately the government decreed a 40-hour week with time and one-half for overtime. Contractors had to comply with New Deal labor legislation—the Walsh-Healey, Fair Labor Standards, and Wagner Acts.

In the second half of 1940, the defense boom began, as the government awarded $10,500,000,000 in contracts. By August, shipyards had already hired 80,000 new workers, and aircraft plants 50,000. Rents rose 40 per cent in Detroit; in Bremerton, Washington, 4,900 workers applied for 600 new housing units. Above all, the boom was one in construction as new aircraft plants, shipyards, and defense plants arose.

Through 1941 it was a limited boom, since, as the Office of Production Management reported in the summer, three fourths of the contracts were going to fifty-six corporations. Most of these, in keeping with the public demand for both guns and butter, continued to turn out automobiles and other consumer goods rather than convert completely to defense production. As the big corporations built new plants and began to bring them into production, they captured through priorities such a large part of the raw materials that thousands of small manufacturers, including most of the 45,000 metal-working firms that lacked defense contracts, could not get metal. They protested vigorously, but only gradually were they able to obtain contracts or subcontracts. Charles E. Wilson of General Motors declared, "This defense program is big business. We might just as well make up our minds to that. . . . Small plants can't make tanks, airplanes or other large complex armaments." The idle machines and men in the small plants could turn out vital components, but as late as December 1942 70 per cent of all war contracts were still going to the hundred largest contractors. Then Congress established the Smaller War Plants Corporation to channel orders to plants employing five hundred or fewer workers.

Stockpiling of strategic materials fared badly, although as early as 1939 Congress had authorized the expenditure of $100,000,000 for the purpose. Jesse Jones, the head of the Reconstruction Finance Corporation, was unprepared to wage economic warfare with his agency, and tried to buy rubber and metals in a frugal and cautious way. As a result, when the Japanese swept into southeast Asia, the United States had no more than a year's normal supply of natural rubber and almost no facilities for producing synthetic rubber.

At the time of Pearl Harbor, the United States still had little armament because it had shipped so much to Great Britain and because so many of the plants had only recently begun production, but the new productive capacity was remarkably large. Despite errors and chaotic conditions, the nation was producing more combat munitions than any of the belligerent countries—indeed almost as much as Germany and Japan combined. Airplane production was up to a rate of almost 25,000 per year. The armed forces already had inducted and were training two million men. This mobilization was only a fraction of what was soon to come, for large scale construction of factories and training camps was underway. While the nation during the debate over neutrality had not built its defenses with the smoothness and speed that critics demanded, it had achieved a substantial degree of preparedness.

The Japanese attack on Pearl Harbor created almost as much chaos indirectly in American war production as it did directly in the fleet in the Pacific. The war agencies in Washington began ordering tremendous quantities—indeed far too much—of everything. No procurement officer wanted the war to be lost through his negligence. In the first six months of 1942 war agencies placed over a hundred billion dollars in contracts, more than the entire American economy had ever produced in its biggest year. Piled on top of twenty billion dollars in outstanding war orders, this placed an impossible burden upon industry. The Bureau of the Budget in its war history, *The United States at War*, has outlined the impasse:

First, . . . The total called for was in excess of our industrial capacity.

Second, there was a resulting collision between the various production programs and between the men who were responsible for them. Merchant ships took steel from the Navy, and landing craft cut into both. . . . The pipe lines took steel from ships, new tools, and the railroads. And at every turn there were foreign demands to be met as well as requirements for new plants.

Third, all semblance of balance in the production program disappeared because of the different rates of contracting and of production that resulted from the scramble to place orders. If there ever had been a planned balance between men, ships, tanks, planes, supplies, weapons, ammunition and new facilities, and there is no evidence that there was, that balance disappeared in the differential time required to develop the orders, the differential energies of the various procurement officers, and the differential difficulties of getting production out.

Fourth, there was terrific waste in conversion. After a tragically slow start, many a plant was changed over to war production when its normal product was more needed than its new product. Locomotive plants went

*The mushrooming of war plants: Two pictures taken in the same spot in
1941* (top) *and 1942 indicate the speed of construction of the Morgan-
town, West Virginia, ordnance plant* (DU PONT)

into tank production, when locomotives were more necessary—but the Tank Division did not know this. . . .

Fifth, we built many new factories, and expanded many others, which we could not use and did not need. Many of these factories we could not supply with labor or with raw materials, or if we had, we would not have been able to fly the planes or shoot the ammunition that would have come out of them. But in the process we used up critical materials and manpower which might better have gone into something else. . . .

Finally, the priority system broke down because of "priority inflation." People with military contracts had the right to take more scarce materials and components than there were, so that a priority or an allocation became nothing more than a "hunting license."

The problem of restoring some order to war production, then raising it to astronomical totals, was a joint one. The armed forces, the Maritime Commission, and other procurement agencies did the ordering. The War Production Board tried to control the size of the procurement program and to allocate materials between the armed forces and the civilians. The W.P.B. was thus trying to control the entire economy and inevitably coming into sharp clash with the armed forces over the size and nature of war orders as opposed to what was to be reserved for civilians. Internecine warfare among the agencies and personality clashes among the administrators were unavoidable.

Out of the confusion a pattern gradually emerged. The first step, singularly enough, was to cut back the building of plants, although at times this created a furor throughout a region, as when the Higgins Shipyards in New Orleans were abandoned. After the middle of 1942, the amount of new construction being started declined sharply; in another six months, the larger part of the war plants and military facilities had been built.

The major problem of co-ordinating the war production program remained. As late as the summer of 1942, bottlenecks were halting some assembly lines. On July 4, the vital shipbuilding program had to be cut back because of scarcities of raw materials such as steel plate and glass, and of components such as valves, turbines, and engines. The W.P.B. tried to break the bottlenecks by establishing a system of horizontal control of materials for each plant—each was to file a list of its inventories and requirements. This was the Production Requirements Plan. It revealed some hoarding of raw materials, but unfortunately it also tempted manufacturers to overestimate their needs. In October 1942 the armed forces and the W.P.B. turned to a more workable system, which Ferdinand Eberstadt, Chairman of the Army-Navy Munitions Board, had proposed. This was the Controlled Materials Plan, which established a balanced production of finished products and allocated precise quantities of raw materials to each manufacturer. A Component Scheduling Program under Charles Wilson of General Electric prevented, for example, electrical equipment from going to the Navy under top priority for ships that could not be launched for a year, when lack of it was creating an immediate bottleneck in tank production. These two schemes were a splendid improvement upon the simple priorities system of the defense period, and made possible the efficient organization of an enormous war production.

The shortage of rubber became so critical in 1942 that it required special attention. After the W.P.B. failed to solve the problem, Roosevelt in August, 1942, appointed a committee under Baruch to make a special report. It recommended sharp restrictions upon the use of motor vehicles, including a national speed limit of 35 miles per hour, and immediate construction of enormous synthetic rubber plants. Roosevelt ordered the restrictions, and appointed a Rubber Director in the W.P.B., William M. Jeffers, president of the Union Pacific Railroad, to construct the plants. By the end of 1943, the synthetic rubber industry was producing a third again as much rubber as the country had normally used before the war.

Spectacular feuds continued to parade across the front pages of American newspapers, especially the highly publicized quarrel between Jesse Jones and Vice-President Wallace over their agencies' priority purchases abroad. In July 1943 President Roosevelt took authority in the area away from both of them and established a new agency, which after another transmutation became the significant Foreign Economic Administration.

An indispensable adjunct of the war agencies was the Senate War Investigating Committee, headed by Harry S. Truman, previously little known. The Senators consciously patterned it after the Committee on the Conduct of the War, of the Civil War period, but avoided the pitfalls of their predecessors by ruling out questions of military policy. Instead they ferreted out incompetence and corruption in the war-production and military-construction programs: outrageous expense in building army camps, improper inspection of airplane engines, a quixotic scheme to build an Arctic pipeline, and the like. The Truman Committee not only uncovered and stopped hundreds of millions of dollars of waste, but by its vigor led war administrators to be more diligent in preventing further waste. In the wartime expenditure of four hundred billion dollars there was amazingly little corruption.

The Output

BY THE BEGINNING OF 1944, war production reached such high levels that factories had substantially turned out what seemed to be needed to win the war. The output was double that of all Axis countries combined. Cutbacks began, but they were haphazard and ill-planned, and, when the armed forces met reverses, turned out in some instances to have been premature. With the cutbacks came pressure for a resumption of the manufacture of civilian durable goods. The military leaders stanchly opposed this. However, war needs even at their peak took only about a third of American production. While manufacture of such goods as automobiles, most electrical appliances, and non-defense housing had come to a halt in 1942, production of food, clothing, and repair and maintenance goods was continued or even slightly increased. As for war production totals, despite the vicissitudes of mobilization, they were enormous. The nation produced:

86,330 tanks
296,400 airplanes
2,681,000 machine guns
64,500 landing craft
6,500 naval vessels
5,400 cargo ships and transports

Of more significance for postwar America, an enormous upsurge in plant capacity resulted from this huge output, as total production almost doubled between 1939 and 1945. This upsurge meant building a magnesium industry, nearly trebling aluminum productive capacity, increasing machine tool production sevenfold, increasing the output of electricity by nearly one half over the 1937 total, and producing more iron and steel than the entire world had turned out a few years earlier. It meant also a spectacular spread of industry to the Pacific coast; not only shipyards and aircraft plants, but even a steel plant was constructed in southern California. It also meant transformation of the agricultural South, as laborers migrated from farms not only to war plants elsewhere, but also to those in many a Southern city.

As war production grew, the problem of transporting the supplies within the country and overseas became acute. Inside the United States, the Office of Defense Transportation, established in December 1941, coordinated all forms of transport—railroads, trucking, airlines, inland waterways, and pipelines. In contrast to the system in the First World War, railroads remained under private control; but they functioned effectively, carrying double the traffic of 1939 with only 10 per cent more locomotives and 20 per cent more freight cars. Since they could not, however, transport sufficient oil to the East when German submarines began attacking coastal tankers in 1942, the government authorized construction of the Big Inch pipeline from Texas to eastern Pennsylvania.

Transporting troops and supplies overseas required one of the most spectacular construction programs of all. The Germans had sunk more than twelve million tons of shipping by 1942. To replace it, the United States Maritime Commission had to abandon its program of building fast, efficient ships requiring scarce turbines, valves, and electrical equipment. As early as July 1940, Admiral Emory S. Land, head of the Commission, and Knudsen recommended to the President mass production of a freighter that, while slow (sailing only 11 knots), would be simple to construct and not require scarce components. By using the existing designs for an old-fashioned British tramp steamer with a reciprocating engine and steam winches, they saved six months in starting production. This "Ugly Duckling" was the Liberty ship. After a slow beginning, builders substituted welding for riveting and applied prefabrication and subassembly techniques in constructing it. In 1941 construction of Liberty ships required an average of 355 days; by the end of 1942, the time had been cut to 56 days, and one of Henry J. Kaiser's companies completed one in 14 days. During 1942 alone, 8 million tons of shipping were built; by 1945 the United States had over 36 million tons of ships afloat.

It was equally difficult to make effective use of the shipping. In 1941, some American shippers carrying cargo for the British to the Red Sea received out of Lend-Lease funds six times their return of the year before in American coastal trade. Worse still, an acute snarl developed. In April 1942 the War Shipping Administration took over ownership or control of all shipping. At first it made many blunders in loading and handling ships, as its officials candidly admitted. They worked diligently to try to correct them, and although bad tie-ups continued for some time, gradually they improved the efficiency of the shipping pool.

Scientists Race Against Germany

THE MOST revolutionary changes for the future came out of laboratories, as scientists pooled their skill in a race against those of the Axis—above all the Germans—to turn basic knowledge that was available to all into decisive weapons of war. Between the two wars the United States had neglected military research and development, while Germany had sprinted far ahead. One notable exception was radar. In the twenties, the Naval Research Laboratory in Washington had discovered the principle of radar by bouncing back a radio beam directed at a ship on the Potomac. The British had developed radar most highly, and it was their salvation during the air blitz of 1940–41.

Other potential weapons which were in the offing could mean Nazi victory in the war if the Germans developed them first. (This was one of the reasons why the armed forces had decided to concentrate upon defeating Germany first.) The only way in which American scientists could catch up seemed to be through teamwork. The German threat brought creation of the government scientific agency that the New Deal had failed to produce. A leading scientist, Vannevar Bush, persuaded President Roosevelt to create a committee for scientific research in June 1940. A year later, under the direction of Bush, it became the Office of Scientific

Albert Einstein working on a war project (NATIONAL ARCHIVES)

Research and Development, which mobilized scientists with such effectiveness that in some areas they outstripped their German opponents.

The Americans and British developed superior radar, which not only detected enemy airplanes and ships, but helped direct shells against them. In these shells by 1943 they were using one of the most effective American inventions, radio-directed proximity fuses that detonated the shells as they neared their targets. American rocket research produced weapons enormously increasing the fire-power of airplanes, ships, and tanks, but lagged behind the progress made by the Germans, who before the end of the war were blasting London with enormous V-1 and V-2 rockets. The Germans also built the first jet airplanes and snorkel submarines, which would have been an even more serious menace if they had come into full production.

Especially there was the little-publicized danger that Germany might develop an atomic bomb. In the summer of 1939, the physicist Enrico Fermi and the mathematician Albert Einstein got word to President Roosevelt that German physicists had achieved atomic fission in uranium. What had long been theoretically possible had been accomplished; next might come a bomb. The President authorized a small research project, and a race in the dark against the Nazis began. In December 1942 physicists produced a controlled chain reaction in an atomic pile at the University of Chicago. The problem then became the enormous technical one of achieving this release of power in a bomb. Through the Manhattan District of the Army Engineer Corps, the government secretly poured nearly two billion dollars into plants to produce fissionable plutonium, and into another project under the supervision of J. Robert Oppenheimer which undertook to build a bomb. It was an enormous and frightening gamble, against the hazards that the bomb might not work and that the enemy might succeed first. Only after the war did the United States discover that the Germans were far from developing a workable bomb. On July 16, 1945, after the end of the war in Europe, the first bomb exploded with the brightest flash of light ever seen on earth and a huge billowing mushroom cloud. The scientists had triumphed, but in an awesome and frightening way.

Enormous potential good existed in atomic fission; advances in radar and aviation also had valuable peacetime applications. The rapid medical advances forced by the war paid especially high dividends on the horrible human cost: the quick development of penicillin and antibiotics, new techniques in plastic surgery and the use of blood plasma, and the discovery of DDT for the control of insects. These were relatively small returns, however, considering the total cost, for almost the entire scientific and medical research facilities of the nation had been turned away from other research to war-making applications. The great achievement was the negative one of outstripping the Axis.

The American People in Wartime

ALMOST as complex as the scientific problems were the enigmas in integrating the domestic economy into the war machine: manpower, agriculture, production for civilian use, and finance.

The nation, after grappling for years with the problem of millions of unemployed, found itself hard pressed for sufficient people to swell the fighting forces, man the war plants, till the fields, and keep the domestic economy functioning. There were periodic demands for national service legislation or a labor draft, but unions opposed such measures so vehemently that they never passed the Senate. The relatively weak War Manpower Commission tried to coerce workers into remaining at defense jobs at the risk of being drafted, but the war came to an end without any tight allocation of manpower comparable to that of materials. The armed forces had first call upon men through Selective Service, which had been in operation since the fall of 1940. Altogether draft boards registered 31,000,-000 men. Including volunteers, over 15,000,000 men and women served in the armed forces during the war. Nevertheless the working force jumped from 46,500,000 to over 53,000,000 as the 7,000,000 unemployed and many previously considered unemployable, the very young and the elderly, and several million women found jobs. The number of civilian employees of the federal government trebled.

This mobilization of manpower entailed the greatest reshuffling of population within such a short time in the entire history of the nation; altogether 27,300,000 people moved during the war. It meant also a heavy weight of wartime tension on American families. With the return of prosperity and the impending departure of soldiers, both marriage and birth rates jumped. In 1942 and 1943 about three million children were born each year, compared with two million a year before the war. But young wives and mothers fared badly in crowded housing near defense plants or army bases, or, after husbands had been shipped overseas, back home with parents. Draft boards deferred fathers as long as possible, but more than a million were ultimately inducted. More than two and a half million wives were separated from their husbands because of the war. The divorce rate increased slowly. Because men in the armed forces could in effect not be divorced without their consent, and many estranged wives stayed married in order to continue receiving allotment checks, a heavy backlog was built for postwar divorce courts.

When mothers were forced to work, children often suffered neglect, or were upset over the change. Court cases involving juvenile delinquency, especially among children from eight to fourteen, and among girls, the "bobby-soxers," increased 56 per cent. Even among the nondelinquents, a serious price had to be paid at the time and later for the disruption of more American families for a longer perior of time than ever before.

As adolescents found jobs, the percentage between fourteen and nineteen who attended school dropped from 62 in 1940 to 56 in 1944. Teachers also left for the armed forces or better-paying war jobs. Universities kept functioning through military research projects and training programs.

The great migration to war plants was stripping the agricultural South of underprivileged whites and Negroes alike, as 5,000,000 people moved within the South, and another 1,600,000 left the area completely. In the South this exodus led to the false rumor among outraged white housewives that the departing Negro domestics had formed "Eleanor Clubs," named after Mrs. Roosevelt, to "get a white woman in every kitchen by 1943." In the North, it led to explosive tension when Negroes, enjoying their new freedom, were jostled in crowded streetcars against indignant whites newly migrated from the South. A serious riot in which twenty-five Negroes and nine whites were killed shook Detroit in June 1943. New York narrowly averted a similar disaster. At the very time when the United States was fighting a war against the racist doctrines of Hitler, many whites became resentful over the rapid gains Negroes were making. In June 1941, after the head of the Pullman porters' union, A. Philip Ran-

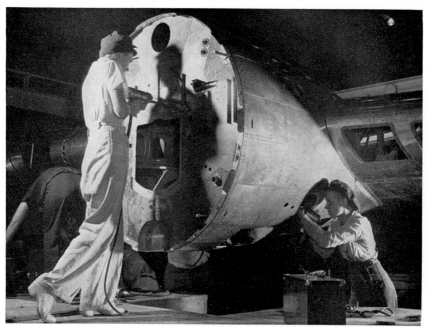

Women riveters in Long Beach, California, aircraft plant, working on a Flying Fortress (NATIONAL ARCHIVES)

dolph, threatened a march on Washington, President Roosevelt established the Fair Employment Practices Committee. It worked diligently throughout the war against discrimination in employment. By 1944, two million Negroes were at work in war industry, and many previous barriers to economic opportunities for Negroes were permanently cracked.

Not everyone shared in the new prosperity. Government economists reported in 1943 that ten million families still received less than the $1,675 per year requisite for a minimum standard of living. Most Americans, however, were relatively more affluent than they had been. The living standard of working people advanced rapidly, due less to wage increases than to payment of time-and-a-half for overtime beyond 40 hours. The average work week lengthened from 40.6 hours in 1941 to 45.2 in 1944. As living costs rose (on a 1935–1939 base of 100) from 100.4 in 1940 to 128.4 in 1945, gross weekly wages went up from $25.20 to $43.39. Working women and children created social problems, but they also brought additional prosperity to millions of families.

Curbing Strikes

LABOR UNIONS rapidly grew in strength during the war, and their unpopularity among Americans of the middle and upper classes grew apace. Union membership increased with the rise in the working force, from about ten and a half million workers in 1941 to over thirteen million in 1945. Keeping these workers satisfied was no easy matter. The administration was determined to prevent strikes and to restrain the formidable pressure of the labor unions from forcing wages, and thus all prices, upward. President Roosevelt followed the procedure of the First World War by establishing a National Defense Mediation Board, in March 1941, made up of representatives of management, labor, and the public. In November 1941 it broke down when the C.I.O. members resigned over the refusal of the Board to recommend a union shop (i.e., one in which all new workers hired must join the union) in coal mines. In January 1942 Roosevelt replaced it with the National War Labor Board, similarly constituted but much stronger. It emerged as a regulatory rather than merely mediatory body, since unions agreed to suspend strikes during the war, and the Board faced the problem of granting unions part of the demands they otherwise would have pressed through collective bargaining. It could set wages, hours, and union conditions, and through the war powers of the President it could enforce these in a final extremity by government seizure and operation of plants.

On the union-shop question, which was creating such hostility between management and labor, the Board arrived at a compromise, the "maintenance of membership" clause. Nonmembers hired into a war plant did not have to join a union, but members had to remain in it, and the union remained the bargaining agent for the duration of the contract. Pressure for wage increases, which might contribute to inflation, was more serious. The Board hit upon a solution in ruling upon the Little Steel cases in July 1942. Taking January 1, 1941, as the base date when workers had received a standard wage, it recognized a 15 per cent rise in the cost-of-living index since then. Consequently, it felt that a proportionate increase for steel workers would be equitable. The Little Steel formula, except for those receiving substandard wages (like some textile workers) served thereafter as a wage ceiling. The Board and the President made a fight to maintain it as part of the over-all stabilization of both wages and prices.

Despite the no-strike pledges of the major unions, there were nearly 15,000 work stoppages during the war, involving the loss of more than thirty-six million man-days. These stoppages involved only one ninth of 1 per cent of the working time (though they indirectly caused more damage than this). Bannered in the newspapers, they angered the public and Congress. When John L. Lewis's United Mine Workers defied the government in their strike against the Little Steel formula in May 1943, Congress reacted by passing over Roosevelt's veto the Smith-Connally or War Labor Disputes Act of June 1943, which required unions to wait thirty days before striking and empowered the President to seize a struck war plant. It merely gave union leaders an additional weapon, the threat to call a strike. Public feeling against unions continued to rise, and many states passed laws to discipline them.

A Bonanza for Agriculture

AT THE BEGINNING of the war, with a two-year supply of wheat, cotton, and corn stored in Secretary Wallace's ever-normal granary, there seemed no danger of food shortages in the United States. But within six months after Pearl Harbor, scarcities of many sorts began to develop. The United States began to feel the increased demand of the armed forces and its allies, and the reduction of supplies due to the loss of fibers and oils from southeast Asia. By 1942, meat production was half again that of depression years, but American consumers with their increased buying power were eager to buy even more. Consumer income in 1943 was 65 per cent above depression levels, and much of it was in the pockets of people who had not eaten adequately for years.

There was a Food Administrator, Chester Davis, but he resigned in protest when his views (and those of the American Farm Bureau Federation) did not prevail; his successor was Marvin Jones. Neither man had the dictatorial powers to provide for agriculture the scarce supplies and manpower that the dominant farm bloc in Congress would have liked to bestow upon agricultural producers. Rather, farmers had to depend upon whatever the War Production Board would allocate to them, and upon a generous draft-exemption program they obtained from Congress. They also received legislation raising the ceiling on commodity prices to 110 per cent of parity. Since this came into conflict with the antiinflation efforts of the administration, a dogged struggle developed between the President and the congressional farm bloc over farm prices. Neither side won entirely.

The 40 per cent of the farmers who produced 85 to 90 per cent of the crops, through their organizations, their supporters in the Department of

Agriculture, and their Congressmen, resisted efforts to break the parity system even though it had been designed to deal with a problem of over-production rather than underproduction. They fought successfully also against Farm Security Administration proposals to concentrate upon in-creasing the production of the 60 per cent of farmers who were marginal and submarginal by supplying them with credit, machinery, fertilizer, and feed. The dominant 40 per cent also blocked schemes to switch their production from traditional staple commodities they customarily grew, or from luxury produce like watermelons which would bring a high price, to other produce more essential in war time. If price incentives were not high enough (as on hogs in 1944), they cut production (not the 20 per cent recommended, but 30 per cent). In other words, the commercial farmers were essentially businessmen, and they acted like other businessmen, neither better nor worse.

At some points the farmers failed to breach the bulwarks the adminis-tration established against higher prices. In April 1943 President Roose-velt used his war powers to try to combat creeping inflation by ordering price rollbacks and a system of consumer price subsidies. These were ex-pensive, but considerably cheaper for taxpayers as a whole than a raising of price ceilings. Twice Congress passed bills destroying the subsidy sys-tem; both times Roosevelt vetoed them. The Office of Price Administra-tion imposed ceilings on meat prices, for example, at the retail rather than farm level and worked backward. This discouraged production, and, by preventing large federally inspected packers from operating at a profit, it diverted meat to small packers who were not inspected and who fed the black market.

The government failed to construct adequate storage facilities and in-stead allowed produce to pour into the domestic market, which by 1944 was consuming 9 per cent more food than in prewar years. Consequently, the United States was barely able to meet food demands in 1945, when the armies liberated large areas in which millions of people were living on no more than a fourth the minimum diet. In the winter of 1945–46 millions actually reached the point of starvation in Asia and Europe. The enormous stocks in storage at the beginning of the war, excellent weather, and boun-tiful harvests enabled the United States to avoid a major world disaster by scraping its granaries empty. The production record of the farmers, like that of the factories, was phenomenal. While farm population dropped 17 per cent as submarginal farmers left their poor fields, the remaining opera-tors of commercial farms, heavily fertilizing their fields, planting hybrid corn, and enjoying plentiful rainfall in the former Dust Bowl, sent the in-dex of all agricultural production up from 108 to 123; increases in food production alone were even higher.

Farmers chafed under shortages and the high prices of machinery, labor, and consumer goods, but they received a substantial return for their production achievement. Agricultural prices more than doubled despite Roosevelt's delaying actions, and net cash income for farmers increased fourfold between 1940 and 1945. Mortgage debt declined two billion dollars, farm tenancy declined from 38.7 per cent to 31.7 per cent, and farmers, in addition to enjoying a higher living standard, amassed eleven billion dollars in savings.

Taxes, Loans, and Inflation

THE PRESSURES OF BUSINESS, farmers, and labor, combined with the scarcity of consumer goods and the burgeoning of buying power, created an almost irresistible trend toward inflation. During the defense period, the Office of Price Administration, under a vigorous New Dealer, Leon Henderson, lacked real coercive power and failed to halt inflation. Between the invasion of Poland and Pearl Harbor, prices of twenty-eight basic commodities rose by nearly 25 per cent. Immediately thereafter, pressures became so acute that prices went up 2 per cent per month. Baruch had recommended placing ceilings upon "every item of commerce or services," prices, rents, wages, commission fees, and interest rates. Instead, Congress hastily passed a bill, drafted six months earlier, authorizing only selective price-fixing and setting ceilings with a preferential trap door for agriculture.

The O.P.A. issued in April 1942 a General Maximum Price Regulation that froze prices of consumer goods, and of rents in defense areas only, at their March 1942 level. The greatest weakness was the rise of farm prices toward 110 per cent of parity which drove food prices—the most conspicuous item in any index—steadily upward. This gave ammunition to labor unions' barrage against fixed wages. In October 1942, Congress, grudgingly responding to the President's demand, passed the Anti-Inflation Act. Under its authority, Roosevelt immediately froze agricultural prices, wages, salaries, and rents throughout the country. Inequities inevitably developed, and every aggrieved group blamed Henderson. When he resigned in December 1942 and was replaced by former Senator Prentiss S. Brown, who was popular with Congress, inflationary forces hailed the new, softer enforcement policies, and redoubled their drive against the ceilings. The President vetoed congressional onslaughts against stabilization; in April 1943 he ordered the O.P.A. and other agencies to "hold the line" against increases; and in May, he rolled back prices of meat, coffee, and butter 10 per cent. A turn in the battle came in July when Roosevelt appointed a former advertising executive with remarkable administrative talents, Chester Bowles, to head the O.P.A. With a small enforcement staff, Bowles braved general unpopularity to hold the increase in living costs during the next two years to 1.4 per cent. Altogether, it had gone up less than 29 per cent from 1939 to the end of the war, compared with 63 per cent between 1914 and the armistice.

Consumers nonetheless suffered numerous irritations and discomforts. The O.P.A., through unpaid local volunteers manning 5,600 price and rationing boards, administered the rationing of canned goods, coffee, sugar meat, butter and other fats, shoes, tires, gasoline, and fuel oil. The O.P.A.

The Home Front Pledge: The OPA urged housewives to put this sticker in their windows

could not, however, control deterioration of quality in clothing; and Congress in 1945 forbade placing ceilings on canned goods on the basis of the government standards of quality—grade labeling. Because of miscalculations, acute shortages developed in 1945, forcing O.P.A. to invalidate quantities of its ration stamps. Black-marketing and overcharging grew in proportions far beyond O.P.A. policing capacity; in 1943 Congress slashed the funds of the enforcement division.

No one liked price-fixing and rationing, and everyone grumbled over the conspicuous 50 per cent increase in food prices. Rents went up only 4 per cent, but this meant little to war workers or military personnel moving into new areas, where they were often gouged mercilessly in renting wretched housing. There was validity to union complaints that the official index figures on the increase in living costs was unrealistically low. Yet for all its shortcomings, the O.P.A. prevented runaway inflation, and was infinitely preferable to no controls at all. Roosevelt may have perpetrated some economic injustices in vetoing inflationary bills, but he would have been guilty of far greater ones if he had signed them.

One of the most important inflationary controls was the sale of war bonds and stamps to channel off some of the excess purchasing power, which for the single year 1945 mounted to nearly sixty billion dollars. Throughout most of the war, personal incomes were at least a third greater than the available civilian goods and services. The Treasury Department, through eight war bond drives and its payroll deduction plans, but with few of the lurid or coercive touches of the First World War, sold forty billion dollars worth of series "E" bonds to small investors, and sixty billion more to individuals and corporate entities other than banks.

Had this been the total of government loans, the effect would have been to quell inflation, but the Treasury had to borrow $87,500,000,000 more

Persons Paying Personal Income Tax, 1939 and 1942

from Federal Reserve and commercial banks. Since in effect the banks created new credits which the government then spent, the effect was to inflate bank credits and the money in circulation by over $100,000,000,000.

Taxes did much more to drain off surplus purchasing power. The government raised 41 per cent of its war costs through taxation, compared with 33 per cent during World War I, and assessed heavy levies against industry and every segment of American society. The Revenue Act of 1942, which Roosevelt hailed as "the greatest tax bill in American history," levied a 94 per cent tax on highest incomes; the President had suggested that no one should net more than $25,000 per year during the war. Also, for the first time the income tax fell upon those in lower income brackets. To simplify payment for these new millions, Congress enacted a withholding system of payroll deductions in 1943. Corporation taxes reached a maximum of 40 per cent on the largest incomes. In addition, excess profits were subject to a 90 per cent tax, reclaiming for the government a large part of the return from war contracts. However, these taxes could be rebated to companies to aid them in reconversion, a provision of future significance. In effect, the government taxed away a large part of the profit of corporations, then returned it later when it was needed. A portfolio of heavy excise taxes on transportation, communication, luxuries, and amusements completed the levies.

With prosperity at a high level, the President in 1943 requested taxes to bring in another $16,000,000,000 in revenue; Congressional leaders balked, and finally in February 1944 voted only $2,200,000,000 additional. Roosevelt vetoed the measure in terms so vehement that the Senate majority leader, Alben Barkley, resigned in protest and recommended overriding the veto. The Senate Democratic caucus unanimously re-elected

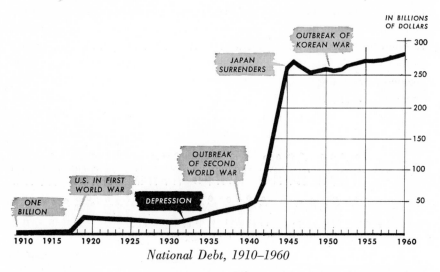

National Debt, 1910–1960

Barkley, and both houses of Congress overrode the veto. Subsequent legislation simplified but did not increase taxes.

Between 1941 and 1945, the government raised $138,000,000,000 through taxation—nearly a $100,000,000,000 of it from income and excess profits taxes. Those in the top 5 per cent of the income scale suffered a serious relative economic loss, as their share of disposable income dropped from 26 per cent in 1940 to 16 per cent in 1944. Few persons or corporations were able to make fortunes out of the war, and a considerable amount of economic leveling—upward more than downward—had taken place. Despite the heavy taxation, by the end of the war consumers possessed an estimated $129,000,000,000 in liquid savings.

From 1941 to 1945, the federal government spent twice as much as the total appropriations from the creation of the government to 1941, and ten times as much as the cost of the First World War—a total of $321,000,-000,000. The national debt rose from $49,000,000,000 in 1941 to $259,-000,000,000 in 1945, yet the black warnings of national bankruptcy which had punctuated the New Deal years had all but disappeared. The phenomenal prosperity and the record savings that consumers were impatiently waiting to spend seemed more significant portents for the postwar world than the huge debt and the threat of inflation.

Selling the War

THE VISION of a postwar America with every husband behind the wheel of his new chromium-trimmed automobile and every wife enthroned in a gleaming kitchen full of miracle-working gadgets seemed the greatest incentive for the winning of the war. In January 1941 Roosevelt had enunciated Four Freedoms as war aims—freedom of speech and worship and freedom from want and fear. These never caught the public imagination as had Wilson's Fourteen Points. Indeed, in the wartime advertising there seemed some danger that "Freedom from Fear" might be confused with something akin to a cure for halitosis. The government depended upon patriotic advertisers, publishers, broadcasting and motion-picture companies to promote its campaigns as a public service. Such companies contributed approximately a billion dollars in space, and in the spring of 1942 were publicizing conversion to war production, rationing, salvage, and "hush hush." Advertising men not able to peddle their usual wares kept the billboards filled with reminders of their products intermingled with war slogans and visions of the chromium age to come. On these weary workers could ponder as they rode home from war plants.

Few people could take exception to the advertising men's interpretation of the war, but that of the government frequently aroused sharp criticism. From Pearl Harbor on, there was the suspicion that through the Office of Censorship, almost immediately established under a competent Associated Press executive, Byron Price, the government was withholding information less because it was vital to the enemy than because it would be damaging to public opinion of the armed forces. Official silence on the Pearl Harbor losses coupled with publication of exaggerated Japanese accounts led the public to discount the official report several weeks later. Diligent newspapermen, aided by Price, exerted pressure on the armed forces to make censorship an instrument for security, not for the concealing of incompetence. Newspapers following Office of Censorship rules censored themselves to withhold local news that might be of value to the enemy.

The overlapping and conflict among government information agencies led to the establishment in June 1942, of the Office of War Information under a shrewd news commentator, Elmer Davis. Although the O.W.I. consolidated four previous organizations, it co-ordinated rather than assumed the information function of domestic war agencies. In the foreign area, Nelson Rockefeller's Office of Inter-American Affairs excluded it from Latin America. It was the Domestic Branch of the O.W.I. that especially aroused the misgivings of Congress, partly because of internal feuding and the mass resignation of the pamphlet writers, mainly because conservatives objected to several of the O.W.I. pamphlets: one opposing inflation, another on Negroes in the war, and another which was a tax primer. A fourth pamphlet intended only for overseas distribution, a cartoon biography of Roosevelt, especially worried antiadministration congressmen. They feared O.W.I. might promote New Dealish policies and the 1944 candidacy of Roosevelt. In 1943, Congress cut funds for the Do-

"Welders" by Ben Shahn, rejected as a poster by the O.W.I., and widely used by the CIO Political Action Committee (COLLECTION MUSEUM OF MODERN ART)

mestic Branch so drastically that it had to stop producing propaganda. Other war agencies proportionately expanded their output.

Overseas, O.W.I. carried on a program employing 8,400 persons by VE day. Through "Voice of America" broadcasts begun in 1941 and propaganda of many sorts it presented an idealistic view of American war aims and aspirations for a peaceful postwar world. As the symbol of this idealism it dramatized President Roosevelt. By the end of the war, Roosevelt was more of a hero overseas than at home, and American aims appeared more idealistic abroad and more materialistic in the United States. But Americans, along with their dreams of a chromium age, were anxious to avoid the dreadful possibility of a third world war. Realistically, they favored American entrance into an organization to preserve the peace.

Japanese-Americans being evacuated from the Pacific Coast (NATIONAL ARCHIVES)

Civil Liberties

ON THE WHOLE, the war produced less hatred and vindictiveness at home than had the First World War. The energy that had gone into crude vigilantism in the earlier war went in the Second World War into serving as air raid wardens and doing similar duties for the Office of Civilian Defense. People continued to eat hamburgers and sauerkraut and listen to Wagner. They demonstrated little animus toward Americans of German background and practically none toward Italians. A few Nazi agents and American fascists were jailed, but the most ambitious effort to punish them, a sedition trial of twenty-eight, ended in a mistrial after the defendants' lawyers had engaged in long weeks of delaying tactics. A few papers like Father Coughlin's *Social Justice* were barred from the mails. But socialists went unpunished, and religious conscientious objectors who were willing to register went to Civilian Public Service camps rather than prison.

In sad contrast to this moderation, the frenzy of public fury turned on the Japanese. The fighting in the Pacific developed a fierce savagery, reflected in the public anger within the United States. On the Pacific Coast, hatred of Americans of Japanese background became extreme. Wild stories circulated about sabotage at Pearl Harbor—later proven 100 per cent untrue. As sandbags were piled around Pacific Coast telephone offices, and barrage balloons were raised over shipyards, fear of Japanese-American espionage and sabotage became intense. Under public pressure, Roosevelt in February 1942 authorized the army to remove all people of Japanese ancestry. Some 117,000 people, two thirds of them United States citizens, were abruptly herded behind barbed wire, and later shipped into ten relocation centers in wild and disagreeable areas. They suffered the financial loss of at least 40 per cent of their possessions and for several years were barred from lucrative employment. Yet Japanese-Americans in Hawaii were left unmolested without incident throughout the war. There were 17,600 Japanese-Americans in the armed forces. Their units, especially in Italy, established outstanding records for bravery under fire.

This persecution of Japanese-Americans was the only major blemish in the wartime civil liberties record, but it represented a serious erosion of civilian rights, since the Supreme Court in 1944 validated the evacuation, and in other decisions upheld military control over civilians. In time of war or national emergency, United States citizens could expect no court protection of their civil rights from military or executive authority. In this way the war had led to a threat to the civil rights of all Americans. During the war, no price seemed too great to pay to win security from the Axis, and restrictions upon the freedom of the individual seemed to be part of the bill.

The United States won the battle of production, even though the economic mobilization fell short of being total and efficient. It succeeded only because of the larger resources and industry of the United States, and because its organization was more effective than that of Germany and Japan. Because of the huge production, the United States could sustain serious losses of supplies at sea yet provide arms for its allies and supply the troops abundantly. Germans were almost incredulous at the abundance of munitions which enabled American troops advancing in France to spray trees with machine gun bullets to drive out snipers. Heavy war production built a margin for victory, and helped make that victory less costly in American lives.

Chapter *17*

TURNING THE TIDE

THE BOMBS DROPPED on Pearl Harbor blasted out of existence the old America living in an illusion of isolation, and the United States found itself not only fighting a global war but also having to assume an irrevocable position of open leadership among the nations. A minority, who earlier had been isolationists, were ready to interpret the war solely as American retaliation for a Japanese attack. The vast majority, even most of those who had opposed entrance, recognized that the nation would never again be able to retreat to the comfortable dream of isolation within the bounds of the Western Hemisphere.

The United States did not fight, as it had during the First World War, as a nation gingerly "associated" with the Allies. Rather it took the initiative in drafting and signing, on January 1, 1942, a Declaration by United Nations, setting forth the war aims of the Atlantic Charter, committing its full resources, both military and economic, to the prosecution of the war, and pledging itself to co-operate with other signators and not to make a separate peace with the enemies. In effect, it was taking the lead in establishing a grand alliance, the United Nations, among the twenty-six signatory powers and the twenty more that signed before the war was over. From this beginning, the United States, as it grew in military strength, took an ever more dominant lead in international diplomacy.

In war strategy, too, the United States played a determining part, very different from its 1917–18 experience. From the outset it took the lead in the Pacific, making the war there preponderantly an American one against the Japanese. At first it deferred to Great Britain in the European area but, as American strength grew, assumed forceful leadership there also.

The United States, Great Britain, Russia, and China formed the "Big Four." China did not determine global policy at all; Russia made its own decisions, influenced only slightly by American and British proposals. The grand alliance was, therefore, basically a close and rather smooth-working entente between the United States and Great Britain, with the British Commonwealth, the Fighting French under General Charles de Gaulle, and some of the lesser powers all contributing vigorously. The powerful Russians were associated with these countries in fighting a common enemy but were semiisolated and suspicious. They made constant demands for Lend-Lease (and received eleven billion dollars worth of vital supplies). They also insisted incessantly that the Western powers open a second front in France. But they participated in no combined strategic planning and seldom divulged their own plans of their knowledge of the Germans.

Postwar considerations influenced the British more than the United States in war planning. Prime Minister Churchill seemed at times to be more concerned with bringing the war to a satisfactory conclusion, President Roosevelt with bringing it to a speedy end. Roosevelt idealistically hoped to supersede power politics in time with a workable international organization. At times Churchill shared his enthusiasm; at times he pessimistically fell back on older thinking. Thus, inevitably, diplomatic problems were closely intertwined with the military during the four years of American participation, and even before the end of the war the shape of the new world was emerging.

The American Military Organization

IN DECEMBER 1941 neither the army nor the navy seemed very well prepared for the enormous tasks ahead, and Pearl Harbor had not improved confidence in their commands. Enormous industrial production alone could not win the war. The military must know what to order, and where and how to use it, on a scale they had not envisaged in their prewar establishments. The navy possessed 300 combat ships—and it was a truism that navies usually fought wars with the ships they had when hostilities commenced—but at the close of the war it had 1,167 major ships and was only employing one of the prewar vessels in the final attacks on Japan.

The army in July 1939 had in theory nine infantry divisions, but actually only the equivalent of about three and a half at half strength. Nor could it organize tactical units larger than a division. By mid-1941 it had twenty-nine infantry and cavalry divisions at nearly full strength, organized into four field armies—still less than half a million men. The army air force, nominally under the army but in practice almost independent, had only 22,000 officers and men and 2,400 aircraft in July 1939.

There was little hint of what was to come. The most important of the war plans, Orange, devised to go into effect in case of conflict with Japan, had presumed primarily a naval war, with the army mobilizing over a million men. In 1940 the more comprehensive Rainbow plans superseded these; by December 1941 a substantial mobilization was underway, though it was still far short of wartime totals.

Vast increases in personnel and equipment forced rapid changes in planning and organization. General George C. Marshall, Chief of Staff of

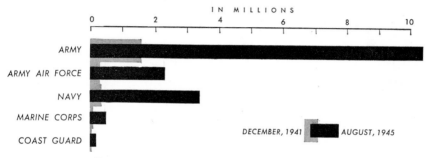

Expansion of U.S. Armed Forces, 1941–1945

the Army, reorganized the army high command in March 1942. That same month, Admiral Ernest J. King, a clear-headed hard driver, became Chief of Naval Operations. Together with General H. H. Arnold of the army air force, these men met with a personal representative of the President, Admiral William D. Leahy, to constitute the Joint Chiefs of Staff. They functioned as the over-all command, and represented the United States in combined planning with the British or occasional negotiations with the Russians.

Over the Joint Chiefs of Staff was the Commander in Chief, President Roosevelt, who bore responsibility for the conduct of the war. Personally, and through assistants like Harry Hopkins and cabinet members, he coordinated the war planning of the Joint Chiefs with war production and manpower, and with foreign policy. In July 1940 the War Plans Division of the Army General Staff had pointed out that civilians should decide the "what" of national policies, and the professional soldiers the "how." Roosevelt, who had always zealously guarded civilian control even in the Navy Department and the War Department, followed this course through the war. Conversely, he depended heavily upon the advice of the Joint Chiefs of Staff, and once major policy had been decided, seldom interfered with their strategy.

The first of the great policy decisions had come in 1940 when the Americans had decided that even if Japan entered the war, their primary goal would be to defeat Germany with its superior military force, war production, and weapons development. The United States confirmed this priority in the initial wartime conference with the British at the end of

WACs washing their mess kits (NATIONAL ARCHIVES)

December 1941. This decision did not mean neglecting the war against Japan. By August 1941, as the buildup of airplanes, especially, was underway in the Philippines, and later when General MacArthur received orders to fight, the strategy was shifting to a two-front war. The war against Germany was to be offensive, while that against Japan was to be defensive. It was difficult to hold to this policy as the Japanese tide in the Pacific swelled far beyond the bounds the most pessimistic planners had anticipated. For the President, furious over Japanese treachery, and the navy, primarily responsible in the Pacific, it was not an easy decision to maintain. General MacArthur, the panic-stricken public on the Pacific Coast, and most Americans elsewhere clamored for prompt and stern action against the Japanese.

During the first chaotic months of shocking reverses, the armed forces alloted their men and supplies piecemeal to try to meet each new Axis threat. Top strategists emphatically warned that such dissipation of effort might lead to defeat. No one was more insistent than Dwight D. Eisenhower, who had been brought to Washington after Pearl Harbor as a Far Eastern expert, and by the spring of 1942 was head of the Operations Planning Division under General Marshall. In emphatic memoranda he hammered away at the need to build up men and supplies in Europe for the invasion of North Africa that Roosevelt and Churchill had decided upon in their December 1941 meeting. Because of his vigor and his important role in developing an invasion plan, Eisenhower became the logical man to send to England in June, 1942, as Commanding General in the European theater.

Stopping the Axis Drives

WHILE THE UNITED STATES was building and equipping its fighting forces, it had to depend upon the Russians and the British to hold back the Germans as best they could. During the discouraging first six months of American participation it had to stand perilously on the defensive in both the Atlantic and the Pacific. There even seemed danger of a breakthrough in Egypt and the Caucasus which might enable the Germans and Japanese to join forces in the Middle East or India.

Ten hours after the strike at Pearl Harbor, Japanese airplanes hit the airfields at Manila, destroying half the American bombers and two thirds of the fighter planes. That same day they sank two British warships off Malaya, the only Allied warships in the Far East. There was no sea, air, or land power of consequence to hold back the Japanese as they methodically went about their conquests. Three days later Guam fell; then, in the weeks that followed, Wake Island and Hong Kong. The great British fortress of Singapore in Malaya surrendered in February 1942, the East Indies in March, and Burma in April. In the Philippines, on May 6, the exhausted Philippine and American troops, having made brave withdrawals to the Battan peninsula and the Island of Corregidor in Manila Bay, ran down the last American flag in the Far East.

Only one weak outpost, Port Moresby in southern New Guinea, stood as a bulwark against the invasion of Australia. It seemed likely to fall, but there containment began through the efforts on land of Australian and American troops, and on the sea of American aircraft carriers. As early as January and February 1942 the two remaining carrier task forces in the Pacific discovered they could strike Japanese bases without serious loss. They began serious harrying that slowed the southward and eastward

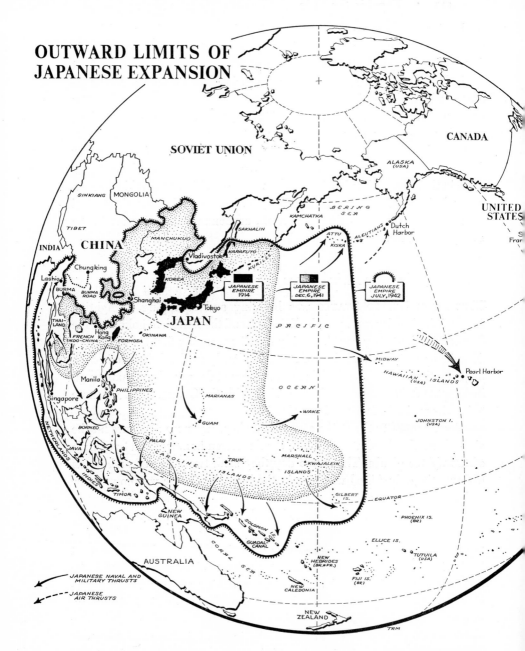

OUTWARD LIMITS OF JAPANESE EXPANSION

SOVIET UNION

CANADA

SINKIANG MONGOLIA

TIBET

INDIA **CHINA** MANCHUKUO

ALASKA (USA)

KAMCHATKA

BERING SEA

SAKHALIN

Chungking

KARAFUTO

ATTU ALEUTIANS Dutch Harbor

UNITED STATES

Lashio

Vladivostok

KISKA

Fran

BURMA BURMA ROAD

KOREA

JAPANESE EMPIRE 1914

JAPANESE EMPIRE DEC. 6, 1941

JAPANESE EMPIRE JULY, 1942

Shanghai

Tokyo

THAI-LAND

FRENCH INDO-CHINA FORMOSA

JAPAN

OKINAWA

Hong Kong

PACIFIC

MIDWAY

Pearl Harbor

HAWAIIAN (USA) ISLANDS

Manila

PHILIPPINES

MARIANAS

OCEAN

Singapore

WAKE

JOHNSTON I. (USA)

BORNEO

GUAM

PALAU

NETHERLANDS

JAVA

CAROLINE ISLANDS

TRUK

MARSHALL

KWAJALEIN

ISLANDS

INDIES

TIMOR

GILBERT IS.

EQUATOR

PHOENIX IS. (BR)

NEW GUINEA

SOLOMON IS.

GUADAL-CANAL

CORAL SEA

ELLICE IS.

NEW HEBRIDES (BR.#FR.)

TUTUILA (USA)

AUSTRALIA

FIJI IS. (BR)

NEW CALEDONIA

→ JAPANESE NAVAL AND MILITARY THRUSTS

--→ JAPANESE AIR THRUSTS

NEW ZEALAND

TRM

expansion. In the Battle of the Coral Sea on May 6–7, 1942, American carriers heavily damaged and turned back Japanese invasion forces threatening Port Moresby. Under General MacArthur, who had escaped from the Philippines, American and Australian troops began pushing back the Japanese. They were inadequately trained and equipped, often badly led, and suffered all the tortures of savage jungle warfare. By 1943, they had cleared the Japanese from New Guinea, but it was scarcely the cheap victory the final press communiqué proclaimed. Almost 90 per cent of the men were either dead, wounded, or sick.

After the Battle of the Coral Sea, the Navy, having intercepted Japanese messages, knew the next move and rushed every available plane and vessel into the central Pacific. Near Midway Island, June 3–6, 1942, they inflicted such heavy damage to a Japanese invasion fleet that a drive to capture the island and neutralize Hawaii was turned back. The Japanese

Japanese airplanes attacking the carrier Yorktown, *Battle of Midway*
(OFFICIAL U.S. NAVY PHOTO)

lost nearly all their well-trained carrier pilots and had left only the light carriers used in a raid of the Aleutians. Nor were they able quickly to replace their losses as more and more new American carriers and airplanes moved into the Pacific. The United States had achieved its goal of containment in the Pacific, and as men and supplies could be spared from the operations against the Nazis, it could assume the offensive against Japan.

In the Atlantic during the early months of 1942, the Nazis tried by means of submarines to confine the Americans to the Western Hemisphere. By mid-January, the Germans had moved so many submarines to the Atlantic coast, where at night they torpedoed tankers silhouetted against the lights of cities, that they created a critical oil shortage. In the summer, they moved into the Caribbean and sank additional quantities of tankers.

Against convoys bound for Europe they made attacks with devastating success. In the first eleven months, they sank over 8,000,000 tons of shipping—1,200,000 more than the United Nations had constructed—and threatened to delay indefinitely the large scale shipment of supplies and men to Europe.

By 1943 the submarines had developed a new and effective "wolf pack" technique for attacking convoys. Throughout the war every major troop convoy had to fight through the submarines; twice transports went

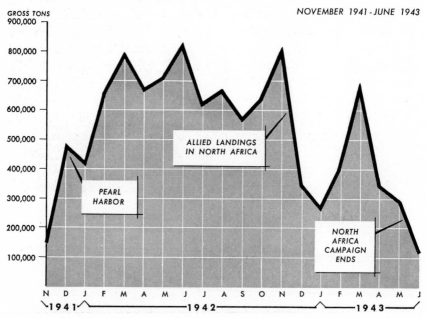

Merchant Ships Sunk by German Submarines, 1941–1943

down with heavy losses. Gradually the United States countered by developing effective antisubmarine vessels, air patrols, detecting devices, and weapons. Small escort carriers were especially effective in keeping wolf packs at bay. Through 1943 the submarines fought back fiercely with improved techniques, but by September of that year the Allies had destroyed ninety submarines in as many days. Ship construction began to run substantially ahead of sinkings, and the enormous American supply line to Europe was functioning.

The submarines had made it difficult to send assistance to the British and Russians in the summer of 1942 when they needed it most. The German *Afrika Corps* raced to El Alamein, only seventy-five miles from Alexandria, Egypt, threatening the Suez Canal and the Middle East. At the same time, German armies in Russia were plunging toward the Caucasus.

Welcoming Molotov, 1942: (left to right) *Chief of Staff George C. Marshall, Secretary of State Hull, Chief of Naval Operations Ernest J. King, Foreign Commissar V. M. Molotov, Ambassador Maxim Litvinoff* (NATIONAL ARCHIVES)

In May, the Russian foreign minister, Vyacheslav Molotov, visited Washington to demand an immediate second front that would divert at least forty German divisions from Russia; the alternative might be Russian collapse. Roosevelt promised to do everything possible to divert the Germans by invading France in 1942. But Churchill arrived the next month during the crisis when the Germans threatened Egypt, and strongly urged an invasion of North Africa instead. In later conferences, Chief of Staff Marshall and General Eisenhower, the American commander in Europe, favored a limited invasion of France which could gradually be enlarged. The British so stubbornly opposed it that the Americans agreed to a North African landing in the late fall of 1942. The discouraging months of containment were almost over.

Attacking in the Mediterranean

SINCE THE LOSSES in the August 1942 raid on Dieppe, France, were overwhelming, although the battle was mostly fought with more experienced

Canadian troops, it seemed wiser to make the first landing on a relatively unprotected flank. Through advance negotiations with officials of the Vichy government of defeated France the Americans hoped to make a bloodless landing in French North Africa. At the end of October 1942 the British opened a counteroffensive at El Alamein which sent the *Afrika Corps* reeling back. On November 8, Anglo-American forces landed at Oran, Algiers, and Casablanca, Morocco, with some bungling and gratifyingly few losses. They met determined French resistance only at Casablanca.

Admiral Jean Darlan, earlier one of the most notorious collaborators with the Nazis, signed an armistice with the Allies on November 12. He ordered a cease-fire and promised the aid of 50,000 French colonial troops. Outraged American liberals protested against the deal with the Vichyites and complained that the United States should have co-operated only with the French resistance forces under General Charles de Gaulle. They quieted somewhat a few weeks later when Darlan was assassinated. Unquestionably the Vichy gamble, unsavory though it was to idealists, saved lives and speeded the liberation of North Africa.

The Germans tried to counter the invasion by ferrying troops from Sicily into Tunisia at the rate of a thousand a day. Early in 1943, the *Afrika Corps*, which had retreated westward across Tripoli, joined these troops and threw the full weight of its armor against the green American troops. The Americans lost heavily, but with the aid of the British held onto their bases and gained in experience. Allied airpower and the British navy so seriously harassed the Axis supply line from Sicily that Germany decided not to make a major stand in Tunisia. From March into May the British army in the east and the armies in the west under Eisenhower gradually closed a vise on the German and Italian troops. On May 12, 1943, the last Axis troops surrendered; altogether they had lost fifteen divisions. The Mediterranean had been reopened and the Americans had learned lessons that would be useful for a successful invasion of France.

That invasion, despite the continued clamoring of the Russians, was not to take place in 1943. The lengthy fighting in Tunisia had tied up too large a part of the Allied combat resources for too long. Nazi submarines were still taking too heavy a toll of the Allies' inadequate shipping. Some of the ships and production had to be diverted to the antisubmarine war, and others to the prosecution of the Pacific campaigns. Also, the planners in London had come to recognize that an enormous buildup was necessary for a successful cross-channel invasion. Fortunately for the Allies, the tide had turned for the Russians also during the winter of 1943, when they had successfully held the Germans at Stalingrad in the Ukraine, eliminating an army of 250,000 men. They were no longer desperately in need of a second front in France, but this did not mean that they moderated their demands. An attack on Sicily, Stalin asserted in March 1943, would not be the equivalent of a second front in France. He warned vaguely but ominously of the "serious danger in any further delay" and "alarm which I cannot suppress." During these same months, Stalin was repeatedly refusing American requests for preliminary staff talks to plan joint Pacific operations if Japan should attack Siberia.

As early as mid-January 1943, Roosevelt and Churchill and their staffs, while conferring at Casablanca, looked ahead to the next move. This was to

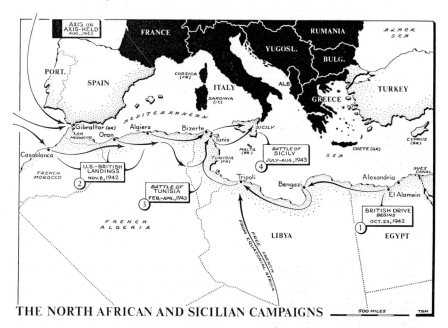

THE NORTH AFRICAN AND SICILIAN CAMPAIGNS

be an invasion of Sicily, even though General Marshall feared it might delay the invasion of France. Churchill argued persuasively that the operation in Sicily might knock Italy out of the war and lead the Germans to tie up many divisions in defense of Italy and the Balkans. Already, at Casablanca, as the United Nations moved to the offensive, the political decisions rivaled the military ones in importance. Roosevelt tried to bring together there the two rival French leaders, General Henri H. Giraud, whom he had established as head of the French forces in Africa, and General Charles de Gaulle, head of the Fighting French. The result was not altogether successful. In the eighteen months that followed, the influence of the American protégé, Giraud, waned, and De Gaulle emerged as leader of resurgent France.

With equally uncertain results Roosevelt enunciated at Casablanca, after previous planning, and consultation with Churchill, the doctrine of unconditional surrender of the Axis. He declared:

The elimination of German, Japanese, and Italian war power means the unconditional surrender by Germany, Italy, and Japan. That means a reasonable assurance of future world peace. It does not mean the destruction of the population of Germany, Italy, or Japan, but it does mean the destruction of the philosophies in those countries which are based on conquest and the subjugation of other people.

What Roosevelt seemed to desire was to avoid the sort of negotiations that had marred the 1918 armistice, causing bickerings among the Allies at the time and German misunderstandings afterwards. As the war progressed, it became clear that "unconditional surrender" left the United Nations free to state to enemy nations the peace terms they might expect. Roosevelt and Churchill both emphasized in speeches through 1943 that it did not mean, as the Nazi propagandists charged, that extremely severe terms would be imposed.

After the war, some historians charged that the "unconditional surrender" doctrine seriously discouraged the German underground, stiffened the Nazi will to fight, and thus lengthened the war. Even the Morgenthau plan for turning Germany into a pastoral area after the war, briefly accepted by Roosevelt and Churchill in September 1944, did not seem to affect Nazi actions, at least until the very end of the war. Rather, the Nazi leaders' knowledge that they would be held accountable for their war crimes, including the murder of several million Jews, spurred them to fight on and on.

As Allied fortunes sharply improved during the summer of 1943, discussions about surrender gained in immediacy. On the night of July 9, 1943, American and British armies landed in the extreme southeast of Sicily, where defenses were comparatively light. It was an effective rehearsal for the main invasion of the continent a year later. The Americans made grievous errors, the worst being to shoot down twenty-three planeloads of their own paratroops, but learned from their mistakes. In thirty-eight days the Allies conquered the island and looked toward the Italian mainland. Before the end of July 1943 the German command asserted that the Italian peninsula could not be held and, while evacuating the bulk of their troops from Sicily, recommended establishing a new defense line in the mountains just south of the industrial Po valley of northern Italy. As the Germans departed, Mussolini fell from power to be replaced by the pro-Allied Marshall Pietro Badoglio. At once Badoglio opened complicated negotiations to switch Italy to the side of the United Nations. As the negotiations went on, the Nazis moved eight strong divisions into northern Italy, concentrated other troops near Rome, and turned the country into an occupied defense bastion.

In previous months, Churchill had argued so effectively in favor of moving onto the Italian mainland that he had overcome American misgivings that it might delay a cross-channel invasion. It was, he pointed out, the only action of first magnitude open to them in 1943. The Americans came to agree, but only on the proviso that the campaign should not interfere with preparations for the invasion of France. Thus a limited but long and punishing campaign opened on the Italian peninsula on September 3,

THE ITALIAN CAMPAIGN

1943. It started with the greatest optimism, for that same day the Italian government signed an armistice agreement and the Allies quickly seized bases and airfields in southern Italy. But the Nazi defenders fought so fiercely from hilly redoubts that by early 1944 they had stopped the slow and deliberately moving Allies at Monte Cassino. When the Allies tried to break behind the line by landing at Anzio, also south of Rome, they were almost thrown back into the sea. With relatively few divisions, the Nazis were tying down the Allies and concentrating upon Russia.

Finally, in May 1944, the Allies captured Cassino, pressed on from the Anzio beachhead, and on June 4 captured Rome, just before the cross-

channel invasion began. The Italian campaign had cost far more than estimated and had brought smaller returns. The men in the field were bitter
because they felt neglected, and the American high command was disappointed. On the positive side, the campaign had, as Churchill pointed
out, engaged eight full-scale German divisions, so that "there has been
cause for rejoicing as well as bitter disappointment."

A Start Back in the Pacific

In the Pacific, as in Italy, Allied commands were mounting limited
offensives with meager allotments of men and equipment. In these campaigns also troops and commanders felt they were forgotten as they struggled across perilous beaches and through tropical pestholes against the

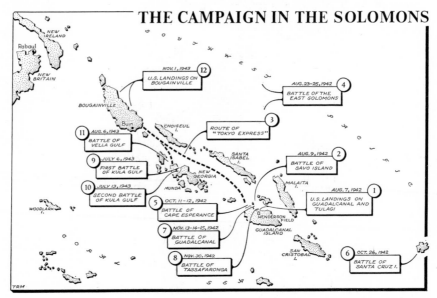

THE CAMPAIGN IN THE SOLOMONS

Japanese. At Casablanca, Admiral King had pointed out that only 15 per
cent of the Allied resources were being used against Japan. He wanted
the allotment doubled in order to drive the Japanese back before they
could establish themselves firmly in their advanced positions and then
strike further, but the other Chiefs of Staff insisted on concentrating on
the cross-channel invasion of Europe. King had to be satisfied with permission to conduct offensives "with the resources available in the theater."

The offensive strategy against the Japanese had already been launched
the previous August. It involved most of the American fleet and a considerable amount of American shipping, landing vessels, and aircraft. It
brought the United States into amphibious warfare of a type which the
marine corps had been developing since the early twenties. In the Pacific

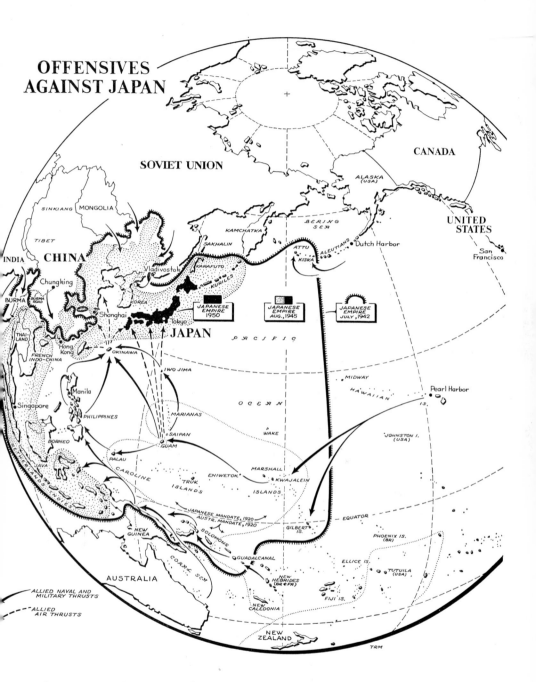

OFFENSIVES
AGAINST JAPAN

these new tactics came to be so perfected that troops were able to cross and seize vigorously defended beaches. Preferably, of course, the United States picked unexpected objectives that would bypass and immobilize advanced Japanese strong points. The American strategy was "Hit 'em where they ain't."

The southern Solomon Islands to the east of New Guinea were being developed as a Japanese base for air raids against American communications with Australia. In August 1942 the navy and marines opened an offensive which apparently would involve limited commitments, against three of these islands, Gavutu, Tulagi, and Guadalcanal. Around and on Guadalcanal a struggle of unprecedented fierceness developed as the United States and Japanese navies battled for control in a series of large-scale engagements. By the time the struggle was over, the United States and its allies had lost heavily in cruisers, carriers, and destroyers, but had sunk 47 Japanese vessels. They meted out such serious punishment to Japanese carrier groups that they never again risked air-sea battles, even though the Japanese switched to the building of additional new carriers. The Japanese navy had lost its offensive strength and thereafter concentrated upon defensive operations.

During the months when the great naval battles had been going against the United States, the Americans had gained control of the air and thus were able to sustain the marines, and subsequently the army, in their precarious jungle onslaught. By February 1943 Guadalcanal had been won. Through the year the island-hopping continued around the enormous Japanese-held perimeter: in the South Pacific through the northern Solomons to New Georgia and, in November, to Bougainville; in the Central Pacific, also in November, the Marine landing on Makin and the bloody assault on Tarawa in the Gilberts; in the Northern Pacific, the inexpert reconquest of Kiska and Attu in the Aleutians.

Victories in the Marshall Islands in February 1944 cracked the Japanese outer perimeter, and before the month was out the Navy had plunged far within it to wreck the bastion at Truk and raid Saipan in the Marianas. American submarines were increasingly harassing Japanese shipping, and thus hampering the economy. In 1943 they sank 284 ships; in 1944 they sank 492—necessitating by summer a cut of nearly a quarter in skimpy Japanese food rations and creating a crucial gasoline shortage. The inner empire of Japan was coming under relentless siege.

Relations with Allies

ONLY THE IMMINENT THREAT of Axis victory had forced an uneasy and not too satisfactory unity between Russia and its Western allies, Great Britain and the United States. As the threat began to lift in 1943, it became an increasingly difficult and dangerous task to keep the alliance cemented until victory had been achieved, and to plan for a postwar world in which a decent peace could be maintained. Against considerable odds Roosevelt and Churchill succeeded in the first of these tasks, but, as was almost inevitable, they failed in the second. Long before the final Nazi surrender—indeed, well before the Yalta conference—the grim outline of postwar Europe was beginning to take shape.

Bad as that outline was, it could have been worse had the Americans and British squabbled seriously among themselves. Clashes of policy and personality did, of course, develop at SHAEF (Supreme Headquarters of the Allied Expeditionary Forces, Europe) in London, and in the field, but General Eisenhower was gifted in reconciling differences. Roosevelt and Churchill held each other in esteem and even personal affection so deep that it overrode their policy clashes. There was, however, irritation among the British over Roosevelt's strong feeling that in the postwar world colonies must become trusteeships and then, in time, independent nations. Churchill publicly announced in November 1942: "We mean to hold our own. I have not become the King's first Minister in order to preside over the liquidation of the British Empire." De Gaulle felt the same about French possessions. The American attitude was of significance after the war, but for the moment was no more than a matter for debate.

Not so the differences between the Americans and British on military operations on the Continent. There Churchill, fearing to risk all on a cross-channel invasion which might end disastrously, pressed incessantly for further and still further ventures in the south of Europe. In a conference with Roosevelt in Washington in May 1943 he had agreed to a direct invasion of France on May 1, 1944—a date the British considered tentative and the Americans firm. In keeping with this agreement, Churchill at the time pressed for a campaign in southern Italy and no more than this. Two months later, he was insisting the Allies must take Rome and march as far north as possible, while "our right hand must give succour to Balkan patriots." These things, he argued, could be done without delaying the invasion of France. The American staff thought otherwise. With reason they stood firm upon earlier plans, since at the end of July 1943 there was only a single American division in Great Britain; almost all the men and supplies were going to the Mediterranean. The American staff, thinking in terms of speediest and cheapest ending of the war, argued doggedly for a cross-channel invasion. Roosevelt firmly backed them.

Up to this point Churchill seemed to have thought almost entirely in military terms, but with the disintegration of Italy leading to the weakening of Axis forces in the Balkans, he and the British began to worry about political considerations. If rival resistance forces in countries like Greece began to fight each other, Communists might win. Roosevelt at times found debate with Churchill over these strategic questions to be exhausting. In April 1944 he was so tired that he refused to meet Churchill at Bermuda for a conference and instead went to South Carolina to recuperate. As he passed historic markers from the Revolutionary War on the way, he wise-cracked that another should be added, commemorating the path of Roose-velt in 1944 as he too fled from the British.

This difference between British and American strategy—with the British misgivings about a channel invasion and predilection for further cam-paigns in southern and eastern Europe—affected the two nations' dealings with the Russians. To a certain extent the United States seemed nearer to the Russian position in insisting with them upon an early invasion of France. Roosevelt personally tried hard to establish a warm relationship with Stalin, and in his efforts seemed at times to take a middle position be-tween Stalin and Churchill. But Roosevelt was never on as convivial terms with Stalin as Churchill had been in Moscow in August 1942. The differ-ences between Churchill's views and Roosevelt's were by no means danger-ous, and were minor compared with the bedrock foundation of their unity.

As the Nazi tide began to recede, the postwar patterns would quickly emerge throughout eastern Europe, even as they were already appearing in Italy. Firm political agreements were necessary if these areas were not to fall entirely under Russian hegemony, just as firm military plans were essential to the achievement of final victory. Roosevelt, in order to obtain these, had to talk directly with Stalin, who had declined earlier invitations to conferences. As a preliminary, Secretary Hull, although he was seventy-two and in precarious health, flew to Moscow in October 1943 to confer with the British and Russian foreign ministers. The Russians, in a jocular mood, hinted that at the proper time they would enter the war against Ja-pan, and seemed to Hull ready to be co-operative in European matters.

Hull, whose faith in Wilsonian idealism was almost limitless, returned from Moscow elated because the Russians had agreed to a Declaration of Four Nations on General Security. (China was the fourth nation.) This was a pledge to continue the united action of wartime "for the organization and maintenance of peace and security," and to create, as soon as practi-cable, a general international organization. Hull's hopes carried him so far beyond reality that he declared in an address to both houses of Con-gress upon his return:

> As the provisions of the Four-Nation Declaration are carried into effect, there will no longer be need for spheres of influence, for alliances, for balance of power, or any other of the special arrangements through which, in the unhappy past, the nations strove to safeguard their security or to promote their interests.

Roosevelt thought the conference a "tremendous success," and Church-ill pronounced the results "prodigious," but Ambassador Averell Harriman and State Department Russian experts like Charles Bohlen warned them not to assume too much. Indeed, it soon became clear in Russian pronouncements that Hull's generalizations were the thinnest of ice bridges over a broad and deep chasm of eastern-European questions.

Nevertheless, it was with an air of optimism that Roosevelt and Churchill traveled eastward in November 1943 for the long-awaited meeting with Stalin at Teheran, Iran. On the way they stopped at Cairo to confer with Chiang Kai-shek and to prepare a statement (released after

Stalin, Roosevelt, and Churchill at Teheran (NATIONAL ARCHIVES)

the Teheran conference) drawing a map for the postwar Far East. They proposed stripping Japan of her empire in order to restore Manchuria, the Pescadores, and Formosa to China, and to create in due course a free and independent Korea. Japan was to lose, in addition, all other territory she had acquired since 1914.

At Teheran, Roosevelt undertook to establish a cordial, intimate relationship with Stalin of the sort he enjoyed with Churchill, because he felt that if a satisfactory peace were to follow the war, Stalin must understand and trust the Americans. Roosevelt tried hard to ingratiate himself with Stalin, even to the extent of poking fun at some of Churchill's suggestions. Stalin seemed to respond. Roosevelt, well pleased, subsequently reported to Congress, "We are going to get along fine with him and the Russian people—very well indeed." It was the high point of cordiality in relations with Russia.

Churchill at Teheran stood by his commitment to invade France in May 1944—indeed, the imminent danger of rocket and guided-missile attacks from the French coast guaranteed that he would not waver long. He failed to sell his plans for a Balkan campaign of one sort or another, primarily because of the resistance of Roosevelt's military advisers. Their interest was in concentrating upon the cross-channel invasion of France, together with a supporting landing on the French Mediterranean coast. They wished to avoid a campaign of dubious military worth in a terrain even more rugged than that blocking the Allied advance in Italy. As for Churchill, his motives through the Teheran conference seem to have been military rather than political. He too seemed to assume that relations with Russia would continue to be friendly, and consented to support Tito in Yugoslavia, which meant allowing that country to fall within the Communist orbit after the war. Stalin reaffirmed his intention to bring Russia into the Pacific war as soon as hostilities ended in Europe, and expressed his satisfaction with the Cairo communiqué on Japan. As for Russia's reward, Stalin hinted it might be a warm-water port; Roosevelt suggested that Dairen, Manchuria, might be made a free port.

In a cordial way the three leaders discussed means through an international organization of keeping Germany from ever again becoming a menace. Roosevelt remarked trustingly that if trouble developed in Europe, the United States would send ships and airplanes, but would have to depend upon the armies of Great Britain and Russia. In this atmosphere of expectation of friendship the Big Three discussed the touchy problems of eastern Europe. Russia wished to retain the areas she had seized in her period of collaboration with Germany, including eastern Poland as far as the so-called Curzon line proposed in 1919. Roosevelt and Churchill agreed to the Polish boundary; Poland could be compensated with German lands stretching to the Oder River. As for Germany, Churchill proposed a mild scheme for partition, and Roosevelt a drastic one to divide it into five independent states and two internationally controlled areas—one of the latter to include the industrial Ruhr and Saar mines. Both were so preoccupied with their fear of Germany, against which a costly assault was yet to come, that they ignored portents in the wind. Russian propaganda broadcasts beamed to Germany were hinting at leniency at the same time that Stalin at Teheran was suggesting the liquidation of 50,000 to 100,000 of "the German commanding staff."

In over-all policy toward central Europe, the British were ready to allow Russia what seemed to be legitimate claims based on history or security, but to stand firm against Soviet encroachments beyond their border areas. They wished to avoid the "pulverisation" of Europe that Russian territorial claims seemed to threaten. The Americans, altruistic and still slightly isolated, were trying to avoid redrawing the European map until the war was over and military considerations were no longer involved. Roosevelt again and again refused to commit the United States on European matters; he assumed that Congress would not support him.

Roosevelt, and even Churchill in his temporary ebullience, seem not to have recognized realistically the nature of the peace that was being foreshadowed at Teheran. In the general rejoicing over the apparent accord among the Big Three, and in their assumption that Russia would be content within its new boundaries, they overlooked the appraisal one of the American participants at Teheran wrote a few days later: "The result would be that the Soviet Union would be the only important military and political force on the continent of Europe. The rest of Europe would be reduced to military and political impotence."

The Russian newspapers and radios were enthusiastic over the conference. Stalin wrote Roosevelt, "Now it is assured that our peoples will act together jointly and in friendship both at the present time and after the end of the war." But within a few weeks, the Russian press was hostile, and officials obdurate. In January 1944 Ambassador Harriman wired Churchill, "The Russian Bear is demanding much and yet biting the hands that are feeding it."

Chapter **18**

VICTORY

WITHOUT PEACE

As the United States gathered its forces for the great drives that should bring the Axis powers crashing down into final defeat, it idealistically expected that the Russians would forebear from rushing into the great European and Asiatic power vacuums that the defeat of Germany and Japan would create. This miscalculation led the Americans into a tragic victory —a triumph without peace.

Driving the Germans out of France

By the time of the Teheran Conference in the fall of 1943, Germany was already reeling under the incessant blows from the growing Allied air power. Great Britain had begun its mass bombings of German industrial centers in the late spring of 1942 with a thousand-plane night raid on Cologne. In August, the Americans made their first experimental daytime raids on the continent. By the summer of 1943, the British by night and the Americans by day were bombing heavily. The Americans suffered such serious losses that they had to discontinue daytime raids until February 1944, when they obtained long-range fighter support. Despite these difficulties, the Allies dropped four times as many tons of bombs on the continent in 1943 as they had in 1942.

Bombing began almost around the clock on a gigantic scale in February 1944, first against the German aviation industry, then against French and Belgian railroad yards and bridges. Later, the principal targets were synthetic oil and chemical plants. Since one of the objects of these bombing raids was to draw German fighter planes into battle, the air force in selecting targets often chose what it thought the Germans would fight hardest to protect. Its purpose was to increase Allied air su-

Ninth Air Force P-47 hitting German ammunition truck (OFFICIAL U.S. AIR FORCE PHOTO)

periority for the cross-channel attack and the breakthrough in France. By the end of the war, the Americans were flying over 7,000 bombers and 6,000 fighters in Europe, had dropped nearly a million and a half tons of bombs, and had lost nearly 10,000 bombers. British figures were similar. Especially in the last year of the war, the bombing drastically cut production and impeded transportation, but as early as the winter of 1944 it so seriously demoralized the German people that 77 per cent of them regarded the war as lost.

The bombing attacks upon the aviation industry and then upon transportation did much to clear the way for the invasion in the late spring. By May 1944, combined with the direct onslaught of fighter planes, they measurably weakened the *Luftwaffe*. It was incapable of beating off the Allied air cover for an invasion. The bomber attacks upon railroads were so effective that the Nazis feared they could not successfully move armies into the areas where landings might occur. They decided to rely primarily upon defending the ports they felt the Allies would have to possess in order to supply an invading army.

Aware of this Nazi strategy, the Allies sought a way to supply armies through beachheads in an area ordinarily washed by rough seas. They planned to ferry across the channel worn-out ships and special caissons to build the breakwaters for two artificial harbors. The other problem was

The Invasion of Normandy (OFFICIAL COAST GUARD PHOTO)

to obtain sufficient landing craft. General Marshall remarked at the end of 1943, "Prior to the present war I never heard of any landingcraft except a rubber boat. Now I think about little else." As D-day approached, the invasion was postponed from the beginning of May until early June despite the likelihood of worsening weather, in order to obtain an additional month's production.

A sudden storm delayed the operation for a day, but on the morning of June 6, 1944, the invasion came, not at the narrowest part of the English Channel where the Nazis expected it, but along sixty miles of the Cotentin peninsula on the Normandy coast. While airplanes and battleships offshore incessantly bombarded the Nazi defenses, 4,000 vessels, stretching as far as the eye could see, poured troops ashore. Many ships were damaged or sunk by mines, but others sailed in to unload men and cargo. The

British made good their landings to the east of the Americans, and the United States forces captured one of their two beaches, known by the code name Utah, against relatively light resistance. Unluckily, a German division was on anti-invasion maneuvers at the other beach (which had the code name Omaha), turning the landing there into a precarious and expensive affair. Americans lost 7,300 men in establishing the beachheads. Holding them was also a difficult and dangerous matter, as the Germans fought vigorously from behind the natural defenses of fields and lanes lined with tall hedgerows. The Allied strategy necessitated the ferrying across the channel of hundreds of thousands of men and tons of supplies with which to cut off the peninsula tipped with the port of Cherbourg, and to capture the port itself. Through it and other ports had to come the millions of troops and mountains of munitions with which to strike a death blow at the Nazis.

Beginning June 18, a gale of top wind velocity churned the channel for four days, destroying one of the artificial harbors and damaging the other. Despite this setback, within two weeks after the initial landings the Allies had put ashore a million men and the equipment for them. They also had captured Cherbourg, only to find that the Germans had blocked its harbor so skillfully that it could not be used until August.

Well into July, the Allies fought mile by mile through the Norman hedgerows until General Omar Bradley's troops on July 19, 1944, captured St. Lô, a hub from which railroads and roads stretched into the heart of France. The initial slow, grinding phase of the invasion was over. Marshall Gerd von Rundstedt, the competent German commander, recommended falling back to a defense line along the Seine; Hitler in a fury removed him and ordered the German positions maintained. The breakthrough came on July 25, 1944, when the Third Army under General George Patton, using its armor as cavalry had been used in earlier wars, smashed the German lines in an enormous sweep that moved southward into Brittany, then westward around the left flank of the German army. With the British and Canadians pressing hard from the north, the Americans fought through August to try to complete encirclement of the Germans. They did not succeed in capturing the entire German army, but only remnants of it escaped across the Seine on August 24.

In rapid and spectacular fashion, the rest of France was freed as the remaining German troops retreated at top speed to the Westwall or Siegfried Line within their own country. The invasion on the Mediterranean coast, beginning on August 15, quickly seized new ports (also seriously blocked) and opened new supply lines for the Allies. On August 25, French forces rode into Paris, jammed with cheering throngs. By mid-September, the Allied armies had driven the Germans from almost all of

France and Belgium, including the port of Antwerp, and had come to a halt against a firm line of German defenses.

The Allies were short of supplies and the fall rains hampered air support. Efforts failed to outflank the Germans through landing paratroopers across the great northern river barriers in Holland. Tantalizingly, victory seemed just beyond grasp, since by every means of measurement the Nazis

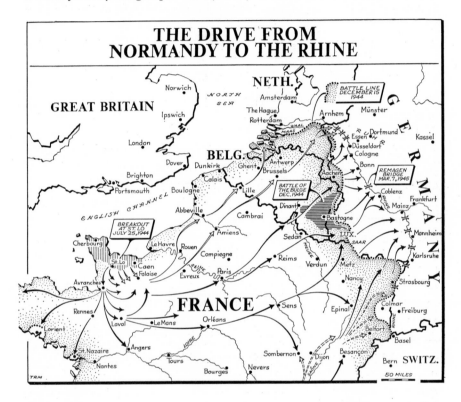

THE DRIVE FROM
NORMANDY TO THE RHINE

were thoroughly trounced. An officers' plot to assassinate Hitler had failed in July 1944, and the Fuehrer was determined to defend Germany to the extreme end, regardless of the destruction it might bring to Germany. Another season of fighting still lay ahead.

The Impasse in China

IN THE DISCOURAGING FALL OF 1944, less-publicized events on the other side of the world were leading already toward what was to be one of the most shocking of the postwar debacles. The tangle in China was becoming snarled almost irreparably. On paper, at least, the United States had elevated China after Pearl Harbor to the status of a great power. In January 1943 the United States signed a treaty restoring the extraterritorial

rights and other special privileges for American citizens, which the United
States like other powers had wrested from China during the previous
century. The United States wished also to build China's strength so that
it could help maintain stability in the postwar Far East.

Early in 1942 this became a serious logistic problem as the Japanese
forced General Joseph H. Stilwell out of Burma and brought their troops
as far west as the mountains bordering on India. China was so isolated
that the United States could send in meager supplies only through an

THE BURMA CAMPAIGN

aerial ferry over the "hump" of the Himalayas. On the return trip, the
planes brought Chinese troops for Stilwell to train and arm. Through 1943
Stilwell, with Chinese, Indian, and a few American troops, fought back
through northern Burma, constructing a road and parallel pipeline across
the rugged mountains into Yunnan province, China. The Ledo or Stilwell
Road was not open until the fall of 1944, but meanwhile the Air Transport
Command managed to fly in sufficient supplies to enable the Fourteenth
Air Force (before Pearl Harbor, the "Flying Tigers") to harass the Japanese. The Command undertook a still larger task, when, in June 1944,
from Chinese bases, B-29 bombers struck the Yawata steel mills in Japan.
The Japanese retaliated in the next few months by overrunning the bases
from which the bombers operated, and clearing the coastal area so they
could bring supplies northward from southeast Asia by rail or road. They
drove so far into the interior that they threatened the Chinese terminus

of the Ledo Road, and perhaps even the center of government at Chungking.

The great Japanese offensive precipitated a long-simmering crisis in Chinese-American affairs, centering around the relations between General Stilwell and Chiang Kai-shek. Stilwell was indignant because Chiang was using many of his troops to maintain an armed frontier against the Chinese Communists and would not deploy them against the Japanese. Further, Chiang was allowing the number of Chinese troops in Burma to dwindle to a degree that might allow Japanese reconquest. The State Department and General Patrick J. Hurley, Roosevelt's representative in China, pressed Chiang to unify his army with that of the Communists or at least to co-operate with it. Ultimately the State Department wished him to establish a constitutional government that would include the Communists.

From Quebec in September 1944, President Roosevelt, on the advice of the Joint Chiefs of Staff, strongly urged Chiang to place Stilwell in effective command of the Chinese Army. Chiang, shocked, instead asked to have Stilwell replaced. By so doing he threw away an opportunity to let the United States in effect take responsibility for the Chinese army, a step that surely would have led to far quicker and stronger aid for him in the postwar period. As it was, the United States had seriously misgauged the nature and strength of the Chinese Communists and the weakness of Chiang's government. In order to have bolstered Chiang adequately, it would have had to send such substantial immediate support that the campaigns against Germany and directly against Japan might have had to be slowed down or postponed.

Quite the reverse occurred, for in the next few months the direct assaults upon the Japanese Empire quickly lessened the pressure on China, and the United States made less of an effort to increase Chiang's military power.

Smashing Japan's Defense Ring

DURING 1944 Japan came under heavy blockade from the sea and bombardment from the air. American submarines, firing torpedoes and laying mines, continued to bring heavy losses to the dwindling Japanese merchant marine. American landings had already cracked the outer Japanese defense perimeter, but at the beginning of 1944 strong bases still guarded a ring around Japan almost as wide as the Atlantic Ocean. The B-29 raids from China were the first effective attack on Japan from within the ring. The liquidation of the air bases was an empty victory for Japan, since by

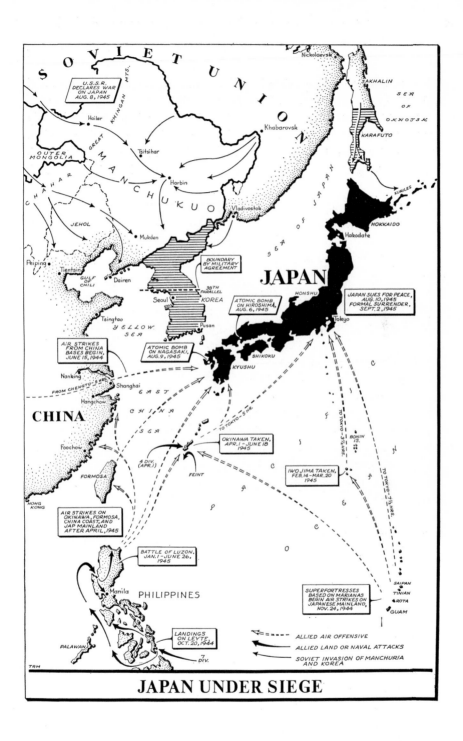

JAPAN UNDER SIEGE

midsummer the Americans had penetrated far within the defense perimeter. From new island airstrips they were able, beginning in November 1944, to mount an increasing bombing attack upon Japanese cities and industries.

In mid-June 1944, an enormous American armada struck the heavily fortified Mariana Islands, quickly but expensively capturing Tinian, Guam, and Saipan, 1,350 miles from Tokyo. These were among the bloodiest operations of the war. The Japanese tried to repel the invaders with

The top admirals: Admiral King, Secretary of the Navy James V. Forrestal, Admiral Halsey, and Admiral Nimitz (NATIONAL ARCHIVES)

their dwindling ships and aircraft, and sustained losses in two engagements. In September, the Americans landed on the Western Carolines. The way was being paved for the return to the Philippines. For weeks in advance, Navy craft swept the central Pacific, and airplanes ranged over the Philippines and Formosa. Finally, on October 20, 1944, General MacArthur's troops landed on Leyte Island in the Philippines. The Japanese, threatened with being fatally cut off from their new empire in Southeast Asia, threw their remaining fleets against the invaders in three major encounters—together comprising the decisive Battle of Leyte Gulf, the largest naval engagement in history—and lost almost all their remaining sea power. Through the winter of 1944–45 the lengthy land campaigns in the Philippines proceeded, not ending until July 1945.

A Wartime Presidential Election

DURING THE MONTHS of alternating rejoicing and gloom in the summer and fall of 1944, the American people were also fighting out a presidential election. The Republicans faced a difficult problem in trying to defeat Roosevelt, because of the enormous prestige his war leadership carried.

As a wartime Presidential candidate, Governor Thomas E. Dewey inspects a medium tank (NATIONAL ARCHIVES)

Nevertheless, dissatisfaction with wartime regimentation and smoldering resentments still glowing from the prewar debate over intervention seemed to give the Republicans an opportunity. They had seen auguries of a national shift toward the right in the congressional election of 1942. In their vigorous young candidate, Governor Thomas E. Dewey of New York, who ran with Governor John W. Bricker of Ohio, they seemed to have an answer to Roosevelt and the aging New Dealers. Their platform was internationalist and progressive; they could claim that they were offering sensible moderation and youthful efficiency.

As for President Roosevelt, it was a foregone conclusion that he would be nominated for a fourth term if he so desired. There was none of the suspense that had preceded the third term nomination. Rather, since he was visibly aging, and thinning so that his clothes ill fit him, there was much speculation over his choice for the Vice-Presidential nominee. Vice-President Wallace was, during the war, the hero of most advanced New Dealers and much of the C.I.O. membership. But he was sneered at by party bosses and some Southern Democrats as a visionary who wished to extend the New Deal to the entire globe, to bring "a quart of milk for

every Hottentot." They rallied behind James F. Byrnes of South Carolina, who had been functioning ably as unofficial assistant president—but
Byrnes was unacceptable to organized labor. Out of the skirmishing among
the rival factions within the Democratic party came Roosevelt's proposal
of a compromise candidate acceptable to most of them, Senator Harry S.
Truman of Missouri. Truman had won newspaper approval as chairman
of the Senate War Investigating Committee, was a consistent New Dealer
in his voting record, and was from a border state. He was popular in the

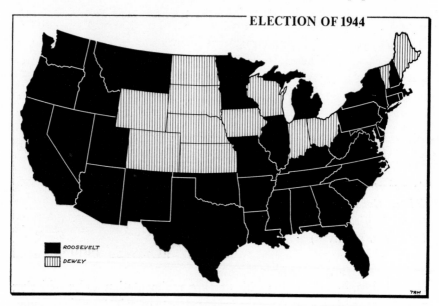

ELECTION OF 1944

ROOSEVELT
DEWEY

Senate, and it may be that Roosevelt saw in him a useful lieutenant to
obtain ratification of postwar treaties.

The campaign showed signs of being dull, and perhaps of ending in a
Republican victory. President Roosevelt again inspected war installations,
traveled to Hawaii to confer with Admiral Chester W. Nimitz, commander
of the Pacific fleet, and General MacArthur. On his return, speaking at
Bremerton, Washington, precariously balanced on the slanting deck of a
vessel while the wind ruffled his manuscript, he spoke haltingly and
seemed old and tired. Dewey, in contrast, was crisp, young, and vigorous
but, having no issue he could develop effectively, had to confine himself to
statesmanlike addresses. He had been told that the United States had possessed the Japanese code at the time of Pearl Harbor, but an envoy from
General Marshall persuaded him not to use this information, since it would
hamper the war in the Pacific. Even without this issue, the election promised to be close—partly because the vote was likely to be small, and presumably a light vote would aid the Republicans.

The possibility was like an injection of adrenalin into Roosevelt. At the end of September 1944, addressing a raucously appreciative audience of Teamsters Union members, he was at his sardonic best. He followed this triumph with a strenous campaign in Chicago and throughout the East. This he climaxed with a day-long drive in an open car through New York City in a soaking rain. Everyone was drenched, and all but Roosevelt were exhausted.

This *tour de force*, seemingly proving Roosevelt's capacity to serve four more years, his international leadership, and his promise to return to the New Deal after the war, were a winning combination. Many middle-class and upper-class people again voted for him on international issues —not because he differed from Dewey but because he was more experienced. Organized labor, working through the C.I.O. Political Action Committee, brought out the workers' votes. The President defeated Dewey by a margin of 432 electoral votes to 99, and a popular vote of 25,602,000 to 22,006,000. The Democrats lost one seat in the Senate, but gained twenty in the House. The Democratic victory seemed to mean a revival of the New Deal at home; and the campaign promises of both parties indicated that the United States would continue to take a lead in international affairs.

The False Promise of Yalta

NO ONE could have grasped even in the fall of 1944 how strong American leadership overseas would have to be in order to maintain even the most uneasy peace. While the Allies had been fighting their way through France to the Westwall (German defense line) and up the Italian peninsula, the Russian armies were sweeping westward into central Europe and the Balkans. As they passed beyond the new boundaries they were claiming for the Soviet Union and liberated portions of other countries from the Nazis, the question became urgent whether the Russians were ready to co-operate with the British and the United States in establishing freely chosen democratic governments in these areas, or whether they intended to turn them into Soviet satellites.

Secretary Hull, despite warnings from the embassy in Moscow, continued to think idealistically that the world had outgrown spheres of influence and power balance. Many State Department officials were only slightly less optimistic in thinking that wrongs could be rectified through the new postwar international organization. A conference held at Dumbarton Oaks in Washington in September 1944 drafted plans for it.

That same month Hull finally took alarm over the Russian insistence that they and they alone could make policy for Hungary, Romania, and

Bulgaria. He asked the American embassy in Moscow why the Russians were reversing their friendly agreements made at Moscow and Teheran. Ambassador Harriman explained he was not sure this was a reversal—that the Russians were ready to make the most of participation in an international organization, but were also ready, now that they felt they could win the war, to override all opposition in establishing their domination over neighboring countries. The United States, he suggested, might be able to counter the Russian policies by taking a firm, decisive, and minute interest in European power politics.

In the fall of 1944 the State Department was not yet ready to intervene strongly. Until the Presidential election was over, Roosevelt did not want to grapple with the thorny Polish problem, so upsetting to Americans of Polish antecedents. Military advisers had other reasons for being hesitant. When the Russians at the Dumbarton Oaks conference insisted upon an absolute veto in an international organization, representatives of the armed forces did not want to debate the question too firmly for fear sharp disagreement might cause Russia to stay out of the war against Japan.

Tacitly, but only tacitly, Roosevelt backed Churchill in October 1944 when the prime minister visited Moscow to negotiate a division of power in the Balkans. Stalin agreed that the British were to exercise a predominance of 90 per cent in Greece, and the Russians 90 per cent in Romania and 75 per cent in Bulgaria. Influence in Yugoslavia and Hungary was to be 50–50. Roosevelt was noncommittal when he heard of this arrangement. The State Department continued to urge that settlements be postponed until after the fighting was over so that military considerations would not distort them and principle could reign.

Churchill's mood fluctuated with the ebb and flow of Russian good will. Upon leaving Moscow, he wrote Stalin, "This memorable meeting . . . has shown that there are no matters that cannot be adjusted between us when we meet together in frank and intimate discussion." By January 1945 he was so chagrined by Russian failure to make good on the October agreements that he wrote Roosevelt concerning the forthcoming Yalta meeting, "This may well be a fateful Conference, coming at a moment when the Great Allies are so divided and the shadow of the war lengthens out before us. At the present time I think the end of this war may well prove to be more disappointing than was the last."

This was the bleak and unpromising setting for the great conference at Yalta in the Crimea in February 1945. The military background of the conference was also far from cheerful. Cold weather, rain, and floods had aided the Germans, who with a hundred divisions were blocking about the same number of Allied divisions in the west and in Italy. In December, the Nazis struck with desperate fury along a seventy-five mile front in the

Ardennes Forest, driving twenty miles toward Antwerp before they were stopped at Bastogne. Before the Yalta conference, the offensive was over and had spent most of the remaining German strategic reserve, but the bulge had not yet been flattened.

In contrast, the Russian armies had advanced more rapidly than had been expected, and in late January launched an offensive of over one hundred and fifty divisions toward the Oder River, deep in Germany. The continued advance of the Russians still seemed desirable in order to gain a victory in Europe, even though they probably would penetrate far into Germany. The line of demarcation between the western and Russian zones of occupation in Germany, which had been agreed upon by a European Advisory Commission five months before the invasion of France, would put Russia far to the west in Germany. This had not worried the United States and Great Britain—and it still seemed as though the troops might meet in that area.

As for the Far East, the Japanese Navy was too weak to fight further major engagements; Japanese shipping had been cut from seven million to two million tons; air resistance could not prevent a 120-plane raid which wrecked Kobe. The United States planned to operate 1,800 bombers against Japan. Another weapon was on the horizon. General Leslie R. Groves, head of the Manhattan Project, wrote General Marshall at the end of 1944 that it should have an atomic bomb ready in August, and another before the end of the year. The first should have an explosive force equal to 500 tons of TNT, and the next, double this amount. This was impressive, but was no more than the total destructive force unleashed in each big bombing raid over Germany. (By comparison, the two bombs actually dropped on Japan had an explosive force equivalent to 10,000 to 20,000 tons of TNT.)

The Joint Chiefs of Staff were of no disposition to depend upon a weapon not yet constructed or proven. Nor did the few bombs likely to be available in the first year give indication of being decisive. The Japanese units, wherever encountered, were continuing their literally suicidal resistance. American forces were having to reduce Germany mile by mile; there seemed no reason to think Japan would be different. General MacArthur insisted on the necessity for Russian aid, taking the position that otherwise the United States would have to fight a series of difficult and expensive campaigns to overcome the Japanese in Manchuria. Consequently the Joint Chiefs did not revise their timetable calling for the defeat of Japan eighteen months after German surrender, and they continued to regard Russian aid as desirable. Roosevelt expressed to Stalin his hope that Japan could be bombed into submission without invasion—but the Americans could not count upon it.

These were the limitations upon the Americans in their bargaining at Yalta. In return for Stalin's reiterated promise to enter the Far Eastern war two or three months after German surrender, Roosevelt and Churchill promised him the Kurile Islands north of Japan and the restoration of "the former rights of Russia" lost in the Russo-Japanese War. This meant the return of southern Sakhalin Island, the return of a lease on Port Arthur as a naval base and internationalizing of the port of Dairen, Manchuria (in both instances with recognition of Russia's pre-eminent interests), and joint operation with China of the Chinese Eastern and South Manchurian Railroads feeding into the ports. China was to retain sovereignty over Manchuria, but Roosevelt did not clarify what "pre-eminent interests" meant. Further, he promised to seek the concurrence of Chiang Kai-shek. Such concurrence appeared likely, since according to reports from Chungking, Chiang felt he would be amply compensated by a Soviet-Chinese mutual assistance pact promised by Stalin. The Americans considered the pact of marked significance. For many months these clauses remained secret because Russia was still at peace with Japan. When they became public, conditions had changed so drastically that to the harshest critics the United States seemed to be acting as the accomplice to a thief. Obviously, Stalin could have wrested whatever he pleased in Manchuria directly from Chiang, but it was unfortunate that the United States, which ordinarily placed so much emphasis upon moral principle, should underwrite his demands.

In its disposition of central European questions, the Yalta conference for the most part ratified previous decisions. Germany was to be divided into zones of occupation previously agreed upon. Since Berlin was to be deep in the Russian zone, the Americans and British proposed an accord providing freedom of transit into Berlin. The Russians held back, and in the general spirit of amity at Yalta, the matter was postponed. At the time, the Russian demands for heavy reparations in the form of German factories, goods, and labor seemed far more important. The British tried to scale down the Russian demand for $20 billion in such reparations, of which Russia was to obtain half. This would so strip and starve the Germans, Churchill pointed out, that the United States and Great Britain would have to feed them. Consequently they agreed to the Russian figure only as a basis for discussion by a reparations commission. Already, in the light of reality the West had left far behind the Morgenthau plan for the pastoralization of Germany.

One of the touchiest questions was to define a democratic government for Poland, a matter over which Russia and the West had negotiated for months. The Russians did not wish to allow the Polish government in exile in London or the Polish underground to assume any substantial share of power with a government the Russians established at Lublin. At the beginning of August 1944, as the Red army drove within ten miles of Warsaw, the underground in the city arose against the Germans. The Russians halted, ignored the revolt, and despite the strong pleas of the United States and Great Britain, stood by while the Polish patriots in sixty-three days of fighting were annihilated. The Russian explanation was military exigency, but the situation seemed to show the sort of government Stalin was determined to establish in Poland.

At Yalta, the West managed to obtain Stalin's agreement that the Lublin (Communist) government should be broadened to include demo-

The final meeting at Yalta (NATIONAL ARCHIVES)

cratic leaders from Poland and abroad. What the percentage should be was not specified. Subsequently the new government should hold "free and unfettered elections as soon as possible on the basis of universal suffrage and secret ballot." It would have been a satisfactory arrangement for the West had the terms been interpreted in their Western meaning. As for the Polish boundary, it was to follow the Curzon line in the east, and the Poles should receive territorial compensation in the north and west.

For the rest of liberated or defeated Europe, the Big Three agreed to establish interim governments "broadly representative of all democratic elements," to be followed by free elections which would create "governments responsible to the will of the people."

In years after the war, disappointed Americans harshly criticized the Yalta agreements, especially for their violations of the Atlantic Charter. The morality of the Far Eastern arrangements is open to challenge. Their purpose was to obtain Russian aid, which top military leaders thought would shorten the war against Japan and perhaps prevent a million American casualties. They promised nothing to Stalin except the Kurile Islands that he could not have taken anyway. The morality of the European arrangements (except perhaps for the ethnic dislocations wrought by the new Polish boundaries) was defensible if the terms received their customary Western interpretation. Roosevelt may be most severely criticized for not insisting at every point upon absolutely clear, sharply defined agreements which could receive only one interpretation in Russia, and that the same as in the West. This was especially true of the question of entry into Berlin. Experience with the Russians long before Yalta pointed to the need of precise understandings.

Roosevelt was careless in this area because he pinned his hopes upon the good faith of the Russians and their willingness to enter into and participate actively in an international organization for the preservation of the peace. He saw clearly that the future of the postwar world depended upon this. The presence of Red divisions in eastern Europe meant that the only way to counter the Russians there would be with armed force, and the Western world was long since sick of bloodletting.

It has been argued that Roosevelt should have fallen in with Churchill's earlier schemes and sent American troops into the "soft underbelly" of Europe, liberating the Balkans and establishing Western-style democracies there. Roosevelt in his optimism saw no political need for this serious military diversion, and probably it would only have meant that the Russians would have moved proportionately further west in Germany. Perhaps for this reason, Stalin in October 1944 had encouraged Churchill's proposal to send troops from the Adriatic to assist the Russians in their drive through Hungary into Austria.

The spirit of Yalta was one of friendly accomodation. Stalin seemed to be meeting Roosevelt and Churchill at least halfway. He agreed to participate in the United Nations, although the West would obviously dominate it, and he seemed committed to the creation of democratic governments throughout shattered Europe. The military arrangements at Yalta were favorable and the Russians were more co-operative than ever before. Understandably the American people hailed the news of Yalta with enthusiasm and hope. A new era in international relations seemed to be dawning—an age in which Roosevelt hoped the new international organization, backed by the great powers, would maintain peace. It depended, he realized, upon the co-operation of Russia, and this he and Churchill seemed to have obtained.

Victory and Tension in Europe

IN THE MONTHS AFTER the Yalta conference, the war came to a triumphant conclusion with unexpected speed, leaving as its aftermath grim difficulties with the Soviet Union. It was a dark victory.

In liquidating the German thrust into the Ardennes, which had almost exhausted the Nazi fighting capacity, the Allied armies pushed on to the Rhine. The Americans captured Cologne on the west bank March 6, 1945, and on the next day, through remarkable luck, captured a bridge across the Rhine at Remagen. Troops poured across it. By the end of March the last great drives were underway as the British Field Marshal Montgomery, with a million troops, pushed across the north, while Bradley's army, sweeping through central Germany, completed the encirclement and trapping of 300,000 German soldiers in the Ruhr. Russian troops were about to mount a spring offensive only 35 miles from Berlin.

Although there were fears that the Nazis were preparing for a last stand in an Alpine redoubt centering around Berchtesgaden on the Austrian border, the German western front had in effect been demolished. The only question was where the Americans would next drive, and where they would join the Russians. They were capable of moving much further eastward than had been anticipated, and could have beaten the Russians to Berlin and Prague. This would have cost American lives, but reaped political gain in Europe. General Eisenhower decided instead to send American troops to capture the Alpine redoubt, and to halt along the Elbe River in central Germany to meet the Russians. The American generals refused to be swayed by political considerations. Stalin was pleased and Churchill dismayed.

Already the implications of the Russian postwar position were becoming apparent as, in the disillusioning weeks after Yalta, Stalin ignored his fair promises there and proceeded to maintain or establish Communist puppet governments in Poland and the Balkan countries. In his attitude toward Americans delivering Lend-Lease supplies, Air Force units in Russia, and American prisoners being liberated in Poland he seemed more to be disciplining potential enemies than co-operating with generous allies. By mid-March 1945, Churchill, whose high hopes of February had already evaporated, wrote Roosevelt his dismay at the "great failure and . . . utter breakdown of what was settled at Yalta." Worse followed, as Stalin unjustly accused the United States of trickery in conducting negotiations for the surrender of the Nazis in Italy. Roosevelt, shocked, retorted to Stalin:

> It would be one of the great tragedies of history if at the very moment of the victory now within our grasp, such distrust, such lack of faith,

should prejudice the entire undertaking after the colossal losses of life, material, and treasure involved.

Roosevelt lived to see neither the final triumph nor the ultimate tragedy. Since the early months of 1944 his vigor had been gradually drained away. Badly needing a rest but optimistic as always, he went to Warm Springs early in April to prepare for the San Francisco conference to establish the United Nations organization upon which he pinned his best hopes. Suddenly, on the afternoon of April 12, 1945, he died of a cerebral hemmorhage.

The new President, Truman, who had been in no way briefed for his enormous responsibilities, had to take over leadership of the war and negotiations with the Russians. During the next few weeks, while he learned rapidly from Roosevelt's advisors, he largely followed policies that had already been established.

On May 8, 1945, the remaining German forces surrendered unconditionally. VE day arrived amidst monster celebrations in western Europe, and rejoicing in the United States tempered only by knowledge of the continuing war against Japan. The public was not yet really aware of the growing difficulties with the Russians. Churchill was trying to impress upon President Truman the necessity for maintaining a strong military frontier against the Russians until the British and Americans could come to a firm understanding with them. None of the American policy makers agreed. The armed forces still wanted Russian aid against Japan. A new factor was also present. All indications were that the atomic bomb was not only successful but more devastatingly powerful than had been earlier anticipated. Those few who knew it was being constructed wished to wait until it had been proven before risking a test of strength with Russia which might lead to war. President Truman, regardless of the success of the bomb, aspired to settle questions with the Russians by peaceful negotiations rather than by the threat of force.

The Atomic Bomb and Japanese Surrender

WITH REMARKABLE SPEED but grievous losses the American forces had cut still deeper into the Japanese empire during the early months of 1945. While fighting continued in the Philippines, the marines landed in February 1945 on the tiny volcanic island of Iwo Jima, only 750 miles from Tokyo. It was needed to provide fighter cover for Japan-bound bombers and a landing place for crippled ones. The Japanese defended it so grimly that the marines suffered over 20,000 casualties. It was the bloodiest battle in the history of the marine corps.

The battle for Okinawa, an island 65 miles long, began on April 1, 1945 and was even bloodier. The island was 370 miles south of Japan, and its conquest clearly would be a prelude to an invasion of the main islands. On land and from the air, the Japanese fought with literally a suicidal fury. Week after week they sent *kamikaze* suicide planes against the American and British ships, losing 3,500 of them, but inflicting great damage. Ashore, Japanese troops launched equally desperate attacks at night on the American lines. The United States and its allies suffered nearly 50,000 casualties on land and afloat before the battle came to an end in late June 1945. The Japanese lost 110,000 killed and 7,800 prisoners.

This same sort of bitter fighting seemed to await the Americans when they invaded Japan—if indeed they had to invade. There were signs that the Japanese might instead surrender, for they had almost no ships and few airplanes with which to fight. In July 1945 American warships stood offshore shelling industrial targets with impunity. Most of these were already in ruins from the heavy bombing attacks. Long since, moderate Japanese leaders had regarded the war as lost. Upon the invasion of Okinawa, the Emperor had appointed a new premier and charged him with suing for peace. The Premier could not persuade the army leaders to lay down their arms, but nevertheless he, and in early summer the Emperor himself, tried to obtain mediation through Russia—which did not notify the United States.

Apparently the Russians were determined to enter the war at their own time. But the atomic bomb rather than Russian intervention was to be decisive in ending it. At the final meeting of the Big Three in Potsdam, Germany, in mid-July 1945, President Truman received word that the first atomic test was successful. He and Prime Minister Clement Attlee (who had succeeded Churchill) issued the Potsdam Declaration urging the Japanese to surrender or face utter devastation. The Premier wished to accept the ultimatum, but the army leaders would not surrender. President Truman had set August 3 as the deadline; when it passed and the Japanese fought on, he ordered an atomic bomb to be dropped on one of four previously selected Japanese cities.

On August 6, 1945, a B-29 dropped an atomic bomb on Hiroshima. It exploded with a destructiveness never before known in human history. The United States Strategic Bombing Survey later reported:

> A single atomic bomb, the first weapon of its type ever used against a target, exploded over the city of Hiroshima at 0815 on the morning of 6 August 1945. Most of the industrial workers had already reported to work, but many workers were enroute and nearly all the school children and some industrial employees were at work in the open on the program

The mushroom cloud over Nagasaki, August 9, 1945 (OFFICIAL U.S. AIR
FORCE PHOTO)

of building-removal. . . . The explosion came as an almost complete surprise, and the people had not taken shelter. Many were caught in the open, and most of the rest in flimsily constructed homes or commercial establishments. The bomb exploded slightly northwest of the center of the city. Because of this accuracy and the flat terrain and circular shape of the city, Hiroshima was uniformly and extensively devastated. Practically the entire densely or moderately built-up portion of the city was leveled by blast and swept by fire. . . . The surprise, the collapse of many buildings, and the conflagration contributed to an unprecedented casualty rate. Seventy to eighty thousand people were killed, or missing and presumed dead, and an equal number were injured.

Even after the horror of Hiroshima, the Japanese army remained adamant. But the bomb apparently caused Russia to enter the war hastily

Hiroshima, Japan, October 1945 (NATIONAL ARCHIVES)

while there was still time; it declared war on Japan as of August 9. That same day, the Air Force dropped a second bomb on Nagasaki. It was the final blow. After frantic negotiations, on August 14 the Japanese government agreed to surrender. On September 2, 1945, aboard the battleship *Missouri* in Tokyo bay, the Japanese signed the articles of surrender.

The Second World War was at an end. The price in lives and suffering had been low for the United States compared with the estimated total 14,000,000 men under arms who had been killed, and the countless millions of civilians who had died. In comparison, about 322,000 Americans had been killed or were missing; total United States casualties were about 1,120,000. Despite this frightful expenditure in lives and an astronomical cost in material resources, the American people faced a future made uncertain and perilous by the tensions with the Russians and the threat of nuclear warfare.

Chapter **19**

THE MENACE OF
COLD WAR

THE MONTHS AFTER the final defeat of Germany and Japan brought the beginnings of a new titanic struggle with Russia, a conflict beginning with relatively minor tensions and mounting to the recurring threat of a new all-out war. Americans were psychologically as unprepared for this crisis as they had been for Pearl Harbor. As it continued with endless variations during the years that followed it created more difficult problems and posed a more serious menace to the United States than had even the Axis onslaught. The Cold War, as it came to be called, split most of the world into two power blocs. The maintenance of world stability came to depend upon a difficult and tenuous balance of power, not, as the United States had planned, upon an international organization.

Well before the Second World War finally came to an end the American people seemed united in feeling that the United States must continue to exercise some degree of positive leadership in world affairs. Most of them agreed that there must be no repetition of the fiasco of Senate rejection of the Versailles Treaty, with the tragic train of events which followed. Some Americans even felt that the breakdown of the peace in the interlude between the two wars had come as a direct result of the isolationism of the United States.

During the long months of planning for a new international organization, when public opinion was being enlisted, there was little inkling how large a role the United States would have to play to preserve world peace. After the war a series of Russian thrusts into weak areas in Europe and Asia gave Americans rude shocks that halted each of the periodic drifts back toward relative isolation and united the nation in preservation of an armed peace. Again and again the normal desire of the American people to enjoy the high living standard and unprecedented prosperity of the postwar years was threatened by these crises; each time the people accepted heavier armaments, firmer international commitments, and even, if need be, the fighting of brushfire wars.

It was a comfortable era at home, but a frightening one in relation to Russia. There were those who in their prejudices and voting habits expressed an understandable nostalgia for the old safer America of the twenties or thirties, but the majority recognized that it was gone forever, and felt that their only safety lay in armed international co-operation.

Establishing the United Nations

A FEW MONTHS after war broke out in Europe, long before Pearl Harbor, Secretary of State Cordell Hull took the first step toward proposing a new international organization in which the United States would participate. In January 1940 he appointed an Advisory Committee on Problems of Foreign Relations. On it served Congressmen from both parties and distinguished experts from within and without the State Department, rather like President Wilson's "inquiry" of the First World War. Several private organizations, such as the Council on Foreign Relations, also prepared numerous studies for the State Department.

President Roosevelt, firmly determined to avoid Wilson's failure, encouraged Hull to include Republicans in the planning for the peace. However, Roosevelt did not consult Congress before making his most famous statements of war aims; Senator Robert A. Taft asserted in Congress in November 1943 that he did not believe "that we went to war to establish the 'four freedoms' or any other freedom throughout the world," nor "for the purposes set forth in the Atlantic Charter." The administration, to counter this sort of resentment, included prominent Republicans in at least sketchy briefing on wartime diplomacy and let them participate more fully in postwar planning of many kinds. In this way it won their support. In March 1943 four Senators, two Republican and two Democratic, none of whom were serving on the Foreign Relations Committee, introduced a resolution calling for American leadership in establishing a United Nations organization. Public opinion polls indicated a general enthusiasm for the resolution; the Senate passed a similar declaration 85 to 5. In this fashion

sound political strategy and wise statesmanship led to bipartisan development of the new foreign policy.

Senator Arthur H. Vandenberg of Michigan, previously one of the
most forthright isolationists, assumed Republican leadership in helping
mold postwar international policy. He thus gained for himself and the Republican party new power and stature. In 1943, when the administration
planned an international food relief organization, the United Nations Relief and Rehabilitation Administration (UNRRA), it framed an executive
agreement not requiring ratification. It would ask Congress only for appropriations. When Vandenberg demurred, Secretary Hull agreed to total
congressional consultation, included Republican reservations in the agreement, and submitted it to Congress for passage as a joint resolution.

The Big Four powers, conferring in the summer and fall of 1944 at
Dumbarton Oaks, a Harvard-owned estate in Washington, drafted tentative outlines for a new international organization. These and some of the
Yalta agreements were the starting points for the drafting of a United Nations charter at a conference of fifty nations in San Francisco, opening
April 25, 1945. President Roosevelt had earlier appointed a bipartisan
delegation headed by his new Secretary of State, Edward R. Stettinius, Jr.
One of its most effective members was Senator Vandenberg, who helped to
wrest concessions from the Russians at San Francisco and to win the votes
of reluctant Republicans for ratification in the Senate.

Basically the charter of the United Nations was a refurbishing of the
old Wilsonian League covenant with the former American objections
removed through giving a veto to each of the five main powers. The Americans and British had insisted upon the veto as a seemingly necessary protection of their sovereignty. Thus, the United Nations would be unable to
act against American national interests. Thus also, it was rendered utterly
impotent to deal with any major quarrel among the big powers. The Russians also wished to protect their self-interest in this fashion and to vest
power, at least negative power, in the big nations. They had wanted almost
all authority placed in the Security Council, made up of the big five plus
six other members elected by the General Assembly. Also, Russia had
wanted the veto power of the permanent members on the Council to
extend even to discussion. The United States insisted upon, and finally obtained, freedom of debate. In addition, the United States, led by Vandenberg, succeeded in obtaining for the small nations in the General Assembly
freedom to discuss and make recommendations—in effect creating "a
town meeting of the world." Although any of the five major powers could
veto a proposed Security Council action, the United Nations went well
beyond the League of Nations in providing for police action against aggression. The Security Council could ask member nations to sever diplo-

matic relations with an aggressor or apply economic or military pressure. It even could have at its disposal military units to form a standing international police force—which never came into existence because the United States and Russia could not agree upon its composition.

This was typical of the great rift which hampered the United Nations in its aim to prevent war and in much of the work of its commissions and specialized agencies. The Senate quickly ratified the Charter on July 28,

The United States representative signing the United Nations Charter: (left to right) *President Truman, Secretary of State Stettinius, Senator Tom Connally, Senator Vandenburg, Harold Stassen* (NATIONAL ARCHIVES)

1945, by a vote of 89 to 2, in remarkable contrast to the slow and painful death it had administered to American adherence in the League of Nations. But the great and growing gulf between Russia and the West seemed destined to make the United Nations, like its predecessor, the League, a town meeting for international discussion or a sounding board for national views, rather than the prototype of a world government.

Truman vs. Stalin

DURING THE LAST MONTHS of his life President Roosevelt had helped build the idealistic hopes of the American people for an effective United Nations that would preserve the peace through the co-operation of the Russians and the Americans. In his message to Congress, January 6, 1945, he had asserted:

> The nearer we come to vanquishing our enemies the more we inevitably become conscious of differences among the victors. We must not let those differences divide us and blind us to our more important and continuing interests in winning the war and building the peace.

This was the spirit in which the American people accepted the reports of emerging difficulties with the Russians. It was the spirit also of Vice-President Harry S. Truman; Roosevelt did not share with him or with the public his growing disillusion with Stalin. Rather, the last lines he added to a speech he was drafting at the time of his death were a call to optimistic idealism: "The only limit to our realization of tomorrow will be our doubts of today. Let us move forward with strong and active faith."

President Truman tried to maintain this level of idealism at the same time that he had to face pragmatically the unco-operativeness of the Russians. His task was a frightening one in suddenly taking control of the intricate machinery for concluding the war and fabricating the peace. No one doubted his sincerity when he remarked to reporters the day after he had suddenly taken his oath of office, "I felt like the moon, the stars, and all the planets had fallen on me. I've got the most terribly responsible job a man ever had." Immediately those administrators who had been closest to Roosevelt began to give the new President an intensive briefing. Secretary of State Stettinius on April 13, 1945, gave him an outline of foreign problems that declared, "Since the Yalta Conference the Soviet Government has taken a firm and uncompromising position on nearly every major question that has arisen in our relations." Ambassador Averell Harriman flew from Moscow to report that he thought Russia would not break with the United States because it needed American aid in reconstruction, but that it was violating all its agreements and threatening a "barbarian invasion of Europe."

President Truman replied to Harriman that he was not afraid of the Russians and intended to be firm but fair. It was in a spirit of idealism tempered by considerable worry over Russian intransigeance that he continued the shift already begun under Roosevelt toward a gradually stiffer policy toward Russia. From a perspective of years, it appears that Truman did not become firm enough soon enough because of two flaws in the 1945 estimate. One was that the Russians in the end would be reasonable in order to obtain American aid in repairing the vast war damage from the Russian border to the Caucasus Mountains. The other was that as long as the United States held a monopoly on atomic secrets she basically had nothing to fear from Russia. Because the public shared these misapprehensions, it was a slow and difficult task to persuade a war-weary and overoptimistic nation to remain on its armed guard in a new era of tension. During the first phase of his relations with the Russians, into 1947, Truman was moderately firm but tried to give the Soviet government no cause for protest. He was chagrined when in May 1945 the Foreign Economic Administration enforced his order ending Lend-Lease so precipitately that it even called back some ships at sea. The British were most hard-hit, but Stalin complained most bitterly. The United States at once softened the order, wishing to give the Russians no offense that would keep them from entering the war against Japan.

Indeed, it was to obtain reassurance that Russia would aid in defeating Japan that President Truman went to the last of the big conferences at Potsdam, outside Berlin, with Stalin and Churchill (later Clement Attlee), beginning on July 17, 1945. He quickly obtained a general pledge, but could secure few satisfactory agreements on questions involving occupied and liberated countries. It was too obvious to the Russians that the United States would want to withdraw most of its troops from Europe for use in the Pacific theater. They worked out rather unsatisfactory arrangements concerning reparations and the occupation of Germany; outward pleasantness cloaked deep disagreements. The Russians finally agreed to allow American and British observers free movement in several of the eastern European countries in return for Western acceptance of Polish occupation of German territory to the Neisse River. This occupation and the Russian annexation of eastern Poland faced President Truman as accepted facts; he later called them "a high-handed outrage."

Despite the failure at Potsdam, Truman's Secretary of State, James F. Byrnes, continued in a conciliatory fashion to seek accomodation with the Russians. The Potsdam conferees established a Council of Foreign Ministers to draft treaties with Italy and the former Axis satellites. During the tedious and depressing round of meetings of the Council in London, Moscow, Paris, and New York between September 1945 and December 1946, relations between the West and Russia steadily deteriorated. But five treaties were concluded. That with Italy reflected Western demands; those with Finland, Hungary, Rumania, and Bulgaria in effect incorporated Soviet armistice terms. The United States, by ratifying the three latter treaties, acquiesced in the Russian domination of these nations. Concerning Austria, the Big Three could come to no agreement at all. During the war they had agreed that Austria, as the first victim of Hitler's aggression, should be reconstituted, free and independent. In 1946 negotiations for a peace treaty began, but the Russians steadily put one or another block in its way; it suited their purpose to continue to occupy part of the nation and exploit the economic resources of their zone.

The greatest obstacle to a satisfactory settlement in Europe was Germany. There a four-power Allied Control Council began sessions in Berlin marked by the same blocking and delaying tactics that made other joint conferences with the Russians so dismal. The Western nations had visualized a unified, standardized control of Germany to prevent its resurgence. To further this control, Secretary Byrnes twice proposed at meetings of the Council of Foreign Ministers in 1945 that the Russians join in a 25-year or even a 40-year guarantee of German disarmament. At first the Russians agreed, then in the spring of 1946 reneged. They also blocked Byrnes when he proposed in September 1946 that Germany should be united both economically and politically. Instead the Russians were using the Potsdam agreement to drain the eastern zone of Germany of its factories and resources, and to claim an additional 25 per cent of those of the western zones. Further, they were organizing the eastern zone as another Communist satellite. Clearly the Russians had no interest in a Germany reunified in a manner acceptable to the West; Germany was to remain split indefinitely.

As early as January 1946 President Truman, upset over Russian delay in withdrawing troops from Iran and threats toward Turkey, had written his Secretary of State: "Unless Russia is faced with an iron fist and strong language another war is in the making. Only one language do they understand—'how many divisions have you?' . . . I'm tired of babying the Soviets."

Although during the war and after, never less than 38 per cent of those queried by public opinion polls expressed a distrust of Russia, Truman faced a peculiarly difficult task in trying to persuade the American public that a truly deep and serious rift was developing between Russia and the West. For too many war years they had listened to publicists ranging from that advanced New Dealer Henry Wallace to the Republican president of the United States Chamber of Commerce, Eric Johnston, praising the Russians and picturing Stalin as a sympathetic figure. Many had come to imagine him as a benign, pipe-smoking sage, "good old Uncle Joe." In addition, idealists had too long placed all their hopes upon the "one world" which Wendell Willkie had preached so eloquently. Even long months of disturbing overseas dispatches barely dented this optimistic complacency, so badly did Americans want to believe that they could settle back to uninterrupted enjoyment of an abundant personal life in a safe unitary world. Nor could a nation which had acquired the twelve-year habit of listening to President Roosevelt with keen attention, whether positive or negative, as yet accord much stature to President Truman and take heed of his warnings. Not even the revered Churchill could shift American opinion. In March 1946, through Truman's arrangement,

Churchill spoke at Westminister College in Fulton, Missouri, and proclaimed a grim warning:

> From Stettin in the Baltic to Trieste in the Adriatic an iron curtain has descended across the Continent. . . . I do not believe that Soviet Russia desires war. What they desire is the fruits of war and the indefinite expansion of their power and doctrines. . . . From what I have seen of our Russian friends and allies during the war, I am convinced that there is nothing they admire so much as strength, and there is nothing for which they have less respect than for weakness, especially military weakness.

President Truman had intended Churchill's admonition as a trial balloon; it collapsed miserably. It frightened the public much as had Roosevelt's "quarantine speech" nine years earlier. Yet Americans accepted "iron curtain" as part of their new vocabulary, and slowly, reluctantly, switched toward the view it implied. Within six months they were jeering Wallace, whose fervent adherence to the "one world" philosophy led him out of Truman's cabinet and into public denunciation of American foreign policy. Within a year after the "iron curtain" speech, President Truman, with the support of the American people, was fabricating a new strong stand against Russian encroachment.

Tragedy in China

IN THE FAR EAST, several years elapsed before the bewildered Americans could even be sure Communism was a threat. By the time they were certain, it was too late. Never had molders of American foreign policy faced a more complex and tragic puzzle than in China in the months after Japan was conquered.

Decisions that were perhaps the fatal ones had been made as early as 1943 at the Cairo Conference. There was an agreement to strip Japan to her limited island domain, thereby guaranteeing she would be an impotent nation, at the same time that Roosevelt, at Churchill's insistence, canceled plans for campaigns in the Burma area which should have been the prelude to building strength in China. The surrender of Japan arrived as a surprise to a Nationalist China ill prepared to take over vast territories from the Japanese occupying forces or to fend off the challenge of the Chinese Communists. To add to the complications, during the two preceding weeks the Russian armies had cut deeply into Manchuria and Korea. Under General Order No. 1 that General MacArthur directed the Emperor of Japan to issue, all Japanese troops in China were to surrender to the Chinese Nationalists, and all those in Manchuria, to the Russians. At this critical juncture Stalin, in return for concessions from Chiang, promised the Chinese Nationalists that he would give moral support and military supplies only to them; apparently Russian forces in Manchuria would give way to Chinese Nationalists. The War Department sent a directive to General Albert C. Wedemeyer, commanding general in China, to help transport the Chinese armies into territories they were to claim, but not to become involved in any land campaign. If the Chinese Nationalists were to engage in civil war with the Communists, the United States was to take no part in it.

In 1945 the Chinese Communists appeared to the Americans as no menace. Indeed, many journalists were picturing them as democratic agrarian reformers in pleasing contrast to Chiang's inefficient, corrupt, and all too dictatorial *Kuomintang*. Molotov had asserted in 1944 that Russia would not come to the aid of the Chinese Communists; this relieved one American fear. If the Communists were not of the Russian variety, it seemed logical enough for the United States to urge Chiang to form a coalition government with them. This was a policy which Ambassador Patrick J. Hurley wholeheartedly pressed upon him. Chiang continued to refuse.

After the Japanese surrender, American forces aided Chiang in occupying all of the large cities of China by the end of the year, but were hampered by the Russians and the Chinese Communists in trying to move Nationalist troops into Manchuria in keeping with earlier Russian agreements. In addition, the Chinese Communists in many sections had strong support in the countryside, and were able to cut the communications of the Nationalist troops, and even, if need be, to keep them bottled in the cities, much as they had harassed the Japanese. Further, the Communists' morale was higher and they were less subject to defection than the Nationalists. Open civil war threatened, and Chiang seemed likely not to fare well. To prevent civil war and to effect a coalition government, the Truman administration, in December 1945, sent General George C. Marshall to China. At first he obtained a cease-fire and encouraging signs of accommodation, but irreconcilable differences divided the two Chinese governments. The Communists delayed while building up their strength. Finally, in January 1947, Marshall returned to Washington disgusted with both governments and all factions except a handful of powerless *Kuomintang* liberals.

Full-scale war broke out. Although the Nationalist armies were larger and better equipped, they soon began to fall back before the better trained, more vigorous Communist forces. As the inept *Kuomintang* government failed both on the fighting front and at home, where inflation and inefficiency were rampant, by the middle of 1947 it was plunging toward defeat. Thus it was that within two years after the end of the war, Communism was advancing militantly in both Asia and Europe. Further, there were close ties between the Russian and Chinese Communists. The United States faced the need for drastic new policies both toward the Communists and toward the areas they were occupying.

Relief and Retribution

THE PRIMARY PROBLEM in both occupied and liberated areas had been to keep millions of people from starving. At the same time, Americans wished to punish the vanquished foes. Between 1945 and 1947 the United States gave four billion dollars to UNRRA for relief in ravished areas in both Europe and Asia. In addition the government directly provided relief through the army in Japan and in the American zone of Germany. Private charity provided several hundred million dollars more in food and clothing. Through other means, the government spent additional billions. By 1947, the total was about eleven billion dollars in western Europe alone. Other expedients, such as loans through the Export-Import Bank and a 1946 credit of $3,750,000,000 to the British government, helped prevent foreign trade from collapsing. In total, these expenditures bolstered the European economic structure, even though as late as 1948 they had not brought rehabilitation.

In occupied Germany and Japan the United States pursued firm but conflicting policies compounded of harshness and idealism. During the war the American people had come to hate the enemy leaders and were insistent that they be punished for their war crimes, especially those Nazis who were responsible for the maintenance of frightful concentration camps like Buchenwald and for the gas-chamber murder of millions of Jews. This led to the trials of thousands of Nazis and war criminals, capped by that of twenty-two key Nazi leaders before an International Military Tribunal at Nuremberg in 1945–46. Eleven were sentenced to death.

There was an equally sweeping purge of Japan, and a trial was held for twenty-five former top Japanese military and civil officials. Seven of them, including two premiers, were executed. The Japanese people understood the punishment of military men found guilty of atrocities, but felt sympathy for the civilian leaders who seemed to them primarily punished for wrong judgment. These trials satisfied the righteous American desire for retribution; they also, however, raised serious questions. In effect they created new international law, bringing civilians as well as military men before specially created military tribunals, breaking with Anglo-American rules of jurisprudence, and establishing the doctrine that officials could be punished for carrying out orders. The dangerous precedent seemed to

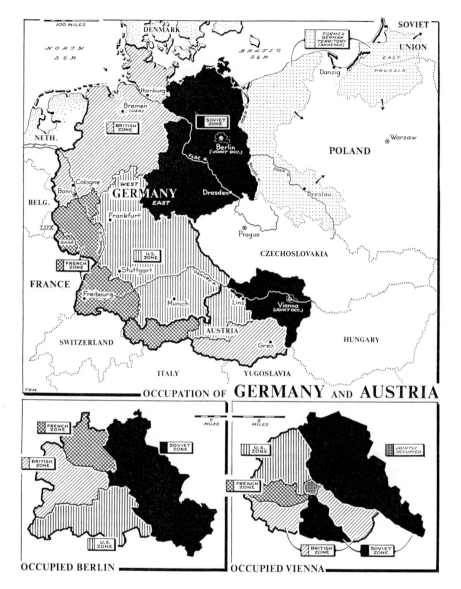

OCCUPATION OF **GERMANY** AND **AUSTRIA**

OCCUPIED BERLIN — **OCCUPIED VIENNA**

be established, Churchill pointed out, that "the leaders of a nation defeated in war shall be put to death by the victors."

At first also the Americans seemed bent on the pastoralization as well
as reform of conquered Germany. They banned all industry directly or indirectly contributing to German war potential, including even the construction of seagoing ships, drastically cut steel and chemical production,
destroyed munition plants, and allowed the dismantling of some factories
for shipment to the Russians. They disbanded cartels and encouraged only
agriculture and peaceful domestic industries. Along with this, they wished

to foster American-style democracy in place of the repudiated Nazism. These economic policies, coming at a time when so much of German housing and industry was rubble, and when several million exiles were making their way from the East or Czechoslovakia, reduced western Germany to not much better than the level of a giant relief camp. The army undertook to feed the German people between 1945 and 1948 at a subsistence level of 950–1,550 calories per day.

Even this near-starvation diet cost the British and Americans nearly half a billion dollars per year. The Russians were adding further to the economic burden by taking out of their zone (and from the western zones to the extent agreed at Potsdam) reparations totaling one and a half to three billion dollars per year. They were siphoning out of Germany more than the Americans and British could pump in. Once more the British saw, as in the early twenties, that the breakdown and stagnation of the great German industrial complex was seriously hampering recovery in all of Europe. Now the added complication of the growing hostility of the Russians led the United States along with the British to modify rapidly their German policies. Humanitarianism and realism both dictated that the United States should help rehabilitate the German economy and build a stable, democratic government as a means of bringing prosperity and reinforcing democracy through most of western Europe. A new program for Germany became an integral part of the development of a new American foreign policy in 1947.

In Japan, American occupation policy suffered fewer obstacles, and profited from the initial errors in Germany. During the first critical weeks General MacArthur, the Supreme Commander for the Allied Powers (SCAP), set up an overwhelmingly American occupation, based on a directive radioed him from Washington, on August 29, 1945. Truman refused Stalin's demand that Russians occupy part of the northern Japanese island, Hokkaido. The irritated Russians had a voice, but no real power, on an eleven-country Far Eastern Commission in Washington and on a four-power Allied Council to advise MacArthur in Tokyo. These bodies did little to swerve American policy; the Russians protested continuously, but did not obstruct the SCAP program.

The American occupation in Japan acted rapidly to demilitarize and democratize the country. From the outset it recognized that Japan must be left with a healthy economy, but in practice—by limiting the nation's war potential—it reduced Japan like Germany to a relief state. The Japanese seemed eager to oblige their occupiers. They had been arrogant as victors throughout southeast Asia; they were humble and co-operative as vanquished. Americans greeted this conformity with friendly enthusiasm that increased in proportion to the Chinese Communist threat on the Asiatic mainland. When that danger became sufficiently great, policy in Japan, as in Germany, underwent important modifications.

Demobilization in a Dangerous World

IN THE FACE OF the growing menaces in Europe and Asia, the United States in the eighteen months after Japan capitulated speedily dismantled its army, air force, and navy. At the end of the war, the army planned to move five and a half million men back to the United States by July 1, 1946, but this was too slow to suit the voters. They brought heavy pressure upon Congressmen, who in turn brought pressure on the administration. President Truman promised that the rate of demobilization would increase to 25,000 men per day by January 1946.

By the end of October, Secretary of War Robert P. Patterson and Secretary of the Navy James V. Forrestal were warning the President that acceleration of demobilization was threatening the strategic position of the United States; privately Forrestal referred to it as the evisceration of the armed forces. President Truman agreed. He slowed down discharges early in 1946, but rioting among soldiers overseas and a new barrage of letters, telegrams, and pleas from Congressmen again forced his hand. In April, he announced that nearly 7,000,000 men had been released from the army, "the most remarkable demobilization in the history of the world, or 'disintegration,' if you want to call it that." A few months later, the army was down to 1,500,000 men and the navy to 700,000.

President Truman proposed a system of universal military training, but Congress did no more between 1946 and 1948 than to pass limited Selective Service measures. Except for temporary increases at two points of crisis, the gradual whittling of the armed forces continued, until by the spring of 1950 the army was down to 600,000 men, and the ceiling on defense expenditures, to thirteen billion dollars. President Truman recognized that Stalin was interested only in the military strength a rival power possessed, but the United States on the eve of the Korean War had only ten active divisions.

Lacking land armies, the United States sought to balance the Soviet power with atomic bombs and an air force that could deliver them. The retention of this weapon was more the result of Russian truculence than American intent. Since September 1945 the administration had been ready to negotiate an agreement with Russia which would, as Secretary of War Stimson had proposed just before resigning, "control and limit the use of the atomic bomb as an instrument of war and so far as possible . . . direct and encourage the development of atomic power for peaceful and humanitarian purposes." Great Britain and Canada joined with the

United States in proposing international control of atomic energy. The United Nations Assembly responded by creating in January 1946 the United Nations Atomic Energy Commission, to which the American member, Bernard Baruch, submitted a plan in June 1946. This proposed a thoroughgoing system of control and inspection of atomic energy development through a United Nations agency. When the system became effective, the United States would liquidate its stockpile and join in an international ban on atomic bombs.

The Russians refused to accept the Baruch plan for international inspection and control of atomic development; instead they constantly and vociferously demanded that the United States unilaterally destroy its atom bombs. Through their wide propaganda they tried to marshal world indignation against the United States while they rushed ahead with their own research on atomic weapons. American scientists and military leaders, not aware as yet of the successful Russian espionage, and underrating Russian scientific and technical proficiency, predicted that it would be many years before the Soviet Union could produce a successful bomb. Meanwhile it served as the jealously guarded mainstay of American defense. During the year after the war ended, Congress lengthily debated the domestic control of American atomic energy. Democrats wished to vest it in civilians; Senator Vandenberg and the Republicans urged giving a full voice to the heads of the armed forces. They compromised in the Atomic Energy Act of August 1946. It created a five-man civilian Atomic Energy Commission with complete control over research and development of fissionable materials; linked to it was a Military Liaison Committee.

Under the protection of an atomic umbrella, military leaders indulged in the luxury of a vigorous and prolonged controversy over unification of the various armed forces. This measure, proposing to bring greater efficiency and effectiveness, led instead to heightened rivalry, as the generals pushed for it and the admirals feared for the loss of the marine corps and the relative weakening of the navy. Both sides brought the utmost pressure upon Congress. Finally, in July 1947, the National Security Act provided for a Secretary of Defense to preside over separate Departments of the Army, Navy, and Air Force, with the Joint Chiefs of Staff serving as advisers to him and to the President. (It was not until 1949 that a Department of Defense was created.) To co-ordinate diplomacy and military planning, the 1947 act also provided for a National Security Council to consist of the President, certain cabinet members, and other advisers on foreign and military policy. This Council, which one writer called "Mr. Truman's Politburo," was to have a staff of its own, resembling the British

Cabinet Secretariat, and was to be served by two other new agencies, a National Security Resources Board and a Central Intelligence Agency.

Within the reorganized Pentagon Building the old rivalries continued. Indeed, through the creation of a separate air force there now appeared to be three separate services where there had been only two previously. The first Secretary of Defense, Forrestal, exhausted by the struggle to make unification effective, resigned in March 1949, and shortly committed suicide. His successor, Louis A. Johnson, became embroiled in a violent quarrel over cancellation of construction of a huge new aircraft carrier, culminating in the resignation of the Secretary of the Navy and replacement of the Chief of Naval Operations. This crisis led to amendments to the National Security Act in August 1949, forcing greater unification and formally establishing a Department of Defense.

Johnson's watchword as Secretary of Defense was "economy," but it was difficult to insist upon a balanced budget in an unbalanced world. Nevertheless, as President Truman formulated a new policy, he did balance it for several years through what seemed at the time to be limited, judicious expenditures.

Economic and Military Containment

THE NEW TRUMAN POLICY for countering Communist aggression began to unfold in the spring of 1947. Already George F. Kennan, counselor of the American embassy in Moscow, was warning the administration that it faced "a political force committed fanatically to the belief that with the U.S. there can be no permanent *modus vivendi.*" The only answer, Kennan wrote anonymously in the July 1947 number of *Foreign Affairs*, must be "a long-term, patient but firm and vigilant containment of Russian expansive tendencies." Russian pressure on Turkey and support of Communist guerilla forces in Greece emphasized the immediacy of the Soviet threat. The British had been aiding the Greek government, but could no longer carry the burden. Unless Stalin were contained quickly, he might achieve the centuries-old Russian prize of the straits leading from the Black Sea into the Mediterranean. Already Russia controlled Albania on the Adriatic.

On March 12, 1947, President Truman appeared before Congress to request $400,000,000 for bolstering the armed forces of Greece and Turkey, and to enunciate the doctrine that came to bear his name:

> I believe that it must be the policy of the United States to support free peoples who are resisting attempted subjugation by armed minorities or by outside pressures.

In support of the new doctrine, Truman declared:

> I believe that our help should be primarily through economic and financial aid which is essential to economic stability and orderly political processes. . . . The seeds of totalitarian regimes are nurtured by misery and want. They spread and grow in the evil soil of poverty and strife. They reach their full growth when the hopes of a people for a better life has died. We must keep that hope alive. The free peoples of the world look to us for support in maintaining their freedoms.

Angry remnants of the isolationists charged that President Truman was acting as a dupe of the British in the eastern Mediterranean, but Senator Vandenberg again supported him, and the Republican Congress voted the Greek-Turkish Aid Act of May, 1947. The initial military aid and subsequent appropriations eased Russian pressure upon Turkey, and by the fall of 1949 brought to an end the long civil war against Communists in Greece.

Military aid was not enough. The Truman Doctrine logically led to a program of economic reconstruction to bolster the stability of Europe and help eradicate the misery out of which the Communist parties in western European countries were gaining recruits. Secretary of State George C. Marshall returned in April 1947 from the Conference of Foreign Ministers in Moscow convinced that the Russians were interested only in profiting from the economic plight of Europe, not in ameliorating it. The solution, he and President Truman agreed, lay in State Department plans to aid European nations that were willing to co-operate with each other in rebuilding their economies. Speaking at the Harvard University commencement in June 1947, Secretary Marshall offered aid to all those European nations (including Russia) who would join in drafting a program for recovery.

Russia denounced the Marshall Plan as American imperialism, and intimidated the satellites and Finland and Czechoslovakia into staying away from the planning conference. Germany had no government, and Spain was not invited. Sixteen other nations of Europe joined a Committee of European Economic Co-operation, which in September 1947 presented specifications for reconstruction to create by 1951 a self-sufficient Europe. Once more opposition formed in Congress, but it was embarrassed from the start by possessing as unwelcome allies the American Communists, and in February 1948 it was overwhelmed by a shocked and aroused public opinion when Czech Communists seized power in Prague. Congress in April established the Economic Co-operation Administration. It cut the administration's request, but did vote an initial four billion dollars.

Over a three-year period the United States spent twelve billion dollars through the ECA, which helped stimulate a remarkable recovery in Europe. By the end of 1950 industrial production was up 64 per cent, economic activity was well above prewar levels, and Communist strength among voters in most areas was dwindling.

President Truman took the next logical step in his inaugural address, January 20, 1949. His predecessor, Roosevelt, twelve years earlier had sounded a call for the aid of the underprivileged third within the United

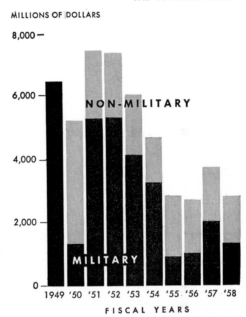

THE ANNUAL TREND

MILLIONS OF DOLLARS

NON-MILITARY

MILITARY

U.S. Foreign Aid, 1949–1958

1949 '50 '51 '52 '53 '54 '55 '56 '57 '58

FISCAL YEARS

States. Truman challenged the nation to come to the succor of the "more than half the people of the world . . . living in conditions approaching misery." He pointed out: "Their food is inadequate. They are victims of disease. Their economic life is primitive and stagnant. Their poverty is a handicap and a threat both to them and to more prosperous areas." Point Four of his proposals for aiding them was technical assistance and the fostering of capital investment for their development. The Point Four or Technical Co-operation program began in 1950 with an appropriation of only $35,000,000, but spent $400,000,000 in the next three years. The United States had made at least a token commitment to battle against world poverty.

Soviet leaders, who had been profiting from the prolonged crisis in the European economy, reacted vigorously against the American efforts. They had organized their own Warsaw Alliance of nine satellite nations,

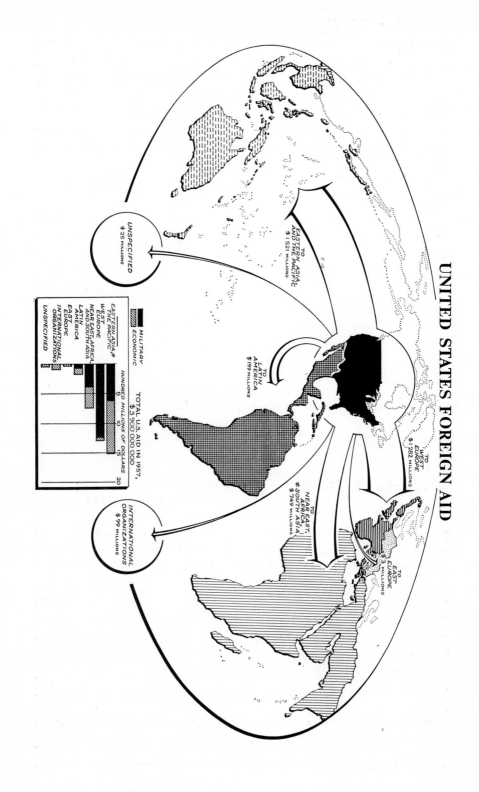

UNITED STATES FOREIGN AID

UNSPECIFIED
$ 25 MILLIONS

EASTERN ASIA
AND THE PACIFIC
$ 1,521 MILLIONS

TO
LATIN
AMERICA
$ 199 MILLIONS

TO
WEST
EUROPE
$ 1,282 MILLIONS

TO
NEAR EAST,
AFRICA
AND SOUTH ASIA
$ 749 MILLIONS

TO
EAST
EUROPE
$ 3 MILLIONS

INTERNATIONAL
ORGANIZATIONS
$ 99 MILLIONS

MILITARY
ECONOMIC

EASTERN ASIA,*
THE PACIFIC
WEST
EUROPE
NEAR EAST, AFRICA,
AND SOUTH ASIA
LATIN
AMERICA
EAST
EUROPE
INTERNATIONAL
ORGANIZATIONS
UNSPECIFIED

HUNDRED MILLIONS OF DOLLARS
5   10   15   20

TOTAL U.S. AID IN 1957,
$ 3,900,000,000

in September 1947, to combat "American imperialism." Through a new Cominform (Communist Information Bureau) they sought to eradicate traces of noncomformity throughout eastern Europe. Their greatest triumph was the successful coup in democratic Czechoslovakia in February 1948. Because it was as horrifying to western Europeans as it was to Americans, it helped unify the Western world against the Communist countries. Later in the year, the pressure of Stalin and the Cominform on Marshal Tito led him to pull Communist Yugoslavia out of their orbit, and with American aid to embark upon an independent course between Russia and the West. In western Europe, Communist parties tried to thwart Marshall Plan recovery, especially by calling out on strike the unions they controlled in Italy and France. Despite the strikes, progress continued.

The struggle between the West and Russia centered upon Germany. After the failure of the Moscow conference of the spring of 1947, the United States step by step moved with the British and the rather reluctant French toward the creation of a self-governing, economically strong West Germany. The culmination came on June 7, 1948, when they announced plans for a new federal West German government with sovereignty over domestic matters and full membership in the European Recovery Program. They also reformed the currency to stop the inflationary flood of marks from the Soviet zone, which was hampering recovery.

Even as the new program for West Germany unfolded in the spring of 1948, the Russians were retaliating. Taking advantage of the lack of a written guarantee of land transit across the Soviet zone into Berlin, beginning on April 1 they began to hamper traffic. On June 23, a few days after the Western powers announced a change in currency, Russia clamped a tight blockade around western sectors of Berlin. They made it clear that they intended to force the Western powers to abandon either Berlin or the proposed West German republic. Withdrawal would have meant an incalculable psychological defeat for the United States and Western nations. President Truman told his military advisers it was unthinkable. Neither was he willing to risk war by ordering in armed convoys by land. Instead he ordered the supplying of Berlin by increasing on a massive scale the airlift begun in April. By the time bad weather hampered flights in the late fall, adequate stockpiles had been established in Berlin. Through the winter and into the spring, the airlift continued. It was a remarkable demonstration to Europeans—especially to the Germans—of what the Americans and British could achieve. Altogether they flew over 277,000 flights to bring in nearly 2,500,000 tons of food, fuel, and other supplies to maintain two million people. They carried in more than had previously been brought by train.

In the spring of 1949, the Russians backed down. In return for the mild concession that the Western nations would agree to another foreign ministers' meeting on May 12, 1949, the Russians ended the blockade. In October 1949, the German Federal Republic came into existence at Bonn in West Germany, and the Soviets established a German Democratic Republic for East Germany.

The failure of the Berlin blockade dealt the Russians a serious defeat. At the same time, the consolidation of the Western countries into a new grand alliance forced the Russians militarily to act less aggressive toward

The Berlin Airlift (OFFICIAL U.S. AIR FORCE PHOTO)

western Europe. In January 1948 the British inaugurated steps leading a year later to the Council of Europe. In June, the Senate passed the Vandenberg Resolution, promising United States co-operation with the new alliance. This led to negotiations culminating in the North Atlantic Treaty, signed April 4, 1949, by twelve nations, and subsequently also by Greece and Turkey. It declared that an armed attack against one would be considered an attack upon all, and provided for the creation of joint military forces. Under it, the signatory powers established the North Atlantic Treaty Organization to construct a defense force that, while not equal to that of the Russians, would be large enough to make an attack highly costly.

The United States began to shift from economic to military aid as the Mutual Defense Act of 1949 appropriated an initial billion dollars for armaments for the signators. The governing body of NATO, the North Atlantic Council, established military headquarters near Paris early in 1951 under the supreme command of General Dwight Eisenhower. This was SHAPE (Supreme Headquarters, Allied Powers in Europe). The number of divisions and airplanes under NATO command began gradually to grow, but while its power was still relatively feeble, its chief significance was the commitment the United States had made with the nations of western Europe to stand firm against Russian threats. That these threats were not to be taken lightly became even more clear on September 23, 1949, when President Truman issued a press statement: "We have evidence that within recent weeks an atomic explosion occurred in the U.S.S.R." The years of relative safety for the American people were already at an end.

The Rise of Red China

WHILE THE UNITED STATES was struggling to contain Russia in Europe between 1947 and 1949, the Chinese Communists were destroying the armies of Chiang Kai-shek. Already by the summer of 1947 defeatism was serious among the Nationalist troops in Manchuria. President Truman sent General Wedemeyer, who had been Chiang's chief of staff, to investigate. Wedemeyer warned that Communist control of China would imperil American interests, since the Communists were in fact closely tied to the Soviet Union. The only way to save Manchuria, he reported, would be to place it under a five-nation United Nations trusteeship. He believed that the United States could rescue Chiang only by sending 10,000 army officers and other advisers to introduce reforms, together with massive material support.

President Truman did not request large scale aid for Chiang, and for this omission critics subsequently castigated him. But to do so might have interfered with the program of containment in Europe; it would have been unpopular; and in any event, it probably would have been too late. Truman did ask Congress to provide $570,000,000; in April 1948 it voted $400,000,000, of which China could spend only $125,000,000 for military supplies. Basically the administration decided, as Secretary Marshall made clear, that the United States could not salvage the Nationalist government so that it would be "capable of re-establishing and then maintaining its control throughout all of China."

The collapse was rapid, and it came through lack of morale rather than shortages of arms and supplies. In October 1948 the Communists seized Mukden, Manchuria, and as Nationalist troops surrendered or defected, the Reds swept on with captured American arms into central and southern China. At the end of 1949, Chiang and the Nationalists fled to Formosa. All of China was under the new People's Republic, which ruthlessly consolidated its strength by liquidating several million dissidents, harrying out American businessmen, teachers, and missionaries, and proclaiming its propaganda to all of East Asia.

The new challenge to the United States was frightening. It stirred angry repercussions at home, especially among those who during the war and after had remained Asia-firsters. They placed responsibility upon allegedly disloyal men in the administration, assuming that the United States was omnipotent enough to have stopped the collapse in China had these advisers not intervened. They also wished the United States to concentrate its military and economic strength against Red China rather than Russia. Instead, American military leaders continued to give priority to opposing Russia with its relatively enormous war potential. Against Red China the administration took less drastic precautions. Even though Great Britain and some of the western European nations recognized the new government, the United States refused to do so and blocked its entry into the United Nations. Also, beginning in 1947, it introduced new economic policies in Japan to strengthen that nation in a manner similar to the rebuilding of Germany.

The administration would by no means capitulate to the demands of the so-called China Lobby that the government send military and naval aid to Chiang on Formosa which might lead the nation into a war against Red China. On the contrary, the State Department issued a white paper (unfortunately not complete) charging the Nationalists with responsibility for their debacle. In January 1950 Secretary of State Dean Acheson publicly outlined a Pacific defense perimeter which did not include Formosa or Korea. To the foes of the administration it seemed further proof that the State Department was being run by subversives who, charged Senator Taft, had "surrendered to every demand of Russia . . . and promoted at every opportunity the Communist cause in China." Taft, together with Senators Joseph R. McCarthy, Kenneth S. Wherry, and others, engaged in an onslaught against the administration so violent that it submerged the bipartisan foreign policy that the dying Senator Vandenberg was struggling to maintain. Then, within a few months, East Asia became the focal point of American foreign policy as the cold war became hot in Korea.

Chapter 20

THE TRUMAN ERA

AGAINST THE MELANCHOLY BACKDROP of permanent crisis in international affairs, Americans after 1945 settled into a life of precarious prosperity at home. They had, in the words of a political slogan, never had it so good, but because of foreign threats and domestic strains, they were never sure how long prosperity would last. At first there were the tensions and problems of reconversion to face, and, for a generation that had known more than a decade of depression, the fears that the economy would collapse. But it was a boom era. Problems at many points were the reverse of those of the prewar years: inadequate rather than surplus production, inflation rather than deflation, and shortages of workers and of housing, automobiles, and almost every sort of consumer durable goods.

Some of the prewar problems came to the forefront in more acute form. This was especially true of civil-rights questions. Some problems were new and especially troublesome, above all the fear that the menace from without was matched by subversion within. The nation engaged in a hunt for traitors so widespread and loud that at times it monopolized the headlines of the newspapers and commanded the emotions of many millions. Other domestic questions seemed less exciting and important than they had before the war. President Truman was able to translate his Fair Deal program into law only with tedious difficulty, yet actually many of the New Deal advances were consolidated and became commonplace. Some new measures were incorporated into the program. What resulted was neither progressivism nor a continuation of the New Deal so much as it was the gradual, pragmatic development of a new American society and polity.

The architect of the new program, President Harry S. Truman, superficially at least was in marked contrast to his predecessor, Roosevelt. During much of his nearly eight years in the White House, he was an underrated President. He was of such unspectacular background and average appearance that it was easy to dismiss him as a person of no unusual qualifications or talents. Many people who had regarded President Roosevelt as the patron of the common man looked upon Truman as being himself the common man.

President Harry S. Truman (UNITED PRESS PHOTO)

And so, in some externals, he was. He had been born in 1884, the son of a horsetrader in a small Missouri town and had grown up on a farm near Kansas City. He had not gone to college. During the First World War he acquitted himself well as an artillery officer, but after his return failed in the men's clothing business. In 1922, his fellow-veterans helped elect him a county commissioner (the title was Judge). Except for the 1924 term when the Ku Klux Klan defeated him, he remained in office until 1934. Although he allied himself with the notorious Kansas City boss, Tom Pendergast, he retained an impeccable reputation for honesty and sound administration. He was elected to the United States Senate in

1934 and, without the support of the Roosevelt administration, re-elected in 1940. The chairmanship of a war investigating committee brought him favorable attention from the public and President Roosevelt. As a border-stater with a consistent New Deal voting record and warm friendships in the Congress, he was an ideal compromise candidate for the Vice-Presidency in 1944.

As President, Truman retained many of the habits of thought and action growing out of his background, and in some minor ways made himself vulnerable to criticism. In facing problems, he studied diligently, read omnivorously, and came firmly to decisions which set postwar policy. The Truman Doctrine, Marshall Plan, and Fair Deal domestic programs were his monuments.

Although Truman had been chosen for the Vice-Presidency because of his moderate, middle-of-the-road background, immediately after the war he aligned himself with the more liberal wing of the Democratic party. On September 6, 1945, only four days after the Japanese surrender ceremonies, the President sent to Congress a twenty-one point domestic program outlining what he later called the "Fair Deal." It called for the expansion of social security, the raising of the legal minimum wage from 40 to 65 cents an hour, a full employment bill, a permanent Fair Employment Practices Act, public housing and slum clearance, long-range planning for the protection of natural resources and building of public works (like TVA), and government promotion of scientific research. Within ten weeks, he sent additional recommendations to Congress for federal aid to education, health insurance, and prepaid medical care, for the St. Lawrence seaway project, and for nationalization of atomic energy. The twenty-one point message, Truman later wrote, "symbolizes for me my assumption of the office of President in my own right."

Despite its preoccupation with reconversion and inflation, Congress did act upon several of the President's recommendations. It passed the Atomic Energy Act in August 1946, and debated unification of the armed forces; in foreign policy it maintained a considerable degree of bipartisanship. One other important measure was passed in modified form, establishing machinery to help maintain full employment. Congress pared the aims of the Murray-Wagner Full Employment Bill to eliminate Federal responsibility for employment and a pledge to resort to deficit spending in time of recession. The measure, with its title changed to the Maximum Employment Act, became law in February 1946. It established a three-man Council of Economic Advisers to aid the President and issue an annual economic report. Although the experts frequently disagreed, and the supposedly nonpartisan reports inevitably became involved in politics, the advisers became an integral part of the governmental machinery. They formed the very agency that the conservatives had previously feared, a unit to engage in economic planning for the general welfare. They were close to the President and carried, because of their reports, great prestige in the press. During the years that followed, they did much to accustom the public to the new economics that had been emerging during the New Deal and the war.

Rapid Reconversion

PRESIDENT TRUMAN worked for enactment of additional parts of his program, but the pressing need in the fall of 1945 was to rush reconversion for a war-weary nation. Congressional conservatives, who by then had abandoned hope that President Truman would be one of them, tried to steer Congress and the public away from the Fair Deal program by concentrating upon reconversion. In the process of dismantling the war machinery they sought to break up as much more as possible of the old New Deal. The President had laid down several points to follow in a rapid return to an expanded peacetime industry, trade, and agriculture. These involved, first, speedily removing all possible controls that would hamper reconversion, and second, preventing increases in prices, rents, and wages. The two aims could easily conflict.

Little conflict arose over rapid reconversion, and it was carried out much more smoothly than after the First World War. As early as 1943 the War Production Board had begun its planning; in 1944 Bernard Baruch and John M. Hancock made a report for the office of War Mobilization which President Roosevelt and Congress translated into national policy. Steps were to be taken to remove government machines and materials from factories as speedily as possible, to pay quickly or extend credit to contractors for work done, and to establish a centralized agency to sell surplus property. Taxes should be reduced to help provide funds for reconversion, and public works should give jobs to those temporarily unemployed.

After Germany surrendered, cutbacks began, and after Japan capitulated, thirty-five billion dollars in contracts was suddenly cancelled. Speedy settlement followed; by June 1946 three fourths of the contracts had been cleared. The War Production Board dropped 229 controls, but retained 150 on commodities still critically scarce. Within a few months, President Truman abolished many of the war agencies, which meant still further lifting of controls. The War Production Board gave way in October 1945 to a Civilian Production Administration. In November, Congress passed a new revenue bill cutting taxes nearly six billion dollars. The War Assets Administration, established in January 1946, sold several hundred war plants, mostly to the corporations which had been operating them, and disposed of mountains of surplus, some of which enabled veterans with priorities to start small businesses. Members of the armed forces, who were being demobilized at an unparalleled pace, found their problems of readjustment to civilian life eased by the Servicemen's Readjustment Act of 1944 (the "G.I. Bill of Rights") which provided them with further education and training, or aid while unemployed or starting in business or farming.

Industry reconverted to civilian production with more speed and less economic dislocation than had been predicted. The gloomy expectations that there might be as many as eight million unemployed did not materialize. By the end of November 1945 peacetime employment was up to the end-of-the-war total, and 93 per cent of the war plants had been reconverted.

The Spiral of Inflation

THE EXPECTED GLUT of surplus goods did not materialize either. Instead, acute problems of scarcity led to such pressures upon prices and wages that the economy embarked upon an inflationary spiral. Within the United States, businessmen of all sorts sought new buildings and equipment; farmers were interested in new machinery and barns; and consumers bought homes, automobiles, and all the many kinds of goods they had done without during the war. Shortages ranged from durable goods to men's suits, nylon stockings, and beefsteak. Consumers alone commanded some $140,000,000 in savings and billions more in credit with which to back their demands. Added to these were the needs of the rest of the world, much of which was devastated by the war, for American goods and foodstuffs. Against these pressures, it was impossible for the Office of Price Administration to hold prices down to the 1941–42 level.

If prices were to be checked, wages must be also, but workingmen were unhappy over their shift from high-paying war work to less well-paying jobs, or from war overtime pay to a 40-hour week. President Truman dissolved the War Labor Board, which had handled wartime labor disputes. Spokesmen for labor, which could no longer be asked to make wartime sacrifices, claimed companies could pay larger wages out of their profits; employers were anxious to go in the other direction to weaken the collective bargaining power of unions. The Labor-Management Conference which met in late 1945 could not agree on reconversion wage policies. By January 1946 workers had gone on strike in a number of the nation's critical industries: steel, automobiles, electrical manufacturing, and others. These strikes increased the direct pressure for raises in prices.

When Philip Murray demanded a 25-cent-an-hour increase for the United Steelworkers to bring them up to their wartime take-home pay, President Benjamin F. Fairless of United States Steel, acting as spokesman for the industry, refused unless the government would allow a $7.00-per-ton increase in the price of steel. President Truman countered by offering increases of $4.00 per ton and 18½ cents an hour. The union accepted the proposal, but the companies refused. The strike cut steel production to 1 per cent of the wartime level, thus hitting most of the American economy.

The President sought a new compromise, while even his own advisers disagreed. Chester Bowles, the head of the Office of Price Administration, opposed any large price increases; he felt the existing ceilings allowed ample profits. John Snyder, Director of Reconversion, argued that higher

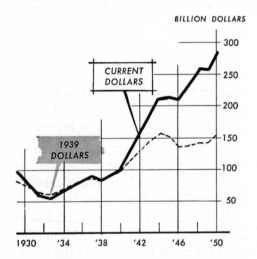

Gross National Product, 1929–1950

prices would bring great production, which, because it would end shortages, would prevent inflation. He called peacetime price controls "police state methods." Behind Snyder was aligned much of Congress, the National Association of Manufacturers and similar organizations, and an increasing portion of the public. The President compromised in Snyder's direction to allow what he called a "bulge in the line." He announced in February 1946 that labor was entitled to the 33 per cent that living costs had gone up since January 1941. The Wage Stabilization Board must approve the increase; but if it cut profits below the prewar level, the companies might obtain corresponding price increases. Ultimately there was a steel settlement allowing raises of 18½ cents an hour and $5.00 per ton.

Throughout industry, the "bulge" led to a round of similar raises in wages and prices, but in April 1946, John L. Lewis precipitated a fresh crisis. He demanded that the bituminous coal workers receive, even before wage increases, drastic improvement in safety rules and substantial contributions to a health and welfare fund. Refusing White House suggestions of compromise, he led out 400,000 miners on April 1, 1946. Within six weeks, as coal supplies dwindled, much of the nation's industrial production had to be cut back. Senator Harry F. Byrd proclaimed that Lewis was "drunk with power." In mid-May Lewis allowed his workers back for twelve days' mining; in the interim a railroad strike threatened. The President, by broadcasting a warning that the army would run the railroads, managed to avert the strike. The government took over the coal mines and provided the workers with most of what Lewis had demanded.

John L. Lewis (NATIONAL ARCHIVES)

An impatient public, plagued with scarcities and rising prices, readily followed the lead of those who blamed the troubles on organized labor. At the height of the railroad crisis, President Truman had asked for drastic curbs on labor disputes in essential industries if the government took them over. Workers might be drafted; corporate profits would go to the government. The House quickly passed the measure, but in the Senate, liberals objected to the disciplining of labor, conservatives to the penalty on business. Instead, Congress passed a mediation bill that the President vetoed on the grounds that it would not have prevented any of the 1946 strikes. Congress had adjourned, but many of its members were of a mood to capitalize upon the strong public resentment against strikes.

While unions were going on strike for higher wages, businessmen and farmers were exerting almost equal pressure upon Congress to end price controls so they could obtain higher prices. Controls, they argued, were preventing full production, encouraging a black market, and robbing producers of a fair profit. Despite the campaign, a majority in Congress wished to retain limited price controls. After long debate, they passed a circumscribed price-control bill on June 27, 1946, just three days before the old act would expire. Bowles, the head of OPA, denounced as booby traps the Taft and Wherry amendments to the bill which would allow manufacturers and distributors to raise their prices, and resigned in protest. President Truman unexpectedly vetoed it as "a sure formula for inflation," and price controls expired.

"Weather Clear, Track Fast" by D. R. Fitzpatrick, for the St. Louis Post-Dispatch

During the first sixteen days of July 1946 the index of prices of twenty-eight basic commodities jumped 25 per cent, compared with 13 per cent during the previous three years. On the first day of free trade at the Chicago stockyards, prime beef jumped from $18 to $22 per hundredweight. As prices soared, stock raisers, who had been holding back their cattle, rushed them to market. Congress rushed through a new price-control bill only slightly stronger than the vetoed one, and on July 25 President Truman signed it. The decontrol board it created studied meat prices, decided they were unreasonable, and ordered prices rolled back to the old levels. Stockmen once again held back cattle until they could force abandonment of controls; angry consumers chafed in near-empty butcher shops.

For several weeks, President Truman stood firm, but as public discontent focused on the Democratic party, politicians already fearful of the worst in the congressional elections of 1946 persuaded him to relent. On October 14, 1946, he announced the immediate ending of meat controls. Meat came back, but like many other commodities, with new price tags so high that the old black-market price seemed to have become the new legal standard. Millions of consumers on small, inflexible salaries or pensions were hurt, and felt little more tender toward the Democrats. Real earnings dropped 12 per cent below July 1945.

In March 1946 President Truman had declared, "If certain interests were not so greedy for gold, there would be less pressure and lobbying to induce Congress to allow the Price Control Act to expire, or to keep down minimum wages, or to permit further concentration of economic power." Few people listened to him.

From the high point of sympathy and popularity President Truman had enjoyed when he first took office in April 1945 he had sunk into a trough of unpopularity by the fall of 1946, the butt of many a joke. People gibed, "To err is Truman." Within his own party, labor was angry with him because of his disciplining of railroad workers and miners. Many of the idealistic New Dealers had dropped him when Secretary of the Interior Ickes had resigned over the nomination of a wealthy oilman as Undersecretary of the Navy. Others had departed when he fired Secretary of Commerce Wallace over foreign policy.

Republicans Win the Congress

ALL THAT THE REPUBLICANS NEEDED in the fall of 1946 was the slogan, "Had Enough? Vote Republican." Emblazoned on buttons, and in folders handed to consumers queuing for meat, it pinned on the Democrats the opprobrium for all the irritations of the war and postwar years. The Republicans finally succeeded in turning the tables on the Democrats, who for so many years had been successfully blaming them for the depression. They captured both houses of Congress, controlling the House 246 to 188, and the Senate 51 to 45. In addition they could command the votes of many Southern Democrats. Governor Dewey swept New York by a margin of 680,000, retaining his standing as a national leader. Jubilant Republicans, confident they would win the Presidency in two years, speculated only whether Dewey or someone else would be the nominee.

President Truman, accepting the returns as a mandate to liquidate regulations, dropped almost all remaining controls on wages and prices and on the channeling of construction into low-cost homes. Congress continued rent control to March 1, 1948, but allowed rents to go up 15 per cent. Retail prices moved upward 3 per cent per month, canceling the gains organized labor had won in the spring of 1946. Unions fought for, and obtained, a second round of increases in 1947, and in 1948 as prices still went upward, a third round. The spiral of inflation was creeping upward relentlessly. Workers and others in modest circumstances began to notice that it was taking place under a Republican Congress whose spokesmen had asserted that laissez faire would cure the nation's ills.

The 1946 election gave leadership in establishing Republican policy to the leaders of the Eightieth Congress rather than to the moderate Governor Dewey. While Senator Vandenberg fought stanchly to maintain bipartisan foreign policy, the most conspicuous spokesman on domestic matters was the conservative Senator Taft of Ohio. At the height of the controversy over meat prices, he demonstrated his faith in the laws of supply and demand by advising succinctly, "Eat less." Taft wanted to return to the "traditional American heart of things, liberty" for a nation that under the New Deal had looked to the government to provide it with positive benefits. He declared:

> We have got to break with the corrupting idea that we can legislate prosperity, legislate equality, legislate opportunity. All of these good things came in the past from free Americans freely working out their destiny. . . . That is the only way they can continue to come in any genuine sense.

The Chairman of the House Appropriations Committee, John Taber, proclaimed that he would apply a "meat-axe to government frills." He did so. Congress refused to appropriate funds for public housing, even of the moderate sort championed by Taft. It would not aid education, or extend social security; it slashed budget allowances for reclamation and power projects in the West. It passed a tax bill that, as President Truman pointed out in vetoing it, reduced the taxes of families receiving $2,400 or less by only 3 per cent, but of those receiving $100,000 or more from 48 to 65 per cent. It passed a second tax cut, which the President again vetoed, and finally, in April 1948, enacted over his veto a third bill more beneficial to those with low incomes. It cut appropriations for the Department of Agriculture and failed to provide adequate commodity storage facilities for farmers who needed them to qualify for price-support payments. It refused to raise the minimum wage from 40 to 75 cents an hour. It extended the reciprocal trade agreements program, but only for one year rather than for the three-year period previously customary.

One of the few noncontroversial domestic achievements of this Congress was authorization of a commission on reorganization of the executive departments. President Truman appointed former President Hoover chairman of the commission. In 1949, it issued eighteen extensive reports recommending 350 changes, mostly consolidations and elimination of overlapping authority. Congress through the Reorganization Act of 1949 authorized President Truman to submit plans of reorganization, which would automatically go into effect unless it acted adversely. In the next two years, it approved thirty-five plans he submitted, defeating only a proposal for a Department of Welfare, which Congress feared might be an opening wedge for a national health insurance program. In 1946, Congress voted to improve its own procedures and to reorganize its committees, cutting those in the House from 48 to 19, and in the Senate from 33 to 15.

The principal positive handiwork of the Eightieth Congress was a new basic labor law to supplant the pro-labor Wagner Act of 1935. The Taft-Hartley Labor-Management Relations Act loosened some of the previous restrictions upon employers and added several prohibitions against the unions. It:

Outlawed "closed shop" (which required that one must be a union member to be hired), but permitted "union shop" (which meant that, if the contract so provided, one had to join the union after being hired).

Provided "cooling off" periods and empowered the President to issue injunctions to prevent strikes imperiling national safety or health.

Prohibited as "unfair" union practices: jurisdictional strikes, refusal to bargain in good faith, secondary boycotts, exaction of pay for work not performed, and union contributions to political campaign funds.

Prohibited certification of unions as bargaining agents with employers until officers had filed affidavits that they were not Communists.

Required unions to register with the Secretary of Labor and submit annual financial reports to him.

Allowed employers to present their side during organizational campaigns, petition the National Labor Relations Board for elections to determine bargaining agents, and sue unions for breach of contract.

President Truman stingingly vetoed the Taft-Hartley bill on June 20, 1947. That same day Republicans and Southern Democrats in the House overrode his veto, 331 to 83; the Senate followed three days later, 68 to 25.

In practice, the Taft-Hartley Act did not cripple organized labor. President Truman appointed to the National Labor Relations Board members sympathetic toward labor. The prohibition of the "closed shop" had little effect upon the skillful leaders of strong unions, who through small changes in their rules obtained the same end. The prime target of the act, John L. Lewis and the United Mine Workers, obtained their most favorable contracts after its passage.

On the other hand, the Taft-Hartley Act did hamper weak unions in relatively lightly organized areas like chemicals, textiles, and retailing, and did complicate new organizing, especially in the South. The provisions against the secondary boycott circumscribed one of the unions' economic weapons, the right to refuse to work on materials produced under non-union conditions. The Act increased the number and scope of injunctions in labor disputes. Indirectly it led the way for eighteen states to pass more stringent "right-to-work" laws undermining the collective bargaining power of unions. Politically its effect was to turn most of organized labor against the Republicans and back to the support of President Truman.

A columnist for the *New Republic,* contemplating the Eightieth Congress, wrote, "Victories fought and won years ago were suddenly in doubt. Everything was debatable again." It still remained to be seen if this was what the American electorate had wanted when it had turned out the Democrats in Congress in 1946.

The Election of Truman in 1948

SIGNIFICANTLY, when the Republicans met at Philadelphia in June 1948 to nominate a presidential candidate, they rejected Taft, the vigorous leader of the Eightieth Congress, although he was the idol of many businessmen. Taft was hampered by his prewar isolationism and his lack of glamor as a campaigner. Instead, on the third ballot, they again nominated Governor Thomas E. Dewey, who favored the new role of the United States in world affairs, and whose stand on domestic issues came closer to the Fair Deal than to the Republican record in Congress. His running mate was Governor Earl Warren of California, who was even more liberal. Their platform was a promise to continue all the things the Democrats had established, but do them more efficiently and cheaply.

It seemed a winning ticket and program, especially since a double schism split the Democratic party, and much of the remainder of it nominated President Truman only as a last resort. A faction to the left followed Henry A. Wallace out of the party. Wallace, who during the war had assumed increasing leadership over advanced New Dealers, at the end of 1947 announced he would run on a third-party ticket to fight for thoroughgoing reform at home and more friendly relations with Communists overseas. His was an indigenous idealistic approach, as his selection of the old label "Progressive" indicated. Around him rallied a sprinkling of Americans who felt the Truman domestic policies were too slow and ineffective, and above all, who feared the foreign policies would lead to a third World War. He further won the support of groups whose fathers had never thrilled to the word "Progressive"—the American Communists and fellow-travelers. These radicals came to wield power in the new Progressive party, and turned its convention into a meeting quite different in spirit from the Bull Moose convention of 1912. It was leadership that in the end proved lethal to the Wallace vote, but early in the campaign he was expected to pull five million or more votes from the Democrats.

Despairing Democratic liberals in an organization formed after the war, the Americans for Democratic Action, together with some urban leaders, sought some more glamorous candidate than President Truman. The one candidate they could be sure would win votes by the million, General Eisenhower, rejected their overtures. At their convention in July 1948, they gloomily accepted the inevitable, the nomination of President Truman. They chose Senator Alben W. Barkley of Kentucky for Vice-President. Certain of defeat, the liberals salvaged what they could by fighting through a platform containing a strong civil rights plank that proposed federal legislation to prevent discrimination in employment, penalize lynching, and outlaw poll taxes. The platform would help Northern and city Democrats in their local and state elections, but it drove Southern Democrats, already angered by President Truman's espousal of a strong civil-rights program, into open revolt. Waving Confederate flags, a number of them met at Birmingham, Alabama, in July 1948 to form the States Rights' Democratic Party and nominate Governor J. Strom Thurmond of South Carolina and Governor Fielding L. Wright of Mississippi. They captured the party organization in Alabama, Louisiana, Mississippi, and South Carolina.

The revolts from both the left and the right seemed to leave President Truman in a pathetically hopeless position; all the public opinion polls showed him trailing far behind. Governor Dewey, campaigning in a statesmanlike way, aroused as little animosity as possible, and seemed to be delivering previews of his inaugural. Only President Truman himself did not seem to expect defeat. In accepting the nomination, he brought fire back into the discouraged and exhausted delegates by delivering a fighting speech. Choosing not to campaign against the impeccable Governor Dewey, who stood for so much the same in domestic and foreign policy, he launched his attack instead at the Republican Congress. In his acceptance address he announced he was calling it back into session on "Turnip Day" (July 26, the day turnips are planted in Missouri) to enact the measures in the Republican platform so at variance with its previous policies. Congress met for two weeks and did almost nothing; the point was not lost upon voters.

Because he felt the press was giving a hostile impression of his administration, Truman embarked upon a strenuous personal tour of the United States, traveling 31,700 miles to speak 356 times directly to the American people. In this "whistle stop" tour, he spoke only a few times from manuscripts, preferring his far more effective, rather blunt extemporaneous style. He had told Senator Barkley, "I'm going to fight hard. I'm going to give them hell." He did. Wherever he spoke, he denounced the "do-nothing" Congress, and strongly urged his own positive program: new or

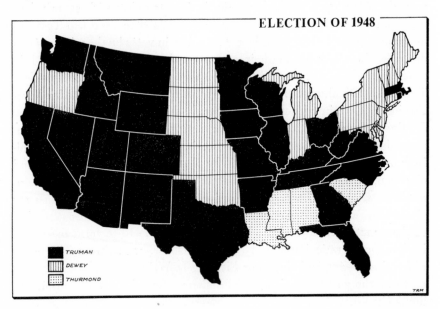

ELECTION OF 1948

TRUMAN

DEWEY

THURMOND

strengthened welfare legislation of a wide variety, repeal of the Taft-Hartley Act for labor, high price supports for farmers, and strong civil rights protection for minorities. He was the first President to campaign in Harlem. To all those groups who could be convinced they had a grievance against the Republican Congress, he appealed effectively, winning the strong support of organized labor, disgruntled farmers, and northern Negroes. To everyone's amazement but his, President Truman defeated Dewey 24,106,000 to 21,969,000 in the popular vote, and 304 to 189 in the electoral vote. Thurmond's Dixiecrat ticket received 1,169,000 popular and 38 electoral votes. Wallace polled only 1,156,000 votes. The Democrats also regained both houses of Congress by a margin of 93 seats in the House and 12 in the Senate.

The Struggle for the Fair Deal

PRESIDENT TRUMAN, in his January 1949 message to Congress, called upon it to enact what he by then was calling the Fair Deal. At times the Democratic Eighty-first Congress seemed much like its Republican predecessor, since again Southern Democrats allied themselves with Republicans to block some legislation. The President obtained less than the program he felt a majority of the voters had approved at the polls, but more than during his first years in office.

For organized labor, the President and his supporters in Congress tried to obtain repeal of the Taft-Hartley Act. Even Senator Taft was willing to offer concessions, but the administration refused to accept compromise amendments voted by the Senate, and failed to win repeal. Congress did raise the minimum wage under the Fair Labor Standards Act to 75 cents an hour. It also voted amendments to the Social Security Act, increasing the benefits to retired workers by three quarters and extending coverage to ten million additional people.

For farmers, Truman's Secretary of Agriculture, Charles Brannan, proposed a new program in April 1949 which came to be known as the Brannan Plan. It put the emphasis upon high income for farmers rather than high prices for farm products. The parity formula for storable commodities was to be changed. Perishables would be sold on the market for whatever price they would bring (presumably a lower price for the consumer); if the price was below an estimated fair return to the farmer, the government would reimburse him. Payments would go to family-size farms rather than to the huge commercial farms representing only 2 per cent of all farms but receiving 25 per cent of farm income. Each farm would be limited to a number of units of protected products equivalent in 1949 values to $20,000. The Farm Bureau Federation, the Grange, and large farmers attacked the Brannan Plan as despotism and socialism, and Congress continued the existing system of price supports. In October 1949 it voted for supports through 1950 at 90 per cent of parity, to be followed by flexible supports at 75 to 90 per cent of parity.

For minorities, President Truman continued to press his civil rights program upon Congress. Southerners, through the threat of filibuster, were able to prevent action in the Senate. In March 1950, Senate supporters of Fair Employment Practices legislation were twelve votes short of the requisite two-thirds majority to vote closure of debate. President Truman as early as 1948 through administrative orders began to attack segregation within the government and in the armed forces and to provide positive aid to minorities. Congress did vote the Displaced Persons Act of 1950, liberalizing the 1948 legislation which the President had denounced as discriminatory against Catholics and Jews because its quotas were unfavorable to people from southern and eastern Europe. It increased the number of persons to be admitted from 205,000 to 415,000 —but even this latter figure was a total, not a yearly number.

The new Congress also strongly implemented some of the New Deal reforms. The National Housing Act of 1949 provided for the construction over the succeeding six years of 810,000 housing units for lower-income families, together with a subsidy for forty years to bridge the gap between costs and the rents the tenants could afford to pay. It also provided grants for slum clearance and rural housing. It voted increased appropriations for power development and reclamation in the West, for TVA, and for the Farmers Home Administration (which carried on the rehabilitation work of the earlier Resettlement Administration and Farm Security Administration). In contrast, the Fair Deal health insurance program went down to crashing defeat under the vigorous opposition of the American Medical Association, which raised three million dollars to combat it. Federal aid for education failed because of dissension over whether aid should go to parochial schools.

Altogether, the congressional votes for Fair Deal measures, together with the public support of Congress in these actions, seemed to indicate that the earlier reforms that had been questioned by the Eightieth Congress were indeed ones that the American people did not wish to reverse. Right-wing Republicans basically failed in their challenge to the Democrats on domestic policy as they had also on foreign policy. But in the question of loyalty they found a successful issue.

Loyalty in a Frightened Nation

IN THE DISAPPOINTING MONTHS and years after the war, as the warm feelings toward Russia turned into apprehension and even alarm, the public became increasingly afraid that traitors within the government were betraying it to the Russians. Especially after a small Communist minority in Czechoslovakia achieved a coup in February 1948 that threw that formerly democratic nation behind the Iron Curtain, Americans began to listen seriously to those who had long warned of an internal Red menace in the United States. As the Western world suffered setbacks from the Communists, it was easy to blame these disasters upon alleged Reds high in the counsels of the government.

During the period of the New Deal and the war there had been some Communists and Communist sympathizers in the government. At a time when the Russians and the United States were allied this seemed of little consequence, but in 1942 and 1943 President Roosevelt established loyalty checks. Few people heeded the flamboyant warnings of the House Un-American Activities Committee, which through the war seemed more alarmed about Communists than about the Nazi enemy, and made charges often wide of the mark. Early in 1945, a government raid on the offices of *Amerasia*, a Communist-sponsored magazine, recovered quantities of classified documents; two of the editors of the magazine received light fines. By 1946, Russia seemed more a potential enemy than an ally. The Canadian government discovered that at least twenty-three of its employees in positions of trust had turned over secrets, some of them concerning nuclear fission, to Russian spies. Several of the spy rings had operated across the boundary in the United States.

The federal government began extensive efforts to ferret out Communists. President Truman in November 1946 established a Temporary Commission on Employee Loyalty to recommend loyalty investigation systems and safeguards of fair hearings. This led, in March 1947, to the establishment of loyalty boards to undertake a sweeping investigation of all federal employees. In August 1950 the President authorized the dismissal in sensitive departments of even those deemed no more than "bad security risks." By 1951 more than 3,000,000 government employees had been cleared, over 2,000 had resigned, and 212 had been dismissed. The thoroughness of the investigations is demonstrated by the fact that the Republicans, when they came into power in 1953, could not ferret out a single additional Communist in the government. President Truman's program was so rigorously administered that if it erred, it was on the side of driving some employees out of the government on very flimsy grounds. "Some reports showed that people were being fired on false evidence," Truman has written. He tried to modify the program in 1950 to safeguard civil liberties, but Congress was moving in the opposite direction.

Congress not only refused to co-operate, but against the recommendations of the Departments of Defense and Justice and of the Central Intelligence Agency, it passed over the President's veto the McCarran Internal Security Act of September 1950. This law rolled together many of the restrictions upon Communists that congressmen had been advocating. Communist organizations were not outlawed but were required to publish their records. Communists could be punished for working toward a totalitarian dictatorship in the United States; they were barred from employment in defense plants, and blocked from obtaining passports. A bipartisan Subversive Activities Control Board was to be established to aid in their exposure. The provisions applying to immigrants were especially objectionable to those responsible for national security; they barred from the United States anyone who had once been a member of a totalitarian organization—thus discouraging in advance those who might be tempted to defect from behind the Iron Curtain. President Truman in his veto message asserted, "In a free country, we punish men for the crimes they commit, but never for the opinions they have."

The temper of the nation and even of the Supreme Court seemed to be against the President. There were those who felt that his own actions belied his words. In 1948 his Attorney General obtained indictments against eleven key Communist leaders for violation of the Smith Act of 1940 which prohibited groups from conspiring to teach the violent overthrow of the government and penalized membership in such groups. During their nine-month trial in 1949, the Communists engaged in elaborate harassing tactics which further aroused the public against them. They were convicted. In June 1951, in the case of *Dennis* v. *United States*, the Supreme Court in a 6-to-2 decision rejected their appeal. Chief Justice Fred Vinson held that advocating or teaching revolution in the existing state of the world, or even conspiring to do so, fell within Justice Holmes's earlier definition of what was punishable—that it constituted a "clear and present danger." Justice Hugo Black in dissenting remarked, "There is hope that in calmer times, when the present pressures, passions, and fears subside, this or some later court will restore the First Amendment liberties to the high preferred place where they belong in a free society."

While the Supreme Court was solemnly deciding that civil liberties must be circumscribed to protect the modern state, some less careful politicians were capitalizing upon the growing public hysteria over several spectacular cases. Above all there was the case of Alger Hiss, in which these politicians seemed to put on trial and condemn a whole generation of liberal intellectuals. Hiss, a handsome and ambitious young man, had risen rapidly in the government during the thirties to become a high-ranking member of the State Department. He had been present at the Yalta conference, but had in no way influenced policy there; he had helped arrange the San Francisco conference. In 1947, he resigned to head the Carnegie Endowment for International Peace. A self-avowed former Communist agent, Whittaker Chambers, had denounced Hiss as early as 1939, but because he provided no details and no supporting evidence, he was ignored. In 1948, he repeated his accusations before the House Un-American Activities Committee; when Hiss sued him for slander, Chambers produced microfilms of classified State Department documents Hiss allegedly had given him in 1937 and 1938.

Hiss was brought to trial for perjury (the statute of limitations prevented indictment for espionage). At his trial, he called upon a number of the nation's most distinguished liberals to bear witness to his character

—including Justice Felix Frankfurter and Governor Adlai E. Stevenson of Illinois. They testified to his good character, within the scope of their knowledge. Throughout the nation, the liberal intellectuals for the most part sided with Hiss as the case was vehemently debated. The first trial ended with a hung jury in July 1949; the second ended with conviction in January 1950. There were several things Hiss had not been able to explain convincingly to the jury; the most important was how the prosecution could produce a typewriter identified as his, the keys of which matched the typing irregularities in Chambers's documents. Hiss went to the penitentiary still protesting his innocence; in his downfall he seemed to have pulled with him the cause of the liberal intellectuals.

More important in convincing Americans that a real Communist menace existed was the revelation that a young British scientist, Dr. Klaus Fuchs, had turned over to Russian agents full details on the manufacture of atomic bombs. His confession led to the trial and ultimate execution of Julius and Ethel Rosenberg, Americans who were alleged to have been his accomplices—and who were hailed as martyrs by Communists throughout the world.

Among the politicians who capitalized upon these apprehensions, none was more sensational in his rise than Senator Joseph McCarthy of Wisconsin. At the beginning of 1950 he was a freshman Senator of not very savory reputation in need of an issue. Already some other politicians were winning fame through crusading against Communism. Representative Richard Nixon, who had helped keep the Hiss affair alive until Chambers produced the incriminating microfilms, was on his way to the Senate and a national reputation. McCarthy decided to exploit the same issue, and did so in February 1950 by charging that there were a large number of Communists and men loyal to the Communist party still shaping foreign policy in the State Department. In his first speech, listeners swore he had claimed he held in his hand a list of 205 names; in later speeches the number was 57. Whether 205 or 57, when a subcommittee of the Senate Foreign Relations Committee took up his charges, they found not a single Communist or fellow-traveler. The Democratic majority on the Committee ultimately reported that McCarthy's charges were "the most nefarious campaign of half-truths and untruths in the history of the Republic."

An excited public numbering many millions eagerly swallowed McCarthy's new claims as he went on from sensation to sensation more rapidly than his detractors could refute his earlier, unsubstantiated charges. Millions wanted to believe McCarthy when he attacked as Communists the "whole group of twisted-thinking New Dealers [who] have led America near to ruin at home and abroad." McCarthy was providing a troubled nation with a scapegoat, and the Republican party with a winning issue.

Attacks on the Fair Deal

IN 1950 the electorate was upset over the charges of subversion at home and the involvement of the United States in the Korean War, which many of them regarded as the result of a conspiracy in the State Department. When Hiss was convicted in January, his former acquaintance Secretary of State Dean Acheson declared he would not turn his back on him, meaning, Acheson later explained, that he was following "Christ's words setting forth compassion as the highest of Christian duties." But Acheson's remark, together with President Truman's early reference to the Hiss case as a red herring, served as Republican campaign texts. Representative Nixon declared, "Traitors in the high councils of our own government have made sure that the deck is stacked on the Soviet side of the diplomatic tables."

Bipartisanship in foreign policy disappeared as the Republicans pressed their issue. They did not capture Congress in November 1950, but they gained 28 seats in the House and 5 in the Senate. Neo-isolationists, heartened by the election results and no longer restrained by Senator Vandenberg, who was fatally ill, opened in December a "great debate" in the Senate over foreign policy. They succeeded in passing a resolution in April 1951 restraining the President from sending troops to western Europe without congressional authorization.

Republicans further undermined the Truman administration with charges of favor-peddling and corruption, which, while they did not involve the President personally, did implicate men in the White House. The President's military aide had received as a gift a $520 deep-freeze unit; the wife of an examiner of loans for the Reconstruction Finance Corporation had acquired a $9,540 mink coat. These became the symbols of a moral malaise in Washington, of those who could obtain contracts in return for a 5 per cent fee, others who could arrange RFC loans, and still others who could take care of tax difficulties in the Bureau of Internal Revenue. President Truman reorganized the RFC and reformed the Bureau of Internal Revenue and the Department of Justice, but much too slowly to satisfy his Republican critics. Added to this, the Democratic Senator Kefauver of Tennessee gained a national television following as his Special Crime Investigation Committee brought gang leaders to the screen and revealed ties between them and many an urban Democratic politician. The Republicans did not allow voters to overlook the significance of these hearings.

The most serious casualty of the onslaught against the Fair Deal was the reputation of President Truman, so whittled down by his opponents and most of the press that it was easy to overlook his monumental achievements in the realm of foreign policy and his substantial contributions to the general welfare of the nation in the Fair Deal program. As the election of 1952 approached there was no indication that the majority of voters wished to reverse either Truman's foreign policy or his domestic program. They did want to "clean up the mess in Washington," and above all they wanted to see an end to the drawn-out, wearying Korean War.

Chapter *21*

THE KOREAN WAR
AND ITS AFTERMATH

WHILE THE UNITED STATES was struggling to build a cold war balance against the forces of Communism pressing from Eastern Europe, it unexpectedly had to lead the United Nations in armed intervention to force back Communist expansion in Asia. Despite its strength in nuclear weapons, the United States could not prevent a limited armed conflict from breaking out, and had to fight one of the most serious wars in American history.

War in Korea

IT WAS IN KOREA that the cold war flared into a shooting conflict, and threatened to turn into large-scale nuclear war. The locale was not one in which many Americans had expected trouble; it had seemed not worth armed defense. During the hectic days at the end of the war in the Pacific, the United States had hastily proposed that it accept the surrender of the Japanese in the lower half of Korea, up to the 38th parallel, and that the Russians occupy the northern half. At the moment it actually was an arrangement beneficial to the United States since it was unable to unload troops at Inchon until nearly a month after the Russians first entered Korea. President Truman later pointed out, "Even the 38th parallel was too far for any American troops to reach if the Russians had chosen to disagree."

The division left most of the electric power, mineral resources, and industry of the country in the Russian area, while the United States occupied the capital city, Seoul, and most of the agricultural area containing two thirds of the population. In any case, the distribution seemed of little moment in August 1945, since the United States expected Korea to be quickly reunited under the terms of the Cairo declaration of 1943. But Korean patriots were displeased because the Cairo statement declared that "in due course Korea shall become free and independent"—which meant that Roosevelt wished for the time being to place Korea under an international trusteeship. This involved immediate difficulties with some seventy political organizations clamoring for immediate independence. Very quickly it became apparent that the Russians threatened even more serious trouble than did Korean nationalists, as the familiar Russian pattern of occupation developed in north Korea. There were reports that they had trained two divisions of Koreans in Siberia which could easily dominate a united country. Consequently, the United States felt Korea could be protected only under a trusteeship, repugnant though it might be to Korean nationalists. At Moscow in December 1945 the Russians agreed to a four-power trusteeship over a reunited Korea. All political factions in South Korea except the Communists opposed the trusteeship. Yet when the Russians negotiated in Korea to establish a common government, they insisted that all Korean parties be excluded except those that had agreed to a trusteeship. In effect, they were ready to accept a united Korea only if it were Communist-dominated. On this point discussions collapsed in 1946 and again in 1947 just when agreement seemed possible.

The 38th parallel became more and more an impenetrable barrier. To the north of it, the Communists developed a "peoples' government" with a strong aggressive army. To the south, the United Nations held elections that led to a government under the ardently nationalistic Dr. Syngman Rhee, previously long an exile in the United States. Rhee would have liked to extend his government to the north, but the United States provided the South Korean army only with relatively light defensive weapons. Consequently when the United States withdrew its forces from below the 38th parallel in June 1949, South Korea was left militarily weaker than its even more aggressive northern twin. Only the United States Military Advisory Group of about five hundred remained in South Korea. The Army considered Korea of no military significance, and feared being caught by Red armies in a peninsular mousetrap. Almost immediately sporadic shooting began northwest of Seoul, but the United States limited itself in the winter of 1950 to the passage of a bill granting Korea $120,000,000 in economic aid. Then on January 12, 1950, Secretary of State Dean Acheson, speaking for the military leaders, publicly outlined the area the United States felt committed to defend in the Far East. It did not include either Formosa or Korea. If these areas were attacked, he declared, the people invaded must rely upon themselves to resist, "and then upon the commitments of the entire civilized world."

The United States thus proclaimed that it would not automatically resist an attack upon Korea. At the time, the possibility of Chiang or Rhee provoking a conflict and counting upon United States support seemed greater than the possibility that the North Koreans or Chinese Communists might launch an attack. In retrospect, critics of the Truman administration denounced Acheson's statement as a colossal blunder, an invitation to the North Koreans to transform their border skirmishing into an easy invasion. Foolish though the statement later seemed, it was no guarantee

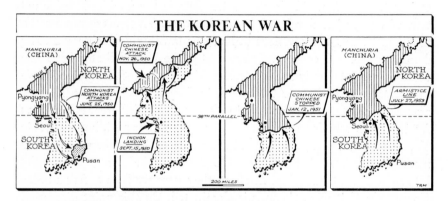

that the United States and Union Nations would not act. This was equally true along the entire troubled border between the Communist territories and the West.

The North Koreans acted swiftly, on June 24, 1950, launching a full-scale invasion that caught the South Koreans and Americans completely by surprise. Almost immediately President Truman and Congress reversed the policy of withdrawal from the Asiatic mainland. The President brought the question of the invasion before the United Nations Security Council. It could act more quickly than the Assembly, and at the moment the Russians were boycotting it, and hence were not present to vote a paralyzing veto. The Council on June 25 passed an American resolution demanding that the North Koreans withdraw behind the 38th parallel, and two days later called upon members of the United Nations to "furnish such assistance to the Republic of Korea as may be necessary to repel the armed attack."

President Truman, on June 27, sent United States air and sea forces to the aid of the South Koreans; on June 30, he ordered ground forces into Korea, and sent the Seventh Fleet to act as a barrier between the Chinese mainland and Formosa. Truman later recalled that as he and his military and diplomatic advisers came to these momentous decisions, there was "complete, almost unspoken acceptance on the part of everyone that whatever had to be done to meet this aggression had to be done. There was no suggestion from anyone that either the United Nations or the United States could back away from it."

For the moment this was the mood of both Congress and the American nation. Even Senator Taft, while excoriating President Truman and Secre-

U.S.S. Missouri *bombarding North Korean installations* (OFFICIAL U.S. NAVY PHOTO)

tary Acheson, proclaimed his approval of armed intervention in Korea to maintain collective security. To this extent by 1950 the United States had come to reverse its position of the thirties, and was willing to support what President Truman called "police action by the United Nations." Technically this was what the Korean war was. The Council of the United Nations on July 7, 1950, requested those nations providing troops to place them under a unified command headed by the United States. President Truman appointed General MacArthur commander-in-chief. Some fifteen nations besides the United States and the Republic of Korea provided troops, but these never comprised more than 9 per cent of the total fighting force. The United States sent about 48 per cent; South Korea mustered

43 per cent. What was officially a United Nations action came to most Americans to seem a war on the part of the United States.

The first phase, during the summer of 1950, was discouraging. General MacArthur, who at first could draw upon only four understrength divisions in Japan, rushed in troop units piecemeal to slow the rapidly advancing North Koreans as they rushed southward past Seoul, threatening to envelop the entire tip of the peninsula. By thus sacrificing themselves, these forces gave MacArthur an opportunity to build stable defenses around the Port of Pusan in the extreme southeast. When the North Koreans struck there in force early in August, strong army and marine reinforcements fresh from the United States hurled them back at each point of assault. As men and supplies poured into Pusan, marine officers devised a bold plan of attack which General MacArthur reluctantly accepted. Rather than try to push the North Koreans back mile by mile, on September 15, 1950, while the United Nations troops around Pusan opened a sharp counteroffensive, he launched an amphibious assault far behind the North Korean lines at Inchon, near Seoul. It caught the Communists almost completely unprepared. The United Nations troops quickly recaptured Seoul; within two weeks the North Korean armies, disrupted and demoralized, were fleeing as best they could to north of the 38th parallel.

Amid jubilation, the United States and United Nations had to make new decisions. Should they capitalize upon their spectacular victory and move into North Korea? The premier of Red China on October 1 warned that the Chinese would "not allow seeing their neighbors being invaded by imperialists." A few days later, he announced the Chinese would send troops, and dispatched a warning to the United Nations through India. These warnings worried American strategists, but there was a possibility that they were bluff, and there was the probability that the North Koreans, unless pursued, would recoup their strength and strike new blows.

The Joint Chiefs of Staff on September 27, 1950, ordered MacArthur to destroy the North Korean armed forces, but under no circumstances to cross the borders of China or Russia. The United Nations Assembly gave its sanction to the project on October 7, reiterating its aim to create "a unified, independent and democratic Korea." Two days later, the United Nations forces poured across the 38th parallel toward the Yalu River, which marked the boundary with Manchuria. They met little resistance. As they rushed northward, General MacArthur flew to Guam, where on October 14, he met President Truman to give him a first-hand briefing. According to a transcript later released by Senate committees, President

Truman asked General MacArthur, "What are the chances for Chinese or Soviet interference?" MacArthur replied:

> Very little. Had they interfered in the first or second months it would have been decisive. We are no longer fearful of their intervention. We no longer stand hat in hand. The Chinese have 300,000 men in Manchuria. Of these probably not more than 100/125,000 are distributed along the Yalu River. Only 50/60,000 could be gotten across the Yalu River. They have no air force. Now that we have bases for our Air Force in Korea, if the Chinese tried to get down to Pyongyang there would be the greatest slaughter.

Eighth Army fighting Chinese Communists, February 1951 (U.S. ARMY PHOTO)

It was a tragic miscalculation. For several weeks the advance into northern Korea went well. On October 19, the capital, Pyongyang, fell, and parachutists landed thirty miles beyond to trap much of the remaining North Korean army. The only remaining objective was the Yalu River. But on October 26, a Chinese Communist soldier was captured; four days later, fourteen more were taken. By November 4, eight Chinese divisions had been identified, and Russian-made MIG fighter planes had briefly engaged the United Nations air force.

General MacArthur issued a special communiqué warning that "a new and fresh army now faces us," and excoriated the Chinese for their international lawlessness in intervening without notice, and "massing a great concentration of possible reinforcing divisions with adequate supply behind the privileged sanctuary of the adjacent Manchurian border." Both in his private communications to the Joint Chiefs of Staff and in the encouragement he gave to pressure groups in the United States, MacArthur engaged in a vigorous campaign for permission to bomb this "privileged sanctuary." President Truman refused to allow all-out military action against China, because, he later explained, "if for no other reason . . . it was a gigantic booby trap."

In the two weeks after they first sighted Chinese troops, the United Nations forces marched into a trap that was serious enough. General MacArthur failed to detect the movement by night of some 200,000 Chinese soldiers into the area around the 40th parallel, and spread his forces in a thin line along a 300-mile front. On November 24, 1950, he began an offensive to end the war. The Chinese suddenly appeared in overwhelming numbers, stalled the offensive, and hurled back advance units. MacArthur immediately recommended that the United Nations accept 33,000 troops from Chiang Kai-shek. President Truman rejected the recommendation, which might not only have spread the conflict but also have disrupted the unity among the Western nations. If need be, MacArthur must retreat back to the beachheads.

Through December 1950, in bitter weather, the outnumbered Eighth Army and X Corps fought a heroic withdrawal from North Korea. The United Nations tried to negotiate peace with the Chinese, but the Communists as they swept below the 38th parallel and recaptured Seoul set impossibly stiff terms. General MacArthur continued to recommend measures that might involve full-scale war against China; when the high command rejected these, he pessimistically predicted that his position in Korea would ultimately become untenable, and recommended withdrawal from the peninsula as rapidly as was tactically feasible. Two members of the Joint Chiefs of Staff hurried to Korea. Far from finding a military disaster impending, they reported on January 17, 1951, that the Eighth Army under General Matthew B. Ridgway was holding firmly to its new positions and planning a new offensive. Through February it inflicted punishing losses upon the Chinese Communists. In March they counterattacked, for a second and final time capturing Seoul and recrossing the 38th parallel. President Truman was ready again to seek a negotiated peace.

MacArthur is Dismissed

GENERAL MACARTHUR, far from ready to accept the position of his commander in chief, repeatedly made public his eagerness to win total victory in Korea at the risk of full involvement in war with China. On March 20, 1951, he wrote the Republican minority leader in the House of Representatives, Joseph W. Martin:

> It seems strangely difficult for some to realize that here in Asia is where the Communist conspirators have elected to make their play for global conquest, and that we have joined the issue thus raised on the battlefield; that here we fight Europe's war with arms while the diplomats there still fight it with words; that if we lose the war to communism in Asia the fall of Europe is inevitable; win it and Europe most probably would avoid war and yet preserve freedom. As you pointed out, we must win. There is no substitute for victory.

This Asia-first policy was excitingly popular among many in Congress and among some of the electorate who earlier had opposed American intervention against the Nazis, had urged more vigorous prosecution of the war against Japan, and had accepted with reluctance American participation in the United Nations. It was a rallying position for many who emotionally still clung to old, outmoded isolationist feelings. President Truman held to his thesis that, in the great struggle against Communism, western Europe with its concentration of heavy industry, not industrially weak Asia, was the main potential battlefield. Had he wished, he could not have won the support of western European partners in the United Nations for a more militant policy in Asia; he would not accept the arguments of the Asia-firsters that the United States should undertake unilateral action —"go it alone."

General MacArthur thus emerged as a major figure in American politics, trying to reverse the administration policies. Five days after Representative Martin released MacArthur's letter to the press, President Truman, on April 11, 1951, relieved General MacArthur of his commands. A groundswell of outrage swept the United States; a Gallup poll reported that 69 per cent of those interviewed favored the General, only 29 per cent the President. MacArthur upon his return was greeted hysterically wherever he appeared; millions watched their television sets as he addressed Congress. "Why, my soldiers asked of me, surrender military advantages to an enemy in the field?" he declaimed, and after pausing dramatically added, "I could not answer."

For the moment the country was with General MacArthur, but during long weeks of congressional hearings that followed, the fever pitch of emotionalism declined perceptibly as the Joint Chiefs of Staff also presented their reasoning. Their chairman, General Omar N. Bradley, declared that all-out war against China would be "the wrong war at the wrong place, at the wrong time and with the wrong enemy." General Mac-

Arthur, at the conclusion of his address to Congress, had referred to the barracks-ballad lines, "Old soldiers never die; they just fade away." As his fervid patriotic oratory went on before gradually dwindling audiences, it remained only for the aged Mencken to comment several years later that MacArthur was "fading satisfactorily."

More significantly, President Truman's policy of fighting a limited war of containment continued to baffle and exasperate a considerable part of the American people. It went too completely against the American tradition of total victory; it was too hard to explain to much of the public or even to many of the soldiers fighting endlessly through the rice paddies

General MacArthur addressing Congress (U.S. ARMY PHOTO)

and on the hilltops of Korea. This was true even though the President's policies bore promise of ultimate success.

In June 1951 the Russian delegate to the United Nations hinted that settlement was possible. Armistice negotiations began on July 10, 1951, near the 38th parallel, and continued for many weary months at Panmunjom. They came to revolve around the difficult questions of locating the cease-fire line, enforcing the armistice, and repatriating prisoners of war. By the spring of 1952, agreements had been reached upon all but the last question; upon it, negotiations made no progress, and finally, in October 1952, were recessed. By then the nation was in the midst of a Presidential campaign, and although there was no large scale fighting in Korea, the interminable negotiations, interminable skirmishing, and ever-growing casualties had worn out the patience of the American people.

Election of Eisenhower

THUS FOREIGN POLICY was probably the key factor in the election of 1952. The nature of the electorate had been rapidly changing in the years of prosperity after the war, but more important, it was increasingly disturbed over the drawn-out Korean War and over charges that in this and other ways the administration was demonstrating a softness toward Communism. There were also domestic concomitants: discontent over rising prices and taxes, and disgust over revelations of corruption in Washington. It was not surprising that in times so troubled the voters overwhelmingly turned to a popular American general who they felt could lead them to a new security in a frightening world. It was significant that they turned not to MacArthur but to Dwight D. Eisenhower, so closely linked to the military and foreign policies of the Roosevelt and Truman administrations.

Partly this was the logic of politics. The wing of the Republican party holding to the views of MacArthur was committed to Senator Robert A. Taft—but it was a minority within the party, even though it controlled the Republican National Committee. The majority (knowing they could count upon the votes of most of the minority) sought a candidate who could pull strong support from many who had favored the Democratic foreign and domestic policy. Consequently, they turned to General Eisenhower—whom some liberal Democrats had sought to draft in 1948.

In the struggle for delegates, Eisenhower easily carried the eastern states, and Taft the middle west. Later, in a violent struggle on the floor of the convention, the Eisenhower forces won contested delegations and, with them, the nomination on the first ballot. Senator Richard M. Nixon of California, who was more acceptable to conservative Republicans, was nominated for the Vice-Presidency. The platform was ambiguous enough to cover disagreements between the two wings of the party. Early in September, Eisenhower went still further to mollify the Midwestern Republicans by conferring with Taft. He promised patronage to the Taft followers, and avowed that the main issue of the campaign was "liberty against creeping socialization"—but he did not compromise on foreign policy. Later in Wisconsin he was conciliatory toward Senator McCarthy. Thus he was able to campaign with the diverse factions of the party unified behind him.

As for the Democrats, the Northern wing of the party was in control at the convention. President Truman had announced on March 30 that he would not run again; the most vigorous campaigner in the primaries, Senator Estes Kefauver of Tennessee, won little support among party leaders; Vice-President Alben Barkley was deserted by labor spokesmen, who declared he was too old. Instead the Northern leaders drafted Governor Adlai E. Stevenson of Illinois, who had earlier declared he would not run. His running mate was the liberal Senator John J. Sparkman of Alabama. The platform stated the positions of the Northern Democrats: endorsement of the Truman foreign policies, civil rights, repeal of the Taft-Hartley Act, and high price supports for farmers.

To the delight of most intellectuals, Governor Stevenson began delivering speeches brilliant in their phraseology and eloquence, clever in their wit, and startling in their candor. He drew the hearty support of a group

The Democratic nominees in 1952: Governor Adlai E. Stevenson and Senator John Sparkman (NATIONAL ARCHIVES)

that came to be known derisively by their opposition as "the eggheads" as he promised to "talk sense to the American people." But General Eisenhower appealed much more effectively to businessmen and the masses by promising to end their various frustrations. In a later speech he summed up succinctly what had been his campaign positions:

Americans wanted an end to the war in Korea—a war allowed to become futile, seemingly without end. . . . Americans wanted a Government thrifty and frugal with the public's money. They wanted a stop to the endless rise in taxes, taking more and more of the family income to support an overgrown Washington bureaucracy. They wanted something done about inflation—to end the growing discouragement, as, day by day, pensions and savings and the weekly paycheck bought less and less at the corner store. Americans were determined to eliminate penetration by the Communist conspiracy in our Government and in our whole society. They did not consider it a red herring.

Above all it was the festering problem of Korea that brought a landslide for Eisenhower. Since the previous June, General Mark Clark had been trying to make the war as costly as possible for the Communists. By blowing up a power dam on the Yalu, the largest in the Far East, he had been for a time successful. Then, in October, with the permission of Washington, he recessed the armistice talks and began a limited offensive that produced little but heavy casualties on both sides—a "grim, face-saving slugging match," he later called it. Against this discouraging background,

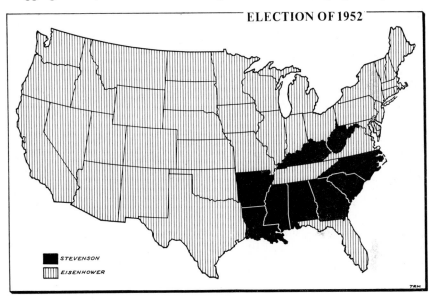

ELECTION OF 1952

STEVENSON
EISENHOWER

General Eisenhower, speaking in Detroit on October 24, 1952, promised to bring the war to "an early and honorable end." To help do so, he promised he would make a personal trip to Korea. The response at the polls was overwhelming. Eisenhower polled 33,824,000 votes to 27,315,000 for Stevenson; the electoral vote was 442 to 89. Despite Eisenhower's sweeping victory, the Republicans surprisingly obtained only an even split in the Senate (which they organized with the vote of the Vice President) and won a majority of only eight seats in the House. The Republican candidate was far more popular than his party.

Armistice in Korea

SHORTLY AFTER HIS ELECTION, General Eisenhower flew to Korea to talk to commanders about means of obtaining an honorable truce. He issued a press statement there asserting, "We have no panaceas, no trick ways of settling any problems." In his inaugural he committed himself to a firm policy in Korea and elsewhere in the struggle against Communists. "In the final choice," he declared, "a soldier's pack is not so heavy a burden as a prisoner's chains." He informed Congress that the United States would encourage the strengthening of the South Korean armed forces, and would no longer use the Seventh Fleet to shield Red China from Chiang Kai-shek.

Fighter pilots on their way to combat, April 1953 (U.S. AIR FORCE PHOTO)

Less than two months after President Eisenhower took office, Stalin died. This opened the possibility of an end to the Korean war and perhaps some moderation of the cold war. When the new Soviet premier, Georgi Malenkov, inaugurated more conciliatory policies, the President called upon Russia to show its good faith by signing an Austrian peace treaty and supporting an armistice in Korea. Through the spring of 1953, negotiations for an armistice proceeded rather smoothly. By June, when they were almost completed, President Rhee disrupted them by freeing unilaterally 27,000 North Korean troops who did not wish to be repatriated.

Nevertheless, on July 27, 1953, a final armistice agreement was signed at Panmunjom. It provided for a cease-fire and withdrawal of both armies two kilometers back of the existing battle line, which ran from coast to coast, from just below the 38th parallel in the west to thirty miles north of it in the east.

In succeeding months, the United Nations sent northward more than 70,000 North Korean and Chinese Communist prisoners, and received in return only 3,597 Americans, 7,848 South Koreans, and 1,315 prisoners of other nationalities. A political conference to seek peaceful unification of Korea was to be held within three months after the signing of the armistice agreement, but it never took place. Instead, the armistice turned into an uneasy and indefinite armed truce. In 1957, after the Communists had long been violating armistice prohibitions against introducing new armaments, the United States announced it also was sending more modern weapons into Korea. The United States not only continued to face a threat from North Korea, but had to restrain President Rhee, who bitterly threatened to unify Korea by force. The Senate ratified a mutual defense treaty in 1954, but warned that the United States would not support South Korean military aggression.

The Korean war (officially only a police action) had lasted more than three years and cost the United States alone 25,000 dead, 115,000 other casualties, and twenty-two billion dollars. For Americans who liked to think in terms of total victory, it seemed painfully inconclusive. Soldiers at the front supposedly had greeted the news of the armistice with remarks like, "Don't forget where you put your gun. You'll need it next week." The war had settled no problems in the Far East except to prevent the Communist conquest of South Korea. It had proven that the United States through the United Nations would fight to prevent the further spread of Communism. It had also shown that Communist China, with its enormous population and its rapid industrialization and militarization, would pose a continuing and growing threat from the East.

Building a Bulwark against China

THE PRESENT and future threat that China posed meant that the United States in Asia as in Europe tried to transform a former enemy into a new military ally. Thus it gradually changed Japan, as it had Germany, from an occupied nation into a partner in the defense system.

In the years before the Korean war, the American occupying forces in Japan under General MacArthur had tried to bring about political, social, and economic reforms. These meant a democratization of the government, extension of rights to women and underprivileged groups, expansion of the educational system (from a starting point as high as the goal of educational reform in China), land reform as drastic as that in China, a curbing of the power of the monopolistic *zaibatsu* industrial system, an improvement of the economic status of labor, and a mushroom growth of labor unions. In Japan more than anywhere else in Asia the United States helped develop a dynamic alternative to Communism. E. O. Reischauer, in *The United States and Japan,* wrote:

> Our attitude toward human rights both in individual and collective terms and our righting of the balance of economic and political power in Japan go far beyond anything the Chinese Communists can at present attempt or perhaps even conceive. American democratic concepts as they have continued to grow through the decades represent an ideal to Asia which makes Communist theories seem old-fashioned and unimaginative by comparison.

The Japanese industrial comeback was so slow that in 1949 the United States ended its reparations and stopped the dismantling of industrial combinations. There was no possibility that Japan could again threaten the West militarily, yet it remained the major industrial power in Asia, and its production was badly needed in non-Communist areas. In addition, Japan had to enjoy a measure of prosperity if it were to remain relatively democratic and not turn to Communism.

Negotiation of a Japanese peace treaty began in 1950 through the skilled offices of a Republican, John Foster Dulles, whom President Truman appointed to undertake the task. Aside from the fact that it stripped Japan of all her possessions, including the Ryukyu Islands (most notably Okinawa) directly south of Japan, it was a generous treaty. By recognizing the right of the sovereign Japanese nation to self-defense, it opened the way to rearmament. Thanks partly to its negotiation by a Republican, the treaty easily received Senate ratification, and went into effect April 28, 1952. A security treaty, signed at the same time, permitted the United States to maintain armed forces in Japan. Two years later, a mutual defense assistance pact provided for Japanese rearmament with American aid, but the building of armed forces proceeded slowly. Disarmament had been one of MacArthur's most cherished reforms, and the Japanese constitution had banned war forever. This had encouraged such a strong pacifist sentiment that as late as 1957 only 100,000 Japanese had joined the armed forces. The task of defending Japan continued to rest largely with the United States.

Several nations to the south which had suffered during the war either invasion or the threat of invasion viewed with some concern the rebuilding of Japan as a military power. To reassure them, the United States in 1951 signed a security treaty with the Philippines, and the ANZUS pact with Australia and New Zealand. Neither the ANZUS and other pacts nor the rearmament of Japan could serve as more than slight deterrents against Communist China. Any effective counter-force must continue to come from the United States, which seemed committed indefinitely to the burden of maintaining an Asiatic power balance.

Chapter **22**

EISENHOWER
REPUBLICANISM

IN THE PROSPEROUS but uncertain years of the early fifties, Americans above all else sought security in domestic as well as foreign policy. A majority of voters were more interested in preserving their economic gains than in adventuring toward new governmental programs or in retreating toward earlier dogmas. It was a nation moderate in its views that looked for its security to the moderate President, Dwight D. Eisenhower.

Throughout his presidency, Eisenhower took only brief excursions to the right or the left of his firm moderate principles. He never deviated far from the position he had stated as early as 1949 when, as president of Columbia University, he had addressed the American Bar Association: "The path to America's future," he declared, "lies down the middle of the road between the unfettered power of concentrated wealth . . . and the unbridled power of statism or partisan interests." He reiterated after five years in the White House, "I still believe in that philosophy; I try to practice it and live by those principles."

President Eisenhower thought that the majority of the Republican party believed in these things too—"those are the kind of people which I will do my best to help elect." But there were times during the Eisenhower administration when it was by no means clear that his Modern Republicanism would win over the more conservative ideas of some Republican leaders in Congress. Neither was it always certain that the businessmen who took a leading part in his administration would subscribe to his "middle of the road" philosophy.

A Businessmen's Administration

PRESIDENT EISENHOWER established a businessmen's administration in Washington. He appointed the president of General Motors, Charles E. Wilson, to be Secretary of Defense; George Humphrey, president of M. A. Hanna and Co. (once Mark Hanna's firm) to be Secretary of the Treasury; a New England manufacturer, Sinclair Weeks, to be Secretary of Commerce; and two automobile distributors, Douglas McKay and Arthur E. Summerfield, to be Secretary of the Interior and Postmaster General, respectively. The new Secretary of State, John Foster Dulles, had been one of the highest-paid corporation lawyers in the country. The Secretary of Agriculture was Ezra T. Benson, a conservative specialist in farm marketing; the Secretary of Health, Education and Welfare (when that department came into existence in April 1953) was Mrs. Oveta Culp Hobby, wartime commander of the WAC's and wife of a wealthy Texas publisher; the Attorney General was Herbert Brownell, who had been legal aide to Governor Dewey; the Secretary of Labor, who resigned before the year was out, was Martin Durkin, the pro-Stevenson president of the plumbers' union. "Eight millionaires and a plumber," the *New Republic* disrespectfully remarked. Wilson, at the hearing on his appointment, played into the hands of Democratic critics by testifying that he had long assumed that "what was good for our country was good for General Motors, and vice versa." A few days later, Stevenson declared in a speech, "While the New Dealers have all left Washington to make way for the car dealers, I hasten to say that I, for one, do not believe the story that the general welfare has become a subsidiary of General Motors."

President Eisenhower's system of administering the government gave special importance to this cabinet preponderantly made up of businessmen. In the techniques that he developed, he borrowed from earlier army experience. He established his assistant, Sherman Adams, former Governor of New Hampshire, as a sort of chief of staff, and from Adams he established a chain of command downward. Through the cabinet, and through numerous new committees, administrators arrived at important policy decisions which they referred to the President. He relied heavily upon these recommendations, which extended into fields well transcending routine matters. Since many of the men who formulated them, in addition to the cabinet officers, were business leaders the President had brought to Washington, over-all policies came to bear strongly the stamp of business. The businessmen's administration was on trial; if it gave way to an impulse to turn the clock back to the twenties, or allowed a depression to come, the electorate might react as sharply against it as against the ill-fated Hoover administration. Republican businessmen did not want to face another twenty years out of power. Secretary Humphrey placed Andrew Mellon's portrait behind his desk in the Treasury Department, but in his earlier dealings with the United Mine Workers he had been as generous as Mark Hanna. In the first phase of the Eisenhower administration the trend in domestic policy was toward the right, but it was a new right of the fifties.

"Eisenhower Prosperity"

THE IMMEDIATE NAGGING WORRY of Americans in the months following the Korean armistice of July 1953 was the possibility that the curtailing of arms expenditures might lead to an economic recession or even depression. When the administration came into power, although the Korean War was continuing, it dropped almost all controls immediately. Secretary Humphrey instead substituted sound-money policies to restrict credit, and thus try to prevent inflation. By the fall of 1953, the threat was of deflation. Already farm income was dropping seriously, and many economists feared that the decline might spread throughout business in general. By March 1954 the Federal Reserve Board index of industrial production had dropped 10 per cent below the previous July, and estimates of unemployment ranged upward from three million.

During the early months of 1954, a debate between the business-minded administrators and their Democratic critics swirled around questions as to the seriousness of the economic setback and the size and timing of the measures the government must take to counter it. All the principals in the debate assumed that the government must play a key role in the economy. Republicans tried to counter the pessimism of Senator Paul Douglas, who had been an economics professor at the University of Chicago, by denouncing "peddlers of gloom and doom." Nevertheless, they went in the directions Douglas recommended, only not so fast or far. When the economy slackened, Secretary of the Treasury Humphrey and the Federal Reserve Board reversed the scarce-money policies and eased credit. A $3,000,000,000 cut in taxes, and a $2,500,000,000 increase in unemployment compensation, in social security payments, and in interest and dividend payments went far to counteract the $6,500,000,000 drop in wage and salary income between July 1953 and February 1954. Consumer confidence remained remarkably high. Housing continued to boom, and this too did much to stem the recession. By the summer of 1954, the President's Council of Economic Advisors was able to report that the threatened recession had turned out to be no more than a contraction and was already over. The Republican administration's first venture with the built-in stabilizers of social security and the expedients of Keynesian economics was a success.

By the summer of 1955 the American economy was again booming. Steel production was up to 95 per cent of capacity from a recession low of 64 per cent. Employment went up to an all-time high; factory workers, thanks to overtime pay, were receiving average weekly wages of $76.52. Salaries and stock dividends were up too. At the same time, prices had remained relatively stable since the inflation that had accompanied the Korean War. Consumers, enjoying a higher living standard than ever before, went on the biggest buying spree in history. They used their large incomes to buy without restraint, and borrowed to buy still more. The Federal Reserve Board again placed restrictions upon credit in order to restrain the boom.

In order to avoid strikes which might unsettle economic conditions, several large industries, led by the automobile manufacturers, made new concessions to organized labor. As early as 1948, Walter Reuther, the president of the United Automobile Workers, had obtained from General Motors, and later from other manufacturers, an "escalator clause" in contracts, providing for automatic increases or decreases in wages every three months as the consumers' price index rose or fell. In 1955, he demanded from the Ford Automobile Company a guaranteed annual wage. Ford compromised by agreeing that workers should receive 65 per cent of their net weekly wages for the first four weeks they were unemployed, and 60 per cent for the next twenty-two weeks. General Motors followed. A few months later, steel workers received from the American Can Company and the Continental Can Company the first genuine guarantee of an annual wage.

The round of wage increases continued through 1956. After a five-week strike, steel workers won a substantial increase; the United Mine Workers, without a strike, obtained a 30-cent-an-hour increase. Factory workers' wages went up to approximately $80.00 per week. These wage increases, together with other factors, led to widespread wholesale price increases and a renewed threat of inflation. Steel prices went up 6.25 per cent after the strike; other increases followed.

Luckily for the Eisenhower administration, the full impact of the increases, leading to higher retail prices, was not felt until after the election of 1956. Through 1957, prices continued to rise, while productivity, which in the years since the war had increased at an average annual rate of 3.7 per cent, dropped in 1956 and 1957 to a 1.4 per cent annual increase.

From this plateau, the United States, at the close of 1957, skidded into the most serious recession since the war. By the late spring of 1958, industrial production had dropped 14 per cent below the level of a year earlier, and approximately five million workers were unemployed. Again the so-called "built-in stabilizers" of the economy, such as unemployment insurance payments to those out of work, somewhat softened the blow of the recession. The Eisenhower administration could also point to other antirecession factors—the easing of credit, and of the size of down payments on houses, the speeding up and increase of spending for defense, and the building of public works, especially highways. The administration would not go beyond these mild steps, which to a considerable degree were in operation anyway; with the co-operation of the Democratic leaders of Congress it blocked tax cuts. The price index was still rising slightly to new highs, which made the administration leaders fearful that any substantial pump-priming would lead to a new spiral of inflation. And they were optimistic enough to think that in a few months the economy would right itself, so that the nation could again enjoy the boom that had marked most of the fifties. By the end of the decade, the economy was again operating at a high level, but the nation was plagued with a problem of chronic unemployment of more than 3,000,000 workers.

For most workers, the dominant pattern of the fifties was prosperity, which until 1958 led many of them to vote Republican even though their leaders for the most part backed the Democratic party. In December 1955, the American Federation of Labor and the Congress of Industrial Organizations merged at the top into a new giant federation, the AFL-CIO. Its leaders tried to direct the unions toward social and political ends rather than merely concentrating upon wage increases. They endorsed the candidacy of Stevenson in 1956, and threw their energy into many state and local political contests through a Committee on Political Education.

"Everything's booming but the guns," Republican politicians proclaimed during the campaign of 1956. Not quite. The farmers were in increasingly serious straits. The technical age both benefited the farmer and caused him to lag further and further behind his urban brother. The farmers' fields were 30 per cent, sows and ewes nearly a third, and cattle nearly half again more productive than thirty years previously. One major result was that fewer farmers raised more produce. The great staples piled up in surplus, and from 1948 to 1956 farm prices dropped a third while the national income went up by half. In 1948 farmers received 8.9 per cent of the national income, in 1956 only 4.1 per cent. The per-capita income of the farm population was $632 (plus $285 of non-farm income) compared with a national per-capita income of $1,629. The average income of the lowest 1,250,000 of farm families was only a quarter that of the average factory worker's family. Farm population dropped steadily, to 22,300,000 in 1956—only a ninth of the nation. In that single year, one out of every eleven of the farm population either moved to a city or was absorbed in an expanding city.

While farm produce prices fell, consumer food prices continued to rise; they went up 2.4 per cent between July 1955, and July 1956. Mainly this was because distribution costs were steadily rising. The farmer was caught in a squeeze, as prices for his produce slipped while prices of what he bought gradually went up. It seemed an anomaly that he did not share in the general prosperity. An Iowa banker pointed out that a packing-plant worker, who earned $6,600 a year taking the bones out of hogs, was receiving more than twice as much as the man who grew them.

As surpluses of such agricultural staples as wheat and cotton piled up, the government sought to bolster the prices through eight billion dollars worth of purchases. In the two years between June 1953 and June 1955, the government thus lost over $1,200,000,000 through the deterioration of the foods in storage or their sale overseas. This was more than had been lost in the previous eighteen years of price supports. Neither price supports nor the fact that the government took thirty-eight million acres out of production of these crops solved the problem.

In 1954, President Eisenhower and Secretary of Agriculture Benson proposed a shift away from rigid price supports to a flexible sliding-scale program. The purpose was to cut government losses and end artificiality in production and distribution. The 1955 harvest was the first to be grown under the new flexible system, but already Democratic politicians were denouncing flexible supports as ones that could only "flex" downward. Seeking to win the farm vote, in 1956 they wrote a bill providing for high price supports and a subsidy for farmers who let land lie fallow. They thought they had put President Eisenhower in an impossible position, and as they expected, he vetoed the bill. But in May 1956 he pulled out of the vetoed bill the provision for a "soil bank" of fallow land, and threw it back at the congressional Democrats. In this form, Congress passed the bill and it became law. Under the 1956 program, farmers took 12,300,000 acres out of production in return for payments of over a quarter billion dollars. And Northern farmers again voted heavily for Eisenhower.

At the close of the fifties, as mechanization, hybridization, and antibiotics made it possible for farmers to grow still more crops and to raise still more wheat than ever before, the farm problem was as far as ever from being solved. The superabundance of American farms had sent surpluses higher than ever at the same time that taxpayers were having to pay six billion dollars a year for price supports. Democrats, controlling Congress, were arguing that the way out was a stricter limitation on acreage and higher supports; the Eisenhower administration continued to advocate less limitation and lower supports.

With greater success, the Eisenhower administration fostered benign tax policies for businessmen to encourage corporate initiative. In August 1954, Congress passed a tax reform bill almost a thousand pages long. For political reasons it contained some relief for individuals, but above all it corrected purported injustices hampering corporations. It granted more rapid depreciation allowances to business, and made it easier for businessmen to obtain tax reductions over a period of years to compensate for losses.

In the realm of public power development, the administration also demonstrated its friendliness toward private enterprise. The President in 1953 referred to expansion of the Tennessee Valley Authority as "creeping socialism." These words of opprobrium brought protests, and he quickly rescinded them. He demonstrated, nevertheless, that he favored Federal development of power only when private enterprise or local governments were incompetent for the task. Throughout the nation there was much agitation because the administration sought to circumvent the T.V.A. by contracting with the Dixon-Yates syndicate in 1954 to build a huge steam power plant on the banks of the Mississippi. The administration declared the contract would save taxpayers immediately $100,000,000 in construction costs, but opponents pointed to the large profits the syndicate would collect over many years. The power would cost the government $3,500,000 per year more than T.V.A. power. Ultimately, in 1955, when the city of Memphis, Tennessee, offered to build the plant, the President retreated to the principle of decentralization and canceled the Dixon-Yates contract.

The Eisenhower administration departed from its predecessors in power development policy through proposing federal "partnership" in power construction when the projects were too large for local public or private enterprise to undertake alone. Secretary of the Interior McKay thus permitted a private power company to plan three smaller power dams in Hell's Canyon on the Snake River, rather than obtain appropriations for one large federal multipurpose dam. In keeping with his feeling that development of resources should be decentralized, President Eisenhower signed a bill turning over to the adjacent states offshore oil lands along the Gulf of Mexico and the Pacific Coast.

To the satisfaction of bankers, the Reconstruction Finance Corporation was liquidated, rather than kept inoperative for a future emergency. Accompanying the tax cuts, serious slashes in the budget, even in the strength of the armed forces and the extent of foreign aid, helped keep the budget nearly balanced.

Even while the Eisenhower administration was moving toward the right, and going far toward conciliating the Taft wing of the Republican party in Congress, the President retained the basic general welfare programs that had been enacted during the previous twenty years. Senator Taft was so co-operative that President Eisenhower later declared he had taken the liberal approach on many issues, but Taft died in the summer of 1953 and many of his followers were less co-operative. Nevertheless, the President proposed measures that on the surface resembled those of his Democratic predecessors in the White House but that embodied the principles of decentralization, very limited liability on the part of the federal government, and stimulation of private enterprise.

Thus President Eisenhower took a firm stand against so-called "socialized medicine," but proposed a public health insurance program that would not involve much more than limited underwriting of private insurance companies issuing health policies. Secretary Hobby of the Department of Health, Education, and Welfare objected to proposals to provide the nation's children with free Salk polio vaccine as being socialized medicine by the back door. The public became alarmed over the chaotic distribution of the vaccine; belatedly the government imposed strict controls, and Congress voted funds for distributing the vaccine. Secretary Hobby, in July 1955, resigned because of her husband's ill health; her successor, Marion B. Folsom, followed more liberal policies. Congress passed no health insurance legislation but, in 1954, did extend social security to ten million more people, and unemployment compensation to an additional four million.

The public housing program, as Congress finally enacted it in July 1955, involved building only 45,000 units a year for four years in a nation of 160,000,000 people. The nation, burgeoning with 32,800,000 school children already, with a 50 per cent increase likely within a decade, was short some quarter million schoolrooms. Local authorities were running out of building funds and reaching their debt limits. In February 1955 the President rushed to Congress a message urging a federal expenditure of $1,100,000,000 over a period of years. This aid was to be in the form of underwriting school bonds and similar methods which would limit federal responsibility; and every state school official who testified in congressional hearings declared that each of the intricate alternatives of the bill was unworkable. The same month, the President also proposed a highway building program, based on rather similar principles. It would establish a Federal Highway Corporation that would sell thirty-year bonds. Thus the national debt would not be increased. In 1955, Congress did not act on either proposal; in 1956, it did authorize a forty billion dollar ten-year high-way building program, for which it would allocate $24,825,000,000.

This concept of the limited role of the federal government in providing for the general welfare was an integral part of the Eisenhower policies, to which he sometimes referred as "dynamic conservatism." It appealed to many members of Congress. During his first two years in office, when Congress was narrowly Republican, the President was supported more often than not by a coalition of liberal Republicans and Democrats. Of 83 key issues brought to a vote in the 1953 session of Congress, the administration won 74, but succeeded in 58 of these only through Democratic support.

Traffic interchange, Dallas, Texas (DEPARTMENT OF COMMERCE)

The congressional elections of 1954 veered slightly toward the Democrats. They controlled the House of Representatives 232 to 203, and the Senate 49 to 47. Although they thus took over committee chairmanships, congressional policy changed little as a result of the election. While liberal Democrats criticized the President's program as not going far enough, conservative ones were ready to band with right-wing Republicans to kill or mutilate much of it.

Civil Liberties and Civil Rights

DESPITE THE CONTINUED POWER of right-wing members of Congress, Americans after the Korean armistice moved away from the excesses of McCarthyism. The hunt for subversives in the government, however, was intensified early in the Eisenhower administration. Large numbers of employees resigned or were dismissed; the administration at one point gave their total as 2,200. But most of the serious security risks had already been ousted in the Truman administration. A study of some four hundred of the Eisenhower administration cases by the Fund for the Republic of the Ford Foundation indicated that in a majority of them the charges had been insupportable, and often reinstatement ultimately followed. In July 1955 the Congress established a bipartisan Commission on Government Security to re-evaluate the security program.

Senator Joseph McCarthy himself plummeted from the national limelight to relative obscurity. His downfall followed his serious blunder in obliquely attacking President Eisenhower and directly assailing Secretary of the Army Robert Stevens. Before the attacks, in January 1954, the Gallup poll showed that 50 per cent of Americans questioned favored him, and only 29 per cent opposed him. His attacks led to congressional hearings, and even before they began, the Gallup polls showed 46 per cent opposing him. For the first few days the hearings were a great national spectacle viewed by millions over television. Many people for the first time saw McCarthy in action, as for thirteen days he bullied and harried Secretary Stevens, evading issues through irrelevant countercharges and insinuations, and interrupting to object at every point. As the public watched, McCarthy seemed to change from a national hero into something of a villain, then into a low buffoon. Soon many people began to laugh. Nothing could have more rapidly deflated his demagogic power. Within a few days a bored public turned to other diversions, and television stations reduced their coverage of the hearings. In December 1954 the Senate voted 67 to 22 to condemn McCarthy, but his hold over the American public had already largely disintegrated. He died in May 1957, a has-been, symbolic of the degree to which the nation had left behind the era of McCarthyism.

Remnants of the attitudes that had made possible the rise of McCarthy remained. There was, for example, the case of a consultant to the Atomic Energy Commission, J. Robert Oppenheimer, who had directed the wartime laboratory at Los Alamos which made the first atomic bomb. In 1950, he had opposed the development of a hydrogen bomb. The F.B.I., in November 1953, distributed to the White House and several government departments a report on Oppenheimer detailing his prewar associations with Communists. On order from President Eisenhower, a "blank wall" was placed between Oppenheimer and government secrets, pending hearings. A three-man board voted two to one against granting him security clearance; the A.E.C. ratified the decision four to one. Scientists were bitterly split over the wisdom of the decision.

The Supreme Court, as a result of the appointments of the Republican President, seemed to be moving toward a more liberal rather than conservative policy. In one case in 1957 it ruled that the government could not use secret F.B.I. evidence against a defendant unless it was made available to his lawyers. Congress quickly passed legislation safeguarding F.B.I. files. In four other cases the Court protected individuals who were suspected of being subversive against undue encroachment by federal or state power. In 1958 the Court ruled five to four that the State Department, in the absence of an act of Congress, was exceeding its authority in refusing passports to persons who failed to file affidavits "with respect to present or past membership in the Communist party." These decisions attracted relatively little attention compared with the Supreme Court rulings on desegregation.

A series of cases before the Supreme Court breaking down bit by bit racial segregation in public education had been pressed by the National Association for the Advancement of Colored People since the late thirties. Their target was a Supreme Court decision of 1896, *Plessy* v. *Ferguson*, which had interpreted the requirement of the Fourteenth Amendment that states give "equal protection of the laws" to mean that separate but equal facilities could be furnished to Negroes. Finally, the Supreme Court reversed this doctrine in the case of *Brown* v. *Board of Education of Topeka* in May 1954. Chief Justice Earl Warren (who had been appointed by President Eisenhower in September 1953, after the death of Chief Justice Vinson) delivered the unanimous opinion of the Court: "We conclude that in the field of public education the doctrine of 'separate but equal' has no place. Separate educational facilities are inherently unequal." The Court granted that Southern states might move gradually toward desegregation.

States in the deep South and several border states resorted to every possible legal device to try to prevent integration from taking place. Each September, mob action against integration in a few communities within the South attracted widespread attention throughout the world. Of some 3,000 biracial school districts in the South, a total of 684 had been integrated by the fall of 1957. Schools within these districts in large cities in the upper South or the border area, such as Washington, Baltimore, Louisville, and St. Louis, opened quietly on a desegregated basis. But 2,300 districts, including all those in the deep South and Virginia, remained segregated. Some 23 districts attempted desegregation—most of them on a very slow, token basis. One of these was Little Rock, Arkansas, where intervention by the governor and mob threats led President Eisenhower to send federal troops to maintain order. Protests and disorders reached their height in 1957. Thereafter, opposition remained solid in five states of the deep South: Alabama, Georgia, Louisiana, Mississippi, and South Carolina. Gradually other Southern states, prodded by the Federal courts, moved toward at least token integration.

Pressure from growing blocs of Negro voters in the North, Negroes rising in economic status in the South, and their supporters helped bring other changes. President Eisenhower completed the desegregation of the armed forces, and tried to bring about greater integration in the government and the District of Columbia. "There must be no second-class citizens in this country," he wrote the Negro Representative Adam Clayton Powell. Representative Powell ironically, was instrumental in killing President Eisenhower's school-aid program of 1956, which provided for grants of a quarter-billion dollars a year for five years to match state funds. Powell succeeded in amending the bill to ban racial segregation; Southern segregationists aligned themselves with Northern conservatives to defeat it.

In August 1957, after debating sixty-three days, Congress passed a new civil rights law—the first since Reconstruction—to give federal protection to Negroes wanting to vote. In eight Southern states with an adult Negro population of over 3,750,000, only 850,000 or 23 per cent were even registered, and still fewer went to the polls. In a 1955 election in Mississippi, only about 1 per cent of the adult Negroes voted. The civil rights act empowered the federal government to remove some of the obstacles that state and local officials were allegedly placing in the way of Negro registration and voting. Federal judges were empowered to enjoin state officials from refusing to register qualified persons, and might fine recalcitrant officials up to $300 and sentence them to forty-five days in jail without jury trial.

The Re-election of Eisenhower

IN SEPTEMBER 1955, thanks to his apparent triumphs at the Geneva summit conference, President Eisenhower was at the height of his popularity. A second term would clearly be his for the choosing. Only the Twenty-second Amendment, prohibiting a third term and ratified in 1951 as a belated slap at Roosevelt, seemed to bar him from staying in the White House as long as he chose. Apparently his health was excellent, but while vacationing in Denver, on the morning of September 24, he suffered a heart attack.

The President began to make a promising recovery, but no one expected he could possibly run for another term. In the weeks that followed, he demonstrated that despite his illness he was keeping a skillful grip upon the political reins. He maintained public confidence by keeping the press informed frankly of the most intimate details of his health. During his long hospitalization in Denver and his convalescence in Gettysburg, he began to "ease" rather than "bulldoze" his way back into his presidential duties. Even while in the hospital, Eisenhower consulted with many of his cabinet members and advisers, weeks earlier than customary, on his State of the Union message to Congress. He gave the impression that he was continuing personally to make vital policy decisions. No one objected

Vice-President Richard Nixon
(NATIONAL ARCHIVES)

because he delegated many of his ceremonial functions to Vice-President Nixon and his routine duties to other subordinates. He cut drastically and permanently the unnecessarily large number of times he had to sign his name.

In his message to Congress of January 1956, the President called for a number of measures to build "an ever-stronger, ever-better America." Those of an economic nature included aid to farmers, development of Western water resources, and federal highway building. Those relating to human welfare included aid to education, expansion of social security for the aged and ill, promotion of voluntary health insurance and medical research, continued building of public housing, reform of immigration laws, improved labor legislation, and investigation of state discrimination against Negroes. It was a comprehensive program that, in scope if not in dimensions of proposals, was very much like that of the Democratic leaders in Congress. They were quick to proclaim that the President had become a New Dealer or Fair Dealer. Nonetheless, Eisenhower retained the confidence of more conservative Republicans through promising a balanced budget and continued encouragement to business.

The President followed this pronouncement with a budget message in which he discarded the retrenchment policies so forcefully followed in the first two years of his administration. He proposed 15 to 30 per cent larger funds for numerous appropriation-starved Federal agencies, such as the Federal Trade Commission and the Securities and Exchange Commission, which badly needed the money in order to police corporations properly. He proposed federal aid to states to help fight juvenile delinquency and for improvement of airports. Altogether, he proposed more public spending than his Democratic predecessors, a total of $66,300,000,000, and this in an election year. The rapidly expanding American economy was bringing in such a heavy tax yield that it was possible for him to do all this yet achieve what to millions of American voters was still a vital goal, a balanced budget.

A panel of doctors met with the press in February 1956 to state that the scar on the President's heart muscle had healed. It was almost an anticlimax when Eisenhower stated that he would run again. In June, stricken a second time, he was operated upon for ileitis. Although the operation was serious, Eisenhower's advisers never let the question arise whether he would continue as a candidate—and except among some Democrats it seemed a matter above debate. At the Republican convention in San Francisco at the end of August, Eisenhower and Vice-President Nixon were renominated by acclamation. The proceedings seemed to some observers to reflect more the atmosphere of a coronation than a party convention. Even while the President was recuperating from his heart attack, public-opinion polls attested to his overwhelming popularity. Regardless of this, Stevenson and Kefauver fought vigorously for the Democratic nomination in state primary after primary. In the end, Stevenson triumphed at the Democratic convention and Kefauver became the Vice-Presidential nominee.

The campaign foreshadowed the outcome, in that it made clear how relatively middle-of-the-road the leadership was in each party. Republicans and Democrats alike pledged to advance the personal security and living standards of individuals (especially farmers), to ameliorate racial discrimination, to improve education, and most important of all, to foster international peace. It was a rather dull campaign, conducted in an unusually gentlemanly fashion. The novelty of both candidates was gone, in contrast to four years earlier. The urgency of the 1952 campaign, conducted amidst fighting in Korea and fear of Stalin overseas, combined with McCarthyism and charges of a "mess in Washington" at home—all this was gone. The new problems were too complex for the average voter to fathom, and most voters considered them of little real importance. Administration supporters fostered this atmosphere of complacency.

On domestic policy, the main differences were ones of degree rather than principle. Democrats declared that Republicans had sabotaged welfare legislation and had favored the rich at the expense of the poor,

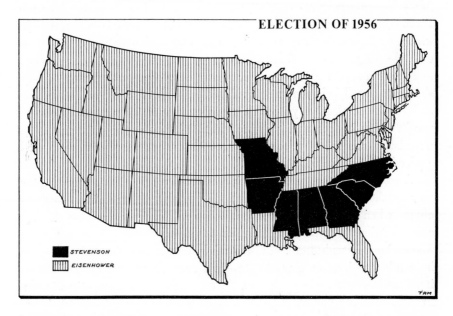

ELECTION OF 1956

STEVENSON
EISENHOWER

but on this issue failed to persuade the electorate to vote for Stevenson. In the realm of foreign policy, Stevenson proposed that the United States agree to end hydrogen bomb tests, and warned that the administration's foreign policy had reached a point of total bankruptcy. Voters were confused or indifferent until the closing days of the campaign. The average voter, relieved because the stalemate in nuclear weapons seemed to rule out a third world war, refused to worry about the new tactics of Moscow (and Cairo) until actual shooting in the Suez area just before election day sent him to seek refuge with Eisenhower as commander in chief. Altogether, about 58 per cent of the voters marked their ballots for Eisenhower, although he was 66, the oldest man ever to be re-elected to the Presidency, and had suffered two serious illnesses in little more than a year past. He received 35,582,000 votes to 26,029,000 for Stevenson, and carried 41 states.

While the Eisenhower landslide was a conservative victory insofar as it indicated the wish of voters to retain what they had previously enjoyed, it was not much of a triumph for the Republican party. It was a vote less for the party than for the President, who had done much to consolidate the changes of the previous twenty-four years in domestic and foreign policy. In the country as a whole, in state and local elections, the people voted Democratic by a slim margin. The prestige of the President pulled some Republican Congressmen to narrow victories, but the Democrats won control over both houses of Congress, and by almost the same margin as in 1954. The Senate had 50 Democrats and 46 Republicans; the House of Representatives, 233 Democrats and 202 Republicans. This enabled the Democrats to organize both houses and continue to hold the important chairmanships of committees. The new Congress, like the old, was dominated by men of both parties fairly co-operative with the President.

Eisenhower's Second Administration

THE ELECTION, which had done so much to confirm the status quo, was the prelude to President Eisenhower's second administration, in which, on domestic matters, little changed. In 1957, Congress, in addition to passing a civil rights act, occupied itself largely with trying to slash the President's $71,800,000,000 budget, the largest in peacetime history. Even Secretary of the Treasury Humphrey (who resigned a few months later) joined in the onslaught against the "terrific" expenditures. He added that if taxes were not cut, "I will predict that you will have a depression that will curl your hair." Considering the rate at which the nation's economy had expanded, the budget did not seem exorbitant to liberal Democrats or to Eisenhower's wing of the Republican party.

At first President Eisenhower seemed acquiescent as conservatives in both major parties, abetted by some liberal Democrats, began trimming appropriations. Then, in May 1957, he began to fight for the budget, especially for mutual-aid appropriations. At first his press and television statements met little but public indifference, but gradually he won back some of the funds. "The road to this disaster [of war]," he declared, "could easily be paved with the good intentions of those blindly striving to save the money that must be spent as the price of peace." Nevertheless, the cuts in the final budget totaled about $4,000,000,000, of which the President had agreed to about half and the remainder were in large part bookkeeping devices.

Domestic considerations seemed trivial by January 1958, in the shadow of the new Russian intercontinental ballistic missiles and satellites. President Eisenhower again presented Congress with a large budget: a billion dollars more than the one which had produced such a great outcry. It emphasized missiles defense and scientific research and development at the expense of more conventional armaments and domestic spending. The President declared that it established a "priority of national security over lesser needs." Military critics complained that it would increase the nation's strength in the event of nuclear war but weaken its capacity for limited war. Some Democrats criticized the cutbacks in domestic programs. While the National Science Foundation received a large increase for basic research, and the President recommended funds for scientific education, he deleted his request for school buildings. The combination of heavy defense expenditures and a sharp recession led to a deficit of nearly thirteen billion dollars by the end of the 1959 fiscal year, a new peacetime high.

Intermittently, the President exercised his leadership to obtain what he wanted from Congress. He helped push through defense and foreign-aid appropriations, a measure reorganizing the Department of Defense, and an unprecedented four-year extension of the reciprocal trade program. For the most part he left leadership to the Democrats in Congress, which meant especially to two moderate Texans, Speaker of the House Sam Rayburn and Senate Majority Leader Lyndon B. Johnson. They obtained passage of bills embodying the President's requests but containing Democratic modifications. In addition to laws already mentioned, Congress passed measures creating a Federal space agency, lowering the price supports on cotton, rice, and corn, and regulating labor union welfare and pension funds. It voted statehood for Alaska, which in January 1959 became the forty-ninth and largest state. The following Congress quickly voted statehood for Hawaii, which in August 1959, became the fiftieth state.

Outside of the South, a variety of state or regional issues, together with the national one of economic distress, set the tone of the campaign of 1958. President Eisenhower, who through his years in the White House had demonstrated little love for politics, late in the campaign made a series of speeches in which he charged the Democrats with being radicals who were ready to steer the economy toward socialism. Vice-President Nixon campaigned in a similarly militant fashion. The charges were so far at variance with the obvious moderation of the Democratic leadership in Congress and of most Democratic candidates that the warnings did not impress the voters.

Some of the more conservative Republican candidates, most notably

Senate Minority Leader William Knowland, running for governor of California, centered their campaigns around attacks on organized labor. In some states they sought "right-to-work" laws to outlaw union shops (plants in which every employee hired must join the union). This sort of onslaught in most states succeeded only in insuring a large labor vote for Democratic candidates. The Republican party was also weakened by the revelation in the spring of 1958 that Sherman Adams, in effect the President's chief of staff, had received gifts from a New England textile manufacturer. Adams resigned in September, too late to benefit the party. In contrast, the Democratic party was less plagued with factional quarrels (like that which wrecked the Republicans in California), was better organized, and presented more attractive and more liberal candidates.

The result on November 4, 1958, was a Democratic landslide of impressive proportions. The Democrats won 13 additional seats in the Senate, giving them a 62 to 34 majority. They gained an added 47 seats in the House of Representatives, providing a majority of 282 to 153—the largest margin since Roosevelt's 1936 victory. Two weeks later Alaska held its first congressional election, adding 2 Senators and 1 Representative to the Democratic totals. The Democrats also won additional governorships and control of several more state legislatures. Many right-wing Republicans, such as Knowland, running for Governor of California, and Senator John Bricker of Ohio, were defeated, while the personable and liberal Republican candidate for Governor of New York, Nelson Rockefeller, won by a margin of more than a half-million votes.

The electorate seemed to have moved decisively, as in New Deal–Fair Deal years, to a position slightly to the left of center. It was primarily an urban shift, research experts of the Republican National Committee concluded. "The reaction against Republicans was manifested particularly (though by no means exclusively) in areas of heavy unemployment," they reported. In seventeen large cities other than New York the Republican congressional vote had dropped 17 per cent. Taking a broader view, Walter Lippmann inquired, "What is this tide which has brought in both Rockefeller and a great Democratic majority?" His answer was, "It is propelled by the growing conviction, based on personal experience of living in countless American communities, that our public needs are not being adequately met."

The voter reaction in 1958 had slight effect upon the national administration in the two years that followed. President Eisenhower presented Congress in January 1959 with a $77,000,000,000 budget, which he promised would be in balance—a budget which northern Democrats decried as not sufficiently large in an expanding economy and not providing the services the nation needed. At first the Democrats in Congress gave promise of pushing far beyond the President's limited requests. But as a renewed sweep of prosperity wiped out the recession in the spring of 1959, public opinion began to react to the incessant warnings of the President and of conservative publicists that budget balancing was the only way to avoid another ruinous round of inflation. Eisenhower, acting more vigorously than in previous years, was able to marshal much public support and congressional voting strength for his conservative course. Speaker Sam Rayburn and Senate Majority Leader Lyndon Johnson were more disposed to compromise than to throw their large Democratic majorities against him. Again and again he vetoed measures, and with one exception (an omnibus public works "pork barrel" bill) sufficient northern Republicans and southern Democrats coalesced to uphold his vetoes. Indeed, the Democratic leaders in Congress themselves engaged in budget-cutting. As a result, Eisenhower succeeded in keeping at a low level expenditures for inexpensive public housing for families displaced from slums, and for other similar social services.

The most notable piece of legislation passed by the first session of the Eighty-sixth Congress was a relatively conservative revision of the Taft-Hartley Act. This was the result of a congressional investigation of labor racketeering begun in 1957. Union-controlled welfare funds to provide benefits for workers had mushroomed into millions of dollars, which in the absence of government regulation could provide tempting spoils for a few dishonest officials, and these few in turn provided a field of activity for notorious racketeers and gangsters.

The investigation focused on the powerful and conservative Teamsters' Brotherhood. The Senate committee charged the president of the Teamsters, David Beck, with the possible misappropriation of over $320,000 in union funds. When Beck appeared before the committee, he refused to answer questions, invoking the Fifth Amendment against self-incrimination. Ultimately the committee brought forth so much evidence against Beck that he did not stand for re-election as president of the Teamsters. But at their convention the Teamsters defiantly elected as their new president James Hoffa, also under attack by the Senate Committee. His election led to the eviction of the Teamsters, the largest union in the United States, from the AFL-CIO.

On the basis of evidence gathered in the hearings, Senator John Kennedy framed a bill primarily protecting the rights of the rank-and-file members of unions. More conservative members of Congress, with strong White House backing, forced into the final measure disciplinary restraints against unions. The main provisions of the Labor Reform Act of 1959 were:

A "bill of rights" for union members to guarantee them secret elections of union officials, fair and public hearings in union disciplinary actions against them, protection of union funds through trusteeship regulations and the filing of detailed reports with the Secretary of Labor, and the banning of Communists and those convicted of certain crimes from union offices.

Restraints upon unions through an expansion of the Taft-Hartley restrictions on secondary boycotting, the prohibition of picketing to obtain union recognition if an employer had legally entered into an agreement with another union, and a granting to state labor boards of jurisdiction over disputes between unions and small businesses of a sort previously rejected by the National Labor Relations Board.

The over-all effect of the Labor Reform Act of 1959 seemed to be rather like that of the Taft-Hartley Act—not harmful for strong unions, even the Teamsters. Few employers would dare invoke the law against them. Indeed, the picketing provision was more likely to lead to increased collusion in the signing of contracts between employers and dishonest union officials. On the other hand, the new measure would handicap relatively weak unions and the spread of unions into unorganized industries. The sharing of jurisdiction with state labor boards would stimulate restrictive state legislation.

Altogether, President Eisenhower had succeeded in restricting the course of the heavily Democratic Congress within markedly conservative bounds.

The American People in Midcentury

IN THE FIFTIES the American people were enjoying a living standard far beyond any they had previously known. The output of goods and services, measured in dollars of equal purchasing power, had doubled since the twenties. Even allowing for inflation and heavy taxation, the average American had 16 per cent more income by 1956 than in 1947, and 53 per cent more than in 1929. Family income had more than tripled since the boom year 1918. A remarkable redistribution of the wealth had taken place also. In 1929, the top 5 per cent of the population received a third of the income; by 1956, they received only 18 per cent. Among city families, in 1929 only 15 per cent earned the equivalent of $4,000 to $7,500 per year (in dollars of the fifties); in 1956, 43 per cent did.

Labor's share of the national income rose from 18 per cent in 1929 to 29 per cent in 1956, while the average work week decreased from 44 hours to 40 hours. The industrial worker enjoyed 15 or 20 hours a week more free time than had his father or grandfather at the turn of the century. Unlike them, upon retirement he could look forward to a pension; welfare and pension plans had increased twentyfold since 1929.

Because of their higher income, workers in the fifties were spending a smaller percentage of their wages for food, clothing, and housing, and more for automobiles, medical care, recreation, and vacations. The statistics on national consumption in 1956 in total were staggering: food, $71,300,000,000; housing, $48,100,000,000; automobile transportation,

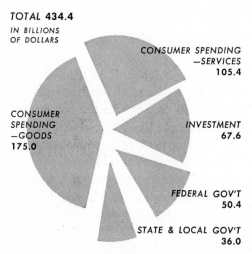

TOTAL 434.4
IN BILLIONS
OF DOLLARS

CONSUMER SPENDING
—SERVICES
105.4

CONSUMER
SPENDING
—GOODS
175.0

INVESTMENT
67.6

FEDERAL GOV'T
50.4

STATE & LOCAL GOV'T
36.0

Disposition of Gross National Product, 1956

$27,000,000,000. Ninety-six per cent of American families had refrigerators; four out of five, a television set; three out of four, at least one car; three out of five owned their own home; and one in ten even had air conditioning. In 1945 there were only 9,000 swimming pools in use; in 1957 alone 55,000 were installed.

But the picture was not entirely cheerful. As late as 1951, one family in six was living on only $1,500 per year or less. This meant existence in dwellings little better than shacks in the country, or in slums in the cities. For many millions more, adequate housing was either a dream or an extravagance. The National Housing Conference estimated in 1957 that only one city family in six was earning enough to buy satisfactory housing without spending over one fifth of its income.

Since the turn of the century, women had entered the working force in increasing numbers. In 1900, half the adult women had never in their lives held jobs; by the fifties, one third of the women over fourteen were working, and nine tenths had worked at one time or another. The old-fashioned "career woman," refusing marriage, was nearly gone; only 7 per

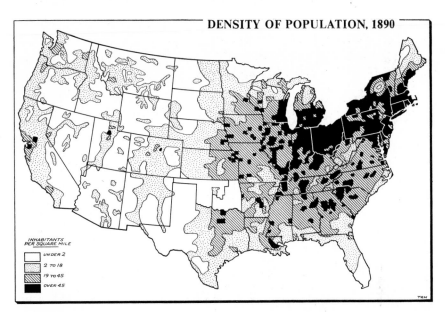

DENSITY OF POPULATION, 1890

INHABITANTS
PER SQUARE MILE

UNDER 2
2 TO 18
19 TO 45
OVER 45

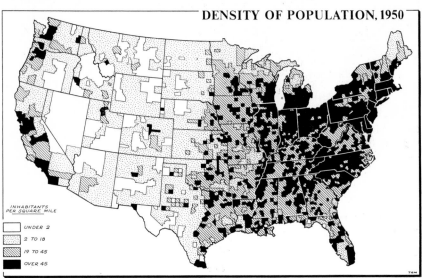

DENSITY OF POPULATION, 1950

INHABITANTS
PER SQUARE MILE

UNDER 2
2 TO 18
19 TO 45
OVER 45

cent of women failed to marry. The modern counterpart of the girls who had worked in the Lowell textile mills in the 1830's were the airline hostesses; on one of the largest airlines they stayed an average of only twenty-six months, and 85 per cent of them left to be married. Women were filling an increasing number of professional positions, but still were not being trained in keeping with their potentialities. Only a quarter of those capable of finishing college were doing so; only 1 in 300 of those qualified was earning a Ph.D. degree.

Instrument panel in a chemical plant (DU PONT)

Negroes rapidly were improving their working and economic status. By 1957 the average Negro wage-earner was receiving four and a half times as much as in 1940; the number in professional work had increased 103 per cent; skilled workers, 181 per cent, and clerical and sales workers, 223 per cent. More than 98 per cent of Negro children between seven and thirteen were attending school, and Negro college enrollment was increasing six times as fast as white enrollment. A third of the Negroes owned their own homes. Compared with the population of Italy, which was about the same size as the American Negro population, they were affluent, but their incomes still averaged far below those of white Americans.

The key to continued future prosperity seemed to be a rapidly expanding population and increased productivity. In the thirties the expectation was that the population would be 140,000,000 in 1960; actually it was well past 170,000,000 before that date. A tidal wave of children was hitting schools and colleges in the late fifties. They would soon be marrying, raising their own families, and buying ever-increasing quantities of consumer goods. The way to increase production to supply them seemed to lie in more and more automation. The precision machinery being installed in Detroit and elsewhere could turn out high-quality products far more rapidly than previous methods. The problem was one of keeping costs down. In Detroit the cost of tooling—preparing the machines and dies to turn out the models of a single year—went up from $1,400,000,000 for 1954 to nearly $2,000,000,000 for the year 1956. The reason for the increase was almost entirely automation.

Along with the increase in production the United States began to change from a "have" to a "have-not" nation in natural resources. Between 1900 and 1950 the production of bituminous coal rose two and a half times, of copper three times, of iron ore three and a half times, and of crude oil thirty times. Now the largest importer of copper, lead, and zinc, the United States was becoming dependent upon other nations for its raw materials, leading to a flow of dollars overseas. Within the United States, producers were having to learn methods of conservation or were turning to the development of synthetics. As the rich iron deposits began to dwindle, steel companies developed processes to make use of lower-grade ore, and opened new ore deposits in Labrador and elsewhere.

Already the United States was beginning to develop electric power from atomic energy. Two small power plants were completed in 1957, and fourteen more were planned or under construction. Altogether they had a capacity of more than 1,000,000 kilowatts of electric power—compared with the 900,000 kilowatts comprising the United States share from the great St. Lawrence water-power project being constructed at the same time. Economical nuclear reactors had yet to be developed, but with few major hydroelectric sites remaining in the United States, atomic energy seemed to be the key to future expansion of electric power.

Applications of scientific knowledge, both civilian and military, were being developed at such a rapid pace that they created a sharp pressure for additional basic research. A Department of Defense research officer declared in 1957, "We have been chewing up the findings of basic research since World War II at a speed faster than they are being produced in the labs and ivory towers." In 1945 Dr. Vannevar Bush, who was wartime director of the Office of Scientific Research and Development, had proposed establishment of a peacetime government agency to promote basic research. The United States could no longer depend upon Europe, Bush warned; Congress in 1950 established the National Science Foundation but limited its annual appropriations to $15,000,000 per year, and appropriated less than that until the 1956 fiscal year. In the 1959 budget, after the "sputnik crisis," President Eisenhower asked for $140,000,000 for the National Science Foundation. Meanwhile, through a number of other agencies, the federal government by 1957 was spending $3,377,000,000 for research and development. Of each dollar, 60 cents was spent for development, 32 cents for applied research, and only 8 cents for basic research. Industry by 1953–54 was spending an additional $3,900,000,000 for research—only 4 per cent of it for basic research.

The most comprehensive and spectacular of basic research enterprises, in which the United States co-operated with sixty-two other countries including Russia, was the International Geophysical Year, running from

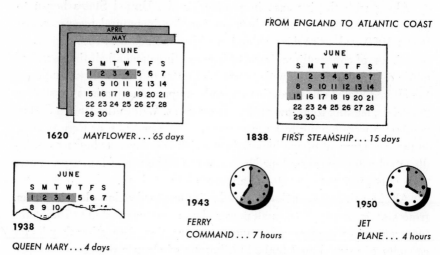

Time Needed to Cross the Atlantic, 1620–1950

July 1, 1957 to the end of 1958. It involved exploring the globe from pole to pole, and from ionosphere to core, and included the launching of earth satellites and the establishment of an American base at the South Pole itself.

In medical research, the most important advance was the development of an effective polio vaccine by Dr. Jonas Salk of the University of Pittsburgh. The vaccine was first used on a large scale in 1955, and within two years the polio rate in the United States dropped 80 per cent. Advances in medical research, extensive public health programs, private health insurance plans covering 73 per cent of the people—all these contributed to a lengthening life span. In 1900, life expectancy had been forty-nine years; by 1955, it was seventy years.

Improved technology made air travel, a luxury before the Second World War, a commonplace in the decade afterward. Travelers abandoned passenger trains for private automobiles and buses for short distances, and for airplanes for long distances. While railroads cut back their passenger service, airlines rapidly expanded. By 1954 they were carrying 32,000,000 passengers a year. The air lanes were already so crowded, despite a safety interval of ten minutes between airplanes, that near-collisions were frequent. One spectacular collision over the Grand Canyon killed 128 persons. Airlines rushed to install more electronic safety equipment as they switched to faster airplanes to carry far more passengers.

The postwar decade marked the advent of television, as the twenties did that of radio. In 1947 fewer than 10,000 people owned television sets with which they could view programs a few hours a day from a handful of stations. A decade later over 40,000,000 sets in American homes, hotels, and bars were tuned in to 467 stations. Motion-picture attendance dropped from a wartime high of 90,000,000 a week to about 40,000,000. Television, even more than radio, meant mass communication to nationwide audience. One musical show presented over 245 stations one night in March 1957 reached an estimated audience of 100,000,000—enough people to fill a Broadway theater every night for 165 years. In the 1952 campaign, television seemed to have remade presidential elections as both candidates made extensive and expensive use of the new medium. By 1956 the effect had somewhat worn off. President Eisenhower received an audience rating one night of only 17.9 compared with 27.6 for his TV adviser, Robert Montgomery, appearing on another network. While television served as the great outlet for the new leisure of many people, more persons than ever before were engaging in outdoor recreation and do-it-yourself home crafts. Patronage of the arts flourished—attendance at the theater, concerts, and exhibitions, and participation in theatrical and musical groups and "Sunday painting." Sales of good books as well as trash in paper covers, and of inexpensive phonograph records, both classics and rock-and-roll, mounted astronomically. Never had so many people participated so deeply and enthusiastically in the arts.

Pioneers in the arts of the twenties and thirties became the accepted pillars of the fifties. Frank Lloyd Wright appeared on TV, and modern architecture became commonplace. Eugene O'Neill's plays enjoyed long runs on Broadway after his death. Ernest Hemingway and William Faulkner became two of the patriarchs of writing for the Western world as well as the United States. Hemingway at times seemed to be parodying his earlier virile, trenchant style; Faulkner retained his master's touch in portraying the deep South he knew so well, and through it seeing the world. New novelists created temporary sensations and achieved best-selling success with their interpretations of the war and the postwar world, but to their contemporaries in the fifties, none seemed to approach

William Faulkner (BROWN BROTHERS)

the talent of the leaders of the "lost generation." Faulkner, when he received the Nobel Prize in 1950, set forth what he considered to be the novelist's task:

> It is [his] privilege to help man endure by lifting his heart, by reminding him of the courage and honor and pride and compassion and pity and sacrifice which have been the glory of his past. The poet's voice need not merely be the record of man, it can be one of the props, the pillars to help him endure and prevail.

One task of all responsible citizens in the fifties was to improve the schools of the nation. A serious teacher shortage existed as the nation prepared for an influx of students well beyond the existing teaching and classroom capacity. State and local school authorities, spending approximately two billion dollars a year on new schools, were doing no more than keeping up, not eliminating the accumulated shortages or preparing for future needs. Universities likewise faced problems of expansion of their student

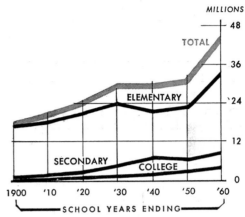

School Enrollment, 1900–1960

bodies and their physical plants without sacrificing the level of their teaching. Men and women of high quality were needed as instructors in institutions ranging from kindergarten through graduate schools.

In the new technical age, when the United States was having to assume positive leadership in the world, the demands upon American youth, whatever their backgrounds, whether they were preparing for farming, the trades, or the professions, were far more exacting than ever before. Standards had been constantly raised, and must be raised steadily higher.

Chapter **23**

A NUCLEAR BALANCE
OF TERROR

DURING THE EISENHOWER ADMINISTRATION, the perils and challenge of the clash between the Western democracies and the Communist world overshadowed all else. The basic policies of the United States toward Russia had already been well established by the beginning of the fifties and those toward China had evolved rapidly during the Korean war. The new administration, which had come into power in part at least through capitalizing upon popular discontent with the Truman-Acheson foreign policy, tried to formulate new approaches. These gave little promise of the firm security which the public so anxiously sought. Instead the United States and the Western nations continued to maintain only a precarious balance in the seesawing power struggle with Russia, China, and their satellites. Upon the maintenance of the balance depended the fate of the nation—indeed, perhaps even the very survival of mankind.

Regardless of the new doctrines enunciated by Secretary of State John Foster Dulles, diplomacy between the United States and Russia centered in a race for superiority in nuclear weapons. Although the Russians had exploded an atomic bomb as early as 1949, the United States continued to hold a lead sufficiently impressive to deter the Communist bloc from launching a full-scale war even though the Communist nations had a preponderance of manpower and conventional weapons. In turn, Russian might was a counterdeterrent against the West. At the end of the Korean war, Secretary Dulles committed the Eisenhower administration to move from the earlier policy of containment of Communism toward a more dynamic one promising liberation of satellite countries. He soon had to back down and turned instead to issuing warnings that the United States would meet aggression with "massive retaliation." Through reliance upon atomic weapons rather than huge land armies, the administration sought to contain Russia and China yet balance the budget. It failed to halt further penetration because the Russians countered with a more flexible foreign policy of their own, and year by year narrowed the American lead in nuclear weapons. By the crisis year 1957, Russia appeared in some categories to assume the lead.

Secretary Dulles and Policy Toward China

THE MAN who assumed a large degree of responsibility for countering the threats from Russia and China during the first six years of the Eisenhower administration was Secretary of State Dulles. Although he had reputedly been the highest paid corporation lawyer in the history of New York, his whole career to 1953 had led toward serving as head of the State Department. He was the grandson of one Secretary, John Foster, under Benjamin Harrison, and nephew of another, Robert Lansing under Wilson. He accompanied his grandfather to the Hague Conference of 1907 when he was only 19, attended the Versailles Conference, was foreign policy adviser to the Republican candidate, Dewey, in the campaigns of 1944 and 1948, helped found the United Nations, negotiated the Japanese peace treaty, and wrote a castigation of Democratic foreign policy into the Republican platform of 1952. As Secretary of State from 1953 to 1959 he gave the impression of formulating policy decisions out of his own head. He was a sturdy moralist, a skilled and stubborn advocate, and a tireless worker. He seemed to feel that he must participate personally in innumerable top-level negotiations all over the globe. Since as Secretary he flew 479,286 miles outside of the United States, his detractors liked to wisecrack that he was demonstrating an infinite capacity for taking planes. Assuming much of the normal functions of State Department officials, diplomats, and even the President, he dominated the determination and negotiation of foreign policy. President Eisenhower was said to have remarked once, "If anything happened to Foster, where could I find a man able to replace him?" To the President, he was a trusted, almost indispensable man.

The policies which Dulles had to revise most vigorously were those concerning Asia, which had been under the most sharp attack from the right wing of the Republican party, and which posed acute problems because of the continuing pressures from Communist China. The Eisenhower administration had come into office firmly committed to existing collective-security arrangements and a Europe-first priority. Nevertheless it maintained a tenuous compromise with the ardently nationalistic Asia-first wing of the party. This group was exploiting at home the thesis that setbacks in Asia were due to internal subversion in the Truman administration, that Communist aggression in Asia must be met with military force, and that economic aid to remove the grievances the Communists were exploiting was a waste of money. Their hero was Chiang Kai-shek, and their enemy Red China, which must be curbed or destroyed at all

Secretary of State John Foster Dulles reporting to President Eisenhower and to the nation over television, May 17, 1955 (DEPARTMENT OF STATE)

costs. Concurring with this group at some points were the business leaders dominant in the Eisenhower administration, who were determined that defense expenditures must fit within a balanced budget.

The pressures of these groups helped lead to significant decisions in 1953. An immediate, minor one was Dulles's refusal to support those in the State Department who had incurred the wrath of the Asia-firsters. When the cases of two such career officers came before him for review, although there was nothing in their records indicating lack of loyalty, he retired them anyway. More important was a basic shift in foreign policy necessitated because again, as before the Korean war, a movement began to reduce the military establishment. At the same time, the Eisenhower administration wished to meet the Communist challenge in Indochina and elsewhere. The solution seemed to lie in a "new look" in defense policy, equally pleasing to the Secretaries of Defense, the Treasury, and State. This meant a cutting of the expensive army ground forces, and low expenditures on unproven missiles research and basic scientific research. Secretary of Defense Charles E. Wilson, an expert on practical matters of automobile production, defined basic research as "when you don't know what you are doing." Instead the United States would depend especially upon its thermonuclear weapons and their delivery by the air force. Popularized, this was the policy of "more bang for a buck." The new administration thus reduced defense expenditures by about 10 per cent and assured the public it was producing more security than before.

A new foreign policy was necessary to make the "new look" in defense operate adequately. Secretary of the Treasury George M. Humphrey, looking at it from a standpoint of cost, asserted that the United States had "no business getting into little wars." If the nation had to intervene, he declared, "let's intervene decisively with all we have got or stay out." This was the economic basis for Secretary of State Dulles's policy of "massive retaliation." The United States would depend less on local defense, he declared in an address on January 12, 1954, and depend more on "the deterrent of massive retaliatory power . . . a great capacity to retaliate instantly, by means and at times of our own choosing." Upon occasion, so Dulles declared two years later, this policy brought the United States close to war, but it brought the desired results. In January 1956, *Life* magazine quoted him:

> The ability to get to the verge without getting into the war is the necessary art. If you cannot master it, you inevitably get into war. If you try to run away from it, if you are scared to go to the brink, you are lost. We've had to look it square in the face—on the question of enlarging the Korean War, on the question of getting into the Indochina war, on the question of Formosa. We walked to the brink and we looked it in the face. We took strong action.

Critics of Dulles, within the United States and abroad, suggested that "brinkmanship" had not worked in this salutary fashion. Rather, they suggested, war-weariness on both sides and mutual fear of atomic retaliation led to compromise solutions in Korea and Indochina and to a continued *modus vivendi* over Formosa.

The Indochina crisis was the first important illustration of the new Eisenhower-Dulles policies in operation. Undoubtedly the end of the Korean war did enable the Chinese Reds to provide at least indirect aid to the Communist general in Indochina at a time when the French were tottering on the edge of military disaster. The French, who had been slow and reluctant in giving firm guarantees of independence, for eight years had been fighting the Indochinese Communist leader, Ho Chi Minh. Even before the Korean armistice, President Eisenhower and Secretary of State Dulles had voiced warnings that an armistice must not release Chinese troops or supplies for use in either Indochina or Malaya, but had done nothing. In the spring of 1954, the Communist forces besieged a French and Vietnamese army of 12,000 in the frontier fortress of Dienbienphu. Already the United States was underwriting 70 per cent of the French financial cost of the war, but without direct military aid, Dienbienphu and perhaps all of Indochina would be lost.

At a press conference, President Eisenhower likened the nations in Southeast Asia to a row of dominoes. The moral was implicit; the first domino must not be allowed to fall. Many of the President's advisers favored at least bombing the besieging army with carrier-based planes, but Dulles failed to gain support among allied nations. Congressional leaders had no stomach for an intervention which might soon involve more ground troops than the Korean war, and in which the United States might have to fight alone. The United States did not intervene; Dienbienphu fell on May 7, 1954. At a conference in Geneva, the United States, stripped of bargaining power (except for the threat of unilateral intervention), had to stand by, neither associating itself with negotiations with Red China nor approving of agreements, in July 1954, which provided for a cease-fire and partitioning of Indochina.

After the Geneva Conference, Secretary Dulles succeeded in building a Southeast Asia Treaty Organization (SEATO) in September 1954 to serve as a counterpart of NATO and help contain Communism. It was far less impressive, since the terms of the Geneva conference kept the nations of Indochina (Vietnam, Laos, and Cambodia) from participating. Nationalist China was no longer recognized by Great Britain and could not join for that reason; several of the most important Asiatic states (India, Ceylon, Burma, and Indonesia) refused to join because they were committed to neutralism. This left only three nations of Southeast Asia, Pakistan, Thailand, and the Philippines, to join with the United States, Great Britain, France, Australia, and New Zealand. They drew up a pact, weaker than the North Atlantic Treaty, providing only that an attack upon one would be regarded as a threat to the others. It did open the way for economic and military aid, but without the key nations of Southeast Asia participating it remained a relatively ineffective organization.

The United States continued to function in Asia as best it could on a virtually unilateral basis. Trouble with Communist China developed over some islands immediately off the mainland which Chiang continued to garrison—Quemoy, and the Matsu and Tachen Islands. Occasionally Chiang's air force attacked the Communists from them. Since the Mutual

Defense Treaty with Chiang, signed at the end of 1954, did not include these islands, Red China in January 1955 began air attacks upon the Tachens and bombardment of Quemoy. Before invasion could follow, Congress granted President Eisenhower rather indefinite emergency powers to aid Chiang. These sufficed to maintain a precarious status quo.

Intermittently, the Chinese Communists renewed their pressure upon Quemoy and Matsu. In August 1958 they began a serious bombardment of Quemoy. Secretary Dulles, although not always clear in what he said, implied repeatedly that the United States would help Chiang defend the islands. Because these were so close to the mainland, the United States could not count upon the support of other Western nations if a large-scale struggle with Red China developed. Consequently, there was much criticism of Dulles within the United States. In October 1958 he shifted somewhat, implying that if Chinese Communist shelling ceased, the islands might be demilitarized or even abandoned. But even after the attack practically stopped, Chiang failed to follow Dulles's advice to reduce his large forces on the islands. They remained a weak point where the Chinese Communists could exert pressure whenever they wished and force the United States to the point of war. Instead, the militant Chinese Communists in 1959 pressed on other borders. After crushing a revolt in Tibet, they pushed troops across several ill-defined frontiers into areas claimed by India. Of much more serious concern to the United States, they backed a Communist penetration deep into Laos, one of the nations of Indochina.

In the involved and unending struggle with Communist China, the American arsenal of atomic weapons was of relatively little effect even against a nation which as yet did not possess any. In the struggles against Russia with its rapidly expanding nuclear strength this was clearer. The threat of massive thermonuclear retaliation would not alone suffice to keep the Communists at bay.

Underwriting NATO Defenses

FORTUNATELY, the United States and its allies did not depend upon nuclear superiority alone. The concept of the North Atlantic Treaty Organization was embodied in its emblem of a sword and a shield. The sword stood for atomic weapons, the striking force, and the shield for conventional ground forces, to deter or withstand attack. During the Korean war, the United States began to rebuild its military establishment at home and gradually to pour funds into NATO, to strengthen its defenses in terms of ground forces as well as atomic weapons.

Several complications hindered the building of NATO forces. The Congressional bloc led by Senators Taft and Wherry whittled away at economic aid ("defense support") for the western European nations, and the Truman administration, in order to ease the strain on the economy, spent far less than Congress allocated. From 1949 to the fall of 1952, the United States shipped only $2,600,000,000 of military supplies, although $11,000,000,000 had been appropriated. Further, although the Senate in April 1951 approved the sending of four additional divisions to Europe, it specified that no more might be sent without its explicit approval. Within the United States this reluctance to send troops and supplies was reinforced by the slowness of European nations to rebuild their armies, and the resistance to rearmament among many non-Communist left-wing political leaders (such as Aneurin Bevan, who had a large following in the Labor Party in Great Britain).

Reciprocally, Europeans worried over the slowness of the United States to provide arms and men, its failure (partly because of constitutional limitations) to commit itself clearly in advance to resist any armed attack on western European nations, and the American desire to rearm Germany. Rearmament was far more of a strain on living standards in western Europe, where the average annual income was about $600, than in the United States, where it was $1,800. While the French were still afraid of the Germans, the Germans themselves were so war-weary that it was difficult to persuade them to arm again. Between 1950 and 1954 the Germans were able to win back step by step almost all of their sovereignty in return for rearming.

During these years the vexing problem was how the new western European defense force would be constituted. The French proposed a European Defense Community consisting of France, Italy, the Benelux countries (Belgium, The Netherlands, and Luxemburg) and West Germany. It would build a supranational army in which each division would have no more than 12,000 men from the same country and would be under the NATO supreme command. This fragmentation of national forces would circumvent the building of a large German army. But the United States and Germany favored larger national army units, and succeeded in obtaining a provision that integration would be at the level of army corps made up of several divisions. The specter of a resurgent German army led the French Communist deputies and the right-wing nationalists in the French Assembly to unite in August 1954 to defeat ratification of the European Defense Community treaty.

Some new way had to be found to make the rearming of Germany acceptable to France. Great Britain, in October 1954, placated the French by promising to keep four divisions and a tactical air force on the Continent as long as its allies wanted them. With this assurance, France agreed to a treaty that same month restoring full sovereignty to Germany (except for the stationing of allied troops in West Berlin until Germany was reunified). To take the place of the European Defense Community a weak and limited treaty organization, created earlier, was expanded and strengthened into the Western European Union, including all the European Defense Community nations plus Great Britain. National armies would not be scrambled as had been earlier planned, but the West German army was to be limited to twelve divisions, which would be supplied to NATO. Germany promised not to seek reunification or extension of her boundaries through force, and was prohibited from manufacturing atomic, biological, or chemical weapons. Germany joined NATO and thus directly became a military ally of the United States. In 1957, it contributed its first forces, five divisions totaling 120,000 men.

The remilitarization of western Germany, adding as it did to the strength of the allies, led to increased complications with Russia—complications which took new forms in the years after the death of the rigid Stalin.

The Summit Conference: The Russians Shift Tactics

THE COMING INTO POWER of a new group of Russian leaders in the spring of 1953 brought to an end one phase of Russian policy and led to the evolution of a new, more supple one, in some ways even more of a challenge to the United States. Throughout 1953 there were increasing signs that changes were taking place in the Kremlin which might lead to more freedom behind the Iron Curtain and some relaxation of tensions with the Western powers. Russia extended an olive branch to Tito of Yugoslavia, returned a key base to Finland, recognized the Federal Republic of West Germany, and signed a peace treaty with Japan. Most important of all, it joined with Western powers in signing a peace treaty with Austria, making it a neutral state, and terminating the long military occupation.

The softening of Soviet policy and the increase in international exchanges brought pressure from western Europe, Asia, and even within the United States for a conference among the heads of state. In May 1955 the United States agreed to a "summit conference" to consider means of easing international tensions. The State Department later announced:

> The success of Western policies coupled with the consequent apparent change of attitude on the part of the Soviet Union indicated that the time had come when a meeting at the level of Heads of Government might usefully be held.

But the greatest single factor operating within the United States was the knowledge that both the United States and Russia were manufacturing

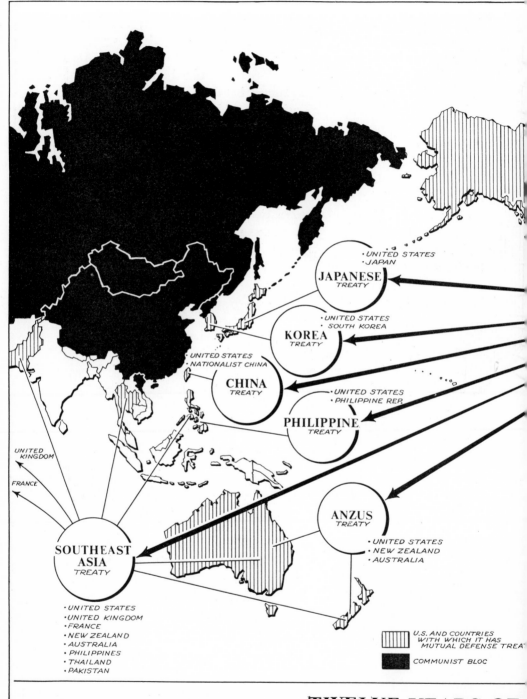

· UNITED STATES
· JAPAN

JAPANESE
TREATY

· UNITED STATES
· SOUTH KOREA

KOREA
TREATY

· UNITED STATES
· NATIONALIST CHINA

CHINA
TREATY

· UNITED STATES
· PHILIPPINE REP.

PHILIPPINE
TREATY

UNITED
KINGDOM

FRANCE

ANZUS
TREATY

· UNITED STATES
· NEW ZEALAND
· AUSTRALIA

**SOUTHEAST
ASIA**
TREATY

· UNITED STATES
· UNITED KINGDOM
· FRANCE
· NEW ZEALAND
· AUSTRALIA
· PHILIPPINES
· THAILAND
· PAKISTAN

U.S. AND COUNTRIES
WITH WHICH IT HAS
MUTUAL DEFENSE TREAT

COMMUNIST BLOC

TWELVE YEARS OF

TRM

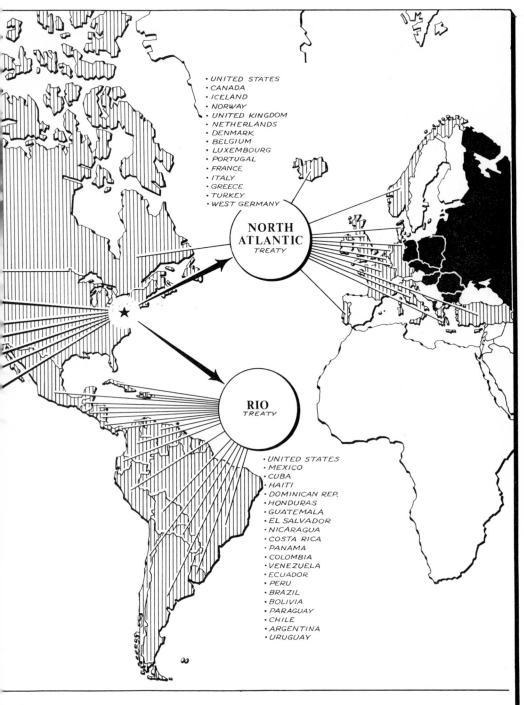

- UNITED STATES
- CANADA
- ICELAND
- NORWAY
- UNITED KINGDOM
- NETHERLANDS
- DENMARK
- BELGIUM
- LUXEMBOURG
- PORTUGAL
- FRANCE
- ITALY
- GREECE
- TURKEY
- WEST GERMANY

NORTH ATLANTIC TREATY

RIO TREATY

- UNITED STATES
- MEXICO
- CUBA
- HAITI
- DOMINICAN REP.
- HONDURAS
- GUATEMALA
- EL SALVADOR
- NICARAGUA
- COSTA RICA
- PANAMA
- COLOMBIA
- VENEZUELA
- ECUADOR
- PERU
- BRAZIL
- BOLIVIA
- PARAGUAY
- CHILE
- ARGENTINA
- URUGUAY

U.S. CONTAINMENT

hydrogen bombs of staggering destructive power. In August 1953 the Russians had exploded a hydrogen bomb. President Eisenhower warned a few weeks later that the physical security of the United States had "almost totally disappeared before the long-range bomber and the destructive power of a single bomb." The meaning of this became dramatically clear in the spring of 1954 when the United States announced that it had exploded a bomb in the Pacific so powerful that it would have destroyed or put out of commission all of New York City.

Against this background, the American people, after an initial wariness, became enthusiastic about the meeting of the heads of the United States, Great Britain, France, and Russia at Geneva in July 1955. President Eisenhower, hopeful that he could wage "a war for peace," proposed at the meetings that the Russians and the United States exchange blueprints of their armed forces and permit inspection of their military installations from the air. He declared to Premier Nicolai A. Bulganin, "The United States will never take part in an aggressive war." Bulganin replied, "Mr. President, we believe that statement."

The affability of Bulganin and Nikita S. Khrushchev at Geneva immensely relieved the American people, who were hopeful for the moment that a real change of policy had come about. This "Geneva spirit," as newspapermen called it, led to a general feeling on the part of most Western nations that a nuclear war between Russia and the United States would not develop. Secretary Dulles declared hopefully that the conference had avoided "creating an illusion that all was now so well that we could safely relax our efforts to build individual and collective self-defense." But in fact, creation of such an illusion for a few brief weeks was the most tangible product of the Geneva Conference. All proposals from both sides had been referred to a foreign ministers' conference that was to meet at the end of October 1955; even before it could meet, several nations began to scale down their NATO obligations.

President Eisenhower upon his return from Geneva warned, "We must never be deluded into believing that one week of friendly, even fruitful negotiations can wholly eliminate a problem arising out of the wide gulf that separates East and West." The American public, less inclined to caution, greeted the President with unrestrained acclaim. He was at the height of his popularity.

The subsequent foreign ministers' conference failed dismally to agree upon German unification, disarmament, or lowering of barriers between Communist nations and the West. Even before it adjourned, the "Geneva spirit" was rapidly evaporating throughout the West. In the United States the new apprehension had been heightened when, at the end of September, President Eisenhower suffered a serious heart attack which required

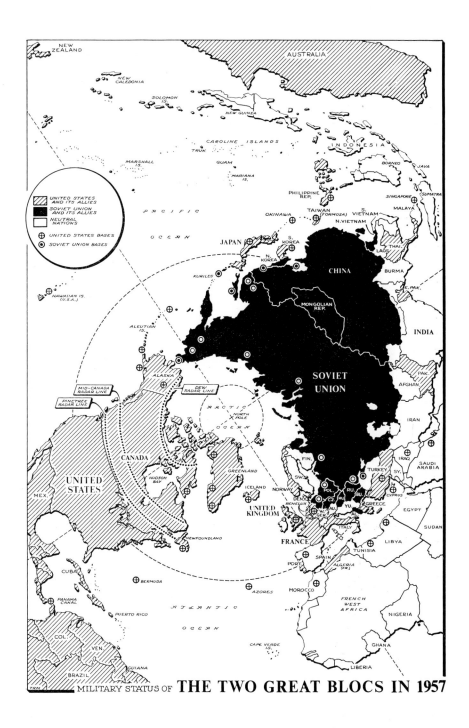

MILITARY STATUS OF **THE TWO GREAT BLOCS IN 1957**

weeks of convalescence. For the time being he could give only limited leadership, as a new Soviet challenge began to take form.

Menace in the Middle East

THE NEW RUSSIAN drive came toward the Middle East, where the United States had long been deeply involved because of its conflicting interests in the populace of the new state of Israel and in the oil of the Arabs. In addition, the State Department strongly desired peace in the whole area in order to develop pro-Western support there. In this aim it was frustrated, and the Middle East in the years after the Second World War continued to be an unstable region from which it was difficult to exclude Russia.

During the war, the British, in order not to offend the Arabs, had continued restrictions upon immigration to Palestine; both political parties in the United States favored lifting these restrictions and creating a Jewish state. After the war, the British brought the problem to the United Nations, which recommended partitioning Palestine between Jews and Arabs. The Jews successfully fought off military attacks from the Arabs, and on the day the British mandate ended, May 14, 1948, proclaimed a new government. President Truman recognized it within a few minutes, thus ending United Nations proposals to put Palestine under a temporary trusteeship. The new nation, Israel, fought off armies from surrounding Arab nations until the United Nations established an unstable truce in 1949. Although the United States tried to promote amity, relations between Israel and its neighbors continued close to the point of explosion, and other quarrels in the Middle East persisted.

Gradually the United States did win over some of the Arab nations to the Western defense system. It leased air bases from Saudi Arabia; and through the Baghdad Pact of February 1955 Secretary Dulles managed to bring the northern bloc of Arab states, Iraq, Iran, and Pakistan, into the defense perimeter.

Countering these successes was the festering sore of Egypt, which for years had quarreled with the British over the Sudan and British bases along the Suez Canal. The United States tried to mediate; in 1954, the British agreed to remove its troops from the Suez area. After Gamal Abdel Nasser came to power, the State Department tried to woo him, although he was proclaiming emphatic neutralist and Arab nationalist policies and striving for leadership of the entire Arab world. Secretary Dulles tried to win him with offers of economic aid—even the sum needed to construct an enormous dam on the Nile. The Russians also offered aid, which was accepted, to the dismay of Western people filled with the "Geneva spirit."

They concluded a deal, made public in September 1955, trading large quantities of armaments in exchange for cotton.

With sufficient Communist arms, Nasser might destroy Israel. He could also threaten the security system the United States was trying to build in the Middle East, since with the arms that went to Nasser and his close ally, Syria, would also go Russian experts to show Egyptians how to use them. Secretary Dulles met the challenge. Instead of continuing to be conciliatory toward Egypt and continuing plans for economic aid, in July 1956 he suddenly withdrew his promise to provide funds for a dam. A week later, Nasser retaliated by seizing the Suez Canal, purportedly to obtain money for the dam. It gave him a stranglehold on the main oil line to Europe, since two thirds of the proven oil reserves of the world were in the Middle East, and four fifths of the oil for western Europe was flowing from there.

During the tedious months of negotiations with Nasser which followed, Great Britain, France, and Israel all came to feel that they were not obtaining as much support as they should from the United States. Meanwhile, the armed strength of Egypt was growing rapidly. On October 29, 1956, Israeli forces struck a preventive blow at Egypt; the next day the British and French intervened to try to drive the Egyptian forces from the Suez Canal zone. They were militarily successful, but not before the Egyptians had thoroughly blocked the canal. The United States led the United Nations in denouncing the military intervention; the Western alliances seemed in danger of dissolving; Russia threatened to send "volunteers" to the aid of Egypt. Under these pressures, the British and French issued a cease-fire order on November 6. Another prolonged truce between Egypt and Israel began under the supervision of the United Nations.

The power vacuum in the Middle East in the weeks after the Suez cease-fire created new opportunities for the spread of Communism. Once again the American public was alarmed and incensed, since coincident with the Suez crisis came brutal Soviet suppression of an uprising in Hungary. Because of the nuclear stalemate, the United States could not intervene in Hungary. It limited itself to fostering United Nations resolutions of censure and to admitting tens of thousands of refugees. In the Middle East it might be possible to take more positive action. The public was receptive when the President appeared before Congress January 5, 1957, to enunciate what came to be called the "Eisenhower Doctrine": "If power-hungry Communists should either falsely or correctly estimate that the Middle East is inadequately defended," the President pointed out, "they might be tempted to use open measures of armed attack. If so, they would start a chain of circumstances which would almost surely involve the United States in military action." He asked Congress to authorize military and economic aid "to secure and protect the territorial independence" of Middle Eastern nations "against overt armed aggression from any nation controlled by international communism."

The Eisenhower Doctrine marked a shift away from Secretary Dulles's "massive retaliation" concept. The United States in 1957 had to recognize that capacity to counter the Soviet Union with nuclear weapons was not enough; in addition it must be prepared to meet aggression in small wars. Congress authorized the President to use armed force as he deemed necessary, and to spend $200,000,000 (without the restrictions of the Mutual Security Act) on economic aid in the area.

As an instrument of pressure upon Egypt, the Eisenhower Doctrine was of little effect. Nasser reopened the Suez Canal on his own terms, and with Soviet aid continued penetration of his neighbors. In April 1957 American policy seemed more successful when the United States rushed its Sixth Fleet to the eastern Mediterranean to bolster the government of Jordan. Three other states, Saudi Arabia, Iraq, and Lebanon, seemed to give at least tacit support to the Eisenhower Doctrine.

Soviet penetration in the next few months, both through feeding Arab nationalism and providing arms to Egypt, Syria, and Yemen, effectively countered the American policy. In August 1957, the Russians negotiated a $500,000,000 arms-and-aid pact with Syria. In its aftermath, a pro-Soviet army clique seized power. Since the clique of course did not ask for American aid, the Eisenhower Doctrine was inoperative in Syria, but the State Department, declaring that Syria's neighbors were alarmed, sent them weapons. The strong tone of the United States led to an unfavorable reaction among the Arab nations, and they reaffirmed their solidarity.

Russia seemed to be moving toward a position of ascendancy in the Middle East. Secretary Dulles told the United Nations:

> The Soviet rulers [have] again made the Middle East the center of their external efforts . . . [and] appear to be engaging in 'acts, direct or indirect, aimed at impairing the freedom, independence or integrity' of certain Near Eastern nations. . . . This is a risky business.

The Russians retorted that the Soviet Union refused to be an impartial observer in the area—and, charging that the United States was trying to incite Turkey to war upon Syria, precipitated a crisis that lasted for several weeks.

Egypt and Syria, combining to form the United Arab Republic, continued to exert pressure on their neighbors. When in July 1958 a pro-Nasser clique took over Iraq, it appeared that Lebanon and Jordan might also come under Nasser's domination. The pro-Western government of Lebanon requested aid against rebels, and the United States rushed in troops. At the same time Great Britain sent forces into Jordan. In the fall of 1958, when conditions became stabilized in Lebanon the United States withdrew its troops. Iraq continued to be a serious problem. Secretary Dulles, in order to balance its loss from the Baghdad Pact mutual defense organization, announced that the United States would assume full partnership in the alliance. But the withdrawal of Iraq from the alliance did not lead the country into Nasser's United Arab Republic as expected. The elements favoring this course soon fell from power in Iraq, and the danger in 1959 seemed to be that the country would swing into the Communist bloc. Reacting against the Communist trend in Iraq, Nasser veered back more toward the West, and the United States began again plying him with favors. Conditions were thus unstable and uncertain in much of the Middle East.

The Disgruntled Neighbors

THE INCESSANT THREATS against so many areas close to the Communist perimeter so occupied the American government and people that they paid scant attention to an area of vital worth to the United States and of growing vulnerability to Communist influence, the nations to the south. One of the minor ironies of this hectic age was the erosion of the Good Neighbor feeling between Latin American nations and the United States during the very years when this country was extending much of the Good Neighbor policy to Europe and Asia.

On paper there was no deterioration. Quite the contrary; the Latin American nations became signators of new pacts and the recipients of additional forms of aid. They had participated in the war except for Argentina, which under pressure did declare war just before the San Francisco Conference. They all became members of the United Nations. In 1947, at a conference at Rio de Janeiro, they drafted an Inter-American Treaty of Reciprocal Assistance, and the following year established an Organization of American States. The United States had abandoned every vestige of the old unilateral Monroe Doctrine in entering into pacts and organizations providing for mutual action whether in defense, settlement of disputes, or economic co-operation.

Yet the overwhelming military and economic power of the "colossus of the North" remained. Latin Americans were not pleased when the United States brought its prestige to bear against the totalitarian dictator of Argentina, Juan D. Perón, in 1946–47, even though the pressure failed. They were not much more pleased when it successfully brought pressure against a pro-Communist regime in Guatemala in 1954. But in the late fifties when many of the nations overthrew dictators as they tried to move toward democratization, the more common complaint was that the United

States had been too friendly toward despots, as in Venezuela, and not enthusiastic enough about rebels like Fidel Castro, who came into power in Cuba in 1959.

Above all, the problems from which Latin American peoples were suffering were economic. After the close of the war, they could no longer sell raw materials from their farms and mines to the United States in such large quantities or at such favorable prices as before. The soaring costs of the American manufactured goods they imported further hurt them. At home they were undergoing a rapid industrial revolution, accompanying social evolution, and an explosive population increase at the highest rate in the world, as much as 2.5 per cent per year. Already their combined population had passed that of the United States. All these factors helped create acute internal problems.

Inevitably the United States would have to be involved in the solution of economic questions because the hostility of neighbors to the South would be potentially ruinous, and because since the Second World War the two areas had become increasingly interdependent economically. Trade with Latin America exceeded eight billion dollars a year by the end of the fifties, and accounted for a third of the imports and a quarter of the exports of the United States. Eighty per cent of the foreign capital in Latin America was American; it had a book value of about nine and a half billion dollars. (This figure was second only to the thirteen billion dollars invested in Canada, which was also unhappy about its economic relations with the United States.)

It seemed to Latin Americans that, despite these close economic ties, the United States was doing little specific to help them solve their problems—to provide adequate capital for large-scale development, to stabilize raw materials at a profitable level, and to conquer inflation. They felt neglected as the American government poured billions into Europe and Asia while giving Latin America only a comparative pittance. Secretary Dulles was occupied elsewhere, and the Eisenhower administration, under the influence of two successive conservative Secretaries of the Treasury, was cold to requests for government loans for development. The festering economic ills and other grievances which could easily be focused against the United States were ready-made for the Communists. Exercising an influence out of proportion to their small numbers, they were active from Guatemala to Argentina.

Despite riots and disorders the Latin American discontent received little notice in the United States until May 1958, when Vice President Nixon was mobbed in Lima and Caracas. In the aftermath of the national shock, the State Department speeded changes in policy which were already slowly under way. It helped Latin American nations negotiate export quota pacts among themselves to raise the price of coffee and some metals and it expedited negotiations toward the establishment of a regional common market among the republics. More important, it took heed of the President of Brazil when in June 1958 he called for an Operation Pan-America to speed economic development, and agreed to furnish nearly half the capital for a new billion-dollar Inter-American Bank to make development loans. It also tried to improve public relations in a way Nixon had suggested by giving no more than a correct handshake to dictators but offering a warm embrace to democratic leaders.

The administration was increasing its attention to Latin America none too soon, since it was obvious that the well-disciplined, widely pervasive Communist activities throughout the area were receiving direction from Russia. Latin American Communist leaders returned early in 1959 from attending the twenty-first party congress in Moscow to begin the systematic denunciation at every point of the new program of the United States.

The full import of the Communist challenge to the south became clear in 1960. Fidel Castro, whose revolutionary accession to power had been cheered by Americans at the beginning of 1959, turned his administration increasingly to the left and indulged in shrill tirades against the United States. The Eisenhower administration, acting with restraint, did not retaliate economically. But in February 1960, Soviet Deputy Premier Anastas I. Mikoyan paid a nine-day visit to Cuba, which he climaxed by signing an agreement to purchase five million tons of sugar in the following five years, and to extend to Cuba a $100,000,000 credit. The treaty seemed to bring Soviet influence to within ninety miles of the United States.

The Missiles Race with Russia

WHAT MADE THE ONSLAUGHT of Communist ideology and power so frightening was the failure of the United States to keep pace with the Soviet Union in the development of intercontinental ballistic missiles, a weakness which Russia tried to exploit throughout the world. In early 1957 the United States appeared to be abreast or ahead of Soviet Russia in the development of guided missiles with nuclear warheads. Because of the potential horror of these weapons, both nations seemed ready to reach disarmament agreements during seven months of discussions in 1957 at a meeting of the United Nations subcommittee in London. Both sides apparently wanted to stop experiments with nuclear weapons, establish controls over them, cut conventional armaments, and regulate long-range missiles and satellites. Then trouble ensued. As an integral part of any disarmament plan, the United States and the West insisted upon schemes of strict inspection, including proposals for aerial photography over strips of each other's territory. To this the Soviet Union would not agree. By fall, the optimism of spring had changed to a melancholy recognition that because of rapid Russian advances in weapons development, the world was reaching what *The New York Times* called a "balance of terror."

Through the summer of 1957, American experts had complacently held that the United States was ahead of Russia in missile development. Then, in August, Russia announced that she had successfully tested an intercontinental ballistic missile. In contrast, the United States had successfully tested only intermediate-range missiles that had traveled from 1,500 to 3,000 miles. The Russian claims received sobering confirmation in October when Soviet scientists, using a rocket booster engine more powerful than any yet developed in the United States, launched the first successful satellite.

In the weeks following the launching of the satellite, Khrushchev, who in a series of bold moves had just consolidated his power in the Kremlin, issued a series of strong statements. The intent of his "sputnik diplomacy" was clearly to shake the Western alliance and impress neutral nations. The reaction within the United States, especially when the first American attempt to launch a much smaller satellite failed, was more one of angry fear than of congratulations to the Russian scientists. Three months later the United States began launching its own, smaller satellites. Moves began to overhaul the teaching of science and to provide greater financial support for basic scientific research. The public insisted, and the President agreed, that dissensions and interservice rivalries in the Department of Defense must come to an end. Congress in 1958 debated a measure to overhaul the defense organization.

As an indication of his concern, President Eisenhower, although he was just recuperating from a mild stroke, flew to Paris in December 1957 to lend strong moral support at a NATO conference. In January 1958 he devoted almost the entirety of his annual message to Congress to the armaments crisis and to the need to surpass Russia in providing aid for underdeveloped countries. He called upon an acquiescent Congress for heavy additional expenditures to rush development and construction of long-range missiles and of submarines and cruisers that could launch missiles. The first task confronting the nation was "to ensure our safety through strength," he pointed out. "But we could make no more tragic mistake than merely to concentrate on military strength. For if we did only this, the future would hold nothing for the world but an age of terror."

As a means of ameliorating the tension, lengthy negotiations went on with Russia over arrangements for another summit conference. In December 1957 Soviet Premier Bulganin asked for a meeting to sign a non-

Launching the first American satellite, January 31, 1958 (U.S. ARMY PHOTO)

aggression pact between the two power blocs, prohibit nuclear tests and the use of nuclear weapons, and establish a zone in Central Europe in which production of nuclear weapons and stockpiles would be banned. In ensuing correspondence, the Russians insisted upon a meeting upon terms favorable to them; the Americans insisted upon American terms. There seemed to be little common ground.

Meanwhile, extensive nuclear testing after 1954 by both the United States and Russia, climaxed by the Russian explosion of several "dirty" bombs, greatly increased the fallout of radioactive isotopes. Even though as yet exposure of populations was relatively slight compared to the radiation to which human beings were normally exposed, throughout the world there was a fear of the harmful effects from radioactive fallout. "Any dose, however small, produces some biological effect and . . . this effect is harmful," the Joint Congressional Committee on Atomic Energy granted in a 1959 report. If testing were to continue at the same rate as that of the previous five years over the next two generations, the report warned, the predicted average concentration of radioactive strontium in bone would be close to what scientists had estimated would be the maximum permissible body burden. This threat, well before 1959, was bringing popular pressure for the curtailing of nuclear tests.

In the spring of 1958, Khrushchev announced a unilateral abstention of nuclear tests in Russia. This left Eisenhower faced with the choice of two courses: He could follow the reasoning of most officials in the Defense Department who held that nuclear weapons were the only way in which the United States could counter the enormous land armies of Russia and China—and continue tests. Or he could promise to stop tests provided Russia would agree to adequate inspection, and perhaps an end to production of nuclear components of weapons.

He decided upon the latter course, and announced that the United States and its allies would suspend tests for one year beginning October 31, 1958. The suspension would continue on a year-to-year basis, provided a proper system of control could be developed and substantial progress could be made on disarmament negotiations. Russia, proclaiming that this was a Western trick, announced that it would resume testing. Nevertheless, President Eisenhower declared that the United States for the time being would continue its suspension of tests as it sought some workable agreement with the Soviet Union. Representatives of the United States, Great Britain, and Russia met in Geneva and slowly, laboriously, tried to construct a regulatory treaty.

In 1959, Khrushchev made much propaganda use of the failure of the United States to catch up with Russia in astronautical feats. "You send up oranges while we send up tons," he characteristically boasted, calling attention to the difference in the sizes of warheads that could be mounted on Soviet rockets and American ones. These feats helped obscure the fact that the missiles gap between the two nations was not as great as had been feared two years earlier. Russia was, as its shots into outer space continued to prove, well ahead in rocketry, but apparently the number of intercontinental ballistic missiles it possessed was not large enough to destroy the growing retaliatory arsenal of American missiles. The United States was successfully producing and testing its own missiles, and developing plans for hiding and spreading the launching sites so that it would require ten times as many Russian missiles to destroy them. The success of the Navy in constructing atomic-powered submarines which

Atomic-powered submarine U.S.S. Skate *surfacing through the ice near the North Pole* (U.S. NAVY PHOTO)

could launch missiles, and in bringing the submarines up through the ice at the North Pole, was a dramatic example of American achievement. The naval development of "Project Tepee," a radio-monitoring system which could detect any missile launchings anywhere in the world, was an indication of the technical advance of American defense. If the Russians were to attack the United States they could not expect their own cities to remain unscathed. The reverse held equally true, that American nuclear power would be incapable of destroying all the sites from which the Russians could launch missiles.

An attack upon the United States, if it came, the Congressional Joint Committee on Atomic Energy reported in August 1959, might kill fifty million people, seriously injure twenty million more, and destroy or render unuseable for months half of the dwellings in the country. Crops would be contaminated and swept by fire. The only hopeful note was that bomb shelters for the entire population could reduce casualties 25 or 30 per cent. The conclusion of the report was that the nation could survive, but it was not of a nature to give cheer to its readers. As for the Russians, they were aware that in the event of nuclear warfare they could expect a similar holocaust. A nuclear "balance of terror" seemed to be operating and, if the United States could keep sufficiently narrow the gap between its strength in missiles and that of Russia, was likely to continue.

The balancing of American and Russian atomic force meant that the United States could scarcely rely upon this power as an effective deterrent except against a possible Communist nuclear attack. That meant a new American strategy must be developed to counter the pressures of the conventional military forces of the Communists. Already, in Europe, the Russian superiority in intermediate range missiles was beginning to neutralize American bases, and seemed to embolden Khrushchev to reopen the question of the status of Berlin which had been in abeyance since the crisis of nearly a decade earlier.

Khrushchev and Eisenhower Exchange Views

Suddenly, in November 1958, Khrushchev precipitated a new crisis over Berlin, where the West's position was, as always, vulnerable. He asserted that conditions had changed so markedly in Berlin since the end of the war that the occupation agreements no longer applied. In six months he proposed to sign a separate peace treaty with the government of East Germany, turning over to it all the Russian occupation functions in Berlin including control over the access routes stretching 110 miles to West Germany.

The United States insisted that its treaty rights still held, and undertook the twofold task of trying to maintain unity regarding Berlin among its western allies, and of insisting upon concessions from the Soviet government corresponding to any it might make. Neither task was easy. Russia made alternate proposals as unacceptable as the first demand had been, and Khrushchev manipulated the issue to try to force a summit meeting. The United States was not willing to go further than a foreign ministers' meeting at Geneva, unless the Russians became more conciliatory; but the sessions beginning in May 1959 were discouragingly unfruitful. An exchange of visits between Eisenhower and Khrushchev seemed to offer the only slight possibility of accomodation.

Meanwhile, the burden of conducting American foreign policy had shifted to a new Secretary of State, Christian Herter, when Dulles, dying of cancer, resigned in April 1959. Herter was a strong successor. He had capped his foreign service record as a young man with a successful career in politics. But he by no means perpetuated the one-man determination of foreign policy that had distinguished Dulles. President Eisenhower seemed to assume a larger measure of responsibility, and this also pointed toward new interchanges at the top with the Russians.

Exchanges at lower levels had been going on at an increasing rate since the Geneva thaw of 1956. One of its few positive effects had been personal and cultural interchanges of musicians, dancers, students, and delegations of all kinds, climaxed in the summer of 1959 by a visit to the United States of Anastas Mikoyan, a Soviet deputy premier, and to Russia of Vice President Nixon. The Russians demonstrated their wares at a fair in New York City, and the Americans at a corresponding fair in Moscow showed crowds of Russians the components of the high standard of living in the United States. While Nixon was at the fair he engaged in informal debate with Khrushchev. The Russian press was for the most part hostile, but the crowds were friendly, and Khrushchev himself, while holding dogmatically to Soviet positions, seemed to demonstrate a keen interest in things American.

In August, 1959, President Eisenhower announced he would exchange visits with the Russian leader. The purpose in inviting Khrushchev, Eisenhower explained, was "to give him the opportunity to see what Americans are like" and "to give him, face to face, the basic convictions of our people on the major issues of the day."

Khrushchev's hectic, tumultuous thirteen-day tour of the United States must indeed have given him insights into the American people and their way of life. And through the extensive radio and press reports and display of motion pictures in the Soviet Union, it gave the Russian masses glimpses at American vistas. As for the curious American crowds who greeted Khrushchev with a rather wary coolness and the many millions who watched him on television—they acquired a new, more realistic impression of the formidable Soviet premier, as he repeatedly and emphatically explained the Russian position on the issues dividing the two nations. The American people did not again fall into the euphoric "Geneva spirit" of 1956, but were hopeful that firm bargaining with Russia would be possible.

Long private talks between Premier Khrushchev and President Eisenhower gave promise of further negotiations. Khrushchev agreed to drop the deadline for settlement of the Berlin problem, but with the stipulation that an agreement must not be delayed indefinitely. Khrushchev had spectacularly proposed before the United Nations in New York that the world totally disarm in four years. Observers were skeptical, since Russia had previously blocked every American suggestion for gradual disarmament.

But between Khrushchev's visit in September 1959 and the end of the year, arrangements were made for the resumption of disarmament negotiations in Geneva in March 1960, and for the holding of a summit conference in Paris later in the spring.

President Eisenhower planned to visit Russia, in return for Khrushchev's visit, in June 1960. Meanwhile he undertook a series of unprecedented, spectacular tours of the nations of the world. In December, he visited eleven nations stretching from Spain to India on a nineteen-day, 22,000-mile trip. In February, he made a similar tour of Latin America. His purpose was to try to win the goodwill of uncommitted nations, develop unity among the Allies, and to convince people everywhere of the sincerity of the United States in seeking peace. Before he left on the first of his trips, he set forth his aims, which in themselves embraced the foreign policy of President Eisenhower as the 1960's opened:

> Now, I have relatively few months left [as President], and I decided to . . . make an effort that no President ever was called on before to make, but I do feel a compulsion to visit a number of countries . . . and tell them exactly what I believe the United States is trying to do; that our basic aspiration is to search out methods by which peace in the world can be assured with justice for everybody. I want to prove that we are not aggressive, that we seek nobody else's territories or possessions; we do not seek to violate anybody else's rights. We are simply trying to be a good partner in this business of searching out for peace.

Books for Further Reading

THE PARAGRAPHS WHICH FOLLOW list some of the more important books on the specific topics covered in each chapter, and following these is a list of paperback editions. Many of these books contain bibliographies of their own which guide the reader to more specialized books and magazine articles. In addition, there are topical bibliographies covering books and articles published through 1950 in Oscar Handlin, *et al.* (eds.), *Harvard Guide to American History* (1954). A detailed bibliography of American literature appears in R. E. Spiller, *et al., Literary History of the United States* (1946), and R. M. Ludwig, *Bibliography Supplement [to] Literary History of the United States* (1959). For reviews of more recent books and lists of historical articles, see the *American Historical Review* and the *Mississippi Valley Historical Review*.

1. The Legacy of the Nineteenth Century

Two excellent brief surveys of the period are S. P. Hays, *The Response to Industrialism, 1885–1914* (1957), and H. U. Faulkner, *Politics, Reform and Expansion, 1890–1900* (1959). On industrialization, see Ida M. Tarbell's readable but rather uncritical *The Nationalizing of Business, 1878–1898* (1936); Matthew Josephson, *The Robber Barons* (1934), a hostile treatment; and three significant interpretations: T. C. Cochran and William Miller, *The Age of Enterprise* (1942); L. M. Hacker, *The Triumph of American Capitalism* (1940); and N. S. B. Gras, *Business and Capitalism* (1946). On the impact of industrialization upon American thinking, see Sidney Fine, *Laissez Faire and the General-Welfare State: A Study of Conflict in American Thought, 1865–1901* (1956). An equally penetrating analysis, covering up to 1903, is H. B. Thorelli, *The Federal Antitrust Policy: Origination of an Amer-ican Tradition* (1955). The ideology of businessmen is delineated in E. C. Kirkland, *Dream and Thought in the Business Community, 1860–1900* (1956). On individual business leaders, see B. J. Hendrick, *Andrew Carnegie* (2 vols., 1932), an official biography; Allan Nevins, *Study in Power: John D. Rockefeller* (2 vols., 1953), which is sympathetic; and Julius Grodinsky, *Jay Gould: His Business Career, 1867–1892* (1957), which treats Gould over-all as a public benefactor. On railroads, see R. E. Riegel, *The Story of Western Railroads* (1926); J. F. Stover, *Railroads of the South, 1865–1900* (1955); G. R. Taylor and I. D. Neu, *The American Railroad Net-work, 1861–1890* (1956), on railroad integration; and T. C. Cochran, *Rail-road Leaders, 1845–1890* (1953), on their ideology.

On conservative and liberal thinking, see Richard Hofstadter, *Social Dar-winism in American Thought* (1944), and Eric Goldman, *Rendezvous with Destiny: A History of Modern American Reform* (1952), which covers through the New Deal. On urbanization, see A. M. Schlesinger, *The Rise of the City* (1933); B. L. Pierce, *The Rise of a Modern City, 1871–1893* (1957), Vol. 3 of her *A History of Chicago;* and Ray Ginger, *Altgeld's America: The Lincoln Ideal versus Changing Realities* (1958), a study of intellectual cross-currents in Chicago, 1892–1905. On urban protest, see Arthur Mann, *Yankee Reformers in the Urban Age* (1954).

The standard history of agriculture in the period is F. A. Shannon, *The Farmer's Last Frontier* (1945). On the populists, see J. D. Hicks, *The Populist Revolt* (1955 ed.), and Richard Hofstadter, *The Age of Reform* (1955). A definitive analysis deflating one of the farmers' grievances is A. G. Bogue, *Money at Interest: The Farm Mortgage on the Middle Border* (1955). On the rise of the A.F.L., see Philip Taft, *The A.F. of L. in the Time of Gompers* (1957), which defends Gompers at every point; on difficulties in the nineties, see Almont Lindsey, *The Pullman Strike* (1942). Among the especially useful biographies are: H. S. Merrill, *Bourbon Leader: Grover Cleveland and the Democratic Party* (1957); C. V. Woodward, *Tom Watson, Agrarian Radical* (1938); D. W. Grantham, *Hoke Smith and the Politics of the New South* (1958); Elmer Ellis, *Henry More Teller* (1941); J. L. Lambert, Jr., *Ar-thur Pue Gorman* (1953); J. F. Wall, *Henry Watterson, Unreconstructed Rebel* (1956); and C. A. Barker, *Henry George* (1955). A readable popular picture is Margaret Leech, *In the Days of McKinley* (1959).

On the background of the Spanish-American War, see J. W. Pratt, *Ex-pansionists of 1898* (1936), and M. M. Wilkerson, *Public Opinion and the Spanish-American War* (1932). Two popular accounts of the war are Walter Millis, *The Martial Spirit* (1931), and Frank Freidel, *The Splendid Little War* (1958). America's acquisitions are described in J. W. Pratt, *America's Colo-nial Experiment* (1950), and W. H. Haas (ed.), *The American Empire* (1940).

The diplomacy of the McKinley and Roosevelt administrations is discussed in Tyler Dennett, *John Hay* (1933). A useful survey is F. R. Dulles, *The Im-*

perial Years (1956). On the Open Door policy, see A. W. Griswold, *The Far Eastern Policy of the United States* (1938); C. S. Campbell, Jr., *Special Business Interest and the Open Door Policy* (1951); and P. A. Varg, *Open Door Diplomat: The Life of W. W. Rockhill* (1952).

2. Technics and Reform

A popular comparison of America at the turn of the century and at mid-century, emphasizing American optimism and progress, is F. L. Allen, *The Big Change* (1952). Hays, *The Response to Industrialism*, is an original survey covering to 1914. For the intellectual history of the Progressive era, see chapters in Hofstadter, *The Age of Reform*, and Goldman, *Rendezvous with Destiny*. H. U. Faulkner's *The Decline of Laissez-Faire* (1951) and *Quest for Social Justice* (1931) are, respectively, economic and social histories of the era. A popular social history of the years 1900–1925, useful for portraying contemporary attitudes, is Mark Sullivan, *Our Times* (6 vols., 1926–35). A disillusioned view of Progressivism is John Chamberlain, *Farewell to Reform* (1932); an exciting but sometimes misleading political history is Matthew Josephson, *The President Makers* (1940); an account of the journalists is C. C. Regier, *The Era of the Muckrakers* (1932). For biographical sketches of some Progressives, see Louis Filler, *Crusaders for American Liberalism* (1950); chapters 7–8 of Aaron, *Men of Good Hope* (1951); D. W. Noble, *The Paradox of Progressive Thought* (1958); and Mann, *Yankee Reformers in the Urban Age*. A brief interpretation of business history is T. C. Cochran, *The American Business System: A Historical Perspective, 1900–1955* (1957). See also Mabel Newcomer, *The Big Business Executive: The Factors That Made Him, 1900–1950* (1955). On working women, see R. W. Smuts, *Women and Work, 1890 to Today* (1958). F. L. Allen's *The Lords of Creation* (1935) is on business leaders. Allan Nevins, F. E. Hill, *et al.*, *Ford* (2 vols., 1954–1957), has much detail on mass production; on changes in industrial technique also see Kendall Birr, *Pioneering in Industrial Research: The Story of the General Electric Research Laboratory* (1957), and M. J. Nadworny, *Scientific Management and the Unions, 1900–1932* (1955). On labor, see Taft, *The A.F. of L. in the Time of Gompers* (1957); on urban poverty, R. H. Bremner, *From the Depths: The Discovery of Poverty in the United States* (1955). On the religious response to poverty, see C. H. Hopkins, *The Rise of the Social Gospel in American Protestantism, 1865–1915* (1940); H. F. May, *Protestant Churches and Industrial America* (1949), covering an earlier period; and H. A. Wisbey, *Soldiers Without Swords: A History of the Salvation Army in the United States* (1955). On the rise of Reform Judaism, see Israel Knox, *Rabbi in America: The Story of Isaac M. Wise* (1957). On women's rights, Eleanor Flexner, *Century of Struggle: The Woman's Rights Movement in the United States* (1959). On social work, see F. J. Bruno and Louis Towley, *Trends in Social Work, 1874–1956* (2nd ed., 1957), and R. H. Shryock, *National Tuberculosis Association, 1904–1954: A Study of the Vol-*

untary Health Movement in the United States (1957). On the "new" immigration and the restriction movement, see Oscar Handlin, *The Uprooted* (1951) ; John Higham, *Strangers in the Land* (1955) ; and B. M. Solomon, *Ancestors and Immigrants* (1956). On the South, see C. V. Woodward, *Origins of the New South* (1951).

3. Roosevelt Progressivism

A brilliant survey of the Roosevelt and Taft administrations is G. E. Mowry, *The Era of Theodore Roosevelt, 1900–1912* (1958). Carleton Putnam is writing a four-volume study of Roosevelt. The first volume, more detailed than critical, is *Theodore Roosevelt, the Formative Years, 1858–1886* (1958). Henry Pringle's readable, highly critical *Theodore Roosevelt* (1931) has appeared also in a revised paperback edition. J. M. Blum, *The Republican Roosevelt* (1954), briefly and brilliantly revises upward the earlier estimates. Roosevelt himself is highly readable in his *Autobiography* (1913) and in Elting Morison *et al.* (eds.), *The Letters of Theodore Roosevelt* (8 vols., 1951–1954). On other leading political figures see: Belle and Fola La Follette, *Robert M. La Follette* (2 vols., 1953), and La Follette's *Autobiography* (1913) ; J. A. Garraty, *Henry Cabot Lodge* (1953) ; C. G. Bowers, *Beveridge and the Progressive Era* (1932) ; Jessup, *Elihu Root* and the briefer treatment by Richard Leopold, *Elihu Root and the Conservative Tradition* (1954).

Among the studies of members of Congress are: N. W. Stephenson, *Nelson W. Aldrich* (1930) ; W. R. Gwinn, *Uncle Joe Cannon* (1957) ; L. L. Sage, *William Boyd Allison* (1956); O. D. Lambert, *Stephen Benton Elkins* (1955) ; F. B. Simkins, *Pitchfork Ben Tillman* (1944) ; and Woodward, *Watson.*

Two newspapermen wrote especially fascinating autobiographies: *The Autobiography of Lincoln Steffens* (2 vols., 1931) and *The Autobiography of William Allen White* (1946). See also Walter Johnson, *William Allen White's America* (1947). On trusts, see Thorelli, *The Federal Antitrust Policy,* and H. R. Seager and C. A. Gulick, Jr., *Trust and Corporation Problems* (1929). A valuable survey of labor during these years is Marc Karson, *American Labor Unions and Politics, 1900–1918* (1958). On a key labor episode, see R. J. Cornell, *The Anthracite Coal Strike of 1902* (1957). F. L. Allen's *The Great Pierpont Morgan* (1949) is a personal portrait of the dominant financier, and Elsie Gluck's *John Mitchell, Miner* (1929) the story of the labor leader. A path-breaking study of conservation is S. P. Hays, *The Gospel of Efficiency: The Progressive Conservation Movement, 1890–1920* (1959). On the Pure Food and Drug Act, see O. E. Anderson, *The Health of a Nation: Harvey W. Wiley and the Fight for Pure Food* (1958).

4. The Assault on the Old Guard

Henry Pringle, *William Howard Taft* (2 vols., 1939), is a full and appreciative account. The Midwest insurgents are analyzed in Kenneth Hechler,

Insurgency: Personalities and Policies of the Taft Era (1940), and the much broader survey by Russell Nye, *Midwestern Progressive Politics, 1870–1958* (1959 ed.). On the Ballinger-Pinchot controversy, see A. T. Mason, *Bureaucracy Convicts Itself* (1941), and on the far-ranging activities of Brandeis, see Mason's biography of him (1946). On Pinchot, see the forthcoming biography by Nelson McGeary. Hays, *The Gospel of Efficiency*, gives a new interpretation of the controversy.

Biographies of leading insurgents are: Belle and Fola La Follette, *La Follette;* Claude Bowers, *Beveridge and the Progressive Era* (1932); T. R. Ross, *Jonathan Prentiss Dolliver; A Study in Political Integrity and Independence* (1958); and G. W. Norris's autobiography, *Fighting Liberal* (1945). On their conservative opponents, see again Stephenson, *Aldrich;* Gwinn, *Cannon;* and Blair Bolles's journalistic account of Cannon, *Tyrant from Illinois* (1951). On the incipient Progressive revolt, George Mowry, *Theodore Roosevelt and the Progressive Movement* (1946), is essential. For an account of Progressive politics on the state level, see Mowry, *California Progressives* (1951); A. D. Kirwan, *Revolt of the Rednecks* (1951); R. S. Maxwell, *La Follette and the Rise of the Progressives in Wisconsin* (1956); E. A. Fitzpatrick, *McCarthy of Wisconsin* (1944). On the municipal level, see Walton Bean, *Boss Ruef's San Francisco* (1952), and Harold Zink, *City Bosses in the United States* (1930). On Socialism see Howard Quint, *The Forging of American Socialism* (1953); Ira Kipnis, *The American Socialist Movement, 1897–1912* (1952); David Shannon, *The Socialist Party of America* (1955); and Ray Ginger, *The Bending Cross* (1949).

5. The New Freedom Triumphs

A. S. Link is writing what promises to be the definitive biography of Woodrow Wilson. The first volume, *The Road to the White House* (1947), covers Wilson's career to his inauguration; the second, *The New Freedom* (1956), brilliantly reinterprets Wilson's domestic program. A briefer version is Link's *Woodrow Wilson and the Progressive Era, 1910–1917* (1954). A useful full biography is A. C. Walworth, *Woodrow Wilson* (2 vols., 1958); a condensed interpretation of Wilson and his administration is J. M. Blum, *Woodrow Wilson and the Politics of Morality* (1956); a sketch of personality, rich in psychological insights, is J. A. Garraty, *Wilson;* an affectionate short biography is H. C. F. Bell, *Woodrow Wilson and the People* (1945). William Diamond, *The Economic Thought of Woodrow Wilson* (1943), is especially good on the years before 1913. J. M. Blum, *Joe Tumulty and the Wilson Era* (1951), is excellent on the politics of the period. Two biographies of Southern Democratic leaders are Simkins, *Tillman*, and G. C. Osborn, *John Sharp Williams* (1943).

There are numerous autobiographies, collections of writings, and popular biographies of Wilson's cabinet members, but few scholarly biographies. Charles Seymour (ed.), *The Intimate Papers of Colonel House* (4 vols., 1926–

1928) is a well-edited collection. A careful account of the Wilson era is F. L. Paxson, *American Democracy and the World War* (3 vols., 1936–1948). Two biographies of Hughes, one lengthy and one brief, are M. J. Pusey, *Charles Evans Hughes* (2 vols., 1951), and Dexter Perkins, *Hughes and American Democratic Statesmanship* (1956). Contemporary expositions of the Progressive ideology are Herbert Croly, *The Promise of American Life* (1909), and L. D. Brandeis, *Other People's Money* (1933).

6. Militant Progressivism

Two thought-provoking essays on twentieth-century diplomacy are: G. F. Kennan, *American Diplomacy, 1900–1950* (1951), and R. E. Osgood, *Ideals and Self-Interest in America's Foreign Relations: The Great Transformation of the Twentieth Century* (1953). A concise, useful survey is F. R. Dulles, *America's Rise to World Power, 1898–1954* (1955).

On the building of a modern American navy, see D. W. Mitchell, *History of the Modern Navy, from 1883 through Pearl Harbor* (1946); the enthusiastic Harold and Margaret Sprout, *The Rise of American Naval Power* (1942); the critical G. T. Davis, *A Navy Second to None* (1940); Elting Morison, *Admiral Sims and the Modern American Navy* (1942); and W. R. Braisted, *The United States Navy in the Pacific, 1897–1909* (1958). A biography of a significant imperialist is W. D. Puleston, *Mahan* (1939).

A thoughtful interpretation of American foreign policy during the Roosevelt administration is H. K. Beale, *Theodore Roosevelt and the Rise of America to World Power* (1956). On Panama, see Gerstle Mack, *The Land Divided: A History of the Panama Canal and Other Isthmian Canal Projects* (1944), and D. C. Miner, *The Fight for the Panama Route* (1940). On Caribbean policy, see W. H. Callcott, *The Caribbean Policy of the United States, 1890–1920* (1942), and Dexter Perkins, *The United States and the Caribbean* (1947). On Latin America, see S. F. Bemis, *The Latin American Policy of the United States* (1943). On Great Britain, see C. S. Campbell, *Anglo-American Understanding, 1898–1903* (1957); L. M. Gelber, *The Rise of Anglo-American Friendship: A Study in World Politics, 1898–1906* (1938); and R. H. Heindel, *The American Impact on Great Britain, 1898–1914* (1940). On the Far East, see Griswold, *Far Eastern Policy*; P. J. Treat, *Diplomatic Relations between the United States and Japan, 1895–1905* (1938); T. A. Bailey, *Theodore Roosevelt and the Japanese-American Crises* (1934); E. H. Zabriskie, *American-Russian Rivalry in the Far East, 1895–1914* (1946); J. K. Fairbank, *The United States and China* (1958 ed.); F. H. Harrington, *God, Mammon and the Japanese: Horace N. Allen and Korean-American Relations, 1884–1905* (1944); and P. A. Varg, *Missionaries, Chinese, and Diplomats: The American Protestant Missionary Movement in China, 1890–1952* (1958). On the background of the American involvement in the Mexican Revolution, see D. M. Pletcher, *Rails, Mines, and Progress: Seven American Promoters in Mexico, 1867–1911* (1959).

On Taft's foreign policies, see Pringle, *Taft*. On those of Wilson, see Link, *Woodrow Wilson and the Progressive Era* (1954) and *Wilson the Diplomatist* (1957), and the bibliography below for Chapter 8.

7. The New Enlightenment

A fresh and brilliant interpretation of intellectual movements before the first World War is H. F. May, *The End of American Innocence* (1959). On social history see again Faulkner, *The Quest for Social Justice* and Sullivan, *Our Times,* a mine of material on popular culture. Chapters 22–24 of Merle Curti, *The Growth of American Thought* (1943), contain an excellent survey of intellectual developments and useful bibliography. On pragmatism, see Morton White, *The Age of Analysis* (1955), chs. 9–11, for excerpts from the pragmatists with succinct introductions to them, and Herbert W. Schneider, *A History of American Philosophy* (1946), ch. 39, with a detailed bibliography on pps. 572–82. See also R. B. Perry, *The Thought and Character of William James* (1935); Sidney Hook, *John Dewey* (1939); G. R. Geiger, *John Dewey in Perspective* (1958); and R. B. Perry, *The Thought and Character of William James* (1935). There are sections on the progressive era in E. W. Knight, *Education in the United States* (1951 ed.); Merle Curti, *The Social Ideas of American Educators* (1935); A. E. Meyer, *The Development of Education in the Twentieth Century* (1939); I. L. Kandel, *American Education in the Twentieth Century* (1957); and Richard Hofstadter and C. DeWitt Hardy, *The Development and Scope of Higher Education in the United States* (1952). On the ideas of some of the leading scholars and thinkers of the era, see Morton White, *Social Thought in America* (1949); Goldman, *Rendezvous with Destiny;* and Hofstadter, *Age of Reform.* Some of the more specialized studies are: Joseph Dorfman, *Thorstein Veblen and His America* (1934); David Riesman, *Thorstein Veblen: A Critical Interpretation* (1953); H. K. Beale (ed.), *Charles A. Beard* (1954); M. D. Howe, *Oliver Wendell Holmes* (1957–); and Paul Sayre, *Roscoe Pound* (1948). On emerging science, little of value has been written as yet, but see Bernard Jaffe, *Men of Science in America* (1944), a popular account. On medicine and medical research, in contrast, there are first-rate studies: R. H. Shryock, *The Development of Modern Medicine* (1947 ed.) and *American Medical Research* (1947); and two brilliant biographies, Simon and J. T. Flexner's *William Henry Welch and the Heroic Age of American Medicine* (1941); and Donald Fleming's briefer *William H. Welch and the Rise of Modern Medicine* (1954). A valuable study of one city is T. N. Bonner, *Medicine in Chicago, 1850–1950* (1958). On literature, see Robert E. Spiller, *et al., Literary History of the United States* (1946), ch. 63–72 and bibliographies; Alfred Kazin, *On Native Grounds: An Interpretation of Modern American Prose Literature* (1942), Part I; Van Wyck Brooks, *The Confident Years, 1885–1915* (1952); Grant C. Knight, *The Strenuous Age in American Literature* (1954); K. S. Lynn, *The Dream of Success* (1955); Maxwell Geismar, *Rebels and Ancestors: The Modern American*

Novel, 1890–1915 (1953) ; and F. J. Hoffman, Charles Allen, and C. F. Ulrich, *The Little Magazine* (1946). On music, see Gilbert Chase, *America's Music* (1955), chs. 21–27 and bibliography; J. H. Mueller, *The American Symphony Orchestra: A Social History of Musical Taste* (1951) ; David Ewen, *Panorama of American Popular Music* (1957) ; and Rudi Blesh, *Shining Trumpets, A History of Jazz* (1958 ed.). On the arts, see O. W. Larkin, *Art and Life in America* (1949), pp. 321–69 and bibliography; J. I. H. Baur, *Revolution and Tradition in Modern American Art* (1951) ; Samuel Hunter, *Modern American Painting and Sculpture* (1959) ; and F. L. Wright, *Modern Architecture* (1931). On motion pictures, see Lewis Jacobs, *The Rise of the American Film* (1939), chs. 1–9.

8. To Make the World Safe for Democracy

On the occasion of Wilson's centenary, a number of essays appeared, most of which centered on Wilson's leadership during the war and his fight for a League of Nations. Among the most interesting of these are: Link, *Wilson the Diplomatist;* E. H. Buehrig (ed.), *Wilson's Foreign Policy in Perspective* (1957) ; and A. P. Dudden (ed.), *Woodrow Wilson and the World of Today* (1957). On American entrance into the First World War, a group of books popular in the thirties emphasize the isolationist viewpoint: Walter Millis, *Road to War: America, 1914–1917* (1935) ; C. H. Grattan, *Why We Fought* (1929) ; E. M. Borchard and W. P. Lage, *Neutrality for the United States* (1937) ; and C. C. Tansill, *America Goes to War* (1938). A view more favorable to the intervention is Charles Seymour's in *American Diplomacy during the World War* (1934) and *American Neutrality, 1914–1917* (1935). An interesting discussion of the issues is included in Osgood, *Ideals and Self-Interest in America's Foreign Relations.* On propaganda, see H. C. Peterson, *Propaganda for War* (1939), and Armin Rappaport, *The British Press and Wilsonian Neutrality* (1950). The most useful survey of the war administration is in Paxson, *American Democracy and the World War,* vol. 2. See also Sullivan, *Our Times,* vol. 5. Some specialized studies are: J. M. Clark, *The Costs of the World War to the American People* (1931) ; Bernard M. Baruch, *American Industry in War* (1941 ed.) ; W. C. Mullendore, *History of United States Food Administration* (1941) ; and Herbert Stein, *Government Price Policy during the World War* (1939). A readable account of Baruch's activities is included in Margaret Coit, *Mr. Baruch* (1957) ; a revealing memoir is Herbert Hoover's *The Ordeal of Woodrow Wilson* (1958).

9. Victory and Isolation

J. R. Mock and Cedric Larson, *Words That Won the War* (1939), is an account of the Committee on Public Information. Zechariah Chafee, Jr., *Free Speech in the United States* (1941), contains a classic account of wartime restrictions on civil liberties; H. C. Peterson and G. C. Fite, *Opponents of War, 1917–1918* (1957), is an equally powerful treatise. On military and naval operations, see Paxson, *American Democracy and the World War*, vol. 2, and these specialized accounts and memoirs: Cyril Falls, *The Great War* (1959); T. G. Frothingham, *The Naval History of the World War* (3 vols., 1924–26); Morison, *Admiral Sims;* D. W. Mitchell, *History of the Modern American Navy* (1946); J. J. Pershing, *My Experiences in the World War* (2 vols., 1931); and J. G. Habord, *The American Army in France, 1917–1919* (1936).

On the end of the fighting, see H. R. Rudin, *Armistice, 1918* (1944). On Wilson as a peacemaker, see the essays cited for Chapter 8; L. W. Martin, *Peace Without Victory: Woodrow Wilson and the British Liberals* (1958); T. A. Bailey's *Woodrow Wilson and the Lost Peace* (1944), on the Versailles conference, and his *Woodrow Wilson and the Great Betrayal* (1945), on the Treaty fight in the Senate. On the background of League of Nations senti-ment, see R. J. Bartlett, *The League to Enforce Peace* (1944). See also Gar-raty, *Lodge*, and Hoover, *Ordeal of Wilson*.

On American foreign relations, see also L. A. R. Yates, *United States and French Security, 1917–1921* (1957) and a brilliant multivolume study in process by G. F. Kennan, *Soviet-American Relations, 1917–1920*.

10. The New Era

A superbly written critical view of the twenties is the first volume of A. M. Schlesinger, Jr.'s *Age of Roosevelt*, subtitled *The Crisis of the Old Order* (1957). An equally distinguished short account of the era is W. E. Leuchten-berg, *The Perils of Prosperity, 1914–32* (1958). A scathing journalistic ac-count of the politics is Karl Schriftgiesser, *This Was Normalcy* (1948); a lively social history is F. L. Allen, *Only Yesterday* (1931); the standard eco-nomic history, George Soule, *Prosperity Decade* (1947); and a useful sober survey, Harold Faulkner, *From Versailles to the New Deal* (1950). Among the entertaining popular accounts are: Isabel Leighton (ed.), *The Aspirin Age* (1949); Lloyd Morris, *Postcript to Yesterday* (1947) and *Not So Long Ago* (1949); Laurence Greene, *The Era of Wonderful Nonsense* (1939); H. M. Robinson, *Fantastic Interim* (1943); Paul Sann, *The Lawless Decade* (1957); M. R. Werner and John Starr, *Teapot Dome* (1959); and Sullivan, *Our Times*, vols. 5–6. A careful contemporary survey is Preston Slosson, *The Great Crusade and After* (1930); a significant study of American society is by The President's Research Committee on Social Trends, *Recent Social Trends in the United States* (1933); Robert and Helen Lynd make a classic examination of society in a typical small city in *Middletown* (1929); and a distillation of British travelers' accounts is *The Jazz Age Revisited* (1955), by G. H. Knoles.

On reconversion, see J. R. Mock and Evangeline Thurber, *Report on Demobilization* (1944). On the red scare, Chafee, *Free Speech in the U.S.;* Robert Murray, *Red Scare* (1955); Theodore Draper, *The Roots of Ameri-can Communism* (1957); G. L. Joughin and E. M. Morgan, *The Legacy of*

Sacco and Vanzetti (1948); and Weeks (ed.), *Commonwealth vs. Sacco and Vanzetti* (1958). The election of 1920 is covered in Bailey, *Wilson and the Great Betrayal*, and Frank Freidel, *Franklin D. Roosevelt: The Ordeal* (1954). S. H. Adams, *Incredible Era* (1939) is a popular account of Harding and his administration verging on the sensational. A state study of wide implications is J. J. Huthmacher, *Massachusetts People and Politics 1919–1933* (1959). On foreign policy, see Pusey, *Hughes;* Perkins, *Hughes;* J. C. Vinson, *The Parchment Peace* (1955), on the Washington Conference; Vinson, *Borah and the Outlawry of War* (1957), and Robert Ferrell, *Peace in Their Time* (1952), on the Kellogg-Briand Pact. On the reaction against war, see Selig Adler, *The Isolationist Impulse* (1957); on foreign economic policy, Herbert Feis, *The Diplomacy of the Dollar* (1950).

11. A Precarious Prosperity

In addition to the general surveys cited in the bibliography for Chapter 10, the following more specialized works are of value. The most readable interpretation of Coolidge is W. A. White, *Puritan in Babylon* (1938). Claude Fuess, *Calvin Coolidge* (1940) is sympathetic and well documented. On the election of 1924, see Kenneth MacKay, *The Progressive Movement of 1924* (1947), and B. C. and Fola La Follette, *La Follette*, vol. 2; on the Democratic convention, Freidel, *Franklin D. Roosevelt*, vol. 2. Hoover has described his work as Secretary of Commerce in his *Memoirs*, vol. 2. Among the economic analyses of the twenties are Soule, *Prosperity Decade*, and the following specialized works: Frederick Mills, *Economic Tendencies in the United States* (1932); Harold Barger, *Outlay and Income in the United States, 1921–1938* (1942); Joseph Schumpeter, *Business Cycles* (1939); Edwin Nourse and others, *America's Capacity to Produce* (1934); Maurice Leven and others, *America's Capacity to Consume* (1934); and Simon Kuznets, *National Income and Its Composition, 1919–1938* (1941). On technological innovations, see Siegfried Giedion, *Mechanization Takes Command* (1948). On labor, Philip Taft, *The A.F. of L. from the Death of Gompers to the Merger* (1959). On agriculture, see J. H. Shideler, *Farm Crisis, 1919–1923* (1957); W. T. Hutchinson, *Lowden of Illinois* (2 vols., 1957); Robert Morlan, *Political Prairie Fire: The Nonpartisan League, 1915–1922* (1955); Theodore Saloutos and J. D. Hicks, *Agricultural Discontent in the Middle West, 1900–1939* (1951); Gilbert Fite, *George Peek and the Fight for Farm Parity* (1954); and Russell Lord, *The Wallaces of Iowa* (1947). On the intellectual history of the twenties, see Kazin, *On Native Grounds;* John Hutchens, *The American Twenties* (1952), a literary anthology; Edmund Wilson, *Shores of Light* (1952) and *The American Earthquake* (1958), contemporary essays; Malcolm Cowley, *Exile's Return* (1951 ed.); Edgar Kemler, *The Irreverent Mr. Mencken* (1950); Walter Lippmann, *A Preface to Morals* (1929); Frederick Hoffman, *Freudianism and the Literary Mind* (1945); Ray Ginger, *Six Days or Forever?* (1958), about the Scopes trial; N. F. Furniss, *The Fundamen-*

talist Controversy, 1918–1931 (1954) ; Paul Carter, *The Decline and Revival of the Social Gospel* (1956) ; R. M. Miller, *American Protestantism and Social Issues, 1919–1939* (1958) ; Otis Pease, *The Responsibilities of American Advertising: Private Control and Public Influence, 1920–1940* (1958) ; and J. W. Protho, *Dollar Decade* (1954).

12. The Great Engineer and the Great Depression

Most writings on President Hoover and his administration are adulatory or denunciatory. The one balanced, judicious account is H. G. Warren, *Herbert Hoover and the Great Depression* (1959). Among the defenses, see Hoover's *Memoirs*, vols. 2–3; W. S. Myers and W. H. Newton, *The Hoover Administration* (1936) ; and R. L. Wilbur and Arthur Hyde, *The Hoover Policies* (1937). Hofstadter, *American Political Tradition*, contains a thoughtful critical essay. On the election of 1928, see Edmund Moore, *A Catholic Runs for President* (1956), and Roy Peel and Thomas Donnelly, *The 1928 Campaign: An Analysis* (1931). Oscar Handlin, *Al Smith and His America* (1958), is a brief biography written with sympathetic insight and verve. On prohibition, see three popular books: Herbert Asbury, *The Great Illusion* (1950) ; Charles Merz, *The Dry Decade* (1931) ; and Virginius Dabney, *Dry Messiah: The Life of Bishop Cannon* (1949). On the crash and depression, see Broadus Mitchell, *Depression Decade* (1947), the standard economic history; J. K. Galbraith, *The Great Crash* (1955), both lively and sound; J. A. Morris, *What a Year!* (1956), a popular account of 1929; and Dixon Wecter, *Age of the Great Depression, 1929–1941* (1948), readable and sound social history. A contemporary economic analysis of considerable influence is A. A. Berle and G. C. Means, *The Modern Corporation and Private Property* (1932). On Hoover foreign policy, see R. N. Current, *Secretary Stimson* (1954), a critical evaluation; R. H. Ferrell, *American Diplomacy in the Great Depression* (1957) ; W. S. Myers, *The Foreign Policies of Herbert Hoover* (1940) ; Sara Smith, *The Manchurian Crisis, 1931–1932* (1948) ; H. L. Stimson and McGeorge Bundy, *On Active Service in Peace and War* (1948) ; and Alexander De Conde, *Herbert Hoover's Latin American Policy* (1951). On the election of 1932, see R. V. Peel and T. C. Donnelly, *The 1932 Campaign* (1935), and Freidel, *Franklin D. Roosevelt*, vol. 3.

13. The Roosevelt Revolution

The most perceptive, lively study of the early years of the New Deal is the second volume of A. M. Schlesinger, Jr., *The Age of Roosevelt*, entitled *The Coming of the New Deal* (1959). Readable brief accounts of the New Deal are Dexter Perkins, *The New Age of Franklin Roosevelt* (1957), which includes a balanced summary of foreign policy; D. W. Brogan, *The Era of Franklin D. Roosevelt* (1950), a favorable account from a British viewpoint; and Mario Einaudi, *The Roosevelt Revolution* (1959), aimed primarily at

European readers. E. E. Robinson, *The Roosevelt Leadership* (1955), measures it against Hoover and finds Roosevelt lacking at every point. Basil Rauch, *The History of the New Deal* (1944), is a pioneering work. Among the biographies of Roosevelt, J. M. Burns, *Roosevelt: The Lion and the Fox* (1956) is a well-written Keynesian interpretation; R. G. Tugwell, *The Democratic Roosevelt* (1957), shrewdly interprets the effect of Roosevelt's early years upon his personality and policies; John Gunther, *Roosevelt in Retrospect* (1950), is an affectionate journalistic estimate; Freidel, *Roosevelt,* is a projected six-volume study, of which the three already in print carry Roosevelt through 1932. Bernard Bellush, *Roosevelt as Governor of New York* (1955), is a definitive monograph. Some of the most useful and readable of the many memoirs are: Frances Perkins, *The Roosevelt I Knew* (1946), friendly but realistic; Raymond Moley, *After Seven Years* (1939), best of the hostile memoirs and indispensable on the early New Deal; J. A. Farley, *Behind the Ballots* (1938), on political maneuvering; S. I. Rosenman, *Working for Roosevelt* (1952), on speech-writing. H. L. Ickes, *Secret Diary* (3 vols., 1953–54), is a tart hodgepodge, not always reliable.

On the recovery program, the following books are suggested. For the N.R.A., see L. S. Lyon and others, *The National Recovery Administration* (1935), and H. S. Johnson, *The Blue Eagle from Egg to Earth* (1935). For A.A.A., see Lord, *The Wallaces of Iowa;* E. G. Nourse and others, *Three Years of the Agricultural Adjustment Administration* (1937); and J. D. Black, *Parity, Parity, Parity* (1942). For monetary policy and a wide variety of New Deal matters, J. M. Blum, *From the Morgenthau Diaries: Years of Crisis, 1928–1938* (1959) is indispensable; see also G. G. Johnson, Jr., *Treasury and Monetary Policy, 1933–1938* (1939), and A. S. Everest, *Morgenthau, New Deal and Silver* (1950). For railroads, see Earl Latham, *The Politics of Railroad Coordination, 1933–1936* (1959). On the R.F.C., see Jesse Jones, *Fifty Billion Dollars* (1951). On the T.V.A., see D. E. Lilienthal, *TVA: Democracy on the March* (1953 ed.).

14. The New Deal Shifts Toward Reform

On the politics of the New Deal, see the surveys for Chapter 13, and H. Gosnell, *Champion Campaigner, Franklin D. Roosevelt* (1952). The continuing poverty of millions of Americans is discussed in Wecter, *Age of the Great Depression;* L. V. Armstrong, *We Too Are People* (1938); T. J. Woofter, Jr., and E. Winston, *Seven Lean Years* (1939); Vance Johnson, *Heaven's Tableland: The Dust Bowl Story* (1947); and M. D. Lane and Francis Steegmuller, *America on Relief* (1938). On pressures from the left, see A. P. Sindler, *Huey Long's Louisiana* (1956); H. T. Kane, *Louisiana Hayride* (1941); and Twentieth Century Fund, *Townsend Crusade* (1936). On the New Deal reform program, see Grace Abbott, *From Relief to Social Security* (1941); H. L. Hopkins, *Spending to Save* (1936); W. O. Douglas, *Democracy and Finance* (1940), concerning the Holding Company Act and the Securities and Exchange Commission; M. S. Eccles, *Beckoning Frontiers* (1951), regarding the Banking Act of 1935 and the Federal Reserve System; G. G. Johnson, Jr., *Public Works Expenditures 1933–1938* (1940) ; and Nathan Straus, *Seven Myths of Housing* (1944). Milton Derber *et al.*, *Labor under the New Deal* (1957), is a comprehensive group of excellent essays; see also Irving Bernstein, *New Deal Collective Bargaining Policy* (1950), essential on the background of the Wagner Act; Herbert Harris, *Labor's Civil War* (1940) ; Selig Perlman, *Labor in the New Deal Decade* (1945) ; and M. M. Kampelman, *The Communist Party vs. the C.I.O.* (1957). On Republican opposition to the New Deal, see Herbert Hoover, *Challenge to Liberty* (1934), and Alf M. Landon, *America at the Crossroads* (1936). On third party movements, see D. R. McCoy, *Angry Voices: Left-of-Center Politics in the New Deal Era* (1958). On the Supreme Court controversy, see Joseph Alsop and Turner Catledge, *168 Days* (1938) ; R. H. Jackson, *The Struggle for Judicial Supremacy* (1941) ; and M. J. Pusey, *The Supreme Court Crisis* (1937). On the new Court, see C. H. Pritchett, *The Roosevelt Court* (1948), and A. T. Mason, *Harlan Fiske Stone* (1956). On New Deal ideology, see Thurman Arnold, *Folklore of Capitalism* (1937), and on antitrust policy, Arnold, *Bottlenecks of Business* (1940). Keynesian overviews of New Deal economics are: J. K. Galbraith and G. G. Johnson, Jr., *The Economic Effects of the Federal Public Works Expenditures* (1940), and Arthur Burns and Donald Watson, *Government Spending and Economic Expansion* (1940). On the social and intellectual history of the thirties, see Wecter, *Age of the Great Depression;* F. L. Allen, *Since Yesterday* (1940) ; Charles and Mary Beard, *America in Midpassage* (2 vols., 1939) ; Leo Gurko, *Angry Decade* (1947) ; and Milton Crane (ed.), *Roosevelt Era* (1947).

15. America Faces the World Crisis

There is a compact survey of foreign policy in Allan Nevins, *The New Deal and World Affairs* (1950), and an even briefer one in Perkins, *The New Age of Roosevelt.* The opening pages of W. L. Langer and S. E. Gleason, *The Challenge to Isolation, 1937–1940* (1952), contains a thoughtful evaluation of the techniques of Roosevelt and Hull. Hull's own account, with extensive quotation from documents, is in his *Memoirs* (2 vols., 1948) ; Robert Sherwood, *Roosevelt and Hopkins* (1948), is a readable account which takes Hopkins's viewpoint. On the Good Neighbor policy, see E. O. Guerrant, *Roosevelt's Good Neighbor Policy* (1950), and H. F. Cline, *The United States and Mexico* (1953) ; on the recognition of Russia, R. P. Browder, *The Origins of Soviet-American Diplomacy* (1953), and W. A. Williams, *American-Russian Relations, 1781–1947* (1952) ; on neutrality legislation, E. M. Borchard and W. P. Lage, *Neutrality for the United States* (1940 ed.). The most comprehensive account of the developing war crisis and American entrance is in Langer and Gleason, *Challenge to Isolation* and *Undeclared War* (1953). A careful evaluation is D. F. Drummond, *The Passing of American Neutrality*

(1955). More specialized monographs are: F. Jay Taylor, *The United States and the Spanish Civil War, 1936–1939* (1956); Herbert Feis, *The Spanish Story* (1948) and *The Road to Pearl Harbor* (1950); and P. W. Schroeder, *The Axis Alliance and Japanese-American Relations, 1941* (1958). Accounts highly critical of Roosevelt's policies are C. A. Beard, *American Foreign Policy, 1932–1940* (1946) and *President Roosevelt and the Coming of the War* (1948); and C. C. Tansill, *Back Door to War* (1952). Basil Rauch, *Roosevelt from Munich to Pearl Harbor* (1950), is a detailed refutation of Beard's charges. On the great debate over intervention, see Walter Johnson, *Battle Against Isolationism* (1944), and W. S. Cole, *America First* (1953). Two general analyses of isolationism are Selig Adler's indictment, *The Isolationist Impulse: Its Twentieth-Century Reaction* (1957); and a symposium, Alexander De Conde (ed.), *Isolation and Security: Ideas and Interests in Twentieth-Century American Foreign Policy* (1957). On the election of 1940, see M. E. Dillon, *Wendell L. Willkie* (1952). On the Japanese attack, see Walter Millis, *This is Pearl!* (1947).

16. Outproducing the Axis

Unfortunately there is no readable, dispassionate account of the battle for production. Eliot Janeway, *The Struggle for Survival* (1951), concentrates on conflicts in Washington; Donald M. Nelson's *Arsenal of Democracy* (1946) is his view of the War Production Board; Bruce Catton, *War Lords of Washington* (1948), emphasizes the influence of big business. The best over-all survey is Bureau of the Budget, *The United States at War* (1946); an interesting compilation is Jack Goodman (ed.), *While You Were Gone: A Report on Wartime Life in the United States* (1946). More specialized studies are: J. P. Baxter III, *Scientists Against Time* (1946); E. R. Stettinius, Jr., *Lend-Lease, Weapon of Victory* (1944); R. H. Connery, *The Navy and Industrial Mobilization in World War II* (1951); J. K. Galbraith, *Theory of Price Control* (1952); W. A. Nielander, *Wartime Food Rationing in the United States* (1947); W. W. Willcox, *The Farmer in the Second World War* (1947); Fred Witney, *Wartime Experiences of the National Labor Relations Board* (1949); Randolph E. Paul, *Taxation for Prosperity* (1947); E. S. Corwin, *Total War and the Constitution* (1947); M. Q. Sibley and P. E. Jacob, *Conscription of Conscience: The Conscientious Objector, 1940–1947* (1952); Jacobus ten Broek *et al.*, *Prejudice, War and the Constitution: Japanese American Evacuation and Resettlement* (1958); D. S. Thomas and others, *Salvage: Japanese American Evacuation and Resettlement* (1952); Morton Grodzins, *Americans Betrayed* (1949), on Japanese-Americans; M. B. Clinard, *Black Market* (1952); Reuben Hill, *Families Under Stress* (1949); W. F. Ogburn (ed.), *American Society in Wartime* (1943); and J. S. Bruner, *Mandate from the People* (1944), on public opinion. On politics, see Jonathan Daniels, *Frontier on the Potomac* (1946); Joseph Gaer, *First Round: The CIO Political Action*

Committee (1944) ; and Roland Young, *Congressional Politics in the Second World War* (1955).

17. Turning the Tide

A short, eloquent exposition of American wartime strategy is S. E. Morison, *Strategy and Compromise* (1958) ; more critical is H. W. Baldwin, *Great Mistakes of the War* (1950). A brief account of the war is Fletcher Pratt, *War for the World* (1950) ; a good pictorial account, *Life's Picture History of World War II* (1950) ; for studies of key decisions, K. R. Greenfield (ed.), *Command Decisions* (1959). A brilliant memoir and history is Winston S. Churchill, *Second World War* (6 vols., 1948–53) ; and a challenging account of the war in Europe from the British viewpoint is Chester Wilmot, *Struggle for Europe* (1952). Brief, clear reports are *General Marshall's Report: The Winning of the War in Europe and the Pacific* (1945) and *U.S. Navy at War, 1941–1945* (1946). The following multivolume histories are well under way or completed: S. E. Morison, *History of United States Naval Operations in World War II* (14 vols., 1947–   ) ; *United States Army in World War II* (91 vols., 1947–   ) ; W. F. Craven and J. L. Cate (eds.), *Army Air Forces in World War II* (5 vols., 1948–53) ; and *Operational Narratives of the Marine Corps in World War II* (1947–   ). A checklist of 150 paperbacks on modern warfare compiled by H. O. Werner is in the *United States Naval Institute Proceedings*, August, 1959. Among the memoirs are: Sherwood, *Roosevelt and Hopkins;* Stimson and Bundy, *On Active Service in Peace and War;* Dwight D. Eisenhower, *Crusade in Europe* (1948) ; Omar N. Bradley, *A Soldier's Story* (1951) ; Henry H. Arnold, *Global Mission* (1949) ; and E. J. King and W. M. Whitehill, *Fleet Admiral King* (1952). On the organization and functioning of the military establishment, see R. S. Cline, *Washington Command Post* (1951) ; Mark S. Watson, *Chief of Staff* (1950) ; and S. M. Rosen, *Combined Boards of the Second World War* (1951).

A monumental account of wartime diplomacy is Herbert Feis, *Churchill, Roosevelt, Stalin* (1957). In addition to the memoirs of Churchill and Hull, and Sherwood's *Roosevelt and Hopkins,* see Sumner Welles, *Seven Decisions That Shaped History* (1951), and W. L. Langer, *Our Vichy Gamble* (1947).

18. Victory Without Peace

In addition to the books cited above, see E. R. Stettinius, Jr., *Roosevelt and the Russians* (1949), on Yalta; J. F. Byrnes, *Speaking Frankly* (1947) ; H. S. Truman, *Memoirs* (2 vols., 1955) ; and Arthur Vandenberg, Jr. (ed.), *The Private Papers of Senator Vandenberg* (1952), on foreign policy from Yalta to the Japanese surrender; and Herbert Feis, *The China Tangle* (1953), on wartime and postwar relations with China. A valuable compilation on Yalta is R. F. Fenno, Jr. (ed.), *The Yalta Conference* (1955). On the effects of the atomic bomb, see John Hersey, *Hiroshima* (1946).

19. The Menace of Cold War

On postwar foreign policy, see William Reitzel and others, *United States Foreign Policy, 1945–1955* (1956), a scholarly analysis; H. B. Westerfield, *Foreign Policy and Party Politics: Pearl Harbor to Korea* (1955); the annual surveys by the Brookings Institution, beginning in 1947, *Major Problems of United States Foreign Policies;* and the surveys of the Council on Foreign Relations, *The United States in World Affairs*. On Truman's policies, see Truman, *Memoirs;* Byrnes, *Speaking Frankly;* Vandenberg, *Papers;* and Walter Millis (ed.), *The Forrestal Diaries* (1951). On the United Nations, see L. M. Goodrich and Edvard Hambro, *Charter of the United Nations* (1949), and E. P. Chase, *The United Nations in Action* (1950); on atomic control, J. R. Newman and B. S. Miller, *The Control of Atomic Energy* (1948). W. B. Smith, *My Three Years in Moscow* (1950), describes growing tensions with Russia; L. D. Clay, *Decision in Germany* (1950), depicts the struggle with Russia there. On occupation policy in Europe, see Hajo Holborn, *American Military Government* (1947); R. H. Jackson, *The Case Against Nazi War Criminals* (1946) and *The Nurnberg Case* (1947); and Drew Middleton, *The Struggle for Germany* (1949). On Japan, see E. O. Reischauer, *The United States and Japan* (1957 ed.); and R. A. Fearey, *Occupation of Japan* (1950). On the Philippines, see R. A. Smith, *Philippine Freedom* (1958). Economic policy is described in S. E. Harris (ed.), *Foreign Economic Policy* (1948); R. F. Mikesell, *United States Economic Policy and International Relations* (1952); Department of State, *Point Four* (1950) and *Point Four Pioneers* (1951).

20. The Truman Era

E. F. Goldman, *The Crucial Decade: America 1945–1955* (1956), is a colorful survey; Herbert Agar, *The Price of Power: America since 1945* (1957), is a very brief interpretation; Allen, *The Big Change*, draws a contrast with the turn of the century. On the Truman administration, in addition to Truman's *Memoirs*, see Jonathan Daniels, *The Man from Independence* (1950), on Truman's background; and L. W. Koenig (ed.), *The Truman Administration* (1956). On domestic problems after 1945, see R. J. Havighurst and others, *The American Veteran Back Home* (1951); L. V. Chandler, *Inflation in the United States, 1940–1948* (1950); G. A. Steiner, *The Government's Role in Economic Life* (1953); H. A. Millis and E. C. Brown, *From the Wagner Act to Taft-Hartley* (1950); C. O. Gregory, *Labor and the Law* (1949); C. W. Mills, *The New Men of Power* (1948), on labor leaders; C. C. Taylor, *et al., Rural Life in the United States* (1949); R. A. Dahl and R. S. Brown, *Domestic Control of Atomic Energy* (1951). On questions of individual rights and loyalty, see The President's Committee on Civil Rights, *To Secure These Rights* (1947); Alan Barth, *The Loyalty of Free Men* (1951); Clair Wilcox (ed.), *Civil Liberties under Attack* (1951); H. D. Lasswell, *National Security and Individual Freedom* (1950) ; C. H. Pritchett, *Civil Liberties and the Vinson Court* (1954); J. R. McCarthy, *McCarthyism* (1952) ; Jack Anderson and R. W. May, *McCarthy* (1952) ; and a brilliant later view, R. H. Rovere, *Senator Joe McCarthy* (1959).

An indispensable interpretation of the political revolution of the era is Samuel Lubell, *The Future of American Politics* (1952). On corruption, see Blair Bolles, *How to Get Rich in Washington* (1952), and P. H. Douglas, *Ethics in Government* (1952). A. M. Rose's *The Negro in Postwar America* (1950) is a competent survey. Significant regional economic studies are: C. B. Hoover and B. U. Ratchford, *Economic Resources and Policies of the South* (1951) ; Wendell Berge, *Economic Freedom for the West* (1946) ; and S. E. Harris, *The Economics of New England*.

21. The Korean War and Its Aftermath

On the background in Korea, see G. M. McCune and A. L. Grey, Jr., *Korea Today* (1950) ; a summary of the military and diplomatic phases of the war is Carl Berger, *The Korea Knot, a Military-Political History* (1957). Military histories are Department of the Army, *Korea—1950* (1952) ; and M. W. Cagle and F. A. Manson, *The Sea War in Korea* (1957). R. H. Rovere and A. M. Schlesinger, Jr., *The General and the President* (1951), is a contemporary but still cogent account of the war and especially the Truman-MacArthur controversy. A dispassionate scholarly appraisal of the controversy is J. W. Spanier, *The Truman-MacArthur Controversy and the Korean War* (1959). For a spirited defense of MacArthur, see Major General Courtney Whitney, *MacArthur: His Rendezvous with History* (1956).

On the debate over foreign policy, Norman Graebner's *The New Isolationism* (1956) is a keen analysis; see also McGeorge Bundy (ed.), *Pattern of Responsibility* (1952), on Secretary Acheson's views; and R. A. Taft, *A Foreign Policy for Americans* (1951). Two criticisms of Asia policy, the first anti-Chiang and the second pro-Chiang, are: E. O. Reischauer, *Wanted: An Asian Policy* (1955), and Geraldine Fitch, *Formosa Beachhead* (1953). A useful case study is B. C. Cohen, *The Political Process and Foreign Policy: The Making of the Japanese Peace Settlement* (1957).

Concerning the 1952 campaign, see Kevin McCann, *The Man From Abilene* (1952), on Eisenhower; N. F. Busch, *Adlai E. Stevenson* (1952) ; and Stevenson, *Major Campaign Speeches* (1953).

22. Eisenhower Republicanism

On President Eisenhower and his policies, see R. J. Donovan, *Eisenhower, The Inside Story* (1956) ; the highly favorable M. J. Pusey, *Eisenhower the President* (1956) ; the more critical Marquis Childs, *Eisenhower: Captive Hero* (1958) ; R. H. Rovere, *Affairs of State: The Eisenhower Years* (1956) ; and A. Merriman Smith, *Meet Mr. Eisenhower* (1955). A study covering from Wilson to Eisenhower is R. F. Fenno, *The President's Cabinet* (1959). A thoughtful interpretation of politics from 1952 to 1956 is Samuel Lubell, *The Revolt of the Moderates* (1956). A study of auto workers, at variance with Lubell's findings, is Kornhauser and others, *When Labor Votes* (1956). On modern Republicanism as a credo, see Arthur Larson, *A Republican Looks at His Party* (1956). The first volume of a government publication is *Public Papers of the Presidents of the United States. Dwight D. Eisenhower: Containing the Messages, Speeches, and Statements of the President, January 1 to December 31, 1957* (1958).

Two brief but cogent analyses of the changing role of the Supreme Court are Alpheus Mason, *The Supreme Court from Taft to Warren* (1958), and C. B. Swisher, *The Supreme Court in Modern Role* (1958). On desegregation, see H. S. Ashmore, *The Negro and the Schools* (1954) ; C. C. Ferguson, *Desegregation and the Law* (1957) ; Wilma Dykeman and James Stokely, *Neither Black nor White* (1957) ; and an account of Citizens Councils in Mississippi, Hodding Carter, *The South Strikes Back* (1959). A survey of the erosion of civil liberties, carrying into the post-McCarthy period, is J. W. Caughey, *In Clear and Present Danger* (1958). Michael Straight, *Trial by Television* (1954), details the Army-McCarthy hearings. J. L. O'Brian, *National Security and Individual Freedom* (1955), analyzes the Eisenhower program; C. P. Curtis, *The Oppenheimer Case* (1955), deals with a *cause célèbre*. Civil liberties questions are seen in perspective in H. M. Hyman, *To Try Men's Souls: Loyalty Tests in American History* (1959).

On the problems of Puerto Ricans and Negroes in the New York City area, see Oscar Handlin, *The Newcomers* (1959). J. K. Galbraith, *The Affluent Society* (1958), explains new economic thinking; and A. A. Berle, *Power Without Property* (1959), analyzes significant recent changes in American economic life. On the Teamsters, see C. R. Mollenhoff, *Tentacles of Terror: The Teamsters Defy the Government* (1959). On agricultural problems, see M. R. Benedict and O. C. Stine, *The Agricultural Commodity Programs: Two Decades of Experience* (1956). An invaluable survey of modern educational problems is J. B. Conant, *The American High School Today* (1959). On art, see again Hunter, *Modern American Painting and Sculpture* (1959). Among the sociological analyses of the postwar generation are C. W. Mills, *White Collar* (1951) and *Power Elite* (1956) ; David Riesman, *Lonely Crowd* (1950) ; W. H. Whyte, *Organization Man* (1956) ; Robert C. Wood, *Suburbia: Its People and Their Politics* (1959) ; Eleanor Clymer and Lillian Erlich, *Modern American Career Women* (1959) ; and Margaret Cussler, *The Woman Executive* (1958).

23. *A Nuclear Balance of Terror*

A useful contemporary overview of the early policies of President Eisenhower and Secretary Dulles is in R. C. Snyder and E. S. Furniss, Jr., *American Foreign Policy* (1954), and in Reitzel *et al.*, *United States Foreign Policy*,

1945–1955. See also the yearly volumes prepared by Richard P. Stebbins for the Council on Foreign Relations, *The United States in World Affairs,* and the yearly surveys by the Brookings Institution, *Major Problems of United States Foreign Policies.* There is much on foreign policy in Donovan, *Eisenhower;* Pusey, *Eisenhower;* Childs, *Eisenhower;* and Rovere, *Affairs of State.* Many of the documents are in *Public Papers of . . . Eisenhower.* Three critical studies of the Eisenhower-Dulles policies are C. L. Sulzberger, *What's Wrong with U.S. Foreign Policy* (1959); W. A. Williams, *The Tragedy of American Diplomacy* (1959); and Arnold Wolfers (ed.), *Alliance Policy in the Cold War* (1959). Dulles's views before he became Secretary of State are in J. F. Dulles, *War or Peace* (1950). A significant analysis of the effect of new weapons is H. A. Kissinger, *Nuclear Weapons and Foreign Policy* (1957). On civil-military relations see Walter Millis *et al., Arms and the State* (1958). On Middle Eastern background and policies, see F. E. Manuel, *Realities of American-Palestine Relations* (1949); E. A. Speiser, *The United States and the Near East* (1949); and L. V. Thomas and R. N. Frye, *The United States and Turkey and Iran* (1951). On Germany, Eugene Davidson, *The Death and Life of Germany: An Account of the American Occupation* (1959).

Paperback Editions

Numerous books treating at least in part with the United States since 1900, most of which are listed in the chapter bibliographies, are available in soft-cover editions at moderate prices. If not obtainable at local bookstores they may be ordered directly from the publisher. In addition to the list below, see H. O. Werner, "Paperbacks on Modern Warfare," *United States Naval Institute Proceedings,* August 1959, a checklist of approximately 150 titles "of generally good quality and great variety."

Adams, C. F., Jr. and Henry, *Chapters of Erie* (Cornell).
Agar, Herbert, *The Price of Power: America Since 1945* (Chicago).
Allen, F. L., *The Great Pierpont Morgan* (Bantam).
——, *Only Yesterday* (Bantam).
American Heritage Reader (Dell).
Arnold, T. W., *The Folklore of Capitalism* (Yale).
Bowen, C. D., *Yankee from Olympus* (Bantam).
Brockway, T. P., *Basic Documents in United States Foreign Policy* (Anvil).
Brooks, Van Wyck, *America's Coming of Age* (Anchor).
Buck, P. H., *The Road to Reunion* (Vintage).
Burlingame, Roger, *Henry Ford* (New American Library).
Butcher, M. J., *The Negro in American Culture* (New American Library).
Cash, W. J., *The Mind of the South* (Anchor).
Commager, H. S., *America in Perspective* (New American Library).
——, *The American Mind* (Yale).
Dollard, John, *Caste and Class in a Southern Town* (Anchor).

Editors of *Fortune, The Exploding Metropolis* (Anchor).

Ellis, J. T., *American Catholicism* (Chicago).

Farmer, Frances (ed.), *The Wilson Reader* (Oceana).

Geismar, Maxwell, *American Moderns* (Hill and Wang).

———, *The Last of the Provincials* (Hill and Wang).

Glazer, Nathan, *American Judaism* (Chicago).

Goldman, E. F., *Rendezvous with Destiny* (Vintage).

Grodzins, Morton, *The Metropolitan Area as a Racial Problem* (Pittsburg).

Handlin, Oscar, *Immigration as a Factor in American History* (Prentice-Hall).

———, *Race and Nationality in American Life* (Anchor).

———, *The Uprooted* (Universal).

Hays, S. P., *The Response to Industrialism: 1885–1914* (Chicago).

Heffner, R. D., *A Documentary History of the United States* (New American Library).

Hofstadter, Richard, *The American Political Tradition* (Vintage).

——— (ed.), *Great Issues in American History: A Documentary Record*, Vol. II (Vintage).

———, *Social Darwinism in American Thought* (Beacon).

Hunter, Samuel, *Modern American Painting and Sculpture* (Dell).

Kazin, Alfred, *On Native Grounds* (Anchor).

Kemmerer, D. L., and Hunter, M. H., *Economic History of the United States* (Littlefield, Adams & Co.).

Kennan, G. F., *American Diplomacy: 1900–1950* (New American Library).

Kissinger, Henry, *Nuclear Weapons and Foreign Policy* (Anchor).

Leuchtenberg, William, *Perils of Prosperity* (Chicago).

Lilienthal, David, *Big Business* (Pocketbooks).

Logan, R. W., *The Negro in the United States* (Anvil).

Lord, Walter, *Day of Infamy* (Bantam).

Lubell, Samuel, *The Future of American Politics* (Anchor).

Lynd, R. S. and H. M., *Middletown* (Harvest).

Marke, Julius (ed.), *The Holmes Reader* (Oceana).

Miller, Perry (ed.), *American Thought from the Civil War to First World War* (Rinehart).

Millis, Walter, *Arms and Men* (New American Library).

Mills, C. W., *The Power Elite* (Galaxy).

———, *White Collar* (Galaxy).

Morris, R. B., *Basic Documents in American History* (Anvil).

Osgood, E. S., *The Day of the Cattleman* (Phoenix).

Perkins, Dexter, *The New Age of Franklin Roosevelt* (Chicago).

Potter, David, *People of Plenty, Economic Abundance and the American Character* (Phoenix).

Pringle, H. F., *Theodore Roosevelt* (Harvest).

Rauch, Basil (ed.), *F. D. Roosevelt, Speeches, Messages, Press Conferences and Letters* (Rinehart).

Richards, W. C., *The Last Billionaire: Henry Ford* (Bantam).

Riesman, David, *The Lonely Crowd* (Anchor).

Rose, Arnold, *The Negro in America* (Beacon).

Roosevelt, F. D., *The American Way. F. D. Roosevelt* (Wisdom Library).

Rossiter, Clinton, *American Presidency* (New American Library).

Steffens, Lincoln, *The Shame of the Cities* (Sagamore).

Swisher, C. B., *Historic Decisions of the Supreme Court* (Anvil).

Warren, R. P., *Segregation* (Modern Library).

Washington, B. T., *Up from Slavery* (Bantam).

Webb, W. P., *The Great Plains* (Universal).

Weeks, R. P. (ed.), *Commonwealth vs. Sacco and Vanzetti* (Prentice-Hall).

White, Morton, *The Age of Analysis: 20th Century Philosophers* (New American Library).

———, *Social Thought in America: The Revolt Against Formalism* (Beacon).

Whyte, W. H., *The Organization Man* (Anchor).

Woodward, C. V., *Reunion and Reaction* (Anchor).

Index

A NOTE ON THE TYPE

THIS BOOK *was set on the Linotype in* Bodoni Book, *a printing-type so called after Giambattista Bodoni, a celebrated printer and type designer of Rome and Parma* (1740–1813). Bodoni Book *as produced by the Linotype company is not a copy of any one of Bodoni's fonts, but is a composite, modern version of the Bodoni manner. Bodoni's innovations in printing-type style were a greater degree of contrast in the "thick and thin" elements of the letters, and a sharper and more angular finish of details.*

The book was composed, printed, and bound by The Kingsport Press, Inc., Kingsport, Tennessee. Paper manufactured by S. D. Warren Company, Boston. Typography and binding design by GUY FLEMING.